Bhagavad Gita

Bhagavad Gita

THE SONG OF GOD

COMMENTARY BY

Swami Mukundananda

First published by Westland Publications Private Limited in 2021

1st Floor, A Block, East Wing, Plot No. 40, SP Infocity, Dr MGR Salai, Perungudi, Kandanchavadi, Chennai 600096

Westland and the Westland logo are the trademarks of Westland Publications Private Limited, or its affiliates.

ISBN: 9789391234140

10 9 8 7 6 5 4 3 2

Typeset in Radha Govind Dham

Printed at Thomson Press (India) Ltd

This elucidation of the Bhagavad Gita is dedicated to my beloved Spiritual Master, Jagadguru Shree Kripaluji Maharaj, who illuminated humankind with the purest rays of divine knowledge. He was immersed in the divine love and bliss of God and engaged in inundating the entire planet with it. This commentary on the Bhagavad Gita has been written to fulfil his instruction to spread the knowledge of the Vedic scriptures. I pray that by his blessings it will be helpful in guiding sincere seekers of the Truth on the path of enlightenment.

Swami Mukundananda

CONTENTS

Introduction 1

Chapter 1: ***Arjun Viṣhād Yog***
Lamenting the Consequences of War 28

Chapter 2: ***Sānkhya Yog***
The Yog of Analytical Knowledge 59

Chapter 3: ***Karm Yog***
The Yog of Action 149

Chapter 4: ***Jnana Karm Sanyas Yog***
The Yog of Knowledge and the Disciplines of Action 202

Chapter 5: ***Karm Sanyas Yog***
The Yog of Renunciation 255

Chapter 6: ***Dhyān Yog***
The Yog of Meditation 291

Chapter 7: ***Jnana Vijnana Yog***
Yog through the Realisation of Divine Knowledge 346

Chapter 8: ***Akṣhar Brahma Yog***
The Yog of the Eternal God 385

Chapter 9: ***Raja Vidyā Yog***
Yog through the King of Sciences 419

Chapter 10: ***Vibhūti Yog***
Yog through Appreciating the Infinite Opulences of God 467

Chapter 11: ***Viśhwaroop Darshan Yog***
Yog through Beholding the Cosmic Form of God 515

Chapter 12: ***Bhakti Yog***
The Yog of Devotion 572

Chapter 13: ***Kṣhetra Kṣhetrajña Vibhāg Yog***
Yog through Distinguishing the Field and the Knower of the Field 600

Chapter 14: ***Guna Traya Vibhāg Yog***
Yog through Understanding the Three Modes of Material Nature 644

Chapter 15: ***Puruṣhottam Yog***
The Yog of the Supreme Divine Personality 669

Chapter 16: ***Daivāsura Sampad Vibhāg Yog***
Yog through Discerning the Divine and Demoniac Natures 701

Chapter 17: ***Śhraddhā Traya Vibhāg Yog***
Yog through Discerning the Three Divisions of Faith 727

Chapter 18: ***Moksha Sanyas Yog***
Yog through the Perfection of Renunciation and Surrender 753

Pronunciation Guide 841

Glossary 844

Appellations used for Shree Krishna and Arjun 862

Subject Index 864

Index of Verses Quoted in the Commentary 869

Other Books by the Author 877

Let's Connect 878

Introduction

Invocation

prathamaṁ sadguruṁ vande śhrī kṛiṣhṇa tadanantaram
guruḥ pāpātmanāṁ trātā śhrī kṛiṣhṇastvamalātmanām

mukundānanda prapannohaṁ guru pādāravindayoḥ
tasya preraṇayā tasya divyādeśhaṁ vadāmyaham

'I first offer my respectful obeisance to my gurudev, Jagadguru Shree Kripaluji Maharaj, and then to the Supreme Lord Shree Krishna. While Shree Krishna embraces the pure-hearted, my gurudev is so merciful that he offers shelter even to the spiritually destitute. This insignificant inconsequential soul, who goes by the name of Mukundananda in the world, is surrendering at the lotus feet of his Spiritual Master. With his guru's permission, inspiration, and grace, he is humbly going to elucidate on spiritual topics.'

vande vṛindāvanānandāṁ rādhikāṁ parameśhvarīm
gopikāṁ paramāṁ śhūddhāṁ hlādinīṁ śhakti rūpiṇīm

'I offer my respectful obeisance to Radha Rani, the Supreme Goddess and the bliss-giving power of God. She is the purest of the *gopis* and embodies the bliss of Vrindavan.'

kadā drakṣhyāmi nandasya bālakaṁ nīpamālakam
pālakaṁ sarva sattvānāṁ lasattilaka bhālakam

'When will my eyes see the wonderful form of the Supreme Lord Shree Krishna who appeared on this earth as the son of Nand? He is adorned with a flower garland around His neck and the holy tilak mark on His forehead; He is the protector of virtuous people.'

ajāta pakṣhā iva mātaraṁ khagāḥ
satanyaṁ yathā vatsatarāḥ kṣhudhārtāḥ
priyaṁ priyeva vyuṣhitaṁ viṣhaṇṇā
manoravindākṣha didṛikṣhate tvām

'O Lord! As a baby bird yearns for its mother, as a famished infant longs to suckle the mother's breast, and as a lover craves for the beloved, may my mind always long for Your divine vision.'

The Ascending and Descending Processes of Knowledge

There are two ways of acquiring knowledge. The first is the ascending process, in which we utilise our senses, mind, and intellect to explore, discover, and conclude about the nature of the Truth. Second is the descending process where we simply receive the knowledge from a proper source. The ascending process of gaining knowledge is inherently prone to defects. Since our senses, mind, and intellect are made from the material energy, they are imperfect and limited. As a result, we can never be completely sure about the accuracy and reliability of the knowledge we gain through them.

As the pursuit of material science is based upon the ascending process, even the most acclaimed and undisputed scientific theories of the past are overthrown and superseded by newer ones. For example, the Greek concept of matter as consisting of indivisible atoms was invalidated by Rutherford when he demonstrated that atoms consist of electrons, protons, neutrons, and vast regions of empty space. Rutherford's theory was overthrown by the Quantum theory which stated that electrons and protons are not solid particles but vibrating patterns of energy with a dual particle wave nature. This makes us wonder whether what we believe to be true today will also be proven utterly incorrect after a few centuries.

The other process of knowledge, the descending process, on the other hand, is completely free from such defects. When we receive knowledge from a perfect source, we can be assured that it is flawless. For example, if we wish to know who our father is, we do not conduct experiments. We simply ask our mother as she is the authority on this piece of information. Likewise in spiritual matters too, the descending process immediately gives us access to vast reservoirs of knowledge which would have taken ages of self-effort to unveil. The only criterion here is that the source from which we receive the knowledge must be infallible and trustworthy. The Vedas are one such source of knowledge.

The Vedas are not the name of any book. They refer to the eternal knowledge of God which he manifests when He creates the world. In this cycle of creation, He first revealed them in the heart of the first-born Brahma. These Vedas were passed on for thousands of years by oral tradition, from master to disciple, and hence another name for them is *śhruti* (knowledge received by hearing). They are also called *apauruṣheya* (not created by any human). For this reason, in Indian philosophy, the Vedas are considered the ultimate authority for validating any spiritual principle. The validity of any spiritual tenet, whether in the context of the past, present, or future, must be established on the basis of the Vedas. To elaborate their meaning, many more scriptures have been written. These scriptures do not deviate from the authority of the Vedas; rather, they attempt to expand and explain the knowledge contained in them. Together, all these are termed 'Vedic scriptures.'

The Vedic scriptures are vast, but three of them have traditionally been called the *Prasthān Trayī* (three points of commencement for understanding Vedic thought). These are the Upanishads, the Brahma Sutras, and the Bhagavad Gita.

The Upanishads are the section of the Vedas that deal with philosophical knowledge and are considered the cream of the Vedas. On reading them, the German philosopher, Arthur Schopenhauer said, 'There is no philosophy in the world as elevating as that of the Upanishads. It has been the solace of my life and it shall be the solace of my death.' Paul Deussen, another German philosopher, expressed himself thus: 'Eternal philosophical truth has seldom found a more striking and decisive expression than in the emancipating knowledge of the philosophy of the Upanishads.' However, for a lay person the Upanishads are difficult to fathom.

The Brahma Sutras is a synopsis of the Upanishads. It was written by Sage Ved Vyas to provide the philosophical conclusion of Vedic knowledge. Thus, it is also called 'Vedant', meaning 'the culmination of Vedic thought'. Like the Upanishads, the Brahma Sutras is also hard to comprehend, and its conciseness often leads to ambiguity and subjective interpretation.

The Bhagavad Gita is more accessible than the above two scriptures. It provides a comprehensive and easy-to-understand summary of the Vedic philosophy. Bhagavad means 'of God', and Gita means 'song'. Hence, the Bhagavad Gita literally means 'Song of God'. It is a dialogue that took place between the Supreme Lord Shree Krishna and His devotee Arjun, on the verge of the Mahabharat war.

In the course of history, hundreds of theories in economics, psychology, sociology, philosophy, and many other subjects were first propounded and then discarded as inaccurate or incomplete. These were all the products of ascending knowledge, and consequently, imperfect and subject to error. If the Bhagavad Gita had also been the creation of a mortal and finite intellect, with the passage of fifty centuries, it would have become outdated and irrelevant. However, the perennial wisdom of the Gita has continued to inspire famous thinkers even in modern times, such as Mahatma Gandhi, Robert Oppenheimer, Carl Jung, Herman Hesse, and Aldous Huxley, to name just a few, thereby substantiating its divine origin.

Embedded in the Mahabharat

The Bhagavad Gita was originally compiled by Ved Vyas as a separate text. Later, when he wrote the Mahabharat, he embedded the Bhagavad Gita in it. The Mahabharat contains one hundred thousand verses, and is therefore, the largest poem in the world. It is seven times bigger than the Iliad and Odyssey put together and three times bigger than the Bible. Along with the Ramayan, it is accorded the status of *Itihās*, meaning, historical manuscript of India. Its stories and moral instructions have fashioned the fabric of Indian culture for thousands of years. The Mahabharat is divided into eighteen sections. The Bhagavad Gita is set in the sixth section which is called the *Bheeshma Parva*. It covers eighteen chapters of the section, from chapter twenty-five to chapter forty-two.

Since the Bhagavad Gita encapsulates most of the important aspects of the knowledge of the Vedas, it is also called *Gitopanishad* or the *Gitā Upaniṣhad*. It serves two important purposes as described below.

It Imparts Brahma Vidyā

As humankind boldly marches forward expanding its frontiers of knowledge, the realisation is dawning that the more we discover and learn, the more there is yet to be known. New sciences emerge every year, leading to the inevitable conclusion that the quest for comprehending the whole truth of creation is a never-ending endeavour. This makes one wonder if there is any one body or source of knowledge that can easily explain everything that exists. According to the Vedas, there is such a branch of knowledge, and it is the science of realising the Absolute Truth. There is one Absolute Truth, which has been referred to by many names, such as Ishwar, Bhagavan, God, Lord, Allah, Khuda, Yahweh, Ahur Mazda, Alakh Niranjan, Shunya, and Ikomkar, among others. All other truths have emanated from it and find their position in the scheme of things from it. Thus, the Vedas state: *ekasmin vijñāte sarvamidaṁ vijñātaṁ bhavati* 'One who comes to know the Absolute Truth attains knowledge of everything.' The science of knowing the Absolute Truth is called *brahma vidyā*. The purpose of the Bhagavad Gita, above everything else, is to impart *brahma vidyā*, the science of God-realisation.

Knowledge that helps a person resolve immediate problems is one kind of enlightenment while knowledge that dispels the root of ignorance to solve all problems in one strike is another kind of enlightenment. The Bhagavad Gita aims at the second kind of enlightenment by destroying the darkness of ignorance that has enveloped the soul since endless lifetimes. Unable to deal with the immediate problem at hand, Arjun approached Shree Krishna for a palliative to overcome the anguish he was experiencing. Shree Krishna did not just advise him on his immediate problem but went beyond that to give Arjun a profound discourse on the philosophy of life.

It Teaches the Practice of Yog

For any science to be useful, it must address two aspects—theory and practice. Even the best of theoretical knowledge is insufficient in itself to solve the problems of life. And if knowledge is not put into practice, it only serves the purpose of intellectual entertainment.

The Bhagavad Gita is not content with providing a lofty philosophical understanding; it also describes clear-cut techniques to implement its spiritual precepts for everyday life. These techniques of applying the science of spirituality in our lives are termed 'Yog'. Hence, the Bhagavad Gita is also called *Yog Shastra*, meaning, 'the scripture that teaches the practice of Yog'.

Inexperienced spiritual practitioners often separate spirituality from temporal life; some look on beatitude as something to be attained in the hereafter. But the Bhagavad Gita makes no such distinction and aims at the consecration of every aspect of human life in this world itself. As a result, all its eighteen chapters are designated as different types of Yog because they deal with methodologies for the application of spiritual knowledge to practical life. These chapters also describe various systems of Yog, such as karm yog, jnana yog, and bhakti yog.

The Setting of the Bhagavad Gita

Though the Truth is one and eternal, in different ages it expresses itself in varied locales that impart their unique flavor to its presentation. The teaching of the Bhagavad Gita must, therefore, not be regarded merely in the light of a generalised philosophy or ethical doctrine. It is the practical application of ethics to human life in a specific situation of crisis that serves as its setting. Since its teachings are exceedingly profound, the Bhagavad Gita required an equally problematic and insurmountable crisis as its setting. Thus, in order to fully appreciate the value of its ideas, the historical flow of events that led to the articulation of the divine message to Arjun by Lord Krishna on the battlefield of Kurukshetra must also be known.

The setting in which the Bhagavad Gita was spoken was the onset of the Mahabharat, a colossal war that was about to begin between two sets of cousins, the Kauravas and the Pandavas. The Pandavas—Yudhishthir, Bheem, Arjun, Nakul, and Sahadev—were five noble brothers. Their father, King Pandu, had suffered an unfortunate death while his five sons were still very young. Pandu's throne had been usurped by his step brother, Dhritarashtra, who was blind from birth. Dhritarashtra had a hundred sons, called the Kauravas, the eldest of whom was Duryodhan. For years, the Kauravas, led by Duryodhan, had victimised their cousins, the Pandavas, and governed over the kingdom of Hastinapur which did not rightfully belong to them.

The Kauravas embodied cruelty, injustice, vice, oppression, and irreligion. On the other hand, the Pandavas were saintly and virtuous—the epitome of morality, sacrifice, devotion, and compassion. Most importantly, they were great devotees of the Supreme Lord Shree Krishna. Due to the oppression meted out to them by the Kauravas, the miseries of the Pandavas had become so unbearable that a war between the two sides had become imminent. Realising the unavoidability of the war, both sides had canvassed for support from the scores of kingdoms that littered the landscape of Bharat (India) at that time. The two groups of cousins were so powerful that the war would impact the whole of Bharat. Thus, all the kings in the land were obliged to align themselves with one side or the other.

As a part of the vigorous mobilisation attempts, both Arjun and Duryodhan arrived at Dwaraka to request the help of Lord Krishna. Being omniscient, Shree Krishna knew that they were coming to entreat His help. He created a situation that set the didactical tone for the approaching battle.

He posed to be sleeping in His chamber. Arjun entered the chamber and, with reverence and humility, sat by the side of Shree Krishna's feet, waiting for Him to wake up. In the meantime, Duryodhan also arrived, and in his characteristic arrogance, sat on a chair behind Shree Krishna's head. When Shree Krishna awoke, His eyes naturally fell first upon Arjun, and later, He was made aware of the presence of Duryodhan as well. Both parties sought His assistance in the war. Since Arjun and Duryodhan were both Shree Krishna's cousins, He did not wish to be blamed of partiality. So, He offered that to one side He would give His huge army of the kingdom of Dwaraka, while to the other side, He would Himself be on their side but without any weapons. Since Shree Krishna had seen Arjun first upon waking up, He gave him the first choice. Arjun elected to have Shree Krishna on His side albeit without weapons. He decided that if God was with Him, He could never lose. Duryodhan was pleased by Arjun's choice for he believed solely in material strength based upon military might. The Supreme Lord Shree Krishna thus became Arjun's charioteer in the war.

On the verge of the battle, huge armies had gathered on either side upon the battlefield of Kurukshetra. This was the impending war of Mahabharat (the great battle of India). The situation was extremely grave, as an era was about to self-destruct itself in internecine warfare. Just before the combat was about to begin, Arjun requested Lord Krishna to pull his chariot between the two armies. On seeing the warriors who had arrayed themselves for the war, Arjun lost heart. In a fit of despondency, he threw down his bow and refused to fight.

Arjun was a victim of a moral paradox. On the one hand, he was facing people who deserved his respect and veneration, such as his grandfather, Bheeshma, his teacher, Dronacharya, among other elders. On the other hand, his duty as a warrior was to fight the war of righteousness. Yet, no fruits of victory seemed to justify such a heinous act. It seemed like a dilemma without solution because even the fruits of victory could not justify such a heinous act. Bewildered, demoralised, disappointed with life, and dejected with the events, Arjun surrendered to the Supreme Lord and supplicated for guidance on what the proper course of action for him should be. In this state of Arjun's moral confusion that Shree Krishna set out to enlighten him.

Historicity of Events

Questions are raised about the historical accuracy of the events described in the Mahabharat. Similar controversies have raged in Europe over the historicity of Christ and events of his life as described in the Bible. Such a debate may have significance for historians but is not important from a spiritual perspective. It doesn't really matter whether Jesus was actually born in Nazareth or Bethlehem, as long as we can benefit from his teachings and live a sacred life in alignment with his instructions. Likewise, in seeking the kernel of thought of the Gita, we need not concern ourselves with the details of history, but with the spiritual principles that it conveys and their usefulness in walking the path of enlightenment.

Even if we maintain divine sentiments toward a stone deity, we become purified. It is our own divine sentiments purify our mind. Then there is absolutely no reason for us to doubt the purifying effect of contemplating upon the pastimes of God with divine sentiments.

When I mentioned to devotees that I intended to write a commentary on the Bhagavad Gita, some in the West suggested that I should make an allegorical interpretation of the Mahabharat and explain the Gita accordingly. They referred me to many of the commentaries popular in the West which have interpreted the whole situation as an allegory. Making such an allegorical interpretation is the easiest thing to do, but the problem with such an approach is that it destroys the beautiful basis of devotion, which the Mahabharat presents us with and pulls it down to the level of dry intellectual analysis. It is like ordering a field to be bulldozed for agricultural cultivation without knowledge of the wonderful flower garden that is already growing in it. Similarly, the intention of Sage Ved Vyas in revealing these scriptures was not only to provide us with treasure chests of divine knowledge but also to present the reader with the enchanting Names, Forms, Virtues, Pastimes, Associates, and Abodes of God, which provide a sweet basis for attaching the mind to the Supreme Lord.

So, let us not succumb to the temptation of reducing everything to lifeless allegorical interpretations. As the Bhagavad Gita already contains in its original form fathomless knowledge to provide abundant nourishment for the intellect, any attempt to explain it with dry intellectualisation on behalf of commentators would be an unnecessary endeavour. Sage Ved Vyas too was aware of the allegory as a literary tool, and he has used it effectively in his writings. Hence, let us allow him to reveal his own allegories wherever necessary as he takes us on a journey of both head and heart, and relates the pastimes and message of the Supreme Lord when He descended in the human form upon the earth.

The Language of the Gita

The Bhagavad Gita was recorded and presented to us in Sanskrit, India's historic language. This is decidedly befitting as Sanskrit possesses a highly evolved vocabulary for expressing spiritual concepts. Among all the languages of the world, it has the most perfect grammar that has remained unchanged for thousands of years. Recently, NASA scientists developing a computer language for work in Artificial Intelligence were astonished to discover that Sanskrit has a perfect computer-compatible grammar for the purpose. Rick Briggs at the NASA Ames Research Center, CA, wrote in his paper 'Knowledge Representation in Sanskrit and Artificial Intelligence' (*The AI Magazine Spring*, 1985 #39): 'There is at least one language, Sanskrit, which for the duration of almost one thousand years was a living spoken language with a considerable literature of its own. Besides works of literary value, there was a long philosophical and grammatical tradition that has continued to exist with undiminished vigor until the present century. Among the accomplishments of the grammarians can be reckoned a method for paraphrasing Sanskrit in a manner that is identical not only in essence but in form with current work in Artificial Intelligence.'

As the medium of the Bhagavad Gita, the Sanskrit language imparts both profoundness and sophistication. At the same time, it is flexible and provides scope for all traditions to see their perspective included in the divine dialogue.

Worldwide popularity of the Gita

From the time of Shankaracharya, great philosophers customarily wrote their respective commentaries on the Bhagavad Gita. It was also translated from Sanskrit into many other Indian languages, such as the *Jñāneśhwarī*, written by Saint Jnaneswar in Marathi in the thirteenth century.

During the British Raj, the popularity of the Gita spread worldwide. It was first translated in English by Charles Wilkins, a merchant with the East India Company. His rendition made a deep impression on the American Transcendentalists, a group of independent thinkers in New England. Ralph Waldo Emerson made it the basis of his poem *Brahma*. Emerson made the Gita required reading for all those who objected to evangelical Christianity. His friend, Henry David Thoreau, was also a tremendous enthusiast of the Gita and incorporated its teachings on karm yog in his own lifestyle and philosophy. And so, for the first time it became a part of the counter culture. A century later, T.S. Eliot had a lifelong interest in Indian philosophy and incorporated it in his poetry. The Gita also appealed to the German Romantics, notably Schlegel, Humboldt, and Goethe.

Back home in India, leaders of the independence movement, who were winning the respect of the nation, began attributing the source of their inspiration to the Bhagavad Gita. Bal Gangadhar Tilak, the leader of the freedom struggle before Mahatma Gandhi and a respected karm yogi, wrote an extensive and scholarly commentary on the Gita. After him, Mahatma Gandhi declared that whenever he faced disappointments, he turned to the Gita for guidance and solace. Gandhi's thinking inspired two other giants of the twentieth century in the West, Martin Luther King Jr. and Nelson Mandela. This cross-seeding of ideas that took place between east and west further enhanced the popularity of the Gita. In the 1960s another wave of counter culture swept America. Continuing in the tradition of Swami Vivekananda and Paramhansa Yogananda, who had visited the western world earlier, many Indian gurus began arriving in America, such as Swami Satchitananda and Swami Prabhupada. They all referred to the Gita as the authoritative reference for their teachings. As a result, the Bhagavad Gita rapidly reached the status it possesses today as one of the most popular and well-read books of wisdom in the history of humankind.

Its Teachings are Above Cult and Creed

There is one kind of teaching that propagates a dogma, cult or creed. There is another kind of teaching that propagates ideals and life principles that are supremely above all cults and creeds. Scholars who regard the Gita as the fruit of some particular religious system do injustice to the universality of its message. The ideas it presents are not the speculations of a philosophic intellect; rather, they are the enduring truths of spiritual realities that are verifiable in our own existence and sojourn through life. Thus, when the first English edition of the Gita was published, Warren Hastings, the then Governor General of India, wrote in his foreword: 'These (writings of the inhabitants of India) will survive when the British dominion of India shall have long ceased to exist, and when the sources which it yielded of wealth and power are lost to remembrance.'

Our approach in studying the Gita must therefore not be a scholastic or academic scrutiny of its message, nor an effort to place its philosophy in the context of contending schools of thought. The Gita is not a treatise of metaphysical philosophy despite the profusion of metaphysical ideas that arise from its pages. Instead, it seeks the highest truth for the highest practical utility, not for intellectual or even spiritual satisfaction, but as the truth that saves and opens to us the passage from our present mortal imperfection to an immortal perfection. Consequently, we must approach it for help and light in receiving the living message that can benefit human beings attain the highest welfare and spiritual perfection.

Commentaries on the Gita

Books of divine knowledge naturally invite several commentaries to be written on them. These commentaries serve to elucidate the eternal edicts they contain, just as countries have their respective law books, such as the constitution. In addition, there are commentaries published by lawyers that assist in studying these books. Similarly, commentaries on the scriptures help in bringing forth the gems of knowledge embedded in these holy books. Due to its vast popularity, the Bhagavad Gita has had hundreds of commentaries written on it. Some of the important commentators in history have been Jagadguru Shankaracharya, Jagadguru Ramanujacharya, Jagadguru Madhvacharya, Jagadguru Nimbarkacharya, and Mahaprabhu Vallabhacharya, who were all founders of major Vedantic traditions. In the Shaiva tradition, the renowned philosopher Abhinavgupta wrote a commentary, with a slightly variant rescension, called *Gitarth Samagraha*.

The beauty about divine knowledge is that the more it is churned, the more nectar it produces, with these insightful commentaries, undoubtedly, enriching the world. Simultaneously, we must be aware that commentaries by the great pontiffs conform to their respective life missions. These great acharyas preached the Absolute Truth according to time, place, and circumstance, always with the aim of humankind's well-being. Thus, they maintained a missionary zeal to propagate their favorite ideas and portrayed their respective perspectives in all the verses of the Bhagavad Gita.

While according full respect to their accomplished works, we should bear in mind that Shree Krishna was not an *Advaita vādī* (non-dualist), *Viśhiṣhṭ advaita vādī* (qualified non-dualist), *Dwait vādī* (dualist), or *Dwait advaita vādī* (dual non-dualist). He was beyond the polemics of philosophers and so was His message. Thus, we see how the principles of theism, asceticism, dualism, pragmatism, karm, jnana, bhakti, hatha, and *Sānkhya*, among other concepts, are all woven into His teachings. We must therefore be wary of limiting the meaning of the Bhagavad Gita within the perspective of one philosophic tradition, and instead, view it as a window to the whole Absolute Truth.

This is the manner of thinking of Jagadguru Shree Kripaluji Maharaj, who freely quotes from the works of wisdom of all the famous Indian saints and even Western ones without getting mired in any one *sampradāya* (religious tradition) or *paramparā* (disciplic succession). When he was asked which of the four *Vaiṣhṇav sampradāyas* he belonged to, he humbly pointed out that the Absolute Truth is one and does not restrict itself to any particular *sampradāya*. All genuine *sampradāyas* have begun from God. So, if there is only one *sampradāya*, which is the *sampradāya* of God, then why should we divide them into four? And if we choose to divide the Truth in this manner, the divisions will only keep multiplying. This is exactly what has happened to the *sampradāyas*, as each of the four original ones has further divided into branches and sub-branches, all claiming sole ownership over the entire region of the Absolute Truth. This tendency has partitioned the one *Sanātan Dharma* (Eternal Religion) into numerous *sāmpradāyic* fragments.

As boundaries in the world break down and the flow of information among people enhances, the idea that one creed, race, sect, or religion is the sole guardian of the Universal Truth is getting fewer and fewer buyers. Let us align ourselves with this surge of broad-mindedness of the intellect and permit the shining light of knowledge from the Bhagavad Gita to illumine the whole indivisible, untainted Truth. This is, after all, the original pristine purpose not only of the Bhagavad Gita, but also of all the Vedic scriptures.

About Jagadguru Shree Kripaluji Maharaj

Jagadguru Shree Kripaluji Maharaj was a descended saint who reestablished ancient Vedic knowledge in modern times. At the age of thirty-four, he lectured for ten days in sophisticated Sanskrit, before the Kashi Vidvat Parishat, the supreme body of five hundred Vedic scholars in the holy city of Kashi. In his lectures, he quoted masterfully from hundreds of Vedic scriptures to reveal the simple, straightforward path to God-realisation for the present times. When the esteemed body of erudite scholars realised that Kripaluji Maharaj's knowledge was deeper than the combined knowledge of all of them together, they honoured him with the title of Jagadguru or 'Spiritual Master of the World'. He thus became the fifth saint in Indian history to receive the original title of Jagadguru, after Jagadguru Shankaracharya, Jagadguru Nimbarkacharya, Jagadguru Ramanujacharya, and Jagadguru Madhvacharya.

The scholars were so impressed with his command of the ancient Vedic texts that they showered many more accolades upon him, such as:

Jagadguruttam—The supreme Jagadguru of Indian history.

Ved Mārga Pratiṣhṭhāpanāchārya—The establisher of the true path revealed by the Vedas.

***Nikhil Darshan Samanvayāchārya*—The reconciler of the import of all the scriptures.**

Sanātan Vaidik Dharmapratiṣhṭhāpanāchārya—The re-establisher of the eternal Vedic religion in this world.

Satsampradāya Paramāchārya—The founder of the true tradition of spiritual knowledge.

This commentary on the Bhagavad Gita is based upon the insightful understanding of its verses as revealed to me by my Spiritual Master. The objective of this commentary is not to propose a new interpretation but simply to bring forth the meaning of the verses spoken by Shree Krishna. For this objective, I have not hesitated to quote from the books of wisdom and the teachings of saints, holy personalities, and luminaries from around the world.

Constraints in Translation

It is often well-nigh impossible to find terms in English that are semantically coextensive with the Indic terms. The word meanings of any language are forged by the cultural and philosophical framework of the people who speak that language. Thus, Sanskrit words derive their meanings from the conceptual system of thought in India. Being much different from the western system of thought that has shaped the meanings of English words, there are unavoidable constraints in any work of translation. All renditions of Sanskrit terms in English are, therefore, approximations.

For example, there is no English word that accurately conveys the meaning of 'Brahman' (the formless, attributeless, all-pervading aspect of God). The same problem typically arises with translating 'dharma' into English; path of righteousness, one's incumbent duty, virtue, and prescribed duties, among other phrases, are all gross approximations of its meaning. In all such cases where suitable English phrases were not available, the original Sanskrit terms have been retained. Such words and phrases have been italicised for identification, and the important ones included in the Glossary at the back of the book, with detailed explanations.

Helpful Points to Make the Reading Easier

Understanding a couple of things will make it easier to read this commentary. First, the Gita is a conversation within a conversation within a conversation. The *Bheeshma Parva* of the Mahabharat, of which the Bhagavad Gita is a part, is related by Sage Vaishampayan to King Janmejaya. Vaishampayan is thus the one who tells Janmejaya: *Sanjaya uvācha* 'Sanjay said', *Dhritarashtra uvācha* 'Dhritarashtra said', and so on. However, Vaishampayan and Janmejaya do not figure directly as speakers in the Bhagavad Gita.

The Gita begins as a dialogue between King Dhritarashtra and his minister Sanjay. Since Dhritarashtra was blind, he could not be personally present on the battlefield. Dhritarashtra initiates the conversation by asking Sanjay about the proceedings in the battlefield; he does not speak again in the Gita. He is answered by Sanjay, who relates the happenings. Sanjay was a disciple of Sage Ved Vyas, and by the grace of his teacher, possessed the mystic ability of distant vision. Thus, he could see from afar all that transpired on the battleground and was giving Dhritarashtra a first-hand account of the events on the warfront. Sanjay pops in and out throughout the book as he relates to Dhritarashtra what he sees and hears. Thus, he says: *Śhrī Bhagavān uvācha* 'The Supreme Lord said', and *Arjun uvācha* 'Arjun said', and so on.

The major portion of the dialogue is between Lord Krishna and Arjun. Arjun asks questions and Shree Krishna answers. The conversation is a somewhat one-sided as Shree Krishna does most of the talking.

Second, there is a profusion of appellations also known as epithets. For example, Shree Krishna is referred to by many names, such as Hrishikesh, Keshav, Govind, Madhusudan, Achyut, and many more.

Similarly, Arjun is called Dhananjaya, Gudakesh, Kaunteya, Parantapa, and others. Often, these names are deliberately chosen to convey a particular meaning or flavour to the conversation. Such emphasis has been explained in the commentary whenever necessary.

Important Terms in the Bhagavad Gita

A synopsis of the entire Bhagavad Gita is beyond the scope of this introduction, first because it will preempt your reading pleasure in discovering it for yourself, and second because it is impossible to summarise everything that Lord Krishna has said in it. However, a few common terms in the Bhagavad Gita and the rest of the Vedic literature are explained here to help the reader easily grasp the concepts presented therein.

God (Bhagavan): In the Vedic scriptures, including the Bhagavad Gita, God refers to the one Supreme Entity. He is all-powerful, all-knowing, and omnipresent. He is the Creator, Maintainer, and Dissolver of this creation. He possesses innumerable contradictory attributes at the same time. Thus, He is near and yet far, big and yet small, formless and yet possessing a form, without qualities and yet possesses innumerable qualities.

People approach the Supreme Entity in three ways. Some relate to Him in His formless all-pervading aspect called Brahman. Others choose to worship Him as the Paramatma, who is seated within the hearts of all living beings. Yet others seek to worship Him in His personal form, as Bhagavan. All these three—Brahman, Paramatma, and Bhagavan—are different aspects of the one Ultimate Being.

Occasionally, out of His causeless grace, God descends upon the earth and engages in divine pastimes to uplift the souls. Such a descension is called an Avatar. Shree Ram and Shree Krishna are both Avatars of the Supreme Divine Personality. Since God is all-powerful, He is not limited to one form; He can manifest in innumerable forms. But we must remember that all these are different forms of the one Divine Lord, and not different Gods.

Soul (atma): The individual soul is a tiny fragmental part of God. It is spiritual in nature, and hence distinct from the material body. The presence of the soul imparts consciousness to the body, which is made from insentient matter. When the soul leaves, the body becomes dead matter again. The body is perishable while the soul is eternal.

According to the Vedic understanding, the soul is without beginning or end; it neither originated on birth nor will it be destroyed when the body dies. What we term as death in worldly parlance is merely the soul changing bodies. The Bhagavad Gita likens this to a person changing clothes to put on new ones. The soul is not free to choose its next birth; that is decided by God based upon the Law of Karma.

Why has the material energy, maya, enveloped us in the first place? This is because we have turned away from God. God is of the nature of light, while the material energy is of the nature of darkness. One who turns away from light is naturally overcome by darkness. Likewise, the souls who have turned their backs towards Him have been covered by material energy.

An understanding of the Vedic terminology regarding the word 'atma' will be helpful. The soul that is in the embodied state is called jivatma because it keeps the body alive (*jīvit*). These words, atma and jivatma, are interchangeably used while referring to souls in the material realm. Along with the individual soul (jivatma), God is also seated within the body. He is called Paramatma (Supreme Soul). He accompanies the jivatma life after life, into whichever bodily form it goes. The Paramatma does not interfere with the activities of the living entity, but remains as a silent Witness. The jivatma is forgetful of its eternal friend and is struggling to enjoy the material energy.

The word atma, which literally means soul, occurs regularly in the Gita, for a variety of usages. In some places, atma is used to refer to the jivatma, without including the body, mind, and intellect (e.g. verse 6.20). At times, it refers to the entire personality of the living being, including the soul and the body, mind, intellect (e.g. verse 6.20). Occasionally, atma refers to the mind (e.g. verse 6.5); in a couple of places, atma is used for the intellect (e.g. verse 5.7). And in some places, it is used for Paramatma (Supreme Soul or God, e.g. verse 6.29).

Material Nature (prakriti or maya): The material energy, called prakriti, is not antithetical to God; rather, it is one of His innumerable powers. At the time of dissolution, prakriti remains latent within the being of God. When He wishes to create the world, He glances at it, and it begins to unwind from its latent state. It then manifests the various gross and subtle elements of creation.

While one aspect of the material energy, maya, is responsible for creating the world, its second aspect is instrumental in keeping the souls bound to the samsara of life and death (repeated cycle of life and death that the soul undergoes in the material world). Maya makes us forget our identity as divine souls and puts us under the illusion of being the material body. Hence, we pursue bodily pleasures in the world. After innumerable lifetimes of endeavouring in the material realm, the soul comes to the realisation that the infinite divine bliss it seeks will not be attained from the world but from God. Then, it must follow the path of Yog to reach the stage of perfection. When the soul achieves perfect union with God, it becomes liberated from the clutches of the material energy.

Modes of Nature (Guṇas): The material energy has three constituent modes: sattva guna (mode of goodness), rajo guna (mode of passion), tamo guna (mode of ignorance). These gunas exist in varying proportions in our personality and influence us. The mode of ignorance induces laziness, stupor, ignorance, anger, violence, and addiction, thereby, pulling the soul deeper into the darkness of material illusion. The mode of passion inflames the desires of the mind and senses and induces one to endeavour passionately for fulfilling worldly ambitions. The mode of goodness illumines a person with knowledge and nourishes virtuous qualities, such as kindness, patience, and tolerance. It makes the mind peaceful and suitable for spiritual practice. A *sādhak* (spiritual practitioner) must strive to reduce the modes of ignorance and passion by cultivating the mode of goodness, and then transcend even sattva guna. God is transcendental to the three guṇas; by attaching the mind to Him, we too can ascend to the transcendental platform.

Yajna (Sacrifice): Generally, the term yajna refers to fire sacrifice. In the Bhagavad Gita, yajna includes all the prescribed actions laid down in the scriptures, when they are done as an offering to the Supreme.

The elements of nature are integral parts of the system of God's creation. All parts of the system naturally draw from and give back to the whole. The sun lends stability to the earth and provides heat and light necessary for life to exist. Earth creates food from its soil for our nourishment and also holds essential minerals in its womb for a civilised lifestyle. Air moves the life force in our body and enables transmission of sound energy. We humans too are an integral part of the entire system of God's creation. The air that we breathe, the earth that we walk upon, the water that we drink, and the light that illumines our day, are all gifts of Creation to us. While we partake of these gifts to sustain our lives, we also have our duties towards the integral system. The Bhagavad Gita states that we are obliged to participate with the creative force of nature by performing our prescribed duties in the service of God. That is the yajna God expects from us.

Consider the example of a hand. It is an integral part of the body. It receives its nourishment—blood, oxygen, nutrients, and so on—from the body, and in turn, it performs necessary functions for the body. If the hand looks on this service as burdensome and decides to get severed from the body, it cannot sustain itself for even a few minutes. It is in the performance of its yajna towards the body that the self-interest of the hand is also fulfilled. Similarly, we individual souls are tiny parts of the Supreme, and we all have our role to play in the grand scheme of things. When we perform our yajna towards Him, our self-interest is naturally satiated.

Sacrifice, or yajna, should be performed in divine consciousness as an offering to the Supreme Lord. However, people vary in their understanding, and hence perform sacrifice in different manners with dissimilar consciousness. Persons with lesser understanding and a desire for material rewards make offerings to the celestial gods.

***Devatās* (Celestial gods):** These are beings that live in the higher planes of existence within this material world, called *swarg* (the celestial abodes). These celestial beings (*devatās*) are not God; rather, they are souls like us. They occupy specific positions in the system of God's administration and oversee specific aspects of the material world.

Consider the Federal government of a country. There is a Secretary of State, a Finance Secretary, a Secretary of Commerce, an Agriculture Secretary, and so on. These are positions which select people occupy for a limited tenure. At the end of its tenure, when the government changes, all these leaders change too. The positions remain but the people holding these positions change. Similarly, in the governance of the affairs of the world, there are positions such as *Agni Devatā* (god of fire), *Vayu Devatā* (god of wind), *Varun Devatā* (god of ocean), *Indra Devatā* (king of the celestial gods), and many other gods. Souls selected by virtue of their deeds in past lives occupy these seats for a certain amount of time. Once their time is up, they fall from these positions and others occupy these seats. Thus, souls become celestial gods only temporarily and, as a result, we cannot compare them to the Supreme Lord.

Many people worship the celestial gods for material rewards. However, we must remember that these *devatās* cannot grant either liberation from material bondage or God-realisation. Even if they do bestow material benefits, it is only by the powers they have received from God. Hence, the Bhagavad Gita repeatedly discourages people from worshipping the celestial gods and states that those who are situated in knowledge worship the Supreme Lord alone.

Divine Abode of God: This material realm including all the celestial abodes, the earth planet, and the hellish planes of existence, is only one-fourth of God's entire creation. It is for those souls who have not yet attained spiritual perfection. Here, we experience suffering in various forms, such as birth, disease, old age, and death. Beyond this entire material realm is the spiritual dimension consisting of three-fourths of God's creation. It contains innumerable divine abodes of God that are referred to in Vedic literature as *Saket Lok* (abode of Lord Ram), *Golok* (abode of Lord Krishna), *Vaikunth Lok* (abode of Lord Narayan), *Shiv Lok* (abode of Lord Shiv), *Devi Lok* (abode of Mother Durga), and so on. The Bhagavad Gita repeatedly mentions that one who attains God-realisation goes to the divine abodes of God and does not return to cycle of life and death in the material world again.

***Śharaṇāgati* (Surrender):** God is divine and cannot be comprehended by our material intellect. Similarly, He cannot be perceived by our material senses—the eyes cannot see Him, the ears cannot hear Him, and so on. However, if He decides to bestow His grace on someone, He grants His divine energy to that fortunate soul. On receiving His divine grace, one can see Him, know Him, and attain Him. This grace of God is not a whimsical act from His side. He bestows His divine grace on those who surrender to Him. Thus, the Bhagavad Gita emphasises that the soul must learn the secret of surrendering to the Supreme Lord.

Yog: The word Yog has been used in the Gita in almost one hundred fifty places, for multiple purposes. It is formed from the root *yuj*, which means 'to unite'. From the spiritual perspective, the union of the individual soul with God is called Yog (e.g. verse 5.21). However, the science of accomplishing that union is also called Yog (e.g. verse 4.1). Again, the state of perfection achieved through the process is also referred to as Yog (e.g. 6.18). Union with God naturally disentangles one from misery born of contact with material nature. Hence, the state of freedom from suffering is referred to as Yog as well (verse 6.23). Since perfection is accompanied by evenness of mind, such equanimity has also been called Yog (verse 2.48). One who is in the state of Yog performs all activities perfectly, in a spirit of devotion to God, and hence dexterity at work is also referred to as Yog (verse 2.50).

One may enquire about the necessity of Yog. The answer is that searching for happiness in the material world is like chasing a mirage in the desert. The nature of material desires is such that fulfilling them is like quenching a fire by pouring oil on it. For a moment, the fire is subdued, but then it flares up with an even greater intensity. Similarly, fulfilling the desires of the mind and senses leads to greed. But obstructing them is also detrimental because it leads to anger. We must, thus, understand the root cause of why desires arise and then seek to address it.

It all begins when we contemplate that there is happiness in some person or object. Repeated contemplation results in attachment of the mind, and attachment gives rise to desire. So if we can firmly decide that the divine bliss the soul is seeking is not in material objects, these desires will stop arising. However, the desire for happiness is intrinsic to the nature of the soul because it is a tiny part of the infinite ocean of divine bliss. This nature can only be satisfied when the soul attains the infinite bliss of God. Hence, knowingly or unknowingly, every soul is struggling to reach that state of divine consciousness or Yog.

The various paths of achieving union with God are referred to as different systems of Yog, such as karm yog, jnana yog, ashtang yog, and bhakti yog. Thus, spiritual practitioners are in general called yogis (e.g. verse 4.25) or *sādhaks*. Occasionally, the word Yog refers specifically to the process of ashtang yog e.g. verse 4.28. In such instances, yogi specifically denotes the practitioner of ashtang yog.

Jnana yog (Path of Knowledge): In this system of Yog, the emphasis is on self-knowledge. The Gita occasionally mentions it as *Sānkhya Yog* as well. Through the practice of intellectual discrimination, the jnani focusses on realising the self, which is distinct from all physical designations and contaminations. Self-realisation is considered as the ultimate goal of perfection. The practice of jnana yog is based on self-effort without support of God's grace. Hence, it is a difficult path, and there is danger of downfall at every step.

Ashtang yog (The eight-fold path): It involves a gradual process of purification beginning with mechanical practices and progressing to the control of the mind. In it, the life force is raised through the *suṣhumṇā* channel in the spinal column. It is brought between the eyebrows, which is the region of the third eye (the inner eye). It is then made to focus on the Supreme Lord with great devotion.

This process was presented in a structured system of practice containing eight stages by Maharshi Patanjali in the famous text written by him, called *Yog Sutras*. Thereby, it came to be known as ashtang yog or the eight-fold system of Yog. A variation of this is hatha yog, in which the emphasis is on austerities. The hatha yogi strives to gain mastery over the mind and senses by exercising the force of willpower.

In many places, Vedic literature also states that there are only three paths to God-realisation—karm yog, jnana yog, and bhakti yog. In such a classification, ashtang yog is included in jnana yog.

Bhakti yog (Path of Devotion): This path involves attaching the mind to the Abodes, Associates, Names, Forms, Virtues, and Pastimes of God through selfless and exclusive love. One develops a loving relationship with God by seeing Him as the eternal Father, Mother, Friend, Master, and Soul Beloved. By surrendering to Him and uniting the individual will with the divine will, the devotee attracts the grace of God and achieves the goal of spiritual perfection more easily than by the other paths. Although the Bhagavad Gita embraces all the systems of Yog, it consistently emphasises the path of bhakti as the superior system of Yog. This repeated pronouncement by Shree Krishna that He can only be known through bhakti is highlighted in the commentary to dispel the misconception amongst some about bhakti being an inferior system of Yog.

Karm-yog (Path of Action): Karm refers to performing one's worldly obligations and responsibilities, while Yog refers to union with God. So the practice of uniting the mind with God even while doing one's obligatory duties in the world is karm yog. This requires detaching the mind from the fruits of actions by developing a resolute conviction of the intellect that all work is meant solely for the pleasure of God. Thus, the Gita occasionally refers to it as *buddhi yog* or the 'Yog of the intellect'. Since most people practice spirituality while living in household life and discharging their worldly duties, karm yog becomes necessary for them alongside with any other system of Yog they may pursue.

With this brief explanation of some important terms, I now leave it to the reader to go through the 'Song of God' and discover first-hand the wonderful divine wisdom offered by the Supreme Lord Shree Krishna.

Gratitude

I offer my deepest and heartfelt gratitude to my gurudev, Jagadguru Shree Kripaluji Maharaj, who was an ocean of divine love and transcendental knowledge. It is only by his grace that an unqualified soul like me has been able to receive a drop of knowledge from the infinite reservoir of wisdom that he possesses. This humble effort is in pursuance of his instruction to preach the Vedic knowledge in the service of humankind.

I express the indebtedness of all humankind to that most benevolent and munificent sage, Ved Vyas, who bestowed upon us the auspicious scripture, the Mahabharat, with the 'Song of God' embedded in it.

I hope the book will fulfill the sincere objective with which it has been published and help seekers in their quest for the Absolute Truth and in their journey to God-realisation.

In the service of the Lord,

Swami Mukundananda

Useful Note

The Bhagavad Gita has eighteen chapters, each with multiple verses. For every verse, the content has been organised in the following manner:

1. **Sanskrit Verse.** First, the original Sanskrit verse is presented in Devanagari script.
2. **Transliteration.** A transliteration of the verse in English script is given, with diacritical marks denoting the exact pronunciation.
3. **Word Meanings.** The English meanings of individual Sanskrit words and phrases are given.
4. **Translation.** Next comes the English meaning of the Sanskrit verse.
5. **Commentary.** Finally, an explanation of the verse follows.
6. **Link.** Occasionally, at the end of the explanation, a sentence or two has been italicised. The italicised sentences, wherever they occur, help the reader establish the link to the subject matter of the subsequent verses.

Diacritical marks have been used with Sanskrit words to depict their exact pronunciation. In the appendices, you will find a **Pronunciation Guide** for the English transliteration. Diacriticals have not been used with Sanskrit words that are now a part of English language, such as 'samsara'. For the sake of elegance of presentation and ease of reading, diacritical marks have not been used for many proper nouns as well, such as 'Shree Krishna'. Where Sanskrit words do not have equivalent English phrases that convey the meaning accurately, the original Sanskrit terms have been retained. These have been included for in the **Glossary of Sanskrit Words** at the back of the book with detailed explanations. Sometimes for ease of reading, directly after the word, its meaning is presented in brackets.

Since various appellations have been used for Shree Krishna and Arjun in the Bhagavad Gita, a **List of Appellations** and their meanings is given for easy reference.

The **Chapter Headings** for the eighteen chapters reveal the content of the chapter and are self-explanatory.

If you wish to locate a particular subject in the book, you can look up the **Subject Index** in the appendices.

A similar **Index of the Verses Quoted** in the commentary is also presented.

CHAPTER 1

Arjun Viṣhād Yog

Lamenting the Consequences of War

The Bhagavad Gita was spoken on the battleground of the colossal Mahabharat war that was just about to begin between two sets of cousins, the Kauravas and the Pandavas. A detailed description of developments that led to the gigantic war is given in the *Introduction* to this book, in the section *The Setting of the Bhagavad Gita*.

The Bhagavad Gita begins to unfold as a dialogue between King Dhritarashtra and his minister Sanjay. Since Dhritarashtra was blind, he could not be personally present on the battlefield. Hence, Sanjay was giving him a first-hand account of the events on the warfront. Sanjay was the disciple of Sage Ved Vyas, the celebrated writer of the Mahabharat. Ved Vyas possessed the mystic power of being able to see what was happening in distant places. He bestowed the same power to Sanjay so that Sanjay could narrate the events of the battlefield to Dhritarashtra.

धृतराष्ट्र उवाच ।
धर्मक्षेत्रे कुरुक्षेत्रे समवेता युयुत्सवः ।
मामकाः पाण्डवाश्चैव किमकुर्वत सञ्जय ।।1।।

dhṛitarāśhtra uvācha
dharma-kṣhetre kuru-kṣhetre samavetā yuyutsavaḥ
māmakāḥ pāṇḍavāśhchaiva kimakurvata sañjaya

dhṛitarāśhtraḥ uvācha—Dhritarashtra said; *dharma-kṣhetre*—the land of dharma; *kuru-kṣhetre*—at Kurukshetra; *samavetāḥ*—having gathered; *yuyutsavaḥ*—desiring to fight; *māmakāḥ*—my sons; *pāṇḍavāḥ*—the sons of Pandu; *cha*—and; *eva*—certainly; *kim*—what; *akurvata*—did they do; *sañjaya*—Sanjay.

Dhritarashtra said: O Sanjay, after gathering on the holy field of Kurukshetra, and desiring to fight, what did my sons and the sons of Pandu do?

King Dhritarashtra, apart from being blind from birth, was also bereft of spiritual wisdom. His attachment to his sons made him deviate from the path of virtue and usurp the rightful kingdom of the Pandavas. He was conscious of the injustice he had done toward his own nephews, the sons of Pandu. His guilty conscience worried him about the outcome of the battle, consequently, he inquired from Sanjay about the events on the battlefield of Kurukshetra, where the war was to be fought.

In this verse, the question he asked Sanjay was, having gathered on the battlefield, what did his sons and the sons of Pandu do? Now, it was obvious that they had assembled there with the sole purpose of fighting. So, it was natural that they would fight. Why did Dhritarashtra feel the need to ask what they did?

His doubt can be discerned from the words he used—*dharma kṣhetre,* meaning, the land of dharma (virtuous conduct). Kurukshetra was a sacred land. In the *Shatapath Brahman* of the *Yajur Veda*, it is described as: *kurukṣhetraṁ deva yajanam.* 'Kurukshetra is the sacrificial arena of the celestial gods.' It was thus the land that nourished dharma. Dhritarashtra apprehended that the influence of the holy land of Kurukshetra would arouse the faculty of discrimination in his sons, and they would regard the massacre of their relatives, the Pandavas, as improper. Thinking in this manner, they might agree to a peaceful settlement. Dhritarashtra felt great dissatisfaction at this possibility. He thought if his sons negotiated a truce, the Pandavas would continue to remain an impediment for them. Hence, it was preferable that the war take place. At the same time, he was uncertain of the consequences of the war and wished to ascertain the fate of his sons. Consequently, he asked Sanjay about the events at the battleground of Kurukshetra where the two armies had gathered.

सञ्जय उवाच ।
दृष्ट्वा तु पाण्डवानीकं व्यूढं दुर्योधनस्तदा ।
आचार्यमुपसङ्गम्य राजा वचनमब्रवीत् ।।2।।

sañjaya uvācha
dṛiṣhṭvā tu pāṇḍavānīkaṁ vyūḍhaṁ duryodhanastadā
āchāryamupasaṅgamya rājā vachanamabravīt

sanjayaḥ uvācha—Sanjay said; *dṛiṣhṭvā*—on observing; *tu*—but; *pāṇḍava-anīkam*—the Pandava army; *vyūḍham*—standing in a military formation; *duryodhanaḥ*—King Duryodhan; *tadā*—then; *āchāryam*—teacher; *upasaṅgamya*—approached; *rājā*—the king; *vachanam*—words; *abravīt*—spoke.

Sanjay said: On observing the Pandava army standing in military formation, King Duryodhan approached his teacher Dronacharya, and said the following words.

Dhritarashtra was looking for an affirmation that the battle would still be fought by his sons. Sanjay understood Dhritarashtra's intent behind the question and confirmed that there would definitely be war by saying that the Pandavas were standing in military formation ready for war. He further turned the conversation to the subject of what Duryodhan was doing.

Duryodhan, the eldest son of Dhritarashtra, possessed a very evil and cruel nature. Since Dhritarashtra was blind, Duryodhan practically ruled the kingdom of Hastinapur on his behalf. He had a strong dislike for the Pandavas, and was determined to eliminate them, so that he could rule unopposed. He had assumed that the Pandavas would not be able to mobilize an army that could face his. But what happened was to the contrary, and beholding the extent of military might they had gathered, he was perturbed and unnerved.

Duryodhan's move to approach his military guru, Dronacharya, revealed that he was feared the outcome of the war. He went to Dronacharya with the pretense of offering respect, but his actual purpose was to palliate his own anxiety. It was then that Duryodhan spoke nine verses beginning with the next one.

पश्यैतां पाण्डुपुत्राणामाचार्य महतीं चमूम् ।
व्यूढां द्रुपदपुत्रेण तव शिष्येण धीमता ।।3।।

paśhyaitāṁ pāṇḍu-putrāṇām āchārya mahatīṁ chamūm
vyūḍhāṁ drupada-putreṇa tava śhiṣhyeṇa dhīmatā

paśhya—behold; *etām*—this; *pāṇḍu-putrāṇām*—of the sons of Pandu; *āchārya*—respected teacher; *mahatīm*—mighty; *chamūm*—army; *vyūḍhām*—arrayed in a military formation; *drupada-putreṇa*—son of Drupad, Dhrishtadyumna; *tava*—by your; *śhiṣhyeṇa*—disciple; *dhī-matā*—intelligent.

Duryodhan said: Respected teacher! Behold the mighty army of the sons of Pandu so expertly arrayed for battle by your own gifted disciple, the son of Drupad.

Duryodhan diplomatically pointed to his military preceptor, Dronacharya, the mistake committed by him in the past. Dronacharya had once had a political quarrel with King Drupad. Angered by the quarrel, Drupad performed a sacrifice and received a boon to beget a son who would be able to kill Dronacharya. As a result of this boon, Dhrishtadyumna was born to him.

Although Dronacharya knew the purpose of Dhrishtadyumna's birth, yet out of his large-heartedness, when Dhrishtadyumna was entrusted to him for military education, he did not hesitate to impart all his knowledge to him. Now, in the battle, Dhrishtadyumna had taken the side of the Pandavas as the commander-in-chief of their army, and he was the one who had arranged their military phalanx. Duryodhan thus hinted to his teacher that his leniency in the past had gotten them into the present trouble, and that he should not display any further leniency in fighting the Pandavas now.

अत्र शूरा महेष्वासा भीमार्जुनसमा युधि ।
युयुधानो विराटश्च द्रुपदश्च महारथः ।।4।।

धृष्टकेतुश्चेकितानः काशिराजश्च वीर्यवान् ।
पुरुजित्कुन्तिभोजश्च शैब्यश्च नरपुङ्गवः ।।5।।

युधामन्युश्च विक्रान्त उत्तमौजाश्च वीर्यवान् ।
सौभद्रो द्रौपदेयाश्च सर्व एव महारथाः ।।6।।

atra śhūrā maheṣhvāsā bhīmārjuna-samā yudhi
yuyudhāno virāṭaśhcha drupadaśhcha mahā-rathaḥ

dhṛiṣhṭaketuśhchekitānaḥ kāśhirājaśhcha vīryavān
purujit kuntibhojaśhcha śhaibyaśhcha nara-puṅgavaḥ

yudhāmanyuśhcha vikrānta uttamaujāśhcha vīryavān
saubhadro draupadeyāśhcha sarva eva mahā-rathāḥ

atra—here; *śhūrāḥ*—powerful warriors; *mahā-iṣhu-āsāḥ*—great bowmen; *bhīma-arjuna-samāḥ*—equal to Bheem and Arjun; *yudhi*—in military prowess; *yuyudhānaḥ*—Yuyudhan; *virāṭaḥ*—Virat; *cha*—and; *drupadaḥ*—Drupad; *cha*—also; *mahā-rathaḥ*—warriors who could single handedly match the strength of ten thousand ordinary warriors; *dhṛiṣhṭaketuḥ*—Dhrishtaketu; *chekitānaḥ*—Chekitan; *kāśhirājaḥ*—Kashiraj; *cha*—and; *vīrya-vān*—heroic; *purujit*—Purujit; *kuntibhojaḥ*—Kuntibhoj; *cha*—and; *śhaibyaḥ*—Shaibya; *cha*—and; *nara-puṅgavaḥ*—best of men; *yudhāmanyuḥ*—Yudhamanyu; *cha*—and; *vikrāntaḥ*—courageous; *uttamaujāḥ*—Uttamauja; *cha*—and; *vīrya-vān*—gallant; *saubhadraḥ*—the son of Subhadra; *draupadeyāḥ*—the sons of Draupadi; *cha*—and; *sarve*—all; *eva*—indeed; *mahā-rathāḥ*—warriors who could single handedly match the strength of ten thousand ordinary warriors.

Behold in their ranks are many powerful warriors, like Yuyudhan, Virat, and Drupad, wielding mighty bows and equal in military

prowess to Bheem and Arjun. There are also accomplished heroes like Dhrishtaketu, Chekitan, the gallant King of Kashi, Purujit, Kuntibhoj, and Shaibya—all the best of men. In their ranks, they also have the courageous Yudhamanyu, the gallant Uttamauja, the son of Subhadra, and the sons of Draupadi, who are all great warrior chiefs.

Due to the fear of the looming catastrophe, Duryodhan perceived the Pandavas army to be larger than it actually was. Expressing his anxiety, he identified the *mahārathīs* (warriors who could single handedly match the strength of ten thousand ordinary warriors) present on the Pandavas' side. Duryodhan mentioned these exceptional heroes amidst the Pandavas ranks, who were all great military commanders equal in strength to Arjun and Bheem, and who would be formidable in the battle.

अस्माकं तु विशिष्टा ये तान्निबोध द्विजोत्तम ।
नायका मम सैन्यस्य संज्ञार्थं तान्ब्रवीमि ते ।।7।।

asmākaṁ tu viśhiṣhṭā ye tānnibodha dwijottama
nāyakā mama sainyasya sanjñārthaṁ tānbravīmi te

asmākam—ours; tu—but; *viśhiṣhṭāḥ*—special; *ye*—who; *tān*—them; *nibodha*—be informed; *dwija-uttama*—best of Brahmins; *nāyakāḥ*—principal generals; *mama*—our; *sainyasya*—of army; *sanjñā-artham*—for information; *tān*—them; *bravīmi*—I recount; *te*—unto you.

O best of Brahmins, hear too about the principal generals on our side, who are especially qualified to lead. These I now recount unto you.

Duryodhan addressed Dronacharya, the military guru of the Kaurava army, as *dwijottam* (best amongst the twice-born or Brahmins). He deliberately used this word to address his teacher. Dronacharya was not really a warrior by profession; he was only a teacher of military science. As a deceitful leader, Duryodhan even entertained shameless doubts about the loyalty of his own preceptor. The hidden meaning in Duryodhan's words was that if Dronacharya did not fight courageously, he would merely be a Brahmin interested in eating fine food served at Duryodhan's palace.

Having said that, Duryodhan now desired to boost his own morale and that of his teacher, so, he started enumerating the great generals in his own army.

भवान्भीष्मश्च कर्णश्च कृपश्च समितिञ्जयः ।
अश्वत्थामा विकर्णश्च सौमदत्तिस्तथैव च ।।8।।

bhavānbhīṣhmaśhcha karṇaśhcha kṛipaśhcha samitiñjayaḥ
aśhvatthāmā vikarṇaśhcha saumadattis tathaiva cha

bhavān—yourself; *bhīṣhmaḥ*—Bheeshma; *cha*—and; *karṇaḥ*—Karn; *cha*—and; *kṛipaḥ*—Kripa; *cha*—and; *samitim-jayaḥ*—victorious in battle; *aśhvatthāmā*—Ashwatthama; *vikarṇaḥ*—Vikarn; *cha*—and; *saumadattiḥ*—Bhurishrava; *tathā*—thus; *eva*—even; *cha*—also.

There are personalities, like yourself, Bheeshma, Karn, Kripa, Ashwatthama, Vikarn, and Bhurishrava, who are ever victorious in battle.

अन्ये च बहवः शूरा मदर्थे त्यक्तजीविताः ।
नानाशस्त्रप्रहरणाः सर्वे युद्धविशारदाः ।।9।।

anye cha bahavaḥ śhūrā madarthe tyaktajīvitāḥ
nānā-śhastra-praharaṇāḥ sarve yuddha-viśhāradāḥ

anye—others; *cha*—also; *bahavaḥ*—many; *śhūrāḥ*—heroic warriors; *mat-arthe*—for my sake; *tyakta-jīvitāḥ*—prepared to lay down their lives; *nānā-śhastra-praharaṇāḥ*—equipped with various kinds of weapons; *sarve*—all; *yuddha-viśhāradāḥ*—skilled in the art of warfare.

Also, there are many other heroic warriors who are prepared to lay down their lives for my sake. They are all skilled in the art of warfare and equipped with various kinds of weapons.

अपर्याप्तं तदस्माकं बलं भीष्माभिरक्षितम् ।
पर्याप्तं त्विदमेतेषां बलं भीमाभिरक्षितम् ॥10॥

aparyāptaṁ tadasmākaṁ balaṁ bhīṣhmābhirakṣhitam
paryāptaṁ tvidameteṣhāṁ balaṁ bhīmābhirakṣhitam

aparyāptam—unlimited; *tat*—that; *asmākam*—ours; *balam*—strength; *bhīṣhma*—by Grandsire Bheeshma; *abhirakṣhitam*—safely marshalled; *paryāptam*—limited; *tu*—but; *idam*—this; *eteṣhām*—their; *balam*—strength; *bhīma*—Bheem; *abhirakṣhitam*—carefully marshalled.

The strength of our army is unlimited, and we are safely marshalled by Grandsire Bheeshma, while the strength of the Pandava army, carefully marshalled by Bheem, is limited.

Duryodhan's words of self-aggrandizement were the typical utterances of a vainglorious person. When their end draws near, instead of making a humble evaluation of the situation, self-aggrandizing people egotistically indulge in vainglory. This tragic irony of fate was reflected in Duryodhan's statement when he said that their strength, secured by Bheeshma, was unlimited.

Grandsire Bheeshma was the commander-in-chief of the Kaurava army. He had received the boon that he could choose his time of death which made him practically invincible. On the Pandavas' side, the army was secured by Bheem, who was Duryodhan's sworn enemy. In this manner, Duryodhan compared the strength of Bheeshma with the might of Bheem.

Bheeshma, however, was the grand-uncle of both the Kauravas and the Pandavas and was genuinely concerned about the welfare of all of them. His compassion for the Pandavas would prevent him from fighting the war wholeheartedly. Also, he knew that in this holy war, where Lord Krishna Himself was present, no power on earth could make the side of *adharma* win. To honor his ethical commitment to the subjects of Hastinapur and the Kauravas, he chose to fight against the Pandavas. This decision underscores the enigmatic character of Bheeshma's personality.

अयनेषु च सर्वेषु यथाभागमवस्थिताः ।
भीष्ममेवाभिरक्षन्तु भवन्तः सर्व एव हि ।।11।।

ayaneṣhu cha sarveṣhu yathā-bhāgamavasthitāḥ
bhīṣhmamevābhirakṣhantu bhavantaḥ sarva eva hi

ayaneṣhu—at the strategic points; *cha*—also; *sarveṣhu*—all; *yathā-bhāgam*—in respective position; *avasthitāḥ*—situated; *bhīṣhmam*—to Grandsire Bheeshma; *eva*—only; *abhirakṣhantu*—defend; *bhavantaḥ*—you; *sarve*—all; *eva hi*—even as.

Therefore, I call upon all the generals of the Kaurava army now to give full support to Grandsire Bheeshma, even as you defend your respective strategic points.

Duryodhan looked upon Bheeshma's unassailability as the inspiration and strength of his army. Thus, he asked his army generals to rally around Bheeshma, while defending their respective vantage points in the military phalanx.

तस्य सञ्जनयन्हर्षं कुरुवृद्धः पितामहः ।
सिंहनादं विनद्योच्चैः शङ्खं दध्मौ प्रतापवान् ।।12।।

tasya sañjanayan harṣhaṁ kuru-vṛiddhaḥ pitāmahaḥ
siṁha-nādaṁ vinadyochchaiḥ śhaṅkhaṁ dadhmau pratāpavān

tasya—his; *sañjanayan*—causing; *harṣham*—joy; *kuru-vṛiddhaḥ*—the grand old man of the Kuru dynasty (Bheeshma); *pitāmahaḥ*—grandfather; *sinha-nādam*—lion's roar; *vinadya*—sounding; *uchchaiḥ*—very loudly; *śhaṅkham*—conch shell; *dadhmau*—blew; *pratāpa-vān*—the glorious.

Then, the grand old man of the Kuru dynasty, the glorious patriarch Bheeshma, roared like a lion, and blew his conch shell very loudly giving joy to Duryodhan.

Grandsire Bheeshma understood the fear in his grand-nephew's heart, and out of his natural compassion for him, tried to cheer him by blowing his conch shell very loudly. He knew that Duryodhan had no chance of victory due to the presence of the Supreme Lord Shree Krishna on the other side, yet Bheeshma let his nephew know that he would perform his duty. In the code of war at that time, this was the inauguration of the battle.

ततः शङ्खाश्च भेर्यश्च पणवानकगोमुखाः ।
सहसैवाभ्यहन्यन्त स शब्दस्तुमुलोऽभवत् ।।13।।

tataḥ śhaṅkhāśhcha bheryaśhcha paṇavānaka-gomukhāḥ
sahasaivābhyahanyanta sa śhabdastumulo 'bhavat

tataḥ—thereafter; *śhaṅkhāḥ*—conches; *cha*—and; *bheryaḥ*—bugles; *cha*—and; *paṇava-ānaka*—drums and kettledrums; *go-mukhāḥ*—trumpets; *sahasā*—suddenly; *eva*—indeed; *abhyahanyanta*—blared forth; *saḥ*—that; *śhabdaḥ*—sound; *tumulaḥ*—overwhelming; *abhavat*—was.

Thereafter, conches, kettledrums, bugles, trumpets, and horns suddenly blared forth, and their combined sound was overwhelming.

Seeing the great eagerness of Bheeshma for battle, the Kaurava army also became eager and began creating a tumultuous sound. *Paṇav* means drums, *ānak* means kettledrums, and *go-mukh* means blowing horns. These are all musical instruments, and the sounds of all these combined together caused a great uproar.

ततः श्वेतैर्हयैर्युक्ते महति स्यन्दने स्थितौ ।
माधवः पाण्डवश्चैव दिव्यौ शङ्खौ प्रदध्मतुः ।।14।।

tataḥ śhvetairhayairyukte mahati syandane sthitau
mādhavaḥ pāṇḍavaśhchaiva divyau śhaṅkhau pradadhmatuḥ

tataḥ—then; *śhvetaiḥ*—by white; *hayaiḥ*—horses; *yukte*—yoked; *mahati*—glorious; *syandane*—chariot; *sthitau*—seated; *mādhavaḥ*—Shree Krishna, husband of the goddess of fortune, Lakshmi; *pāṇḍavaḥ*—Arjun; *cha*—and; *eva*—also; *divyau*—divine; *śhaṅkhau*—conch shells; *pradadhmatuḥ*—blew.

Then, from amidst the Pandava army, seated in a glorious chariot drawn by white horses, Madhav and Arjun blew their divine conch shells.

After the sound from the Kaurava army had subsided, the Supreme Lord Shree Krishna and Arjun, seated on a magnificent chariot, intrepidly blew their conch shells powerfully, igniting the eagerness of the Pandavas for battle as well.

Sanjay uses the name 'Madhav' for Shree Krishna. *Mā* refers to the goddess of fortune; *dhav* means husband. Shree Krishna in His form as Lord Vishnu is the husband of the goddess of fortune, Lakshmi. The verse indicates that the grace of the goddess of fortune was on the side of the Pandavas, and they would soon be victorious in the war to reclaim the kingdom.

Pandavas means sons of Pandu. Any of the five brothers may be referred to as Pandava. Here the word is being used for Arjun. The glorious chariot on which he was sitting had been gifted to him by Agni, the celestial god of fire.

पाञ्चजन्यं हृषीकेशो देवदत्तं धनञ्जयः ।
पौण्ड्रं दध्मौ महाशङ्खं भीमकर्मा वृकोदरः ।।15।।

pāñchajanyaṁ hṛiṣhīkeśho devadattaṁ dhanañjayaḥ
pauṇḍraṁ dadhmau mahā-śhaṅkhaṁ bhīma-karmā vṛikodaraḥ

pāñchajanyam—the conch shell named Panchajanya; *hṛiṣhīka-īśhaḥ*—Shree Krishna, Lord of the mind and senses; *devadattam*—the conch shell named Devadutta; *dhanañjayaḥ*—Arjun, winner of wealth; *pauṇḍram*—the conch named Paundra; *dadhmau*—blew; *mahā-śhaṅkham*—mighty conch; *bhīma-karmā*—one who performs Herculean tasks; *vṛika-udaraḥ*—Bheem, the voracious eater.

Hrishikesh blew His conch shell, called Panchajanya, and Arjun blew the Devadutta. Bheem, the voracious eater and performer of Herculean tasks, blew his mighty conch, called Paundra.

The word 'Hrishikesh' means Lord of the mind and senses and has been used for Shree Krishna. He is the Supreme Master of everyone's mind and senses, including His own. Even while performing amazing pastimes on the planet Earth, He maintained complete mastery over His own mind and senses.

अनन्तविजयं राजा कुन्तीपुत्रो युधिष्ठिरः ।
नकुलः सहदेवश्च सुघोषमणिपुष्पकौ ।।16।।

काश्यश्च परमेष्वासः शिखण्डी च महारथः ।
धृष्टद्युम्नो विराटश्च सात्यकिश्चापराजितः ।।17।।

द्रुपदो द्रौपदेयाश्च सर्वशः पृथिवीपते ।
सौभद्रश्च महाबाहुः शङ्खान्दध्मुः पृथक् पृथक् ।।18।।

anantavijayaṁ rājā kuntī-putro yudhiṣhṭhiraḥ
nakulaḥ sahadevaśhcha sughoṣha-maṇipuṣhpakau

kāśhyaśhcha parameṣhvāsaḥ śhikhaṇḍī cha mahā-rathaḥ
dhṛiṣhṭadyumno virāṭaśhcha sātyakiśh chāparājitaḥ

drupado draupadeyāśhcha sarvaśhaḥ pṛithivī-pate
saubhadraśhcha mahā-bāhuḥ śhaṅkhāndadhmuḥ pṛithak pṛithak

ananta-vijayam—the conch named Anantavijay; *rājā*—king; *kuntī-putraḥ*—son of Kunti; *yudhiṣhṭhiraḥ*—Yudhishthir; *nakulaḥ*—Nakul; *sahadevaḥ*—Sahadev; *cha*—and; *sughoṣha-maṇipuṣhpakau*—the conch shells named Sughosh and Manipushpak; *kāśhyaḥ*—King of Kashi; *cha*—and; *parama-iṣhu-āsaḥ*—the excellent archer; *śhikhaṇḍī*—Shikhandi; *cha*—also; *mahā-rathaḥ*—warriors who could single handedly match the strength of ten thousand ordinary warriors; *dhṛiṣhṭadyumnaḥ*—Dhrishtadyumna; *virāṭaḥ*—Virat; *cha*—and; *sātyakiḥ*—Satyaki; *cha*—and; *aparājitaḥ*—invincible; *drupadaḥ*—Drupad; *draupadeyāḥ*—five sons of Draupadi; *cha*—and; *sarvaśhaḥ*—all; *pṛithivī-pate*—Ruler of the earth; *saubhadraḥ*—Abhimanyu, son of Subhadra; *cha*—also; *mahā-bāhuḥ*—the mighty-armed; *śhaṅkhān*—conch shells; *dadhmuḥ*—blew; *pṛithak pṛithak*—individually.

King Yudhishthir blew the Anantavijay, while Nakul and Sahadev

blew the Sughosh and Manipushpak. The excellent archer and king of Kashi, the great warrior Shikhandi, Dhrishtadyumna, Virat, and the invincible Satyaki, Drupad, the five sons of Draupadi, and the mighty-armed Abhimanyu, son of Subhadra, all blew their respective conch shells, O Ruler of the earth.

Yudhishthir was the eldest of the Pandava brothers. Here, he is being called 'King'; he had earned the right to that title after performing the *Rājasūya Yajna* and receiving tribute from all the other kings. Also, his bearing exuded royal grace and magnanimity, whether he was in the palace or in exile in the forest.

Dhritarashtra is being called 'Ruler of the earth' by Sanjay. To preserve a country or engage it in a ruinous warfare is all in the hands of the ruler. So the hidden implication in the appellation is, 'The armies are heading for war. O Ruler, Dhritarashtra, you alone can call them back. What are you going to decide?'

स घोषो धार्तराष्ट्राणां हृदयानि व्यदारयत् ।
नभश्च पृथिवीं चैव तुमुलोऽभ्यनुनादयन् ।।19।।

sa ghoṣho dhārtarāṣhṭrāṇāṁ hṛidayāni vyadārayat
nabhaśhcha pṛithivīṁ chaiva tumulo 'bhyanunādayan

saḥ—that; *ghoṣhaḥ*—sound; *dhārtarāṣhṭrāṇām*—of Dhritarashtra's sons; *hṛidayāni*—hearts; *vyadārayat*—shattered; *nabhaḥ*—the sky; *cha*—and; *pṛithivīm*—the earth; *cha*—and; *eva*—certainly; *tumulaḥ*—terrific sound; *abhyanunādayan*—thundering.

The terrific sound thundered across the sky and the earth and shattered the hearts of your sons, O Dhritarashtra.

The sound from the conch shells of the Pandava army shattered the hearts of the Kaurava army. However, no such effect on the Pandava army was mentioned when the Kaurava army blew on their conches. Since the Pandavas had taken the shelter of the Lord, they were confident of being preserved. On the other hand, the Kauravas, relying on their own strength and pricked by the guilty conscience of their crimes, became fearful of defeat.

अथ व्यवस्थितान्दृष्ट्वा धार्तराष्ट्रान् कपिध्वजः ।
प्रवृत्ते शस्त्रसम्पाते धनुरुद्यम्य पाण्डवः ।।20।।
हृषीकेशं तदा वाक्यमिदमाह महीपते ।

atha vyavasthitān dṛiṣhṭvā dhārtarāṣhṭrān kapi-dhwajaḥ
pravṛitte śhastra-sampāte dhanurudyamya pāṇḍavaḥ
hṛiṣhīkeśhaṁ tadā vākyam idam āha mahī-pate

atha—thereupon; *vyavasthitān*—arrayed; *dṛiṣhṭvā*—seeing; *dhārtarāṣhṭrān*—Dhritarashtra's sons; *kapi-dwajaḥ*—the Monkey -bannered; *pravṛitte*—about to commence; *śhastra-sampāte*—to use the weapons; *dhanuḥ*—bow; *udyamya*—taking up; *pāṇḍavaḥ*—Arjun, son of Pandu; *hṛiṣhīkeśham*—to Shree Krishna; *tadā*—at that time; *vākyam*—words; *idam*—these; *āha*—said; *mahī-pate*—King.

At that time, the son of Pandu, Arjun, who had the insignia of Hanuman on the flag of his chariot, took up his bow. Seeing your sons arrayed against him, O King, Arjun then spoke the following words to Shree Krishna.

Arjun is called by the name *Kapi Dhwaj*, denoting the presence of the powerful Hanuman on his chariot. There is a story behind this.

Arjun once became proud of his skill in archery and told Shree Krishna that he could not understand why, in the time of Lord Ram, the monkeys labored so much to make the bridge from India to Lanka. Had he been there, he would have made a bridge of arrows. Shree Krishna asked him to demonstrate how he would do this. Arjun made the bridge by releasing a shower of arrows. Shree Krishna called Hanuman to come and test the bridge. When the great Hanuman began walking on it, the bridge started crumbling. Arjun realized that his bridge of arrows would never have been able to uphold the weight of the vast army of Lord Ram and apologized for his mistake. Hanuman then taught Arjun the lesson to never become proud of his skills. He benevolently gave the boon to Arjun that he would sit on his chariot during the battle of Mahabharat. As a result, Arjun's chariot carried the insignia of Hanuman on its flag, from which he got the name 'Kapi Dhwaj' or the 'Monkey Bannered'.

अर्जुन उवाच ।
सेनयोरुभयोर्मध्ये रथं स्थापय मेऽच्युत ।।21।।

यावदेतान्निरीक्षेऽहं योद्धुकामानवस्थितान् ।
कैर्मया सह योद्धव्यमस्मिन् रणसमुद्यमे ।।22।।

arjuna uvācha
senayor ubhayor madhye rathaṁ sthāpaya me 'chyuta

yāvadetān nirīkṣhe 'haṁ yoddhu-kāmān avasthitān
kairmayā saha yoddhavyam asmin raṇa-samudyame

arjunaḥ uvācha—Arjun said; *senayoḥ*—armies; *ubhayoḥ*—both; *madhye*—in the middle; *ratham*—chariot; *sthāpaya*—place; *me*—my; *achyuta*—Shree Krishna, the infallible One; *yāvat*—as many as; *etān*—these; *nirīkṣhe*—look; *aham*—I; *yoddhu-kāmān*—for the battle; *avasthitān*—arrayed; *kaiḥ*—with whom; *mayā*—by me; *saha*—together; *yoddhavyam*—must fight; *asmin*—in this; *raṇa-samudyame*—great combat.

Arjun said: O Infallible One, please take my chariot to the middle of both armies, so that I may look at the warriors arrayed for battle, whom I must fight in this great combat.

Arjun was a devotee of Shree Krishna, who is the Supreme Lord of the entire creation. Yet, in this verse, Arjun instructed the Lord to drive his chariot in to the desired place. This reveals the sweetness of God's relationship with His devotees. Indebted by their love for Him, the Lord becomes the servant of His devotees.

ahaṁ bhakta-parādhīno hyasvatantra iva dvija
sādhubhir grasta-hṛidayo bhaktair bhakta-jana-priyaḥ

(Bhagavatam 9.4.63)

'Although I am Supremely Independent, yet I become enslaved by My devotees. They are very dear to Me, and I become indebted to them for their love.' Obliged by Arjun's devotion, Shree Krishna took the position of the chariot driver, while Arjun sat comfortably on the passenger seat instructing Him.

योत्स्यमानानवेक्षेऽहं य एतेऽत्र समागताः ।
धार्तराष्ट्रस्य दुर्बुद्धेर्युद्धे प्रियचिकीर्षवः ॥23॥

yotsyamānān avekṣhe 'haṁ ya ete 'tra samāgatāḥ
dhārtarāṣhṭrasya durbuddher yuddhe priya-chikīrṣhavaḥ

yotsyamānān—those who have come to fight; *avekṣhe aham*—I desire to see; *ye*—who; *ete*—those; *atra*—here; *samāgatāḥ*—assembled; *dhārtarāṣhṭrasya*—of Dhritarashtra's son; *durbuddheḥ*—evil-minded; *yuddhe*—in the fight; *priya-chikīrṣhavaḥ*—wishing to please.

I desire to see those who have come here to fight on the side of the evil-minded son of Dhritarashtra wishing to please him.

The evil-minded sons of Dhritarashtra had usurped the kingdom rightfully due the Pandavas, so the warriors fighting from their side were also naturally ill-intentioned. Arjun desired to see those whom he would have to fight in this war. To begin with, Arjun was valiant and eager for the battle. This is why, he referred to the evil-minded sons of Dhritarashtra, conveying how Duryodhan had conspired several times to destroy the Pandavas. Arjun's attitude was, 'We are the lawful owners of half the empire, but he wants to usurp it. He is evil-minded and these kings have assembled to help him, so they are also evil. I want to observe the warriors who are so impatient to wage war. They have favored injustice, and so they are sure to be destroyed by us.'

सञ्जय उवाच ।
एवमुक्तो हृषीकेशो गुडाकेशेन भारत ।
सेनयोरुभयोर्मध्ये स्थापयित्वा रथोत्तमम् ॥24॥

sañjaya uvācha
evam ukto hṛiṣhīkeśho guḍākeśhena bhārata
senayor ubhayor madhye sthāpayitvā rathottamam

sañjayaḥ uvācha—Sanjay said; *evam*—thus; *uktaḥ*—addressed; *hṛiṣhīkeśhaḥ*—Shree Krishna, Lord of the senses; *guḍākeśhena*—

by Arjun, the conqueror of sleep; *bhārata*—descendant of Bharat; *senayoḥ*—armies; *ubhayoḥ*—the two; *madhye*—between; *sthāpayitvā*—having drawn; *ratha-uttamam*—magnificent chariot.

Sanjay said: O Dhritarashtra, having thus been addressed by Arjun, the conqueror of sleep, Shree Krishna then drew the magnificent chariot between the two armies.

भीष्मद्रोणप्रमुखतः सर्वेषां च महीक्षिताम् ।
उवाच पार्थ पश्यैतान्समवेतान्कुरूनिति ।।25।।

bhīṣhma-droṇa-pramukhataḥ sarveṣhāṁ cha mahī-kṣhitām
uvācha pārtha paśhyaitān samavetān kurūn iti

bhīṣhma—Grandsire Bheeshma; *droṇa*—Dronacharya; *pramukhataḥ*—in the presence; *sarveṣhām*—all; *cha*—and; *mahī-kṣhitām*—other kings; *uvācha*—said; *pārtha*—Arjun, son of Pritha; *paśhya*—behold; *etān*—these; *samavetān*—gathered; *kurūn*—descendants of Kuru; *iti*—thus.

In the presence of Bheeshma, Dronacharya, and all the other kings, Shree Krishna said: O Parth, behold these Kurus gathered here.

The word *Kuru* includes both the Kauravas and the Pandavas, because they both belong to the Kuru dynasty. Shree Krishna deliberately uses this word to enthuse the feeling of kinship in Arjun and make him feel that they are all one. He wants the feeling of kinship to lead to attachment, which would confuse Arjun, and give Shree Krishna the opportunity to preach the gospel of the Bhagavad Gita for the benefit of human beings of the forthcoming age of *Kali*. Thus, instead of using the word *dhārtarāṣhṭrān* (sons of Dhritarashtra), he uses the word *kurūn* (descendants of Kuru). Just as a surgeon first gives medicine to a patient suffering from a boil, to suppurate it, and then performs surgery to remove the diseased part; the Lord is working in the same way to first arouse the hidden delusion of Arjun, only to destroy it later.

तत्रापश्यत्स्थितान् पार्थः पितॄनथ पितामहान् ।
आचार्यान्मातुलान्भ्रातॄन्पुत्रान्पौत्रान्सखींस्तथा ।।26।।
श्वशुरान्सुहृदश्चैव सेनयोरुभयोरपि ।

tatrāpaśhyat sthitān pārthaḥ pitṝīn atha pitāmahān
āchāryān mātulān bhrātṝīn putrān pautrān sakhīns tathā
śhvaśhurān suhṛidaśh chaiva senayor ubhayor api

tatra—there; *apaśhyat*—saw; *sthitān*—stationed; *pārthaḥ*—Arjun; *pitṝīn*—fathers; *atha*—thereafter; *pitāmahān*—grandfathers; *āchāryān*—teachers; *mātulān*—maternal uncles; *bhrātṝīn*—brothers; *putrān*—sons; *pautrān*—grandsons; *sakhīn*—friends; *tathā*—also; *śhvaśhurān*—fathers-in-law; *suhṛidaḥ*—well-wishers; *cha*—and; *eva*—indeed; *senayoḥ*—armies; *ubhayoḥ*—in both armies; *api*—also.

There, Arjun could see stationed in both armies, his fathers, grandfathers, teachers, maternal uncles, brothers, cousins, sons, nephews, grand-nephews, friends, fathers-in-law, and well-wishers.

तान्समीक्ष्य स कौन्तेयः सर्वान्बन्धूनवस्थितान् ।।27।।
कृपया परयाविष्टो विषीदन्निदमब्रवीत् ।

tān samīkṣhya sa kaunteyaḥ sarvān bandhūn avasthitān
kṛipayā parayāviṣhṭo viṣhīdann idam abravīt

tān—these; *samīkṣhya*—on seeing; *saḥ*—they; *kaunteyaḥ*—Arjun, son of Kunti; *sarvān*—all; *bandhūn*—relatives; *avasthitān*—present; *kṛipayā*—by compassion; *parayā*—great; *āviṣhṭaḥ*—overwhelmed; *viṣhīdan*—deep sorrow; *idam*—this; *abravīt*—spoke.

Seeing all his relatives present there, Arjun, son of Kunti, was overwhelmed with compassion, and with deep sorrow, spoke the following words.

Seeing his relatives together in the battlefield, for the first time, Arjun realised the consequences of this fratricidal war. The valiant warrior who had arrived for battle, mentally prepared to dispatch his enemies to the gates of death and to avenge the wrongs that had been committed against the Pandavas, suddenly had a change of heart. Seeing his fellow Kurus assembled in the enemy ranks, his heart sank, his intellect became confused, his bravery was replaced by cowardice towards his duty, and his stoutheartedness gave way to softheartedness. Hence, Sanjay calls him the son of Kunti, his mother, referring to the softhearted and nurturing side of his nature.

अर्जुन उवाच ।
दृष्ट्वेमं स्वजनं कृष्ण युयुत्सुं समुपस्थितम् ।।28।।
सीदन्ति मम गात्राणि मुखं च परिशुष्यति ।

arjuna uvācha
dṛiṣhṭvemaṁ sva-janaṁ kṛiṣhṇa yuyutsuṁ samupasthitam
sīdanti mama gātrāṇi mukhaṁ cha pariśhuṣhyati

arjunaḥ uvācha—Arjun said; *dṛiṣhṭvā*—on seeing; *imam*—these; *sva-janam*—kinsmen; *kṛiṣhṇa*—Krishna; *yuyutsum*—eager to fight; *samupasthitam*—present; *sīdanti*—quivering; *mama*—my; *gātrāṇi*—limbs; *mukham*—mouth; *cha*—and; *pariśhuṣhyati*—is drying up.

Arjun said: O Krishna, seeing my own kinsmen arrayed for battle here and intent on killing each other, my limbs are giving way and my mouth is drying up.

Affection can be either a material or a spiritual sentiment. Attachment for one's relatives is a material emotion arising from identification with the physical body. In this manner, thinking of oneself as the body, one gets attached to its relatives. This attachment is based on ignorance and drags one further into materialistic consciousness. Ultimately, such attachment ends in pain, because at the time of death, the familial relationships end too.

On the other hand, the Supreme Lord is the Father, Mother, Friend, Master, and Beloved of our soul. Consequently, attachment to Him is a spiritual sentiment, at the platform of the soul, which elevates the consciousness and illumines the intellect. Love for God is oceanic and all-encompassing, while love for physical relations is narrow and differentiating. Here, Arjun was experiencing material attachment, which was drowning his mind in an ocean of gloom and making him tremble at the thought of doing his duty.

वेपथुश्च शरीरे मे रोमहर्षश्च जायते ।।29।।

गाण्डीवं स्त्रंसते हस्तात्त्वक्चै व परिदह्यते ।
न च शक्नोम्यवस्थातुं भ्रमतीव च मे मनः ।।30।।

निमित्तानि च पश्यामि विपरीतानि केशव ।
न च श्रेयोऽनुपश्यामि हत्वा स्वजनमाहवे ।।31।।

vepathuśh cha śharīre me roma-harṣhaśh cha jāyate

gāṇḍīvaṁ sraṁsate hastāt tvak chai va paridahyate
na cha śhaknomy avasthātuṁ bhramatīva cha me manaḥ

nimittāni cha paśhyāmi viparītāni keśhava
na cha śhreyo 'nupaśhyāmi hatvā sva-janam āhave

vepathuḥ—shuddering; *cha*—and; *śharīre*—on the body; *me*—my; *roma-harṣhaḥ*—standing of bodily hair on end; *cha*—also; *jāyate*—is happening; *gāṇḍīvam*—Arjun's bow; *sraṁsate*—is slipping; *hastāt*—from (my) hand; *tvak*—skin; *cha*—and; *eva*—indeed; *paridahyate*—is burning all over; *na*—not; *cha*—and; *śhaknomi*—am able; *avasthātum*—remain steady; *bhramati iva*—whirling like; *cha*—and; *me*—my; *manaḥ*—mind; *nimittāni*—omens; *cha*—and; *paśhyāmi*—I see; *viparītāni*—misfortune; *keśhava*—Shree Krishna, killer of the Keshi demon; *na*—not; *cha*—also; *śhreyaḥ*—good; *anupaśhyāmi*—I foresee; *hatvā*—from killing; *sva-janam*—kinsmen; *āhave*—in battle.

My whole body shudders; my hair is standing on end. My bow, the *Gāṇḍīv*, is slipping from my hand, and my skin is burning all over. My

mind is in a quandary and whirling in confusion; I am unable to hold myself steady any longer. O Krishna, killer of the Keshi demon, I only see omens of misfortune. I do not foresee how any good can come from killing my own kinsmen in this battle.

As Arjun thought of the consequences of the war, he grew worried and sad. The same *Gāṇḍīv* bow, the sound of which had terrified powerful enemies, began dropping from his hand. His mind was reeling, thinking it was a sin to wage the war. In this unsteadiness of mind, he even descended to the level of accepting superstitious omens portending disastrous failures and imminent consequences.

न काङ्क्षे विजयं कृष्ण न च राज्यं सुखानि च ।
किं नो राज्येन गोविन्द किं भोगैर्जीवितेन वा ।।32।।

येषामर्थे काङ्क्षितं नो राज्यं भोगाः सुखानि च ।
त इमेऽवस्थिता युद्धे प्राणांस्त्यक्त्वा धनानि च ।।33।।

na kāṅkṣhe vijayaṁ kṛiṣhṇa na cha rājyaṁ sukhāni cha
kiṁ no rājyena govinda kiṁ bhogair jīvitena vā

yeṣhām arthe kāṅkṣhitaṁ no rājyaṁ bhogāḥ sukhāni cha
ta ime 'vasthitā yuddhe prāṇāṁs tyaktvā dhanāni cha

na—nor; *kāṅkṣhe*—do I desire; *vijayam*—victory; *kṛiṣhṇa*—Krishna; *na*—nor; *cha*—as well; *rājyam*—kingdom; *sukhāni*—happiness; *cha*—also; *kim*—what; *naḥ*—to us; *rājyena*—by kingdom; *govinda*—Krishna, He who gives pleasure to the senses, He who is fond of cows; *kim*—what; *bhogaiḥ*—pleasures; *jīvitena*—life; *vā*—or; *yeṣhām*—for whose; *arthe*—sake; *kāṅkṣhitam*—coveted for; *naḥ*—by us; *rājyam*—kingdom; *bhogāḥ*—pleasures; *sukhāni*—happiness; *cha*—also; *te*—they; *ime*—these; *avasthitāḥ*—situated; *yuddhe*—for battle; *prāṇān*—lives; *tyaktvā*—giving up; *dhanāni*—wealth; *cha*—also.

O Krishna, I do not desire victory, kingdom, or the happiness accruing to it. Of what avail will be a kingdom, pleasures, or even life itself,

when the very persons for whom we covet them, are standing before us for battle?

Arjun's confusion arose from the fact that killing itself was considered a sinful act; then to kill one's relatives seemed an even more grossly evil act. Even if he did engage in such a heartless act for the sake of the kingdom, Arjun felt that victory would not give him eventual happiness. He would be unable to share its glory with his friends and relatives, whom he would have to kill to achieve this victory.

Here, Arjun is displaying a lower set of sensibilities and confusing them for noble ones. Indifference to worldly possessions and material prosperity is a praiseworthy spiritual virtue, but Arjun is not experiencing spiritual sentiments. Rather, his delusion is masquerading as words of compassion. Virtuous sentiments bring internal harmony, satisfaction, and the joy of the soul. If Arjun's compassion was at the transcendental platform, he would have been elevated by the sentiment. But his experience is quite to the contrary—he is feeling discord in his mind and intellect, dissatisfaction with the task at hand, and deep unhappiness within. The effect of the sentiment upon him indicates that his compassion is stemming from delusion.

आचार्याः पितरः पुत्रास्तथैव च पितामहाः ।
मातुलाः श्वशुराः पौत्राः श्यालाः सम्बन्धिनस्तथा ।।34।।

एतान्न हन्तुमिच्छामि घ्नतोऽपि मधुसूदन ।
अपि त्रैलोक्यराज्यस्य हेतोः किं नु महीकृते ।।35।।

āchāryāḥ pitaraḥ putrās tathaiva cha pitāmahāḥ
mātulāḥ śhvaśhurāḥ pautrāḥ śhyālāḥ sambandhinas tathā

etān na hantum ichchhāmi ghnato 'pi madhusūdana
api trailokya-rājyasya hetoḥ kiṁ nu mahī-kṛite

āchāryāḥ—teachers; *pitaraḥ*—fathers; *putrāḥ*—sons; *tathā*—as well; *eva*—indeed; *cha*—also; *pitāmahāḥ*—grandfathers; *mātulāḥ*—maternal uncles; *śhvaśhurāḥ*—fathers-in-law; *pautrāḥ*—grandsons;

śhyālāḥ—brothers-in-law; *sambandhinaḥ*—kinsmen; *tathā*—as well; *etān*—these; *na*—not; *hantum*—to slay; *ichchhāmi*—I wish; *ghnataḥ*—killed; *api*—even though; *madhusūdana*—Shree Krishna, killer of the demon Madhu; *api*—even though; *trai-lokya-rājyasya*—dominion over three worlds; *hetoḥ*—for the sake of; *kim nu*—what to speak of; *mahī-kṛite*—for the earth.

Teachers, fathers, sons, grandfathers, maternal uncles, grandsons, fathers-in-law, grand-nephews, brothers-in-law, and other kinsmen are present here, staking their lives and riches. O Madhusudan, I do not wish to slay them, even if they attack me. Even if we kill the sons of Dhritarashtra, what satisfaction will we derive from the dominion over the three worlds, what to speak of this earth?

Dronacharya and Kripacharya were Arjun's teachers; Bheeshma and Somadatta were his grand-uncles; people like Bhurishrava (son of Somdatta) were like his father; Purujit, Kuntibhoj, Shalya, and Shakuni were his maternal uncles; the hundred sons of Dhritarashtra were his cousin brothers; Lakshman (Duryodhan's son) was like his child. Arjun refers to all his various relatives present on the battlefield. He uses the word *api,* which means 'even though', twice. First, 'Why would they wish to kill me, even though I am their relative and well-wisher?' Second, 'Even though they may desire to slay me, why should I wish to slay them?'

निहत्य धार्तराष्ट्रान्नः का प्रीतिः स्याज्जनार्दन ।
पापमेवाश्रयेदस्मान्हत्वैतानाततायिनः ।।36।।

तस्मान्नार्हा वयं हन्तुं धार्तराष्ट्रान्स्वबान्धवान् ।
स्वजनं हि कथं हत्वा सुखिनः स्याम माधव ।।37।।

nihatya dhārtarāṣhṭrān naḥ kā prītiḥ syāj janārdana
pāpam evāśhrayed asmān hatvaitān ātatāyinaḥ

tasmān nārhā vayaṁ hantuṁ dhārtarāṣhṭrān sva-bāndhavān
sva-janaṁ hi kathaṁ hatvā sukhinaḥ syāma mādhava

nihatya—by killing; *dhārtarāṣhṭrān*—the sons of Dhritarashtra; *naḥ*—our; *kā*—what; *prītiḥ*—pleasure; *syāt*—will there be; *janārdana*—He who looks after the public, Shree Krishna; *pāpam*—vices; *eva*—certainly; *āśhrayet*—must come upon; *asmān*—us; *hatvā*—by killing; *etān*—all these; *ātatāyinaḥ*—aggressors; *tasmāt*—hence; *na*—never; *arhāḥ*—behove; *vayam*—we; *hantum*—to kill; *dhārtarāṣhṭrān*—the sons of Dhritarashtra; *sva-bāndhavān*—along with friends; *sva-janam*—kinsmen; *hi*—certainly; *katham*—how; *hatvā*—by killing; *sukhinaḥ*—happy; *syāma*—will we become; *mādhava*—Shree Krishna, the husband of *Yogmaya*.

O Maintainer of all living entities, what pleasure will we derive from killing the sons of Dhritarashtra? Even though they may be aggressors, sin will certainly come upon us if we slay them. Hence, it does not behove us to kill our own cousins, the sons of Dhritarashtra, and friends. O Madhav (Krishna), how can we hope to be happy by killing our own kinsmen?

Having said 'even though' twice in the last verse to justify his intention not to slay his relatives, Arjun again says, 'Even though I were to kill them, what pleasure would I derive from such a victory?'

In most situations, fighting and killing is an ungodly act that generates feelings of repentance and guilt. The Vedas state that non-violence is a great virtue, and except in the extreme cases, violence is a sin: *mā hinsyāt sarvā bhūtāni* 'Do not kill any living being.' Here, Arjun does not wish to kill his relatives, for he considers it to be a sin. However, the *Vasiṣhṭh Smṛiti* (verse 3.19) states that there are six kinds of aggressors against whom we have the right to defend ourselves: those who set fire to one's property, those who poison one's food, those who seek to murder, those who wish to steal wealth, those who come to kidnap one's wife, and those who usurp one's kingdom. The *Manu Smṛiti* (8.351) states that it is not considered a sin if one kills such an aggressor in self-defence.

यद्यप्येते न पश्यन्ति लोभोपहतचेतसः ।
कुलक्षयकृतं दोषं मित्रद्रोहे च पातकम् ।।38।।

कथं न ज्ञेयमस्माभिः पापादस्मान्निवर्तितुम् ।
कुलक्षयकृतं दोषं प्रपश्यद्भिर्जनार्दन ।।39।।

yady apy ete na paśhyanti lobhopahata-chetasaḥ
kula-kṣhaya-kṛitaṁ doṣhaṁ mitra-drohe cha pātakam

kathaṁ na jñeyam asmābhiḥ pāpād asmān nivartitum
kula-kṣhaya-kṛitaṁ doṣhaṁ prapaśhyadbhir janārdana

yadi api—even though; *ete*—they; na—not; *paśhyanti*—see; *lobha*—greed; *upahata*—overpowered; *chetasaḥ*—thoughts; *kula-kṣhaya-kṛitam*—in annihilating their relatives; *doṣham*—fault; *mitra-drohe*—to wreak treachery upon friends; *cha*—and; *pātakam*—sin; *katham*—why; *na*—not; *jñeyam*—should be known; *asmābhiḥ*—we; *pāpāt*—from sin; *asmāt*—these; *nivartitum*—to turn away; *kula-kṣhaya*—killing the kindered; *kṛitam*—done; *doṣham*—crime; *prapaśhyadbhiḥ*—who can see; *janārdana*—He who looks after the public, Shree Krishna.

Their thoughts are overpowered by greed, and they see no wrong in annihilating their relatives or wreaking treachery upon friends. Yet, O Janardan (Krishna), why should we, who can clearly see the crime in killing our kindred, not turn away from this sin?

Although a warrior by occupation, Arjun abhorred unnecessary violence. An incident at the end of the battle of Mahabharat reveals this side of his character.

The hundred Kauravas had been killed, but in revenge, Ashwatthama, son of Dronacharya, crept into the Pandava camp at night and killed the five sons of Draupadi while they were sleeping. Arjun caught Ashwatthama, tied him like an animal, and brought him to the feet of Draupadi, who was crying. Being soft-hearted and forgiving, she said that because Ashwatthama was the son of their guru, Dronacharya, he should be forgiven. Bheem, on the other hand, wanted Ashwatthama to be killed immediately. In a dilemma, Arjun looked for a solution towards Shree Krishna, who said, 'A respect-worthy Brahmin must be forgiven even if he may have temporarily fallen from virtue. But a person who approaches to kill with a lethal weapon must certainly be punished.' Arjun understood Shree Krishna's equivocal instructions. He did not kill Ashwatthama; instead, he cut the Brahmin tuft behind his head, removed the jewel from his forehead, and expelled him from the camp. So, Arjun's very nature is to shun violence wherever possible. In this particular situation, he says that he knows it is improper to kill kindred and elders:

ṛitvikpurohitāchāryair mātulātithisanśhritaiḥ
bālavṛiddhāturair vaidyair jñātisambandhibāndhavaiḥ

(*Manu Smṛiti* 4.179)

'One should not quarrel with the Brahmin who performs the fire sacrifice, the family priest, teacher, maternal uncle, guest, those who are dependent upon one, children, elders, doctor, and relatives.' Arjun thus concluded that being overpowered by greed, the Kauravas might have deviated from propriety and had lost their sense of discrimination, but why should he, who did not have any sinful motive, engage in such an abominable act?

कुलक्षये प्रणश्यन्ति कुलधर्माः सनातनाः ।
धर्मे नष्टे कुलं कृत्स्नमधर्मोऽभिभवत्युत ।।40।।

kula-kṣhaye praṇaśhyanti kula-dharmāḥ sanātanāḥ
dharme naṣhṭe kulaṁ kṛitsnam adharmo 'bhibhavaty uta

kula-kṣhaye—in the destruction of a dynasty; *praṇaśhyanti*—are vanquished; *kula-dharmāḥ*—family traditions; *sanātanāḥ*—eternal; *dharme*—religion; *naṣhṭe*—is destroyed; *kulam*—family; *kṛitsnam*—the whole; *adharmaḥ*—irreligion; *abhibhavati*—overcome; *uta*—indeed.

When a dynasty is destroyed, its traditions get vanquished, and the rest of the family becomes involved in irreligion.

Families have age-old traditions and time-honored customs, in accordance with which, elders in the family pass on noble values and ideals to their next generation. These traditions help family members follow honourable values and religious propriety. If the elders die prematurely, their succeeding generations become bereft of family guidance and training. Arjun points this out by saying that when dynasties get destroyed, their traditions die with them, and the remaining members of the family develop irreligious and wanton habits, thereby losing their chance for spiritual emancipation. Thus, according to him, the elders of the family should never be slain.

अधर्माभिभवात्कृष्ण प्रदुष्यन्ति कुलस्त्रियः ।
स्त्रीषु दुष्टासु वार्ष्णेय जायते वर्णसङ्करः ।।41।।

adharmābhibhavāt kṛiṣhṇa praduṣhyanti kula-striyaḥ
strīṣhu duṣhṭāsu vārṣhṇeya jāyate varṇa-saṅkaraḥ

adharma—irreligion; *abhibhavāt*—preponderance; *kṛiṣhṇa*—Shree Krishna; *praduṣhyanti*—become immoral; *kula-striyaḥ*—women of the family; *strīṣhu*—of women; *duṣhṭāsu*—immorality; *vārṣhṇeya*—descendant of Vrishni; *jāyate*—are born; *varṇa-saṅkaraḥ*—unwanted progeny.

With the preponderance of vice, O Krishna, the women of the family become immoral; and from the immorality of women, O descendent of Vrishni, unwanted progeny are born.

The Vedic civilization accorded a very high place in society to women and emphasised the need for women to be virtuous. Hence, the *Manu Smṛiti* states: *yatra nāryas tu pūjyante ramante tatra devatāḥ* (3.56) 'Wherever women lead chaste and virtuous lives, and for their purity they are worshipped by the rest of society, there the celestial gods become joyous.' However, when women become immoral, then irresponsible men take advantage by indulging in adultery, and consequently, unwanted children are born.

सङ्करो नरकायैव कुलघ्नानां कुलस्य च ।
पतन्ति पितरो ह्येषां लुप्तपिण्डोदकक्रियाः ॥42॥

saṅkaro narakāyaiva kula-ghnānāṁ kulasya cha
patanti pitaro hy eṣhāṁ lupta-piṇḍodaka-kriyāḥ

saṅkaraḥ—unwanted children; *narakāya*—hellish; *eva*—indeed; *kula-ghnānām*—for those who destroy the family; *kulasya*—of the family; *cha*—also; *patanti*—fall; *pitaraḥ*—ancestors; *hi*—verily; *eṣhām*—their; *lupta*—deprived of; *piṇḍodaka-kriyāḥ*—performances of sacrificial offerings.

An increase in unwanted children results in hellish life both for the family and for those who destroy the family. Deprived of sacrificial offerings, the ancestors of such corrupt families also fall.

दोषैरेतैः कुलघ्नानां वर्णसङ्करकारकैः ।
उत्साद्यन्ते जातिधर्माः कुलधर्माश्च शाश्वताः ॥43॥

doṣhair etaiḥ kula-ghnānāṁ varṇa-saṅkara-kārakaiḥ
utsādyante jāti-dharmāḥ kula-dharmāśh cha śhāśhvatāḥ

doṣhaiḥ—through evil deeds; *etaiḥ*—these; *kula-ghnānām*—of those who destroy the family; *varṇa-saṅkara*—unwanted progeny; *kārakaiḥ*—causing; *utsādyante*—are ruined; *jāti-dharmāḥ*—social and family welfare activities; *kula-dharmāḥ*—family traditions; *cha*—and; *śhāśhvatāḥ*—eternal.

Through the evil deeds of those who destroy the family tradition and thus give rise to unwanted progeny, a variety of social and family welfare activities are ruined.

उत्सन्नकुलधर्माणां मनुष्याणां जनार्दन ।
नरकेऽनियतं वासो भवतीत्यनुशुश्रुम ॥44॥

utsanna-kula-dharmāṇāṁ manuṣhyāṇāṁ janārdana
narake 'niyataṁ vāso bhavatītyanuśhuśhruma

utsanna—destroyed; *kula-dharmāṇām*—whose family traditions; *manuṣhyāṇām*—of such human beings; *janārdana*—He who looks after the public, Shree Krishna; *narake*—in hell; *aniyatam*—indefinite; *vāsaḥ*—dwell; *bhavati*—is; *iti*—thus; *anuśhuśhruma*—I have heard from the learned.

O Janardan (Krishna), I have heard from the learned that those who destroy family traditions dwell in hell for an indefinite period of time.

अहो बत महत्पापं कर्तुं व्यवसिता वयम् ।
यद्राज्यसुखलोभेन हन्तुं स्वजनमुद्यताः ।।45।।

यदि मामप्रतीकारमशस्त्रं शस्त्रपाणयः ।
धार्तराष्ट्रा रणे हन्युस्तन्मे क्षेमतरं भवेत् ।।46।।

aho bata mahat pāpaṁ kartuṁ vyavasitā vayam
yad rājya-sukha-lobhena hantuṁ sva-janam udyatāḥ

yadi mām apratīkāram aśhastraṁ śhastra-pāṇayaḥ
dhārtarāṣhṭrā raṇe hanyus tan me kṣhemataraṁ bhavet

aho—alas; *bata*—horrible results; *mahat*—great; *pāpam*—sins; *kartum*—to perform; *vyavasitāḥ*—have decided; *vayam*—we; *yat*—because; *rājya-sukha-lobhena*—driven by the desire for kingly pleasure; *hantum*—to kill; *sva-janam*—kinsmen; *udyatāḥ*—intending; *yadi*—if; *mām*—me; *apratīkāram*—unresisting; *aśhastram*—unarmed; *śhastra-pāṇayaḥ*—those with weapons in hand; *dhārtarāṣhṭrāḥ*—the sons of Dhritarashtra; *raṇe*—on the battlefield; *hanyuḥ*—shall kill; *tat*—that; *me*—to me; *kṣhema-taram*—better; *bhavet*—would be.

Alas! How strange it is that we have set our mind to perform this great sin with horrifying consequences. Driven by the desire for kingly pleasures, we are intent on killing our own kinsmen. It would be better if, with weapons in hand, the sons of Dhritarashtra kill me unarmed and unresisting on the battlefield.

Arjun mentioned a number of evils that would come from the impending battle, but he was not able to see that evil would actually prevail if these wicked people were allowed to thrive in society. He uses the word *aho* to express surprise. The word *bata* means 'horrible results.' Arjun is saying, 'How surprising it is that we have decided to commit sin by engaging in this war, even though we know of its horrifying consequences'.

As often happens, people are unable to see their own mistakes and instead attribute them to situations and to others. Similarly, Arjun felt that the sons of Dhritarashtra were motivated by greed; he could not see that his outpouring of compassion was not a transcendental sentiment, but materialistic infatuation based on the ignorance of being the body. The problem with all of Arjun's arguments was that he was using them to justify his delusion that had been created from his physical attachment, weakness of heart, and dereliction of duty. Shree Krishna explains the reasons why Arjun's arguments were untenable in subsequent chapters.

सञ्जय उवाच ।
एवमुक्त्वार्जुनः सङ्ख्ये रथोपस्थ उपाविशत् ।
विसृज्य सशरं चापं शोकसंविग्नमानसः ।।47।।

sañjaya uvācha
evam uktvārjunaḥ saṅkhye rathopastha upāviśhat
visṛijya sa-śharaṁ chāpaṁ śhoka-saṁvigna-mānasaḥ

sañjayaḥ uvācha—Sanjay said; *evam uktvā*—speaking thus; *arjunaḥ*—Arjun; *saṅkhye*—in the battlefield; *ratha upasthe*—on the chariot; *upāviśhat*—sat; *visṛijya*—casting aside; *sa-śharam*—along with arrows; *chāpam*—the bow; *śhoka*—with grief; *saṁvigna*—distressed; *mānasaḥ*—mind.

Sanjay said: Speaking thus, Arjun cast aside his bow and arrows, and sank into the seat of his chariot, his mind in distress and overwhelmed with grief.

Often while speaking, a person gets carried away by the sentiments, and Arjun's despondency, which he began expressing in verse 1.28, has now reached a climax. He has given up the struggle to engage in his *dhārmic* duty in desperate resignation, which is entirely opposite to the state of self-surrender to God in knowledge and devotion. It is appropriate to clarify at this point that Arjun was not a novice bereft of spiritual knowledge. He had been to the celestial abodes and had received instructions from his father Indra, the king of heaven. In fact, he was Nar in his past life and as a result, situated in transcendental knowledge (Nar-Narayan were twin descensions, where Nar was a perfected soul and Narayan was the Supreme Lord). The proof of this was the fact that before the battle of Mahabharat, Arjun chose Shree Krishna on his side, leaving the entire Yadu army for Duryodhan. He possessed the firm conviction that he would never lose if the Lord was on his side. However, Shree Krishna desired to deliver the message of the Bhagavad Gita for the benefit of posterity, and so at the opportune moment, He deliberately created confusion in Arjun's mind.

CHAPTER 2

Sānkhya Yog

The Yog of Analytical Knowledge

In this chapter, Arjun reiterates his utter inability to cope with the situation he finds himself in and refuses to perform his duty in the impending battle. He then formally asks Shree Krishna to be his spiritual teacher, and beseeches Him for guidance on the proper path of action in the situation he finds himself in. The Supreme Lord begins imparting divine knowledge by teaching him about the immortal nature of the self, which is not destroyed when the body perishes; it merely changes bodies from lifetime to lifetime just as a person puts on new garments and discards the old ones. Shree Krishna then moves on to the topic of social responsibilities. He reminds Arjun of his duty as a warrior which is to fight for upholding righteousness. He explains that the performance of one's social duty is a virtuous act that will open to him the stairway to celestial abodes, while dereliction of duty will only bring him humiliation and infamy.

Having motivated Arjun from the mundane level, Shree Krishna moves deeper into the science of work. He asks Arjun to work without attachment to the fruits of his actions. He terms the science of working without desire for rewards as *buddhi yog* or 'yog of the intellect'. The intellect must be used to restrain the mental yearning for the rewards of work. By acting in such consciousness, bondage-creating karmas will be transformed into bondage-breaking karmas, and Arjun will attain the state beyond sorrows.

Arjun enquires about the signs of those who are situated in divine consciousness. In response, Shree Krishna describes how persons situated in transcendence are free from attachment, fear, and anger; they are equipoised and undisturbed in all situations; their senses are subdued; and their minds are ever absorbed in God. He also gives a step-by-step explanation of how the afflictions of the mind—lust, anger, and greed—develop, and how they may be eradicated.

सञ्जय उवाच ।
तं तथा कृपयाविष्टमश्रुपूर्णाकुलेक्षणम् ।
विषीदन्तमिदं वाक्यमुवाच मधुसूदनः ।।1।।

sañjaya uvācha
taṁ tathā kṛipayāviṣhṭamaśhru pūrṇākulekṣhaṇam
viṣhīdantamidaṁ vākyam uvācha madhusūdanaḥ

sañjayaḥ uvācha—Sanjay said; *tam*—to him (Arjun); *tathā*—thus; *kṛipayā*—with pity; *āviṣhṭam*—overwhelmed; *aśhru-pūrṇa*—full of tears; *ākula*—distressed; *īkṣhaṇam*—eyes; *viṣhīdantam*—grief-stricken; *idam*—these; *vākyam*—words; *uvācha*—said; *madhusūdanaḥ*—Shree Krishna, slayer of the Madhu demon.

Sanjay said: Seeing Arjun overwhelmed with pity, his mind grief-stricken, and his eyes full of tears, Shree Krishna spoke the following words.

To describe Arjun's feelings, Sanjay uses the word *kṛipayā*, meaning pity or compassion. Compassion is of two kinds. One is the divine compassion that God and the saints feel towards the souls in the material realm on seeing their suffering in separation to God. The other is the material compassion that we feel upon seeing the bodily distress of others. Material compassion is a noble sentiment that is not perfectly directed. It is like being obsessed with the health of the car while the driver sitting within is famished. Arjun is experiencing this second kind of sentiment. He is overwhelmed with material pity toward his enemies gathered for battle. The fact that Arjun is overcome by grief and despair shows that he himself is in dire need of compassion. Therefore, to believe he is being merciful upon others is meaningless.

In this verse, Shree Krishna is addressed as 'Madhusudan'. He had killed the demon Madhu and got the name Madhusudan or 'slayer of the Madhu demon'. Here, He is about to slaughter the demon of doubt that has arisen in Arjun's mind, which is preventing him from discharging his duty.

श्रीभगवानुवाच ।
कुतस्त्वा कश्मलमिदं विषमे समुपस्थितम् ।
अनार्यजुष्टमस्वर्ग्यमकीर्तिकरमर्जुन ।।2।।

śhrī bhagavān uvācha
kutastvā kaśhmalamidaṁ viṣhame samupasthitam
anārya-juṣhṭamaswargyam akīrti-karam arjuna

śhrī-bhagavān uvācha—the Supreme Lord said; *kutaḥ*—wherefrom; *tvā*—to you; *kaśhmalam*—delusion; *idam*—this; *viṣhame*—in this hour of peril; *samupasthitam*—overcome; *anārya*—crude person; *juṣhṭam*—practiced; *aswargyam*—which does not lead to the higher abodes; *akīrti-karam*—leading to disgrace; *arjuna*—Arjun.

The Supreme Lord said: My dear Arjun, how has this delusion overcome you in this hour of peril? It is not befitting an honorable person. It leads not to the higher abodes but to disgrace.

The word *Ārya* in our sacred books does not refer to any race or ethnic group. The *Manu Smriti* defines an Aryan as a highly evolved and cultured person. 'Aryan' implies goodness, like the term 'perfect gentleman'. The aim of the Vedic scriptures is to induce humans to become Aryans in all respects. Shree Krishna finds Arjun's present condition in conflict with that ideal and reprimands him by calling attention to his confusion on how to live up to this ideal state of being given his current state of mind.

The Bhagavad Gita or 'Song of God', effectively begins from here because Shree Krishna, who was quiet until now, starts speaking. The

Supreme Lord first begins by inducing in Arjun a hunger for knowledge. He does this by pointing out that his state of confusion is dishonourable and inappropriate for virtuous persons. He then goes on to remind Arjun of the consequences of delusion, which are pain, infamy, failure in life, and degradation of the soul.

Rather than comforting him, Shree Krishna is making Arjun uncomfortable about his current state. We all feel uncomfortable when we are confused because it is not the natural condition of the soul. This feeling of discontentment, if properly channeled, can become a powerful impetus to search for true knowledge. The appropriate resolution of doubt helps a person acquire a deeper understanding than before. Thus, God sometimes deliberately puts a person in turmoil, so that he or she may be forced to search for knowledge to address the confusion. And when the doubt is finally resolved, one reaches a higher level of understanding.

क्लैब्यं मा स्म गमः पार्थ नैतत्त्वय्युपपद्यते ।
क्षुद्रं हृदयदौर्बल्यं त्यक्त्वोत्तिष्ठ परन्तप ।।3।।

klaibyaṁ mā sma gamaḥ pārtha naitat tvayyupapadyate
kṣhudraṁ hṛidaya-daurbalyaṁ tyaktvottiṣhṭha parantapa

klaibyam—unmanliness; *mā sma*—do not; *gamaḥ*—yield to; *pārtha*—Arjun, son of Pritha; *na*—not; *etat*—this; *tvayi*—to you; *upapadyate*—befitting; *kṣhudram*—petty; *hṛidaya*—heart; *daurbalyam*—weakness; *tyaktvā*—giving up; *uttiṣhṭha*—arise; *param-tapa*—conqueror of enemies.

O Parth, it does not befit you to yield to this unmanliness. Give up such petty weakness of heart and arise, O vanquisher of enemies.

Successfully treading the path of enlightenment requires high spirits and morale. One needs to be optimistic, enthusiastic, and energetic to overcome the negativities of the material mind, such as sloth, the rut of habit, ignorance, and attachment. Shree Krishna is a skilful teacher, and having reprimanded Arjun, He now enhances Arjun's internal strength to tackle the situation by encouraging him.

By addressing Arjun as the son of Pritha (another name for Kunti), Shree Krishna invokes him to remember his mother Kunti. She had worshipped Indra, chief of the celestial gods, and with his blessings Arjun was born. Hence, he was endowed with extraordinary might and valour, similar to Indra. Shree Krishna is reminding him of this and inspiring him to not yield to this impotence, which does not befit his illustrious parentage. Again, He addresses Arjun as Parantapa, or conqueror of enemies, exhorting him to vanquish the enemy that has arisen within him, visible by his desire to shun his dutiful action as a Kshatriya or a warrior class prince.

Shree Krishna goes on to explain that the way he is feeling is neither moral duty nor true compassion; rather, it is lamentation and delusion. It has its roots in the weakness of the mind. If his behaviour was truly based on wisdom and mercy, then he would experience neither confusion nor grief.

अर्जुन उवाच ।
कथं भीष्ममहं सङ्ख्ये द्रोणं च मधुसूदन ।
इषुभिः प्रतियोत्स्यामि पूजार्हावरिसूदन ।।4।।

arjuna uvācha
kathaṁ bhīṣhmam ahaṁ sankhye droṇaṁ cha madhusūdana
iṣhubhiḥ pratiyotsyāmi pūjārhāvari-sūdana

arjunaḥ uvācha—Arjun said; *katham*—how; *bhīṣhmam*—Bheeshma; *aham*—I; *sankhye*—in battle; *droṇam*—Dronacharya; *cha*—and; *madhu-sūdana*—Shree Krishna, slayer of the Madhu demon; *iṣhubhiḥ*—with arrows; *pratiyotsyāmi*—shall I shoot; *pūjā-arhau*—worthy of worship; *ari-sūdana*—destroyer of enemies.

Arjun said: O Madhusudan, how can I shoot arrows in battle on men like Bheeshma and Dronacharya, who are worthy of my worship, O destroyer of enemies?

In response to Shree Krishna's call for action, Arjun presents his confusion. He states that Bheeshma and Dronacharya are worthy of his respect and adoration. Bheeshma was the embodiment of chastity and remained a lifelong celibate to fulfill the vow he had made to his father. Arjun's military preceptor, Dronacharya, was a genius in the science of warfare, and it was from him that Arjun mastered the art of archery. Kripacharya was another respectable person on the other side whom Arjun had always held in veneration. To treat these men of high merit as enemies now seemed abominable to the noble-minded Arjun. If even arguing with these venerable elders was improper, then how could he ever think of attacking them with weapons? His statement thus implies, 'O Krishna, please do not doubt my courage. I am prepared to fight. But from the perspective of moral duty, my duty is to respect my teachers and to show compassion to the sons of Dhritarashtra.'

गुरूनहत्वा हि महानुभावान्
श्रेयो भोक्तुं भैक्ष्यमपीह लोके ।
हत्वार्थकामांस्तु गुरूनिहैव
भुञ्जीय भोगान् रुधिरप्रदिग्धान् ।।5।।

gurūnahatvā hi mahānubhāvān
śhreyo bhoktuṁ bhaikṣhyamapīha loke
hatvārtha-kāmāṁstu gurūnihaiva
bhuñjīya bhogān rudhira-pradigdhān

gurūn—teachers; *ahatvā*—not killing; *hi*—certainly; *mahā-anubhāvān*—noble elders; *śhreyaḥ*—better; *bhoktum*—to enjoy life; *bhaikṣhyam*—by begging; *api*—even; *iha loke*—in this world; *hatvā*—killing; *artha*—gain; *kāmān*—desiring; *tu*—but; *gurūn*—noble elders; *iha*—in this world; *eva*—certainly; *bhuñjīya*—enjoy; *bhogān*—pleasures; *rudhira*—blood; *pradigdhān*—tainted with.

It would be better to live in this world by begging than to enjoy life by killing these noble elders, who are my teachers. If we kill them, the wealth and pleasures we enjoy will be tainted with blood.

It could be argued that Arjun needed to fight and win the kingdom to maintain his livelihood. But Arjun refutes that line of thought here. He says that he would prefer to live by begging than commit this heinous crime. He further believes that if he does indulge in this terrible act of killing his elders and relatives, his conscience will not allow him to enjoy any of the fruits of his action in this world, such as riches and power.

Shakespeare's play *Macbeth* carries a telling example of a person not being able to enjoy even the natural state of sleep due to a guilty conscience, let alone enjoy any wealth and power that comes along by immoral conduct. Macbeth was a nobleman of Scotland. Once while travelling, the king of Scotland came to rest during the night at his house. Macbeth's wife incited him to murder the king and usurp his throne. Macbeth got swayed by her advice and assassinated the king, and thereafter, he and Lady Macbeth were crowned as the king and queen of Scotland. However, for years after, Macbeth could be found walking in his palace, fully awake at night. The author writes, 'Macbeth hath killed sleep, and so Macbeth shall sleep no more.' The queen could be found repeatedly washing her hands as if to remove imaginary blood stains. In this verse, Arjun commiserates that if he did kill these noble elders, tainted with their blood, his conscience would not let him enjoy all the royal benefits of ruling the kingdom.

न चैतद्विद्मः कतरन्नो गरीयो
यद्वा जयेम यदि वा नो जयेयुः ।
यानेव हत्वा न जिजीविषाम
स्तेऽवस्थिताः प्रमुखे धार्तराष्ट्राः ।।6।।

na chaitadvidmaḥ kataranno garīyo
yadvā jayema yadi vā no jayeyuḥ
yāneva hatvā na jijīviṣhāmas
te 'vasthitāḥ pramukhe dhārtarāṣhṭrāḥ

na—not; *cha*—and; *etat*—this; *vidmaḥ*—we know; *katarat*—which; *naḥ*—for us; *garīyaḥ*—is preferable; *yat vā*—whether; *jayema*—we may conquer; *yadi*—if; *vā*—or; *naḥ*—us; *jayeyuḥ*—they may conquer; *yān*—whom; *eva*—certainly; *hatvā*—after killing; *na*—not; *jijīviṣhāmaḥ*—we desire to live; *te*—they; *avasthitāḥ*—are standing; *pramukhe*—before us; *dhārtarāṣhṭrāḥ*—sons of Dhritarashtra.

We do not even know which result of this war is preferable for us—conquering them or being conquered by them. Even after killing them, we will not desire to live. Yet they have taken the side of Dhritarashtra, and now stand before us on the battlefield.

When evaluating the most suitable course of action, one considers various alternatives and their consequences. Arjun was debating whether it would be desirable to defeat the Kauravas or to be defeated by them. Both alternatives seemed like defeat, for if he did win the war by slaying the Kauravas, he would have no further desire to live.

However, the fact was that Bheeshma, Dronacharya, and Kripacharya, along with others had acted ignobly by taking the side of the unrighteous Kauravas. The word *arthakām* has been used for them, implying, 'attached to wealth and position', as they had taken the side of the wicked Duryodhan. So, killing them in war would be a natural consequence. In fact, after the war, Bheeshma himself admitted that a teacher who acts ignobly is fit to be abandoned.

Here, special mention needs to be made of Bheeshma. According to the Shreemad Bhagavatam (verse 9.22.19), he was a great devotee of Shree Krishna. He was a master of his senses and an icon of chivalry and generosity. He was a knower of the Absolute Truth and had vowed to always speak the truth. Even death could only come to him when he chose to accept it. For multiple reasons, he is enumerated among the twelve great personalities, or Mahajans, mentioned in the Bhagavatam:

swayambhūr nāradaḥ śhambhuḥ kumāraḥ kapilo manuḥ
prahlādo janako bhīṣhmo balir vaiyāsakir vayam (6.3.20)

'These are the twelve great knowers of religious principles—the first-born Brahma, Sage Narad, Lord Shiv, the four Kumars, Bhagavan Kapil (son of Devahuti), Svayambhuva Manu, Prahalad Maharaj, Janak Maharaj, Grandfather Bheeshma, Bali Maharaj, Shukadev Muni, and Ved Vyas.'

Hence, Bheeshma was an enlightened soul, whose actions could never be against the principles of dharma. However, his profound character was beyond mundane reasoning. Even though he fought on the side of the Kauravas, before the war he said to Yudhishthir (the eldest Pandava brother), 'I am obliged to combat on the side of unrighteousness, but I give you the boon that you will be victorious.' Bheeshma knew that the righteous Pandavas, who had the Supreme Lord Shree Krishna on their side, could never lose. By taking the side of *adharma* (unrighteousness), he showed that even the biggest forces on heaven and earth could not make unholiness win in this holy war. He thus offered the biggest sacrifice of laying down his life, to assist in the divine pastimes of Lord Krishna.

Shree Krishna was well aware of Bheeshma's deep devotion towards Him despite his fighting from the side of the Kauravas. That is why He upheld Bheeshma's vow by breaking His own. Bheeshma resolved on a particular day during the war that before sunset on the next day, he would either kill Arjun, the foremost Pandava warrior, or else to save him, Shree Krishna would have to break His own vow of not lifting weapons in the battle of Mahabharat. Poets describe the vow that Bheeshma made:

āju jo harihiṅ na śhastra gahāūñ,
tau lājahuñ gaṅgā jananī ko śhāntanu suta na kahāūñ

(Saint Tulsidas)

'If I do not make the Supreme Lord Shree Krishna lift weapons, then I will shame my mother Ganga, and I am not the son of King Shantanu.' Bheeshma fought so valiantly that Arjun's chariot was shattered, and he was stranded on the ground. At that stage, Shree Krishna lifted the chariot wheel and came forward to prevent Bheeshma from killing Arjun. Bheeshma saw the Lord with the chariot wheel in His hand as a weapon and broke into a big smile. He understood that *Bhaktavatsala Bhagavan* (God who gives pleasure to His devotees) had broken His own vow to honour the vow of His devotee.

In fact, Bheeshma's devotion to Lord Krishna had a very *rasik* (full of sweetness) flavour to it. He used to meditate on Shree Krishna's pastimes in Vrindavan. There, in the evening when the Lord would return to the village after grazing the cows in the forest, the dust raised from the hooves of the cows would cover His charming face, increasing its beauty and allure. During the battle of Mahabharat, the dust raised from the hooves of the horses too added to Shree Krishna's beauty, and he loved having darshan (divine vision) of his Lord there.

In the last stage of his life, as he lay for six months on a bed of arrows, he meditated on that very vision of God, offering the following prayer to Him:

yudhi turaga-rajo-vidhūmra-viṣhvak-
kacha-lulita-śhramavāry-alaṅkṛitāsye
mama niśhita-śharair vibhidyamāna-
tvachi vilasat-kavache 'stu kṛiṣhṇa ātmā

(Bhagavatam 1.9.34)

'On the battlefield, Lord Krishna's flowing hair was covered with white dust raised by the hooves of the horses, and His face was covered with sweat beads because of His physical effort in driving the chariot. These were like ornaments enhancing the beauty of my Lord; and the wounds dealt by my sharp arrows further intensified the decorations. Let my mind meditate unto that Shree Krishna.'

Lord Krishna reciprocated his loving devotion by coming to meet Bheeshma on his deathbed of arrows, and with the darshan of God in front of him, Bheeshma, the great mahajan, left his body of his own volition.

कार्पण्यदोषोपहतस्वभावः
पृच्छामि त्वां धर्मसम्मूढचेताः ।
यच्छ्रेयः स्यान्निश्चितं ब्रूहि तन्मे
शिष्यस्तेऽहं शाधि मां त्वां प्रपन्नम् ।।7।।

kārpaṇya-doṣhopahata-svabhāvaḥ
pṛichchhāmi tvāṁ dharma-sammūḍha-chetāḥ
yach-chhreyaḥ syānniśhchitaṁ brūhi tanme
śhiṣhyaste 'haṁ śhādhi māṁ tvāṁ prapannam

kārpaṇya-doṣha—the flaw of cowardice; *upahata*—besieged; *sva-bhāvaḥ*—nature; *pṛichchhāmi*—I am asking; *tvām*—to you;

dharma—duty; *sammūḍha*—confused; *chetāḥ*—in heart; *yat*—what; *śhreyaḥ*—best; *syāt*—may be; *niśhchitam*—decisively; *brūhi*—tell; *tat*—that; *me*—to me; *śhiṣhyaḥ*—disciple; *te*—your; *aham*—I; *śhādhi*—please instruct; *mām*—me; *tvām*—unto you; *prapannam*—surrendered.

I am confused about my duty and am besieged with anxiety and faintheartedness. I am Your disciple and am surrendered to You. Please instruct me for certain what is best for me.

This is a great moment in the Bhagavad Gita, when for the first time, Arjun, who is Shree Krishna's friend and cousin, requests Him to be his guru. Arjun pleads to Shree Krishna that he has been overpowered by *kārpaṇya doṣh*, or the flaw of cowardice in behaviour, and so he requests the Lord to become his guru and instruct him about the path of auspiciousness.

All the Vedic scriptures declare in unison that it is through the medium of a Spiritual Master that we receive divine knowledge for our eternal welfare:

tadvijñānārthaṁ sagurumevābhigachchhet samitpāniḥ
śhrotriyaṁ bhramhaniṣhṭham (*Muṇḍakopaniṣhad* 1.2.12)

'To know the Absolute Truth, approach a guru who is both a knower of the scriptures and is practically situated on the platform of God-realisation.'

tasmād guruṁ prapadyeta jijñāsuḥ śhreya uttamam
śhābde pare cha niṣhṇātaṁ brahmaṇy upaśhamāśhrayam

(Bhagavatam 11.3.21)

'Seekers of the Truth should surrender themselves to a Spiritual Master who has understood the conclusion of the scriptures and taken complete shelter of God, leaving aside all material considerations.'

The Ramayan states:

guru binu bhava nidhi tarai na koī jauṅ biranchi sankara sama hoī

'Not even the most elevated of spiritual aspirants can cross over the material ocean without the grace of the guru.' Shree Krishna states this Himself in the Bhagavad Gita in verse 4.34: 'Learn the Truth by approaching a spiritual master. Enquire from him with reverence and render service unto him. Such an enlightened saint can impart knowledge unto you because he has seen the Truth.'

To demonstrate the need for accepting a guru to gain knowledge, Shree Krishna Himself took this step. In His youth, He went to the hermitage of Sandipani Muni to learn sixty-four sciences from him. His classmate, Sudama, remarked:

yasya chchhando mayaṁ brahma deha āvapanaṁ vibho
śhreyasāṁ tasya guruṣhu vāso 'tyanta viḍambanam

(Bhagavatam 10.80.45)

'O Shree Krishna, the Vedas are like Your body, manifested from the knowledge that You possess (hence, what requirement do You have for making a guru?). Yet, You too pretend You need to learn from a guru; this is only Your divine leela (pastime).'

Shree Krishna is in fact the first guru of the world, because He is the guru of Brahma, the first-born in this material world. He performed this leela for our benefit, to teach by His example that we souls, who are under the influence of maya, will need a guru to dispel our ignorance. In this verse, Arjun takes the step of surrendering to Shree Krishna as His disciple and requests his guru to enlighten him regarding the proper course of action.

न हि प्रपश्यामि ममापनुद्याद्
यच्छोकमुच्छोषणमिन्द्रियाणाम् ।
अवाप्य भूमावसपत्नमृद्धं
राज्यं सुराणामपि चाधिपत्यम् ।।8।।

na hi prapaśhyāmi mamāpanudyād
yach-chhokam uchchhoṣhaṇam-indriyāṇām
avāpya bhūmāv-asapatnamṛiddhaṁ
rājyaṁ surāṇāmapi chādhipatyam

na—not; *hi*—certainly; *prapaśhyāmi*—I see; *mama*—my; *apanudyāt*—drive away; *yat*—which; *śhokam*—anguish; *uchchhoṣhaṇam*—is drying up; *indriyāṇām*—of the senses; *avāpya*—after achieving; *bhūmau*—on the earth; *asapatnam*—unrivalled; *ṛiddham*—prosperous; *rājyam*—kingdom; *surāṇām*—like the celestial gods; *api*—even; *cha*—also; *ādhipatyam*—sovereignty.

I can find no means of driving away this anguish that is drying up my senses. Even if I win a prosperous and unrivalled kingdom on the earth, or gain sovereignty like the celestial gods, I will be unable to dispel this grief.

When we are swamped in misery, the intellect keeps analysing the cause of misery, and when it is able to think no further, then dejection sets in. Since Arjun's problems are looming larger than his feeble intellectual abilities, his material knowledge is insufficient to save him from the ocean of grief that he finds himself in. Having accepted Shree Krishna as his guru, Arjun now pours out his heart to Him revealing his pitiable state.

Arjun's situation is not unique. This is invariably the situation we sometimes find ourselves in as we go through the journey of life. We want happiness but experience misery; we desire knowledge but are unable to lift the cloud of ignorance; we crave perfect love but repeatedly meet with disappointment. Our college degrees, acquired knowledge, and mundane scholarships do not provide solutions to these perplexities of life. We need divine knowledge to solve the puzzle of life. That treasure chest of divine knowledge is opened when we find a true guru, one who is situated in transcendence, provided we have the humility to learn from him. Such is the path Arjun decided to take.

सञ्जय उवाच ।
एवमुक्त्वा हृषीकेशं गुडाकेशः परन्तप ।
न योत्स्य इति गोविन्दमुक्त्वा तूष्णीं बभूव ह ।।9।।

sañjaya uvācha
evam-uktvā hṛiṣhīkeśhaṁ guḍākeśhaḥ parantapa
na yotsya iti govindam uktvā tūṣhṇīṁ babhūva ha

sañjayaḥ uvācha—Sanjay said; *evam*—thus; *uktvā*—having spoken; *hṛiṣhīkeśham*—to Shree Krishna, master of the mind and senses; *guḍākeśhaḥ*—Arjun, conquerer of sleep; *parantapaḥ*—Arjun, chastiser of enemies; *na yotsye*—I shall not fight; *iti*—thus; *govindam*—Krishna, giver of pleasure to the senses; *uktvā*—having addressed; *tūṣhṇīm*—silent; *babhūva*—became; *ha*—he.

Sanjay said: Having thus spoken, Gudakesh, that chastiser of enemies, addressed Hrishikesh, 'Govind, I shall not fight' and became silent.

The sagacious Sanjay, in his narration to Dhritarashtra, uses very apt names for the personalities he refers to. Here, Arjun is called Gudakesh or 'conqueror of sleep'. The power of sleep is such that all living beings succumb to it sooner or later. But with his determination, Arjun had disciplined himself in such a way that sleep would come to him only when he permitted it and only for the amount of time he chose. By using the name Gudakesh for Arjun, Sanjay is subtly hinting to Dhritarashtra, 'Just as this "hero amongst men" conquered sleep, so too will he conquer his despondency.'

And the word he uses for Shree Krishna is Hrishikesh or 'master of the mind and senses'. The subtle hint here is that He who is the master of his senses will definitely ensure that the events are properly managed.

तमुवाच हृषीकेशः प्रहसन्निव भारत ।
सेनयोरुभयोर्मध्ये विषीदन्तमिदं वचः ।।10।।

tam-uvācha hṛiṣhīkeśhaḥ prahasanniva bhārata
senayorubhayor-madhye viṣhīdantam-idaṁ vachaḥ

tam—to him; *uvācha*—said; *hṛiṣhīkeśhaḥ*—Shree Krishna, Master of mind and senses; *prahasan*—smilingly; *iva*—as if; *bhārata*—Dhritarashtra, descendant of Bharat; *senayoḥ*—of the armies;

ubhayoḥ—of both; *madhye*—in the midst of; *viṣhīdantam*—to the grief-stricken; *idam*—this; *vachaḥ*—words.

O Dhritarashtra, thereafter, in the midst of both the armies, Shree Krishna smilingly spoke the following words to the grief-stricken Arjun.

In sharp contrast to Arjun's words of lamentation, Shree Krishna smiled, displaying that the situation was not making Him despair; rather, He was perfectly happy with it. Such is the equanimous attitude exhibited in all situations, by someone with true knowledge.

With our incomplete understanding, we find faults with the situations we are in—we complain and grumble about them, wish to run away from them, and hold them responsible for our misery. But the enlightened souls inform us that the world created by God is perfect in every way, and both good and bad situations come to us for a divine purpose. They all are arranged for our spiritual evolution, to push us upward in our journey towards perfection. Those who understand this secret are never disturbed in difficult circumstances, facing them with serenity and tranquility.

'The snowflakes fall slowly to the ground, each flake in its proper place' is a famous Taoist expression. It beautifully expresses the inherent perfection in the design of the world and the macro events taking place in it even though we are not able to perceive it from our material perspective.

The *Chhāndogya Upanishad* explains why earthquakes, hurricanes, cyclones, floods, and typhoons are created in the world by God, as a part of the grand scheme of things. It states that God deliberately creates difficult situations to prevent people from slowing down in their journey of spiritual progress. When people become complacent, a natural calamity comes along, forcing the souls to strain their abilities to cope with it, which ensures their progress. However, it must be noted that the progress being talked about here is not the external increase of material luxuries, but the internal unfoldment of the glorious divinity of the soul over a continuum of lifetimes.

श्रीभगवानुवाच ।
अशोच्यानन्वशोचस्त्वं प्रज्ञावादांश्च भाषसे ।
गतासूनगतासूंश्च नानुशोचन्ति पण्डिताः ।।11।।

śhrī bhagavān uvācha
aśhochyān-anvaśhochas-tvaṁ prajñā-vādānśh cha bhāṣhase
gatāsūn-agatāsūnśh-cha nānuśhochanti paṇḍitāḥ

śhrī-bhagavān uvācha—the Supreme Lord said; *aśhochyān*—not worthy of grief; *anvaśhochaḥ*—are mourning; *tvam*—you; *prajñā-vādān*—words of wisdom; *cha*—and; *bhāṣhase*—speaking; *gata āsūn*—the dead; *agata asūn*—the living; *cha*—and; *na*—never; *anuśhochanti*—lament; *paṇḍitāḥ*—the wise.

The Supreme Lord said: While you speak words of wisdom, you are mourning for that which is not worthy of grief. The wise lament neither for the living nor for the dead.

Starting with this verse, Shree Krishna initiates His discourse with a dramatic opening statement. Arjun is lamenting for what he feels are very valid reasons. Rather than commiserate with him, Shree Krishna takes the wind out of his arguments. He says, 'Arjun, though you may feel you are speaking words of wisdom, you are actually speaking and acting out of ignorance. No possible reason justifies lamentation. The pandits—those who are wise—never lament, neither for the living nor for the dead. Hence the grief you visualise in killing your relatives is illusory, and it proves that you are not a pandit.'

One does not need to go far into the Gita to find a wise person above lamentation; Grandsire Bheeshma himself was the perfect example. He was a sage who had fathomed the mysteries of life and death and risen above the dualities of circumstances. Serene in any eventuality, he had even consented to taking the side of the wicked, if it served the Lord. He thus demonstrated that those who are surrendered to God simply do their duty in all situations without being affected by outcomes. Such persons never lament because they accept all circumstances as God's grace.

न त्वेवाहं जातु नासं न त्वं नेमे जनाधिपाः ।
न चैव न भविष्यामः सर्वे वयमतः परम् ।।12।।

na tvevāhaṁ jātu nāsaṁ na tvaṁ neme janādhipāḥ
na chaiva na bhaviṣhyāmaḥ sarve vayamataḥ param

na—never; *tu*—however; *eva*—certainly; *aham*—I; *jātu*—at any time; *na*—nor; *āsam*—exist; *na*—nor; *tvam*—you; *na*—nor; *ime*—these; *jana-adhipāḥ*—kings; *na*—never; *cha*—also; *eva*—indeed; *na bhaviṣhyāmaḥ*—shall not exist; *sarve vayam*—all of us; *ataḥ*—from now; *param*—after.

Never was there a time when I did not exist, nor you, nor all these kings; nor in the future shall any of us cease to be.

On the gates of the temple of Apollo at Delphi are inscribed the words, *Gnothi Seuton* or 'Know Thyself'. Even Socrates, the wise old man of Athens, was fond of encouraging people to enquire into the nature of the self. A local legend goes like this:

Once, Socrates was walking on the street, absorbed in deep philosophic contemplation, when he accidentally bumped into someone.

That man blurted in annoyance, 'Can't you see where you walk? Who are you?'

Socrates answered with amusement, 'My dear fellow, I have been pondering over that question for the last forty years. If you ever come to know who I am, please let me know.'

In the Vedic tradition, whenever divine knowledge is imparted, it usually begins with knowledge of the self. Shree Krishna follows the same approach in the Bhagavad Gita with a piece of information that would have swept Socrates off his feet. Shree Krishna begins by explaining that the entity we call the 'self' is really the soul, not the material body, and is eternal, just as God Himself is eternal. The *Śhwetāśhvatar Upanishad* states:

jñājñau dwāvajā vīśhanīśhā-
vajā hyekā bhoktṛi bhogyārtha yuktā
anantaśhchātmā viśhwarūpo hyakartā
trayaṁ yadā vindate brahmametat (1.9)

The above verse states that creation is a combination of three entities—God, soul, and maya—and all the three are eternal. *If we believe the soul is eternal, then it follows logically that there is life after death of the material body. Shree Krishna talks about this in the next verse.*

देहिनोऽस्मिन्यथा देहे कौमारं यौवनं जरा ।
तथा देहान्तरप्राप्तिर्धीरस्तत्र न मुह्यति ।।13।।

dehino 'smin yathā dehe kaumāraṁ yauvanaṁ jarā
tathā dehāntara-prāptir dhīras tatra na muhyati

dehinaḥ—of the embodied; *asmin*—in this; *yathā*—as; *dehe*—in the body; *kaumāram*—childhood; *yauvanam*—youth; *jarā*—old age; *tathā*—similarly; *deha-antara*—another body; *prāptiḥ*—achieves; *dhīraḥ*—the wise; *tatra*—thereupon; *na muhyati*—are not deluded.

Just as the embodied soul continuously passes from childhood to youth to old age, similarly, at the time of death, the soul passes into another body. The wise are not deluded by this.

With immaculate logic, Shree Krishna establishes the principle of transmigration of the soul from lifetime to lifetime. He explains that in one lifetime itself, we change bodies from childhood to youth to maturity and then to old age. In fact, modern science informs us that cells within the body undergo regeneration—old cells die, and new ones take their place. It is estimated that within seven years, practically all the cells of the body change. Further, the molecules within the cells change even more rapidly. With every breath we inhale, oxygen molecules are absorbed into our cells via metabolic processes, and molecules that were earlier locked within the cells are released as carbon dioxide. Scientists estimate that in one year's time, about ninety-eight per cent of our bodily molecules change. And yet, despite the continual change of the body, we perceive that we are the same person. This is because we are not the material body, but the spiritual soul seated within.

In this verse, the word *deha* means 'the body', and *dehi* means 'possessor of the body' or the soul. Shree Krishna draws Arjun's attention to the fact that since the body is constantly changing in one lifetime itself, the soul passes through many bodies. Similarly, at the time of death, it passes into another body. Actually, what we term as 'death' in worldly parlance is merely the soul discarding its old dysfunctional body, and what we call 'birth' is the soul taking on a new body elsewhere. This is the principle of reincarnation.

Most Oriental philosophies accept this concept of reincarnation. It is an integral part of Hinduism, Jainism, and Sikhism. In Buddhism, the Buddha made references to His past lives repeatedly. Many people do not know the extent to which reincarnation was a part of the belief system of the Occidental philosophies as well. In ancient classical Western religious and philosophic circles, famous thinkers, such as Pythagoras, Plato, and Socrates accepted reincarnation to be true, and their views were also reflected in Orphism, Hermeticism, Neoplatonism, Manichaeism, and Gnosticism. Within the mainstream Abrahamic faiths, mystics of the three major religions also supported reincarnation. Examples include Jews who studied the Kabbalah, the Christian Cathars, and Muslim Shia sects, such as the Alawi Shias and the Druze. For example, amongst Occidental religions, Josephus, the great ancient Jewish historian, used language in his writings that seems to ascribe belief in some form of reincarnation among the Pharisees and Essenes of his day. Certainly, the Jewish Kabbalah prescribes to the idea of reincarnation as *gilgul neshamot* or the 'rolling of the soul'. The great Sufi mystic, Maulana Jalaluddin Rumi declared:

> I died out of the stone and I became a plant;
> I died out of the plant and became an animal;
> I died out of the animal and became a man.
> Why then should I fear to die?
> When did I grow less by dying?
> I shall die out of man and shall become an angel!

Many of the early Christians believed in the concept of reincarnation. Christian history informs us that in 325 AD, the Council of Nicaea, a conclave, was held to discuss the principle of reincarnation, and it was thereafter declared a heresy, apparently to increase the authority of the Church over the lives of the people. Until then, it was commonly accepted. Jesus indirectly proclaimed this doctrine when he told his disciples that John the Baptist was Elijah the Prophet reincarnated (Matthew 11:13–14, Matthew 17:10–13). This is also mentioned in the Old Testament (Malachi 4:5). Origen, the most learned of the Christian Fathers, declared: 'Every man receives a body for himself according to his deserts in former lives.' Solomon's *Book of Wisdom* says: 'To be born in sound body with sound limbs is a reward of the virtues of the past lives.' (*Wisdom of Solomon* 8:19–20)

Belief in reincarnation is also found in many tribal societies around the world, such as in Siberia, West Africa, North America, and Australia. Moving to more recent centuries and civilisations, reincarnation has been affirmed by Rosicrucians, Spiritism, Theosophists, and New Age followers. Lately, it has even been studied in serious scientific circles at major universities exemplified by the works of Dr Ian Stevenson and Dr Jim Tucker, both at the University of Virginia.

Without accepting the concept of rebirth, it is difficult to make sense out of the suffering, chaos, and incompleteness of the world, and hence, many famous western thinkers also believed in this principle. Virgil and Ovid regarded this doctrine as self-evident. The German philosophers Goethe, Fichte, Schelling, and Lessing accepted it. Among the more recent philosophers, Hume, Spencer, and Max Müeller, all recognised it as an incontrovertible doctrine. Among Western poets, Browning, Rosetti, Tennyson, and Wordsworth, to mention just a few, believed in it.

Shree Krishna has previously declared that the wise do not lament. But the fact remains that we do experience happiness and distress. What is the reason for this? He now explains this concept.

मात्रास्पर्शास्तु कौन्तेय शीतोष्णसुखदुःखदाः ।
आगमापायिनोऽनित्यास्तांस्तितिक्षस्व भारत ।।14।।

mātrā-sparśhās tu kaunteya śhītoṣhṇa-sukha-duḥkha-dāḥ
āgamāpāyino 'nityās tans-titikṣhasva bhārata

mātrā-sparśhāḥ—contact of the senses with the sense objects; *tu*—indeed; *kaunteya*— Arjun, son of Kunti; *śhīta*—winter; *uṣhṇa*—summer; *sukha*—happiness; *duḥkha*— distress; *dāḥ*—give; *āgama*—come; *apāyinaḥ*—go; *anityāḥ*—non-permanent; *tān*—them; *titikṣhasva*—tolerate; *bhārata*—descendant of Bharat.

O son of Kunti, the contact between the senses and the sense objects gives rise to fleeting perceptions of happiness and distress. These are non-permanent and come and go like the winter and summer seasons. O descendent of Bharat, one must learn to tolerate them without being disturbed.

The human body houses five senses—the senses of sight, smell, taste, touch, and hearing—and these, in contact with their objects of perception, give rise to sensations of happiness and distress. None of these sensations is permanent; they come and go like the changing seasons. Although cool water provides pleasure in the summer, the same water gives distress in the winter. Thus, both the perceptions of happiness and distress experienced through the senses are transitory. If we permit ourselves to be affected by them, we will sway like a pendulum from side to side. A person of discrimination should practice tolerating both the feelings of happiness and distress without being disturbed by them.

The technique of Vipassana, which is the primary technique of self-realisation in Buddhism, is based on this principle of tolerance of sense perceptions. Its practice helps eliminate desire, which, as stated in the four noble truths (the truth of suffering, the truth of the origin of suffering, the truth of the cessation of suffering, and the truth of the path leading to the cessation), is the cause of all suffering. This is not surprising considering that Buddhist philosophy is a subset of the vast Vedic philosophy.

यं हि न व्यथयन्त्येते पुरुषं पुरुषर्षभ ।
समदुःखसुखं धीरं सोऽमृतत्वाय कल्पते ।।15।।

yaṁ hi na vyathayantyete puruṣhaṁ puruṣharṣhabha
sama-duḥkha-sukhaṁ dhīraṁ so 'mṛitatvāya kalpate

yam—whom; *hi*—verily; *na*—not; *vyathayanti*—distressed; *ete*—these; *puruṣham*—person; *puruṣha-ṛiṣhabha*—noblest among men, Arjun; *sama*—equipoised; *duḥkha*—distress; *sukham*—happiness; *dhīram*—steady; *saḥ*—that person; *amṛitatvāya*—for liberation; *kalpate*—becomes eligible.

O Arjun, noblest amongst men, that person who is not affected by happiness and distress, and remains steady in both, becomes eligible for liberation.

In the previous verse, Shree Krishna explained that both the sensations of happiness and distress are fleeting. He now encourages Arjun to rise above these dualities through discrimination. In order to develop this discrimination, we first need to understand the answers to two important questions: 1) Why do we aspire for happiness? 2) Why doesn't material happiness satisfy us?

The answer to the first question is very simple. God is an ocean of infinite bliss, and we souls are His tiny parts. This basically means that we are tiny fragments of an infinite ocean of bliss. Swami Vivekananda would address people by saying, 'O ye children of immortal bliss.' Just as a child is drawn to his or her mother, each part is naturally drawn towards its whole. Similarly, being infinitesimal parts of the ocean of bliss, we souls too are drawn to this bliss. Hence, everything we do in the world is for the sake of happiness. We all may have different views regarding where happiness lies or what form it might take, but all living beings seek nothing apart from it. This answers the first question.

Now, let's understand the answer to the second question. The soul, being a tiny part of God, is divine in nature like God Himself. As a result, the happiness that the soul seeks is also divine. Such happiness must possess the following three characteristics:

- It must be infinite in extent.
- It must be permanent.
- It must be ever-fresh.

Such is the happiness of God, which is described as *sat-chit-anand* or eternal-sentient-ocean of bliss. However, the happiness we experience from the contact of the senses with their objects is the reverse; it is temporary, finite, and insentient. Thus, the material happiness that we perceive through the body can never satisfy the divine soul.

With this discrimination, we must practice tolerating the perception of material happiness. Similarly, we must tolerate the sensation of material distress. (This second aspect is discussed in detail in many future verses, such as 2.48 and 5.20) Only then will we rise above these dualities and the material energy will no longer bind us.

नासतो विद्यते भावो नाभावो विद्यते सतः ।
उभयोरपि दृष्टोऽन्तस्त्वनयोस्तत्त्वदर्शिभिः ।। 16 ।।

nāsato vidyate bhāvo nābhāvo vidyate sataḥ
ubhayorapi dṛiṣhṭo 'nta stvanayos tattva-darśhibhiḥ

na—no; *asataḥ*—of the temporary; *vidyate*—there is; *bhāvaḥ*—is; *na*—no; *abhāvaḥ*—cessation; *vidyate*—is; *sataḥ*—of the eternal; *ubhayoḥ*—of the two; *api*—also; *dṛiṣhṭaḥ*—observed; *antaḥ*—conclusion; *tu*—verily; *anayoḥ*—of these; *tattva*—entity; *darśhibhiḥ*—by the seers.

Of the transient there is no endurance, and of the eternal there is no cessation. This has verily been observed and concluded by the seers of the Truth, after studying the nature of both.

According to the *Śhwetāśhvatar Upanishad*, there are three entities in existence:

bhoktā bhogyaṁ preritāraṁ cha matvā
sarvaṁ proktaṁ trividhaṁ brahmametat (1.12)

kṣharaṁ pradhānamamṛitākṣharaṁ haraḥ
kṣharātmānāvīśhate deva ekaḥ (1.10)

sanyuktametatkṣharamakṣharaṁ cha
vyaktāvyaktaṁ bharate viśhwamīśhaḥ (1.8)

All these Ved mantras state that these three entities—God, the individual soul, and maya—are all eternal.

1. God is everlasting which means He is *sat* (eternally existing). Hence, a name for Him in the Vedas is *sat-chit-anand* (eternal-full of knowledge-ocean of bliss).

2. The soul is imperishable, and therefore, it is *sat*. However, the body will cease to exist one day, and consequently is *asat* (temporary). The soul is also *sat-chit-anand*, but it is also *aṇu* (tiny). Hence, the soul is *aṇu sat*, *aṇu chit*, and *aṇu anand.*

3. The entity maya from which the world has been made is eternal or *sat*. However, all material objects we see around us came into existence and will be destroyed with time. Thus, they can all be termed as *asat* or temporary. So, while the world itself is *asat*, it is only the entity maya that is *sat*.

When we say that the world is *asat*, this should not be confused with *mithyā*. *Asat* (temporary) does not mean *mithyā* (non-existent). Some philosophers claim that the world is *mithyā*. They assert that it is only the ignorance within us that is making us perceive the world, and once we are situated in brahma jnana, (knowledge of the Supreme) the world will cease to exist. However, if this were true, then the world should no longer have remained for the God-realised saints. Since they have destroyed their ignorance, the world should have stopped existing for them. Why and how then did these saints write books even after attaining the state of God-realisation? Where did the paper and pen come from? The fact that brahma jnanis use the objects of the world proves that the world exists even for them. Besides, even brahma jnanis need food to nourish their bodies. The Vedic scriptures state:

paśhvādibhiśhchāviśheṣhat 'Even God-realised saints feel hungry, just as animals do, and need to eat food.' If the world does not exist for them, then how and why should they eat?

Further, the *Taittirīya Upanishad* repeatedly informs us that God is all-pervading in the world:

> *so 'kāmayata bahu syāṁ prajāyeyeti sa tapo 'tapyata sa tapastaptvā idaṁsarvamasṛijata yadidaṁ kiṁ cha tatsṛiṣhtvā tadevānuprāviṣhat tadanupraviśhya sachcha tyachchābhavat niruktaṁ chāniruktaṁ cha nilayanaṁ chānilaynaṁ cha vijñānaṁ chāvijñānaṁ cha satyaṁ chānṛitam cha satyamabhavat yadidaṁ kiṁ cha tatsatyamityāchakṣhate tadapyeṣha śhloko bhavati* (2.6.4)

This Vedic mantra states that God not only created the world, but also permeates every atom of it. If God is truly all-pervading in this world, then how can the world have no existence? To say that the world is *mithyā* is to contradict the fact that God pervades the world. In this verse, Shree Krishna explains that the world does exist, but it is fleeting. Thus, He calls it *asat* or 'temporary'; He does not call it *mithyā* or 'non-existent'.

अविनाशि तु तद्विद्धि येन सर्वमिदं ततम् ।
विनाशमव्ययस्यास्य न कश्चित्कर्तुमर्हति ।।17।।

avināśhi tu tadviddhi yena sarvam idaṁ tatam
vināśham avyayasyāsya na kaśhchit kartum arhati

avināśhi—indestructible; *tu*—indeed; *tat*—that; *viddhi*—know; *yena*—by whom; *sarvam*—entire; *idam*—this; *tatam*—pervaded; *vināśham*—destruction; *avyayasya*—of the imperishable; *asya*—of it; *na kaśhchit*—no one; *kartum*—to cause; *arhati*—is able.

That which pervades the entire body, know it to be indestructible. No one can cause the destruction of the imperishable soul.

Shree Krishna establishes the relationship between the body and the soul by saying that the soul pervades the body. What does He mean by this? The soul is sentient, i.e., it possesses consciousness. The body is made from insentient matter, devoid of consciousness. However, the soul imparts the quality of consciousness to the body as well, by residing in it. Consequently, the soul pervades the body by spreading its consciousness everywhere in it.

Some raise a question here regarding the location of the soul. The Vedas state that the soul resides in the heart:

hṛidi hyeṣha ātmā (*Praśhnopaniṣhad* 3.6)

sa vā eṣha ātmā hṛidi (*Chhāndogya Upanishad* 8.3.3)

The word *hṛidi* indicates that the soul is seated in the region of the heart. Yet, consciousness, which is the quality of the soul, spreads throughout the body. How does this happen? Ved Vyas explains this concept as follows:

avirodhaśhchandanavat (*Brahma Sutra* 2.3.23)

'Just as applying sandalwood to your forehead cools the entire body, similarly, the soul, although residing locally in the heart, infuses its consciousness throughout the body.'

Again, someone may ask that if consciousness is a characteristic of the soul, then how does it spread into the body? This question has also been answered by Ved Vyas:

vyaktireko gandhavat (*Brahma Sutra* 2.3.26)

'Fragrance is a quality of the flower. But the garden where the flower grows also becomes fragrant.' This means that the flower permeates its fragrance to the garden. Likewise, the soul is sentient, and it also makes the dead matter of the body sentient by pervading it with consciousness.

अन्तवन्त इमे देहा नित्यस्योक्ताः शरीरिणः ।
अनाशिनोऽप्रमेयस्य तस्माद्युध्यस्व भारत ।। 18 ।।

antavanta ime dehā nityasyoktāḥ śharīriṇaḥ
anāśhino 'prameyasya tasmād yudhyasva bhārata

anta-vantaḥ—having an end; *ime*—these; *dehāḥ*—material bodies; *nityasya*—eternally; *uktāḥ*—are said; *śharīriṇaḥ*—of the embodied soul; *anāśhinaḥ*—indestructible; *aprameyasya*—immeasurable; *tasmāt*—therefore; *yudhyasva*—fight; *bhārata*—descendant of Bharat, Arjun.

Only the material body is perishable; the embodied soul within is indestructible, immeasurable, and eternal. Therefore, fight, O descendent of Bharat.

The gross body is factually made from mud. It is mud that gets converted to vegetables, fruits, grains, lentils, and grass. Cows graze the grass and produce milk. We humans consume these edibles, and they transform into our body. So, it is not an exaggeration to say that the body is created from mud.

At the time of death, when the soul departs, the body can have one of the three ends: *kṛimi*, *viḍ*, or *bhasma*. Either it is burnt, in which case it is converted to ashes and becomes mud. Or it is buried, in which case insects eat it and transform it into mud. Else, it is thrown into the river, in which case the sea creatures make it their fodder and excrete it as waste, which ultimately merges with the mud of the seabed.

In this manner, mud undergoes an amazing cycle in the world. It gets transformed into edibles, bodies are made from these edibles, and the bodies go back into mud. The Bible states: 'For dust thou are, and unto dust thou shalt return.' (Genesis 3:19) This phrase refers to the material body. Shree Krishna tells Arjun, 'Within that material body is an eternal imperishable entity which is not made of mud. That is the divine soul, the real self.'

य एनं वेत्ति हन्तारं यश्चैनं मन्यते हतम् ।
उभौ तौ न विजानीतो नायं हन्ति न हन्यते ।।19।।

ya enaṁ vetti hantāraṁ yaśh chainaṁ manyate hatam
ubhau tau na vijānīto nāyaṁ hanti na hanyate

yaḥ—one who; *enam*—this; *vetti*—knows; *hantāram*—the slayer; *yaḥ*—one who; *cha*—and; *enam*—this; *manyate*—thinks; *hatam*—slain; *ubhau*—both; *tau*—they; *na*—not; *vijānītaḥ*—in knowledge; *na*—neither; *ayam*—this; *hanti*—slays; *na*—nor; *hanyate*—is killed.

Neither of them is in knowledge—the one who thinks the soul can slay and the one who thinks the soul can be slain. For truly, the soul neither kills nor can it be killed.

The illusion of death is created because we identify ourselves with the body. The Ramayan explains this as follows:

jauṅ sapaneṅ sira kāṭai koī, binu jāgeṅ na dūri dukh hoī

'If we dream of our head getting cut, we will perceive its pain until we wake up.' The incident in the dream is an illusion, but the experience of the pain continues to torment until we wake up and dispel the illusion. Similarly, in the illusion that we are the body, we fear the experience of death. For the enlightened soul whose illusion has been dispelled, this fear of death vanishes.

One may ask that if nobody can kill anyone, then why is murder considered a punishable offence? The answer is that the body is the vehicle of the soul and destroying any living being's vehicle is violence, which is forbidden. The Vedas clearly instruct: *mā hinsyāt sarvabhūtāni* 'Do not commit violence towards anyone.' In fact, the Vedas even consider killing of animals as a crime.

However, there are occasions where the rules change and even violence becomes necessary. For example, in cases where a snake is approaching to bite, or if one is attacked with lethal weapons, or if one's life sustenance is being snatched away, then violence is permitted for self-protection.

In the present situation, what is appropriate for Arjun, violence or non-violence, and why? Shree Krishna will explain this to him in great detail as the dialogue of the Bhagavad Gita progresses. And in the course of the explanation, priceless divine knowledge will be revealed to shed light on the subject.

न जायते म्रियते वा कदाचिन्नायं भूत्वा भविता वा न भूयः ।
अजो नित्यः शाश्वतोऽयं पुराणो न हन्यते हन्यमाने शरीरे ।।20।।

na jāyate mriyate vā kadāchin nāyaṁ bhūtvā bhavitā vā na bhūyaḥ
ajo nityaḥ śhāśhvato 'yaṁ purāṇo na hanyate hanyamāne śharīre

na jāyate—is not born; *mriyate*—dies; *vā*—or; *kadāchit*—at any time; *na*—not; *ayam*—this; *bhūtvā*—having once existed; *bhavitā*—will be; *vā*—or; *na*—not; *bhūyaḥ*—further; *ajaḥ*—unborn; *nityaḥ*—eternal; *śhāśhvataḥ*—immortal; *ayam*—this; *purāṇaḥ*—the ancient; *na hanyate*—is not destroyed; *hanyamāne*—is destroyed; *śharīre*—when the body.

The soul is neither born, nor does it ever die; nor having once existed, does it ever cease to be. The soul is without birth, eternal, immortal, and ageless. It is not destroyed when the body is destroyed.

The eternal nature of the soul has been established in this verse which is everlasting and beyond birth and death. Consequently, it is devoid of the six types of transformations: *asti, jāyate, vardhate, vipariṇamate, apakṣhīyate*, and *vinaśhyati* 'Existence in the womb, birth, growth, procreation, diminution, and death.' These are transformations of the body, not of the self. What we call as death is merely the destruction of the body, but the immortal self remains unaffected by all bodily changes. This concept has been repeatedly emphasised in the Vedas. The *Kaṭhopaniṣhad* contains a mantra almost identical to this verse of the Bhagavad Gita:

na jāyate mriyate vā vipaśhchin
nāyaṁ kutaśhchin na babhūva kaśhchit
ajo nityaḥ śhāśhvato 'yaṁ purāṇo
na hanyate hanyamāne śharīre (1.2.18)

'The soul is not born, nor does it die; it did not spring from something, and nothing sprang from it. It is unborn, eternal, immortal, and ageless. It is not destroyed when the body is destroyed.' The *Bṛihadāraṇyaka Upanishad* states:

sa vā eṣha mahān aja ātmājaro 'maro 'mṛito 'bhayaḥ (4.4.25)

'The soul is glorious, unborn, deathless, free from old age, immortal, and fearless.'

वेदाविनाशिनं नित्यं य एनमजमव्ययम् ।
कथं स पुरुषः पार्थ कं घातयति हन्ति कम् ।।21।।

vedāvināśhinaṁ nityaṁ ya enam ajam avyayam
kathaṁ sa puruṣhaḥ pārtha kaṁ ghātayati hanti kam

veda—knows; *avināśhinam*—imperishable; *nityam*—eternal; *yaḥ*—who; *enam*—this; *ajam*—unborn; *avyayam*—immutable; *katham*—how; *saḥ*—that; *puruṣhaḥ*—person; *pārtha*—Parth; *kam*—whom; *ghātayati*—causes to be killed; *hanti*—kills; *kam*—whom.

O Parth, how can one who knows the soul to be imperishable, eternal, unborn, and immutable kill anyone or cause anyone to kill?

A spiritually elevated soul quells the ego that makes us feel that we are the doers of our actions. In that state, one can see that the soul seated within actually does nothing. Such an elevated soul, though doing all kinds of actions, is never tainted by them. Shree Krishna is advising Arjun that he must elevate himself to that enlightened level, seeing himself as the non-doer, free from egotism, and perform his duty rather than shirk from it.

वासांसि जीर्णानि यथा विहाय नवानि गृह्णाति नरोऽपराणि ।
तथा शरीराणि विहाय जीर्णा न्यन्यानि संयाति नवानि देही ।।22।।

vāsānsi jīrṇāni yathā vihāya navāni gṛihṇāti naro 'parāṇi
tathā śharīrāṇi vihāya jīrṇānya nyāni sanyāti navāni dehī

vāsānsi—garments; *jīrṇāni*—worn-out; *yathā*—as; *vihāya*—sheds; *navāni*—new; *gṛihṇāti*—accepts; *naraḥ*—a person; *aparāṇi*—others; *tathā*—likewise; *śharīrāṇi*—bodies; *vihāya*—casting off; *jirṇāni*—worn-out; *anyāni*—other; *sanyāti*—enters; *navāni*—new; *dehī*—the embodied soul.

As a person sheds worn-out garments and wears new ones, likewise, at the time of death, the soul casts off its worn-out body and enters a new one.

Continuing to explain the nature of the soul, Shree Krishna reiterates the concept of rebirth, comparing it to an everyday activity. When garments become torn and useless, we discard them in favour of new ones, but in doing so, we do not change ourselves. In the same manner, the soul remains unchanged, when it discards its worn-out body and takes birth in a new body elsewhere.

The *Nyaya Darshan* gives the following argument to prove the existence of rebirth:

jātasya harṣhabhayaśhoka sampratipatteḥ (3.1.18)

It states that if you observe a little baby, you will find it sometimes becomes happy, sometimes sad, and sometimes fearful without any apparent reason. According to the *Nyaya Darshan*, the little baby experiences these emotions because it remembers its past life. However, as it grows up, the impressions of the present life are imprinted so strongly upon its mind that they erase most past memories. Besides, the processes of death and birth are also so painful to the soul that they erase a substantial portion of the past life's memories.

The *Nyaya Darshan* gives another argument in support of rebirth: *stanyābhilāṣhāt* (3.1.21) It says that a newborn baby has no knowledge of language. How then can a mother teach her baby to suckle her breast when she inserts it in the baby's mouth? The newborn child has drunk milk in infinite past lifetimes, even in animal forms, from the breasts, teats, and udders of innumerable mothers. Thus, when the mother puts her breast in the baby's mouth, it automatically starts suckling based on past practice.

Without accepting the concept of rebirth, the disparity among human beings becomes inexplicable and irrational. For example, let us suppose one man is blind from birth. If that person asks why he was punished in this way, what logical answer can be given to him? If we say it was the result of his karmas, he may argue that the present life is the only life he has, and therefore, there are no past karmas at the time of birth that should afflict him. If we say it was the will of God, it would also seem implausible, since God is all-merciful and would not unnecessarily want anyone to be blind. The only logical explanation is that the person was born blind as a consequence of karmas from past lives. As a result, from common sense and on the authority of the scriptures, we are obliged to believe in the concept of rebirth.

नैनं छिन्दन्ति शस्त्राणि नैनं दहति पावकः ।
न चैनं क्लेदयन्त्यापो न शोषयति मारुतः ।।23।।

nainaṁ chhindanti śhastrāṇi nainaṁ dahati pāvakaḥ
na chainaṁ kledayantyāpo na śhoṣhayati mārutaḥ

na—not; *enam*—this soul; *chhindanti*—shred; *śhastrāṇi*—weapons; *na*—nor; *enam*—this soul; *dahati*—burns; *pāvakaḥ*—fire; *na*—not; *cha*—and; *enam*—this soul; *kledayanti*—moisten; *āpaḥ*—water; *na*—nor; *śhoṣhayati*—dry; *mārutaḥ*—wind.

Weapons cannot shred the soul, nor can fire burn it. Water cannot wet it, nor can the wind dry it.

Consciousness, which is the symptom of the soul, can be perceived by material instruments, but the soul itself cannot be contacted by any material object. This is so only because the soul is divine, and hence beyond the interactions of material objects. Shree Krishna expresses this vividly by saying that wind cannot wither the soul, nor can water moisten it, nor fire burn it.

अच्छेद्योऽयमदाह्योऽयमक्लेद्योऽशोष्य एव च ।
नित्यः सर्वगतः स्थाणुरचलोऽयं सनातनः ।।24।।

achchhedyo 'yam adāhyo 'yam akledyo 'śhoṣhya eva cha
nityaḥ sarva-gataḥ sthāṇur achalo 'yaṁ sanātanaḥ

achchhedyaḥ—unbreakable; *ayam*—this soul; *adāhyaḥ*—incombustible; *ayam*—this soul; *akledyaḥ*—cannot be dampened;

aśhoṣhyaḥ—cannot be dried; *eva*—indeed; *cha*—and; *nityaḥ*—everlasting; *sarva-gataḥ*—all-pervading; *sthāṇuḥ*—unalterable; *achalaḥ*—immutable; *ayam*—this soul; *sanātanaḥ*—primordial.

The soul is unbreakable and incombustible; it can neither be dampened nor dried. It is everlasting, in all places, unalterable, immutable, and primordial.

The point about immortality is again being driven home here. For the teacher to merely impart perfect knowledge is not enough; for that knowledge to be useful, it must sink deep into the heart of the student. Hence a skillful teacher often repeats a point previously made. In Sanskrit literature, this is called *punarukti* or 'repetition'. Shree Krishna has often used *punarukti*, as a tool in the Bhagavad Gita for stressing the important spiritual principles to ensure that they are grasped deeply by His student.

अव्यक्तोऽयमचिन्त्योऽयमविकार्योऽयमुच्यते।
तस्मादेवं विदित्वैनं नानुशोचितुमर्हसि।।25।।

avyakto 'yam achintyo 'yam avikāryo 'yam uchyate
tasmādevaṁ viditvainaṁ nānuśhochitum arhasi

avyaktaḥ—unmanifested; *ayam*—this soul; *achintyaḥ*—inconceivable; *ayam*—this soul; *avikāryaḥ*—unchangeable; *ayam*—this soul; *uchyate*—is said; *tasmāt*—therefore; *evam*—thus; *viditvā*—having known; *enam*—this soul; *na*—not; *anuśhochitum*—to grieve; *arhasi*—befitting.

The soul is spoken of as invisible, inconceivable, and unchangeable. Knowing this, you should not grieve for the body.

Our eyes, made from material energy, can see only material objects. The soul, being divine and beyond the realm of material energy, is invisible to our eyes. Scientists have conducted experiments to perceive its presence. They put a dying person in a glass case and sealed the case, to see whether the departure of the soul would crack the glass. The soul left the body without the glass box getting cracked. Being subtle, the soul did not need physical space for its movement.

Being subtler than the material energy, the soul is also inconceivable to our intellect. The *Kaṭhopaniṣhad* says:

indriyebhyaḥ parā hyarthā arthebhyaśhcha paraṁ manaḥ
manasastu parā buddhirbhuddherātmā mahān paraḥ (1.3.10)

'Beyond the senses are the objects of the senses; subtler than the objects of the senses is the mind. Beyond the mind is the intellect; and subtler than the intellect is the soul.' The material intellect can only comprehend material concepts but can never reach the divine soul by the power of its contemplation. As a result, knowledge of the self requires external sources, which are the scriptures and the guru.

अथ चैनं नित्यजातं नित्यं वा मन्यसे मृतम् ।
तथापि त्वं महाबाहो नैवं शोचितुमर्हसि ।।26।।

atha chainaṁ nitya-jātaṁ nityaṁ vā manyase mṛitam
tathāpi tvaṁ mahā-bāho naivaṁ śhochitum arhasi

atha—if, however; *cha*—and; *enam*—this soul; *nitya-jātam*—taking constant birth; *nityam*—always; *vā*—or; *manyase*—you think; *mṛitam*—dead; *tathā api*—even then; *tvam*—you; *mahā-bāho*—mighty-armed one, Arjun; *na*—not; *evam*—like this; *śhochitum*—grieve; *arhasi*—befitting.

If, however, you think that the self is subject to constant birth and death, O mighty-armed Arjun, even then you should not grieve like this.

Shree Krishna uses the word *atha* to indicate that Arjun may want to believe the other explanations that exist about the nature of the self. This verse needs to be understood in the context of the philosophical streams existing in India and their divergent understandings about the nature of self. Indian philosophy has historically comprised of twelve schools of thought. Six of these accept the authority of the Vedas and are called *Āstik Darshans*. These are *Mimansa*, *Vedant*, *Nyaya*, *Vaiśheṣhik*, *Sānkhya*, and *Yog*. Within each of these are more branches—for example, the Vedant school of thought is further divided into six schools—*Adavita vāda*, *Dwaita vāda*, *Viśhiṣhṭādvaita vāda*,

Viśhuddhādvaita vāda, Dwaitādvaita vāda, and *Achintya-bhedābheda vāda.* Each of these has further branches, for example, *Advaita vāda* is subdivided into *Dṛiṣhṭi-sṛiṣhṭi vāda, Avachchheda vāda, Bimba-pratibimba vāda, Vivarta vāda, Ajāta vāda,* and so on. We will not go into the details of these schools here. Let it suffice for now to know that all these schools of thought accept the Vedas as the authority of reference. Accordingly, they all accept the eternal, unchangeable soul as the self.

The remaining six schools of Indian philosophy do not accept the authority of the Vedas. These are *Chārvāk vāda,* the four Buddhist schools (*Yogāchār vāda, Mādhyamik vāda, Vaibhāśhik vāda,* and *Sautāntrik vāda*), and Jainism. Each of these has its own explanation for the nature of the self. *Chārvāk vāda* states that the body itself comprises the self, and consciousness is merely a product of the conglomeration of its constituents. Jainism states that the soul is the same size as the body and subject to change from birth to birth. The Buddhist schools of thought do not accept the existence of a permanent soul, and instead, maintain that there is a stream of renewed animation from lifetime to lifetime, which ensures continuity of the individual.

It seems that at the time of Shree Krishna too, versions of the Buddhist philosophy of renewed animation and non-permanence of the soul existed. This is why He is explaining that even if Arjun subscribes to this philosophy of renewed animation of the self from life to life, there is still no reason to lament. *Why should one not lament? This is now explained in the next verse.*

जातस्य हि ध्रुवो मृत्युर्ध्रुवं जन्म मृतस्य च ।
तस्मादपरिहार्येऽर्थे न त्वं शोचितुमर्हसि ।।27।।

jātasya hi dhruvo mṛityur dhruvaṁ janma mṛitasya cha
tasmād aparihārye 'rthe na tvaṁ śhochitum arhasi

jātasya—for one who has been born; *hi*—for; *dhruvaḥ*—certain; *mṛityuḥ*—death; *dhruvam*—certain; *janma*—birth; *mṛitasya*—for the dead; *cha*—and; *tasmāt*—therefore; *aparihārye arthe*—in this inevitable situation; *na*—not; *tvam*—you; *śhochitum*—lament; *arhasi*—befitting.

Death is certain for one who has been born, and rebirth is inevitable for one who has died. Therefore, you should not lament over the inevitable.

In the English language, there is a popular idiom: as sure as death. Benjamin Franklin said: 'The only things certain in life are death and taxes.' The most certain thing in life is that we will meet with death one day. Psychologists categorise the fear of death as the biggest fear in life. In Patanjali's *Yog Darshan* too, *abhiniveśh*, or the instinctive urge to survive at all costs, is mentioned as a trait of the material intellect. But for one who is born, death is inevitable. So, when something is inevitable, why lament over it? The Mahabharat relates an incident regarding this:

During the period of their exile in the forest, one day while wandering, the five Pandavas were thirsty and came across a lake. Yudhishthir asked Bheem to fetch water for them. When Bheem reached the lake, a *yakṣha* (semi-celestial being) began speaking from inside the lake, 'I will only let you take water if you first answer my questions.' Bheem paid no heed and proceeded to drink water. The *yakṣha* pulled him in. After some time when Bheem did not return, a concerned Yudhishthir sent Arjun to see what was happened and fetch water. When Arjun reached the lake, the *yakṣha* warned him too, 'I have already seized your brother. Do not attempt to drink water unless you can answer all my questions correctly.' Arjun also paid no heed, and the *yakṣha* pulled him into the lake as well. The other brothers, Nakul and Sahadev, followed him, but met with the same fate.

Finally, Yudhishthir himself came to the lake. Once again, the *yakṣha* said, 'Answer my questions if you want to drink water from the lake, or I will pull you in, just as I have done with your four brothers.' Yudhishthir agreed to answer the questions. The *yakṣha* was actually the celestial god of death, Yamraj, in disguise. He asked sixty questions, each of which was answered perfectly by Yudhishthir. One of these questions was: *kim āśhcharyaṁ?* 'What is the most surprising thing in this world?' Yudhishthir replied:

ahanyahani bhūtāni gachchhantīha yamālayam
śheṣhāḥ sthiratvam ichchhanti kimāśhcharyamataḥ param

(Mahabharat)

'At every moment, people are dying. Those who are alive are witnessing this phenomenon, and yet they do not think that one day they will also have to die. What can be more astonishing than this?'

Shree Krishna explains in this verse that life is inescapably a dead end, so, a wise person does not lament over the inevitable.

अव्यक्तादीनि भूतानि व्यक्तमध्यानि भारत।
अव्यक्तनिधनान्येव तत्र का परिदेवना।।28।।

avyaktādīni bhūtāni vyakta-madhyāni bhārata
avyakta-nidhanānyeva tatra kā paridevanā

avyakta-ādīni—unmanifest before birth; *bhūtāni*—created beings; *vyakta*—manifest; *madhyāni*—in the middle; *bhārata*—Arjun, scion of Bharat; *avyakta*—unmanifest; *nidhanāni*—on death; *eva*—indeed; *tatra*—therefore; *kā*—why; *paridevanā*—grieve.

O scion of Bharat, all created beings are unmanifest before birth, manifest in life, and again unmanifest on death. So why grieve?

Shree Krishna dispelled the cause of lamentation with respect to the soul in verse 2.20 and with respect to the body in verse 2.27. Now He includes both in this verse. In the Shreemad Bhagavatam, Sage Narad instructed Yudhishthir along similar lines:

yan manyase dhruvaṁ lokam adhruvaṁ vā na chobhayam
sarvathā na hi śhochyās te snehād anyatra mohajāt (1.13.43)

'Whether you consider the personality to be an eternal soul or to be a temporary body, or even if you accept it as an inconceivable mixture of soul and body, you should not lament in any way. The cause for lamentation is only attachment that arises out of illusion.'

In the material realm, each individual soul is bound by three bodies—gross body, subtle body, and causal body.

Gross body: consists of the five gross elements of nature—earth, water, fire, air, and space.

Subtle body: consists of eighteen elements—five life airs, five working senses, five knowledge senses, mind, intellect, and ego.

Causal body: consists of the account of karmas from endless past lives, including the *sanskārs* (tendencies) carried forward from previous lives.

At the time of death, the soul discards its gross body and departs with the subtle and causal bodies. Then, God gives the soul another gross body according to its subtle and causal bodies and sends the soul into a suitable mother's womb for the purpose. After the soul gives up one gross body, there is a transitional phase before it receives a new gross body. This could be a few seconds in duration or a few years long. So, before birth, the soul existed with the unmanifest subtle and causal bodies. After death, it still exists in the unmanifest state. It only becomes manifest in the middle. Therefore, death is no reason for grief.

आश्चर्यवत्पश्यति कश्चिदेन
माश्चर्यवद्वदति तथैव चान्यः ।
आश्चर्यवच्चैनमन्यः शृणोति
श्रुत्वाप्येनं वेद न चैव कश्चित् ।।29।।

āśhcharya-vat paśhyati kaśhchid enan
āśhcharya-vad vadati tathaiva chānyaḥ
āśhcharya-vach chainam anyaḥ śhṛiṇoti
śhrutvāpyenaṁ veda na chaiva kaśhchit

āśhcharya-vat—as amazing; *paśhyati*—see; *kaśhchit*—someone; *enam*—this soul; *āśhcharya-vat*—as amazing; *vadati*—speak of; *tathā*—thus; *eva*—indeed; *cha*—and; *anyaḥ*—other; *āśhcharya-vat*—similarly amazing; *cha*—also; *enam*—this soul; *anyaḥ*—others; *śhṛiṇoti*—hear; *śhrutvā*—having heard; *api*—even; *enam*—this soul; *veda*—understand; *na*—not; *cha*—and; *eva*—even; *kaśhchit*—some.

Some see the soul as amazing, some describe it as amazing, and some hear of the soul as amazing, while others, even on hearing, cannot understand it at all.

The whole world is amazing, from the tiniest atoms to the largest galaxies, for they are all wonderful creations of God. A little rose flower is also amazing—in its texture, smell, and beauty. The most amazing is the Supreme Lord Himself. It is said that Anant Shesh, the divine ten thousand-headed serpent on whom Lord Vishnu resides, has been singing the glories of God since the beginning of creation and has still not completed them.

The soul, as a fragmental part of God, is more amazing than the things of the world because it is transcendental to material existence. Just as God is divine, its fragment, the soul, is also divine. For this reason, mere intellectual prowess is not enough to comprehend the soul since the existence and nature of the soul are difficult to grasp. The *Kaṭhopaniṣhad* states:

śhravaṇāyāpi bahubhiryo na labhyaḥ śhṛiṇvanto 'pi bahavo yaṁ
na vidyuḥ āśhcharyo vaktā kuśhalo 'sya labdhā 'ścharyo jñātā
kuśhalānuśhiṣhṭaḥ (1.2.7)

'A teacher who is self-realised is very rare. The opportunity to hear instructions about the science of self-realisation from such a teacher is even rarer. If, by great good fortune, such an opportunity presents itself, students who can comprehend this topic are the rarest.' Hence, an enlightened teacher is never discouraged when, despite sincere efforts, the majority of the people are either not interested in or cannot understand the science of the soul.

देही नित्यमवध्योऽयं देहे सर्वस्य भारत ।
तस्मात्सर्वाणि भूतानि न त्वं शोचितुमर्हसि ।।30।।

dehī nityam avadhyo 'yaṁ dehe sarvasya bhārata
tasmāt sarvāṇi bhūtāni na tvaṁ śhochitum arhasi

dehī—the soul that dwells within the body; *nityam*—always; *avadhyaḥ*—immortal; *ayam*—this soul; *dehe*—in the body;

sarvasya—of everyone; *bhārata*—descendant of Bharat, Arjun; *tasmāt*—therefore; *sarvāṇi*—for all; *bhūtāni*—living entities; *na*—not; *tvam*—you; *śhochitum*—mourn; *arhasi*—should.

O Arjun, the soul that dwells within the body is immortal; therefore, you should not mourn for anyone.

Often, in the course of His teachings, Shree Krishna explains a concept in a few verses and then states a verse summarizing those teachings. This verse is a summary of the instructions on the immortality of the self and its distinction from the body.

स्वधर्ममपि चावेक्ष्य न विकम्पितुमर्हसि ।
धर्म्याद्धि युद्धाच्छ्रेयोऽन्यत्क्षत्रियस्य न विद्यते ।।31।।

swa-dharmam api chāvekṣhya na vikampitum arhasi
dharmyāddhi yuddhāch chhreyo 'nyat kṣhatriyasya na vidyate

swa-dharmam—one's duty in accordance with the Vedas; *api*—also; *cha*—and; *avekṣhya*—considering; *na*—not; *vikampitum*—to waver; *arhasi*—should; *dharmyāt*—for righteousness; *hi*—indeed; *yuddhāt*—than fighting; *śhreyaḥ*—better; *anyat*—another; *kṣhatriyasya*—of a warrior; *na*—not; *vidyate*—exists.

Besides, considering your duty as a warrior, you should not waver. Indeed, for a warrior, there is no better engagement than fighting for upholding of righteousness.

Swa-dharma is one's duty as an individual, in accordance with the Vedas. There are two kinds of *swa-dharmas* or prescribed duties for the individual—*para dharma* or spiritual duties, and *apara dharma* or material duties. Considering oneself to be the soul, the prescribed duty is to love and serve God with devotion; this is called *para dharma*. However, since a vast majority of humankind does not possess this spiritual perspective, the Vedas also prescribe duties for those who see themselves as the body. These duties are defined according to one's ashram (station in life) and varna (occupation). They are called *apara dharma* or mundane duties. This distinction between spiritual duties and material duties needs to be kept in mind while understanding the Bhagavad Gita and the Vedic philosophy at large.

By occupation, Arjun was a warrior, so his duty was to fight for the protection of righteousness. Shree Krishna is calling this *swa-dharma* or prescribed duty at the bodily level.

यदृच्छया चोपपन्नं स्वर्गद्वारमपावृतम् ।
सुखिनः क्षत्रियाः पार्थ लभन्ते युद्धमीदृशम् ।।32।।

yadṛichchhayā chopapannaṁ swarga-dvāram apāvṛitam
sukhinaḥ kṣhatriyāḥ pārtha labhante yuddham īdṛiśham

yadṛichchhayā—unsought; *cha*—and; *upapannam*—come; *swarga*—celestial abodes; *dvāram*—door; *apāvṛitam*—wide open; *sukhinaḥ*—happy; *kṣhatriyāḥ*—warriors; *pārtha*—Arjun, son of Pritha; *labhante*—obtain; *yuddham*—war; *īdṛiśham*—such.

O Parth, happy are the warriors to whom such opportunities to defend righteousness come unsought, opening for them the stairway to the celestial abodes.

The warrior class has always been necessary in the world for protecting society. The occupational duties of warriors demand that they be brave and even willing to lay down their life, if required, for the protection of society. During Vedic times, while killing animals was forbidden for the rest of society, warriors were allowed to go into the forest and practice warfare by killing animals. Such chivalrous warriors were expected to welcome, with open arms, the opportunity to defend righteousness. Fulfilment of their duty would be rewarded as a virtuous act in this life and in the next.

The proper implementation of one's occupational duties is not a spiritual act in itself and does not result in God-realisation. It is merely a virtuous deed with positive material rewards. Shree Krishna brings His instructions a step lower and says that even if Arjun is not interested in spiritual teachings and wishes to remain at the bodily platform, then also his social duty as a warrior is to defend righteousness.

As we can see, the Bhagavad Gita is a call to action, not to inaction. When people are exposed to lectures on spirituality, they often question, 'Are you asking me to give up my work?' However, verse after verse, Shree Krishna is urging Arjun into action, which is contrary to his desire to shun action. While Arjun wishes to abandon his duty, Shree Krishna repeatedly coaxes him to discharge it. The change that Shree Krishna wishes to see in Arjun is an internal one, in his consciousness, and not an external renunciation of works. *He now explains to Arjun the consequences of giving up his duty.*

अथ चेत्त्वमिमं धर्म्यं संग्रामं न करिष्यसि ।
ततः स्वधर्मं कीर्तिं च हित्वा पापमवाप्स्यसि ।।33।।

atha chet tvam imaṁ dharmyaṁ saṅgrāmaṁ na kariṣhyasi
tataḥ sva-dharmaṁ kīrtiṁ cha hitvā pāpam avāpsyasi

atha chet—if, however; *tvam*—you; *imam*—this; *dharmyam saṅgrāmam*—righteous war; *na*—not; *kariṣhyasi*—act; *tataḥ*—then; *sva-dharmam*—one's duty in accordance with the Vedas; *kīrtim*—reputation; *cha*—and; *hitvā*—abandoning; *pāpam*—sin; *avāpsyasi*—will incur.

If, however, you refuse to fight this righteous war, abandoning your social duty and reputation, you will certainly incur sin.

If a warrior chooses to become non-violent on the battlefield, it will be dereliction of duty, and consequently, classified as a sinful act. This is why Shree Krishna states that if Arjun abandons his duty, considering it to be repugnant and troublesome, he will be committing a sin. The *Parāśhar Smriti* states:

kṣhatriyoḥ hi prajā rakṣhañśhastrapāṇiḥ pradaṇḍavān
nirjitya parasainyādi kṣhitiṁ dharmeṇa pālayet (1.61)

'The occupational duty of a warrior is to protect the citizens of the country from oppression. This requires the application of violence in appropriate cases for the maintenance of law and order. He should thus defeat the soldiers of enemy kings and help rule the country according to the principles of righteousness.'

अकीर्तिं चापि भूतानि कथयिष्यन्ति तेऽव्ययाम् ।
सम्भावितस्य चाकीर्ति मरणादतिरिच्यते ।।34।।

akīrtiṁ chāpi bhūtāni kathayiṣhyanti te 'vyayām
sambhāvitasya chākīrtir maraṇād atirichyate

akīrtim—infamy; *cha*—and; *api*—also; *bhūtāni*—people; *kathayiṣhyanti*—will speak; *te*—of your; *avyayām*—everlasting; *sambhāvitasya*—of a respectable person; *cha*—and; *akīrtiḥ*—infamy; *maraṇāt*—than death; *atirichyate*—is greater.

People will speak of you as a coward and a deserter. For a respectable person, infamy is worse than death.

For respectable people, social prestige is very important. The particular gunas (modes of nature) of warriors make respect and honour especially important for them. For them, dishonour is worse than death. Shree Krishna reminds Arjun of this, so that if he is not inspired by superior knowledge, he may at least be inspired by inferior knowledge.

A warrior who runs away from the battlefield out of cowardice is ostracised from society. That could be the dishonour inflicted upon Arjun if he avoided his duty.

भयाद्रणादुपरतं मंस्यन्ते त्वां महारथाः ।
येषां च त्वं बहुमतो भूत्वा यास्यसि लाघवम् ।।35।।

bhayād raṇād uparataṁ mansyante tvāṁ mahā-rathāḥ
yeṣhāṁ cha tvaṁ bahu-mato bhūtvā yāsyasi lāghavam

bhayāt—out of fear; *raṇāt*—from the battlefield; *uparatam*—have fled; *mansyante*—will think; *tvām*—you; *mahā-rathāḥ*—warriors who could single handedly match the strength of ten thousand ordinary warriors; *yeṣhām*—for whom; *cha*—and; *tvam*—you;

bahu-mataḥ—highly esteemed; *bhūtvā*—having been; *yāsyasi*—you will lose; *lāghavam*—decreased in value.

The great generals who hold you in high esteem will think that you fled from the battlefield out of fear, and thus will lose their respect for you.

Arjun was famous as a mighty warrior and a worthy opponent for even the most valiant of the Kaurava warriors, such as Bheeshma, Dronacharya, Karn, and others. He had attained fame by fighting many celestial gods. He had fought and overwhelmed even Lord Shiv, who had once appeared in the disguise of a hunter. Pleased with his valour and skill, Lord Shiv had rewarded him with a celestial weapon called *Pāshupatāstra.* His archery teacher, Dronacharya, had also bestowed his blessings on him in the form of a special weapon. If Arjun were to withdraw from the battlefield just before the start of the battle, would these gallant warriors ever know that concern for the lives of his relatives had inspired him to flee? They would consider him a coward and assume that he had backed out from the war in dread of their prowess.

अवाच्यवादांश्च बहून्वदिष्यन्ति तवाहिताः ।
निन्दन्तस्तव सामर्थ्यं ततो दुःखतरं नु किम् ।।36।।

avāchya-vādānśh cha bahūn vadiṣhyanti tavāhitāḥ
nindantastava sāmarthyaṁ tato duḥkhataraṁ nu kim

avāchya-vādān—using derogatory words; *cha*—and; *bahūn*—many; *vadiṣhyanti*—will say; *tava*—your; *ahitāḥ*—enemies; *nindantaḥ*—defame; *tava*—your; *sāmarthyam*—might; *tataḥ*—than that; *duḥkha-taram*—more painful; *nu*—indeed; *kim*—what.

Your enemies will defame and humiliate you with unkind words, disparaging your might. Alas, what could be more painful than that?

If Arjun chose to flee from battle, not only would Arjun's estimation wane in the assembly of mighty warriors, but he would also be disparaged. Shree Krishna uses the word *nindataḥ* which means 'to vilify'; *avāchya vādān* means the 'use of derogatory words' such as eunuch. Arjun's enemies, like Duryodhan, would say many unbecoming things about him, such as, 'Look at that impotent Arjun fleeing from the battlefield like a dog with its tail between its legs.' Shree Krishna reminds Arjun that such derision would be very painful to him.

हतो वा प्राप्स्यसि स्वर्गं जित्वा वा भोक्ष्यसे महीम् ।
तस्मादुत्तिष्ठ कौन्तेय युद्धाय कृतनिश्चयः ।।37।।

hato vā prāpsyasi swargaṁ jitvā vā bhokṣhyase mahīm
tasmād uttiṣhṭha kaunteya yuddhāya kṛita-niśhchayaḥ

hataḥ—slain; *vā*—or; *prāpsyasi*—you will attain; *swargam*—celestial abodes; *jitvā*—by achieving victory; *vā*—or; *bhokṣhyase*—you shall enjoy; *mahīm*—the kingdom on earth; *tasmāt*—therefore; *uttiṣhṭha*—arise; *kaunteya*— Arjun, son of Kunti; *yuddhāya*—for fight; *kṛita-niśhchayaḥ*—with determination.

If you fight, you will either be slain on the battlefield and go to the celestial abodes, or you will gain victory and enjoy the kingdom on earth. Therefore arise with determination, O son of Kunti, and be prepared to fight.

Continuing from verse 2.31, Shree Krishna is still giving instructions at the level of occupational duties. He explains to Arjun about the two possibilities arising from the performance of his duty. If Arjun becomes victorious, a kingdom on earth awaits him, and if he is forced to lay down his life in the discharge of his duty, he will go to the celestial abodes.

सुखदुःखे समे कृत्वा लाभालाभौ जयाजयौ ।
ततो युद्धाय युज्यस्व नैवं पापमवाप्स्यसि ।।38।।

sukha-duḥkhe same kṛitvā lābhālābhau jayājayau
tato yuddhāya yujyasva naivaṁ pāpam avāpsyasi

sukha—happiness; *duḥkhe*—in distress; *same kṛitvā*—treating alike; *lābha-alābhau*—gain and loss; *jaya-ajayau*—victory and defeat;

tataḥ—thereafter; *yuddhāya*—for fighting; *yujyasva*—engage; *na*—never; *evam*—thus; *pāpam*—sin; *avāpsyasi*—shall incur.

Fight for the sake of duty, treating alike happiness and distress, loss and gain, victory and defeat. Fulfilling your responsibility in this way, you will never incur sin.

After motivating Arjun at the mundane level, Shree Krishna now moves deeper into the science of work. Arjun had expressed his fear that by killing his enemies he would incur sin. Shree Krishna addresses this apprehension. He advises Arjun to do his duty without attachment to the fruits of his actions. Such an attitude to work will release him from any sinful reactions.

When we work with selfish motives, we create karmas, which bring about their subsequent karmic reactions. The *Māṭhar Shruti* states:

puṇyena puṇya lokaṁ nayati pāpena pāpamubhābhyāmeva manuṣhyalokam

'If you do good deeds, you will go to the celestial abodes; if you do bad deeds, you will go to the nether regions; if you do a mixture of both, you will come back to the planet earth.' In either case, we get bound by the reactions of our karmas. Thus, mundane good deeds are also binding. They result in material rewards, which add to the stockpile of our karmas and thicken the illusion that there is happiness in the world.

However, if we give up selfish motives, then our actions no longer create any karmic reactions. For example, murder is a sin, and the judicial law of every country of the world declares it to be a punishable offence. But if a policeman in the discharge of his duty kills the leader of a gang, he is not punished for it. If a soldier kills an enemy soldier in battle, he is not punished for it. In fact, he can even be awarded a medal for bravery. The reason for apparent lack of punishment is that these actions are not motivated by any ill-will or personal motive; they are performed as a matter of duty to the country. God's law is quite similar. If one gives up all selfish motives and works merely for the sake of duty towards the Supreme, then such work does not create any karmic reactions.

So, Shree Krishna advises Arjun to become detached from outcomes and simply focus on doing his duty. When he fights with the attitude of equanimity, treating victory and defeat, pleasure and pain as the same, then despite killing his enemies, he will never incur sin. This subject is also repeated later in the Bhagavad Gita, in verse 5.10: 'Just as a lotus leaf is untouched by water, those who dedicate all their actions to God while abandoning all attachment, remain untouched by sin.'

Having declared a profound conclusion about work without attachment, Shree Krishna now says that He will explain the science of work in detail to reveal the logic behind what He has said.

एषा तेऽभिहिता साङ्ख्ये बुद्धिर्योगे त्विमां शृणु ।
बुद्ध्या युक्तो यया पार्थ कर्मबन्धं प्रहास्यसि ।। 39 ।।

eṣhā te 'bhihitā sānkhye buddhir yoge tvimāṁ śhṛiṇu
buddhyā yukto yayā pārtha karma-bandhaṁ prahāsyasi

eṣhā—hitherto; *te*—to you; *abhihitā*—explained; *sānkhye*—by analytical knowledge; *buddhiḥ yoge*—by the yog of intellect; *tu*—indeed; *imām*—this; *śhṛiṇu*—listen; *buddhyā*—by understanding; *yuktaḥ*—united; *yayā*—by which; *pārtha*—Arjun, son of Pritha; *karma-bandham*—bondage of karma; *prahāsyasi*—you shall be released from.

Hitherto, I have explained to you *Sānkhya yog* or analytic knowledge regarding the nature of the soul. Now listen, O Parth, as I reveal *buddhi yog* or the Yog of Intellect. When you work with such understanding, you will be freed from the bondage of karma.

The word *Sānkhya* comes from the roots *sāṅ*, meaning, 'complete', and *khyā*, meaning, 'to know'. So *Sānkhya* means 'the complete analytical knowledge of something'. The *Sānkhya Darshan*, which is one of the six philosophical treatises in Indian philosophy, makes an analytical enumeration of the entities in the cosmos. It lists twenty-four entities: *pañcha mahābhūta* (earth, water, fire, air, and sky), *pañcha tanmātrā* (the five abstract qualities of matter—taste, touch, smell, sound, and sight), *pañcha karmendriya* (five working senses), *pañcha jnanendriya* (five knowledge senses), mind, *ahankār* (the entity created by the evolution of *mahān*), *mahān* (the entity created by the evolution of prakriti), prakriti (the primordial form of material energy). Apart from these is purush or the soul, which tries to enjoy prakriti and gets bound in it.

Shree Krishna has just explained to Arjun another form of *Sānkhya* which is the analytical knowledge of the immortal soul. He now says that He is going to reveal the science of working without desire for rewards. This requires detachment from the fruits of actions. Such detachment comes by practising discrimination with the intellect. Hence, Shree Krishna has interestingly called it *buddhi yog* or 'Yog of the Intellect'. In subsequent verses (2.41 and 2.44), He goes on to explain the role of the intellect in bringing the mind to a state of detachment.

नेहाभिक्रमनाशोऽस्ति प्रत्यवायो न विद्यते ।
स्वल्पमप्यस्य धर्मस्य त्रायते महतो भयात् ।।40।।

nehābhikrama-nāśho 'sti pratyavāyo na vidyate
svalpam apyasya dharmasya trāyate mahato bhayāt

na—not; *iha*—in this; *abhikrama*—efforts; *nāśhaḥ*—loss; *asti*—there is; *pratyavāyaḥ*—adverse result; *na*—not; *vidyate*—is; *su-alpam*—a little; *api*—even; *asya*—of this; *dharmasya*—occupation; *trāyate*—saves; *mahataḥ*—from great; *bhayāt*—danger.

Working in this state of consciousness, there is no loss or adverse result, and even a little effort saves one from great danger.

The great danger we face is that we may not get the human form in the next life; instead, we could go into the lower species of life, such as animals, birds, or life forms in the nether regions. We cannot be complacent that the human form will remain reserved for us because the next birth will be determined by our karmas and level of consciousness in this life.

There are 8.4 million species of life in existence. The species below human beings—animals, birds, fishes, insects, and all others—do not have an evolved intellect as we humans do. Yet, they also perform commonplace activities, such as eating, sleeping, defending, and mating. Human beings have been endowed with the faculty of knowledge for a higher purpose, so that they may utilise it to elevate themselves. If humans utilise their intellects merely for doing the animalistic activities of eating, sleeping, mating, and defending, in a deluxe way, it is a misuse of the human form. For example, if someone makes eating the primary pleasure of life, then the body of a pig becomes more suitable for such a person, and thus, that individual receives a pig's body in the next life. If someone makes sleeping the goal of life, then God deems that the body of a polar bear is more suitable for such activity and allots it in the succeeding life. So, the great danger before us is that we may not get a human birth in the next life. The Vedas state:

iha chedavedīdatha satyamasti na chedihāvedīnmahatī vinaṣhṭhiḥ

(*Kenopaniṣhad* 2.5)

'O human being, the human birth is a rare opportunity. If you do not utilise it to achieve your goal, you will suffer great ruin.' Again, they state:

iha chedaśhakad boddhuṁ prākśharīrasya visrasaḥ
tataḥ sargeṣhu lokeṣhu śharīratvāya kalpate

(*Kaṭhopaniṣhad* 2.3.4)

'If you do not strive for God-realisation in this life, you will continue to rotate in the 8.4 million species of life for many births.'

However, once we commence on the journey of spiritual practice, then even if we do not complete the path in this life, God sees that our intention to do so existed. As a result, He grants us human birth again, to enable us to continue from where we had left off. In this way, we avert great danger.

Additionally, Shree Krishna says that no loss ever comes from any endeavour made on this path. This is because whatever material assets we accumulate in the present life must be left behind at the time of death. But if we make any spiritual advancement on the path of Yog, God preserves it and gives us the fruits in the next life, enabling us to start off from where we had left. *Thus, having informed Arjun about its benefits, Shree Krishna now begins instructing him about the science of working without attachment.*

व्यवसायात्मिका बुद्धिरेकेह कुरुनन्दन ।
बहुशाखा ह्यनन्ताश्च बुद्धयोऽव्यवसायिनाम् ।।41।।

vyavasāyātmikā buddhir ekeha kuru-nandana
bahu-śhākhā hyanantāśh cha buddhayo 'vyavasāyinām

vyavasāya-ātmikā—resolute; *buddhiḥ*—intellect; *ekā*—single; *iha*—on this path; *kuru-nandana*—descendent of the Kurus; *bahu-śhākhāḥ*—many-branched; *hi*—indeed; *anantāḥ*—endless; *cha*—also; *buddhayaḥ*—intellect; *avyavasāyinām*—of the irresolute.

O descendent of the Kurus, the intellect of those who are on this path is resolute, and their aim is one-pointed. But the intellect of those who are irresolute is many-branched.

Attachment is a function of the mind. Its manifestation is that the mind repeatedly runs towards the object of its attachment, which could be persons, sensual objects, prestige, physical comfort, situations, and so on. So, if thoughts of a person or an object repeatedly come to the mind, it is a possible indication of the mind being attached to it. However, if it is the mind that gets attached, then why is Shree Krishna bringing the intellect into the topic of attachment? Is there any role of the intellect in eliminating attachment?

Within our body is the subtle *antaḥ karaṇ*, colloquially referred to as the heart. It consists of the mind, the intellect, and the ego. In this subtle machine, the intellect is superior to the mind. It makes decisions while the mind creates desires and gets attached to the object of affection as determined by the intellect. For instance, if the intellect decides that money is the source of happiness, the mind hankers for wealth. If the intellect decides that prestige is the most important thing in life, the mind craves for reputation and fame. In other words, the mind develops desires in accordance with the knowledge of the intellect.

Throughout the day, we humans control our mind with the intellect. While sitting at home, we adopt casual postures in which the mind finds comfort. Yet, we adopt appropriate formal postures while sitting in the office. It is not that the mind enjoys the formality of the office—given its way, it would rather embrace the casualness of home. However, the intellect decides that formal behaviour is necessary in the office. So, the intellect controls the mind, and people sit formally all day long, following the decorum of the workplace against the nature of the mind. Similarly, the mind does not enjoy doing office work—if it had its way, it would rather sit at home and watch television. But the intellect rules that working in the office is necessary to earn a living. Therefore, the intellect again reins in the natural tendency of the mind, and people work eight hours a day or longer.

The above examples illustrate that as human beings, our intellect possesses the ability to control the mind. Thus, we must cultivate the intellect with proper knowledge and use it to guide the mind in the proper direction. *Buddhi yog* is the art of detaching the mind from the fruits of actions by developing a firm conviction of the intellect that all work is meant for the pleasure of God. Such a person of resolute intellect cultivates single-minded focus on the goal and traverses the path like an arrow released from the bow. This resolve becomes so strong in higher stages of sadhana that nothing can deter the *sādhak* from treading the path. He or she thinks, 'Even if there are millions of obstacles on my path, even if the whole world condemns me, even if I have to lay down my life, I will still not give up my sadhana.' But those whose intellect is many-branched find their mind running in various directions. They are unable to develop the focus of mind that is required to tread the path to God.

यामिमां पुष्पितां वाचं प्रवदन्त्यविपश्चितः ।
वेदवादरताः पार्थ नान्यदस्तीति वादिनः ।।42।।

कामात्मानः स्वर्गपरा जन्मकर्मफलप्रदाम् ।
क्रियाविशेषबहुलां भोगैश्वर्यगतिं प्रति ।।43।।

yāmimāṁ puṣhpitāṁ vāchaṁ pravadanty-avipaśhchitaḥ
veda-vāda-ratāḥ pārtha nānyad astīti vādinaḥ

kāmātmānaḥ swarga-parā janma-karma-phala-pradām
kriyā-viśheṣha-bahulāṁ bhogaiśhwarya-gatiṁ prati

yām imām—all these; *puṣhpitām*—flowery; *vācham*—words; *pravadanti*—speak; *avipaśhchitaḥ*—those with limited understanding; *veda-vāda-ratāḥ*—attached to the flowery words of the Vedas; *pārtha*—Arjun, son of Pritha; *na anyat*—no other; *asti*—is; *iti*—thus; *vādinaḥ*—advocate; *kāma-ātmānaḥ*—desirous of sensual pleasure; *swarga-parāḥ*—aiming to achieve the heavenly planets; *janma-karma-phala*—high birth and fruitive results; *pradāṁ*—awarding; *kriyā-viśheṣha*—pompous ritualistic ceremonies; *bahulām*—various; *bhoga*—gratification; *aiśhwarya*—luxury; *gatim*—progress; *prati*—towards.

Those with limited understanding, get attracted to the flowery words of the Vedas which advocate ostentatious rituals for elevation to the celestial abodes and presume no higher principle is described in them. They glorify only those portions of the Vedas that please their senses and perform pompous ritualistic ceremonies for attaining high birth, opulence, sensual enjoyment, and elevation to the heavenly planets.

The Vedas are divided into three sections. These are: *Karm-kāṇḍ* (ritualistic ceremonies), *Jnana-kāṇḍ* (knowledge section), and *Upāsanā-kāṇḍ* (devotional section). The *Karm-kāṇḍ* section advocates the performance of ritualistic ceremonies for material rewards and promotion to the celestial abodes. Those who seek sensual pleasures glorify this section of the Vedas.

The celestial abodes contain a higher order of material luxuries and offer greater facility for sensual enjoyment. But elevation to the heavenly abodes does not imply a concurrent spiritual elevation. These celestial planes are also within the material universe, and after going there, when one's account of good karmas gets depleted, one again returns to planet earth. People with limited understanding strive for the heavenly abodes, thinking this is the whole purpose of the Vedas. In this way, they continue transmigrating in the cycle of life-and-death without endeavouring for God-realisation. However, those with spiritual wisdom do not make even heaven their goal. The *Muṇḍakopaniṣhad* states:

avidyāyāmantare vartamānāḥ svayaṁdhīrāḥ paṇḍitaṁ manyamānāḥ jaṅghanyamānāḥ pariyanti mūḍhā andhenaiva nīyamānā yathāndhāḥ (1.2.8)

'Those, who practice the ostentatious rituals prescribed in the Vedas for enjoying the celestial pleasures of the higher abodes, think themselves to be scholars of the scriptures, but in reality, they are foolish. They are like the blind leading the blind.'

भोगैश्वर्यप्रसक्तानां तयापहृतचेतसाम् ।
व्यवसायात्मिका बुद्धिः समाधौ न विधीयते ।। 44 ।।

bhogaiśwvarya-prasaktānāṁ tayāpahṛita-chetasām
vyavasāyātmikā buddhiḥ samādhau na vidhīyate

bhoga—gratification; *aiśhwarya*—luxury; *prasaktānām*—whose minds are deeply attached; *tayā*—by that; *apahṛita-chetasām*—bewildered in intellect; *vyavasāya-ātmikā*—resolute; *buddhiḥ*—intellect; *samādhau*—fulfilment; *na*—never; *vidhīyate*—occurs.

With their minds deeply attached to worldly pleasures and their intellects bewildered by such things, they are unable to possess the resolute determination for success on the path to God.

People whose minds are attached to sensual enjoyment concern themselves with *bhog* (gratification), and *aiśhwarya* (luxury). They engage their intellects in enhancing their income and contemplating how to increase their material possessions and maximize their enjoyment. Bewildered in this manner, they are unable to develop the firm resolve required for traversing the path to God-realisation.

त्रैगुण्यविषया वेदा निस्त्रैगुण्यो भवार्जुन ।
निर्द्वन्द्वो नित्यसत्त्वस्थो निर्योगक्षेम आत्मवान् ।।45।।

trai-guṇya-viṣhayā vedā nistrai-guṇyo bhavārjuna
nirdvandvo nitya-sattva-stho niryoga-kṣhema ātmavān

trai-guṇya—of the three modes of material nature; *viṣhayāḥ*—subject matter; *vedāḥ*—Vedic scriptures; *nistrai-guṇyaḥ*—above the three modes of material nature, transcendental; *bhava*—be; *arjuna*—Arjun; *nirdvandvaḥ*—free from dualities; *nitya-sattva-sthaḥ*—eternally fixed in truth; *niryoga-kṣhemaḥ*—unconcerned about gain and preservation; *ātma-vān*—situated in the self.

The Vedas deal with the three modes of material nature, O Arjun. Rise above the three modes to a state of pure spiritual consciousness. Freeing yourself from dualities, eternally fixed in Truth, and without concern for material gain and safety, be situated in the self.

The material energy binds the divine soul to the bodily conception of life by its three constituent modes. These modes of material nature are sattva (mode of goodness), rajas (mode of passion), and tamas (mode of ignorance). The relative proportion of the three modes vary for every individual, due to their *sanskārs* (tendencies) from countless past lives, and accordingly, everyone has different inclinations and tendencies.

The Vedic scriptures accept this disparity and give suitable instructions for all kinds of people. If the shastras did not contain instructions for worldly minded people, they would have gone further astray. So, the Vedas offer them material rewards for the performance of rigorous rituals, to help them rise from the mode of ignorance to passion to goodness.

Thus, the Vedas contain both kinds of knowledge—ritualistic ceremonies for the materially attached and divine knowledge for spiritual aspirants. When Shree Krishna tells Arjun to reject the Vedas, the statement needs to be understood in the context of the preceding and following verses. He is implying that Arjun should not be attracted by the section of the Vedas that propounds rules, regulations, and ceremonies for material rewards. Instead, he should use the divine section of Vedic knowledge to elevate himself to the level of Absolute Truth.

यावानर्थ उदपाने सर्वतः सम्प्लुतोदके ।
तावान्सर्वेषु वेदेषु ब्राह्मणस्य विजानतः ।।46।।

yāvān artha udapāne sarvataḥ samplutodake
tāvānsarveṣhu vedeṣhu brāhmaṇasya vijānataḥ

yāvān—whatever; *arthaḥ*—purpose; *uda-pāne*—a well of water; *sarvataḥ*—in all respects; *sampluta-udake*—by a large lake; *tāvān*—that many; *sarveṣhu*—in all; *vedeṣhu*—Vedas; *brāhmaṇasya*—one who realises the Absolute Truth; *vijānataḥ*—who is in complete knowledge.

Whatever purpose is served by a small well of water is naturally served in all respects by a large lake. Similarly, one who realizes the Absolute Truth also fulfills the purpose of all the Vedas.

The Vedas contain one lakh or one hundred thousand mantras describing a variety of rituals, practices, prayers, ceremonies, and gems of knowledge. All these are given with only one aim—to help unite the soul with God.

vāsudeva-parā vedā vāsudeva-parā makhāḥ
vāsudeva-parā yogā vāsudeva-parāḥ kriyāḥ

vāsudeva-paraṁ jñānaṁ vāsudeva-paraṁ tapaḥ
vāsudeva-paro dharmo vāsudeva-parā gatiḥ

(Bhagavatam 1.2.28–29)

'The goal of all Vedic mantras, ritualistic activities, spiritual practices, sacrifices, cultivation of knowledge, and performance of duties is to help the soul reach the divine feet of God.'

However, just as a medicine pill is often sugar-coated to make it more palatable, similarly, to attract materially minded people, the Vedas also give material incentives. The underlying motive is to help the individual gradually get detached from the world and attached to God. Thus, one who is attaching the mind to God is automatically fulfilling the purpose of all Vedic mantras. Shree Krishna advises Uddhav:

ājñāyaivaṁ guṇān doṣhān mayādiṣhṭān api swakān
dharmān santyajya yaḥ sarvān māṁ bhajeta sa sattamaḥ

(Bhagavatam 11.11.32)

'The Vedas prescribe varieties of social and ritualistic duties for individuals. But those who grasp their underlying motive and reject all intermediate instructions, wholeheartedly fulfil their duty towards Me, I consider them to be the highest devotees.'

कर्मण्येवाधिकारस्ते मा फलेषु कदाचन ।
मा कर्मफलहेतुर्भूर्मा ते सङ्गोऽस्त्वकर्मणि ।।47।।

karmaṇy-evādhikāras te mā phaleṣhu kadāchana
mā karma-phala-hetur bhūr mā te saṅgo 'stvakarmaṇi

karmaṇi—in prescribed duties; *eva*—only; *adhikāraḥ*—right; *te*—your; *mā*—not; *phaleṣhu*—in the fruits; *kadāchana*—at any time; *mā*—never; *karma-phala*—results of the activities; *hetuḥ*—cause; *bhūḥ*—be; *mā*—not; *te*—your; *saṅgaḥ*—attachment; *astu*— must be; *akarmaṇi*—in inaction.

You have a right to perform your prescribed duties, but you are not entitled to the fruits of your actions. Never consider yourself to be the cause of the results of your activities, nor be attached to inaction.

This is an extremely popular verse of the Bhagavad Gita, so much so that even most school children in India are familiar with it. It offers deep insight into the proper spirit of work and is often quoted whenever the topic of karm yog is discussed. The verse gives four instructions regarding the science of work: 1) Do your duty, but do not concern yourself with the results. 2) The fruits of your actions are not for your enjoyment. 3) Give up the pride of doership even while working. 4) Do not be attached to inaction.

Do your duty, but do not concern yourself with the results: We have the right to do our duty, but the results are not dependent only upon our efforts. A number of factors come into play to determine the results—our efforts, destiny (based on our past karmas), the will of God, the efforts of others, the cumulative karmas of the people involved, the place, and situation (a matter of luck), and so on. If we become anxious for results, we will experience anxiety whenever they are not according to our expectations. So, Shree Krishna advises Arjun to give up concern for the results and instead focus solely on doing a good job. The fact is that when we are unconcerned about the results, we can focus entirely on our efforts, and the result is even better than before.

A humorous acronym for this is NATO or Not Attached to Outcome. Consider its application to a simple everyday activity, such as playing golf. When people play golf, they are engrossed in the fruits—whether their score is under par, over par, etc. Now if they could merely focus on playing the shots to the best of their ability, they would find it to be the most enjoyable game of golf they have ever played. Additionally, with their complete focus on the shot being played, their game would be raised to a higher level.

The fruits of your actions are not for your enjoyment: To perform action is an integral part of human nature. Having come into this world, we all have various duties determined by our family situation, social position, occupation, and various responsibilites. While performing these actions, we must remember that we are not the enjoyers of the results—the results are meant solely for the pleasure of God. The individual soul is a tiny part of God (verse 15.7), and our inherent nature is to serve Him through all our actions.

dāsa bhūtamidaṁ tasya jagatsthāvara jangamam
śhrīmannārāyaṇa swāmī jagatāṁprabhurīśhwaraḥ

(*Padma Puran*)

'God is the Master of entire creation; all moving and non-moving beings are His servants.'

Material consciousness is characterised by the following manner of thoughts, 'I am the proprietor of all that I possess. All this is mine. It is all meant for my enjoyment. I have the right to enhance my possessions and maximise my enjoyment.' The reverse of this is spiritual consciousness, which is characterised by thoughts, such as 'God is the owner and enjoyer of this entire world. I am merely His selfless servant. I must use all that I have in the service of God.' In this manner, Shree Krishna instructs Arjun not to think of himself as the enjoyer of the fruits of his actions.

Give up the pride of doership even while working: Shree Krishna wants Arjun to give up *kartritwābhimān* or the ego of being the doer. He instructs Arjun to neither chase after preconceived motives attached to his actions nor consider himself as the cause of the results of his actions.

When we perform actions, why should we not consider ourselves as the doers of those actions? The reason is that our senses, mind, and intellect are inert; God energises them with His power and puts them at our disposal. As a result, we are able to work only with the help of the power we receive from Him. For example, the tongs in the kitchen are inactive by themselves, but when energised by someone's hand, they perform even difficult tasks, such as lifting burning coal. It would be erroneous to say that the tongs are the doers of actions. If the hand did not energise them, what would they be able to do? They would merely lie inert on the counter. Similarly, if God did not supply our body-mind-soul mechanism the power to perform actions, we could not have done anything. Thus, we must give up the ego of doing, remembering that God is the only source of the power by which we perform all our actions.

All the above thoughts are very nicely summarised in the following popular Sanskrit verse:

yatkṛitaṁ yatkarişhyāmi tatsarvaṁ na mayā kṛitam
tvayā kṛitaṁ tu phalabhuk tvameva madhusūdana

'Whatever I have achieved and whatever I wish to achieve, I am not the doer of these. O Madhusudan, You are the real doer, and You alone are the enjoyer of their results.'

Do not be attached to inaction: Although the nature of living beings is to work, often situations arise where work seems burdensome and confusing. In such cases, instead of running away from it, we must understand and implement the proper science of work, as explained by Shree Krishna to Arjun. It is highly inappropriate if we consider work as laborious and burdensome and resort to inaction. Becoming attached to inaction is never the solution and is clearly condemned by Shree Krishna.

योगस्थः कुरु कर्माणि सङ्गं त्यक्त्वा धनञ्जय ।
सिद्ध्यसिद्ध्योः समो भूत्वा समत्वं योग उच्यते ॥48॥

yoga-sthaḥ kuru karmāṇi saṅgaṁ tyaktvā dhanañjaya
siddhy-asiddhyoḥ samo bhūtvā samatvaṁ yoga uchyate

yoga-sthaḥ—being steadfast in yog; *kuru*—perform; *karmāṇi*—duties; *saṅgam*—attachment; *tyaktvā*—having abandoned; *dhanañjaya*—Arjun; *siddhi-asiddhyoḥ*—in success and failure; *samaḥ*—equipoised; *bhūtvā*—becoming; *samatvam*—equanimity; *yogaḥ*—Yog; *uchyate*—is called.

Be steadfast in the performance of your duty, O Arjun, abandoning attachment to success and failure. Such equanimity is called Yog.

The equanimity that enables us to accept all circumstances with serenity is so praiseworthy that Shree Krishna calls it 'Yog' or 'union with the Supreme'. This equipoise comes from implementing the knowledge of the previous verse. When we understand that the effort is in our hands, not the results, we then concern ourselves only with doing our duty. Since the results are for the pleasure of God, we dedicate them to Him. Now, if the results are not to our expectations, we calmly accept them as the will of God. In this way, we are able to accept fame and infamy, success and failure, pleasure and pain, as God's will. When we learn to embrace both equally, we develop the equanimity that Shree Krishna talks about.

The verse offers a very practical solution to the vicissitudes of life. If we are sailing in the ocean in a boat, it is natural to expect the waves of the ocean to shake the boat. If we get disturbed each time a wave rocks the boat, our miseries would be endless. And if we do not expect the waves to rise, we would be expecting the ocean to be something other than its natural self. Waves are an inseparable phenomenon of the ocean.

Similarly, as we wade through the ocean of life, it throws up all kinds of waves that are beyond our control. If we keep struggling to eliminate negative situations, we will be unable to avoid unhappiness. But if we can learn to accept everything that comes our way, without sacrificing our best efforts, we will have surrendered to the will of God and that will be true Yog.

दूरेण ह्यवरं कर्म बुद्धियोगाद्धनञ्जय ।
बुद्धौ शरणमन्विच्छ कृपणाः फलहेतवः ।।49।।

dūreṇa hy-avaraṁ karma buddhi-yogād dhanañjaya
buddhau śharaṇam anvichchha kṛipaṇāḥ phala-hetavaḥ

dūreṇa—(discrad) from far away; *hi*—certainly; *avaram*—inferior; *karma*—reward-seeking actions; *buddhi-yogāt*—with the intellect established in divine knowledge; *dhanañjaya*—Arjun; *buddhau*—divine knowledge and insight; *śharaṇam*—refuge; *anvichchha*—seek; *kṛipaṇāḥ*—miserly; *phala-hetavaḥ*—those seeking fruits of their work.

Seek refuge in divine knowledge and insight, O Arjun, and discard reward-seeking actions that are certainly inferior to works performed

with the intellect established in divine knowledge. Miserly are those who seek to enjoy the fruits of their works.

There are two aspects to work: 1) The external activity we do and 2) Our internal attitude towards it. For example, let us say that a temple is being built in the holy land of Vrindavan. The workers are engaged in a sacred activity, but their attitude is mundane. They are concerned with the salary they receive. If another contractor offers higher wages, they will not mind switching their employer. There is also an ascetic living in Vrindavan, who, seeing the glorious temple being built, engages in *kār sevā* (voluntary work) as a service to God. The external work performed by the sadhu and the workers are the same, but their internal attitudes are poles apart.

Here Shree Krishna advises Arjun to move higher in his internal motivation towards work. He declares that those who work with the motivation of self-enjoyment are miserly. Those who are detached from the fruits and dedicate their work to a higher cause are superior. And those who offer the fruits to God are truly in knowledge.

The word *kṛipaṇa* (miserly) has been used here. The Shreemad Bhagavatam describes a *kṛipaṇa*:

na veda kṛipaṇaḥ śhreya ātmano guṇa-vastu-dṛik
tasya tān ichchhato yachchhed yadi so 'pi tathā-vidhaḥ (6.9.49)

'*Kṛipaṇa* are those who think that the ultimate reality consists only of sense objects produced from material energy.' Again, the Shreemad Bhagavatam, states: *kṛipaṇo yo 'jitendriyaḥ* (11.19.44) 'A *kṛipaṇa* is one who has no control over the senses.'

As an individual evolves to higher levels of consciousness, one naturally sheds the desire for enjoying the fruits of work and moves in the direction of service. Bill Gates, having renounced his position in Microsoft Corporation, now dedicates his energy in the service of society. Similarly, after having had his fill of power and position as the President of USA, Bill Clinton now preaches the glories of service to humankind and has even written a book on the topic, *Giving: How Each of Us Can Change the World*. Their engagement in service is praiseworthy, but it is still imperfectly oriented. That service attitude becomes perfect when we learn to do our works for the pleasure of God, dedicating all the fruits to Him.

बुद्धियुक्तो जहातीह उभे सुकृतदुष्कृते ।
तस्माद्योगाय युज्यस्व योगः कर्मसु कौशलम् ।।50।।

buddhi-yukto jahātīha ubhe sukṛita-duṣhkṛite
tasmād yogāya yujyasva yogaḥ karmasu kauśhalam

buddhi-yuktaḥ—endowed with wisdom; *jahāti*—get rid of; *iha*—in this life; *ubhe*—both; *sukṛita-duṣhkṛite*—good and bad deeds; *tasmāt*—therefore; *yogāya*—for Yog; *yujyasva*—strive for; *yogaḥ*—yog is; *karmasu kauśhalam*—the art of working skillfully.

One who prudently practises the science of work without attachment can get rid of both good and bad reactions in this life itself. Therefore, strive for Yog, which is the art of working skillfully (in proper consciousness).

On hearing about the science of karm yog, people often wonder that if they give up attachment to results, will their performance go down? Shree Krishna explains that working without personal motivation does not reduce the quality of our work; instead, we become even more skilful than before.

Consider the example of a sincere surgeon who cuts people with his knife while operating upon them. He performs his duty with equanimity and is undisturbed irrespective of whether the patient survives or dies. This is because he is merely doing his duty unselfishly, to the best of his ability, and is not attached to the results. Hence, even if the patient dies while being operated upon, the surgeon does not feel guilty of murder. However, if the same surgeon's only child needs to be operated, he does not have the courage to do so. Because of attachment to the results, he fears he will not be able to perform the operation skilfully and seeks the help of another surgeon. This shows that attachment to results does not make us more skilful; rather, the attachment affects our performance adversely. Instead, if we work without attachment, we can do so at our maximum skill level, without feeling nervous, jittery, scared, tense, or excited.

Likewise, Arjun's personal example also illustrates the point that giving up attachment to the fruits does not adversely affect performance. Before hearing the Bhagavad Gita, he intended to engage in war with the desire of winning a kingdom. After hearing the Bhagavad Gita, he was fighting because it was his duty to God, and Shree Krishna would be pleased by it. He was still a warrior; however, his internal motivation had changed. The fact that he did his duty without attachment did not make him any less competent than before. On the contrary, he fought with greater inspiration because his work was directly in service of God.

कर्मजं बुद्धियुक्ता हि फलं त्यक्त्वा मनीषिणः ।
जन्मबन्धविनिर्मुक्ताः पदं गच्छन्त्यनामयम् ।।51।।

karma-jaṁ buddhi-yuktā hi phalaṁ tyaktvā manīṣhiṇaḥ
janma-bandha-vinirmuktāḥ padaṁ gachchhanty-anāmayam

karma-jam—born of fruitive actions; *buddhi-yuktāḥ*—endowed with equanimity of intellect; *hi*—as; *phalam*—fruits; *tyaktvā*—abandoning; *manīṣhiṇaḥ*—the wise; *janma-bandha-vinirmuktāḥ*—freedom from the bondage of life and death; *padam*—state; *gachchhanti*—attain; *anāmayam*—devoid of sufferings.

The wise endowed with equanimity of intellect, abandon attachment to the fruits of actions, which bind one to the cycle of life and death. By working in such consciousness, they attain the state beyond all suffering.

Shree Krishna continues to expound on the topic of working without attachment to the fruits of actions and states that it leads one to the state beyond suffering. The paradox of life is that we strive for happiness, but reap misery; we crave love, but we meet with disappointment; we covet life, but know we are moving towards death at every moment. The Bhagavatam states:

sukhāya karmāṇi karoti loko
na taiḥ sukhaṁ vānyad-upāramaṁ vā
vindeta bhūyas tata eva duḥkhaṁ
yad atra yuktaṁ bhagavān vaden naḥ (3.5.2)

'Every human being engages in fruitive works to get happiness but finds no satisfaction. Instead, these activities only aggravate misery.' As a result, practically everyone in this world is unhappy. Some suffer from the miseries of their own body and mind; others are tormented by their family members and relatives; some suffer from scarcity of wealth and the paucity of the necessities of life. Materially minded people know they are unhappy. Yet they continue running in the direction of material growth because they think that others ahead of them must be happy. This blind pursuit has been going on for many lifetimes with or no end in sight. Now, if people could realise that nobody has ever achieved happiness by engaging in fruitive works, they would then understand that the direction in which they are running is futile, and they would think of doing a U-turn towards spiritual life.

Those whose intellects have become steadfast with spiritual knowledge understand that God is the Supreme Enjoyer of everything. Consequently, they renounce attachment to the fruits of their actions, offer everything to Him, and serenely accept everything that comes as His prasad (mercy). In doing so, their actions become free from karmic reactions that bind one to the cycle of life and death.

यदा ते मोहकलिलं बुद्धिर्व्यतितरिष्यति ।
तदा गन्तासि निर्वेदं श्रोतव्यस्य श्रुतस्य च ।।52।।

yadā te moha-kalilaṁ buddhir vyatitariṣhyati
tadā gantāsi nirvedaṁ śhrotavyasya śhrutasya cha

yadā—when; *te*—your; *moha*—delusion; *kalilam*—quagmire; *buddhiḥ*—intellect; *vyatitariṣhyati*—crosses; *tadā*—then; *gantāsi*—you shall acquire; *nirvedam*—indifferent; *śhrotavyasya*—to what is yet to be heard; *śhrutasya*—to what has been heard; *cha*—and.

When your intellect crosses the quagmire of delusion, you will then acquire indifference to what has been heard and what is yet to be heard (about enjoyments in this world and the next).

Shree Krishna had previously said that people who are attached to worldly enjoyment get attracted to the flowery words of the Vedas, which propagate ostentatious rituals for gaining worldly opulence and attaining celestial abodes (verses 2.42–43). However, one whose intellect is illumined with spiritual knowledge no longer seeks material sense pleasures, knowing them to be harbingers of misery. Such a person then loses interest in Vedic rituals. The *Muṇḍakopaniṣhad* states:

parīkṣhya lokānkarmachitānbrāhmaṇo nirvedamāyānnāstyakṛitaḥ kṛitena (1.2.12)

'Realised sages go beyond Vedic rituals after understanding that the pleasures one attains from fruitive karmas, in this life and in the celestial abodes, are temporary and mixed with misery.'

श्रुतिविप्रतिपन्ना ते यदा स्थास्यति निश्चला ।
समाधावचला बुद्धिस्तदा योगमवाप्स्यसि ।।53।।

śhruti-vipratipannā te yadā sthāsyati niśhchalā
samādhāv-achalā buddhis tadā yogam avāpsyasi

śhruti-vipratipannā—not allured by the fruitive sections of the Vedas; *te*—your; *yadā*—when; *sthāsyati*—remains; *niśhchalā*—steadfast; *samādhau*—in divine consciousness; *achalā*—steadfast; *buddhiḥ*—intellect; *tadā*—at that time; *yogam*—Yog; *avāpsyasi*—you will attain.

When your intellect ceases to be allured by the fruitive sections of the Vedas and remains steadfast in divine consciousness, you will then attain the state of perfect Yog.

As *sādhaks* advance on the spiritual path, their relationship with God becomes stronger. At that time, they find Vedic rituals they were previously performing to be cumbersome and time-consuming. They then wonder whether they are obliged to keep performing these rituals, along with their devotion, or would they be committing an offence if they reject the ritual and dedicate themselves fully to their sadhana? Such people will find the answer to their doubt in this verse. Shree Krishna says that to be fixed in sadhana without being allured to the fruitive sections of the Vedas is not an offence; rather, it is a higher spiritual state.

Madhavendra Puri, the famous fourteenth century sage, states this sentiment very emphatically. He was a Vedic Brahmin and used to engage in extensive ritualistic practices, but then took to sanyas (the renounced order) and engaged wholeheartedly in devotion to Shree Krishna. In his later life, he wrote:

sandhyā vandana bhadramastu bhavate
bhoḥ snāna tubhyaṁ namaḥ
bho devāḥ pitaraśhchatarapaṇa vidhau
nahaṁ kṣhamaḥ kṣhamyatām

yatra kvāpi niṣhadya yādava kulot
taasya kansadviṣhaḥ
smāraṁ smāramaghaṁ harāmi tadalaṁ
manye kimanyena me

'I wish to apologise to all kinds of rituals as I have no time to respect them. So dear *Sandhyā Vandan* (a set of rituals performed thrice daily by those who have received the sacred thread), holy baths, sacrifices to the celestial gods, offerings to the ancestors, and so on, please excuse me. Now, wherever I sit, I remember the Supreme Lord Shree Krishna, the Enemy of Kansa, and that is sufficient to release me from material bondage.'

Shree Krishna uses the word *samādhāv-achalā* in this verse to refer to the state of steadfastness in divine consciousness. The word samadhi has been formed from the roots *sam* (equilibrium) and *dhi* (intellect), meaning, 'a state of total equilibrium of the intellect'. One who is steadfast in the higher consciousness, unmoved by material allurements, attains that state of samadhi or perfect Yog.

अर्जुन उवाच ।
स्थितप्रज्ञस्य का भाषा समाधिस्थस्य केशव ।
स्थितधीः किं प्रभाषेत किमासीत व्रजेत किम् ।।54।।

arjuna uvācha
sthita-prajñasya kā bhāṣhā samādhi-sthasya keśhava
sthita-dhīḥ kiṁ prabhāṣheta kim āsīta vrajeta kim

arjunaḥ uvācha—Arjun said; *sthita-prajñasya*—one with steady intellect; *kā*—what; *bhāṣhā*—talk; *samādhi-sthasya*—situated in divine consciousness; *keśhava*—Shree Krishna, killer of the Keshi demon; *sthita-dhīḥ*—enlightened person; *kim*—what; *prabhāṣheta*—talks; *kim*—how; *āsīta*—sits; *vrajeta*—walks; *kim*—how.

Arjun said : O Keshav, what is the disposition of one who is situated in divine consciousness? How does an enlightened person talk? How does he sit? How does he walk?

The designations *sthita prajña* (one with steady intellect) and *samadhi-stha* (situated in trance) apply to enlightened persons. Having heard from Shree Krishna about the state of perfect yog or samadhi, Arjun asks a natural question. He wishes to know the nature of the mind of a person who is in this state. Additionally, he wishes to know how this divine state of mind manifests in a person's behaviour.

Beginning with this verse, Arjun asks Shree Krishna sixteen sets of questions. In response, Shree Krishna reveals the deepest secrets of karm yog, jnana yog, bhakti yog, austerity, and meditation, among other topics. The sixteen sets of questions asked by Arjun are:

1. What is the disposition of one who is situated in divine consciousness? (verse 2.54)
2. If You consider knowledge superior to fruitive works, then why do You ask me to wage this terrible war? (verse 3.1)

3. Why is a person impelled to commit sinful acts, even unwillingly, as if by force? (verse 3.36)

4. You were born much after Vivasvan. How am I to understand that in the beginning You instructed this science to him? (verse 4.4)

5. You praised the path of renunciation of actions, and again You praised work with devotion. Please tell me decisively which of the two is more beneficial? (verse 5.1)

6. O Krishna, the mind is very restless, turbulent, strong, and obstinate. It appears to me that it is more difficult to control than the wind. (verse 6.34)

7. What is the fate of the unsuccessful yogi who begins the path with faith, but whose mind deviates from God due to untamed passions and is unable to reach the highest perfection in this life? (verse 6.37)

8. What is Brahman and what is karm? What is *Adhibhūta*, and who are the *Ādhidaiva*? Who is *Ādhiyajna*, and how does he dwell in this body? O slayer of the Madhu demon, how can those of steadfast mind be united with You at the time of death? (verses 8.1–2)

9. Please describe to me Your divine opulences by which You pervade all the worlds. (verse 10.16)

10. I long to see Your cosmic form, O Supreme Divine Personality. (verse 11.3)

11. You, who existed before all creation, I wish to know who You are, for Your nature and workings mystify me. (verse 11.31)

12. Between those who are steadfastly devoted to Your personal form and those who worship the formless Brahman, whom do You consider to be more perfect in Yog? (verse 12.1)

13. I wish to know about prakriti (nature) and purush (the enjoyer). What is the field of activities and who is the knower of the field? What is the nature of knowledge and the object of knowledge? (verse 13.1)

14. What are the characteristics of those who have gone beyond the three gunas, O Lord? How do they act? How have they passed beyond the bondage of the gunas? (verse 14.21)

15. Where do they stand who disregard the injunctions of the scriptures but still worship with faith? (verse 17.1)

16. I wish to understand the nature of sanyas (renunciation), and how it is distinct from *tyāg* or renouncing the fruits of actions. (verse 18.1)

श्रीभगवानुवाच ।
प्रजहाति यदा कामान्सर्वान्पार्थ मनोगतान् ।
आत्मन्येवात्मना तुष्टः स्थितप्रज्ञस्तदोच्यते ।।55।।

śhrī bhagavān uvācha
prajahāti yadā kāmān sarvān pārtha mano-gatān
ātmany-evātmanā tuṣhṭaḥ sthita-prajñas tadochyate

śhrī-bhagavān uvācha—The Supreme Lord said; *prajahāti*—discards; *yadā*—when; *kāmān*—selfish desires; *sarvān*—all; *pārtha*—Arjun, son of Pritha; *manaḥ-gatān*—of the mind; *ātmani*—of the self; *eva*—only; *ātmanā*—by the purified mind; *tuṣhṭaḥ*—satisfied; *sthita-prajñaḥ*—one with steady intellect; *tadā*—at that time; *uchyate*—is said.

The Supreme Lord said: O Parth, when one discards all selfish desires and cravings of the senses that torment the mind and becomes satisfied in the realization of the self, such a person is said to be transcendentally situated.

Shree Krishna begins answering Arjun's questions here and continues till the end of the chapter. Each fragment is naturally drawn towards its whole, just as a piece of stone is drawn by the force of gravitation towards the earth. The individual soul is a fragment of God, who is infinite bliss. Hence, the soul is a fragment of the ocean of infinite bliss, and it experiences the natural urge for bliss. When it strives to relish the bliss of the soul from God, it is called 'Divine Love'. But when, in ignorance of its spiritual nature, it thinks of itself as the body and seeks to relish the bliss of the body from the world, it is called 'lust'.

This world has been called *mṛiga tṛiṣhṇā* in the scriptures, meaning, like the mirage seen by the deer. The sun rays reflecting on the hot desert sand create an illusion of water for the deer. It thinks there is water ahead of it and runs to quench its thirst. But the more it runs towards the water, the more the mirage fades away. Its dull intellect cannot recognise that it is running after an illusion. The unfortunate deer keeps chasing the illusory water and dies of exhaustion on the desert sand. Similarly, the material energy, maya, too, creates an illusion of happiness, and we run after that illusory happiness in the hope of quenching the thirst of our senses. But no matter how much we try, happiness keeps fading further away from us. The *Garuḍ Puran* states:

chakradharo 'pi suratvaṁ suratvalābhe sakalasurapatitvam
bhavtirum surapatirūrdhvagatitvaṁ tathāpi nanivartate tṛiṣhṇā

(2.12.14)

'A king wishes to be the emperor of the whole world; the emperor aspires to be a celestial god; a celestial god seeks to be Indra, the king of heaven; and Indra desires to be Brahma, the secondary creator. Yet the thirst for material enjoyment does not get satiated.'

But when one learns to turn the mind away from material allurements and renounces the desires of the senses, such a person comes in touch with the inner bliss of the soul and becomes transcendentally situated. The *Kaṭhopaniṣhad* goes to the extent of saying that one who has renounced desires becomes like God:

yadā sarve pramuchyante kāmā ye 'sya hṛidi śhritaḥ
atha martyo 'mṛito bhavatyatra brahma samaśhnute (2.3.14)

'When one eliminates all selfish desires from the heart, then the materially fettered jivatma attains freedom from birth and death and becomes godlike in virtue.' Shree Krishna states in the above verse that a transcendentally situated person is one who has given up selfish desires and cravings of the senses and is satisfied in the self.

दुःखेष्वनुद्विग्नमनाः सुखेषु विगतस्पृहः ।
वीतरागभयक्रोधः स्थितधीर्मुनिरुच्यते ।।56।।

duḥkheṣhv-anudvigna-manāḥ sukheṣhu vigata-spṛihaḥ
vīta-rāga-bhaya-krodhaḥ sthita-dhīr munir uchyate

duḥkheṣhu—amidst miseries; *anudvigna-manāḥ*—one whose mind is undisturbed; *sukheṣhu*—in pleasure; *vigata-spṛihaḥ*—without craving; *vīta*—free from; *rāga*—attachment; *bhaya*—fear; *krodhaḥ*—anger; *sthita-dhīḥ*—enlightened person; *muniḥ*—a sage; *uchyate*—is called.

One whose mind remains undisturbed amidst misery, who does not crave for pleasure, and who is free from attachment, fear, and anger, is called a sage of steady wisdom.

In this verse, Shree Krishna describes sages of steady wisdom as: 1) *Vīta rāga*—they give up craving for pleasure, 2) *Vīta bhaya*—they remain free from fear, 3) *Vīta krodha*—they are devoid of anger.

An enlightened person does not allow the mind to harbour material frailties of lust, anger, greed, envy, and other negative emotions. Only then can the mind steadily contemplate on transcendence and be fixed in the Divine. If one permits the mind to brood over miseries, then the contemplation on the Divine ceases and the mind is dragged down from the transcendental level. The process of torture works in the same manner. More than the present pain itself, it is the memories of past pain and apprehensions of future pain that torment the mind. But when the mind drops these two and simply focuses on the present sensation, the pain surprisingly shrinks to a tolerable size. It is well known that historically Buddhist monks adopted a similar technique for tolerating torture from invading conquerors.

Similarly, if the mind craves external pleasures, it runs to the objects of enjoyment and is again diverted from divine contemplation. So, a sage of steady wisdom is one who does not allow the mind to hanker for pleasure or lament for miseries. Further, such a sage does not permit the mind to succumb to the urges of fear and anger. In this way, the mind becomes situated on the transcendental level.

यः सर्वत्रानभिस्नेहस्तत्तत्प्राप्य शुभाशुभम् ।
नाभिनन्दति न द्वेष्टि तस्य प्रज्ञा प्रतिष्ठिता ।।57।।

yaḥ sarvatrānabhisnehas tat tat prāpya śhubhāśhubham
nābhinandati na dveṣhṭi tasya prajñā pratiṣhṭhitā

yaḥ—who; *sarvatra*—in all conditions; *anabhisnehaḥ*—unattached; *tat*—that; *tat*—that; *prāpya*—attaining; *śhubha*—good; *aśhubham*—evil; *na*—neither; *abhinandati*—delight in; *na*—nor; *dveṣhṭi*—dejected by; *tasya*—his; *prajñā*—knowledge; *pratiṣhṭhitā*—is fixed.

One who remains unattached under all conditions and is neither delighted by good fortune nor dejected by tribulation, he is a sage with perfect knowledge.

Rudyard Kipling, a famous British poet, has encapsulated the essence of this verse on *sthita prajña* (sage of steady intelligence) in his famous poem *If*. Here are a few lines from the poem:

> If you can dream—and not make dreams your master;
> If you can think—and not make thoughts your aim,
> If you can meet with Triumph and Disaster
> And treat those two impostors just the same;
> ...
> If neither foes nor loving friends can hurt you,
> If all men count with you, but none too much:
> If you can fill the unforgiving minute
> With sixty seconds' worth of distance run,
> Yours is the Earth and everything that's in it,
> And—which is more—you'll be a Man, my son!

The popularity of this poem shows the natural urge in people to reach the state of enlightenment, which Shree Krishna describes to Arjun. One may wonder how an English poet expressed the same state of enlightenment that is described by the Supreme Lord. The fact is that the urge for enlightenment is the intrinsic nature of the soul. Hence, knowingly or unknowingly, across all cultures, everyone craves for it. Shree Krishna is describing it here in response to Arjun's question.

यदा संहरते चायं कूर्मोऽङ्गानीव सर्वशः ।
इन्द्रियाणीन्द्रियार्थेभ्यस्तस्य प्रज्ञा प्रतिष्ठिता ।।58।।

yadā sanharate chāyaṁ kūrmo 'ṅgānīva sarvaśhaḥ
indriyāṇīndriyārthebhyastasya prajñā pratiṣhṭhitā

yadā—when; *sanharate*—withdraw; *cha*—and; *ayam*—this; *kūrmaḥ*—tortoise; *aṅgāni*—limbs; *iva*—as; *sarvaśhaḥ*—fully; *indriyāṇi*—senses; *indriya-arthebhyaḥ*—from the sense objects; *tasya*—his; *prajñā*—divine wisdom; *pratiṣhṭhitā*—fixed in.

One who is able to withdraw the senses from their objects, just as a tortoise withdraws its limbs into its shell, is established in divine wisdom.

Attempting to quench the cravings of the senses by supplying them with their desired objects is like trying to dowse a fire by pouring clarified butter on it. The fire may be smothered for a moment, but then it flares up with redoubled intensity. Hence, the Shreemad Bhagavatam states that desires never go away when they are fulfilled; they only come back more strongly:

na jātu kāmaḥ kāmānām upabhogena śhāmyati
haviṣhā kṛiṣhṇa-vartmeva bhūya evābhivardhate (9.19.14)

'Fulfilling the desires of the senses does not extinguish them, just as offering oblations of butter in the fire does not extinguish it; instead, it makes the fire blaze even stronger.'

These desires can be compared to an itch in the body. The itch is troublesome and creates an irresistible urge to scratch. But scratching does not solve the problem. For a few moments, there is relief, and then the itch returns with greater force. Instead, if someone can tolerate the itch for some time, it begins losing its sting and dies down slowly. That is the secret for getting peace from the itch. The same logic applies to desires as well. The mind and senses throw up myriad desires for happiness, but as long as we are in the game of fulfilling them, happiness remains illusive like the mirage. But when we learn to discard all these desires, to find happiness in God, the mind and senses make peace with us.

So, an enlightened sage intelligently masters the senses and the mind. The illustration used in this verse is that of the turtle. Whenever it encounters danger, the turtle protects itself by drawing its limbs and head inside its shell. After the danger passes, the turtle again extracts its limbs and head and continues on its way. The enlightened soul possesses similar control over the mind and senses and can retract and extract them according to the situation.

विषया विनिवर्तन्ते निराहारस्य देहिनः ।
रसवर्जं रसोऽप्यस्य परं दृष्ट्वा निवर्तते ।।59।।

viṣhayā vinivartante nirāhārasya dehinaḥ
rasa-varjaṁ raso 'pyasya paraṁ dṛiṣhṭvā nivartate

viṣhayāḥ—objects of senses; *vinivartante*—restrain; *nirāhārasya*—practicing self restraint; *dehinaḥ*—for the embodied; *rasa-varjam*—cessation of taste; *rasaḥ*—taste; *api*—however; *asya*—person's; *param*—the Supreme; *dṛiṣhṭvā*—on realisation; *nivartate*—ceases to be.

Aspirants may restrain the senses from their objects of enjoyment, but the taste for sense objects remains. However, even this taste ceases for those who realise the Supreme.

When one gives up eating during a fast, the desires of the senses become feeble. Similarly, in sickness one loses interest towards the objects of enjoyment. These states of dispassion are temporary because the seed of desire remains within the mind. Desires return when the fast is terminated or the sickness goes away.

What is this seed of desire? It is the intrinsic nature of the soul for the divine bliss of God, of whom it is a tiny fragment. Until it gets that divine bliss, the soul can never be content, and the search for happiness will continue. *Sādhaks* (spiritual aspirants) may forcibly restrain their senses with their willpower, but such restrain is temporary because it does not extinguish the internal flame of desire. However, when the soul engages in devotion towards God and gets divine bliss, it experiences the higher taste for which it had been craving since infinite lifetimes. The *Taittirīya Upanishad* states:

raso vai saḥ rasaṁ hyevāyaṁ labdhvā 'nandī bhavati (2.7.2)

'God is all-bliss. When the soul attains God, it becomes satiated in bliss.' Then, one naturally develops dispassion towards the lower sensual pleasures. This detachment that comes through devotion is firm and unshakeable.

Thus, the Bhagavad Gita does not teach a dry suppression of desires; instead, it teaches the beautiful path of sublimation of desires by directing them towards God. Saint Ramakrishna Paramahamsa expressed this principle very eloquently, when he said: 'Devotion is love for the highest; and the lowest shall fall away by itself.'

यततो ह्यपि कौन्तेय पुरुषस्य विपश्चितः ।
इन्द्रियाणि प्रमाथीनि हरन्ति प्रसभं मनः ।।60।।

yatato hyapi kaunteya puruṣhasya vipaśhchitaḥ
indriyāṇi pramāthīni haranti prasabhaṁ manaḥ

yatataḥ—while practicing self-control; *hi*—for; *api*—even; *kaunteya*—Arjun, son of Kunti; *puruṣhasya*—of a person; *vipaśhchitaḥ*—one endowed with discrimination; *indriyāṇi*—the senses; *pramāthīni*—turbulent; *haranti*—carry away; *prasabham*—forcibly; *manaḥ*—the mind.

The senses are so strong and turbulent, O son of Kunti, that they can forcibly carry away the mind even of a person endowed with discrimination and who practices self-control.

The senses are like wild horses that have been newly harnessed. They are impetuous and reckless; disciplining them is an important battle that *sādhaks* have to fight within themselves. Therefore, those seeking spiritual growth should carefully strive to tame the indulgent senses, which are coloured with lust and greed, or else they have the power to sabotage and derail the spiritual process of even the most well-intentioned yogis.

The Shreemad Bhagavatam relates a story that perfectly illustrates this statement (canto 9, chapter 6):

Saubhari was a great sage in ancient times. He is mentioned in the *Rig Veda*, where there is a mantra called *Saubhari Sutra*. There is also a scripture called the *Saubhari Samhita*. So, he was no ordinary sage. Saubhari had attained such control over his body that he used to submerge himself in the river Yamuna and meditate under water. One day, he saw two fish mating. This sight carried away his mind and senses, and the desire for sexual connsumation arose in him. He abandoned his spiritual practice and came out of the water, wondering how to fulfil his desire.

At that time, the king of Ayodhya was Mandhata, who was a very illustrious and noble ruler. He had fifty daughters, each more beautiful than the other. Saubhari approached the king and asked for the hand of one of the fifty princesses.

King Mandhata wondered about the sanity of the sage and thought to himself, 'An old man wanting to get married!' The king knew Saubhari to be a powerful sage and feared the sage might curse him if he refused. But if he consented, the life of one of his daughters would be ruined. He was in a dilemma. So, he said, 'O holy one! I have no objection to your request. Please take a seat. I shall bring my fifty daughters before you, and whosoever chooses you will become yours in marriage.' The king was confident that none of his daughters would choose the old ascetic, and in this way, he would be saved from the sage's curse.

Understanding the king's intention, Saubhari told the king that he would return the following day. That evening, he used his yogic powers to turn himself into a handsome young man. Consequently, when he presented himself at the palace the next day, all the fifty princesses chose him as their husband. The king was bound by the word he had given and was compelled to marry all his daughters to the sage.

Now the king was concerned about the fights that would take place among the fifty sisters since they would have to share a husband. However, Saubhari again used his yogic powers. Putting the king's apprehension to rest, he assumed fifty forms and created fifty palaces for his wives and lived separately with each one of them. In this manner, thousands of years passed by. The Puranas state that Saubhari had many children from each of them, and those children had further children until a tiny city had been created.

One day, Saubhari came to his senses, and exclaimed, *'aho imaṁ paśhyata me vināśhaṁ'* (Bhagavatam 9.6.50) 'O humans! Those of you who make plans to attain happiness through material acquisitions, be careful. Look at my degradation—where I was and where am I now. I created fifty bodies by my yogic powers and lived with fifty women for thousands of years. And yet, the senses did not experience fulfilment; they only kept hankering for more. Learn from my downfall and be warned not to venture in this direction.'

तानि सर्वाणि संयम्य युक्त आसीत मत्परः ।
वशे हि यस्येन्द्रियाणि तस्य प्रज्ञा प्रतिष्ठिता ।।61।।

tāni sarvāṇi sanyamya yukta āsīta mat-paraḥ
vaśhe hi yasyendriyāṇi tasya prajñā pratiṣhṭhitā

tāni—them; *sarvāṇi*—all; *sanyamya*—subduing; *yuktaḥ*—united; *āsīta*—seated; *mat-paraḥ*—towards Me (Shree Krishna); *vaśhe*—control; *hi*—certainly; *yasya*—whose; *indriyāṇi*—senses; *tasya*—their; *prajñā*—perfect knowledge; *pratiṣhṭhitā*—is fixed.

They are established in perfect knowledge, who subdue their senses and keep their minds ever absorbed in Me.

In this verse, the word *yuktaḥ* (united) indicates 'absorption in devotion', and *mat paraḥ* means 'towards Lord Krishna'. The word *āsīta* (seated) may be understood figuratively here to mean 'situated or established'. Having said that the impetuous mind and senses need to be tamed, Shree Krishna now reveals the proper engagement for them, which is absorption in devotion to God.

ध्यायतो विषयान्पुंसः सङ्गस्तेषूपजायते ।
सङ्गात्सञ्जायते कामः कामात्क्रोधोऽभिजायते ।।62।।

dhyāyato viṣhayān puṁsaḥ saṅgas teṣhūpajāyate
saṅgāt sañjāyate kāmaḥ kāmāt krodho 'bhijāyate

dhyāyataḥ—contemplating; *viṣhayān*—sense objects; *puṁsaḥ*—of a person; *saṅgaḥ*—attachment; *teṣhu*—to them (sense objects); *upajāyate*—arises; *saṅgāt*—from attachment; *sañjāyate*—develops; *kāmaḥ*—desire; *kāmāt*—from desire; *krodhaḥ*—anger; *abhijāyate*—arises.

While contemplating on the objects of the senses, one develops attachment to them. Attachment leads to desire, and from desire arises anger.

Anger, greed, lust, etc. are labeled as *mānas rog* or diseases of the mind in the Vedic scriptures. The Ramayan states:

mānas roga kachhuka maiṅ gāe
hahiṅ saba keṅ lakhi biralenha pāe

This verse alludes to the fact that we are all aware of the diseases of the body—even a single physical ailment has the power to make one's whole day miserable—but we do not realise that we are being continuously tormented by multiple mental ailments. And since we do not recognise lust, anger, greed, etc. as mental diseases, we do not try to cure them. Psychology is a branch of human knowledge that attempts to analyse these ailments and propose solutions to them. However, both the analysis and the solution presented by western psychology leave much to be desired and appear to be gross approximations of the reality of the mind.

In this and the subsequent verse, Shree Krishna has given a perfect and penetrating insight into the functioning of the mind. He explains that when we repeatedly contemplate that there is happiness in some object, the mind becomes attached to it. For example, in a class there are a number of boys and girls, and they interact innocuously with each other. One day one boy notices something about one girl and starts thinking, 'I would be very happy if she were mine.' As he continuously repeats this thought in his mind, his mind becomes attached to her. He tells his friends that he is madly in love with her, and he is unable to study because his mind repeatedly goes to her. His friends ridicule him, saying that they all interact with her in class, but none of them is crazy about her. Why is he losing his sleep and ruining his future because of her? The fact is that by repeatedly thinking that he would be happy with the girl, his mind became attached to her.

Now, attachment seems quite innocuous by itself. But the problem is that from attachment comes desire. If one is attached to drinks, the desire for drinks comes repeatedly to the mind. If one is attached to cigarettes, then thoughts of the pleasure of smoking cigarettes repeatedly flow in the mind, creating a craving for them. In this way, attachment leads to desire.

Once desire develops, it gives birth to two more problems—greed and anger. Greed comes from the fulfilment of desire. *Jimi pratilābha lobha adhikāī* (Ramayan) 'If you satisfy desire, it leads to greed.' Desire is never eliminated by satiating it:

yat pṛithivyāṁ vrīhi-yavaṁ hiraṇyaṁ paśhavaḥ striyaḥ
na duhyanti manaḥ-prītiṁ puṁsaḥ kāma-hatasya te

(Bhagavatam 9.19.13)

'If one person were to get all the wealth, luxuries, and sensual objects in the world, that person's desire would still not be satiated. Hence, knowing it to be the cause of misery, an intelligent person should renounce desire.'

On the flip side what happens if the fulfilment of desire is obstructed? It gives rise to anger. Bear in mind that anger does not arise by itself but is created from the obstruction of desire; and desire arises from attachment, while attachment comes from contemplation of sense objects. In this manner, we see how the simple act of contemplating the pleasures of sense objects leads downward to the twin diseases of greed and anger. *In the next verse, Shree Krishna continues the chain further and explains the consequences of anger.*

क्रोधाद्भवति सम्मोहः सम्मोहात्स्मृतिविभ्रमः ।
स्मृतिभ्रंशाद् बुद्धिनाशो बुद्धिनाशात्प्रणश्यति ।।63।।

krodhād bhavati sammohaḥ sammohāt smṛiti-vibhramaḥ
smṛiti-bhranśhād buddhi-nāśho buddhi-nāśhāt praṇaśhyati

krodhāt—from anger; *bhavati*—comes; *sammohaḥ*—clouding of judgement; *sammohāt*—from clouding of judgement; *smṛiti*—memory; *vibhramaḥ*—bewilderment; *smṛiti-bhranśhāt*—from bewilderment of memory; *buddhi-nāśhaḥ*—destruction of intellect; *buddhi-nāśhāt*—from destruction of intellect; *praṇaśhyati*—one is ruined.

Anger leads to clouding of judgment, which results in bewilderment of memory. When memory is bewildered, the intellect gets destroyed; and when the intellect is destroyed, one is ruined.

Anger impairs judgement, just as the morning mist creates a hazy covering on the sunlight. In anger, people commit mistakes that they later regret because the intellect gets clouded by a haze of emotions. People say, 'He is twenty years older to me. Why did I speak in this manner to him? What happened to me?' What happened was that the faculty of judgement was affected by anger, and hence the mistake of scolding an elder was made.

When the intellect is clouded, it leads to bewilderment of memory. The person then forgets what is right and what is wrong and flows along with the surge of emotions. The downward descent continues from there, and bewilderment of memory results in destruction of the intellect. And since the intellect is the internal guide, when it gets destroyed, one is ruined. In this manner, the path of descent from divinity to impiety has been described beginning with contemplation on the sense objects to the destruction of the intellect.

रागद्वेषवियुक्तैस्तु विषयानिन्द्रियैश्चरन् ।
आत्मवश्यैर्विधेयात्मा प्रसादमधिगच्छति ।।64।।

rāga-dveṣha-viyuktais tu viṣhayān indriyaiśh charan
ātma-vaśhyair-vidheyātmā prasādam adhigachchhati

rāga—attachment; *dveṣha*—aversion; *viyuktaiḥ*—free; *tu*—but; *viṣhayān*—objects of the senses; *indriyaiḥ*—by the senses; *charan*—while using; *ātma-vaśhyaiḥ*—controlling one's mind; *vidheya-ātmā*—one who controls the mind; *prasādam*—grace of God; *adhigachchhati*—attains.

But one who controls the mind and is free from attachment and aversion, even while using the objects of the senses, attains the grace of God.

The entire downward spiral leading to ruin begins with contemplation of happiness in sense objects. Now, the urge for happiness is as natural to the soul as thirst is to the physical body. It is impossible to think 'I will not contemplate happiness anywhere'. The simple solution then is to envision happiness in the proper direction, i.e., in God. If we repeatedly revise the thought that happiness is in God, we will develop attachment towards Him. This divine attachment will not degrade the mind like material attachment; rather, it will purify it. God is all-pure, and when we attach our mind to Him, the mind will also become pure.

Thus, whenever Shree Krishna asks us to give up attachment and desire, He is referring only to material attachment and desire. Spiritual attachment and desire are not to be given up; in fact, they are most praiseworthy. They are to be cultivated and increased for purification of the mind. The greater the burning desire we develop for God, the purer our mind will become. Jnanis who propound the worship of the undifferentiated attributeless Brahman do not understand this point when they recommend giving up all attachments. However, Shree

Krishna states: 'Those who attach their minds to Me with unadulterated devotion rise above the three modes of material nature and attain the level of the supreme Brahman.' (Bhagavad Gita 14.26) He repeatedly urges Arjun to attach his mind to God in many verses ahead, such as 8.7, 8.14, 9.22, 9.34, 10.10, 11.54, 12.8, 18.55, 18.58, and 18.65.

Attachment and aversion are two sides of the same coin. Aversion is nothing but negative attachment. Just as, in attachment, the object of attachment repeatedly comes to one's mind; similarly, in aversion, the object of hatred keeps popping into the mind. Both, attachment and aversion to material objects, have the same effect on the mind—they dirty it and pull it into the three modes of material nature. When the mind is free from both attachment and aversion and is absorbed in devotion to God, one receives the grace of God and experiences His unlimited divine bliss. On experiencing that higher taste, the mind no longer feels attracted to the sense objects, even while using them. Thus, even while tasting, touching, smelling, hearing, and seeing, like all of us, the *sthita prajña* is free from both attachment and aversion.

प्रसादे सर्वदु:खानां हानिरस्योपजायते ।
प्रसन्नचेतसो ह्याशु बुद्धि: पर्यवतिष्ठते ।।65।।

prasāde sarva-duḥkhānāṁ hānir asyopajāyate
prasanna-chetaso hyāśhu buddhiḥ paryavatiṣhṭhate

prasāde—by divine grace; *sarva*—all; *duḥkhānām*—sorrows; *hāniḥ*—destruction; *asya*—his; *upajāyate*—comes; *prasanna-chetasaḥ*—with a tranquil mind; *hi*—indeed; *āśhu*—soon; *buddhiḥ*—intellect; *paryavatiṣhṭhate*—becomes firmly established.

By divine grace comes the peace in which all sorrows end, and the intellect of such a person of tranquil mind soon becomes firmly established in God.

Grace is divine energy that floods into a person's personality. By grace, God who is *sat-chit-anand* bestows His divine knowledge, divine love, and divine bliss. This entrenches the intellect, like the North Star, in the love, bliss, and knowledge of God. By God's grace, when we experience the higher taste of divine bliss, the agitation for sensual happiness is extinguished. Once that hankering for material objects ceases, one goes beyond all suffering and the mind becomes tranquil. In that state of internal fulfilment, the intellect becomes firm in its decision that God alone is the source of happiness and is the final goal of the soul. Previously, the intellect accepted this only on the basis of knowledge as stated in the scriptures, but now it gets the experience of perfect peace and divine bliss. This convinces the intellect beyond any shadow of doubt, and it becomes steadily situated in God.

नास्ति बुद्धिरयुक्तस्य न चायुक्तस्य भावना ।
न चाभावयतः शान्तिरशान्तस्य कुतः सुखम् ।।66।।

nāsti buddhir-ayuktasya na chāyuktasya bhāvanā
na chābhāvayataḥ śhāntir aśhāntasya kutaḥ sukham

na—not; *asti*—is; *buddhiḥ*—intellect; *ayuktasya*—not united; *na*—not; *cha*—and; *ayuktasya*—not united; *bhāvanā*—contemplation; *na*—nor; *cha*—and; *abhāvayataḥ*—for those not united; *śhāntiḥ*—peace; *aśhāntasya*—of the unpeaceful; *kutaḥ*—where; *sukham*—happiness.

But an undisciplined person, who has not controlled the mind and senses, can neither have a resolute intellect nor steady contemplation on God. For one who never unites the mind with God there is no peace; and how can one who lacks peace be happy?

This verse strengthens the conclusion of the previous verse by stating the reverse and negating it. Previously, Shree Krishna said 'Know God; know peace.' In this verse, He says 'No God; no peace.' A person who has not learnt to discipline the mind and senses can neither meditate upon God nor experience His divine bliss. Without the higher taste, it becomes impossible to renounce the lower taste, and such a person keeps hankering for material happiness, like the bee that finds it impossible to renounce the nectar of the flower:

rātrirgamiṣhyati bhaviṣhyati suprabhātaṁ
bhāsvānudveṣhyati hasiṣhyati paṅkajaśhrīḥ
evaṁ vichintayati koṣha gate dvirephe
hā hanta hanta nalinīṁ gaja ujjahāra (*Sukti Sudhakar*)

This popular verse in Sanskrit literature relates a bee's story. The bee was sitting on a lotus flower, drinking its nectar. As the sun began setting, the petals of the flower began shutting. But the bee was so attached to enjoying the object of its senses that it refused to fly off. It thought, 'There is still time for the flower to close. Let me suck a little more nectar while I can.' In the same way, we can see old age coming as a sure sign of death, but like the bee, we remain engrossed in enjoying worldly pleasures.

In the meantime, it became dark and the lotus flower closed, trapping the bee. It thought, 'Never mind! Let me remain inside my beloved flower for tonight. Tomorrow morning, when its petals open again, I will fly away.' *Kāṣhṭha bhedo nipuṇopi sangṛihī kuṇṭhito bhavati padma vibhede* 'A bee has the power to cut through wood. But look at the attachment to the sense objects that the bee, which can cut through wood, is stuck inside the soft petals of the lotus.' A little later, an elephant came, broke the lotus from the stem, and swallowed it. The bee along with the lotus went into the stomach of the elephant. The bee was thinking, 'My beloved lotus is going somewhere, and I am happily going along with it.' It died shortly thereafter.

Similarly, we humans too remain engrossed in the gratification of the senses and do not heed the message of the saints to engage in devotion to God. Eventually, time overtakes us in the form of death. Here, Shree Krishna says that those who refuse to discipline the senses and engage in devotion continue to be rocked by the three-fold miseries of maya. Material desires are like an itching eczema, and the more we indulge in them, the worse they become. How can we be truly happy in this state of material indulgence?

इन्द्रियाणां हि चरतां यन्मनोऽनुविधीयते ।
तदस्य हरति प्रज्ञां वायुर्नावमिवाम्भसि ।।67।।

indriyāṇāṁ hi charatāṁ yan mano 'nuvidhīyate
tadasya harati prajñāṁ vāyur nāvam ivāmbhasi

indriyāṇām—of the senses; *hi*—indeed; *charatām*—roaming; *yat*—which; *manaḥ*—the mind; *anuvidhīyate*—becomes constantly engaged; *tat*—that; *asya*—of that; *harati*—carries away; *prajñām*—intellect; *vāyuḥ*—wind; *nāvam*—boat; *iva*—as; *ambhasi*—on the water.

Just as a strong wind sweeps a boat off its chartered course on the water, even one of the senses on which the mind focuses can lead the intellect astray.

The *Kaṭhopaniṣhad* states that God has made our five senses outward facing. *Parāñchi khāni vyatṛiṇatsvayambhūḥ* (2.1.1) Hence, they are automatically drawn towards their objects in the external world, and even one of the senses on which the mind focuses has the power to lead it astray.

kuraṅga mātaṅga pataṅga bṛiṅga
　mīnāhatāḥ pañchabhireva pañcha
ekaḥ pramādī sa kathaṁ na hanyate
　yaḥ sevate pañchabhireva pañcha (*Sukti Sudhakar*)

'Deer are attached to sweet sounds. The hunter attracts them by starting melodious music and then kills them. Bees are attached to fragrance. While they suck its nectar, the flower closes at night, and they get trapped within it. Fish are trapped by the desire for eating, and they swallow the bait of the fishermen. Insects are drawn to light. They come too close to the fire and get burnt. The weakness of elephants is the sense of touch. The hunter leverages this to trap the male elephant by using the female elephant as bait to draw it into the pit. On entering the pit to touch the female, the male elephant is unable to get out and is killed by the hunter. All these creatures get drawn towards their death by one of their senses. What then will be the fate of a human being who enjoys the objects of all the five senses?' In this verse, Shree Krishna warns Arjun of the power of these senses in leading the mind astray.

तस्माद्यस्य महाबाहो निगृहीतानि सर्वशः ।
इन्द्रियाणीन्द्रियार्थेभ्यस्तस्य प्रज्ञा प्रतिष्ठिता ।।68।।

tasmād yasya mahā-bāho nigṛihītāni sarvaśhaḥ
indriyāṇīndriyārthebhyas tasya prajñā pratiṣhṭhitā

tasmāt—therefore; *yasya*—whose; *mahā-bāho*—mighty-armed one; *nigṛihītāni*—restrained; *sarvaśhaḥ*—completely; *indriyāṇi*—senses; *indriya-arthebhyaḥ*—from sense objects; *tasya*—of that person; *prajñā*—transcendental knowledge; *pratiṣhṭhitā*—remains fixed.

Therefore, one who has restrained the senses from their objects, O mighty armed Arjun, is firmly established in transcendental knowledge.

Enlightened souls control the intellect through transcendental knowledge. Then, with the purified intellect, they control the mind, and the mind is used to bridle the senses. The reverse takes place in the materially conditioned state: the senses pull the mind in their direction; the mind overpowers the intellect; and the intellect gets derailed from the direction of true welfare. Thus, Shree Krishna says that if the intellect is purified by spiritual knowledge, then the senses will be restrained; and when senses are held in check, the intellect will not be swayed from the path of divine wisdom.

या निशा सर्वभूतानां तस्यां जागर्ति संयमी ।
यस्यां जाग्रति भूतानि सा निशा पश्यतो मुनेः ।।69।।

yā niśhā sarva-bhūtānāṁ tasyāṁ jāgarti sanyamī
yasyāṁ jāgrati bhūtāni sā niśhā paśhyato muneḥ

yā—which; *niśhā*—night; *sarva-bhūtānām*—of all living beings; *tasyām*—in that; *jāgarti*—awake; *sanyamī*—self-controlled; *yasyām*—in which; *jāgrati*—awake; *bhūtāni*—creatures; *sā*—that; *niśhā*—night; *paśhyataḥ*—see; *muneḥ*—sage.

What all beings consider as day is the night of ignorance for the wise, and what all creatures see as night is the day for the introspective sage.

Shree Krishna has used day and night figuratively here. People often confuse the meaning of this verse by taking the words literally. There was once a Khade Shree Baba (the standing ascetic), whose disciples claimed he was a very big sage. He had not slept in thirty-five years! He would stand in his room, resting on a hanging rope under his armpits. He used the rope to help him remain in the standing position. On being asked what his motivation was for this destructive kind of austerity, he would quote this verse of the Bhagavad Gita: 'What all beings see as night, the enlightened sage sees as day.' To practice it, he had given up sleeping at night. What a misunderstanding of the verse! From all that standing, his feet and lower legs were swollen; he could practically do nothing except stand.

Let us try and understand the true meaning of Shree Krishna's words. Those who are in mundane consciousness look to material enjoyment as the real purpose of life. They consider the opportunity for worldly pleasures as the success of life or 'day', and deprivation from sense pleasures as darkness or 'night'. On the other hand, those who have become wise with divine knowledge, see sense enjoyment as harmful for the soul, and hence, view it as 'night'. They consider refraining from the objects of the senses as elevating to the soul, and consequently look on it as 'day'. Using these connotations of the words, Shree Krishna states that what is night for the sage is day for the worldly-minded people and vice versa.

आपूर्यमाणमचलप्रतिष्ठं
समुद्रमापः प्रविशन्ति यद्वत् ।
तद्वत्कामा यं प्रविशन्ति सर्वे
स शान्तिमाप्नोति न कामकामी ।।70।।

āpūryamāṇam achala-pratiṣhṭhaṁ
samudram āpaḥ praviśhanti yadvat
tadvat kāmā yaṁ praviśhanti sarve
sa śhāntim āpnoti na kāma-kāmī

āpūryamāṇam—filled from all sides; *achala-pratiṣhṭham*—

undisturbed; *samudram*—ocean; *āpaḥ*—waters; *praviśhanti*—enter; *yadvat*—as; *tadvat*—likewise; *kāmāḥ*—desires; *yam*—whom; *praviśhanti*—enter; *sarve*—all; *saḥ*—that person; *śhāntim*—peace; *āpnoti*—attains; *na*—not; *kāma-kāmī*—one who strives to satisfy desires.

Just as the ocean remains undisturbed by the incessant flow of waters from rivers merging into it, likewise the sage who is unmoved despite the flow of desirable objects all around him attains peace and not the person who strives to satisfy desires.

The ocean is unique in its ability to maintain its undisturbed state, despite being inundated by the incessant flow of rivers into it. All the rivers of the world constantly empty themselves into the oceans, which neither overflow nor get depleted. Shree Krishna uses the word *āpūryamāṇaṁ* (filled from all sides) to describe that even the rivers pouring all their water during the rainy season into the ocean cannot make it flow over. Similarly, the realised sage remains quiescent and unmoved in both conditions—while utilising sense objects for bodily necessities or being bereft of them. Only such a sage can attain shanti or true peace.

विहाय कामान्यः सर्वान्पुमांश्चरति निःस्पृहः ।
निर्ममो निरहङ्कारः स शान्तिमधिगच्छति ।।71।।

vihāya kāmān yaḥ sarvān pumānśh charati niḥspṛihaḥ
nirmamo nirahankāraḥ sa śhāntim adhigachchhati

vihāya—giving up; *kāmān*—material desires; *yaḥ*—who; *sarvān*—all; *pumān*—a person; *charati*—lives; *niḥspṛihaḥ*—free from hankering; *nirmamaḥ*—without a sense of proprietorship; *nirahankāraḥ*—without ego; *saḥ*—that person; *śhāntim*—perfect peace; *adhigachchhati*—attains.

That person, who gives up all material desires and lives free from a sense of greed, proprietorship, and egoism, attains perfect peace.

In this verse, Shree Krishna lists the things that disturb one's peace, and then asks Arjun to give them up.

Material desires: The moment we harbour a desire, we walk into the trap of greed and anger. Either way, we get trapped. The path to inner peace does not lie in fulfilling desires but in eliminating them.

Greed: First, greed for material advancement is a great waste of time. Second, it is an endless chase. In developed countries, very few people are deprived of sufficient food and clothes, yet they remain disturbed; this is because their hankering is still unsatisfied. Thus, those who possess the wealth of contentment possess one of the biggest treasures of life.

Ego: Most of the quarrels that erupt between people stem from the ego. Mark H McCormack, author of *What They Don't Teach You at Harvard Business School* writes: 'Most corporate executives are one giant ego with a couple of arms and legs sticking out.' Statistics reveal that a majority of executives, who lose their jobs at the senior management level, do so not because of professional incompetence, but because of interpersonal issues. The way to peace is not to nurture and increase pride but to get rid of it.

Proprietorship: The feeling of proprietorship is based upon ignorance because the whole world belongs to God. We came empty-handed in the world and will go back empty-handed. How then can we think of worldly things as ours?

एषा ब्राह्मी स्थितिः पार्थ नैनां प्राप्य विमुह्यति ।
स्थित्वास्यामन्तकालेऽपि ब्रह्मनिर्वाणमृच्छति ।।72।।

eṣhā brāhmī sthitiḥ pārtha naināṁ prāpya vimuhyati
sthitvāsyām anta-kāle 'pi brahma-nirvāṇam ṛichchhati

eṣhā—such; *brāhmī sthitiḥ*—state of God-realisation; *pārtha*—Arjun, son of Pritha; *na*—never; *enām*—this; *prāpya*—having attained; *vimuhyati*—is deluded; *sthitvā*—being established; *asyām*—in this; *anta-kāle*—at the hour of death; *api*—even; *brahma-nirvāṇam*—liberation from maya; *ṛichchhati*—attains.

O Parth, such is the state of an enlightened soul that having attained

it, one is never again deluded. Being established in this consciousness even at the hour of death, one is liberated from the cycle of life and death and reaches the supreme abode of God.

Brahman means 'God', and *brāhmī sthiti* means the 'state of God-realisation'. When the soul purifies the heart (the mind and intellect are sometimes jointly referred to as the heart), God bestows His divine grace, as mentioned in verse 2.64. By His grace, He grants divine knowledge, divine bliss, and divine love to the soul. All these are divine energies that are given by God to the soul at the time of God-realisation.

At the same time, He liberates the soul from the bondage of maya. The *sañchit* karmas (account of karmas of endless lifetimes) are destroyed. The *avidyā*, ignorance within, from endless lifetimes in the material world, is dispelled. The influence of *tri-gunas*, three modes of material nature, ceases. The *tri-doṣhas*, three defects of the materially conditioned state, come to an end. The *pañcha kleśhas*, five defects of the material intellect, are destroyed. The *pañcha kośhas*, five sheaths of the material energy, are burnt. And from that point onward, the soul becomes free from the bondage of maya for the rest of eternity.

When this state of God-realisation is achieved, the soul is said to be *jīvan mukt*, or liberated even while residing in the body. Then, at the time of death, the liberated soul finally discards the corporeal body, and it reaches the supreme abode of God. The *Rig Veda* states:

tadviṣhṇoḥ paramaṁ padaṁ sadā paśhyanti sūrayaḥ (1.22.20)

'Once the soul attains God, it always remains in union with Him. After that, the ignorance of maya can never overpower it again.' That state of eternal liberation from maya is also called nirvana, moksha, etc. As a result, liberation is a natural consequence of God-realisation.

CHAPTER 3

Karm Yog

The Yog of Action

In this chapter, Shree Krishna explains that it is the intrinsic nature of all beings to work, and nobody can remain without action for even a moment. Those who display external renunciation by donning ochre robes, but internally dwell upon sense objects, are in fact hypocrites. Superior to them are those who practise karm yog and continue to engage in action externally but give up attachment from within. Shree Krishna then stresses that all living beings have responsibilities to fulfil as integral parts of the system of God's creation. When we execute our prescribed duties as an obligation to God, such work becomes yajna (sacrifice). The performance of yajna is naturally pleasing to the celestial gods, and they bestow us with material prosperity. Such yajna causes the rains to fall, and rain begets grains which are necessary for sustenance of life. Those who do not accept their responsibility in this cycle are in fact sinful; they live only for the delight of their senses, and their lives are in vain.

Shree Krishna then explains that unlike the rest of humankind, enlightened souls who are situated in the self are not obliged to fulfil bodily responsibilities because they are executing higher responsibilities at the level of the soul. However, if they abandon their social duties, it creates discord in the minds of common people who tend to follow in the footsteps of the great ones. So, to set a good example for the world to emulate, the wise should continue working without any motive for personal reward. This will prevent the ignorant from prematurely abandoning their prescribed duties. It was for this purpose that enlightened kings in the past, such as King Janak and others, performed their works.

Arjun then asks why people commit sinful acts, even unwillingly, as if by force. The Supreme Lord explains that the all-devouring sinful enemy of the world is lust alone. As a fire is covered by smoke and a mirror is masked by dust, in the same way, desire shrouds one's knowledge and drags away the intellect. Shree Krishna then gives the clarion call to Arjun to slay this enemy called desire, which is the embodiment of sin, and bring his senses, mind, and intellect under control.

अर्जुन उवाच ।
ज्यायसी चेत्कर्मणस्ते मता बुद्धिर्जनार्दन ।
तत्किं कर्मणि घोरे मां नियोजयसि केशव ।।1।।

व्यामिश्रेणेव वाक्येन बुद्धिं मोहयसीव मे ।
तदेकं वद निश्चित्य येन श्रेयोऽहमाप्नुयाम् ।।2।।

arjuna uvācha
jyāyasī chet karmaṇas te matā buddhir janārdana
tat kiṁ karmaṇi ghore māṁ niyojayasi keśhava

vyāmiśhreṇeva vākyena buddhiṁ mohayasīva me
tad ekaṁ vada niśhchitya yena śhreyo 'ham āpnuyām

arjunaḥ uvācha—Arjun said; *jyāyasī*—superior; *chet*—if; *karmaṇaḥ*—than fruitive action; *te*—by you; *matā*—is considered; *buddhiḥ*—intellect; *janārdana*—He who looks after the public, Krishna; *tat*—then; *kim*—why; *karmaṇi*—action; *ghore*—terrible; *mām*—me; *niyojayasi*—do you engage; *keśhava*—Krishna, killer of the demon named Keshi; *vyāmiśhreṇa iva*—by your apparently ambiguous; *vākyena*—words; *buddhim*—intellect; *mohayasi*—I am getting bewildered; *iva*—as it were; *me*—my; *tat*—therefore; *ekam*—one; *vada*—please tell; *niśhchitya*—decisively; *yena*—by which; *śhreyaḥ*—the highest good; *aham*—I; *āpnuyām*—may attain.

Arjun said: O Janardan, if You consider knowledge superior to action, then why do You ask me to wage this terrible war? My intellect is bewildered by Your ambiguous advice. Please tell me decisively the one path by which I may attain the highest good.

Chapter one introduced the setting in which Arjun's grief and lamentation arose, creating a reason for Shree Krishna to give spiritual instructions. In chapter two, the Lord first explained knowledge of the immortal self. He then reminded Arjun of his duty as a warrior and said that performing it would result in glory and entry into the celestial abodes. After prodding Arjun to do his occupational work as a Kshatriya, Shree Krishna then revealed a superior principle—the science of karm yog—and asked Arjun to detach himself from the fruits of his works. In this way, bondage-creating karmas would be transformed into bondage-breaking karmas. He termed the science of working without desire for rewards as *buddhi yog* or Yog of the intellect. By this, He meant that the mind should be detached from worldly temptations by controlling it with a resolute intellect made unwavering through the cultivation of spiritual knowledge. He did not suggest that actions should be given up, rather, attachment to the fruits of actions should be renounced.

Arjun misunderstood Shree Krishna's explanation, thinking that if knowledge is superior to action, then why should he perform the ghastly duty of waging this war? Hence, he says, 'By making contradictory statements, You are bewildering my intellect. I know You are merciful and Your desire is not to baffle me, so please dispel my doubt.'

श्रीभगवानुवाच ।
लोकेऽस्मिन्द्विविधा निष्ठा पुरा प्रोक्ता मयानघ ।
ज्ञानयोगेन साङ्ख्यानां कर्मयोगेन योगिनाम् ।।3।।

śhrī bhagavān uvācha
loke 'smin dvi-vidhā niṣhṭhā purā proktā mayānagha
jñāna-yogena sāṅkhyānāṁ karma-yogena yoginām

śhrī-bhagavān uvācha—the Lord said; *loke*—in the world;

asmin—this; *dvi-vidhā*—two kinds of; *niṣhṭhā*—faith; *purā*—previously; *proktā*—explained; *mayā*—by Me (Shree Krishna); *anagha*—sinless; *jñāna-yogena*—through the path of knowledge; *sānkhyānām*—for those inclined towards contemplation; *karma-yogena*—through the path of action; *yoginām*—of the yogis.

The Lord said: O sinless one, the two paths leading to enlightenment were previously explained by Me: the path of knowledge for those inclined towards contemplation, and the path of work for those inclined towards action.

In verse 2.39, Shree Krishna explained the two paths leading to spiritual perfection. The first is the acquisition of knowledge through the analytical study of the nature of the soul and its distinction from the body. Shree Krishna refers to this as *Sānkhya Yog*. People with a philosophic bent of mind are inclined towards this path of knowing the self through intellectual analysis. The second is the process of working in the spirit of devotion to God or karm yog. Shree Krishna also calls this *buddhi yog* as explained in the previous verse. Working in this manner purifies the mind, and knowledge naturally awakens in the purified mind, thereby leading to enlightenment.

Among people interested in the spiritual path, there are those who are inclined towards contemplation and those inclined to action. Hence, both these paths have existed ever since the soul's aspiration for God-realisation has existed. Shree Krishna touches upon both of them since His message is meant for people of all temperaments and inclinations.

न कर्मणामनारम्भान्नैष्कर्म्यं पुरुषोऽश्नुते ।
न च संन्यसनादेव सिद्धिं समधिगच्छति ।।4।।

na karmaṇām anārambhān naiṣhkarmyaṁ puruṣho 'śhnute
na cha sannyasanād eva siddhiṁ samadhigachchhati

na—not; *karmaṇām*—of actions; *anārambhāt*—by abstaining from; *naiṣhkarmyam*—freedom from karmic reactions;

puruṣhaḥ—a person; *aśhnute*—attains; *na*—not; *cha*—and; *sannyasanāt*—by renunciation; *eva*—only; *siddhim*—perfection; *samadhigachchhati*—attains.

One cannot achieve freedom from karmic reactions by merely abstaining from work, nor can one attain perfection of knowledge by mere physical renunciation.

The first line of this verse refers to the karm yogi (follower of the discipline of work), and the second line refers to the *sānkhya yogi* (follower of the discipline of knowledge).

In the first line, Shree Krishna says that mere abstinence from work does not result in a state of freedom from karmic reactions. The mind continues to engage in fruitive thoughts, and since mental work is also a form of karma, it binds one in karmic reactions, just as physical work does. A true karm yogi must learn to work without any attachment to the fruits of actions. This requires cultivation of knowledge in the intellect. Hence, philosophic knowledge is also necessary for success in karm yog.

In the second line, Shree Krishna declares that the *sānkhya yogi* cannot attain the state of knowledge merely by renouncing the world and becoming a monk. One may give up the physical objects of the senses, but true knowledge cannot awaken as long as the mind remains impure. The mind has a tendency to repeat its previous thoughts. Such repetition creates a channel within the mind, and new thoughts flow irresistibly in the same direction. Out of previous habit, the materially contaminated mind keeps running in the direction of anxiety, stress, fear, hatred, envy, attachment, and the whole gamut of material emotions. Thus, realised knowledge will not appear in an impure heart by mere physical renunciation. It must be accompanied by congruent action that purifies the mind and intellect. Therefore, action is also necessary for success in *Sānkhya Yog*.

It is said that devotion without philosophy is sentimentality, and philosophy without devotion is intellectual speculation. Action and knowledge are necessary in both karm yog and *Sānkhya Yog*.

It is only their proportion that varies, thereby creating a difference between the two paths.

न हि कश्चित्क्षणमपि जातु तिष्ठत्यकर्मकृत् ।
कार्यते ह्यवशः कर्म सर्वः प्रकृतिजैर्गुणैः ।।5।।

na hi kaśhchit kṣhaṇam api jātu tiṣhṭhatyakarma kṛit
kāryate hyavaśhaḥ karma sarvaḥ prakṛiti-jair guṇaiḥ

na—not; *hi*—certainly; *kaśhchit*—anyone; *kṣhaṇam*—a moment; *api*—even; *jātu*—ever; *tiṣhṭhati*—can remain; *akarma-kṛit*—without action; *kāryate*—are performed; *hi*—certainly; *avaśhaḥ*—helpless; *karma*—work; *sarvaḥ*—all; *prakṛiti-jaiḥ*—born of material nature; *guṇaiḥ*—by the qualities.

There is no one who can remain without action even for a moment. Indeed, all beings are compelled to act by their qualities born of material nature (the three gunas).

Some people think that action refers only to professional work and not to daily activities, such as eating, drinking, sleeping, waking, and thinking. So when they renounce their profession, they think they are not performing actions. But Shree Krishna considers all activities performed with the body, mind, and tongue as actions. Hence, He tells Arjun that complete inactivity is impossible even for a moment. If we simply sit down, it is an activity; if we lie down, that is also an activity; if we fall asleep, the mind is still engaged in dreaming; even in deep sleep, the heart and other bodily organs are functioning. Thus, Shree Krishna declares that for human beings, inactivity is an impossible state to reach, since the body-mind-intellect mechanism is compelled by its own composition of the three gunas (sattva, rajas, and tamas) to work. The Shreemad Bhagavatam contains a similar verse:

na hi kaśhchit kṣhaṇam api jātu tiṣhṭhaty akarma-kṛit
kāryate hy avaśhaḥ karma guṇaiḥ svābhāvikair balāt (6.1.53)

'Nobody can remain inactive for even a moment. Everyone is forced to act by their modes of nature.'

कर्मेन्द्रियाणि संयम्य य आस्ते मनसा स्मरन् ।
इन्द्रियार्थान्विमूढात्मा मिथ्याचारः स उच्यते ।।6।।

karmendriyāṇi sanyamya ya āste manasā smaran
indriyārthān vimūḍhātmā mithyāchāraḥ sa uchyate

karma-indriyāṇi—organs of action; *sanyamya*—restrain; *yaḥ*—who; *āste*—remain; *manasā*—in the mind; *smaran*—to remember; *indriya-arthān*—sense objects; *vimūḍha-ātmā*—the deluded; *mithyā-āchāraḥ*—hypocrite; *saḥ*—they; *uchyate*—are called.

Those who restrain the external organs of action, while continuing to dwell on sense objects in the mind, certainly delude themselves and are to be called hypocrites.

Attracted by the lure of an ascetic life, people often renounce their work, only to discover later that their renunciation is not accompanied by an equal amount of mental and intellectual withdrawal from the sensual fields. This creates a situation of hypocrisy where one displays an external show of religiosity while internally living a life of ignoble sentiments and base motives. In such instances, it is better to face the struggles of the world as a karm yogi than to lead the life of a false ascetic. Running away from the problems of life by prematurely taking sanyas is not the way forward in the journey of the evolution of the soul. Saint Kabir stated sarcastically:

mana na raṅgāye ho,
raṅgāye yogī kapaṛā
jatavā baḍhāe yogī dhuniyā ramaule,
dahiyā baḍhāe yogī bani gayele bakarā

'O Ascetic Yogi, you have donned the ochre robes, but you have ignored dyeing your mind with the colour of renunciation. You have grown long locks of hair and smeared ash on your body (as a sign of detachment). But without the internal devotion, the external beard you have sprouted only makes you resemble a goat.' Shree Krishna states in this verse that people who externally renounce the objects of the senses while continuing to dwell upon them in the mind are hypocrites, and they delude themselves.

The Puranas relate the story of two brothers, Tavrit and Suvrit, to illustrate this point.

The brothers were walking from their house to hear the Shreemad Bhagavatam discourse at the temple. On the way, it began raining heavily, so they ran into the nearest building for shelter. To their dismay, they found themselves in a brothel where women of disrepute were dancing to entertain their guests. Tavrit, the older brother, was appalled and walked out into the rain to continue to the temple. The younger brother, Suvrit, felt no harm in sitting there for a while to escape getting wet in the rain.

Tavrit reached the temple and sat for the discourse, but in his mind, he became remorseful, 'O how boring this is! I made a dreadful mistake; I should have remained at the brothel. My brother must be enjoying himself greatly in revelry there.' Suvrit, on the other hand, started thinking, 'Why did I remain in this house of sin? My brother is so holy; he is bathing his intellect in the knowledge of the Bhagavatam. I too should have braved the rain and reached there. After all, I am not made of salt that I would have melted in a little bit of rain.'

When the rain stopped, both started out in the direction of the other. The moment they met, lightning struck them and they both died on the spot. The *Yamdoots* (servants of the god of death) came to take Tavrit to hell. Tavrit complained, 'I think you have made a mistake. I am Tavrit. It was my brother who was sitting at the brothel a little while ago. You should be taking him to hell.'

The *Yamdoots* replied, 'We have made no mistake. He was sitting there to avoid the rain, but in his mind, he was longing to be at the Bhagavatam discourse. On the other hand, while you were sitting and hearing the discourse, your mind was yearning to be at the brothel.'

Tavrit was doing exactly what Shree Krishna declares in this verse; he had externally renounced the objects of the senses but was dwelling upon them in the mind. This was the improper kind of renunciation. *The next verse states the proper kind of renunciation.*

यस्त्विन्द्रियाणि मनसा नियम्यारभतेऽर्जुन ।
कर्मेन्द्रियैः कर्मयोगमसक्तः स विशिष्यते ।। 7 ।।

yas-tvindriyāṇi manasā niyamyārabhate 'rjuna
karmendriyaiḥ karma-yogam asaktaḥ sa viśhiṣhyate

yaḥ—who; *tu*—but; *indriyāṇi*—the senses; *manasā*—by the mind; *niyamya*—control; *ārabhate*—begins; *arjuna*—Arjun; *karma-indriyaiḥ*—by the working senses; *karma-yogam*—karm yog; *asaktaḥ*—without attachment; *saḥ*—they; *viśhiṣhyate*—are superior.

But those karm yogis who control their knowledge senses with the mind, O Arjun, and engage the working senses in working without attachment, are certainly superior.

The word karm yog has been used in this verse. It consists of two main concepts: karm (occupational duties) and Yog (union with God). Hence, a karm yogi is one who performs worldly duties while keeping the mind attached to God. Such a karm yogi is not bound by karma even while performing all kinds of works. This is because what binds one to the Law of Karma is not actions but the attachment to the fruits of those actions. And a karm yogi has no attachment to the fruits of action. On the other hand, a false renunciant renounces action, but does not forsake attachment; thus, he remains bound by the Law of Karma.

Here, Shree Krishna says that a person in household life who practises karm yog is superior to the false renunciant who continues to dwell on the objects of the senses in the mind. Jagadguru Shree Kripaluji Maharaj contrasts these two situations very beautifully:

mana hari meṅ tana jagat meṅ, karmayog tehi jāna
tana hari meṅ mana jagat meṅ, yaha mahāna ajñāna

(*Bhakti Śhatak* verse 84)

'When one works in the world with the body but keeps the mind attached to God, know it to be karm yog. When one engages in spirituality with the body but keeps the mind attached to the world, know it to be hypocrisy.'

नियतं कुरु कर्म त्वं कर्म ज्यायो ह्यकर्मणः ।
शरीरयात्रापि च ते न प्रसिद्ध्येदकर्मणः ।।8।।

niyataṁ kuru karma tvaṁ karma jyāyo hyakarmaṇaḥ
śharīra-yātrāpi cha te na prasiddhyed akarmaṇaḥ

niyatam—constantly; *kuru*—perform; *karma*—Vedic duties; *tvam*—you; *karma*—action; *jyāyaḥ*—superior; *hi*—certainly; *akarmaṇaḥ*—than inaction; *śharīra*—bodily; *yātrā*—maintenance; *api*—even; *cha*—and; *te*—your; *na prasiddhyet*—would not be possible; *akarmaṇaḥ*—inaction.

You should thus perform your prescribed Vedic duties, since action is superior to inaction. By ceasing activity, even your bodily maintenance will not be possible.

Until the mind and intellect reach a state where they are absorbed in God-consciousness, physical work performed in an attitude of duty is very beneficial for one's internal purification. Hence, to help them discipline their mind and senses, the Vedas prescribe duties for humans. In fact, laziness is described as one of the biggest pitfalls on the spiritual path:

ālasya hi manuṣhyāṇāṁ śharīrastho mahān ripuḥ
nāstyudyamasamo bandhūḥ kṛitvā yaṁ nāvasīdati

'Laziness is the greatest enemy of humans and is especially pernicious since it resides in their own body. Work is their most trustworthy friend and is a guarantee against downfall.' Even the basic bodily activities like eating, bathing, and maintaining proper health require work. These obligatory actions are called *nitya karm*. To neglect these basic maintenance activities is not a sign of progress, but an indication of slothfulness, leading to emaciation and weakness of both body and mind. On the other hand, a cared for and nourished body is a positive adjunct on the road to spirituality. Thus, the state of inertia does not lend itself either to material or spiritual achievement. For the progress of our own soul, we should embrace the duties that help elevate and purify our mind and intellect.

यज्ञार्थात्कर्मणोऽन्यत्र लोकोऽयं कर्मबन्धनः ।
तदर्थं कर्म कौन्तेय मुक्तसङ्गः समाचर ॥9॥

yajñārthāt karmaṇo 'nyatra loko 'yaṁ karma-bandhanaḥ
tad-arthaṁ karma kaunteya mukta-saṅgaḥ samāchara

yajña-arthāt—for the sake of sacrifice; *karmaṇaḥ*—than action; *anyatra*—else; *lokaḥ*—material world; *ayam*—this; *karma-bandhanaḥ*—bondage through one's work; *tat*—that; *artham*—for the sake of; *karma*—action; *kaunteya*—Arjun, son of Kunti; *mukta-saṅgaḥ*—free from attachment; *samāchara*—perform properly.

Work must be done as a yajna (sacrifice) to the Supreme Lord, otherwise, it causes bondage in this material world. Therefore, O son of Kunti, for the satisfaction of God, perform your prescribed duties without being attached to the results.

A knife in the hands of a robber is a weapon for intimidation or committing murder but in the hands of a surgeon is an invaluable instrument used for saving people's lives. The knife in itself is neither murderous nor benedictory—its effect is determined by how it is used. As Shakespeare said: 'There is nothing either good or bad but thinking makes it so.' Similarly, work in itself is neither good nor bad. Depending upon the state of the mind, it can be either binding or elevating. Work done for the enjoyment of one's senses and the gratification of one's pride is the cause of bondage in the material world, while work performed as yajna for the pleasure of the Supreme Lord liberates one from the bonds of maya and attracts divine grace. Since it is our nature to perform actions, we are forced to work in one of the two modes. We cannot remain without working for even a moment as our mind cannot remain still.

If we do not perform actions as a sacrifice to God, we will be forced to work to gratify our mind and senses. Instead, when we perform work as a sacrifice, we then look upon the whole world and everything in it as belonging to God, and therefore, meant for utilisation in His service. A beautiful ideal for this was established by King Raghu, the ancestor of Lord Ram.

Raghu performed the *Viśhwajit Yajna*, which requires donating all of one's possessions in charity.

sa viśhwajitam ājahre yajñaṁ sarvasva dakṣhiṇam
ādānaṁ hi visargāya satāṁ vārimuchām iva

(*Raghuvanśh* 4.86)

'Raghu performed the *Viśhwajit Yajna* with the thought that just as clouds gather water from the earth, not for their enjoyment, but to shower it back upon the earth, similarly, all he possessed as a king had been gathered from the public in taxes, not for his pleasure, but for the pleasure of God. So, he decided to use his wealth to please God by serving his citizens with it.'

After the yajna, Raghu donated all his possessions to his citizens. Then, donning the rags of a beggar and holding an earthen pot, he went out to beg for his meal. While resting under a tree, he heard a group of people discussing, 'Our king is so benevolent. He has given away everything in charity.'

Raghu was pained on hearing his praise and spoke out, 'What are you discussing?'

They answered, 'We are praising our king. There is nobody in the world as charitable as him.'

Raghu retorted, 'Do not ever say that again. Raghu has given nothing.'

They said, 'What kind of person are you who are criticising our king? Everyone knows that Raghu has donated everything he owned.'

Raghu replied, 'Go and ask your king that when he came into this world, did he possess anything? He was born empty-handed, is it not? Then what was his that he has given away?'

This is the spirit of karm yog, in which we see the whole world as belonging to God, and hence, meant for His satisfaction. We then perform our duties not for gratifying our mind and senses but for the pleasure of God. Lord Vishnu instructed the Prachetas in this fashion:

gṛiheṣhv āviśhatāṁ chāpi puṁsāṁ kuśhala-karmaṇām
mad-vārtā-yāta-yāmānāṁ na bandhāya gṛihā matāḥ

(Bhagavatam 4.30.19)

'The perfect karm yogis, even while fulfilling their household duties, perform all their works as yajna to Me, knowing Me to be the Enjoyer of all activities. They spend whatever free time they have in hearing and chanting My glories. Such people, though living in the world, never get bound by their actions.'

सहयज्ञाः प्रजाः सृष्ट्वा पुरोवाच प्रजापतिः ।
अनेन प्रसविष्यध्वमेष वोऽस्त्विष्टकामधुक् ।। 10 ।।

saha-yajñāḥ prajāḥ sṛiṣhṭvā purovācha prajāpatiḥ
anena prasaviṣhyadhvam eṣha vo 'stviṣhṭa-kāma-dhuk

saha—along with; *yajñāḥ*—sacrifices; *prajāḥ*—humankind; *sṛiṣhṭvā*—created; *purā*—in the beginning; *uvācha*—said; *prajā-patiḥ*—Brahma; *anena*—by this; *prasaviṣhyadhvam*—increase prosperity; *eṣhaḥ*—these; *vaḥ*—your; *astu*—shall be; *iṣhṭa-kāma-dhuk*—bestower of all wishes.

In the beginning of creation, Brahma created humankind along with duties, and said, 'Prosper in the performance of these yajnas, for they shall bestow upon you all you wish to achieve.'

All the elements of nature are integral parts of the system of God's creation. All the parts of the system naturally draw from and give back to the whole. The sun lends stability to the earth and provides heat and light necessary for life to exist. Earth creates food from its soil for our nourishment and also holds essential minerals in its womb for a civilised lifestyle. The air moves the life force in our body and enables transmission of sound energy. We humans too are an integral part of the entire system of God's creation. The air that we breathe, the earth that we walk upon, the water that we drink, and the light that illumines our day, are all gifts of Creation. While we partake of these gifts to sustain our life, we also have our duties towards the integral system. Shree Krishna says that we are obligated to participate with the creative force of nature by performing our prescribed duties in the service of God. That is the yajna He expects from us.

Consider the example of a hand. It is an integral part of the body. It receives its nourishment—blood, oxygen, and nutrients—from the body, and in turn, it performs necessary functions for the body. If the hand looks on this service as burdensome and decides to get severed from the body, it cannot sustain itself for even a few minutes. It is in the performance of its yajna towards the body that the self-interest of the hand is also fulfilled. Similarly, we individual souls are tiny parts of the Supreme Soul and we all have our role to play in the grand scheme of things. When we perform our yajna towards Him, our self-interest is naturally satiated.

Generally, the term yajna refers to fire sacrifice. In the Bhagavad Gita, yajna includes all the prescribed actions laid down in the scriptures, when they are done as an offering to the Supreme.

देवान्भावयतानेन ते देवा भावयन्तु वः ।
परस्परं भावयन्तः श्रेयः परमवाप्स्यथ ।।11।।

devān-bhāvayatānena te devā bhāvayantu vaḥ
parasparaṁ bhāvayantaḥ śhreyaḥ param avāpsyatha

devān—celestial gods; *bhāvayatā*—will be pleased; *anena*—by these (sacrifices); *te*—those; *devāḥ*—celestial gods; *bhāvayantu*—will be pleased; *vaḥ*—you; *parasparam*—one another; *bhāvayantaḥ*—pleasing one another; *śhreyaḥ*—prosperity; *param*—great; *avāpsyatha*—shall achieve.

By your sacrifices, the celestial gods will be pleased, and by cooperation between humans and the celestial gods, great prosperity will reign for all.

The celestial gods, or *devatās*, are in-charge of the administration of the universe. The Supreme Lord does His work of managing the universe through them. These *devatās* live within this material universe in the higher planes of existence called *swarg* or the celestial abodes. The *devatās* are not God; they are souls like us. They occupy specific positions in the affairs of running the world. Consider the Federal government of a country. There is a Secretary of State, a Secretary of the Treasury, a Secretary of Defense, Attorney General, and so on. These are positions and chosen people occupy them for a limited tenure. At the end of the tenure, the government changes and all the post-holders change too. Similarly, in administering the affairs of the world, there are positions such as *Agni Devatā* (god of fire), *Vayu Devatā* (god of the wind), *Varun Devatā* (god of the ocean), *Indra Devatā* (king of the celestial gods), and so on. Souls selected by virtue of their deeds in past lives occupy these seats for a fixed number of ages and administer the affairs of the universe. These are the *devatās*.

The Vedas mention various ceremonies and processes for the satisfaction of the celestial gods, and in turn, these *devatās* bestow material prosperity. However, when we perform our yajna for the satisfaction of the Supreme Lord, the celestial gods are automatically appeased, just as when we water the root of a tree, the water inevitably reaches its flowers, fruits, leaves, branches, and twigs. The *Skand Puran* states:

archite deva deveśhe śhaṅkha chakra gadādhare
architāḥ sarve devāḥ syur yataḥ sarva gato hariḥ

'By worshipping the Supreme Lord Shree Vishnu, we automatically worship all the celestial gods since they all derive their power from Him.' Thus, the performance of yajna is naturally pleasing to the *devatās*, who then create prosperity for living beings by favourably adjusting the elements of material nature.

इष्टान्भोगान्हि वो देवा दास्यन्ते यज्ञभाविताः ।
तैर्दत्तानप्रदायैभ्यो यो भुङ्क्ते स्तेन एव सः ।।12।।

iṣhṭān bhogān hi vo devā dāsyante yajña-bhāvitāḥ
tair dattān apradāyaibhyo yo bhuṅkte stena eva saḥ

iṣhṭān—desired; *bhogān*—necessities of life; *hi*—certainly; *vaḥ*—unto you; *devāḥ*—celestial gods; *dāsyante*—will grant; *yajña-bhāvitāḥ*—satisfied by sacrifice; *taiḥ*—by them; *dattān*—things granted; *apradāya*—without offering; *ebhyaḥ*—to them; *yaḥ*—who; *bhuṅkte*—enjoys; *stenaḥ*—thieves; *eva*—verily; *saḥ*—they.

The celestial gods, being satisfied by the performance of sacrifice, will grant you all the desired necessities of life. But those who enjoy what is given to them, without making offerings in return, are verily thieves.

As administrators of various processes of the universe, the *devatās* provide us with rain, wind, crops, vegetation, minerals, fertile soil, and other resources. We human beings are indebted to them for all that we receive from them. The *devatās* perform their duty and expect us to perform our duty in the proper consciousness too. Since these celestial gods are all servants of the Supreme Lord, they become pleased when someone performs a sacrifice for Him, and in turn assist such a soul by creating favourable material conditions. Thus, it is said that the universe begins to cooperate with us when we strongly resolve to serve God.

However, if we begin looking upon the gifts of nature, not as a means of serving the Lord but as objects for our own enjoyment, Shree Krishna calls it a thieving mentality. Often people ask the question, 'I lead a virtuous life; I do not harm anyone, nor do I steal anything. But I do not believe in God or in worshipping Him. Am I doing anything wrong?' This question is answered in the above verse. Such persons may not be doing anything wrong in the eyes of humans, but they are thieves in the eyes of God. Let us say, we walk into someone's house and without recognising the owner, we sit on the sofa, eat from the refrigerator, and use the restroom. We may claim that we are not doing anything wrong, but we will be considered thieves in the eyes of the law, because the house does not belong to us. Similarly, the world that we live in was made by God and everything in it belongs to Him. If we utilise His creation for our pleasure, without acknowledging His dominion over it, then from the divine perspective, we are certainly committing theft.

The famous king in Indian history, Chandragupta, asked Chanakya Pandit, his guru, 'According to Vedic scriptures, what is the position of the king vis-à-vis his subjects?'

Chanakya Pandit replied, 'The king is the servant of the subjects and nothing else. His God-given duty is to help the citizens of his kingdom progress in their journey towards God-realisation.'

Whether one is a king, a businessperson, a farmer, or a worker, each person, as an integral member of God's world, is expected to do his or her duty as a service to the Supreme.

यज्ञशिष्टाशिनः सन्तो मुच्यन्ते सर्वकिल्बिषैः ।
भुञ्जते ते त्वघं पापा ये पचन्त्यात्मकारणात् ।।13।।

yajña-śhiṣhṭāśhinaḥ santo muchyante sarva-kilbiṣhaiḥ
bhuñjate te tvaghaṁ pāpā ye pachantyātma-kāraṇāt

yajña-śhiṣhṭa—remnants of food offered in sacrifice; *aśhinaḥ*—eaters; *santaḥ*—saintly persons; *muchyante*—are released; *sarva*—all kinds of; *kilbiṣhaiḥ*—from sins; *bhuñjate*—enjoy; *te*—they; *tu*—but; *agham*—sins; *pāpāḥ*—sinners; *ye*—who; *pachanti*—cook (food); *ātma-kāraṇāt*—for their own sake.

The spiritually minded, who eat food that is first offered in sacrifice, are released from all kinds of sin. Others, who cook food for their own enjoyment, verily eat only sin.

In the Vedic tradition, food is cooked with the consciousness that the meal is for the pleasure of God. A serving of the food items is then put in a plate and a verbal or mental prayer is made for the Lord to come and eat it. After the offering, the food in the plate is considered prasad (grace of God). All the food in the plate and the pots is then accepted as God's grace and eaten in that consciousness. Other religious traditions follow similar customs. Christianity has the sacrament of the Eucharist where bread and wine are consecrated and then partaken. Shree Krishna states in this verse that eating prasad (food that is first offered as sacrifice to God) releases one from sin, while those who eat food without offering it first to God commit sin.

The question may arise whether we can offer non-vegetarian items to God and then accept the remnants as His prasad. The answer to this question is that the Vedas prescribe a vegetarian diet for humans, which includes foods such as grains, pulses and beans, vegetables, fruits, and dairy products. Apart from Vedic culture, many spiritually evolved souls in the history of all cultures around the world also rejected a non-vegetarian diet that makes the stomach a graveyard for animals. Even though many of them were born in meat-eating families, they gravitated to a vegetarian lifestyle as they advanced on the path of spirituality. Here are quotations from some famous thinkers and personalities advocating vegetarianism:

> To avoid causing terror to living beings, let the disciple refrain from eating meat ... the food of the wise is that which is consumed by the sadhus; it does not consist of meat.
>
> — *The Buddha*

> If you declare that you are naturally designed for such a diet, then first kill for yourself what you want to eat. Do it, however, only through your own resources, unaided by cleaver or cudgel or any kind of ax.
>
> — *The Roman Plutarch, in the essay, 'On Eating Flesh'*

> As long as men massacre animals, they will kill each other. Indeed, he who sows the seeds of murder and pain cannot reap joy and love.
>
> —*Pythagoras*

> Nonviolence leads to the highest ethics, which is the goal of all evolution. Until we stop harming all living beings, we are all savages.
>
> —*Thomas Edison*

> If he be really and seriously seeking to live a good life, the first thing from which he will abstain will always be the use of animal food, because ... its use is simply immoral, as it involves the performance of an act which is contrary to moral feeling—killing.
>
> —*Leo Tolstoy*

I look my age. It is the other people who look older than they are. What can you expect from people who eat corpses?

—*George Bernard Shaw*

Truly man is the king of beasts, for his brutality exceeds them. We live by the death of others. We are burial places! I have since an early age abjured the use of meat...

—*Leonardo da Vinci*

It may indeed be doubted whether butchers' meat is anywhere necessary of life... Decency nowhere requires that any man should eat butchers' meat.

—*Adam Smith*

A dead cow or sheep lying in a pasture is recognized as carrion. The same sort of carcass dressed and hung up in a butcher's stall passes as food!

—*J. H. Kellogg*

It is my view that the vegetarian manner of living, by its purely physical effect on the human temperament, would most beneficially influence the lot of mankind.

—*Albert Einstein*

I do feel that spiritual progress does demand at some stage that we should cease to kill our fellow creatures for the satisfaction of our bodily wants.

—*Mahatma Gandhi*

In this verse, Shree Krishna goes further and says that even vegetation contains life, and if we eat it for our own sense enjoyment, we get bound in the karmic reactions of destroying life. The word used in the verse is *atma-kāraṇāt*, meaning, 'for one's individual pleasure'. However, if we eat food as remnants of yajna offered to God, then the consciousness changes. We then look upon our body as the property of God, which has been put under our care for His service. And we partake of permitted food, as His grace, with the intention that it will nourish the body. In this sentiment, the entire process is consecrated to the Divine. Bharat Muni states:

vasusato kratu dakṣhau kāla kāmau dṛitiḥ kuruḥ
pururavā madravāśhcha viśhwadevāḥ prakīrtitāḥ

'Violence is caused unknowingly to living entities in the process of cooking, by the use of the pestle, fire, grinding instruments, water pot, and broom. Those who cook food for themselves become implicated in the sin. But yajna nullifies the sinful reactions.'

अन्नाद्भवन्ति भूतानि पर्जन्यादन्नसम्भवः ।
यज्ञाद्भवति पर्जन्यो यज्ञः कर्मसमुद्भवः ।।14।।

annād bhavanti bhūtāni parjanyād anna-sambhavaḥ
yajñād bhavati parjanyo yajñaḥ karma-samudbhavaḥ

annāt—from food; *bhavanti*—subsist; *bhūtāni*—living beings; *parjanyāt*—from rains; *anna*—of food grains; *sambhavaḥ*—production; *yajñāt*—from the performance of sacrifice; *bhavati*—becomes possible; *parjanyaḥ*—rain; *yajñaḥ*—performance of sacrifice; *karma*—prescribed duties; *samudbhavaḥ*—born of.

All living beings subsist on food, and food is produced by rains. Rains come from the performance of sacrifice, and sacrifice is produced by the performance of prescribed duties.

Here, Lord Krishna is describing the cycle of nature. Rain begets grains. Grains are eaten and transformed into blood. From blood, semen is created. Semen is the seed from which the human body is created. Human beings perform yajnas, and these propitiate the celestial gods, who then cause rains. In this way, the cycle continues.

कर्म ब्रह्मोद्भवं विद्धि ब्रह्माक्षरसमुद्भवम् ।
तस्मात्सर्वगतं ब्रह्म नित्यं यज्ञे प्रतिष्ठितम् ।।15।।

karma brahmodbhavaṁ viddhi brahmākṣhara-samudbhavam
tasmāt sarva-gataṁ brahma nityaṁ yajñe pratiṣhṭhitam

karma—duties; *brahma*—in the Vedas; *udbhavam*—manifested; *viddhi*—you should know; *brahma*—the Vedas; *akṣhara*—from the Imperishable (God); *samudbhavam*—directly manifested; *tasmāt*—

therefore; *sarva-gatam*—all-pervading; *brahma*—the Lord; *nityam*—eternally; *yajñe*—in sacrifice; *pratiṣhṭhitam*—established.

The duties for human beings are described in the Vedas, and the Vedas are manifested by God Himself. Therefore, the all-pervading Lord is eternally present in acts of sacrifice.

The Vedas emanated from the breath of God: *asya mahato bhūtasya niśhvasitametadyadṛigvedo yajurvedaḥ sāmavedo 'thavaṅgirasaḥ* (*Bṛihadāraṇyak Upanishad* 4.5.11) 'The four Vedas—*Rig Veda, Yajur Veda, Sama Veda, Atharva Veda*—all emanated from the breath of the Supreme Divine Personality.' In these eternal Vedas, duties of humans have been laid down by God Himself. These duties have been planned in such a way that through their performance, materially engrossed persons may gradually learn to control their desires and slowly elevate themselves from the mode of ignorance to the mode of passion, and then to the mode of goodness. These duties are enjoined to be dedicated to Him as yajna. Hence, duties consecrated as sacrifice to God verily become godly, of the nature of God, and non-different from Him.

The *Tantra Sār* states yajna to be the Supreme Divine Lord Himself:

yajño yajña pumāṁśh chaiva yajñaśho yajña yajñabhāvanaḥ
yajñabhuk cheti pañchātmā yajñeṣhvijyo hariḥ svayaṁ

In the Bhagavatam (11.19.39), Shree Krishna declares to Uddhav: *yajño 'haṁ bhagavattamaḥ* 'I, the Son of Vasudev, am Yajna.' The Vedas state: *yajño vai viṣhṇuḥ* 'Yajna is indeed Lord Vishnu Himself.' Reiterating this principle, Shree Krishna says in this verse that God is eternally present in the act of sacrifice.

एवं प्रवर्तितं चक्रं नानुवर्तयतीह यः ।
अघायुरिन्द्रियारामो मोघं पार्थ स जीवति ।।16।।

evaṁ pravartitaṁ chakraṁ nānuvartayatīha yaḥ
aghāyur indriyārāmo moghaṁ pārtha sa jīvati

evam—thus; *pravartitam*—set into motion; *chakram*—cycle; *na*—not; *anuvartayati*—follow; *iha*—in this life; *yaḥ*—who; *agha-āyuḥ*—sinful living; *indriya-ārāmaḥ*—for the delight of their senses; *mogham*—vainly; *pārtha*—Arjun, son of Pritha; *saḥ*—they; *jīvati*—live.

O Parth, those who do not accept their responsibility in the cycle of sacrifice established by the Vedas are sinful. They live only for the delight of their senses; indeed, their lives are in vain.

Chakra or cycle means an ordered series of events. The cycle from grains to rains has been described in verse 3.14. All members of this universal wheel of action perform their duties and contribute to its smooth rotation. Since we also partake of the fruits of this natural cycle, we too must do our bounden duty in the chain.

We humans are the only ones in this chain who have been bestowed with the ability to choose our actions by our own free will. We can thus either contribute to the harmony of the cycle or bring about discord in the smooth running of this cosmic mechanism. When human society accepts its responsibility to live as an integral part of the universal system, material prosperity abounds and spiritual growth is engendered. Such periods become golden eras in the social and cultural history of humankind. Conversely, when a major section of humankind begins to violate the universal system and rejects its responsibility as an integral part of the cosmic system, then material nature begins to punish, and peace and prosperity become scarce.

The wheel of nature has been set up by God for disciplining, training, and elevating all living beings of varying levels of consciousness. Shree Krishna explains to Arjun that those who do not perform the yajna enjoined of them become slaves of their senses and lead a sinful existence. Thus, they live in vain. But persons conforming to the divine law become pure at heart and free from material contamination.

यस्त्वात्मरतिरेव स्यादात्मतृप्तश्च मानवः ।
आत्मन्येव च सन्तुष्टस्तस्य कार्यं न विद्यते ।।17।।

yas tvātma-ratir eva syād ātma-tṛiptaśh cha mānavaḥ
ātmanyeva cha santuṣhṭas tasya kāryaṁ na vidyate

yaḥ—who; *tu*—but; *ātma-ratiḥ*—rejoice in the self; *eva*—certainly; *syāt*—is; *ātma-tṛiptaḥ*—self-satisfied; *cha*—and; *mānavaḥ*—human being; *ātmani*—in the self; *eva*—certainly; *cha*—and; *santuṣhṭaḥ*—satisfied; *tasya*—his; *kāryam*—duty; *na*—not; *vidyate*—exist.

But those who rejoice in the self, who are illumined and fully satisfied in the self, for them, there is no duty.

Only those who have given up desires for external objects can rejoice and be satisfied in the self. The root of bondage is our material desires, 'This should happen; that should not happen.' Shree Krishna explains a little further ahead in this chapter (in verse 3.37) that desire is the cause of all sins, consequently, it must be renounced. As explained previously (in the purport of verse 2.64), it must be borne in mind that whenever Shree Krishna says we should give up desire, He refers to material desires, and not to the aspirations for spiritual progress or the desire to realise God.

However, why do material desires arise in the first place? When we identify the self with the body, we identify with the yearnings of the body and mind as desires of the self, and these send us spinning into the realm of maya. Sage Tulsidas explains:

jiba jiba te hari te bilagāno taba te deha geha nija mānyo,
māyā basa swarūp bisarāyo tehi brama te dāruṇa duḥkh pāyo

'Since the soul separated itself from God, the material energy covered it in an illusion. By virtue of that illusion, it began thinking of itself as the body, and ever since, in forgetfulness of the self, it has been experiencing immense misery.'

Those who are illumined realise that the self is not material in nature but divine and hence imperishable. The perishable objects of the world can never fulfil the thirst of the imperishable soul, and therefore it is a folly to hanker after those sense-objects. Thus, self-illumined souls learn to unite their consciousness with God and experience His infinite bliss within them.

The karm (duties) prescribed for materially conditioned souls are no longer applicable to such illumined souls because they have already attained the goal of all such karm. For example, as long as one is a college student, one is obliged to follow the rules of the university, but for one who has graduated and earned the degree, the rules now become irrelevant. For such liberated souls, it is said: *brahmavit śhruti mūrdhnī* 'Those who have united themselves with God now walk on the head of the Vedas,' i.e., they have no need to follow the rules of the Vedas any longer.

Take another example where a pandit unites a man and woman in wedlock by performing the wedding ceremony. Once the ceremony is over, he says, 'You are now husband and wife; I am leaving.' His task is over. If the wife says, 'Panditji, the vows you made us take during the wedding ceremony are not being followed by my husband', the pandit will reply, 'That is not my area of expertise. My duty was to get you both united in marriage and that work is over.'

The goal of the Vedas is to help unite the soul with God. Once the soul becomes God-realised, the rules of the Vedas, no longer apply; the soul has transcended their area of jurisdiction.

नैव तस्य कृतेनार्थो नाकृतेनेह कश्चन ।
न चास्य सर्वभूतेषु कश्चिदर्थव्यपाश्रयः ।।18।।

naiva tasya kṛitenārtho nākṛiteneha kaśhchana
na chāsya sarva-bhūteṣhu kaśhchid artha-vyapāśhrayaḥ

na—not; *eva*—indeed; *tasya*—his; *kṛitena*—by discharge of duty; *arthaḥ*—gain; *na*—not; *akṛitena*—without discharge of duty; *iha*—here; *kaśhchana*—whatsoever; *na*—never; *cha*—and; *asya*—of that person; *sarva-bhūteṣhu*—among all living beings; *kaśhchit*—any; *artha*—necessity; *vyapāśhrayaḥ*—to depend upon.

Such self-realised souls have nothing to gain or lose either in discharging or renouncing their duties. Nor do they need to depend on other living beings to fulfil their self-interest.

These self-realised personalities are situated on the transcendental platform of the soul. Their every activity is transcendental, in service of God. So, the duties prescribed for worldly people at the physical level, in accordance with the varnashram dharma, no longer apply to them.

Here, the distinction needs to be made between karm and bhakti. Previously, Shree Krishna was talking about karm or prescribed worldly duties and saying that they must be done as an offering to God. This is necessary to purify the mind and help it rise above worldly contamination. But self-realised souls have already reached absorption in God and developed purity of mind. These transcendentalists are directly engaged in bhakti or pure spiritual activities, such as meditation, worship, kirtan, service to the guru, and so on. If such souls reject their worldly duties, it is not considered a sin. They may continue to perform worldly duties if they wish, but they are not obliged to do them.

Historically, saints have been of two kinds. 1) Those like Prahalad, Dhruv, Ambarish, Prithu, and Vibheeshan, who continued to discharge their worldly duties even after attaining the transcendental platform. These were the karm yogis—externally they were doing their duties with their body while internally their minds were attached to God. 2) Those like Shankaracharya, Madhvacharya, Ramanujacharya, and Chaitanya Mahaprabhu, who rejected their worldly duties and accepted the renounced order of life. These were the karm sanyasis, who were both internally and externally, with both body and mind, engaged only in devotion to God. In this verse, Shree Krishna tells Arjun that both options exist for the self-realised sage. *In the next verse, He states which one of these He recommends to Arjun.*

तस्मादसक्तः सततं कार्यं कर्म समाचर ।
असक्तो ह्याचरन्कर्म परमाप्नोति पूरुषः ।।19।।

tasmād asaktaḥ satataṁ kāryaṁ karma samāchara
asakto hyācharan karma param āpnoti pūruṣhaḥ

tasmāt—therefore; *asaktaḥ*—without attachment; *satatam*—

constantly; *kāryam*—duty; *karma*—action; *samāchara*—perform; *asaktaḥ*—unattached; *hi*—certainly; *ācharan*—performing; *karma*—work; *param*—the Supreme; *āpnoti*—attains; *pūruṣhaḥ*—a person.

Therefore, giving up attachment, perform actions as a matter of duty because by working without being attached to the fruits, one attains the Supreme.

From verses 3.8 to 3.16, Shree Krishna strongly urged those who have not yet reached the transcendental platform to perform their prescribed duties. In verses 3.17 and 3.18, He stated that the transcendentalist is not obliged to perform prescribed duties. So, what path is more suitable for Arjun? Shree Krishna's recommendation for him is to be a karm yogi, and not take karm sanyas. *He explains the reason for this in verses 3.20 to 3.26.*

कर्मणैव हि संसिद्धिमास्थिता जनकादयः ।
लोकसंग्रहमेवापि सम्पश्यन्कर्तुमर्हसि ।।20।।

यद्यदाचरति श्रेष्ठस्तत्तदेवेतरो जनः ।
स यत्प्रमाणं कुरुते लोकस्तदनुवर्तते ।।21।।

karmaṇaiva hi sansiddhim āsthitā janakādayaḥ
loka-saṅgraham evāpi sampaśhyan kartum arhasi

yad yad ācharati śhreṣhṭhas tat tad evetaro janaḥ
sa yat pramāṇaṁ kurute lokas tad anuvartate

karmaṇā—by the performance of prescribed duties; *eva*—only; *hi*—certainly; *sansiddhim*—perfection; *āsthitāḥ*—attained; *janaka-ādayaḥ*—King Janak and other kings; *loka-saṅgraham*—for the welfare of the masses; *eva api*—only; *sampaśhyan*—considering; *kartum*—to perform; *arhasi*—you should; *yat yat*—whatever; *ācharati*—does; *śhreṣhṭhaḥ*—the best; *tat tat*—that (alone); *eva*—certainly; *itaraḥ*—common; *janaḥ*—people; *saḥ*—they; *yat*—whichever; *pramāṇam*—standard; *kurute*—perform; *lokaḥ*—world; *tat*—that; *anuvartate*—pursues.

By performing their prescribed duties, King Janak and others attained perfection. You should also perform your duties to set an example for the good of the world. Whatever actions great persons perform, common people follow. Whatever standards they set, all the world pursues.

King Janak attained perfection through karm yog while discharging his kingly duties. Even after reaching the transcendental platform, he continued to do his worldly duties purely for the reason that it would set a good example for the world to follow. Many other saints did the same.

Humanity is inspired by the ideals that they see in the lives of great people. Such leaders inspire society by their example and become shining beacons for the masses to follow. Leaders of society thus have a moral responsibility to set lofty examples for inspiring the rest of the population by their words, deeds, and character. When noble leaders are in the forefront, the rest of society naturally gets uplifted in morality, selflessness, and spiritual strength. But in times when there is a vacuum of principled leadership, the rest of society has no standards to pursue and slumps into self-centredness, moral bankruptcy, and spiritual lassitude. Hence, great personalities should always act in an exemplary manner to set standards for the world. Even though they themselves may have risen to the transcendental platform and may not need to perform prescribed Vedic duties, by doing so, they inspire others to perform prescribed Vedic actions.

If a great leader of society becomes a karm sanyasi and renounces work, it sets a confusing example for others. The leader may be at the transcendental platform and therefore eligible to renounce work and engage completely in spirituality. However, others in society use their example as an excuse for escapism and to run away from their responsibilities. Such escapists cite the instances of the great karm sanyasis, such as Shankaracharya, Madhvacharya, Nimbarkacharya, and Chaitanya Mahaprabhu. Following their lofty footsteps, these imposters also renounce worldly duties and take sanyas, even though they have not yet attained the purity of mind required for it. In India, we find thousands of such sadhus. They copy examples of great sanyasis and don ochre robes without the simultaneous internal enlightenment and bliss. Though externally renounced, their nature forces them to seek happiness. Then they begin indulging in the lowly pleasure of intoxication because they are devoid of the divine bliss of God. In this way, they slip even below the level of people in household life, as stated in the following verse:

brahma jñāna jānyo nahīṅ, karm diye chhiṭakāya,
tulasī aisī ātmā sahaja naraka mahñ jāya

Sage Tulsidas says: 'One who renounces worldly duties, without the concurrent internal enlightenment with divine knowledge, treads the quick path to hell.'

Instead, if a great leader is a karm yogi, at least the followers will continue to do their karm and dutifully perform their responsibilities. This will help them learn to discipline their mind and senses and slowly rise to the transcendental platform. Hence, to present an example for society to follow, Shree Krishna suggests that Arjun should practice karm yog. *He now gives His own example to illustrate the above point.*

न मे पार्थास्ति कर्तव्यं त्रिषु लोकेषु किञ्चन ।
नानवाप्तमवाप्तव्यं वर्त एव च कर्मणि ।।22।।

na me pārthāsti kartavyaṁ triṣhu lokeṣhu kiñchana
nānavāptam avāptavyaṁ varta eva cha karmaṇi

na—not; *me*—mine; *pārtha*—Arjun; *asti*—is; *kartavyam*—duty; *triṣhu*—in the three; *lokeṣhu*—worlds; *kiñchana*—any; *na*—not; *anavāptam*—to be attained; *avāptavyam*—to be gained; *varte*—I am engaged; *eva*—yet; *cha*—also; *karmaṇi*—in prescribed duties.

There is no duty for Me to do in all the three worlds, O Parth, nor do I have anything to gain or attain. Yet, I am engaged in prescribed duties.

The reason why we all work is because we need something. We all are tiny parts of God, who is an ocean of bliss, and hence, we all seek bliss. Since we have not yet attained perfect bliss, we feel dissatisfied and incomplete. So, whatever we do is for the sake of attaining bliss. However, bliss is one of God's energies and He alone possesses it to an infinite extent. He is perfect and complete in Himself and has no need of anything outside of Himself. Thus, He is also called *Ātmārām* (one who rejoices in the Self), *Ātma-ratī* (one who is attracted to His or Her own Self), and *Ātma-krīḍa* (one who performs divine pastimes with His or Her own Self).

If such a personality does work, there can be only one reason for it—it will not be for oneself; rather, it will be for the welfare of others. Thus, Shree Krishna tells Arjun that although in His personal form as Shree Krishna, He has no duty to perform in the universe, yet He works for the welfare of others. *Next, He explains the welfare that is accomplished when He works.*

यदि ह्यहं न वर्तेयं जातु कर्मण्यतन्द्रितः ।
मम वर्त्मानुवर्तन्ते मनुष्याः पार्थ सर्वशः ।।23।।

yadi hyahaṁ na varteyaṁ jātu karmaṇyatandritaḥ
mama vartmānuvartante manuṣhyāḥ pārtha sarvaśhaḥ

yadi—if; *hi*—certainly; *aham*—I; *na*—not; *varteyam*—thus engage; *jātu*—ever; *karmaṇi*—in the performance of prescribed duties; *atandritaḥ*—carefully; *mama*—my; *vartma*—path; *anuvartante*—follow; *manuṣhyāḥ*—all men; *pārtha*—Arjun, son of Pritha; *sarvaśhaḥ*—in all respects.

For if I did not carefully perform the prescribed duties, O Parth, all men would follow My path in all respects.

In His divine pastimes on the earth, Shree Krishna played the role of a king and a great leader. He appeared in the material world as the Son of King Vasudeva from the Vrishni dynasty, the foremost of the righteous. If Lord Krishna did not perform prescribed Vedic activities, then so many ignorant people would follow in His footsteps thinking that violating them was the standard practice. Lord Krishna states that He would be at fault for leading mankind astray.

उत्सीदेयुरिमे लोका न कुर्यां कर्म चेदहम् ।
सङ्करस्य च कर्ता स्यामुपहन्यामिमाः प्रजाः ।।24।।

utsīdeyur ime lokā na kuryāṁ karma ched aham
sankarasya cha kartā syām upahanyām imāḥ prajāḥ

utsīdeyuḥ—would perish; *ime*—all these; *lokāḥ*—worlds; *na*—not; *kuryām*—I perform; *karma*—prescribed duties; *chet*—if; *aham*—I; *sankarasya*—of uncultured population; *cha*—and; *kartā*—responsible; *syām*—would be; *upahanyām*—would destroy; *imāḥ*—all these; *prajāḥ*—living entities.

If I ceased to perform prescribed actions, all these worlds would perish. I would be responsible for the pandemonium that would prevail and would thereby destroy the peace of the human race.

When Shree Krishna appeared on the earth, seemingly as a human being, He conducted Himself in all ways and manners, appropriate for a member of the royal warrior class. If He had acted otherwise, others would begin to imitate Him, thinking that they must copy the conduct of the worthy Son of the righteous King Vasudev. Had Shree Krishna failed to perform Vedic duties, people following His example would be led away from the discipline of karm into a state of chaos. This would have been a very serious offence and Lord Krishna would be considered at fault. So, He explains to Arjun that if He did not fulfil His occupational duties, it would cause pandemonium in society.

Similarly, Arjun was world-famous for being undefeated in battle and was the brother of the virtuous King Yudhishthir. If Arjun refused to fulfil his duty to protect dharma, then many other worthy and noble warriors could follow his example and also renounce their prescribed duty of protecting righteousness. This would destroy world balance and bring about the rout of innocent and virtuous people. Thus, for the benefit of the entire human race and the world, Shree Krishna coaxed Arjun not to neglect performing his prescribed Vedic activities.

सक्ताः कर्मण्यविद्वांसो यथा कुर्वन्ति भारत ।
कुर्याद्विद्वांस्तथासक्तश्चिकीर्षुर्लोकसंग्रहम् ।।25।।

saktāḥ karmaṇyavidvānso yathā kurvanti bhārata
kuryād vidvāns tathāsaktaśh chikīrṣhur loka-saṅgraham

saktāḥ—attached; *karmaṇi*—duties; *avidvānsaḥ*—the ignorant; *yathā*—as much as; *kurvanti*—act; *bhārata*—scion of Bharat (Arjun); *kuryāt*—should do; *vidvān*—the wise; *tathā*—thus; *asaktaḥ*—unattached; *chikīrṣhuḥ*—wishing; *loka-saṅgraham*—welfare of the world.

As ignorant people perform their duties with attachment to the results, O scion of Bharat, so should the wise act without attachment, for the sake of leading people on the right path.

Previously, in verse 3.20, Shree Krishna had used the expression *loka-saṅgraham evāpi sampaśhyan* meaning, 'with an eye on the welfare of the masses'. In this verse, the expression *loka-saṅgraham chikīrṣhuḥ* means 'wishing the welfare of the world'. Thus, Shree Krishna again emphasises that the wise should always act for the benefit of humankind.

Also, in this verse, the expression *saktāḥ avidvānsaḥ* has been used for people who are as yet in bodily consciousness and attached to worldly pleasures, but who have full faith in the Vedic rituals sanctioned by the scriptures. They are called ignorant because though they have bookish knowledge of the scriptures, they do not comprehend the final goal of God-realisation. Such ignorant people perform their duty scrupulously according to the ordinance of the scriptures without indolence or doubt. They have firm faith that the performance of Vedic duties and rituals will bring the material rewards they desire. If the faith of such people in rituals is broken, without their having developed faith in the higher principle of devotion, they will have nowhere to go. The Shreemad Bhagavatam states:

tāvat karmāṇi kurvīta na nirvidyeta yāvatā
mat-kathā-śhravaṇādau vā śhraddhā yāvan na jāyate (11.20.9)

'One should continue to perform karm as long as one has not developed renunciation from the sense objects and attachment to God.'

Shree Krishna urges Arjun that just as ignorant people faithfully perform ritualistic duties, so also the wise should perform their works dutifully, not for material rewards, but for setting an ideal for the rest of society. Besides, the particular situation in which Arjun finds himself is a *dharma yuddha* (war of righteousness). Thus, for the welfare of society, Arjun should perform his duty as a warrior.

न बुद्धिभेदं जनयेदज्ञानां कर्मसङ्गिनाम् ।
जोषयेत्सर्वकर्माणि विद्वान्युक्तः समाचरन् ।।26।।

na buddhi-bhedaṁ janayed ajñānāṁ karma-saṅginām
joṣhayet sarva-karmāṇi vidvān yuktaḥ samācharan

na—not; *buddhi-bhedam*—discord in the intellects; *janayet*—should create; *ajñānām*—of the ignorant; *karma-saṅginām*—who are attached to fruitive actions; *joṣhayet*—should inspire (them) to perform; *sarva*—all; *karmāṇi*—prescribed; *vidvān*—the wise; *yuktaḥ*—enlightened; *samācharan*—performing properly.

The wise should not create discord in the intellects of ignorant people, who are attached to fruitive actions, by inducing them to stop work. Rather, by performing their duties in an enlightened manner, they should inspire the ignorant also to do their prescribed duties.

Great persons have greater responsibility because common people follow them. So, Shree Krishna urges that wise people should not perform any actions or make any utterances that lead the ignorant towards downfall. It may be argued that if the wise feel compassion for the ignorant, they should give them the highest knowledge—the knowledge of God-realisation. Lord Krishna neutralises this argument by stating, *na buddhi-bhedaṁ janayet*, meaning, the ignorant should not be asked to abandon duties by giving superior instructions they are not qualified to understand.

Usually, people in material consciousness consider only two options. Either they are willing to work hard for fruitive results or they wish to give up all exertions on the plea that all work is laborious, painful, and fraught with evil. Between these, working for results is far superior to the escapist approach. Hence, the spiritually wise in Vedic knowledge should inspire the ignorant to perform their duties with attentiveness and care. If the minds of the ignorant become disturbed and unsettled then they may lose faith in work altogether, and with actions stopped and knowledge not arising, the ignorant will lose out from both sides.

If both the ignorant and the wise perform Vedic actions, then what is the difference between them? Apprehending such a question, Shree Krishna explains this in the next two verses.

प्रकृतेः क्रियमाणानि गुणैः कर्माणि सर्वशः ।
अहङ्कारविमूढात्मा कर्ताहमिति मन्यते ।।27।।

prakṛiteḥ kriyamāṇāni guṇaiḥ karmāṇi sarvaśhaḥ
ahankāra-vimūḍhātmā kartāham iti manyate

prakṛiteḥ—of material nature; *kriyamāṇāni*—carried out; *guṇaiḥ*—by the three modes; *karmāṇi*—activities; *sarvaśhaḥ*—all kinds of; *ahankāra-vimūḍha-ātmā*—those who are bewildered by the ego and misidentify themselves with the body; *kartā*—the doer; *aham*—I; *iti*—thus; *manyate*—thinks.

All activities are carried out by the three modes of material nature. But in ignorance, the soul, deluded by false identification with the body, thinks of itself as the doer.

We can see that the natural phenomena of the world are not directed by us but are performed by prakriti or Mother Nature. Actions of our own body are usually divided into two categories: 1) Natural biological functions, such as digestion, blood circulation, heartbeat, and others, which we do not consciously execute but which occur naturally. 2) Actions such as speaking, hearing, walking, sleeping, working, and so on that we think we perform.

Both these categories of works are performed by the mind-body-senses mechanism. All the parts of this mechanism are made from prakriti or the material energy, which consists of the three modes (gunas)—goodness (sattva), passion (rajas), and ignorance (tamas). Just as waves are not separate from the ocean but a part of it, similarly, the body is a part of Mother Nature from which it is created. Hence, material energy is the doer of everything.

Why then does the soul perceive itself to be doing activities? The reason is: in the grip of the unforgiving ego, the soul falsely identifies itself with the body. Hence, it remains under the illusion of doership. Let us say there are two trains parked side-by-side on the railway platform. A passenger on one train fixes his gaze on the other. When the second train moves, it seems that the first is moving. Likewise, the immobile soul identifies with the mobility of prakriti. Thus, it perceives itself as the doer of actions. The moment the soul eliminates the ego and surrenders to the will of God, it realises itself as the non-doer.

One may question that if the soul is truly the non-doer, then why is it implicated in the Law of Karma for actions performed by the body? The reason is that the soul does not itself perform actions, but it does direct the actions of the senses-mind-intellect. For example, a chariot driver does not pull the chariot himself, but he does direct the horses. Now, if there is any accident, it is not the horses that are blamed but the driver who was directing them. Similarly, the soul is held responsible for the actions of the mind-body mechanism because the senses-mind-intellect work on receiving inspiration from the soul.

तत्त्ववित्तु महाबाहो गुणकर्मविभागयोः ।
गुणा गुणेषु वर्तन्त इति मत्वा न सज्जते ।।28।।

tattva-vit tu mahā-bāho guṇa-karma-vibhāgayoḥ
guṇā guṇeṣhu vartanta iti matvā na sajjate

tattva-vit—knower of the truth; *tu*—but; *mahā-bāho*—mighty-armed one; *guṇa-karma*—from gunas and karma; *vibhāgayoḥ*—distinguish; *guṇāḥ*—modes of material nature in the shape of the senses, mind, and others; *guṇeṣhu*—modes of material nature in the shape of the objects of perception; *vartante*—are engaged; *iti*—thus; *matvā*—knowing; *na*—never; *sajjate*—becomes attached.

O mighty-armed Arjun, illumined persons distinguish the soul as distinct from gunas and karmas. They perceive that it is only the gunas (in the shape of the senses, mind, and others) that move among the gunas (in the shape of the objects of perception), and thus they do not get entangled in them.

The previous verse mentioned that the *ahankāra vimūḍhātmā* (those who are bewildered by the ego and misidentify themselves with the body) think themselves to be the doers. This verse talks about the *tattva-vit* or knowers of the Truth. Having thus abolished the ego, they are free from material identifications and are able to discern their spiritual identity distinct from the corporeal body. Hence, they are not beguiled into thinking of themselves as the doers of their material actions, and instead, they attribute every activity to the movements of the three gunas. Such God-realised saints say: *jo karai so hari karai, hota kabīr kabīr* 'God is doing everything, but people are thinking that I am doing.'

प्रकृतेर्गुणसम्मूढाः सज्जन्ते गुणकर्मसु ।
तानकृत्स्नविदो मन्दान्कृत्स्नविन्न विचालयेत् ।।29।।

prakṛiter guṇa-sammūḍhāḥ sajjante guṇa-karmasu
tān-akṛitsna-vido mandān kṛitsna-vin na vichālayet

prakṛiteḥ—of material nature; *guṇa*—by the modes of material nature; *sammūḍhāḥ*—deluded; *sajjante*—become attached; *guṇa-karmasu*—to results of actions; *tān*—those; *akṛitsna-vidaḥ*—persons without knowledge; *mandān*—the ignorant; *kṛitsna-vit*—persons with knowledge; *na vichālayet*—should not unsettle.

Those who are deluded by the operation of the gunas become attached

to the results of their actions. But the wise who understand these truths should not unsettle such ignorant people who know very little.

The question may be raised that if the soul is distinct from the gunas and their activities, then why are the ignorant attached to sense objects? Shree Krishna explains in this verse that they become bewildered by the gunas of the material energy and think themselves to be the doers. Infatuated by the three modes of material nature, they work for the express purpose of being able to enjoy sensual and mental delights. They are unable to perform actions as a matter of duty, without desiring rewards.

However, the *kṛitsna-vit* (persons with knowledge) should not disturb the minds of the *akṛitsna-vit* (persons without knowledge). This means that the wise should not force their thoughts on ignorant persons by saying, 'You are the soul, not the body, and hence karm is meaningless; give it up.' Rather, they should instruct the ignorant to perform their respective karm, and slowly help them rise above attachment. In this way, after presenting the distinctions between those who are spiritually wise and those who are ignorant, Shree Krishna gives the sober caution not to unsettle the minds of the ignorant.

मयि सर्वाणि कर्माणि संन्यस्याध्यात्मचेतसा ।
निराशीर्निर्ममो भूत्वा युध्यस्व विगतज्वरः ।।30।।

mayi sarvāṇi karmāṇi sannyasyādhyātma-chetasā
nirāśhīr nirmamo bhūtvā yudhyasva vigata-jvaraḥ

mayi—unto me; *sarvāṇi*—all; *karmāṇi*—works; *sannyasya*—renouncing completely; *adhyātma-chetasā*—with the thoughts resting on God; *nirāśhīḥ*—free from hankering for the results of the actions; *nirmamaḥ*—without ownership; *bhūtvā*—so being; *yudhyasva*—fight; *vigata-jvaraḥ*—without mental fever.

Performing all works as an offering unto Me, constantly meditate on Me as the Supreme. Become free from desire and selfishness, and with your mental grief departed, fight!

In His typical style, Shree Krishna expounds on a topic and then finally presents the summary. The words *adhyātma chetasā* mean 'with the thoughts resting on God'; *sannyasya* means 'renouncing all activities that are not dedicated to Him'; *nirāśhīḥ* means 'without hankering for the results of the actions'. The consciousness of dedicating all actions to God requires forsaking claim to proprietorship and renouncing all desires for personal gain, hankering, and lamentation.

The summary of the instructions in the previous verses is that one should very faithfully reflect, 'My soul is a tiny part of the Supreme Lord Shree Krishna. He is the Enjoyer and Master of all. All my works are meant for His pleasure, and therefore, I should perform my duties in the spirit of yajna or sacrifice to Him. He supplies the energy by which I accomplish works of yajna. Thus, I should not take credit for any actions performed by me.'

ये मे मतमिदं नित्यमनुतिष्ठन्ति मानवाः ।
श्रद्धावन्तोऽनसूयन्तो मुच्यन्ते तेऽपि कर्मभिः ।।31।।

ye me matam idaṁ nityam anutiṣhṭhanti mānavāḥ
śhraddhāvanto 'nasūyanto muchyante te 'pi karmabhiḥ

ye—who; *me*—my; *matam*—teachings; *idam*—these; *nityam*—constantly; *anutiṣhṭhanti*—abide by; *mānavāḥ*—human beings; *śhraddhā-vantaḥ*—with profound faith; *anasūyantaḥ*—free from envy; *muchyante*—become free; *te*—those; *api*—also; *karmabhiḥ*—from the bondage of karma.

Those who abide by these teachings of Mine, with profound faith and free from envy, are released from the bondage of karma.

Very beautifully, the Supreme Lord terms the *siddhānt* (principle) explained by Him as *mata* (opinion). An opinion is a personal view while a principle is a universal fact. Opinions can differ among teachers, but the principle is the same. Philosophers and teachers name their opinion as principle, but in the Gita, the Lord has named the principle explained by Him as opinion. By His example, He is teaching us humility and cordiality.

Having given the call for action, Shree Krishna now points out the virtues of accepting the teachings of the Bhagavad Gita with faith and following them in one's life. Our prerogative as humans is to know the truth and then modify our life accordingly. In this way, our mental fever (of lust, anger, greed, envy, illusion, and other mental diseases) gets pacified.

In the previous verse, Shree Krishna had clearly explained to Arjun to offer all works to Him. But He knows that this statement can cause ridicule from those who have no belief in God and rebuke from those who are envious of Him. So, He now emphasises the need for accepting the teachings with conviction. He says that by faithfully following these teachings, one becomes free from the bondage of karma. *But what happens to those who are faithless? Their position is explained next.*

ये त्वेतदभ्यसूयन्तो नानुतिष्ठन्ति मे मतम् ।
सर्वज्ञानविमूढांस्तान्विद्धि नष्टानचेतसः ।।32।।

ye tvetad abhyasūyanto nānutiṣhṭhanti me matam
sarva-jñāna-vimūḍhāns tān viddhi naṣhṭān achetasaḥ

ye—those; *tu*—but; *etat*—this; *abhyasūyantaḥ*—cavilling; *na*—not; *anutiṣhṭhanti*—follow; *me*—my; *matam*—teachings; *sarva-jñāna*—in all types of knowledge; *vimūḍhān*—deluded; *tān*—they are; *viddhi*—know; *naṣhṭān*—ruined; *achetasaḥ*—devoid of discrimination.

But those who find faults with My teachings, being bereft of knowledge and devoid of discrimination, they disregard these principles and bring about their own ruin.

The teachings presented by Shree Krishna are perfect for our eternal welfare. However, our material intellect has innumerable imperfections, and as a result, we are not always able to comprehend the sublimity of His teachings or appreciate their benefits. If we could, what would be the difference between us tiny souls and the Supreme Divine Personality? Thus, faith becomes a necessary ingredient for accepting the divine teachings of the Bhagavad Gita. Wherever our intellect is unable to comprehend, rather than finding fault with the teachings, we must allow our intellect to give in, and agree, 'Shree Krishna has said it. There must be veracity in it, which I cannot understand at present. Let me accept it for now and engage in spiritual sadhana. I will be able to comprehend it in the future as I progress in my spirituality through sadhana.' This attitude is called *śhraddhā* or faith.

Jagadguru Shankaracharaya defines *śhraddhā* as: *guru vedānta vākyeṣhu dṛiḍho viśhvāsaḥ śhraddhā*. '*Śhraddhā* is strong faith in the words of the guru and the scriptures.' Chaitanya Mahaprabhu explained it similarly: *śhraddhā śhabde viśhwāsa kahe sudṛiḍha niśhchaya* (*Chaitanya Charitāmṛit, Madhya Leela,* 22.62). 'The word *Śhraddhā* means strong faith in God and guru, even though we may not comprehend their message at present.' The British poet, Alfred Tennyson said: 'By faith alone, embrace believing, where we cannot prove.' So, *śhraddhā* means earnestly digesting the comprehensible portions of the Bhagavad Gita, and also accepting the abstruse portions, with the hope that they will become comprehensible in future.

Now, one of the persistent defects of the material intellect is pride. Due to pride, the intellect rejects as incorrect what it cannot comprehend at present. Though Shree Krishna's teachings were presented by the omniscient Lord for the welfare of all souls, people still find fault in them, such as, 'Why is God asking everything to be offered to Him? Is He greedy? Is He an egotist that He asks Arjun to worship Him?' Shree Krishna says that such people are *achetasaḥ* or 'devoid of discrimination' because they cannot distinguish between the pure and the impure, the righteous and the unrighteous, the Creator and the created, the Supreme Master and the servant. Such people 'bring about their own ruin' because they reject the path to eternal salvation and keep rotating in the cycle of life and death.

सदृशं चेष्टते स्वस्याः प्रकृतेर्ज्ञानवानपि ।
प्रकृतिं यान्ति भूतानि निग्रहः किं करिष्यति ।।33।।

sadṛiśhaṁ cheṣhṭate svasyāḥ prakṛiter jñānavān api
prakṛitiṁ yānti bhūtāni nigrahaḥ kiṁ kariṣhyati

sadṛiśham—accordingly; *cheṣhṭate*—act; *svasyāḥ*—by their own; *prakṛiteḥ*—modes of nature; *jñāna-vān*—the wise; *api*—even; *prakṛitim*—nature; *yānti*—follow; *bhūtāni*—all living beings; *nigrahaḥ*—repression; *kim*—what; *kariṣhyati*—will do.

Even wise people act according to their natures, for all living beings are propelled by their natural tendencies. What will one gain by repression?

Shree Krishna again comes back to the point about action being superior to inaction. Propelled by their natures, people are inclined to act in accordance with their individual modes. Even those who are theoretically learned carry with them the baggage of the *sanskārs* (tendencies and impressions) of endless past lives, the *prārabdh* karma (destiny one is allotted at the time of birth based on one's accumulated past karmas of endless lifetimes) of this life, and the individual traits of their minds and intellects. They find it difficult to resist this force of habit and nature. If the Vedic scriptures instructed them to give up all works and engage in pure spirituality, it would create an unstable situation. Such artificial repression would be counterproductive. The proper and easier way for spiritual advancement is to utilise the immense force of habit and tendencies and dovetail it in the direction of God. We have to begin the spiritual ascent from where we stand. Doing so requires that we first accept our present condition and then improve upon it.

We can see how even animals act according to their unique natures. Ants are social creatures that bring food for the community while forsaking it themselves, a quality difficult to find in humans. A cow has such intense attachment for its calf that the moment it goes out of sight, the cow feels disturbed. Dogs display the virtue of loyalty to depths that cannot be matched by the best of humans. Similarly, we humans too are propelled by our natures. Since Arjun was a warrior by nature, Shree Krishna told him, 'Your own nature will compel you to fight.' (Bhagavad Gita 18.59) 'You will be driven to do it by your own inclination, born of your own material nature.' (Bhagavad Gita 18.60) That nature should be sublimated in the spirit of service to God by shifting the goal from worldly enjoyment to God-realisation, and by performing our prescribed duty without attachment and aversion.

इन्द्रियस्येन्द्रियस्यार्थे रागद्वेषौ व्यवस्थितौ ।
तयोर्न वशमागच्छेत्तौ ह्यस्य परिपन्थिनौ ।।34।।

indriyasyendriyasyārthe rāga-dveṣhau vyavasthitau
tayor na vaśham āgachchhet tau hyasya paripanthinau

indriyasya—of the senses; *indriyasya arthe*—in the sense objects; *rāga*—attachment; *dveṣhau*—aversion; *vyavasthitau*—situated; *tayoḥ*—of them; *na*—never; *vaśham*—be controlled; *āgachchhet*—should become; *tau*—those; *hi*—certainly; *asya*—for him; *paripanthinau*—foes.

The senses naturally experience attachment and aversion to the sense objects, but do not be controlled by them for they are way-layers and foes.

Although Shree Krishna previously emphasised that the mind and senses are propelled by their natural tendencies, He now opens up the possibility of harnessing them. As long as we have the material body, we have to utilise the objects of the senses for its maintenance. Shree Krishna is not asking us to stop consuming what is necessary but to practise eradicating attachment and aversion. Definitely *sanskārs* (past life tendencies) do have a deep-rooted influence on all living beings, but we can succeed in correcting the situation if we practice the method taught in the Bhagavad Gita.

The senses naturally run towards the sense objects and their mutual interaction creates sensations of pleasure and pain. For example, the taste buds experience joy in contact with delicious foods and distress in contact with bitter foods. The mind repeatedly contemplates the sensations of pleasure and pain which it associates with these objects. Thoughts of pleasure in the sense objects create attachment while thoughts of pain create aversion. Shree Krishna tells Arjun to succumb neither to feelings of attachment nor aversion.

In the discharge of our worldly duty, we will have to encounter all kinds of likeable and unlikeable situations. We must neither yearn for likeable situations, nor avoid unlikeable situations. We overcome our lower nature when we stop being slaves of both the likes and dislikes of the mind and senses. And when we become indifferent to both pleasure and pain in the implementation of our duty, we become truly free to act from our higher nature.

श्रेयान्स्वधर्मो विगुणः परधर्मात्स्वनुष्ठितात् ।
स्वधर्मे निधनं श्रेयः परधर्मो भयावहः ।।35।।

śhreyān swa-dharmo viguṇaḥ para-dharmāt sv-anuṣhṭhitāt
swa-dharme nidhanaṁ śhreyaḥ para-dharmo bhayāvahaḥ

śhreyān—better; *swa-dharmaḥ*—personal duty; *viguṇaḥ*—tinged with faults; *para-dharmāt*—than another's prescribed duties; *su-anuṣhṭhitāt*—perfectly done; *swa-dharme*—in one's personal duties; *nidhanam*—death; *śhreyaḥ*—better; *para-dharmaḥ*—duties prescribed for others; *bhaya-āvahaḥ*—fraught with fear.

It is far better to perform one's natural prescribed duty though tinged with faults, than to perform another's prescribed duty though perfectly. In fact, it is preferable to die in the discharge of one's duty than to follow the path of another, which is fraught with danger.

In this verse, the word dharma has been used four times. Dharma is a word commonly used in Hinduism and Buddhism. But it is the most elusive word to translate into the English language. Terms like righteousness, good conduct, duty, noble quality, among others only describe an aspect of its meaning. Dharma comes from the root word *dhṛi*, which means *ḍhāraṇ karane yogya* or 'responsibilities, duties, thoughts, and actions that are appropriate for us'. For example, the dharma of the soul is to love God. It is like the central law of our being.

The prefix *swa* means 'the self'. Thus, *swa-dharma* is our personal dharma, which is the dharma applicable to our context, situation, maturity, and profession in life. This *swa-dharma* can change as our context in life changes, and as we grow spiritually. By asking Arjun to follow his *swa-dharma*, Shree Krishna is telling him to follow his profession and not change it because someone else may be doing something else.

It is more enjoyable to be ourself than to pretend to be someone else. The duties born of our nature can be easily performed with stability of mind. The duties of others may seem attractive from a distance and we may think of switching, but it is a risky thing to do. If they conflict with our nature, they will create disharmony in our senses, mind, and intellect. This will be detrimental for our consciousness and will hinder our progress on the spiritual path. Shree Krishna emphasises this point dramatically by saying that it is better to die in the faithful performance of one's duty than to be in the unnatural position of doing another's duty.

अर्जुन उवाच ।
अथ केन प्रयुक्तोऽयं पापं चरति पूरुषः ।
अनिच्छन्नपि वार्ष्णेय बलादिव नियोजितः ।।36।।

arjuna uvācha
atha kena prayukto 'yaṁ pāpaṁ charati pūruṣhaḥ
anichchhann api vārṣhṇeya balād iva niyojitaḥ

arjunaḥ uvācha—Arjun said; *atha*—then; *kena*—by what; *prayuktaḥ*—impelled; *ayam*—one; *pāpam*—sins; *charati*—commit; *pūruṣhaḥ*—a person; *anichchhan*—unwillingly; *api*—even; *vārṣhṇeya*—he who belongs to the Vrishni clan, Shree Krishna; *balāt*—by force; *iva*—as if; *niyojitaḥ*—engaged.

Arjun asked: Why is a person impelled to commit sinful acts, even unwillingly, as if by force, O descendant of Vrishni (Krishna)?

Shree Krishna stated in the previous verse that one should not come under the influence of attraction and aversion. Arjun wishes to lead such a divine life but finds the advice difficult to implement. So, he asks Shree Krishna a question that is very realistic and representative of the human struggle. He asks, 'What force prevents us from reaching this high ideal? What makes one succumb to attachment and aversion?'

We all have a conscience that makes us feel remorseful while committing a sin. The conscience is grounded in the fact that God is the abode of virtues, and as His fragments, we all have an innate attraction for virtue and goodness. The goodness that is the nature of the soul gives rise to the voice of conscience. Thus, we cannot make the excuse that we did not know stealing, swindling, libel, extortion, murder, oppression, and corruption are sinful activities. We intuitively know these deeds to be sinful, and yet we commit such acts, as if some strong power impels us to do them. Arjun wishes to know what that strong force is.

श्रीभगवानुवाच ।
काम एष क्रोध एष रजोगुणसमुद्भवः ।
महाशनो महापाप्मा विद्ध्येनमिह वैरिणम् ।।37।।

śhrī bhagavān uvācha
kāma eṣha krodha eṣha rajo-guṇa-samudbhavaḥ
mahāśhano mahā-pāpmā viddhyenam iha vairiṇam

śhri-bhagavān uvācha—the Supreme Lord said; *kāmaḥ*—desire; *eṣhaḥ*—this; *krodhaḥ*—wrath; *eṣhaḥ*—this; *rajaḥ-guṇa*—the mode of passion; *samudbhavaḥ*—born of; *mahā-aśhanaḥ*—all-devouring; *mahā-pāpmā*—greatly sinful; *viddhi*—know; *enam*—this; *iha*—in the material world; *vairiṇam*—the enemy.

The Supreme Lord said: It is lust alone, which is born of contact with the mode of passion and later transformed into anger. Know this as the sinful, all-devouring enemy in the world.

The Vedas use the word *kām*, or lust, not only for sexual desires but also to include all desires for material enjoyment based on the physical concept of the self. Thus, lust manifests in various ways—the urge for money, physical cravings, hankering for prestige, the drive for power, and so on. This lust is only a perverted reflection of love for God, which is the inherent nature of every living being. Just as the soul, in association with the material energy, identifies with the body, similarly, its divine love for God, in association with the mode of passion, is transformed into lust. Since divine love is the highest power of God, its perversion in the material realm, lust, is also the most powerful force in worldly activities.

Shree Krishna identifies this 'lust' for worldly enjoyment as the cause of sin, as the malignant cancer sitting within us. The mode of passion deludes the soul into believing that worldly objects will give satisfaction. Under this misconception, one creates desires for acquiring them. When desire is satisfied, it gives birth to greed; when it is not satisfied, it gives rise to anger. One commits sins under the influence of all three—lust, greed, and anger. Greed is nothing but intensified desire while anger is frustrated desire. Hence, Shree Krishna labels lust, or desire, as the root of all evil.

धूमेनाव्रियते वह्निर्यथादर्शो मलेन च ।
यथोल्बेनावृतो गर्भस्तथा तेनेदमावृतम् ।।38।।

dhūmenāvriyate vahnir yathādarśho malena cha
yatholbenāvṛito garbhas tathā tenedam āvṛitam

dhūmena—by smoke; *āvriyate*—is covered; *vahniḥ*—fire; *yathā*—just as; *ādarśhaḥ*—mirror; *malena*—by dust; *cha*—also; *yathā*—just as; *ulbena*—by the womb; *āvṛitaḥ*—is covered; *garbhaḥ*—embryo; *tathā*—similarly; *tena*—by that (desire); *idam*—this; *āvṛitam*—is covered.

Just as a fire is covered by smoke, a mirror is masked by dust, and an embryo is concealed by the womb, similarly one's knowledge gets shrouded by desire.

Knowledge of what is right or wrong is called discrimination. This discrimination resides in the intellect. However, lust is such a formidable adversary that it clouds the discriminatory ability of the intellect. Shree Krishna gives three grades of examples to illustrate this principle. Fire, which is the source of light, gets covered by smoke. This partial obscuring is like a thin cloud that sattvic desires create. A mirror, which is naturally reflective, gets obscured by dust. This semi-opacity is like the masking impact of rajasic desires on the intellect. And an embryo gets concealed in the womb. This complete obfuscation is like the consequence of tamasic desires subverting the power of discrimination. Similarly, in proportion to the grade of our desires, the spiritual knowledge we may have heard and read gets shrouded.

There is a beautiful allegorical story to illustrate this point:

A man used to take his evening walk by the side of a forest. One evening, he decided to walk in the forest instead. When he had walked a couple of miles, the sun began setting and the light started fading. He turned around to walk out of the forest, but to his dismay, he found that animals had gathered on the other side. These ferocious animals started chasing him and to escape from them, he ran deeper into the forest.

While running, he found a witch standing in front of him with open arms to embrace him. To escape her, he turned direction and ran perpendicular to the animals and the witch. By then, it had become dark. Unable to see much, he ran over a ditch that was covered by vine hanging from a tree. He fell headlong, but his feet became entangled in the vine. As a result, he found himself hanging upside down above the ditch.

After a few moments he came to his senses and saw a snake sitting at the bottom of the ditch, waiting to bite him should he fall down. In the meantime, two mice appeared—one white and one black—and started nibbling at the branch from which the vine was hanging. To confound his problems, some wasps gathered and began stinging him on his face. In this precarious situation, it was found that the man was smiling. Philosophers gathered to ponder how he could smile in such a dire situation. They looked upwards and found a beehive from which honey was dripping onto his tongue. He was licking the honey and thinking how pleasurable it was; he had forgotten the animals, the witch, the snake, the mice, and the wasps.

The person in the story may seem insane to us. However, this tale depicts the condition of all humans under the influence of desire. The forest in which the man was walking represents the material world in which we live, where there is danger at every step. The animals that chased him represent diseases that appear in life and continue to harass us until death. The witch represented old age that is waiting to embrace us with the passage of time. The snake at the bottom of the pit is like the inevitable death that awaits us all. The white and black mice that were nibbling on the branch represent day and night, which are steadily reducing our life and bringing us closer to death. The wasps that were stinging the face are like the innumerable desires that arise in the mind and agitate it, resulting in pain and distress. Honey represents the sensual enjoyment we experience in the world, which clouds the discrimination of our intellect. Hence, forgetting our precarious position, we remain absorbed in enjoying the temporary delights of the senses. Shree Krishna states that it is this type of lustful desire that is responsible for shrouding our power of discrimination.

आवृतं ज्ञानमेतेन ज्ञानिनो नित्यवैरिणा ।
कामरूपेण कौन्तेय दुष्पूरेणानलेन च ।।39।।

āvṛitaṁ jñānam etena jñānino nitya-vairiṇā
kāma-rūpeṇa kaunteya duṣhpūreṇānalena cha

āvṛitam—covered; *jñānam*—knowledge; *etena*—by this; *jñāninaḥ*—of the wise; *nitya-vairiṇā*—by the perpetual enemy; *kāma-rūpeṇa*—in the form of desires; *kaunteya*—Arjun son of Kunti; *duṣhpūreṇa*—insatiable; *analena*—like fire; *cha*—and.

The knowledge of even the most discerning gets covered by this perpetual enemy in the form of insatiable desire, which is never satisfied and burns like fire, O son of Kunti.

Here, the inimical nature of *kām* or lust is being made even more explicit by Lord Krishna. *Kām* means 'desire', *duṣhpūreṇa* means 'insatiable', and *anala* means 'inexhaustible'. Desire overpowers the discriminatory power of the wise and lures them to fulfil it. However, the more they attempt to dowse the fire of desire, the more strongly it burns. The Buddha states:

na kahāpaṇa vassena, titti kāmesu vijjati
appassādā kāmā dukhā kāmā, iti viññāya paṇḍito

(Dhammapada verse 186)

'Desire burns like an unquenchable fire which never brings happiness to anyone. The wise renounce it, knowing it to be the root of misery.' But those who do not understand this secret waste away their life in the futile pursuit of trying to satiate their lust.

इन्द्रियाणि मनो बुद्धिरस्याधिष्ठानमुच्यते ।
एतैर्विमोहयत्येष ज्ञानमावृत्य देहिनम् ।।40।।

indriyāṇi mano buddhir asyādhiṣhṭhānam uchyate
etair vimohayatyeṣha jñānam āvṛitya dehinam

indriyāṇi—the senses; *manaḥ*—the mind; *buddhiḥ*—the intellect; *asya*—of this; *adhiṣhṭhānam*—dwelling place; *uchyate*—are said to be; *etaiḥ*—by these; *vimohayati*—deludes; *eṣhaḥ*—this; *jñānam*—knowledge; *āvṛitya*—clouds; *dehinam*—the embodied soul.

The senses, mind, and intellect are said to be breeding grounds of desire. Through them, it clouds one's knowledge and deludes the embodied soul.

By revealing the locations where lust resides, Shree Krishna now indicates that there is a method of controlling it. The fortress of the enemy must be spotted before one can lay siege on it. In this verse, Shree Krishna states that the senses, mind, and intellect are the places from where lust exercises its dominion over the soul. Under the sway of lust, the sense objects are desired by the senses, the senses infatuate the mind, the mind misleads the intellect, and the intellect loses its discriminatory powers. When the intellect is clouded, the living being is deluded to become a slave of lust and will do anything to satiate it.

These instruments—senses, mind, and intellect—are not bad in themselves. They were given to us for the purpose of achieving God-realisation, but we have permitted lust in its many forms to lay siege on them. Now, we have to use the same senses, mind, and intellect to uplift ourselves. *In the following verses, Shree Krishna explains the method for it.*

तस्मात्त्वमिन्द्रियाण्यादौ नियम्य भरतर्षभ ।
पाप्मानं प्रजहि ह्येनं ज्ञानविज्ञाननाशनम् ।।41।।

tasmāt tvam indriyāṇyādau niyamya bharatarṣhabha
pāpmānaṁ prajahi hyenaṁ jñāna-vijñāna-nāśhanam

tasmāt—therefore; *tvam*—you; *indriyāṇi*—senses; *ādau*—in the very beginning; *niyamya*—having controlled; *bharata-ṛiṣhabha*—Arjun, best of the Bharatas; *pāpmānam*—the sinful; *prajahi*—slay; *hi*—certainly; *enam*—this; *jñāna*—knowledge; *vijñāna*—realisation; *nāśhanam*—the destroyer.

Therefore, O best of the Bharatas, in the very beginning bring the senses under control and slay this enemy called desire, which is the embodiment of sin and destroys knowledge and realisation.

Now, Shree Krishna explains how to overcome lust, the root of all evil, which is so pernicious to human consciousness. Having identified the repositories of lust, Shree Krishna asks Arjun, at the outset, to curb the desires of the senses. Permitting them to arise is the cause of our miseries, while eliminating them is the way to peace. Consider the following example.

Ramesh and Dinesh were two fellow students sharing the same room in the hostel. At 10 p.m. at night, Ramesh developed the desire to smoke cigarettes. He said, 'I am getting the urge to smoke.'

Dinesh replied, 'It is so late at night. Forget about cigarettes and go to sleep.'

'No...no...I will not be able to sleep until I puff the tobacco,' said Ramesh.

Dinesh went to sleep, but Ramesh went out in search of cigarettes. The shops nearby had closed. It took him two hours to return to the hostel with the cigarette and smoke it.

In the morning, Dinesh asked him, 'Ramesh, when did you sleep at night?'

'At midnight.'

'Really! That means you remained agitated for cigarettes for two hours, and when you had your puffs, you returned to the same state that you were in at 10 p.m.'

'What do you mean by that?' asked Ramesh.

'Look, at 10 p.m. when you did not have any desire for cigarettes, you were peaceful. Then you yourself created the desire for them. From 10 p.m. to midnight, you remained agitated for cigarettes. Finally, when you smoked them, the desire which you had created was satiated, and you went to sleep. I, on the other hand, did not create any desire and slept peacefully at 10 p.m. itself.'

In this way, we create desires for the objects of the senses of the body and then become agitated by them. When we get the cherished object, the disease of our own creation gets eradicated, and we think of it as happiness. However, if we think of ourselves as the soul and our only purpose is happiness of the soul, then it becomes easier to renounce such material desires. Shree Krishna tells Arjun to bring the senses under control, thereby slaying the lust residing in them. *To accomplish this, we must use the higher instruments given by God, as stated in the next verse.*

इन्द्रियाणि पराण्याहुरिन्द्रियेभ्यः परं मनः ।
मनसस्तु परा बुद्धिर्यो बुद्धेः परतस्तु सः ।।42।।

indriyāṇi parāṇyāhur indriyebhyaḥ paraṁ manaḥ
manasas tu parā buddhir yo buddheḥ paratas tu saḥ

indriyāṇi—senses; *parāṇi*—superior; *āhuḥ*—are said; *indriyebhyaḥ*—than the senses; *param*—superior; *manaḥ*—the mind; *manasaḥ*—than the mind; *tu*—but; *parā*—superior; *buddhiḥ*—intellect; *yaḥ*—who; *buddheḥ*—than the intellect; *parataḥ*—more superior; *tu*—but; *saḥ*—that (soul).

The senses are superior to the gross body, and superior to the senses is the mind. Beyond the mind is the intellect, and even beyond the intellect is the soul.

An inferior entity can be controlled by its superior entity. Shree Krishna explains the gradation of superiority among the instruments God has provided to us. He describes that the body is made of gross matter; superior to it are the five knowledge-bearing senses (which grasp the perceptions of taste, touch, sight, smell, and sound); beyond the senses is the mind; superior to the mind is the intellect, with its ability to discriminate; but even beyond the intellect is the divine soul.

This knowledge of the sequence of superiority among the senses, mind, intellect, and soul, can now be used for rooting out lust, as explained in the final verse of this chapter.

एवं बुद्धेः परं बुद्ध्वा संस्तभ्यात्मानमात्मना ।
जहि शत्रुं महाबाहो कामरूपं दुरासदम् ।।43।।

evaṁ buddheḥ paraṁ buddhvā sanstabhyātmānam ātmanā
jahi śhatruṁ mahā-bāho kāma rūpaṁ durāsadam

evam—thus; *buddheḥ*—than the intellect; *param*—superior; *buddhvā*—knowing; *sanstabhya*—subdue; *ātmānam*—the lower self (senses, mind, and intellect); *ātmanā*—by higher self (soul); *jahi*—kill; *śhatrum*—the enemy; *mahā-bāho*—mighty-armed one; *kāma-rūpam*—in the form of desire; *durāsadam*—formidable.

Thus, knowing the soul to be superior to the material intellect, O mighty armed Arjun, subdue the lower self (senses, mind, and intellect)

by the higher self (strength of the soul), and kill this formidable enemy called lust.

In conclusion, Shree Krishna emphasises that we should slay this enemy called lust through knowledge of the self. Since the soul is a part of God, it is divine in nature. Thus, the divine bliss it seeks can only be attained from a divine subject, while the objects of the world are all material. These material objects can never fulfil the innate longing of the soul, so it is futile to create desires for them. We must exert and train the intellect to think in this manner, and then use it to control the mind and the senses.

This is explained very beautifully in the *Kaṭhopaniṣhad* with the help of the model of a chariot:

ātmānagvaṁ rathinaṁ viddhi śharīraṁ rathameva tu
buddhiṁ tu sārathiṁ viddhi manaḥ pragrahameva cha

indriyāṇi hayānāhurviṣhayānsteṣhu gocharān
ātmendriyamanoyuktaṁ bhoktetyāhurmanīṣhiṇaḥ (1.3.3–4)

The Upanishads say there is a chariot which has five horses pulling it; the horses have reins in their mouths which are in the hands of a charioteer; a passenger is sitting at the back of the chariot. Ideally, the passenger should instruct the charioteer, who should then control the reins and guide the horses in the proper direction. However, in this case, the passenger has gone to sleep, and the horses are holding sway.

In this analogy, the chariot is the body, the horses are the five senses, the reins in the mouth of the horses are the mind, the charioteer is the intellect, and the passenger seated behind is the soul residing in the body. The senses (horses) desire pleasurable things. The mind (reins) is not exercising restraint on the senses (horses). The intellect (charioteer) submits to the pull of the reins (mind). In the materially bound state, the sleeping soul does not direct the intellect in the proper direction. Thus, the senses are free to decide the direction in which the chariot should go. The soul experiences the pleasures of the senses vicariously, but these do not satisfy it. Seated on this chariot, the soul (passenger) is moving around in this material world since eternity.

However, if the soul wakes up to its higher nature and decides to take a proactive role, it can exercise the intellect in the proper direction. The intellect will then govern the lower self—the mind and the senses—and the chariot will move in the direction of eternal welfare. In this way, the higher self (soul) must be used to control the lower self (senses, mind, and intellect).

CHAPTER 4

Jnana Karm Sanyas Yog

The Yog of Knowledge and the Disciplines of Action

In Chapter four, Shree Krishna strengthens Arjun's faith in the knowledge He is imparting to him by revealing its pristine origin. He explains how this system of knowledge is an eternal science that He taught in the beginning to the Sun God, and it was passed on in a continuous tradition to saintly kings. He is now revealing the same supreme science of Yog to Arjun, who is a dear friend and devotee. Arjun asks how Shree Krishna, who exists in the present, could have taught this science eons ago to the Sun God. In response, Shree Krishna discloses the divine mystery of His descension. He explains that though God is unborn and eternal, yet by His *Yogmaya* power, He descends on the earth to establish dharma (the path of righteousness). However, His birth and activities are both divine and never tainted by material imperfections. Those who know this secret engage in His devotion with great faith and on attaining Him, do not take birth in this world again.

The chapter then explains the nature of work and discusses three principles—action, inaction, and forbidden action. It discloses how karm yogis are in the state of inaction even while performing the most engaging works, and thus, they are not entangled in karmic reactions. With this wisdom, ancient sages performed their works, merely as an act of sacrifice for the pleasure of God, without being affected by success or failure, happiness or distress, fame or infamy. Sacrifice is of various kinds, and many of them are mentioned here. When sacrifice is properly dedicated, its remnants become like nectar. By partaking of such nectar, performers are cleansed of impurities. Hence, sacrifice must always be performed with proper sentiments and knowledge. With the help of the boat of knowledge, even the biggest sinners can cross over the ocean of material miseries. Such knowledge must be learnt from a genuine spiritual master who has realised the Truth. Shree Krishna, as Arjun's Guru, asks him to pick up the sword of knowledge, and cutting asunder the doubts that have arisen in his heart, stand up and perform his duty.

श्रीभगवानुवाच ।
इमं विवस्वते योगं प्रोक्तवानहमव्ययम् ।
विवस्वान्मनवे प्राह मनुरिक्ष्वाकवेऽब्रवीत् ।।1।।

śhrī bhagavān uvācha
imaṁ vivasvate yogaṁ proktavān aham avyayam
vivasvān manave prāha manur ikṣhvākave 'bravīt

śhrī-bhagavān uvācha—the Supreme Lord Shree Krishna said; *imam*—this; *vivasvate*—to the Sun God; *yogam*—the science of Yog; *proktavān*—taught; *aham*—I; *avyayam*—eternal; *vivasvān*—Sun God; *manave*—to Manu, the original progenitor of humankind; *prāha*—told; *manuḥ*—Manu; *ikṣhvākave*—to Ikshvaku, first king of the Solar dynasty; *abravīt*—instructed.

The Supreme Lord Shree Krishna said: I taught this eternal science of Yog to the Sun God, Vivasvan, who passed it on to Manu; and Manu, in turn, instructed it to Ikshvaku.

Merely imparting invaluable knowledge to someone is not enough. The recipients of that knowledge must appreciate its value and have faith in its authenticity. Only then will they put in the effort required to implement it practically in their lives. In this verse, Shree Krishna establishes the credibility and importance of the spiritual wisdom He is bestowing on Arjun. Shree Krishna informs Arjun that the knowledge being imparted unto him is not newly created for the convenience of motivating him into battle. It is the same eternal science of Yog that He originally taught to Vivasvan, or Surya, Sun God, who imparted it to Manu, the original progenitor of humankind; Manu, in turn, taught it to Ikshvaku, first king of the Solar dynasty. This is the descending process of knowledge where someone who is a perfect authority on the knowledge passes it down to another who wishes to learn.

In contrast to this is the ascending process of acquiring knowledge where one endeavours to enhance the frontiers of understanding through self-effort. The ascending process is laborious, imperfect, and time-consuming. For example, if we wish to learn physics, we could either try to do it by the ascending process, where we speculate about its principles with our own intellect and then reach conclusions, or we could do it by the descending process, where we approach a good teacher of the subject. The ascending process is exceedingly time-consuming, and we may not even be able to complete the enquiry in our lifetime. We can also not be sure about the validity of our conclusions. In comparison, the descending process gives us instant access to the deepest secrets of physics. If our teacher has perfect knowledge of physics, then it is very straightforward—simply listen to the science from him and digest what he says. This descending process of receiving knowledge is both easy and faultless.

Every year, thousands of self-help books are released in the market, which present the authors' solutions to the problems encountered in life. These books may be helpful in a limited way, but because they are based upon the ascending process of attaining knowledge, they are imperfect. Every few years, a new theory comes along that overthrows the current ones. This ascending process is unsuitable for learning about the Absolute Truth. Divine knowledge does not need to be created by self-effort. It is the energy of God, and has existed ever since He has existed, just as heat and light are as old as the fire from which they emanate.

God and the individual soul are both eternal, and so the science of Yog that unites the soul and God is also eternal. There is no need to speculate and formulate new theories about it. An amazing endorsement of this truism is the Bhagavad Gita itself, which continues to astound people with the sagacity of its perennial wisdom that remains relevant to our daily lives even fifty centuries after it was spoken. Shree Krishna states here that the knowledge of Yog, which He is revealing to Arjun, is eternal, and it was passed down in ancient times through the descending process—from guru to disciple.

एवं परम्पराप्राप्तमिमं राजर्षयो विदुः ।
स कालेनेह महता योगो नष्टः परन्तप ।।2।।

evaṁ paramparā-prāptam imaṁ rājarṣhayo viduḥ
sa kāleneha mahatā yogo naṣhṭaḥ parantapa

evam—thus; *paramparā*—in a continuous tradition; *prāptam*—received; *imam*—this (science); *rāja-ṛiṣhayaḥ*—saintly kings; *viduḥ*—understood; *saḥ*—that; *kālena*—with the long passage of time; *iha*—in this world; *mahatā*—great; *yogaḥ*—the science of Yog; *naṣhṭaḥ*—lost; *parantapa*—Arjun, scorcher of foes.

O subduer of enemies, the saintly kings thus received this science of Yog in a continuous tradition. But with the long passage of time, it was lost to the world.

In the descending process of receiving divine knowledge, the disciple understands the science of God-realisation from the guru, who, in turn, received it from his guru. It was in such a tradition that saintly kings like Nimi and Janak understood the science of Yog. This tradition starts from God Himself, who is the first Guru of the world.

tene brahma hṛidā ya ādi-kavaye muhyanti yat sūrayaḥ

(Bhagavatam 1.1.1)

According to this verse, God revealed this knowledge at the beginning of creation in the heart of the first-born Brahma, and the tradition continued from him. Shree Krishna stated in the last verse that He also revealed this knowledge to the Sun God, Vivasvan, from whom the tradition continued as well. However, the nature of this material world is such that with the passage of time, this knowledge got lost. Materially minded and insincere disciples interpret the teachings according to their blemished perspectives. Within a few generations, its pristine purity is contaminated. When this happens, by His causeless grace, God reestablishes the tradition for the benefit of humankind. He may do so, either by Himself descending in the world, or through a great God-realised saint, who becomes a conduit for God's work on earth.

Jagadguru Shree Kripaluji Maharaj, who was the fifth original Jagadguru in Indian history, was such a God-inspired saint who has reestablished the ancient knowledge in modern times. When he was only thirty-four years old, the Kashi Vidvat Parishat, the supreme body of five hundred Vedic scholars in the holy city of Kashi, honoured him with the title of Jagadguru or 'Spiritual Master of the world'. He became the fifth saint in Indian history to receive the original title of Jagadguru, after Jagadguru Shankaracharya, Jagadguru Nimbarkacharya, Jagadguru Ramanujacharya, and Jagadguru Madhvacharya. This commentary on the Bhagavad Gita has been written based upon its insightful understanding, as revealed to me by Jagadguru Shree Kripaluji Maharaj.

स एवायं मया तेऽद्य योगः प्रोक्तः पुरातनः ।
भक्तोऽसि मे सखा चेति रहस्यं ह्येतदुत्तमम् ।।3।।

sa evāyaṁ mayā te 'dya yogaḥ proktaḥ purātanaḥ
bhakto 'si me sakhā cheti rahasyaṁ hyetad uttamam

saḥ—that; *eva*—certainly; *ayam*—this; *mayā*—by me; *te*—unto you; *adya*—today; *yogaḥ*—the science of Yog; *proktaḥ*—reveal; *purātanaḥ*—ancient; *bhaktaḥ*—devotee; *asi*—you are; *me*—my; *sakhā*—friend; *cha*—and; *iti*—therefore; *rahasyam*—secret; *hi*—certainly; *etat*—this; *uttamam*—supreme.

The same ancient knowledge of Yog, which is the supreme secret, I am today revealing unto you, because you are My friend as well as My devotee, who can understand this transcendental wisdom.

Shree Krishna tells Arjun that the ancient science being imparted to him is an uncommonly known secret. Secrecy in the world is maintained for two reasons: either due to selfishness in keeping the truth to oneself, or to protect the truth from the abuse of knowledge. The science of

Yog remains a secret, not for either of these reasons, but because it requires a qualification to be understood. That qualification is revealed in this verse as devotion. The deep message of the Bhagavad Gita is not amenable to being understood merely through scholasticism or mastery of the Sanskrit language. It requires devotion, which destroys the subtle envy of the soul towards God and enables us to accept the humble position as His tiny parts and servitors.

Arjun was a fit student of this science because he was a devotee of the Lord. Devotion to God can be practised in any of the five sequentially higher bhavas or sentiments: 1) *Śhānt bhav*: adoring God as our King. 2) *Dāsya bhav*: the sentiment of servitude towards God as our Master. 3) *Sakhya bhav*: considering God as our Friend. 4) *Vātsalya bhav*: considering God as our Child. 5) *Mādhurya bhav*: worshipping God as our Soul-beloved. Arjun worshipped God as his Friend so, Shree Krishna speaks to him as His friend and devotee.

Without a devotional heart, one cannot truly grasp the message of the Bhagavad Gita. This verse also invalidates the commentaries on the Bhagavad Gita written by scholars, jnanis, yogis, *tapasvīs*, and many others, who lack bhakti (devotion) towards God. According to this verse, since they are not devotees, they cannot comprehend the true import of the supreme science that was revealed to Arjun, and hence, their commentaries are inaccurate and/or incomplete.

अर्जुन उवाच ।
अपरं भवतो जन्म परं जन्म विवस्वतः ।
कथमेतद्विजानीयां त्वमादौ प्रोक्तवानिति ।।4।।

arjuna uvācha
aparaṁ bhavato janma paraṁ janma vivasvataḥ
katham etad vijānīyāṁ tvam ādau proktavān iti

arjunaḥ uvācha—Arjun said; *aparam*—later; *bhavataḥ*—your; *janma*—birth; *param*—prior; *janma*—birth; *vivasvataḥ*—Vivasvan, the Sun God; *katham*—how; *etat*—this; *vijānīyām*—am I to understand; *tvam*—you; *ādau*—in the beginning; *proktavān*—taught; *iti*—thus.

Arjun said: You were born much after Vivasvan. How am I to understand that in the beginning, You instructed this science to him?

Arjun is puzzled by the apparent incongruity of events in Shree Krishna's statement. The Sun god has been present since almost the beginning of creation, while Shree Krishna has only recently been born in the world. If Shree Krishna is the son of Vasudev and Devaki, then His statement that He taught this science to Vivasvan, the Sun God, appears inconsistent to Arjun, and he queries Him about it. *Arjun's question invites an exposition on the concept of the divine descension of God, and Shree Krishna responds to it in the subsequent verses.*

श्रीभगवानुवाच ।
बहूनि मे व्यतीतानि जन्मानि तव चार्जुन ।
तान्यहं वेद सर्वाणि न त्वं वेत्थ परन्तप ।।5।।

śhrī bhagavān uvācha
bahūni me vyatītāni janmāni tava chārjuna
tānyahaṁ veda sarvāṇi na tvaṁ vettha parantapa

śhrī-bhagavān uvācha—the Supreme Lord said; *bahūni*—many; *me*—of mine; *vyatītāni*—have passed; *janmāni*—births; *tava*—of yours; *cha*—and; *arjuna*—Arjun; *tāni*—them; *aham*—I; *veda*—know; *sarvāṇi*—all; *na*—not; *tvam*—you; *vettha*—know; *parantapa*—Arjun, the scorcher of foes.

The Supreme Lord said: Both you and I have had many births, O Arjun. You have forgotten them, while I remember them all, O Parantapa.

Shree Krishna explains that merely because He is standing before Arjun in the human form, He should not be equated with human beings. The president of a country sometimes decides to visit the prison, but if we see the president standing in the jail, we do not erroneously conclude that he is also a convict. We know that he is in the jail merely for an inspection. Similarly, God sometimes descends in the material world, but He is never divested of His divine attributes and powers.

In his commentary on this verse, Shankaracharya states: *yā vāsudeve anīśhvarāsarvajñāśhaṅkā mūrkhāṇāṁ tāṁ pariharan śhrī-bhagavān uvācha* (*Śhārīrak Bhāṣhya* on verse 4.5) 'This verse has been spoken by Shree Krishna to refute foolish people who doubt that He is God.' Non-believers argue that Shree Krishna too was born like the rest of us, and He ate, drank and slept, like we all do, and so He could not have been God. Here, Shree Krishna emphasises the difference between the soul and God by stating that although He descends in the world innumerable times, He still remains omniscient unlike the soul whose knowledge is finite.

The individual soul and the Supreme Soul, God, have many similarities—both are *sat-chit-anand* (eternal, sentient, and blissful). However, there are also many differences. God is all-pervading, while the soul only pervades the body it inhabits; God is all-powerful, while the soul does not even have the power to liberate itself from maya without God's grace; God is the Creator of the laws of nature, while the soul is subject to these laws; God is the Upholder of entire creation, while the soul is upheld by Him; God is all-knowing, while the soul does not have complete knowledge even in one subject.

In this verse, Shree Krishna calls Arjun 'Parantapa', meaning, 'subduer of enemies'. He implies, 'Arjun, you are a valiant warrior who has slayed so many powerful enemies. Now, do not accept defeat before this doubt that has crept into your mind. Use the sword of knowledge that I am giving you to slay it and be situated in wisdom.'

अजोऽपि सन्नव्ययात्मा भूतानामीश्वरोऽपि सन् ।
प्रकृतिं स्वामधिष्ठाय सम्भवाम्यात्ममायया ।।6।।

ajo 'pi sannavyayātmā bhūtānām īśhvaro 'pi san
prakṛitiṁ svām adhiṣhṭhāya sambhavāmyātma-māyayā

ajaḥ—unborn; *api*—although; *san*—being so; *avyaya ātmā*—imperishable nature; *bhūtānām*—of (all) beings; *īśhvaraḥ*—the Lord; *api*—although; *san*—being; *prakṛitim*—nature; *svām*—of myself; *adhiṣhṭhāya*—situated; *sambhavāmi*—I manifest; *ātma-māyayā*—by my *Yogmaya* power.

Although I am unborn, the Lord of all living entities, and have an imperishable nature, yet I appear in this world by virtue of *Yogmaya*, My divine power.

Many people revolt at the idea of a God who possesses a form. They are more comfortable with a formless God, who is all-pervading, incorporeal, and subtle. God is definitely intangible and formless, but that does not mean that He cannot simultaneously have a form as well. Since God is all-powerful, He has the power to manifest in a form if He so wishes. If someone stipulates that God cannot have a form, it means that person does not accept Him as all-powerful. Thus, to say that 'God is formless' is an incomplete statement. On the other hand, to say that 'God manifests in a personal form' is also only a partial truth. The all-powerful God has both aspects to His divine personality—the personal form and the formless aspect. Hence, the *Bṛihadāraṇyak Upanishad* states:

dwe vāva brahmaṇo rūpe mūrtaṁ chaiva amūrtaṁ cha (2.3.1)

'God appears in both ways—as the formless Brahman and as the personal God.' They both are dimensions of His personality.

In fact, the individual soul also has these two dimensions to its existence. It is formless, and hence, when it leaves the body upon death, it cannot be seen. Yet it takes on a body—not once, but innumerable times—as it transmigrates from birth to birth. When the tiny soul is able to possess a body, can the all-powerful God not have a form? Or is it that God says, 'I do not have the power to manifest in a form, and therefore, I am only a formless light.' For Him to be perfect and complete, He must be both personal and formless.

The difference is that while our form is created from the material energy, maya, God's form is created by His divine energy, *Yogmaya*. It is divine and beyond material defects. This has been nicely stated in the *Padma Puran*:

yastu nirguṇa ityuktaḥ śhāstreṣhu jagadīśhvaraḥ
prākṛitairheya sanyuktairguṇairhīnatvamuchyate

'Wherever Vedic scriptures state that God does not have a form, they imply that His form is not subject to the blemishes of the material energy; rather, it is a divine form.'

यदा यदा हि धर्मस्य ग्लानिर्भवति भारत ।
अभ्युत्थानमधर्मस्य तदात्मानं सृजाम्यहम् ।।7।।

yadā yadā hi dharmasya glānir bhavati bhārata
abhyutthānam adharmasya tadātmānaṁ sṛijāmyaham

yadā yadā—whenever; *hi*—certainly; *dharmasya*—of righteousness; *glāniḥ*—decline; *bhavati*—is; *bhārata*—Arjun, descendant of Bharat; *abhyutthānam*—increase; *adharmasya*—of unrighteousness; *tadā*—at that time; *ātmānam*—self; *sṛijāmi*—manifest; *aham*—I.

Whenever there is a decline in righteousness and an increase in unrighteousness, O Arjun, at that time, I manifest Myself on earth.

Dharma is verily the prescribed actions that are conducive to our spiritual growth and progress; the reverse of this is *adharma* (unrighteousness). When unrighteousness prevails, the Creator and Administrator of the world intervenes by descending and reestablishing dharma. Such a descension of God is called an Avatar. The word 'Avatar' has been adopted from Sanskrit into English and is now commonly used to describe various people's images on the media screen. In this text, we will be using it in its original Sanskrit connotation to refer to the divine descension of God. Twenty-four such descensions have been listed in the Shreemad Bhagavatam. However, the Vedic scriptures state that there are innumerable descensions of God:

janma-karmābhidhānāni santi me 'ṅga sahasraśhaḥ
na śhakyante 'nusaṅkhyātum anantatvān mayāpi hi

(Bhagavatam 10.51.37)

'Nobody can count the infinite Avatars of God since the beginning of eternity.' These Avatars are classified in four categories, as stated below:

1. ***Āveśhāvatār:*** when God manifests His special powers in an individual soul and acts through Him. The sage Narad is an example of *Āveśhāvatār*. The Buddha is also an example of *Āveśhāvatār*.

2. ***Prābhavāvatār:*** these are the descensions of God in the personal form where He displays some of His divine powers. *Prābhavāvatārs* are also of two kinds:

   Where God reveals Himself only for a few moments, completes His work, and then departs. Hansavatar is an example of this, where God manifested before the four Kumaras, answered their question, and left.

   Where the Avatar remains on the earth for many years. Ved Vyas, who wrote the eighteen Puranas and the Mahabharat, and divided the Vedas into four parts, is an example of such an Avatar.

3. ***Vaibhavatār:*** when God descends in His divine form and manifests more of His divine powers. Matsyavatar, Kurmavatar, Varahavatar are all examples of *Vaibhavatārs*.

4. ***Parāvasthāvatār:*** when God manifests all His divine powers in His personal divine form. Shree Krishna, Shree Ram, and Nrisinghavatar are all *Parāvasthāvatārs*.

This classification does not imply that any one Avatar is bigger than the other. Ved Vyas, who is himself an Avatar, clearly states this in the *Padma Puran*: *sarve pūrṇāḥ śhāśhvatāśhcha dehāstasya paramātmanaḥ* 'All the descensions of God are replete with all divine powers; they all are perfect and complete.' Hence, we should not differentiate one Avatar as bigger and another as smaller. However, in each descension, God manifests His powers based on the objectives He wishes to accomplish during that particular descension. The remaining powers reside latently within the Avatar. Consequently, the above classifications were created to explain these differences.

परित्राणाय साधूनां विनाशाय च दुष्कृताम्।
धर्मसंस्थापनार्थाय सम्भवामि युगे युगे ।।8।।

paritrāṇāya sādhūnāṁ vināśhāya cha duṣhkṛitām
dharma-sansthāpanārthāya sambhavāmi yuge yuge

paritrāṇāya—to protect; *sādhūnām*—the righteous; *vināśhāya*—to annihilate; *cha*—and; *duṣhkṛitām*—the wicked; *dharma*—the eternal religion; *sansthāpana-arthāya*—to reestablish; *sambhavāmi*—I appear; *yuge yuge*—age after age.

To protect the righteous, to annihilate the wicked, and to reestablish the principles of dharma, I appear on this earth, age after age.

Having stated in the last verse that God descends in the world, He now states the three reasons for doing so: 1) To annihilate the wicked. 2) To protect the pious. 3) To establish dharma. However, if we closely study these three points, none of the three reasons seem very convincing:

To protect the righteous: God is seated in the hearts of His devotees and always protects them from within. There is no need to take an Avatar for this purpose.

To annihilate the wicked: God is all-powerful and can kill the wicked merely by wishing it. Why should He have to take an Avatar to accomplish this?

To establish dharma: Dharma is eternally described in the Vedas. God can reestablish it through a saint; He does not need to descend Himself, in His personal form, to accomplish this.

How then do we make sense of the reasons that have been stated in this verse? Let's delve a little deeper to grasp the import of what Shree Krishna is stating.

The biggest dharma that the soul can engage in is devotion to God. That is what God strengthens by taking an Avatar. When God descends in the world, He reveals His divine Forms, Names, Virtues, Pastimes, Abodes, and Associates. This provides the souls with an easy basis for devotion. The formless aspect of God is very difficult to worship because the mind needs a form to focus upon and to connect with. On the other hand, devotion to the personal form of God is easy for people to comprehend, simple to perform, and pleasing to engage in.

Thus, since the descension of Lord Krishna five thousand years ago, billions of souls have made His divine leelas (pastimes) as the basis of their devotion and purified their minds with ease and joy. Similarly, the Ramayan has provided souls with a popular basis for devotion for innumerable centuries. When the TV show, *Ramayan*, first began airing on Indian national television on Sunday mornings, all the streets of India would become empty. The pastimes of Lord Ram held such fascination for the people that they would be glued to their television sets to see the leelas on the screen. This reveals how Lord Ram's descension provided the basis for devotion to billions of souls in history. The Ramayan says:

rām eka tāpasa tiya tārī, nāma koṭi khala kumati sudhārī

'In His descension period, Lord Ram helped only one Ahalya (Sage Gautam's wife, whom Lord Ram released from the body of stone). However, since then, by chanting the divine name "Ram," billions of fallen souls have elevated themselves.' So, a deeper understanding of this verse is:

To establish dharma: God descends to establish the dharma of devotion by providing souls with His Names, Forms, Pastimes, Virtues, Abodes, and Associates, with the help of which they may engage in bhakti and purify their mind.

To kill the wicked: Along with God, to help facilitate His divine pastimes, some liberated saints descend and pretend to be miscreants. For example, Ravan and Kumbhakarn were Jaya and Vijaya who descended from the divine abode of God. They pretended to be demons and opposed and fought with Ram. They could not have been killed by anyone else since they were divine personalities. So, God slayed such demons as a part of His leelas. And having killed them, He sent them to His divine abode since that was where they originally came from.

To protect the righteous: Many souls had become sufficiently elevated in their sadhana (spiritual practice) to qualify to meet God face-to-face. When Shree Krishna descended in the world, these eligible souls obtained their first opportunity to participate in God's divine pastimes. For example, some *gopis* (cowherd women of Vrindavan, where Shree Krishna manifested His pastimes) were liberated souls who had descended from the divine abode to assist in Shree Krishna's leelas. Other *gopis* were materially bound souls who were awarded their first chance to meet and serve God and participate in His leelas. So, when Shree Krishna descended in the world, such qualified souls got the opportunity to perfect their devotion by directly participating in the pastimes of God.

This is the deeper meaning of the verse. However, it is not wrong if someone wishes to cognise the verse more literally or metaphorically.

जन्म कर्म च मे दिव्यमेवं यो वेत्ति तत्त्वतः ।
त्यक्त्वा देहं पुनर्जन्म नैति मामेति सोऽर्जुन ॥9॥

janma karma cha me divyam evaṁ yo vetti tattvataḥ
tyaktvā dehaṁ punar janma naiti mām eti so 'rjuna

janma—birth; *karma*—activities; *cha*—and; *me*—of mine; *divyam*—divine; *evam*—thus; *yaḥ*—who; *vetti*—know; *tattvataḥ*—in truth; *tyaktvā*—having abandoned; *deham*—the body; *punaḥ*—again; *janma*—birth; *na*—never; *eti*—takes; *mām*—to me; *eti*—comes; *saḥ*—he; *arjuna*—Arjun.

Those who understand the divine nature of My birth and activities, O Arjun, upon leaving the body, do not have to take birth again but come to My eternal abode.

Understand this verse in the light of the previous one. Our mind gets cleansed by engaging in devotional remembrance of God. This devotion can either be towards the formless aspect of God or towards His personal form. Devotion towards the formless is intangible and nebulous to most people. They find nothing to focus upon or feel connected with during such devotional meditation. On the other hand, devotion to the personal form of God is tangible and simple. Such devotion requires divine sentiments towards the personality of God. For people to engage in devotion to Shree Krishna, they must develop divine feelings towards His Names, Form, Virtues, Pastimes, Abodes, and Associates. For example, people purify their minds by worshipping stone deities because they harbour the divine sentiments that God resides in these deities. It is these sentiments that purify the devotee's mind. The progenitor Manu says:

na kāṣhṭhe vidyate devo na śhilāyāṁ na mṛitsu cha
bhāve hi vidyate devastasmātbhāvaṁ samācharet

'God resides neither in wood nor in stone but in a devotional heart. Hence, worship the deity with loving sentiments.'

Similarly, if we wish to engage in devotion to Lord Krishna, we must learn to harbour divine sentiments towards His leelas. Those commentators who give a figurative interpretation to the Mahabharat and the Bhagavad Gita, do grave injustice by destroying the basis of people's faith in devotion to Shree Krishna. For enhancing our devotion, in this verse, Shree Krishna has emphasised the need for divine sentiments towards His pastimes.

To develop such divine feelings, we must understand the difference between God's actions and ours. We materially bound souls have not yet attained divine bliss, and hence, the longing of our soul is not yet satiated. Thus, our actions are motivated by self-interest and the desire for personal fulfilment. However, God's actions have no personal motive because He is perfectly satiated by the infinite bliss of His own personality. He does not need to achieve further personal bliss by performing actions. Therefore, whatever He does is for the welfare of the materially conditioned souls. Such divine actions that God performs are termed as 'leelas' while the actions we perform are called 'work'.

Similarly, God's birth is also divine, and unlike ours, it does not take place physically from a woman. The all-Blissful God has no requirement to hang upside down in a mother's womb. The Bhagavatam states:

tam adbhutaṁ bālakam ambujekṣhaṇaṁ
chatur-bhujaṁ śhaṅkha gadāryudāyudham (10.3.9)

'When Shree Krishna manifested upon birth before Vasudev and Devaki, He was in His four-armed Vishnu form.' This full-sized form could definitely not have resided in Devaki's womb. However, to create in her the feeling that He was there, by His *Yogmaya* power, He simply kept expanding Devaki's womb. Finally, He manifested from the outside, revealing that He had never been inside her:

āvirāsīd yathā prāchyāṁ diśhīndur iva puṣhkalaḥ

(Bhagavatam 10.3.8)

'As the moon manifests in its full glory in the night sky, similarly the Supreme Lord Shree Krishna manifested before Devaki and Vasudev.' This is the divine nature of God's birth. If we can develop faith in the divinity of His pastimes and birth, then we will be able to easily engage in devotion to His personal form and attain the supreme destination.

वीतरागभयक्रोधा मन्मया मामुपाश्रिताः ।
बहवो ज्ञानतपसा पूता मद्भावमागताः ।।10।।

vīta-rāga-bhaya-krodhā man-mayā mām upāśhritāḥ
bahavo jñāna-tapasā pūtā mad-bhāvam āgatāḥ

vīta—free from; *rāga*—attachment; *bhaya*—fear; *krodhāḥ*—anger; *mat-mayā*—completely absorbed in me; *mām*—in me; *upāśhritāḥ*—taking refuge (of); *bahavaḥ*—many (persons); *jñāna*—of knowledge; *tapasā*—by the fire of knowledge; *pūtāḥ*—purified; *mat-bhāvam*—my divine love; *āgatāḥ*—attained.

Being free from attachment, fear, and anger, becoming fully absorbed in Me, and taking refuge in Me, many persons in the past became purified by knowledge of Me, and thus attained My divine love.

In the previous verse, Lord Krishna explained that those who truly know the divine nature of His birth and pastimes attain Him. He now confirms that legions of human beings in all ages became God-realised by this means. They achieved this goal by purifying their minds through devotion. Shree Aurobindo put it very nicely: 'You must keep the temple of the heart clean, if you wish to install therein the living presence.' The Bible states: 'Blessed are the pure in heart, for they shall see God.' (Matthew 5.8)

Now, how does the mind get purified? By giving up attachment, fear, and anger, and absorbing the mind in God. Actually, attachment is the cause of both fear and anger. Fear arises out of apprehension that the object of our attachment will be snatched away from us. And anger arises when there is an obstruction in attaining the object of our attachment. Attachment is thus the root cause of the mind getting soiled.

This world of maya consists of the three modes of material nature—sattva, rajas, and tamas (goodness, passion, and ignorance). All objects and personalities in the world come within the realm of these three modes. When we attach our mind to a material object or person, our mind too becomes affected by the three modes. Instead, when we absorb the same mind in God, who is beyond the three modes of material nature, such devotion purifies the mind. Thus, the sovereign recipe to cleanse the mind from the defects of lust, anger, greed, envy, and illusion, is to detach it from the world and attach it to the Supreme Lord. Hence, the Ramayan states:

prema bhagati jala binu raghurāī,
abhiantara mala kabahuñ na jāī

'Without devotion to God, the dirt of the mind will not be washed away.' Even the ardent propagator of jnana yog, Shankaracharya, stated:

śhuddhayati hi nāntarātmā kṛiṣhṇapadāmbhoja bhaktimṛite

(*Prabodh Sudhākar*)

'Without engaging in devotion to the lotus feet of Lord Krishna, the mind will not be cleansed.'

On reading the previous verse, a question may arise whether Lord Krishna is partial in bestowing His grace upon those who absorb their minds in Him versus the worldly-minded souls. The Supreme Lord addresses this in the next verse.

ये यथा मां प्रपद्यन्ते तांस्तथैव भजाम्यहम् ।
मम वर्त्मानुवर्तन्ते मनुष्याः पार्थ सर्वशः ।।11।।

ye yathā māṁ prapadyante tāns tathaiva bhajāmyaham
mama vartmānuvartante manuṣhyāḥ pārtha sarvaśhaḥ

ye—who; *yathā*—in whatever way; *mām*—unto me; *prapadyante*—surrender; *tān*—them; *tathā*—so; *eva*—certainly; *bhajāmi*—reciprocate; *aham*—I; *mama*—my; *vartma*—path; *anuvartante*—follow; *manuṣhyāḥ*—men; *pārtha*—Arjun, son of Pritha; *sarvaśhaḥ*—in all respects.

In whatever way people surrender unto Me, I reciprocate accordingly. Everyone follows My path, knowingly or unknowingly, O son of Pritha.

Here, Lord Krishna states that He reciprocates with everyone as they surrender to Him. For those who deny the existence of God, He meets them in the form of the Law of Karma—He sits inside their hearts, notes their actions, and dispenses the results. But such atheists too cannot get away from serving Him; they are obliged to serve God's material energy because maya, in its various apparitions, such as wealth, luxuries, relatives, prestige, etc. holds them under the sway of anger, lust, and greed. On the other hand, for those who turn their mind away from worldly attractions and look upon God as their only goal and refuge, He takes care of them just as a mother takes care of her child.

Shree Krishna uses the word *bhajāmi* which means 'to serve'. He serves the surrendered souls by destroying their accumulated karmas of endless lifetimes, cutting the bonds of maya, removing the darkness of material existence, and bestowing divine bliss, divine knowledge, and divine love. And when the devotee learns to love God selflessly, He willingly enslaves Himself to their love. Shree Ram thus tells Hanuman:

ekaikasyopakārasya prāṇān dāsyāmi te kape
śheṣhasyehopakārāṇāṁ bhavām ṛiṇino vayaṁ

(Valmiki Ramayan)

'O Hanuman, to release Myself from the debt of one service you performed for Me, I shall have to offer My life to you. For all the other devotional services done by you, I shall remain eternally indebted.' In this way, God reciprocates with everyone as they surrender to Him.

If God is so merciful upon His devotees, why do some people worship the celestial gods instead? He explains in the following verse.

काङ्क्षन्तः कर्मणां सिद्धिं यजन्त इह देवताः ।
क्षिप्रं हि मानुषे लोके सिद्धिर्भवति कर्मजा ।।12।।

kāṅkṣhantaḥ karmaṇāṁ siddhiṁ yajanta iha devatāḥ
kṣhipraṁ hi mānuṣhe loke siddhir bhavati karmajā

kāṅkṣhantaḥ—desiring; *karmaṇām*—material activities; *siddhim*—success; *yajante*—worship; *iha*—in this world; *devatāḥ*—the celestial gods; *kṣhipram*—quickly; *hi*—certainly; *mānuṣhe*—in human society; *loke*—within this world; *siddhiḥ*—rewarding; *bhavati*—manifest; *karma-jā*—from material activities.

In this world, those desiring success in material activities worship the celestial gods since material rewards manifest quickly.

Persons who seek worldly gain worship the celestial gods and ask them for boons. The boons the celestial gods bestow are material and temporary, and they are given only by virtue of the power they have received from the Supreme Lord Himself. There is a beautiful instructive story in this regard:

Saint Farid went to the court of Emperor Akbar, a powerful king in Indian history. He waited in the court for an audience while Akbar was praying in the next room. Farid peeped into the room to see what was going on and was amused to hear Akbar praying to God for a more powerful army, a bigger treasure chest, and success in battle. Without disturbing the king, Farid returned to the royal court.

After completing his prayers, Akbar came and gave him an audience. He asked the great sage if there was anything that he wanted. Farid replied, 'I came to ask the Emperor for things I required for my ashram. However, I find that the Emperor is himself a beggar before the Lord.

Then why should I ask him for any favours; why not directly ask the Lord Himself?'

The celestial gods give boons only by the powers bestowed upon them by the Supreme Lord. People who lack proper knowledge approach them, but those who are intelligent realise that there is no point in going to the intermediary and they approach the Supreme Lord for the fulfilment of their aspirations. *People are of various kinds, possessing higher and lower aspirations. Shree Krishna now mentions four categories of qualities and works.*

चातुर्वर्ण्यं मया सृष्टं गुणकर्मविभागशः ।
तस्य कर्तारमपि मां विद्ध्यकर्तारमव्ययम् ।।13।।

chātur-varṇyaṁ mayā sṛiṣhṭaṁ guṇa-karma-vibhāgaśhaḥ
tasya kartāram api māṁ viddhyakartāram avyayam

chātuḥ-varṇyam—the four categories of occupations; *mayā*—by me; *sṛiṣhṭam*—were created; *guṇa*—of quality; *karma*—and activities; *vibhāgaśhaḥ*—according to divisions; *tasya*—of that; *kartāram*—the Creator; *api*—although; *mām*—me; *viddhi*—know; *akartāram*—non-doer; *avyayam*—unchangeable.

The four categories of occupations were created by Me according to people's qualities and activities. Although I am the Creator of this system, know Me to be the non-doer and eternal.

The Vedas classify people into four categories of occupations not according to their birth but according to their natures. Such varieties of occupations exist in every society. Even in communist nations where equality is the overriding principle, the diversity in human beings cannot be smothered. There are the philosophers who are the communist party think-tanks; the military men who protect the country; the farmers who engage in agriculture; and the factory workers.

The Vedic philosophy explains this variety in a more scientific manner. It states that the material energy is constituted of three gunas (modes): sattva guna (mode of goodness), rajo guna (mode of passion), and tamo guna (mode of ignorance). The Brahmins are those who have a preponderance of the mode of goodness. They are predisposed towards teaching and worship. The Kshatriyas are those who have a preponderance of the mode of passion mixed with a smaller amount of the mode of goodness. They are inclined towards administration and management. The Vaishyas are those who possess the mode of passion mixed with some mode of ignorance. Accordingly, they form the business and agricultural class. Then there are the Shudras who are predominated by the mode of ignorance and form the working class. This classification was neither meant to be according to birth nor was it unchangeable. Shree Krishna explains in this verse that the classification of the Varnashram system was according to people's qualities and activities.

Although God is the Creator of the system of the world, yet He is the non-doer. This is similar to rain. Just as rainwater falls equally on the forest, yet from some seeds, huge banyan trees sprout; from other seeds, beautiful flowers bloom; and from some, thorny bushes emerge. The rain, which is impartial, is not answerable for this difference. In the same way, God provides the souls with the energy to act, but they are free to determine what they wish to do with it; God is not responsible for their actions.

न मां कर्माणि लिम्पन्ति न मे कर्मफले स्पृहा ।
इति मां योऽभिजानाति कर्मभिर्न स बध्यते ।।14।।

na māṁ karmāṇi limpanti na me karma-phale spṛihā
iti māṁ yo 'bhijānāti karmabhir na sa badhyate

na—not; *mām*—me; *karmāṇi*—activities; *limpanti*—taint; *na*—nor; *me*—my; *karma-phale*—the fruits of action; *spṛihā*—desire; *iti*—thus; *mām*—me; *yaḥ*—who; *abhijānāti*—knows; *karmabhiḥ*—result of action; *na*—never; *saḥ*—that person; *badhyate*—is bound.

Activities do not taint Me, nor do I desire the fruits of action. One who knows Me in this way is never bound by the karmic reactions of work.

God is all-pure, and whatever He does also becomes pure and auspicious. The Ramayan states:

samaratha kahuñ nahiṅ doṣhu gosāīṅ,
rabi pāvaka surasari kī nāīṅ

'Pure personalities and entities, like the sun, the fire, and the Ganges are never tainted by defects even when in contact with impurities.' The sun does not get tainted if sunlight falls on a puddle of urine. The sun retains its purity while also purifying the dirty puddle. Similarly, if we offer impure objects into the fire, it still retains its purity—the fire is pure, and whatever we pour into it also gets purified. In the same manner, numerous gutters of rainwater merge into the holy Ganges, but this does not make the Ganges a gutter—the Ganges is pure, and it transforms all those dirty gutters into the holy Ganges. Likewise, God is not tainted by the activities He performs.

Activities bind one in karmic reactions when they are performed with the attitude of enjoying the results. However, God's actions are not motivated by selfishness; His every act is driven by compassion for the souls. Therefore, although He directly or indirectly governs the world and engages in all kinds of activities in the process, He is never tainted by any reactions. Lord Krishna states here that He is transcendental to the fruitive reactions of work.

Even saints who are situated in God-consciousness become transcendental to the material energy. Since all their activities are effectuated in love for God, such pure-hearted saints are not bound by the fruitive reactions of work. The Shreemad Bhagavatam states:

yat pāda paṅkaja parāga niṣheva tṛiptā
yoga prabhāva vidhutākhila karma bandhāḥ
svairaṁ charanti munayo 'pi na nahyamānās
tasyechchhayātta vapuṣhaḥ kuta eva bandhaḥ (10.33.35)

'Material activities never taint the devotees of God who are fully satisfied in serving the dust of His lotus feet. Nor do material activities stain those wise sages who have freed themselves from the bondage of fruitive reactions by the power of Yog. So where is the question of bondage for the Lord Himself who assumes His transcendental Form according to His own sweet will?'

एवं ज्ञात्वा कृतं कर्म पूर्वैरपि मुमुक्षुभिः ।
कुरु कर्मैव तस्मात्त्वं पूर्वैः पूर्वतरं कृतम्।।15।।

evaṁ jñātvā kṛitaṁ karma pūrvair api mumukṣhubhiḥ
kuru karmaiva tasmāttvaṁ pūrvaiḥ pūrvataraṁ kṛitam

evam—thus; *jñātvā*—knowing; *kṛitam*—performed; *karma*—actions; *pūrvaiḥ*—of ancient times; *api*—indeed; *mumukṣhubhiḥ*—seekers of liberation; *kuru*—should perform; *karma*—duty; *eva*—certainly; *tasmāt*—therefore; *tvam*—you; *pūrvaiḥ*—of those ancient sages; *pūrva-taram*—in ancient times; *kṛitam*—performed.

Knowing this truth, even seekers of liberation in ancient times performed actions. Therefore, following the footsteps of those ancient sages, you too should perform your duty.

The sages who aspire for God are not motivated to work for material gain. Why then do they engage in activities in this world? The reason is that they wish to serve God and are inspired to work for His pleasure. The knowledge of the previous verse assures them that they themselves will never be bound by welfare work that is done in the spirit of devotion. They are also moved by compassion on seeing the sufferings of materially bound souls who are bereft of God consciousness and are inspired to work for their spiritual elevation. The Buddha once said, 'After attaining enlightenment, you have two options—either you do nothing, or you help others attain enlightenment.'

Thus, even sages who have no selfish motive for work still engage in activities for the pleasure of God. Working in devotion also attracts the grace of God. Shree Krishna is advising Arjun to do the same. *Having instructed Arjun to perform actions that do not bind one, the Lord now begins expounding the philosophy of action.*

किं कर्म किमकर्मेति कवयोऽप्यत्र मोहिताः ।
तत्ते कर्म प्रवक्ष्यामि यज्ज्ञात्वा मोक्ष्यसेऽशुभात् ।।16।।

kiṁ karma kim akarmeti kavayo 'pyatra mohitāḥ
tat te karma pravakṣhyāmi yaj jñātvā mokṣhyase 'śhubhāt

kim—what; *karma*—action; *kim*—what; *akarma*—inaction; *iti*—thus; *kavayaḥ*—the wise; *api*—even; *atra*—in this; *mohitāḥ*—are confused; *tat*—that; *te*—to you; *karma*—action; *pravakṣhyāmi*—I shall explain; *yat*—which; *jñātvā*—knowing; *mokṣhyase*—you may free yourself; *aśhubhāt*—from inauspiciousness.

What is action and what is inaction? Even the wise are confused in determining this. Now I shall explain to you the secret of action, by knowing which, you may free yourself from material bondage.

The principles of dharma cannot be determined by mental speculation. Even intelligent persons become confused in the maze of apparently contradictory arguments presented by the scriptures and the sages. For example, the Vedas recommend non-violence. Accordingly, in the Mahabharat, Arjun wishes to follow the same course of action and shun violence, but Shree Krishna advises that his duty here is to engage in violence. If duty varies with circumstance, then to ascertain one's duty in any specific situation is a complex matter. Yamraj, the celestial god of death, stated:

dharmaṁ tu sākṣhād bhagavat praṇītaṁ
na vai vidur ṛiṣhayo nāpi devāḥ (Bhagavatam 6.3.19)

'What is proper action and what is improper action? This is difficult to determine even for the great rishis and the celestial gods. Dharma has been created by God Himself, and He alone is its true Knower.' *Lord Krishna says to Arjun that He shall now reveal to him the esoteric science of action and inaction through which he may free himself from material bondage.*

कर्मणो ह्यपि बोद्धव्यं बोद्धव्यं च विकर्मणः ।
अकर्मणश्च बोद्धव्यं गहना कर्मणो गतिः ।।17।।

karmaṇo hyapi boddhavyaṁ boddhavyaṁ cha vikarmaṇaḥ
akarmaṇaśh cha boddhavyaṁ gahanā karmaṇo gatiḥ

karmaṇaḥ—recommended action; *hi*—certainly; *api*—also; *boddhavyam*—should be known; *boddhavyam*—must understand; *cha*—and; *vikarmaṇaḥ*—forbidden action; *akarmaṇaḥ*—inaction; *cha*—and; *boddhavyam*—must understand; *gahanā*—profound; *karmaṇaḥ*—of action; *gatiḥ*—the true path.

You must understand the nature of all three—recommended action, wrong action, and inaction. The truth about these is profound and difficult to understand.

Work has been divided by Shree Krishna into three categories—action (*karm*), forbidden action (*vikarm*), and inaction (*akarm*).

Action: *Karm* is auspicious action recommended by the scriptures for regulating the senses and purifying the mind.

Forbidden action: *Vikarm* is inauspicious action prohibited by the scriptures since they are detrimental and result in degradation of the soul.

Inaction: *Akarm* is action that is performed without attachment to the results, merely for the pleasure of God. They neither have any karmic reactions, and nor do they entangle the soul.

कर्मण्यकर्म यः पश्येदकर्मणि च कर्म यः ।
स बुद्धिमान्मनुष्येषु स युक्तः कृत्स्नकर्मकृत् ।।18।।

karmaṇyakarma yaḥ paśhyed akarmaṇi cha karma yaḥ
sa buddhimān manuṣhyeṣhu sa yuktaḥ kṛitsna-karma-kṛit

karmaṇi—action; *akarma*—in inaction; *yaḥ*—who; *paśhyet*—see; *akarmaṇi*—inaction; *cha*—also; *karma*—action; *yaḥ*—who; *saḥ*—they; *buddhi-mān*—wise; *manuṣhyeṣhu*—amongst humans; *saḥ*—

they; *yuktaḥ*—yogis; *kṛitsna-karma-kṛit*—performers of all kinds of actions.

Those who see action in inaction and inaction in action are truly wise amongst humans. Although performing all kinds of actions, they are yogis and masters of all their actions.

Action in inaction: There is one kind of inaction where persons look upon their social duties as burdensome and renounce them out of indolence. While they physically give up actions, their mind continues to contemplate upon the objects of the senses. Such persons may appear to be inactive, but their lethargic idleness is actually sinful action. When Arjun suggested that he wishes to shy away from his duty of fighting the war, Shree Krishna explained to him that doing so would be a sin, and he would go to the hellish regions for such inaction.

Inaction in action: There is another kind of inaction performed by karm yogis. They execute their social duties without attachment to results, dedicating the fruits of their actions to God. Although engaged in all kinds of activities, they are not entangled in karmic reactions since they have no motive for personal enjoyment. There were many great kings in Indian history—Dhruv, Prahalad, Yudhishthir, Prithu, and Ambarish—who discharged their kingly duties to the best of their abilities, and yet, because their minds were not entangled in material desires, their actions were termed *akarm* or inaction. Another name for *akarm* is karm yog, which has been discussed in detail in the previous two chapters as well.

यस्य सर्वे समारम्भाः कामसङ्कल्पवर्जिताः ।
ज्ञानाग्निदग्धकर्माणं तमाहुः पण्डितं बुधाः ।।19।।

yasya sarve samārambhāḥ kāma-saṅkalpa-varjitāḥ
jñānāgni-dagdha-karmāṇaṁ tam āhuḥ paṇḍitaṁ budhāḥ

yasya—whose; *sarve*—every; *samārambhāḥ*—undertakings; *kāma*—desire for material pleasures; *saṅkalpa*—resolve; *varjitāḥ*—devoid of; *jñāna*—divine knowledge; *agni*—in the fire;

dagdha—burnt; *karmāṇam*—actions; *tam*—him; *āhuḥ*—address; *paṇḍitam*—a sage; *budhāḥ*—the wise.

The enlightened sages call those persons wise whose every action is free from the desire for material pleasures and who have burnt the reactions of work in the fire of divine knowledge.

The soul, being a tiny part of God who is an ocean of bliss, naturally seeks bliss for itself. However, covered by the material energy, the soul mistakenly identifies itself with the material body. In this ignorance, it performs actions to attain bliss from the world of matter. Since these actions are motivated by the desire for sensual and mental enjoyment, they bind the soul in karmic reactions.

In contrast, when the soul is illumined with divine knowledge, it realises that the bliss it seeks will be attained not from the objects of the senses but in loving service to God. It then strives to perform every action for the pleasure of God. 'Whatever you do, whatever you eat, whatever you offer as oblation to the sacred fire, whatever you bestow as a gift, and whatever austerities you perform, O son of Kunti, do them as an offering to Me.' (Bhagavad Gita 9.27) Since such an enlightened soul renounces selfish actions for material pleasures and dedicates all actions to God, the works performed produce no karmic reactions. They are said to be burnt in the fire of divine knowledge.

त्यक्त्वा कर्मफलासङ्गं नित्यतृप्तो निराश्रयः ।
कर्मण्यभिप्रवृत्तोऽपि नैव किञ्चित्करोति सः ॥20॥

tyaktvā karma-phalāsaṅgaṁ nitya-tṛipto nirāśhrayaḥ
karmaṇyabhipravṛitto 'pi naiva kiñchit karoti saḥ

tyaktvā—having given up; *karma-phala-āsaṅgam*—attachment to the fruits of action; *nitya*—always; *tṛiptaḥ*—satisfied; *nirāśhrayaḥ*—without dependence; *karmaṇi*—in activities; *abhipravṛittaḥ*—engaged; *api*—despite; *na*—not; *eva*—certainly; *kiñchit*—anything; *karoti*—do; *saḥ*—that person.

Such people, having given up attachment to the fruits of their actions,

are always satisfied and not dependent on external things. Despite engaging in activities, they do not do anything at all.

Actions cannot be classified by external appearances. It is the state of the mind that determines what is inaction and action. The minds of enlightened persons are absorbed in God. Being fully satisfied in devotional union with Him, they look upon God as their only refuge and do not depend upon any external support. In this state of mind, all their actions are termed as *akarm* or inactions.

There is a beautiful story in the Puranas to illustrate this point:

The *gopis* (cowherd women) of Vrindavan once kept a fast. The ceremony of breaking the fast required them to feed a sage. Shree Krishna advised them to feed Sage Durvasa, the elevated ascetic, who lived on the other side of River Yamuna. The *gopis* prepared a delicious feast and started off but found the river was very turbulent that day, and no boatman was willing to ferry them across.

The *gopis* turned to Shree Krishna for a solution. He said, 'Tell River Yamuna that if Shree Krishna is an *akhaṇḍ brahmachārī* (perfect celibate since birth), it should give them way.' The *gopis* started laughing because they felt that Shree Krishna used to dote on them, so there was no question of His being an *akhaṇḍ brahmachārī*. Nevertheless, when they requested River Yamuna in that manner, the river gave them way and a bridge of flowers manifested for their passage across the river.

The *gopis* were astonished. They went across to the ashram of Sage Durvasa and requested him to accept the delicious meal they had brought for him. Being an ascetic, he ate only a small portion, which disappointed the *gopis*. So, Durvasa decided to fulfil their expectations, and using his mystic powers, he ate everything they had brought. The *gopis* were amazed to see him eat so much but were very pleased that he had done justice to their cooking.

The *gopis* now asked Durvasa for help to cross the Yamuna and return to the other side. He replied, 'Tell River Yamuna that if Durvasa has not eaten anything today except Doob grass (a kind of grass which was the only thing Durvasa used to eat), the river should give way.'

The *gopis* again started laughing because they had seen him eat such an extravagant meal. Yet to their utmost surprise, when they beseeched River Yamuna in that manner, the river again gave them way.

The *gopis* asked Shree Krishna the secret behind what had happened. He explained that while God and the saints appear to engage in material activities externally, internally they are always transcendentally situated. Thus, even while doing all kinds of actions, they are still considered to be non-doers. Although interacting with the *gopis* externally, Shree Krishna was an *akhaṇḍ brahmachārī* internally. And though Durvasa ate the delectable meal offered by the *gopis*, internally his mind only tasted the Doob grass. Both these were illustrations of inaction in action.

निराशीर्यतचित्तात्मा त्यक्तसर्वपरिग्रहः ।
शारीरं केवलं कर्म कुर्वन्नाप्नोति किल्बिषम् ।।21।।

nirāśhīr yata-chittātmā tyakta-sarva-parigrahaḥ
śhārīraṁ kevalaṁ karma kurvan nāpnoti kilbiṣham

nirāśhīḥ—free from expectations; *yata*—controlled; *chitta-ātmā*—mind and intellect; *tyakta*—having abandoned; *sarva*—all; *parigrahaḥ*—sense of ownership; *śhārīram*—bodily; *kevalam*—only; *karma*—actions; *kurvan*—performing; *na*—never; *āpnoti*—incurs; *kilbiṣham*—sin.

Free from expectations and the sense of ownership, with the mind and intellect fully controlled, they incur no sin even though they perform actions by their body.

Even according to worldly law, acts of violence that happen accidentally are not considered as punishable offences. If one is driving a car in the correct lane, at the correct speed, with eyes fixed ahead, and someone suddenly comes and falls in front of the car and dies as a result, the court of law will not consider it as a culpable offence, provided it can be proven that the person had no intention to maim or kill. It is the intention of the mind that is of primary importance and not the action. Similarly, the mystics who work in divine consciousness are released from all sins, because their mind is free from attachment and proprietorship, and their every act is performed with the divine intention of pleasing God.

यदृच्छालाभसन्तुष्टो द्वन्द्वातीतो विमत्सरः ।
समः सिद्धावसिद्धौ च कृत्वापि न निबध्यते ।।22।।

yadṛichchhā-lābha-santuṣhṭo dvandvātīto vimatsaraḥ
samaḥ siddhāvasiddhau cha kṛitvāpi na nibadhyate

yadṛichchhā—which comes of its own accord; *lābha*—gain; *santuṣhṭaḥ*—contented; *dvandva*—duality; *atītaḥ*—surpassed; *vimatsaraḥ*—free from envy; *samaḥ*—equipoised; *siddhau*—in success; *asiddhau*—failure; *cha*—and; *kṛitvā*—performing; *api*—even; *na*—never; *nibadhyate*—is bound.

Content with whatever gain that comes of its own accord and free from envy, they are beyond the dualities of life. Being equipoised in success and failure, they are not bound by their actions even while performing all kinds of activities.

Just like there are two sides to a coin, so too, God created this world full of dualities—there is day and night, sweet and sour, hot and cold, rain and drought, and so on. The same rose bush that has a beautiful flower also has an ugly thorn. Life too brings its share of dualities—happiness and distress, victory and defeat, fame and notoriety. Lord Ram Himself, in His divine pastimes, was exiled to the forest the day before He was to be crowned as the king of Ayodhya.

While living in this world, nobody can hope to neutralise the dualities to have only positive experiences. Then how can we successfully deal with the dualities that come our way in life? The solution is to take these dualities in our stride by learning to rise above them and remain equipoised in all situations. This happens when we develop detachment to the fruits of our actions, concerning ourselves merely with doing our duty in life without yearning for the results. When we perform works for the pleasure of God, we see both positive and negative fruits of those works as the will of God and gladly accept both.

गतसङ्गस्य मुक्तस्य ज्ञानावस्थितचेतसः ।
यज्ञायाचरतः कर्म समग्रं प्रविलीयते ।।23।।

gata-saṅgasya muktasya jñānāvasthita-chetasaḥ
yajñāyācharataḥ karma samagraṁ pravilīyate

gata-saṅgasya—free from material attachments; *muktasya*—of the liberated; *jñāna-avasthita*—established in divine knowledge; *chetasaḥ*—whose intellect; *yajñāya*—as a sacrifice (to God); *ācharataḥ*—performing; *karma*—action; *samagram*—completely; *pravilīyate*—are free.

They are released from the bondage of material attachments and their intellect is established in divine knowledge. Since they perform all actions as a sacrifice (to God), they are freed from all karmic reactions.

In this verse, Lord Krishna summarises the conclusion of the previous five verses. Dedication of all our actions to God results from the understanding that the soul is the eternal servitor of God. Chaitanya Mahaprabhu said: *jīvera svarūpa haya kṛiṣhṇera nitya-dāsa* (*Chaitanya Charitāmṛit, Madhya Leela*, 20.108) 'The soul is by nature the servant of God.' Those who are established in this knowledge perform all their actions as an offering to Him and are released from the sinful reactions of their work.

What is the kind of vision that such souls develop? Shree Krishna explains this in the next verse.

ब्रह्मार्पणं ब्रह्म हविर्ब्रह्माग्नौ ब्रह्मणा हुतम् ।
ब्रह्मैव तेन गन्तव्यं ब्रह्मकर्मसमाधिना ।।24।।

brahmārpaṇaṁ brahma havir brahmāgnau brahmaṇā hutam
brahmaiva tena gantavyaṁ brahma-karma-samādhinā

brahma—Brahman; *arpaṇam*—the ladle and other offerings; *brahma*—Brahman; *haviḥ*—the oblation; *brahma*—Brahman; *agnau*—in the sacrificial fire; *brahmaṇā*—by that person; *hutam*—offered; *brahma*—Brahman; *eva*—certainly; *tena*—by that; *gantavyam*—to be attained; *brahma*—Brahman; *karma*—offering; *samādhinā*—those completely absorbed in God-consciousness.

For those who are completely absorbed in God-consciousness, the oblation is Brahman, the ladle with which it is offered is Brahman, the act of offering is Brahman, and the sacrificial fire is also Brahman. Such persons, who view everything as God, easily attain Him.

Factually, the objects of the world are made from maya, the material energy of God. Energy is both one with its energetic source and also different from it. For example, light is the energy of fire. It can be considered as different from the fire because it exists outside it. But it can also be reckoned as a part of the fire itself. Hence, when the rays of the sun enter the room through a window, people say, 'The sun has come'. Here, they are bundling the sunrays with the sun. The energy is both distinct from the energetic source and yet a part of it.

The soul too is the energy of God—it is a spiritual energy called *jīva shakti*. Shree Krishna states this in verse 7.5. Chaitanya Mahaprabhu stated:

jīva-tattva śhakti, kṛiṣhṇa-tattva śhaktimān
gītā-viṣhṇupurāṇādi tāhāte pramāṇa

(*Chaitanya Charitāmṛit, Ādi Leela,* 7.117)

'Lord Krishna is the energetic and the soul is His energy. This has been stated in Bhagavad Gita, *Vishnu Puran,* and others.' Thus, the soul is also simultaneously one with and different from God. Hence, those whose minds are fully absorbed in God-consciousness see the whole world in its unity with God as non-different from Him. The Shreemad Bhagavatam states:

sarva-bhūteṣhu yaḥ paśhyed bhagavad-bhāvam ātmanaḥ
bhūtāni bhagavatyātmanyeṣha bhāgavatottamaḥ (11.2.45)

'One who sees God everywhere and in all beings is the highest spiritualist.' For such advanced spiritualists whose minds are completely absorbed in God-consciousness, the person making the sacrifice, the object of the sacrifice, the instruments of the sacrifice, the sacrificial fire, and the act of sacrifice, are all perceived as non-different from God.

Having explained the spirit in which sacrifice is to be done, Lord Krishna now relates the different kinds of sacrifice people perform in this world for purification.

दैवमेवापरे यज्ञं योगिनः पर्युपासते ।
ब्रह्माग्नावपरे यज्ञं यज्ञेनैवोपजुह्वति ।।25।।

daivamevāpare yajñaṁ yoginaḥ paryupāsate
brahmāgnāvapare yajñaṁ yajñenaivopajuhvati

daivam—the celestial gods; *eva*—indeed; *apare*—others; *yajñam*—sacrifice; *yoginaḥ*—spiritual practioners; *paryupāsate*—worship; *brahma*—of the Supreme Truth; *agnau*—in the fire; *apare*—others; *yajñam*—sacrifice; *yajñena*—by sacrifice; *eva*—indeed; *upajuhvati*—offer.

Some yogis worship the celestial gods with material offerings unto them. Others worship perfectly who offer the self as sacrifice in the fire of the Supreme Truth.

Sacrifice or yajna should be performed in divine consciousness as an offering to the Supreme Lord. However, people vary in their understanding, and as a result, perform sacrifice in different manners with dissimilar consciousness. Persons with lesser understanding and desirous of material rewards make offerings to the celestial gods.

Others with deeper understanding of the meaning of yajna offer their own selves as sacrifice to the Supreme. This is called *atma samarpaṇ* or *atmāhutī* or offering one's soul to God. Yogi Shri Krishna Prem explained this very well: 'In this world of dust and din, whenever one makes *atmāhutī* in the flame of divine love, there is an explosion, which is grace, for no true *atmāhutī* can ever go in vain.' But what is the process of offering one's own self as sacrifice? This is performed by surrendering oneself completely to God. Such surrender has six aspects to it, which have been explained in the commentary of verse 18.62. Here, Shree Krishna continues to explain the different kinds of sacrifice that people perform.

श्रोत्रादीनीन्द्रियाण्यन्ये संयमाग्निषु जुह्वति ।
शब्दादीन्विषयानन्य इन्द्रियाग्निषु जुह्वति ।।26।।

śhrotrādīnīndriyāṇyanye sanyamāgniṣhu juhvati
śhabdādīn viṣhayānanya indriyāgniṣhu juhvati

śhrotra-ādīni—such as the hearing process; *indriyāṇi*—senses; *anye*—others; *sanyama*—restraint; *agniṣhu*—in the sacrficial fire; *juhvati*—sacrifice; *śhabda-ādīn*—sound vibration, etc.; *viṣhayān*—objects of sense-gratification; *anye*—others; *indriya*—of the senses; *agniṣhu*—in the fire; *juhvati*—sacrifice.

Others offer hearing and other senses in the sacrificial fire of restraint. Still others offer sound and other objects of the senses as sacrifice in the fire of the senses.

Fire transforms the nature of things consigned into it. In external ritualistic Vedic sacrifices, it physically consumes oblations offered to it. In the internal practice of spirituality, fire is symbolic. The fire of self-discipline burns the desires of the senses.

Here, Shree Krishna distinguishes between two diametrically opposite approaches to spiritual elevation. One is the path of negation of the senses, which is followed in the practice of hatha yog. In this type of yajna, the actions of the senses are suspended except for the bare maintenance of the body. The mind is completely withdrawn from the senses and made introvertive by force of willpower.

Opposite to this is the practice of bhakti yog. In this second type of yajna, the senses are made to behold the glory of the Creator that manifests in every atom of His creation. The senses no longer remain as instruments for material enjoyment; rather, they are sublimated to perceive God in everything. In verse 7.8, Shree Krishna says: *raso 'ham apsu kaunteya* 'Arjun, know Me to be the taste in water.' Accordingly, bhakti yogis practise to behold God through all their senses, in everything they see, hear, taste, feel, and smell. This yajna of devotion is simpler than the path of hatha yog; it is a joy to perform and involves a smaller risk of downfall from the path. For example, if one is riding a bicycle and presses the brakes to stop the forward motion, he will be in an unstable condition, but if the cyclist simply turns the handle to the left or right, the bicycle will very easily stop its forward motion and still remain stable and balanced.

सर्वाणीन्द्रियकर्माणि प्राणकर्माणि चापरे ।
आत्मसंयमयोगाग्नौ जुह्वति ज्ञानदीपिते ।।27।।

sarvāṇīndriya-karmāṇi prāṇa-karmāṇi chāpare
ātma-sanyama-yogāgnau juhvati jñāna-dīpite

sarvāṇi—all; *indriya*—the senses; *karmāṇi*—functions; *prāṇa-karmāṇi*—functions of the life breath; *cha*—and; *apare*—others; *ātma-sanyama yogāgnau*—in the fire of the controlled mind; *juhvati*—sacrifice; *jñāna-dīpite*—kindled by knowledge.

Some, inspired by knowledge, offer the functions of all their senses and their life energy in the fire of the controlled mind.

There are some yogis who follow the path of discrimination, or jnana yog, and take the help of knowledge to withdraw their senses from the world. While hatha yogis strive to restrain the senses with brute willpower, jnana yogis accomplish the same goal with the repeated practice of discrimination based on knowledge. They engage in deep contemplation upon the illusory nature of the world and the identity of the self as distinct from the body, mind, intellect, and ego. The senses are withdrawn from the world, and the mind is engaged in meditation upon the self. The goal is to become practically situated in self-knowledge in the assumption that the self is identical with the Supreme Ultimate reality. As aids to contemplation, they chant aphorisms such as: *tattvamasi* 'I am That,' (*Chhāndogya Upanishad*

6.8.7) and *ahaṁ brahmāsmi* 'I am the Supreme Entity.' (*Bṛihadāraṇyak Upanishad* 1.4.10)

The practice of jnana yog is a very difficult path which requires a very determined and trained intellect. The Shreemad Bhagavatam (11.20.7) states: *nirviṇṇānāṁ jñānayogaḥ* 'Success in the practice of jnana yog is only possible for those who are at an advanced stage of renunciation.'

द्रव्ययज्ञास्तपोयज्ञा योगयज्ञास्तथापरे ।
स्वाध्यायज्ञानयज्ञाश्च यतयः संशितव्रताः ।।28।।

dravya-yajñās tapo-yajñā yoga-yajñās tathāpare
swādhyāya-jñāna-yajñāśh cha yatayaḥ sanśhita-vratāḥ

dravya-yajñāḥ—offering one's own wealth as sacrifice; *tapaḥ-yajñāḥ*—offering severe austerities as sacrifice; *yoga-yajñāḥ*—performance of eight-fold path of yogic practices as sacrifice; *tathā*—thus; *apare*—others; *swādhyāya*—cultivating knowledge by studying the scriptures; *jñāna-yajñāḥ*—those who offer cultivation of transcendental knowledge as sacrifice; *cha*—also; *yatayaḥ*—these ascetics; *sanśhita-vratāḥ*—observing strict vows.

Some offer their wealth as sacrifice while others offer severe austerities as sacrifice. Some practise the eight-fold path of yogic practices, and yet others study the scriptures and cultivate knowledge as sacrifice while observing strict vows.

Human beings differ from each other in their nature, motivation, activities, professions, aspirations, and *sanskārs* (tendencies carrying forward from past lives). Shree Krishna brings Arjun to the understanding that sacrifices can take on hundreds of forms, but when they are dedicated to God, they become means of purification of the mind and senses and elevation of the soul. In this verse, He mentions three such yajnas that can be performed.

Dravya yajna: There are those who are inclined towards earning wealth and donating it in charity towards a divine cause. Although they may engage in large and complicated business endeavours, yet their inner motivation remains to serve God with the wealth they earn. In this manner, they offer their propensity for earning money as a sacrifice to God in devotion. John Wesley, the British preacher and founder of the Methodist Church would instruct his followers: 'Make all you can. Save all you can. Give all you can.'

Yog yajna: In Indian philosophy, the *Yog Darshan* is one of the six philosophical treatises written by six learned sages. Jaimini wrote *Mimansa Darshan*, Ved Vyas wrote *Vedant Darshan*, Gautam wrote *Nyaya Darshan*, Kanad wrote *Vaiśheṣhik Darshan*, Kapil wrote *Sānkhya Darshan*, and Patanjali wrote *Yog Darshan*. *Patanjali Yog Darshan* describes an eight-fold path, called ashtang yog, for spiritual advancement, starting with physical techniques and ending in the conquest of the mind. Some people find this path attractive and practice it as sacrifice. However, *Patanjali Yog Darshan* also clearly states:

samādhisiddhirīśhvara praṇidhānāt (2.45)

'To attain perfection in Yog, you must surrender to God.' So, when persons inclined towards ashtang yog learn to love God, they offer their yogic practice as yajna in the fire of devotion. An example of this is the yogic system Jagadguru Kripaluji Yog, where the physical postures of ashtang yog are practised as yajna to God, along with the chanting of His divine names. Such a combination of yogic postures along with devotion results in the physical, mental, and spiritual purification of the practitioner.

Jnana yajna: Some persons are inclined towards the cultivation of knowledge. This propensity finds its perfect employment in the study of scriptures for enhancing one's understanding and love for God. *sā vidyā tanmatiryayā* (Bhagavatam 4.29.49) 'True knowledge is that which increases our devotion to God.' Thus, studiously inclined *sādhaks* engage in the sacrifice of knowledge, which when imbued with the spirit of devotion, leads to loving union with God.

अपाने जुह्वति प्राणं प्राणेऽपानं तथापरे ।
प्राणापानगती रुद्ध्वा प्राणायामपरायणाः ।।29।।

अपरे नियताहाराः प्राणान्प्राणेषु जुह्वति ।
सर्वेऽप्येते यज्ञविदो यज्ञक्षपितकल्मषाः ।।30।।

apāne juhvati prāṇaṁ prāṇe 'pānaṁ tathāpare
prāṇāpāna-gatī ruddhvā prāṇāyāma-parāyaṇāḥ

apare niyatāhārāḥ prāṇān prāṇeṣhu juhvati
sarve 'pyete yajña-vido yajña-kṣhapita-kalmaṣhāḥ

apāne—the incoming breath; *juhvati*—offer; *prāṇam*—the outgoing breath; *prāṇe*—in the outgoing breath; *apānam*—incoming breath; *tathā*—also; *apare*—others; *prāṇa*—of the outgoing breath; *apāna*—and the incoming breath; *gatī*—movement; *ruddhvā*—blocking; *prāṇa-āyāma*—control of breath; *parāyaṇāḥ*—wholly devoted; *apare*—others; *niyata*—having controlled; *āhārāḥ*—food intake; *prāṇān*—life breaths; *prāṇeṣhu*—life energy; *juhvati*—sacrifice; *sarve*—all; *api*—also; *ete*—these; *yajña-vidaḥ*—knowers of sacrifices; *yajña-kṣhapita*—being cleansed by performances of sacrifices; *kalmaṣhāḥ*—of impurities.

Still others offer as sacrifice the outgoing breath in the incoming breath, while some offer the incoming breath into the outgoing breath. Some arduously practice pranayam and restrain the incoming and outgoing breaths, purely absorbed in the regulation of life energy. Yet others curtail their food intake and offer the breath into the life energy as sacrifice. All these knowers of sacrifice are cleansed of their impurities as a result of such performances.

Some persons are drawn to the practice of pranayam, which is loosely translated as 'control of breath'. This involves:

Pūrak: the process of drawing breath into the lungs.

Rechak: the process of emptying the lungs of breath.

Antar kumbhak: holding the breath in the lungs after inhalation. The outgoing breath gets suspended in the incoming breath during the period of suspension.

Bāhya kumbhak: keeping the lungs empty after exhalation. The incoming breath gets suspended in the outgoing breath during the period of suspension.

Both the *kumbhaks* are advanced techniques and should only be practised under the supervision of qualified teachers, else they can cause harm. Yogis who are inclined towards the practice of pranayam utilise the process of breath control to help tame the senses and bring the mind into focus. Then they offer the controlled mind in the spirit of yajna to the Supreme Lord.

Pran is not exactly breath; it is the subtle life force energy that pervades the breath and varieties of animate and inanimate objects. The Vedic scriptures describe five kinds of *pranas* in the body—*prāṇ, apān, vyān, samān, udān*—that help regulate various physiological bodily functions. Amongst these, *samān* is responsible for the bodily function of digestion. Some people may also be inclined towards fasting. They curtail their eating with the knowledge that diet impacts character and behaviour. Such fasting has been employed as a spiritual technique in India since ancient times and also considered here a form of yajna. When the diet is curtailed, the senses become weak and the *samān*, which is responsible for digestion, is made to neutralise itself. This is the nature of the sacrifice that some people perform.

These are the various kinds of austerities performed for purification. It is the desire for gratification of the senses and the mind which leads to the heart becoming impure. The aim of all these austerities is to curtail the natural propensity of the senses and mind to seek pleasure in material objects. When these austerities are performed as a sacrifice to the Supreme, they result in the purification of the heart (the word 'heart' is often used to refer to the internal machinery of the mind and intellect).

यज्ञशिष्टामृतभुजो यान्ति ब्रह्म सनातनम् ।
नायं लोकोऽस्त्ययज्ञस्य कुतोऽन्यः कुरुसत्तम ।।31।।

yajña-śhiṣhṭāmṛita-bhujo yānti brahma sanātanam
nāyaṁ loko 'styayajñasya kuto 'nyaḥ kuru-sattama

yajña-śhiṣhṭa amṛita-bhujaḥ—they partake of the nectarean remnants of sacrifice; *yānti*—go; *brahma*—Absolute Truth; *sanātanam*—eternal; *na*—never; *ayam*—this; *lokaḥ*—planet; *asti*—is; *ayajñasya*—for one who performs no sacrifice; *kutaḥ*—how; *anyaḥ*—other (world); *kuru-sat-tama*—best of Kurus, Arjun.

Those who know the secret of sacrifice, and engaging in it, partake of its remnants that are like nectar, advance towards the Absolute Truth. O best of the Kurus, those who perform no sacrifice find no happiness either in this world or the next.

The secret of sacrifice, as mentioned previously, is the understanding that it should be performed for the pleasure of God, and then the remnants can be taken as His prasad (grace). For example, devotees of the Lord partake of food after offering it to Him. After cooking the food, they place it on the altar and pray to God to accept their offering. In their mind, they meditate on the sentiment that God is actually eating from the plate. At the end of the offering, the remnants on the plate are accepted as prasad, or the grace of God. Partaking of such nectar-like prasad leads to illumination, purification, and spiritual advancement.

In the same sentiment, devotees offer clothes to God and then wear them as His prasad. They instal His deity in their house, and then live in it with the attitude that their home is a temple of God. When objects or activities are offered as sacrifice to God, then the remnants or prasad, are a nectar-like blessing for the soul. The great devotee Uddhav told Shree Krishna:

tvayopabhukta-srag-gandha-vāso 'laṅkāra-charchitāḥ
uchchhiṣhṭa-bhojino dāsās tava māyāṁ jayema hi

(Bhagavatam 11.6.46)

'I will only eat, smell, wear, live in, and talk about objects that have first been offered to You. In this way, by accepting the remnants as Your prasad, I will easily conquer maya.' Those who do not perform sacrifice remain entangled in the fruitive reactions of work and continue to experience the torments of maya.

एवं बहुविधा यज्ञा वितता ब्रह्मणो मुखे ।
कर्मजान्विद्धि तान्सर्वानेवं ज्ञात्वा विमोक्ष्यसे ।।32।।

evaṁ bahu-vidhā yajñā vitatā brahmaṇo mukhe
karma-jān viddhi tān sarvān evaṁ jñātvā vimokṣhyase

evam—thus; *bahu-vidhāḥ*—various kinds of; *yajñāḥ*—sacrifices; *vitatāḥ*—have been described; *brahmaṇaḥ*—of the Vedas; *mukhe*—through the mouth; *karma-jān*—originating from works; *viddhi*—know; *tān*—them; *sarvān*—all; *evam*—thus; *jñātvā*—having known; *vimokṣhyase*—you shall be liberated.

All these different kinds of sacrifice have been described in the Vedas. Know them as originating from different types of work; this understanding cuts the knots of material bondage.

One of the beautiful features of the Vedas is that they recognise and cater to the wide variety of human nature. Different kinds of sacrifice have thus been described for different kinds of performers. The common thread running through them is that they are to be done with devotion, as an offering to God. With this understanding, one is not bewildered by the multifarious instructions in the Vedas, and by pursuing the particular yajna suitable to one's nature, one can be released from material bondage.

श्रेयान्द्रव्यमयाद्यज्ञाज्ज्ञानयज्ञः परन्तप ।
सर्वं कर्माखिलं पार्थ ज्ञाने परिसमाप्यते ।।33।।

śhreyān dravya-mayād yajñāj jñāna-yajñaḥ parantapa
sarvaṁ karmākhilaṁ pārtha jñāne parisamāpyate

śhreyān—superior; *dravya-mayāt*—of material possessions; *yajñāt*—than the sacrifice; *jñāna-yajñaḥ*—sacrifice performed in knowledge; *parantapa*—subduer of enemies, Arjun; *sarvam*—all; *karma*—works; *akhilam*—all; *pārtha*—Arjun, son of Pritha; *jñāne*—in knowledge; *parisamāpyate*—culminate.

O subduer of enemies, sacrifice performed in knowledge is superior to any mechanical material sacrifice. After all, O Parth, all sacrifices of work culminate in knowledge.

Shree Krishna now puts the previously described sacrifices in proper perspective. He tells Arjun that it is good to do physical acts of devotion but not good enough. Ritualistic ceremonies, fasts, mantra chants, holy pilgrimages, and other such techniques are all fine, but remain mere physical activities if not performed with proper knowledge. While such mechanical activities are better than not doing anything at all, they are insufficient to purify the mind.

Many people chant God's Name on rosary beads, sit in recitations of the scriptures, visit holy places, and perform worship ceremonies, with the belief that the physical act itself is sufficient for liberating them from material bondage. However, Saint Kabir rejects this idea very eloquently:

mālā pherata yuga phirā, phirā na mana kā pher,
kar kā manakā ḍāri ke, manakā manakā pher

'O spiritual aspirant, you have been rotating chanting beads for many ages, but the mischief of the mind has not ceased. Now put those beads down and rotate the beads of the mind.' Jagadguru Shree Kripaluji Maharaj says:

bandhan aur mokṣha kā, kāraṇ manahi bakhān
yāte kauniu bhakti karu, karu man te haridhyān

(*Bhakti Śhatak* verse 19)

'The cause of bondage and liberation is the mind. Whatever form of devotion you do, engage your mind in meditating upon God.'

Devotional sentiments are nourished by the cultivation of knowledge. For example, let us say that it is your birthday party, and people are coming and handing you gifts. Someone comes and gives you a ragged bag. You look at it disdainfully, thinking it is insignificant in comparison to the other wonderful gifts you have received. That person requests you to look inside the bag. You open it and find a stack of one hundred notes of Rs 2,000 denomination. You immediately hug the bag to your chest, and say, 'This is the best gift I have received!' Knowledge of its contents developed love for the object. Similarly, cultivating knowledge of God and our relationship with Him nurtures devotional sentiments. Hence, Shree Krishna explains to Arjun that sacrifices performed in knowledge are superior to the sacrifice of material things. *He now explains the process of acquiring knowledge.*

तद्विद्धि प्रणिपातेन परिप्रश्नेन सेवया ।
उपदेक्ष्यन्ति ते ज्ञानं ज्ञानिनस्तत्त्वदर्शिनः ।।34।।

tad viddhi praṇipātena paripraśhnena sevayā
upadekṣhyanti te jñānaṁ jñāninas-tattva-darśhinaḥ

tat—the truth; *viddhi*—try to learn; *praṇipātena*—by approaching a spiritual master; *paripraśhnena*—by humble enquiries; *sevayā*—by rendering service; *upadekṣhyanti*—can impart; *te*—unto you; *jñānam*—knowledge; *jñāninaḥ*—the enlightened; *tattva-darśhinaḥ*—those who have realised the truth.

Learn the Truth by approaching a spiritual master. Enquire from him with reverence and render service unto him. Such an enlightened saint can impart knowledge unto you because he has seen the Truth.

On hearing that sacrifice should be performed in knowledge, the natural question that follows is, how can we obtain spiritual knowledge? Shree Krishna gives the answer in this verse. He says: 1) Approach a spiritual master. 2) Enquire from him submissively. 3) Render service to him.

The Absolute Truth cannot be understood merely by our own contemplation. The Bhagavatam states:

anādyavidyā yuktasya puruṣhasyātma vedanam
svato na sambhavād anyas tattva-jño jñāna-do bhavet

(11.22.10)

'The intellect of the soul is clouded by ignorance from endless lifetimes. Covered with nescience, the intellect cannot overcome its ignorance simply by its own effort. One needs to receive knowledge from a God-realised saint who knows the Absolute Truth.'

The Vedic scriptures advise us repeatedly on the importance of the guru on the spiritual path.

āchāryavān puruṣho vedaḥ (*Chhāndogya Upanishad* 6.14.2)

'Only through a guru can you understand the Vedas.' The *Pañchadaśhī* states:

tatpādāmburu hadvandva sevā nirmala chetasām
sukhabodhāya tattvasya viveko 'yaṁ vidhīyate (1.2)

'Serve the guru with a pure mind, giving up doubts. He will then bring you great happiness by bestowing knowledge of the scriptures and discrimination.' Jagadguru Shankaracharya stated: *yāvat gururna kartavyo tāvanmuktirna labhyate* 'Until you surrender to a guru, you cannot be liberated from material energy.'

One of the most magnanimous graces of God is when He brings the soul in contact with a true guru. But the process of transfer of spiritual knowledge from the teacher to the student is very different from that of material knowledge. Secular education does not require deep respect for the teacher. The transmission of knowledge can be purchased simply by paying the teacher's fees. However, spiritual edification is neither imparted to the student by a mechanical teaching process nor is it purchased for a price. It is revealed in the heart of the disciple by the guru's grace, when the disciple develops humility and the guru is pleased with the service attitude of the disciple. That is why Prahalad Maharaj said:

naiṣhāṁ matis tāvad urukramāṅghriṁ
spṛiśhatyanarthāpagamo yadarthaḥ

mahīyasāṁ pāda rajo 'bhiṣhekaṁ
niṣhkiñchanānāṁ na vṛiṇīta yāvat (Bhagavatam 7.5.32)

'Until we bathe ourselves in the dust of the lotus feet of a saint, we can never have an experience of the transcendental platform.' Hence, in this verse, Shree Krishna mentions the need for approaching a guru with reverence, enquiring about the Truth from him with humility, and pleasing him by rendering service.

यज्ज्ञात्वा न पुनर्मोहमेवं यास्यसि पाण्डव ।
येन भूतान्यशेषेण द्रक्ष्यस्यात्मन्यथो मयि ।।35।।

yaj jñātvā na punar moham evaṁ yāsyasi pāṇḍava
yena bhūtānyaśheṣheṇa drakṣhyasyātmanyatho mayi

yat—which; *jñātvā*—having known; *na*—never; *punaḥ*—again; *moham*—delusion; *evam*—like this; *yāsyasi*—you shall get; *pāṇḍava*—Arjun, son of Pandu; *yena*—by this; *bhūtāni*—living beings; *aśheṣhāṇi*—all; *drakṣhyasi*—you will see; *ātmani*—within Me (Shree Krishna); *atho*—that is to say; *mayi*—in me.

Following this path and having achieved enlightenment from a guru, O Arjun, you will no longer fall into delusion. In the light of that knowledge, you will see that all living beings are but parts of the Supreme and are within Me.

Just as darkness can never engulf the sun, similarly, illusion can never again overcome the soul who has once attained enlightenment. *Tadviṣhṇoḥ paramaṁ padaṁ sadā paśhyanti sūrayaḥ* (*Rig Veda*) 'Those who have realised God always remain in God-consciousness.'

Under the illusion of maya, we see the world as separate from God and establish friendship or enmity with other human beings depending upon whether they satisfy or harm our self-interest. Divine knowledge that comes with enlightenment changes our perspective and vision of the world. Enlightened saints see the world as the energy of God and utilise whatever comes their way in the service of God. They also see all human beings as parts of God and harbour a divine attitude towards everyone. Thus, Hanuman says:

sīyā rāmamaya saba jaga jānī, karauñ pranāma jori juga pānī

(Ramayan)

'I see the forms of Lord Ram and Mother Sita in everyone, and so I fold my hands and offer my respects to all.'

अपि चेदसि पापेभ्यः सर्वेभ्यः पापकृत्तमः ।
सर्वं ज्ञानप्लवेनैव वृजिनं सन्तरिष्यसि ।।36।।

api chedasi pāpebhyaḥ sarvebhyaḥ pāpa-kṛit-tamaḥ
sarvaṁ jñāna-plavenaiva vṛijinaṁ santariṣhyasi

api—even; *chet*—if; *asi*—you are; *pāpebhyaḥ*—sinners; *sarvebhyaḥ*—of all; *pāpa-kṛit-tamaḥ*—most sinful; *sarvam*—all; *jñāna-plavena*—by the boat of divine knowledge; *eva*—certainly; *vṛijinam*—sin; *santariṣhyasi*—you shall cross over.

Even those who are considered the most immoral of all sinners can cross over this ocean of material existence by seating themselves in the boat of divine knowledge.

Material existence is like a vast ocean, which one is tossed around by the waves of birth, disease, old age, and death. The material energy subjects everyone to three-fold miseries: *ādiātmik*—miseries due to one's own body and mind, *ādibhautik*—miseries due to other living entities, and *ādidaivik*—miseries due to environmental conditions. In this state of material bondage, there is no respite for the soul, and endless lifetimes have been subjected to these conditions. Like a football being kicked around the field, the soul is elevated to the celestial abodes, dropped to the hellish planes of existence, and brought back to the earthly realm, according to its karmas of righteous or sinful deeds.

Divine knowledge provides the boat to cross over the material ocean. The ignorant perform karmas and get bound by them. Performing the same karmas as a yajna to God liberates the knowledgeable. Thus, knowledge becomes the means of cutting material bondage. The *Kaṭhopaniṣhad* states:

vijñānasārathiryastu manaḥ pragrahavān naraḥ
so 'dhvanaḥ pāramāpnoti tadviṣhṇoḥ paramaṁ padam (1.3.9)

'Illumine your intellect with divine knowledge; then with the illumined intellect, control the unruly mind to cross over the material ocean and reach the divine realm.'

यथैधांसि समिद्धोऽग्निर्भस्मसात्कुरुतेऽर्जुन ।
ज्ञानाग्निः सर्वकर्माणि भस्मसात्कुरुते तथा ।।37।।

yathaidhānsi samiddho 'gnir bhasma-sāt kurute 'rjuna
jñānāgniḥ sarva-karmāṇi bhasma-sāt kurute tathā

yathā—as; *edhānsi*—firewood; *samiddhaḥ*—blazing; *agniḥ*—fire; *bhasma-sāt*—to ashes; *kurute*—turns; *arjuna*—Arjun; *jñāna-agniḥ*—the fire of knowledge; *sarva-karmāṇi*—all reactions from material activities; *bhasma-sāt*—to ashes; *kurute*—it turns; *tathā*—similarly.

As a kindled fire reduces wood to ashes, O Arjun, so does the fire of knowledge burn to ashes all reactions from material activities.

Even a spark of fire has the potential to become a major conflagration and burn down a huge heap of combustible material. In 1666, the Great Fire of London began as only a little flame in a small bakery, but as it grew, it consigned to flames 13,200 houses, 87 churches, and most of the offices in the city.

We too have a heap of karmas attached to each of us consisting of the reactions of sinful and righteous deeds performed over infinite lifetimes. If we endeavour to exhaust these karmas by reaping their results, it will take many more lifetimes, and in the meantime, further karmas will accumulate in an endless cycle. But Shree Krishna assures Arjun that correct knowledge has the power to burn our heap of karmas in this lifetime itself. That is because knowledge of the soul and its relationship with God leads us to surrender to Him. When we surrender to God, He burns our stockpile of endless lifetimes of karmas and releases us from material bondage.

न हि ज्ञानेन सदृशं पवित्रमिह विद्यते ।
तत्स्वयं योगसंसिद्धः कालेनात्मनि विन्दति ।।38।।

na hi jñānena sadṛiśhaṁ pavitramiha vidyate
tatsvayaṁ yogasansiddhaḥ kālenātmani vindati

na—not; *hi*—certainly; *jñānena*—with divine knowledge; *sadṛiśham*—like; *pavitram*—pure; *iha*—in this world; *vidyate*—exists; *tat*—that; *svayam*—oneself; *yoga*—practice of yog; *sansiddhaḥ*—he who has attained perfection; *kālena*—in course of time; *ātmani*—within the heart; *vindati*—finds.

In this world, there is nothing as purifying as divine knowledge. One who has attained purity of mind through prolonged practice of Yog, receives such knowledge within the heart, in due course of time.

Knowledge has the power to purify, elevate, liberate, and unite a person with God. It is thus supremely sublime and pure. But a distinction needs to be made between two kinds of knowledge—theoretical information and practical realisation.

There is one kind of knowledge that is acquired by reading the scriptures and hearing from the guru. This theoretical information is insufficient by itself. It is like someone memorising a cookbook but never entering the kitchen. Such theoretical knowledge of cooking does not help in satiating one's hunger. Similarly, one may acquire theoretical knowledge on the topics of the soul, God, maya, karm, jnana, and bhakti from the guru, but that by itself does not make a person God-realised. When one practices sadhana in accordance with the theory, it results in purification of the mind. Then, from within, one gets realisation of the nature of the self and its relationship with God. Sage Patanjali states:

śhrutānumāna-prajñābhyām anya-viṣhayā viśheṣhārthatvāt

(*Yog Darshan* 1.49)

'The knowledge attained by realisation from within through the practice of Yog is far superior to theoretical knowledge of the scriptures.' Such realised knowledge is being extolled by Shree Krishna as the purest sublime thing.

श्रद्धावाँल्लभते ज्ञानं तत्परः संयतेन्द्रियः ।
ज्ञानं लब्ध्वा परां शान्तिमचिरेणाधिगच्छति ।।39।।

śhraddhāvānllabhate jñānaṁ tat-paraḥ sanyatendriyaḥ
jñānaṁ labdhvā parāṁ śhāntim achireṇādhigachchhati

śhraddhāvān—a faithful person; *labhate*—achieves; *jñānam*—divine knowledge; *tat-paraḥ*—devoted (to that); *sanyata*—controlled; *indriyaḥ*—senses; *jñānam*—transcendental knowledge; *labdhvā*—having achieved; *parām*—supreme; *śhāntim*—peace; *achireṇa*—without delay; *adhigachchhati*—attains.

Those whose faith is deep and who have practised controlling their mind and senses attain divine knowledge. Through such transcendental knowledge, they quickly attain everlasting supreme peace.

Shree Krishna now introduces the concept of faith in the context of knowledge. Not all spiritual truths are immediately perceptible; some of them can only be experienced after having attained sufficient elevation on the path. If we only accept what we can presently verify or comprehend, we will be bereft of the higher spiritual secrets. Faith helps us accept what we cannot understand at present. Jagadguru Shankaracharya defined faith as:

guru vedānta vākyeṣhu dṛiḍho viśhvāsaḥ śhraddhā

'Faith means firm confidence in the words of the guru and the scriptures.' When such faith is placed upon a wrong personality, it can lead to disastrous consequences. But when it is placed on the true guru, it opens the pathway for eternal welfare.

However, blind faith is not a desirable thing. Before placing it on any guru, we must use our intellect to confirm that the guru has realised the Absolute Truth, and he is teaching it in accordance with the eternal Vedic scriptures. Once this is confirmed, then we should strive to deepen our faith in such a guru and surrender to God under his guidance. The *Śhwetāśhvatar Upanishad* states:

yasya deve parā bhaktiryathā deve tathā gurau
tasyaite kathitā hyarthāḥ prakāśhante mahātmanaḥ (6.23)

'The imports of all the Vedic knowledge is revealed within the hearts of those who engage with unflinching faith in devotion towards guru and God.'

अज्ञश्चाश्रद्दधानश्च संशयात्मा विनश्यति ।
नायं लोकोऽस्ति न परो न सुखं संशयात्मनः ।।40।।

ajñaśh chāśhraddadhānaśh cha sanśhayātmā vinaśhyati
nāyaṁ loko 'sti na paro na sukhaṁ sanśhayātmanaḥ

ajñaḥ—the ignorant; *cha*—and; *aśhraddadhānaḥ*—without faith; *cha*—and; *sanśhaya*—sceptical; *ātmā*—a person; *vinaśhyati*—falls down; *na*—never; *ayam*—in this; *lokaḥ*—world; *asti*—is; *na*—not; *paraḥ*—in the next; *na*—not; *sukham*—happiness; *sanśhaya-ātmanaḥ*—for the sceptical soul.

But persons who possess neither faith nor knowledge, and who are of a doubting nature, suffer a downfall. For the sceptical souls, there is no happiness either in this world or the next.

The *Bhakti Rasāmṛit Sindhu* classifies *sādhaks* into three classes based on the degree of faith and knowledge:

śhāstre yuktau cha nipuṇaḥ sarvathā dṛiḍha-niśhchayaḥ
prauḍha-śhraddho 'dhikārī yaḥ sa bhaktāvuttamo mataḥ

yaḥ śhāstrādiṣhvanipuṇaḥ śhraddhāvān sa tu madhyamaḥ

yo bhavet komala śhraddhaḥ sa kaniṣhṭho nigadyate

(1.2.17–19)

'The highest *sādhak* (spiritual aspirant) is one who possesses knowledge of the scriptures and is also endowed with firm faith. The medium-class *sādhak* is one who does not have knowledge of the scriptures but is endowed with faith towards God and guru. The lowest-class *sādhak* is one, who neither has scriptural knowledge nor is endowed with faith.' For the third category, Shree Krishna says that such persons cannot attain peace either in this life or hereafter.

Even worldly activities require the exercise of faith. For example, if a woman goes to a restaurant and orders a meal, she has faith that the restaurant will not mix poison in her food. If, however, she is besieged with doubts and wants to subject every food item to a chemical test first, how will she ever enjoy and finish her meal? Similarly, a man goes to a barber shop to get a shave and sits on the chair while the barber moves the sharp edge of his knife over his throat. Now, if the man doubts the barber and fears that he will murder him, he will not be able to sit still for the barber to be able to shave him. Hence, Shree Krishna says in this verse that for the doubting person, there is no happiness either in this world or in the next.

योगसंन्यस्तकर्माणं ज्ञानसञ्छिन्नसंशयम् ।
आत्मवन्तं न कर्माणि निबध्नन्ति धनञ्जय ।।41।।

yoga-sannyasta-karmāṇaṁ jñāna-sañchhinna-sanśhayam
ātmavantaṁ na karmāṇi nibadhnanti dhanañjaya

yoga-sannyasta-karmāṇam—those who renounce ritualistic karm, dedicating their body, mind, and soul to God; *jñāna*—by knowledge; *sañchhinna*—dispelled; *sanśhayam*—doubts; *ātma-vantam*—situated in knowledge of the self; *na*—not; *karmāṇi*—actions; *nibadhnanti*—bind; *dhanañjaya*—Arjun, conqueror of wealth.

O Arjun, actions do not bind those who have renounced karm in the fire of Yog, whose doubts have been dispelled by knowledge, and who are situated in knowledge of the self.

'Karm' is action as per prescribed rituals and social duties; 'sanyas' means 'to renounce' while 'yog' means 'to unite with God'. Here, Shree Krishna has used the word *yogasanyasta karmāṇaṁ* to refer to 'those who renounce all ritualistic karm and dedicate their body, mind, and soul to God'. Such persons do their every action as a service to God. Shree Krishna says that their work performed in devotion do not bind them.

Only those actions which are performed to fulfil one's self-interest bind one in karma. When work is done only for the pleasure of God, such action becomes free from all karmic reaction. This is like multiplying with 0 (zero). If we multiply zero with ten, the result will be zero; if we multiply zero with a thousand, the result will remain zero; and if we multiply zero with one lakh, the result will still be zero. Similarly, the works that enlightened souls perform in the world do not bind them because they are offered to God in the fire of Yog, i.e., they are done for the pleasure of God. Thus, although doing all kinds of works, the saints remain unfettered from the bonds of karma.

तस्मादज्ञानसम्भूतं हृत्स्थं ज्ञानासिनात्मनः ।
छित्त्वैनं संशयं योगमातिष्ठोत्तिष्ठ भारत ।।42।।

tasmād ajñāna-sambhūtaṁ hṛit-sthaṁ jñānāsinātmanaḥ
chhittvainaṁ sanśhayaṁ yogam ātiṣhṭhottiṣhṭha bhārata

tasmāt—therefore; *ajñāna-sambhūtam*—born of ignorance; *hṛit-stham*—situated in the heart; *jñāna*—of knowledge; *asinā*—with the sword; *ātmanaḥ*—of the self; *chhittvā*—cut asunder; *enam*—this; *sanśhayam*—doubt; *yogam*—in karm yog; *ātiṣhṭha*—take shelter; *uttiṣhṭha*—arise; *bhārata*—Arjun, descendant of Bharat.

Therefore, with the sword of knowledge, cut asunder the doubts that have arisen in your heart. O scion of Bharat, establish yourself in karm yog. Arise, stand up, and take action!

The use of the word heart does not imply the physical machine housed in the chest that pumps blood in the body. The Vedas state that one's physical brain resides in the head, but the subtle mind resides in the region of the heart. This is the reason why in love and hatred, one experiences pain in the heart. In this sense, the heart is the source of compassion, love, sympathy, and all the good emotions. So, when

Shree Krishna mentions doubts that have arisen in the heart, He means doubts that have arisen in the mind, which is the subtle machine that resides in the region of the heart.

In the role of being the Spiritual Master of Arjun, the Lord has imparted to His disciple the knowledge of how to gain insightful wisdom from the practice of karm yog. He now advises Arjun to utilise both wisdom and faith to cleave out the doubts from his mind. Then, He gives the call to action and asks Arjun to rise up and do his duty in the spirit of karm yog. The dual instructions to both refrain from action and to engage in action still create confusion in Arjun's mind, which he reveals at the beginning of the next chapter.

CHAPTER 5

Karm Sanyas Yog

The Yog of Renunciation

This chapter compares the path of karm sanyas (renunciation of actions) with the path of karm yog (work in devotion). Shree Krishna explains that we can choose either of them because they both lead to the same goal. However, renunciation of actions cannot be done perfectly until the mind is sufficiently pure, and purification of the mind is achieved by work in devotion. Hence, karm yog is the appropriate option for the majority of humankind. Karm yogis do their worldly duties with purified intellect, abandoning attachment to the fruits of their works and dedicating them to God. In this way, they remain unaffected by sin just as a lotus leaf remains untouched by the water on which it floats.

With the light of knowledge, they realise the body to be like a city of nine gates within which the soul resides. Thus, they neither consider themselves as the doers nor the enjoyers of their actions. They are endowed with equality of vision and see a Brahmin, a cow, an elephant, a dog, and a dog-eater equally. Such truly learned people develop the flawless qualities of God and become seated in the Absolute Truth. Worldly people strive to relish the pleasures that arise from the sense objects without realising that they are verily the source of misery. But karm yogis do not delight in them; instead, they relish the bliss of God within.

The chapter then goes on to describe the path of renunciation. The karm sanyasis perform austerities to control their senses, mind, and intellect. They shut out all thoughts of external enjoyment and become free from desire, greed, and anger. Then, consummating their austerities with devotion to God, they attain abiding peace.

अर्जुन उवाच ।
संन्यासं कर्मणां कृष्ण पुनर्योगं च शंससि ।
यच्छ्रेय एतयोरेकं तन्मे ब्रूहि सुनिश्चितम् ।।1।।

arjuna uvācha
sanyāsaṁ karmaṇāṁ kṛiṣhṇa punar yogaṁ cha śhansasi
yach chhreya etayor ekaṁ tan me brūhi su-niśhchitam

arjunaḥ uvācha—Arjun said; *sanyāsam*—renunciation; *karmaṇām*—of actions; *kṛiṣhṇa*—Shree Krishna; *punaḥ*—again; *yogam*—about karm yog; *cha*—also; *śhansasi*—you praise; *yat*—which; *śhreyaḥ*—more beneficial; *etayoḥ*—of the two; *ekam*—one; *tat*—that; *me*—unto me; *brūhi*—please tell; *su-niśhchitam*—conclusively.

Arjun said: O Shree Krishna, You praised karm sanyas (the path of renunciation of actions), and You also advised to do karm yog (work with devotion). Please tell me decisively which of the two is more beneficial?

This is the fifth of Arjun's sixteen questions. Shree Krishna praised both the concepts of renunciation of works and work with devotion. Arjun is confused by these apparently equivocal instructions and wishes to understand which of the two is more auspicious for him. Let us review the context of the question.

The first chapter described the nature of Arjun's grief and created the context for Shree Krishna to begin to relate spiritual knowledge to him. In the second chapter, Shree Krishna revealed to Arjun the science of the self and explained that since the soul is immortal, nobody would die in the war and it was foolish to lament. He then reminded Arjun that his karm (social duty) as a warrior was to fight the war on the side of righteousness. But, since karm binds one to the fruits of actions, Shree Krishna encouraged Arjun to dedicate the fruits of his works to God. His actions would then become karm yog or 'united with God through work'.

In the third chapter, the Supreme Lord explained that performing one's duties is necessary because it helps to purify the mind. But He also said that a person who has already developed purity of mind is not obliged to perform any social duty (verse 3.17).

In the fourth chapter, the Lord explained the various kinds of sacrifices (works that can be done for the pleasure of God). He concluded by saying that sacrifice performed in knowledge is better than mechanical ritualistic sacrifice. He also said that all sacrifice ends in the knowledge of one's relationship with God. Finally, in verse 4.41, He introduced the principle of karm sanyas, in which ritualistic duties and social obligations are renounced and one engages in devotional service with the body, mind, and soul.

These instructions perplexed Arjun. He thought that karm sanyas (renunciation of work) and karm yog (work in devotion) are opposite in nature, and it is not possible to perform both simultaneously. Hence, he raises doubts before Shree Krishna.

श्रीभगवानुवाच ।
संन्यासः कर्मयोगश्च निःश्रेयसकरावुभौ ।
तयोस्तु कर्मसंन्यासात्कर्मयोगो विशिष्यते ॥2॥

śhrī bhagavān uvācha
sanyāsaḥ karma-yogaśh cha niḥśhreyasa-karāvubhau
tayos tu karma-sanyāsāt karma-yogo viśhiṣhyate

śhrī-bhagavān uvācha—the Supreme Lord said; *sanyāsaḥ*—renunciation; *karma-yogaḥ*—working in devotion; *cha*—and; *niḥśhreyasa-karau*—lead to the supreme goal; *ubhau*—both; *tayoḥ*—of the two; *tu*—but; *karma-sanyāsāt*—renunciation of actions; *karma-yogaḥ*—working in devotion; *viśhiṣhyate*—is superior.

The Supreme Lord said: Both the path of karm sanyas (renunciation of actions) and karm yog (working in devotion) lead to the supreme goal. But karm yog is superior to karm sanyas.

In this verse, Shree Krishna compares karm sanyas and karm yog. It is a very deep verse; so, let's understand it one word at a time.

A karm yogi is one who does both—spiritual and social duties. Social duties are done with the body while the mind is attached to God. Jagadguru Kripaluji Maharaj states:

sochu mana yaha karm mama saba lakhata hari guru pyāre

(*Sadhana Bhakti Tattva*)

'Dear one! Think always that all your actions are being observed by God and guru.' This is the sadhana of karm yog by which we gradually elevate ourselves from bodily consciousness to spiritual consciousness.

Karm sanyas is for elevated souls who have already risen beyond the bodily platform. A karm sanyasi is one who discards social duties due to complete absorption in God and engages entirely in the performance of spiritual duties (devotional service to God). This sentiment of karm sanyas was beautifully expressed by Lakshman, when Lord Ram asked him to fulfil his worldly duties:

more sabai eka tumha swāmī, dīnabandhu ura antarayāmī

(Ramayan)

Lakshman said to Ram, 'You are my Master, Father, Mother, Friend, and Everything. I will only fulfil my duty towards You with all my might. So please do not tell me about any of my material duties.'

Those who practise karm sanyas do not consider themselves to be the body, and as a result, they do not feel obligated to discharge their physical duties. Such karm sanyasis dedicate their full time and energy to spirituality, while karm yogis are required to split their time between worldly and spiritual duties. The karm sanyasis can thus move much faster towards God while the karm yogis are encumbered with social duties.

However, in this verse, Shree Krishna extols karm yog beyond karm sanyas and recommends it to Arjun as the preferred path. This is because karm sanyasis are exposed to a danger. If, having renounced their duties they cannot absorb their mind in God, they are left neither here nor there. In India, there are tens of thousands of such sadhus, who felt they were detached and renounced the world, but their mind was not yet attached to God. Consequently, they could not experience the divine bliss of the spiritual path. And so, although wearing the saffron clothes of mendicants, they indulge in grossly sinful activities such as smoking opium. Only the ignorant mistake their sloth as detachment from the world.

On the other hand, karm yogis do both—their worldly duties and spiritual practice. So, if their mind turns away from spirituality, at least they have their work to fall back upon. Karm yog is thus the safer path for most people, while karm sanyas is only to be pursued under the expert guidance of a guru.

ज्ञेयः स नित्यसंन्यासी यो न द्वेष्टि न काङ्क्षति ।
निर्द्वन्द्वो हि महाबाहो सुखं बन्धात्प्रमुच्यते ।।3।।

jñeyaḥ sa nitya-sanyāsī yo na dveṣhṭi na kāṅkṣhati
nirdvandvo hi mahā-bāho sukhaṁ bandhāt pramuchyate

jñeyaḥ—should be considered; *saḥ*—that person; *nitya*—always; *sanyāsī*—practising renunciation; *yaḥ*—who; *na*—never; *dveṣhṭi*—hate; *na*—nor; *kāṅkṣhati*—desire; *nirdvandvaḥ*—free from all dualities; *hi*—certainly; *mahā-bāho*—mighty-armed one; *sukham*—easily; *bandhāt*—from bondage; *pramuchyate*—is liberated.

The karm yogis, who neither desire nor hate anything, should be considered always renounced. Free from all dualities, they are easily liberated from the bonds of material energy.

Karm yogis continue to discharge their worldly duties while internally practising detachment. They accept both positive and negative outcomes with equanimity, as the grace of God. The Lord has designed this world so beautifully that it makes us experience both happiness and distress for our gradual elevation. If we continue to lead our regular lives and tolerate whatever comes our way while happily doing our duty, the world naturally pushes us towards gradual spiritual elevation.

There is a sweet story that illustrates this concept:

There was once a piece of wood. It went to a sculptor and said, 'Can you please make me beautiful?'

The sculptor said, 'I am ready to do that. But are you ready for it?'

The wood replied, 'Yes, I am also ready.'

The sculptor took out his tools and began hammering and chiselling. The wood screamed, 'What are you doing? Please stop! This is so painful.'

The sculptor replied wisely, 'If you wish to become beautiful, you will have to bear the pain.'

'All right,' said the wood, 'Go ahead and do it. But please be gentle and considerate.'

The sculptor continued his work again. The wood kept screaming, 'Enough for today; I can't bear it any further. Please resume tomorrow.'

The sculptor continued undeterred in his task, and in a few days, the wood was transformed into a beautiful deity, fit to sit on the altar of the temple.

In the same way, our hearts are rough and unfinished because of endless lifetimes of attachment in the world. If we wish to become internally beautiful, we must be willing to tolerate pain and let the world do its job of purifying us. So karm yogis work with devotion, are equipoised in the results, and practice attaching their mind to God.

साङ्ख्ययोगौ पृथग्बालाः प्रवदन्ति न पण्डिताः ।
एकमप्यास्थितः सम्यगुभयोर्विन्दते फलम् ।।4।।

sānkhya-yogau pṛithag bālāḥ pravadanti na paṇḍitāḥ
ekamapyāsthitaḥ samyag ubhayor vindate phalam

sānkhya—renunciation of actions; *yogau*—karm yog; *pṛithak*—different; *bālāḥ*—the ignorant; *pravadanti*—say; *na*—never; *paṇḍitāḥ*—the learned; *ekam*—in one; *api*—even; *āsthitaḥ*—being situated; *samyak*—completely; *ubhayoḥ*—of both; *vindate*—achieve; *phalam*—the result.

Only the ignorant speak of *sānkhya* (renunciation of actions or karm sanyas) and karm yog (work in devotion) as different. Those who are truly learned say that by applying ourselves to any one of these paths, we can achieve the results of both.

Here, Shree Krishna uses the word *sānkhya* to refer to karm sanyas or the renunciation of actions with the cultivation of knowledge. It is important to understand here that renunciation is of two kinds: *phalgu vairāgya* and *yukt vairāgya*. *Phalgu vairāgya* is where people look upon the world as cumbersome and renounce it with the desire of getting rid of responsibilities and hardships. Such *phalgu vairāgya* is an escapist attitude and is unstable. The renunciation of such persons is motivated by the desire to run away from difficulties. When such persons encounter difficulties on the spiritual path, they become detached from there as well and desire to run back to worldly life. *Yukt vairāgya* is where people see the whole world as the energy of God. They do not see what they possess as belonging to them and do not wish to enjoy it for themselves. Instead, they are motivated by the desire to serve God with whatever He has given to them. *Yukt vairāgya* is stable and undeterred by difficulties.

The karm yogis, while conducting their daily duties externally, develop the sentiment of *yukt vairāgya* or stable renunciation. They see themselves as the servants and God as the enjoyer, and hence, they become fixed in the consciousness of doing everything for His pleasure. In this manner, their internal state becomes the same as that of the karm sanyasis who are completely absorbed in divine consciousness. Externally, they may appear to be worldly people, but internally, they are no less than sanyasis.

The Puranas and *Itihās* relate the examples of great kings in Indian history, who, though externally discharging their kingly duties with diligence and living in royal opulence, were mentally completely absorbed in God-consciousness. Prahalad, Dhruv, Ambarish, Prithu, Vibheeshan, Yudhishthir, and others were all such exemplary karm yogis. The Shreemad Bhagavatam states:

gṛihītvāpīndriyair arthān yo na dveṣhṭi na hṛiṣhyati
viṣhṇor māyām idaṁ paśhyan sa vai bhāgavatottamaḥ

(11.2.48)

'The person who accepts the objects of the senses—neither yearning for them nor running away from them—in the divine consciousness that everything is an energy of God and is to be used in His service, is the highest devotee.' Thus, the truly learned see no difference between karm yog and karm sanyas. By following one of them, the results of both are achieved.

यत्साङ्ख्यैः प्राप्यते स्थानं तद्योगैरपि गम्यते ।
एकं साङ्ख्यं च योगं च यः पश्यति स पश्यति ।।5।।

yat sānkhyaiḥ prāpyate sthānaṁ tad yogair api gamyate
ekaṁ sānkhyaṁ cha yogaṁ cha yaḥ paśhyati sa paśhyati

yat—what; *sānkhyaiḥ*—by means of karm sanyas; *prāpyate*—is attained; *sthānam*—place; *tat*—that; *yogaiḥ*—by working in devotion; *api*—also; *gamyate*—is attained; *ekam*—one; *sānkhyam*—renunciation of actions; *cha*—and; *yogam*—karm yog; *cha*—and; *yaḥ*—who; *paśhyati*—sees; *saḥ*—that person; *paśhyati*—actually sees.

The supreme state that is attained by means of karm sanyas is also attained by working in devotion. Hence, those who see karm sanyas and karm yog to be identical, truly see things as they are.

In spiritual practice, the intention of the mind is what matters, not the external activities. One may be living in the holy land of Vrindavan, but if the mind contemplates on eating rasgullas in Kolkata, one will be deemed to be living in Kolkata. Conversely, if a person lives amidst the hubbub of Kolkata and keeps the mind absorbed in the divine land of Vrindavan, he will get the benefit of residing there. All the Vedic scriptures state that our level of consciousness is determined by the state of our mind:

mana eva manuṣhyāṇāṁ kāraṇaṁ bandha mokṣhayoḥ

(*Pañchadaśhī*)

'The mind is the cause of bondage, and the mind is the cause of liberation.' Jagadguru Shree Kripaluji Maharaj states the same principle:

bandhan aur mokṣha kā, kāraṇ manahi bakhān
yāte kauniu bhakti karu, karu mana te haridhyān

(*Bhakti Śhatak* verse 19)

'Bondage and liberation depend upon the state of the mind. Whatever form of devotion you choose to do, keep the mind engaged in meditation upon God.'

Those who do not possess this spiritual vision see the external distinction between a karm sanyasi and a karm yogi and declare the karm sanyasi to be superior because of external renunciation. But those who are learned see that both the karm sanyasi and the karm yogi have absorbed their minds in God, and they both are identical in their internal consciousness.

संन्यासस्तु महाबाहो दुःखमाप्तुमयोगतः ।
योगयुक्तो मुनिर्ब्रह्म नचिरेणाधिगच्छति ।।6।।

sanyāsas tu mahā-bāho duḥkham āptum ayogataḥ
yoga-yukto munir brahma na chireṇādhigachchhati

sanyāsaḥ—renunciation; *tu*—but; *mahā-bāho*—mighty-armed one; *duḥkham*—distress; *āptum*—attains; *ayogataḥ*—without karm yog; *yoga-yuktaḥ*—one who is adept in karm yog; *muniḥ*—a sage; *brahma*—Brahman; *na chireṇa*—quickly; *adhigachchhati*—goes.

Perfect renunciation (karm sanyas) is difficult to attain without performing work in devotion (karm yog), O mighty-armed Arjun, but the sage who is adept in karm yog quickly attains the Supreme.

Living in a cave in the Himalayas, a yogi may feel that he has renounced the world, but the test of that renunciation comes when he returns to the city. For instance, one sadhu practised austerities for twelve years in the mountains of Garhwal. He came down to Haridwar to participate in the holy fair called Kumbh Mela. In the hustle and bustle of the fair, someone accidentally placed his shoe on the sadhu's bare foot. The sadhu was infuriated, and screamed, 'Are you blind? Can you not see where you are going?' Later he repented for permitting anger to overcome him and lamented, 'Twelve years of austerities in the mountains got washed away by living one day in the city!' The world is the arena where our renunciation gets tested.

In this verse, Shree Krishna says that while performing one's duties in the world, a person should slowly learn to rise above anger, greed, and desire. Instead, if one first gives up duties, it is very difficult to purify the mind; and without a pure mind, true detachment remains a distant dream.

We are all propelled to work by our nature. Arjun was a warrior, and if he had artificially renounced his duty to retire to the forest, his nature would make him work there as well. He would probably gather a few tribesmen and declare himself their king. On the other hand, it would be more fruitful to use his natural inclinations and talents in the service of God. Keeping this in mind, the Lord instructs him, 'Continue to fight, but make one change. At first, you came to this battleground on the presumption of saving a kingdom. Now, simply dedicate your service unselfishly to God. In this way, you will naturally purify the mind and achieve true renunciation from within.'

A tender and unripe fruit clings fast to the tree that bears and nourishes it. But the same fruit, when fully ripe, severs its connection from its sustainer. Similarly, from the material existence, the karm yogi gets the experience that matures into wisdom. Just as sound sleep is only possible for those who have worked hard, deep meditation comes to those who have purified their mind through karm yog.

योगयुक्तो विशुद्धात्मा विजितात्मा जितेन्द्रियः ।
सर्वभूतात्मभूतात्मा कुर्वन्नपि न लिप्यते ।।7।।

yoga-yukto viśhuddhātmā vijitātmā jitendriyaḥ
sarva-bhūtātma-bhūtātmā kurvann api na lipyate

yoga-yuktaḥ—united in consciousness with God; *viśhuddha-ātmā*—one with purified intellect; *vijita-ātmā*—one who has conquered the mind; *jita-indriyaḥ*—having conquered the senses; *sarva-bhūta-ātma-bhūta-ātmā*—one who sees the Soul of all souls in every living being; *kurvan*—performing; *api*—although; *na*—never; *lipyate*—entangled.

The karm yogis, who are of purified intellect and who control the mind and senses, see the Soul of all souls in every living being. Though performing all kinds of actions, they are never entangled.

The word atma has been used in multiple ways in Vedic literature: for God, for the soul, for the mind, and for the intellect. This verse typifies all these uses. Shree Krishna describes the karm yogi who is *yog yukt* (united in consciousness with God). He says that such a noble soul is: 1) *viśhuddhātmā* (of purified intellect), 2) *vijitātmā* (who has conquered the mind), and 3) *jitendriya* (one who has controlled the senses).

Such karm yogis, with purified intellect, see God situated in all living beings and behave respectfully towards everyone without attachment. Since their actions are not motivated by the desire for self-enjoyment, their knowledge is progressively clarified. As their desires are eliminated, the senses, mind, and intellect that were being propelled for sense pleasures come under control. These instruments are now available for service of the Lord. Devotional service leads to realised knowledge from within. In this way, karm yog naturally brings about these successive stages of enlightenment, and hence, is no different from karm sanyas.

नैव किञ्चित्करोमीति युक्तो मन्येत तत्त्ववित् ।
पश्यञ्शृण्वन्स्पृशञ्जिघ्रन्नश्नन्गच्छन्स्वपञ्श्वसन् ।।8।।

प्रलपन्विसृजन्गृह्णन्नुन्मिषन्निमिषन्नपि ।
इन्द्रियाणीन्द्रियार्थेषु वर्तन्त इति धारयन् ।।9।।

naiva kiñchit karomīti yukto manyeta tattva-vit
paśhyañ śhṛiṇvan spṛiśhañjighrann aśhnangachchhan svapañśhvasan

pralapan visṛijan gṛihṇann unmiṣhan nimiṣhann api
indriyāṇīndriyārtheṣhu vartanta iti dhārayan

na—not; *eva*—certainly; *kiñchit*—anything; *karomi*—I do; *iti*—thus; *yuktaḥ*—steadfast in karm yog; *manyeta*—thinks; *tattva-vit*—one who knows the truth; *paśhyan*—seeing; *śhṛiṇvan*—hearing; *spṛiśhan*—touching; *jighran*—smelling; *aśhnan*—eating; *gachchhan*—moving; *svapan*—sleeping; *śhvasan*—breathing; *pralapan*—talking; *visṛijan*—giving up; *gṛihṇan*—accepting; *unmiṣhan*—opening (the eyes); *nimiṣhan*—closing (the eyes); *api*—although; *indriyāṇi*—the senses; *indriya-artheṣhu*—in sense-objects; *vartante*—moving; *iti*—thus; *dhārayan*—convinced.

Those steadfast in karm yog always think 'I am not the doer' even while engaged in seeing, hearing, touching, smelling, moving, sleeping, breathing, speaking, excreting, grasping, and opening or closing the eyes. With the light of divine knowledge, they see that it is only the material senses that are moving amongst their objects.

Whenever we accomplish anything substantial, we are overcome with the pride that we have done something great. The pride of being the doer of one's actions is a stumbling block to rising beyond material consciousness. However, the God-conscious karm yogis overcome this obstacle with ease. With purified intellect, they see themselves as separate from the body, and consequently, do not attribute their physical actions to themselves. The body is made from the material energy of God. Keeping this knowledge in mind, they attribute all their works as done by the power of God. Since they have surrendered to the will of God, they depend upon Him to inspire their mind and intellect in accordance with His divine will. So, they remain situated in the understanding that God is the doer of everything.

Along these lines, Sage Vasishth advised Lord Ram:

kartā bahirkartāntarloke vihara rāghava (*Yog Vāsiṣhṭh*)

'O Ram, externally engage in actions diligently, but internally practice to see yourself as the non-doer and God as the prime mover of all your activities.' In this divine consciousness, the karm yogis see themselves as mere instruments in the hands of God. *Shree Krishna explains in the following verse the consequences of work done in this consciousness.*

ब्रह्मण्याधाय कर्माणि सङ्गं त्यक्त्वा करोति यः ।
लिप्यते न स पापेन पद्मपत्रमिवाम्भसा ।।10।।

brahmaṇyādhāya karmāṇi saṅgaṁ tyaktvā karoti yaḥ
lipyate na sa pāpena padma-patram ivāmbhasā

brahmaṇi—to God; *ādhāya*—dedicating; *karmāṇi*—all actions; *saṅgam*—attachment; *tyaktvā*—abandoning; *karoti*—performs; *yaḥ*—who; *lipyate*—is affected; *na*—never; *saḥ*—that person; *pāpena*—by sin; *padma-patram*—a lotus leaf; *iva*—like; *ambhasā*—by water.

Those who dedicate their actions to God, abandoning all attachment, remain untouched by sin, just as a lotus leaf is untouched by water.

Both Hindu and Buddhist scriptures abound with analogies of the lotus flower. The word is used as a respectful appellation while describing various parts of God's divine body. Hence *charaṇ-kamal* means 'lotus-like feet', *kamalekṣhaṇa* means 'lotus-like eyes', *kar-kamal* means 'lotus-like hands', and so on.

Another word for the lotus flower is *paṅkaj* which means 'born from mud'. The lotus flower grows from the mud found at the bottom of the lake, yet it rises above the water and blossoms towards the sun. Thus, the lotus flower is often used in Sanskrit literature as an example of something that is born amidst dirt and rises above it while retaining its beautiful purity.

Further, the lotus plant has large leaves that float atop the water surface of the lake. Lotus leaves are used in Indian villages for plates as they are waterproof; liquid poured on them does not soak through but runs off. The beauty of the lotus leaf is that although the lotus owes its birth, growth, and sustenance to the water, the leaf does not permit itself to be soaked. Water poured on the lotus leaf runs off the side due to the small hair growing on its surface.

With the help of the beautiful analogy of the lotus leaf, Shree Krishna says that just as it floats atop the surface of the lake but does not allow itself to get soaked by the water, similarly, karm yogis remain untouched by sin, although performing all kinds of work because they perform them in divine consciousness.

कायेन मनसा बुद्ध्या केवलैरिन्द्रियैरपि ।
योगिनः कर्म कुर्वन्ति सङ्गं त्यक्त्वात्मशुद्धये ।।11।।

kāyena manasā buddhyā kevalair indriyair api
yoginaḥ karma kurvanti saṅgaṁ tyaktvātma-śhuddhaye

kāyena—with the body; *manasā*—with the mind; *buddhyā*—with the intellect; *kevalaiḥ*—only; *indriyaiḥ*—with the senses; *api*—even; *yoginaḥ*—the yogis; *karma*—actions; *kurvanti*—perform; *saṅgam*—attachment; *tyaktvā*—giving up; *ātma*—of the self; *śhuddhaye*—for the purification.

The yogis, while giving up attachment, perform actions with their body, senses, mind, and intellect only for the purpose of self-purification.

The yogis understand that pursuing material desires in the pursuit of happiness is as futile as chasing a mirage in the desert. Realising this, they renounce selfish desires and perform all their actions for the pleasure of God, who alone is the *bhoktāraṁ yajña tapasām* (Supreme enjoyer of all activities). However, in this verse, Shree Krishna brings a new twist to *samarpaṇ* (dedication of all work to God). He says the enlightened yogis perform their works for the purpose of purification. How then do the works get dedicated to God?

The fact is that God needs nothing from us. He is the Supreme Lord of everything that exists and is perfect and complete in Himself. What can a tiny soul offer to the Almighty God that He does not already possess? Hence, it is customary while making an offering to God to say: *tvadiyaṁ vastu govinda tubhyameva samarpitaṁ* 'O God, I am offering Your item back to You.' Expressing a similar sentiment, Saint Yamunacharya states:

mama nātha yad asti yo 'smyahaṁ
sakalam taddhī tavaiva mādhava
niyata-svam iti prabuddha-dhāir atha vā
kiṁ nu samarpayāmi te (*Śhrī Stotra Ratna*, 50)

'O Lord Vishnu, husband of the Goddess of Fortune, when I was in ignorance, I thought I would give You many things. But now when I have gained knowledge, I realise that everything I own is already Yours. What then can I offer to You?'

However, there is one activity that is in our hands and not in God's hands; it is the purification of our own heart (mind and intellect). When we purify our heart and engage it in devotion to God, it pleases Him more than anything else. Realising this, the great yogis make purification of their heart as the foremost goal, not out of selfishness, rather, for the pleasure of God.

Thus, the yogis understand that the biggest gift they can offer to God is the purity of their own heart, and they strive hard to achieve it. In the Ramayan, there is a beautiful illustration of this principle.

Lord Ram found Sugreev to be somewhat frightened before the battle of Lanka, so He consoled him in the following manner:

piśhāchān dānavān yakṣhān pṛithivyāṁ chaiva rākṣhasān
aṅgugreṇa tānhanyā michchhan harī gaṇeśhvaraḥ

(Valmiki Ramayan)

Lord Ram said, 'If I, the Supreme Lord, merely bend the little finger of My left hand, what to speak of Ravan and Kumbhakarn, all the demons in the world will die.'

Sugreev responded, 'If that is the case, my Lord, then in order to kill Ravan, what is the need for collecting this army?'

The Lord replied, 'That is merely to give you all the opportunity to engage in devotional service for your own purification. However, do not assume that I need your help in annihilating these demons.'

Our only permanent asset is the purity that we achieve. It goes with us into the next life while all material assets get left behind. Hence in the final analysis, the success and failure of our life is determined by the extent to which we manage to achieve purity of heart. With this perspective, elevated yogis welcome adverse circumstances because they use them as opportunities to purify the heart. Saint Kabir states:

nindak niyare rākhiye āngan kuṭi chhabāya
nita sābun pānī binā nirmala kare subhāya

'If you are desirous of quickly cleansing your heart, cultivate the company of a critic. When you tolerate his acrimonious words, your heart will be cleansed without water and soap.' Thus, when purification of the heart is made the prime motive of actions, adversarial circumstances are welcomed as God-sent opportunities for further progress, and one remains equanimous in both success and failure. As we work for the pleasure of God, the heart gets purified; and as the heart gets purified, we naturally offer the results of all our actions to the Supreme Lord.

युक्तः कर्मफलं त्यक्त्वा शान्तिमाप्नोति नैष्ठिकीम् ।
अयुक्तः कामकारेण फले सक्तो निबध्यते ।।12।।

yuktaḥ karma-phalaṁ tyaktvā śhāntim āpnoti naiṣhṭhikīm
ayuktaḥ kāma-kāreṇa phale sakto nibadhyate

yuktaḥ—one who is united in consciousness with God; *karma-phalam*—the results of all activities; *tyaktvā*—giving up; *śhāntim*—

peace; *āpnoti*—attains; *naiṣhṭhikīm*—everlasting; *ayuktaḥ*—one who is not united with God in consciousness; *kāma-kāreṇa*—impelled by desires; *phale*—in the result; *saktaḥ*—attached; *nibadhyate*—becomes entangled.

Offering the results of all activities to God, karm yogis attain everlasting peace. Whereas those who, being impelled by their desires, work with a selfish motive become entangled because they are attached to the fruits of their actions.

How is it possible that by performing the same actions some people are bound to material existence and others are released from material bondage? Shree Krishna gives the answer in this verse. Those who are unattached and unmotivated by material rewards are never bound by karma. But those craving rewards and obsessed with the desire to enjoy material pleasures become entangled in the reactions of work.

The word *yukt* means 'united in consciousness with God'. It can also mean 'not wanting any reward other than purification of the heart'. Persons who are *yukt* relinquish their desire for the rewards of their actions, and instead, engage in works for the purpose of self-purification. Therefore, they soon attain divine consciousness and eternal beatitude.

On the other hand, *ayukt* means 'not united with God in consciousness'. It can also denote 'desiring mundane rewards not beneficial to the soul'. Such persons, incited by cravings, lustfully desire the rewards of their actions. The reactions of work performed in this consciousness bind these *ayukt* persons to the samsara or the cycle of life and death.

सर्वकर्माणि मनसा संन्यस्यास्ते सुखं वशी ।
नवद्वारे पुरे देही नैव कुर्वन्न कारयन् ।।13।।

sarva-karmāṇi manasā sannyasyāste sukhaṁ vaśhī
nava-dvāre pure dehī naiva kurvan na kārayan

sarva—all; *karmāṇi*—activities; *manasā*—by the mind; *sannyasya*—having renounced; *āste*—remains; *sukham*—happily;

vaśhī—the self-controlled; *nava-dvāre*—of nine gates; *pure*—in the city; *dehī*—the embodied being; *na*—never; *eva*—certainly; *kurvan*—doing anything; *na*—not; *kārayan*—causing to be done.

The embodied beings who are self-controlled and detached reside happily in the city of nine gates free from thoughts that they are the doers or the cause of anything.

Shree Krishna compares the body with its openings to a city of nine gates. The soul is like the king of the city whose administration is carried out by the ministry of the ego, intellect, mind, senses, and life energy. The reign over the body continues until time, in the form of death, snatches away the corporeal frame. However, even while the reign continues, the enlightened yogis neither see themselves as the body nor do they consider themselves as the lord of the body. Rather, they hold the body and all activities performed by it as belonging to God. Renouncing all actions through the mind, such enlightened souls remain happily situated in their body. This is also called *sākṣhī bhav* or the attitude of being the detached observer of all that is happening around.

The analogy in this verse is also given in the *Śhwetāśhvatar Upanishad*:

navadwāre pure dehī hanso lelāyate bahiḥ
vaśhī sarvasya lokasya sthāvarasya charasya cha (3.18)

'The body consists of nine gates—two ears, one mouth, two nostrils, two eyes, anus, and genitals. In material consciousness, the soul residing within the body identifies itself with this city of nine gates. Within this body also sits the Supreme Lord who is the Controller of all living beings in the world. When the soul establishes its connection with the Lord, it becomes free like Him even while residing in the body.'

In this verse, Shree Krishna declared that the embodied soul is neither the doer nor the cause of anything. Then the question arises whether God is the actual cause of actions in the world. This is answered in the next verse.

न कर्तृत्वं न कर्माणि लोकस्य सृजति प्रभुः ।
न कर्मफलसंयोगं स्वभावस्तु प्रवर्तते ।।14।।

na kartṛitvaṁ na karmāṇi lokasya sṛijati prabhuḥ
na karma-phala-saṅyogaṁ svabhāvas tu pravartate

na—neither; *kartṛitvam*—sense of doership; *na*—nor; *karmāṇi*—actions; *lokasya*—of the people; *sṛijati*—creates; *prabhuḥ*—God; *na*—nor; *karma-phala*—fruits of actions; *sanyogam*—connection; *svabhāvaḥ*—one's nature; *tu*—but; *pravartate*—is enacted.

Neither the sense of doership nor the nature of actions comes from God; nor does He create the fruits of actions. All this is enacted by the modes of material nature (gunas).

In this verse, the word *Prabhu* has been used for God to indicate that He is the Lord of the world. He is also omnipotent and controls the entire universe. Although He conducts the activities of the universe, He remains the non-doer. He is neither the director of our actions, nor does He decree whether we will perform a particular virtuous or evil deed. Had He been our director, there would be no need for elaborate instructions on good and bad actions. All the scriptures would have ended in three short sentences: 'O souls, I am the Director of all your works. So, you do not need to understand what good or bad action is. I will make you do as I wish.'

Similarly, God is not responsible for our getting stuck with the sense of doership. If He had deliberately created the pride of doing in us, then we could have blamed Him for our misdoings. But the fact is that the soul brings this pride onto itself out of ignorance. If the soul chooses to do away with the ignorance, then God helps dispel it with His grace.

Thus, renunciation of the sense of doership is the responsibility of the soul. The body is constituted of the three modes of material nature, and all actions are performed by these modes. But out of ignorance, the soul identifies with the body and becomes implicated as the doer of actions, which are in fact done by material nature (verse 3.27).

नादत्ते कस्यचित्पापं न चैव सुकृतं विभुः ।
अज्ञानेनावृतं ज्ञानं तेन मुह्यन्ति जन्तवः ।।15।।

nādatte kasyachit pāpaṁ na chaiva sukṛitaṁ vibhuḥ
ajñānenāvṛitaṁ jñānaṁ tena muhyanti jantavaḥ

na—not; *ādatte*—accepts; *kasyachit*—anyone's; *pāpam*—sin; *na*—not; *cha*—and; *eva*—certainly; *su-kṛitam*—virtuous deeds; *vibhuḥ*—the omnipresent God; *ajñānena*—by ignorance; *āvṛitam*—covered; *jñānam*—knowledge; *tena*—by that; *muhyanti*—are deluded; *jantavaḥ*—the living entities.

The omnipresent God does not involve Himself in the sinful or virtuous deeds of anyone. The living entities are deluded because their inner knowledge is covered by ignorance.

God is not responsible either for anyone's virtuous deeds or sinful actions. God's work in this regard is threefold: 1) He provides the soul with the power to act. 2) Once we have performed actions with the power supplied to us, He notes our actions. 3) He gives us the results of our actions (karmas).

The individual soul has the freedom to perform good or bad actions by the exercise of its own free will. That free will is the basis of the play of creation, and it accounts for the varieties of consciousness among the souls in existence. God's work is like that of an umpire in a cricket match. He keeps giving the results, 'Four runs!' 'Six runs!' 'He's out!' The umpire cannot be blamed for the decision, for it was based upon the way the player performed.

One may ask why God granted free will to the soul. It is because the soul is a tiny part of God and it possesses His qualities to a minuscule extent. God is *abhijña swarāṭ* (supremely independent), and so, the soul also possesses a tiny amount of independence to utilise its senses, mind, and intellect in the manner it wishes.

Also, there can be no love without free will. A machine cannot love since it has no independence to choose. Only a personality that has the ability to choose possesses the option to love. Since God created us to love Him, He has endowed us with free will. The exercise of our own free will results in good and bad deeds, and we must not blame God for them.

In ignorance, some souls do not even realise that they possess the freedom to choose their actions and hold God responsible for their mistakes. Others realise they possess a free will, but they harbour the pride of doership in the egoistic notion of being the body. This is again a sign of ignorance. *Shree Krishna explains next how such ignorance can be dispelled.*

ज्ञानेन तु तदज्ञानं येषां नाशितमात्मनः ।
तेषामादित्यवज्ज्ञानं प्रकाशयति तत्परम् ।।16।।

jñānena tu tad ajñānaṁ yeṣhāṁ nāśhitam ātmanaḥ
teṣhām āditya-vaj jñānaṁ prakāśhayati tat param

jñānena—by divine knowledge; *tu*—but; *tat*—that; *ajñānam*—ignorance; *yeṣhām*—whose; *nāśhitam*—has been destroyed; *ātmanaḥ*—of the self; *teṣhām*—their; *āditya-vat*—like the sun; *jñānam*—knowledge; *prakāśhayati*—illumines; *tat*—that; *param*—Supreme Entity.

But for those whose ignorance is destroyed by divine knowledge, the Supreme Entity is revealed, just as the sun illumines everything when it rises.

The sun's power in removing the darkness of night is incomparable. The Ramayan states:

rākāpati ṣhoṛasa uahiñ tārāgana samudāi
sakala girinha dava lāia binu rabi rāti na jāi

'Despite the combined light of the full moon and all the visible stars in a cloudless sky, the night does not go. But the moment the sun rises, the night makes a hasty exit.' The light of the sun is such that darkness cannot remain before it. The light of God's knowledge has a similar effect in dispelling the darkness of ignorance.

Darkness is responsible for creating illusions. In the darkness of the cinema hall, the light falling on the screen creates the illusion of reality and people get absorbed in watching it. However, when the main lights in the cinema hall are turned on, the illusion is dispelled, and people wake up from their reverie to realise that they were only watching a movie. Similarly, in the darkness of ignorance, we identify ourselves with the body and consider ourselves to be the doers and enjoyers of our actions. When the light of God's knowledge begins shining brightly, the illusion beats a hasty retreat, and the soul wakes up to its true spiritual identity even while it continues to live in the city of nine gates. The soul had fallen into illusion because God's material energy (*avidyā shakti*) had covered it in darkness. The illusion is dispelled when God's spiritual energy (*vidyā shakti*) illumines it with the light of knowledge.

तद्बुद्धयस्तदात्मानस्तन्निष्ठास्तत्परायणाः ।
गच्छन्त्यपुनरावृत्तिं ज्ञाननिर्धूतकल्मषाः ।।17।।

tad-buddhayas tad-ātmānas tan-niṣhṭhās tat-parāyaṇāḥ
gachchhantyapunar-āvṛittiṁ jñāna-nirdhūta-kalmaṣhāḥ

tat-buddhayaḥ—those whose intellect is directed towards God; *tat-ātmānaḥ*—those whose heart (mind and intellect) is solely absorbed in God; *tat-niṣhṭhāḥ*—those whose intellect has firm faith in God; *tat-parāyaṇāḥ*—those who strive for God as the supreme goal and refuge; *gachchhanti*—go; *apunaḥ-āvṛittim*—not returning; *jñāna*—by knowledge; *nirdhūta*—dispelled; *kalmaṣhāḥ*—sins.

Those whose intellect is fixed in God, who are completely absorbed in God, with firm faith in Him as the supreme goal, such persons quickly reach the state from which there is no return, their sins having been dispelled by the light of knowledge.

Just as ignorance causes one to suffer in samsara, the perpetual cycle of life and death, knowledge has the power to release one from material bondage. Such knowledge is always accompanied with devotion to

God. This verse makes very emphatic use of words denoting complete God-consciousness.

Tadbuddhayaḥ means the intellect is directed towards God.

Tadātmanaḥ means the heart (mind and intellect) is solely absorbed in God.

Tanniṣhṭhāḥ means the intellect has firm faith in God.

Tatparāyaṇaḥ means striving for God as the supreme goal and refuge.

Thus, the sign of true knowledge is that it leads to love for God. *Imbued with such love, devotees see Him everywhere. Such a divine vision is described in the next verse.*

विद्याविनयसम्पन्ने ब्राह्मणे गवि हस्तिनि ।
शुनि चैव श्वपाके च पण्डिताः समदर्शिनः ।।18।।

vidyā-vinaya-sampanne brāhmaṇe gavi hastini
śhuni chaiva śhva-pāke cha paṇḍitāḥ sama-darśhinaḥ

vidyā—divine knowledge; *vinaya*—humbleness; *sampanne*—equipped with; *brāhmaṇe*—a Brahmin; *gavi*—a cow; *hastini*—an elephant; *śhuni*—a dog; *cha*—and; *eva*—certainly; *śhva-pāke*—a dog-eater; *cha*—and; *paṇḍitāḥ*—the learned; *sama-darśhinaḥ*—see with equal vision.

The truly learned, with the eyes of divine knowledge, see with equal vision a Brahmin, a cow, an elephant, a dog, and a dog-eater.

When we perceive things through the perspective of knowledge, it is called *prajñā chakṣhu* which means 'with the eyes of knowledge'. Shree Krishna uses the words *vidyā sampanne* to the same effect, but He also adds *vinaya,* meaning, 'humbleness'. The sign of divine knowledge is that it is accompanied by a sense of humility while shallow bookish knowledge is accompanied with the pride of scholarship.

Shree Krishna reveals in this verse how divine knowledge bestows a vision so different from physical sight. Endowed with knowledge, devotees see all living beings as souls who are fragments of God and are therefore divine in nature. The examples given by Shree Krishna are of diametrically contrasting species and life forms. A Vedic Brahmin who conducts worship ceremonies is respected, while a dog-eater is usually looked down upon as an outcaste; a cow is milked for human consumption, but not a dog; an elephant is used for ceremonial parades, while neither the cow nor the dog are. From the physical perspective, these species are sharp contrasts in the spectrum of life on our planet. However, a truly learned person endowed with spiritual knowledge sees them all as eternal souls, and consequently, views them with an equal eye.

The Vedas do not support the view that the Brahmins (priestly class) are of higher caste, while the Shudras (labour class) are of lower caste. The perspective of knowledge is that even though the Brahmins conduct worship ceremonies, the Kshatriyas administer society, the Vaishyas conduct business, and the Shudras engage in labour, yet they all are eternal souls, who are tiny parts of God, and therefore, alike.

इहैव तैर्जितः सर्गो येषां साम्ये स्थितं मनः ।
निर्दोषं हि समं ब्रह्म तस्माद् ब्रह्मणि ते स्थिताः ।।19।।

ihaiva tair jitaḥ sargo yeṣhāṁ sāmye sthitaṁ manaḥ
nirdoṣhaṁ hi samaṁ brahma tasmād brahmaṇi te sthitāḥ

iha eva—in this very life; *taiḥ*—by them; *jitaḥ*—conquer; *sargaḥ*—the creation; *yeṣhām*—whose; *sāmye*—in equanimity; *sthitam*—situated; *manaḥ*—mind; *nirdoṣham*—flawless; *hi*—certainly; *samam*—in equality; *brahma*—God; *tasmāt*—therefore; *brahmaṇi*—in the Absolute Truth; *te*—they; *sthitāḥ*—are seated.

Those whose minds are established in equality of vision conquer the cycle of birth and death in this very life. They possess the flawless qualities of God and are therefore seated in the Absolute Truth.

Sri Krishna uses the word *sāmye* to mean 'one possessed of an equal vision towards all living beings', as explained in the previous verse.

Further, equality of vision also means to rise beyond likes and dislikes, happiness and misery, fame and infamy. Shree Krishna says that those who are able to do so transcend the samsara of repeated birth and death.

So long as we think of ourselves as the body, we cannot attain this equality of vision because we will experience continued desires and aversions for physical pleasures and discomforts. Saints rise above bodily consciousness and absorb their minds in God, giving up all worldly attachments. The Ramayan states:

sevahiṅ lakhanu sīya raghubīrahi, jimi abibekī puruṣha sarīrahi

'Lakshman served Lord Ram and Sita, just as an ignorant person serves his body.'

When one's mind is situated in this divine consciousness, attachment to bodily pleasures and pains get transcended, and one reaches a state of equanimity. This equipoise that comes through the sacrifice of selfish material desires makes one godlike in demeanour. The Mahabharat states: *yo na kāmayate kiñchit brahma bhūyāya kalpate* 'One who gives up desires becomes like God.'

न प्रहृष्येत्प्रियं प्राप्य नोद्विजेत्प्राप्य चाप्रियम् ।
स्थिरबुद्धिरसम्मूढो ब्रह्मविद् ब्रह्मणि स्थितः ।।20।।

na prahṛiṣhyet priyaṁ prāpya nodvijet prāpya chāpriyam
sthira-buddhir asammūḍho brahma-vid brahmaṇi sthitaḥ

na—neither; *prahṛiṣhyet*—rejoice; *priyam*—the pleasant; *prāpya*—obtaining; *na*—nor; *udvijet*—become disturbed; *prāpya*—attaining; *cha*—also; *apriyam*—the unpleasant; *sthira-buddhiḥ*—steady intellect; *asammūḍhaḥ*—firmly situated; *brahma-vit*—having a firm understanding of divine knowledge; *brahmaṇi*—established in God; *sthitaḥ*—situated.

Established in God, having a firm understanding of divine knowledge and not hampered by delusion, they neither rejoice in getting something pleasant nor grieve on experiencing the unpleasant.

The section of this verse—neither rejoicing in pleasure nor lamenting the unpleasant—is the highest ideal of the Vipassana tradition of meditation in Buddhism. Rigorous training is undertaken to reach this state of clarity and precision, ultimately leading to equanimity and destruction of self-will. However, the same state is naturally reached in devotion to God when we surrender our will to the divine. In accordance with verse 5.17, when we unite our will to the will of God, then both pleasure and pain are serenely accepted as His grace. A beautiful story illustrates this attitude.

A wild horse once ran into a farm. People congratulated the farmer on his good luck. He said, 'Good luck, bad luck, who knows? It is all the will of God.'

A few days later, the horse ran away, back into the forest. His neighbours commiserated with his bad luck. He said, 'Bad luck, good luck, who knows? It is all God's will.'

A few more days went by, and the horse returned with twenty more wild horses. Again, people congratulated the farmer on his stroke of good luck. He wisely reflected, 'What is good or bad luck? This is all God's will.'

A few days later, the farmer's son broke his leg while riding one of the horses. The neighbours came to express grief. The wise farmer responded, 'Pleasant or unpleasant, it is only God's will.'

Some more days went by, and the king's soldiers came to recruit all young men into the army for the war that had just broken out. All the young men in the neighbourhood were taken into the army, but the farmer's son was left behind because his leg was broken.

Divine knowledge brings the understanding that our self-interest lies in giving pleasure to God. This leads to surrender to the will of God, and when self-will gets merged into divine will, one develops the equanimity to serenely accept both pleasure and pain as His grace. This is the sign of a person situated in transcendence.

बाह्यस्पर्शेष्वसक्तात्मा विन्दत्यात्मनि यत्सुखम् ।
स ब्रह्मयोगयुक्तात्मा सुखमक्षयमश्नुते ।।21।।

bāhya-sparśheṣhvasaktātmā vindatyātmani yat sukham
sa brahma-yoga-yuktātmā sukham akṣhayam aśhnute

bāhya-sparśheṣhu—external sense pleasure; *asakta-ātmā*—those who are unattached; *vindati*—find; *ātmani*—in the self; *yat*—which; *sukham*—bliss; *saḥ*—that person; *brahma-yoga yukta-ātmā*—those who are united with God through yog; *sukham*—happiness; *akṣhayam*—unlimited; *aśhnute*—experiences.

Those who are not attached to external sense pleasures realise divine bliss in the self. Being united with God through Yog, they experience unending happiness.

The Vedic scriptures repeatedly describe God as an ocean of unlimited divine bliss:

ānando brahmeti vyajānāt (*Taittirīya Upanishad* 3.6)

'Know God to be bliss.'

kevalānubhavānanda svarūpaḥ parameśhvaraḥ

(Bhagavatam 7.6.23)

'God's form is made of pure bliss.'

ānanda mātra kara pāda mukhodarādi (*Padma Puran*)

'God's hands, feet, face, stomach, etc. are all made of bliss.'

jo ānand sindhu sukharāsī (Ramayan)

'God is an ocean of bliss and happiness.'

All these mantras and verses from the scriptures emphasise that divine bliss is the nature of God's personality. The yogi, who absorbs the senses, mind, and intellect in God, begins to experience the infinite bliss of God who is seated within.

ये हि संस्पर्शजा भोगा दुःखयोनय एव ते ।
आद्यन्तवन्तः कौन्तेय न तेषु रमते बुधः ।।22।।

ye hi sansparśha-jā bhogā duḥkha-yonaya eva te
ādyantavantaḥ kaunteya na teṣhu ramate budhaḥ

ye—which; *hi*—verily; *sansparśha-jāḥ*—born of contact with the sense objects; *bhogāḥ*—pleasures; *duḥkha*—misery; *yonayaḥ*—source of; *eva*—verily; *te*—they are; *ādya-antavantaḥ*—having beginning and end; *kaunteya*—Arjun, son of Kunti; *na*—never; *teṣhu*—in those; *ramate*—takes delight; *budhaḥ*—the wise.

The pleasures that arise from contact with the sense objects, though appearing as enjoyable to worldly-minded people, are verily a source of misery. O son of Kunti, such pleasures have a beginning and an end, so the wise do not delight in them.

The senses create sensations of pleasure in contact with the sense objects. The mind, which is like the sixth sense, derives pleasure from honour, praise, circumstances, success, and other such intangibles. All these pleasures of body and mind are known as *bhog* (material enjoyment). Such worldly pleasures cannot satisfy the soul for the following reasons:

Worldly pleasures are finite, and hence, the feeling of deficiency remains inherent in them. One may feel happiness on becoming a millionaire, but the same millionaire becomes discontented on seeing a billionaire, and thinks, 'If only I also had one billion, then I too would be happy.' In contrast, the bliss of God is infinite, and so it gives complete satisfaction.

Worldly pleasures are temporary. Once they finish, they again leave one with the feeling of misery. For example, an alcoholic enjoys the pleasure of drinking alcohol at night, but the next morning, the hangover gives him a splitting headache. However, the bliss of God is eternal, and once attained, remains forever.

Worldly pleasures are transient and get exhausted quickly. When people see a new Academy Award prize-winning movie, they are overjoyed, but if they have to see the movie a second time to give company to a friend, their joy dries up. And if a second friend insists that they see it a third time, they say, 'Give me any punishment, but don't ask me to see that movie again.' The pleasure from material objects keeps decreasing as we enjoy it. In economics, this is defined as the Law of Diminishing Returns. But the bliss of God is ever-fresh; it is *sat-chit-anand* (eternal, ever-fresh, divine bliss). Hence, we can go on chanting the same divine name of God all day long and relish ever-new devotional satisfaction in it.

No sane person enjoying a delicious dessert would be willing to give it up and eat mud. Similarly, when one begins to enjoy divine bliss, the mind loses all taste for material pleasures. Those endowed with the faculty of discrimination understand the above- mentioned drawbacks of material pleasures and restrain their senses from them. *Shree Krishna emphasises this in the next verse.*

शक्नोतीहैव यः सोढुं प्राक्शरीरविमोक्षणात् ।
कामक्रोधोद्भवं वेगं स युक्तः स सुखी नरः ।।23।।

śhaknotīhaiva yaḥ soḍhuṁ prāk śharīra-vimokṣhaṇāt
kāma-krodhodbhavaṁ vegaṁ sa yuktaḥ sa sukhī naraḥ

śhaknoti—is able; *iha eva*—in the present body; *yaḥ*—who; *soḍhum*—to withstand; *prāk*—before; *śharīra*—the body; *vimokṣhaṇāt*—giving up; *kāma*—desire; *krodha*—anger; *udbhavam*—generated from; *vegam*—forces; *saḥ*—that person; *yuktaḥ*—yogi; *saḥ*—that person; *sukhī*—happy; *naraḥ*—person.

Those persons are yogis, who before giving up the body are able to check the forces of desire and anger; and they alone are happy.

The human body presents a golden opportunity for the soul to reach the supreme goal of God-realisation. In this body, we possess the faculty of discrimination while animals are driven by their nature. Shree Krishna emphasises that this power of discrimination should be exercised to restrain the impulses of desire and anger.

One meaning of the word *kām* is lust, but in this verse, *kām* is used for all kinds of desires of the body and mind for material pleasures. When the mind does not attain the object of its desire, it modifies its state to exhibit anger. The urges of desire and anger are very powerful like the strong current of a river. Even animals are subject to these urges, but unlike humans, they are not bestowed with the discrimination to restrain them. However, the human intellect has been bestowed with the power of discrimination.

The word *sodhum* means 'to withstand'. This verse instructs us to withstand the urges of desire and anger. Sometimes one restrains the urges of the mind out of embarrassment. Let us say there is a man sitting at the airport. A beautiful lady comes and sits by his side. His mind desires the pleasure of putting his arm around her, but the intellect resists with the thought, 'This is improper conduct. The lady may even slap me for it.' He restrains himself to avoid the shame of censure. Here Shree Krishna is not asking Arjun to restrain the mind out of embarrassment, fear, or apprehension, but through discrimination based on knowledge.

The resolute intellect should be used to check the mind. As soon as the thought of savouring a material pleasure comes to the mind, one should bring the knowledge to the intellect that these are sources of misery. The Shreemad Bhagavatam states:

nāyaṁ deho deha-bhājāṁ nṛiloke
kaṣhṭān kāmān arhate viḍ-bhujāṁ ye
tapo divyaṁ putrakā yena sattvaṁ
śhuddhyed yasmād brahma-saukhyaṁ tvanantam (5.5.1)

'In the human form, one should not undertake great hardships to obtain sensual pleasures, which are available even to creatures that eat excreta (hogs). Instead, one should practice austerities to purify one's heart and enjoy the unlimited bliss of God.' This opportunity to practice discrimination is available only while the human body exists, and one who is able to check the forces of desire and anger while living, becomes a yogi. Such a person alone tastes the divine bliss within and becomes happy.

योऽन्तःसुखोऽन्तरारामस्तथान्तर्ज्योतिरेव यः ।
स योगी ब्रह्मनिर्वाणं ब्रह्मभूतोऽधिगच्छति ।।24।।

yo 'ntaḥ-sukho 'ntar-ārāmas tathāntar-jyotir eva yaḥ
sa yogī brahma-nirvāṇaṁ brahma-bhūto 'dhigachchhati

yaḥ—who; *antaḥ-sukhaḥ*—happy within the self; *antaḥ-ārāmaḥ*—enjoying within the self; *tathā*—as well as; *antaḥ-jyotiḥ*—illumined by the inner light; *eva*—certainly; *yaḥ*—who; *saḥ*—he; *yogī*—yogi; *brahma-nirvāṇam*—liberation from material existence; *brahma-bhūtaḥ*—united with the Lord; *adhigachchhati*—attains.

Those who are happy within themselves, enjoying the delight of God within, and are illumined by the inner light, such yogis are united with the Lord and are liberated from material existence.

'Inner light' is the divine knowledge that is bestowed by the grace of God from within in the form of realisation, when we surrender to Him. The *Yog Darshan* states:

ṛitambharā tatra prajñā (1.48)

'In the state of samadhi, one's intellect becomes filled with realisation of the Truth.'

After instructing Arjun about the need to withstand the impulses of desire and anger, Shree Krishna reveals the confidential means of practising this. The words *yo'ntah sukho* mean 'one who is internally happy'. There is one kind of happiness that we get from external objects, and another kind of happiness that we experience from within when we absorb the mind in God. If we do not experience happiness within, we will not be able to permanently resist external temptations. But when the bliss of God starts flowing within the heart, then the fleeting external pleasures seem trivial in comparison and are easy to renounce.

Saint Yamunacharya states:

yadāvadhi mama chetaḥ kṛiṣhṇa-padāravinde
nava-nava-rasa-dhāmanudyata rantum āsīt
tadāvadhi bata nārī-saṅgame smaryamāne
bhavati mukha-vikāraḥ suṣhṭu niṣhṭhīvanaṁ cha

'Ever since I have begun meditating upon the lotus-like feet of Lord Krishna, I have been experiencing ever-increasing bliss. If by chance the thought of sex pleasure comes to my mind, I spit at the thought and curl my lips in distaste.'

लभन्ते ब्रह्मनिर्वाणमृषयः क्षीणकल्मषाः ।
छिन्नद्वैधा यतात्मानः सर्वभूतहिते रताः ।।25।।

labhante brahma-nirvāṇam ṛiṣhayaḥ kṣhīṇa-kalmaṣhāḥ
chhinna-dvaidhā yatātmānaḥ sarva-bhūta-hite ratāḥ

labhante—achieve; *brahma-nirvāṇam*—liberation from material existence; *ṛiṣhayaḥ*—holy persons; *kṣhīṇa-kalmaṣhāḥ*—whose sins have been purged; *chhinna*—annihilated; *dvaidhāḥ*—doubts; *yata-ātmānaḥ*—whose minds are disciplined; *sarva-bhūta*—for all living entities; *hite*—in welfare work; *ratāḥ*—rejoice.

Those holy persons whose sins have been purged, whose doubts are annihilated, whose minds are disciplined, and who are devoted to the welfare of all beings, attain God and are liberated from material existence.

In the preceding verse, Shree Krishna explained the state of the sages who experience the pleasure of God within themselves. In this verse, He describes the state of the sages who are actively engaged in the welfare of all beings. The Ramayan states:

para upakāra bachana mana kāyā,
santa sahaja subhāu khagarāyā

'The trait of compassion is the intrinsic nature of saints. Motivated by it, they use their words, mind, and body for the welfare of others.'

Human welfare is a praiseworthy endeavour. However, welfare schemes that merely focus on physical care only result in temporary welfare. For example, if a hungry person is given food, his hunger is satiated. But after four hours, again, he is hungry. Spiritual welfare goes right to the root of all material suffering and endeavours to revive the God-consciousness of the soul. Hence, the highest welfare activity is to help unite a person's consciousness with God. This is the kind of welfare work that elevated souls with purified minds engage in. Such welfare activity further attracts God's grace which elevates them even further on the path. Finally, when they have achieved complete purification of the mind and perfected their surrender to God, they are liberated to the spiritual realm and the divine abode.

Thus far in this chapter, Shree Krishna has extolled the path of karm yog. He now speaks the remaining verses for karm sanyasis, revealing that they too attain the final goal.

कामक्रोधवियुक्तानां यतीनां यतचेतसाम् ।
अभितो ब्रह्मनिर्वाणं वर्तते विदितात्मनाम् ।।26।।

kāma-krodha-viyuktānāṁ yatīnāṁ yata-chetasām
abhito brahma-nirvāṇaṁ vartate viditātmanām

kāma—desires; *krodha*—anger; *vimuktānām*—of those who are liberated; *yatīnām*—of the saintly persons; *yata-chetasām*—those self-realised persons who have subdued their mind; *abhitaḥ*—from every side; *brahma*—spiritual; *nirvāṇam*—liberation from material existence; *vartate*—exists; *vidita-ātmanām*—of those who are self-realised.

For those sanyasis who have broken out of anger and lust through constant effort, who have subdued their mind, and are self-realised, liberation from material existence is both here and hereafter.

As previously explained in verse 5.2, karm yog is the safer path for most people, and that is why Shree Krishna strongly recommended it to Arjun. However, for someone who is truly detached from the world, karm sanyas is also suitable. It is advantageous in that there is no diversion of time and energy towards worldly duties, and one can dedicate oneself fully to the practice of spirituality. There have been many accomplished sanyasis in history. Shree Krishna states that such true karm sanyasis also make rapid progress and experience peace everywhere. By eliminating the urges of desire and anger and subduing their mind, they attain perfect peace both in this life and hereafter.

We often harbour the misconception that external circumstances are at fault for the lack of peace in our lives, and we hope for the day when the situation will become conducive to peace of mind. However, peace is not dependent upon external situations; it is a product of purified senses, mind, and intellect. The sanyasis, with their mind and thoughts turned inward, find the ocean of peace within, independent of external circumstances. And then, with the internal machinery in order, they experience the same peace everywhere and are liberated in this world itself.

स्पर्शान्कृत्वा बहिर्बाह्यांश्चक्षुश्चैवान्तरे भ्रुवोः ।
प्राणापानौ समौ कृत्वा नासाभ्यन्तरचारिणौ ।।27।।

यतेन्द्रियमनोबुद्धिर्मुनिर्मोक्षपरायणः ।
विगतेच्छाभयक्रोधो यः सदा मुक्त एव सः ।।28।।

sparśhān kṛitvā bahir bāhyānśh chakṣhuśh chaivāntare bhruvoḥ
prāṇāpānau samau kṛitvā nāsābhyantara-chāriṇau

yatendriya-mano-buddhir munir mokṣha-parāyaṇaḥ
vigatechchhā-bhaya-krodho yaḥ sadā mukta eva saḥ

sparśhān—contacts (through senses); *kṛitvā*—keeping; *bahiḥ*—outside; *bāhyān*—external; *chakṣhuḥ*—eyes; *cha*—and; *eva*—certainly; *antare*—between; *bhruvoḥ*—of the eyebrows; *prāṇa-apānau*—the outgoing and incoming breaths; *samau*—equal; *kṛitvā*—keeping; *nāsa-abhyantara*—within the nostrils; *chāriṇau*—moving; *yata*—controlled; *indriya*—senses; *manaḥ*—mind; *buddhiḥ*—intellect; *muniḥ*—the sage; *mokṣha*—liberation; *parāyaṇaḥ*—dedicated; *vigata*—free; *ichchhā*—desires; *bhaya*—fear; *krodhaḥ*—anger; *yaḥ*—who; *sadā*—always; *muktaḥ*—liberated; *eva*—certainly; *saḥ*—that person.

Shutting out all thoughts of external enjoyment, with the gaze fixed on the space between the eyebrows, equalising the flow of the incoming and outgoing breath in the nostrils, and thus controlling the senses,

mind, and intellect, the sage who becomes free from desire and fear always lives in freedom.

Often renunciants are more inclined towards ashtang yog or hatha yog along with their practice of asceticism. Their extreme detachment makes them disinterested in the path of devotion which requires meditation on the Names, Forms, Pastimes, Virtues, Abodes, and Associates of God. Here, Shree Krishna describes the path that the ascetics take.

He says that such ascetics shut out thoughts of sense objects by controlling their sight and breath. They focus their gaze between their eyebrows. If the eyes are fully closed, sleep may overtake one; and if they are wide open, they may get distracted by the objects around them. In order to avoid both these defects, the ascetics concentrate their gaze, with eyes half-open between the eyebrows or the tip of the nose. They also harmonise the pran (outgoing breath) with the *apān* (incoming breath) until both become suspended in yogic trance. This yogic process enables the controlling of the senses, mind, and intellect. Such persons make liberation from material energy as their only goal.

Such ascetic practices lead to atma jnana (knowledge of the self), not to brahma jnana (knowledge of God). Hence, the ascetic path must also be consummated through devotion to God, as stated in the next verse.

भोक्तारं यज्ञतपसां सर्वलोकमहेश्वरम् ।
सुहृदं सर्वभूतानां ज्ञात्वा मां शान्तिमृच्छति ।।29।।

bhoktāraṁ yajña-tapasāṁ sarva-loka-maheśhvaram
suhṛidaṁ sarva-bhūtānāṁ jñātvā māṁ śhāntim ṛichchhati

bhoktāram—the enjoyer; *yajña*—sacrifices; *tapasām*—austerities; *sarva-loka*—of all worlds; *mahā-īśhvaram*—the Supreme Lord; *su-hṛidam*—the selfless friend; *sarva*—of all; *bhūtānām*—the living beings; *jñātvā*—having realised; *mām*—me (Lord Krishna); *śhāntim*—peace; *ṛichchhati*—attains.

Having realised Me as the enjoyer of all sacrifices and austerities, the Supreme Lord of all the worlds and the selfless Friend of all living beings, My devotee attains peace.

The ascetic sadhana, explained in the previous two verses, can lead to atma jnana (knowledge of the self). But brahma jnana (knowledge of God) requires the grace of God which comes through devotion. The words *sarva loka maheśhwaram* mean 'Sovereign Lord of all the worlds', and *suhṛidaṁ sarva-bhūtānāṁ* means 'benevolent well-wisher of all living beings'. In this way, He emphasises that the ascetic path too is consummated in surrender to God with the knowledge that the Supreme Lord is the enjoyer of all austerities and sacrifices. Jagadguru Shree Kripaluji Maharaj has put this very nicely:

hari kā viyogī jīva govind rādhe,
sañcho yog soī jo hari se milāde (*Radha Govind Geet*)

'The soul is disconnected from God since eternity. True Yog is that which unites the soul with the Lord.' Hence, no system of Yog is complete without the inclusion of bhakti.

In His 'Song of God', Shree Krishna beautifully includes all the genuine paths of spiritual practice, but each time, He concludes by stating that success in these paths also requires bhakti. For example, He uses this system of presentation in verses 6.46–47, 8.22, 11.53–54, 18.54–55, etc. Here too, Shree Krishna ends the topic revealing the necessity of devotion.

CHAPTER 6

Dhyan Yog

The Yog of Meditation

In this chapter, Shree Krishna continues the comparative evaluation of karm yog (practising spirituality while continuing worldly duties) and karm sanyas (practising spirituality in the renounced order) from chapter five and recommends the former. When we perform work in devotion, it purifies the mind and deepens our spiritual realisation. Then when the mind becomes tranquil, meditation becomes the primary means of elevation. Through meditation, yogis strive to conquer their mind, for while the untrained mind is the worst enemy, the trained mind is the best friend. Shree Krishna cautions Arjun that one cannot attain success on the spiritual path by engaging in severe austerities, and hence, one must be temperate in eating, working, recreation, and sleeping. He then explains the sadhana for uniting the mind with God. Just as a lamp in a windless place does not flicker, likewise, the *sādhak* too must hold the mind steady in meditation. The mind is indeed difficult to restrain, but by practice and detachment, it can be controlled. So, wherever it wanders, one should bring it back and continually focus it upon God. When the mind gets purified, it becomes established in transcendence. In that joyous state called samadhi, one experiences boundless divine bliss.

Arjun then questions Shree Krishna about the fate of the aspirant who begins on the path but is unable to reach the goal due to an unsteady mind. Shree Krishna reassures him that one who strives for God-realisation is never overcome by evil. God always keeps account of our spiritual merits accumulated in previous lives and reawakens that wisdom in future births, so that we may continue the journey from where we had left off. With the accrued merits of many past lives, yogis are able to reach God in their present life itself. The chapter concludes with a declaration that the yogi (one who strives to unite with God) is superior to the *tapasvī* (ascetic), the jnani (person of learning), and the karmi (ritualistic performer). And among all yogis, one who engages in bhakti (loving devotion to God) is the highest of all.

श्रीभगवानुवाच ।
अनाश्रितः कर्मफलं कार्यं कर्म करोति यः ।
स संन्यासी च योगी च न निरग्निर्न चाक्रियः ।।1।।

śhrī bhagavān uvācha
anāśhritaḥ karma-phalaṁ kāryaṁ karma karoti yaḥ
sa sanyāsī cha yogī cha na niragnir na chākriyaḥ

śhrī-bhagavān uvācha—the Supreme Lord said; *anāśhritaḥ*—not desiring; *karma-phalam*—results of actions; *kāryam*—obligatory; *karma*—work; *karoti*—perform; *yaḥ*—one who; *saḥ*—that person; *sanyāsī*—in the renounced order; *cha*—and; *yogī*—yogi; *cha*—and; *na*—not; *niḥ*—without; *agniḥ*—fire; *na*—not; *cha*—also; *akriyaḥ*—without activity.

The Supreme Lord said: Those who perform prescribed duties without desiring the results of their actions are actual sanyasis (renunciates) and yogis, not those who have merely ceased performing sacrifices such as *Agnihotra yajna* or abandoned bodily activities.

The ritualistic activities described in the Vedas include fire sacrifices, such as Agnihotra yajna. The rules for those who enter the renounced order of sanyas state that they should not perform the ritualistic *karm kāṇḍ* activities; in fact, they should not touch fire at all, not even for the purpose of cooking. And they should subsist on alms instead. However, Shree Krishna states in this verse that merely giving up the sacrificial fire does not make one a sanyasi (renunciant).

Who are true yogis, and who are true sanyasis? There is much confusion in this regard. People say, 'This swamiji is *phalāhārī* (one who eats only fruits and nothing else), so he must be an elevated yogi.' 'This *bābājī* (renunciant) is *dūdhāhārī* (subsists on milk alone), hence, he must be an even higher yogi.' 'This guruji is *pavanāhārī* (does not eat, lives only on the breath), therefore, he must definitely be God-realised.' 'This sadhu is a *nāgā bābā* (ascetic who does not wear clothes), thus, he is perfectly renounced.' However, Shree Krishna dismisses all these concepts. He says that such external acts of asceticism do not make anyone either a sanyasi or a yogi. Those who can renounce the fruits of their actions by offering them to God are the true renunciants and yogis.

Nowadays, yoga has become the buzzword in the western world. Numerous yoga studios have sprung up in every town of every country around the world. Statistics reveal that one out of every ten persons in America is practising yoga. But the word 'yoga' does not exist in the Sanskrit scriptures; the actual word is 'Yog' which means 'union'. It refers to the union of individual consciousness with Divine Consciousness. In other words, a yogi is one whose mind is fully absorbed in God. It also follows that such a yogi's mind is naturally detached from the world. As a result, the true yogi is also the true sanyasi.

Persons who perform karm yog do all activities in the spirit of humble service to God without any desire whatsoever for rewards. Even though they may be *gṛihasthas* (householders), such persons are true yogis and real renunciants.

यं संन्यासमिति प्राहुर्योगं तं विद्धि पाण्डव ।
न ह्यसंन्यस्तसङ्कल्पो योगी भवति कश्चन ॥2॥

yaṁ sanyāsam iti prāhur yogaṁ taṁ viddhi pāṇḍava
na hyasannyasta-saṅkalpo yogī bhavati kaśhchana

yam—what; *sanyāsam*—renunciation; *iti*—thus; *prāhuḥ*—they say; *yogam*—yog; *tam*—that; *viddhi*—know; *pāṇḍava*—Arjun, son of

Pandu; *na*—not; *hi*—certainly; *asannyasta*—without giving up; *saṅkalpaḥ*—desire; *yogī*—a yogi; *bhavati*—becomes; *kaśhchana*—anyone.

What is known as sanyas is non-different from Yog, for none become yogis without renouncing worldly desires.

A sanyasi is one who renounces pleasures of the mind and senses. But mere renunciation is not the goal, nor is it sufficient to reach the goal. Renunciation means that our running in the wrong direction has stopped. We were searching for happiness in the world, and we understood that there is no happiness in material pleasures. So, we stopped running for worldy gratification. However, the destination is not reached just by stopping. The purpose of the soul's journey is God-realisation. The process of going towards God—taking the mind towards Him—is the path of Yog. Those who have incomplete knowledge of the goal of life look upon renunciation as the highest goal of spirituality. On the other hand, those who truly understand the goal of life regard God-realisation as the ultimate goal of their spiritual endeavours.

In the purport to verse 5.4, it was explained that there are two kinds of renunciation—*phalgu vairāgya* and *yukt vairāgya*. *Phalgu vairāgya* is that where worldly objects are seen as objects of maya, the material energy, and hence, renounced because they are detrimental to spiritual progress. *Yukt vairāgya* is that where everything is seen as belonging to God, and therefore, meant to be used in His service. In the first kind of renunciation, one would say, 'Give up money. Do not touch it. It is a form of maya and an impediment on the path of spirituality.' In the second kind of renunciation, one would say, 'Money is also a form of the energy of God. Do not waste it or throw it away; utilise whatever you have in the service of God.'

Phalgu vairāgya is unstable and can easily revert to attachment for the world. The name Phalgu comes from a river in the city of Gaya, in the state of Bihar in India. The river Phalgu runs below the surface. From atop, it seems as if there is no water, but if you dig a few feet, you encounter the stream below. Similarly, many people renounce the world to go and live in monasteries, only to find that in a few years, the renunciation has vanished and the mind is again attached to the world. Their detachment was *phalgu vairāgya.* Finding the world to be troublesome and miserable, they desired to get away from it by taking shelter in a monastery. But when they found spiritual life also to be difficult and arduous, they became detached from spirituality as well. Then there are others who establish their loving relationship with God. Motivated by the desire to serve Him, they renounce the world to live in a monastery. Their renunciation is *yukt vairāgya.* They usually continue the journey even in the face of difficulties.

In the first line of this verse, Shree Krishna states that a real sanyasi (renunciant) is one who is a yogi, i.e., one whose mind is united with God in loving service. In the second line, Shree Krishna states that one cannot be a yogi without giving up material desires. If there are material desires in the mind, then it will naturally run towards the world. Since it is the mind that has to be united with God, this is only possible if the mind is free from all material desires. Thus, to be a yogi one must be a sanyasi from within; and one can only be a sanyasi if one is a yogi.

आरुरुक्षोर्मुनेर्योगं कर्म कारणमुच्यते ।
योगारूढस्य तस्यैव शमः कारणमुच्यते ॥3॥

ārurukṣhor muner yogaṁ karma kāraṇam uchyate
yogārūḍhasya tasyaiva śhamaḥ kāraṇam uchyate

ārurukṣhoḥ—a beginner; *muneḥ*—of a sage; *yogam*—Yog; *karma*—working without attachment; *kāraṇam*—the cause; *uchyate*—is said; *yoga ārūḍhasya*—of those who are elevated in Yog; *tasya*—their; *eva*—certainly; *śhamaḥ*—meditation; *kāraṇam*—the cause; *uchyate*—is said.

To the soul who is aspiring for perfection in Yog, work without attachment is said to be the means; to the sage who is already elevated in Yog, tranquillity in meditation is said to be the means.

In chapter 3, verse 3, Shree Krishna mentioned that there are two paths for attaining welfare—the path of contemplation and the path of action. Between these, He recommended to Arjun to follow the path of action. Again, in chapter 5, verse 2, He declared it to be the better path. Does this mean that we must keep doing work all our life? Anticipating such a question, Shree Krishna sets the limits for it. When we perform karm yog, it leads to purification of the mind and ripening of spiritual knowledge. But once the mind has been purified and we advance in Yog, then we can leave karm yog and take to karm sanyas. At this stage, material activities serve no purpose, and meditation becomes the means.

So, the path we must follow filters down to a matter of our eligibility, and Shree Krishna explains the criteria of eligibility in this verse. He says that for those who are aspiring for Yog, the path of karm yog is more suitable; and for those who are elevated in Yog, the path of karm sanyas is more suitable.

The word Yog refers to both the goal and the process to reach the goal. When we talk of it as being the goal, we use Yog to mean 'union with God'. And when we talk of it as being the process, we use Yog to mean the 'path' to union with God.

In this second context, Yog is like a ladder we climb to reach God. At the lowest rung, the soul is caught in worldliness with the consciousness absorbed in mundane matters. The ladder of Yog takes the soul from that level to the stage where consciousness is absorbed in the Divine. The various rungs of the ladder have different names, but Yog is a term common to them all. *Yog-ārurukṣhu* are those *sādhaks* who aspire for union with God and have just begun climbing the ladder. *Yog-ārūḍha* are those who have become elevated on the ladder.

So, how do we understand when one is elevated in the science of Yog? Shree Krishna explains this next.

यदा हि नेन्द्रियार्थेषु न कर्मस्वनुषज्जते ।
सर्वसङ्कल्पसंन्यासी योगारूढस्तदोच्यते ।।4।।

yadā hi nendriyārtheṣhu na karmasv-anuṣhajjate
sarva-saṅkalpa-sanyāsī yogārūḍhas tadochyate

yadā—when; *hi*—certainly; *na*—not; *indriya-artheṣhu*—for sense-objects; *na*—not; *karmasu*—to actions; *anuṣhajjate*—is attachment; *sarva-saṅkalpa*—all desires for the fruits of actions; *sanyāsī*—renouncer; *yoga-ārūḍhaḥ*—elevated in the science of Yog; *tadā*—at that time; *uchyate*—is said.

When one is neither attached to sense objects nor to actions, such a person is said to be elevated in the science of Yog, having renounced all desires for the fruits of actions.

As the mind becomes attached to God in Yog, it naturally becomes detached from the world. So, an easy criterion of evaluating the state of one's mind is to check whether it has become free from all material desires. A person will be considered detached from the world when one no longer craves for sense objects nor is inclined to perform any actions for attaining them. Such a person ceases to look for opportunities to create circumstances to enjoy sensual pleasures, eventually extinguishes all thoughts of enjoying sense objects, and also dissolves the memories of previous enjoyments.

The mind now no longer rushes into self-centred activities at the urge of the senses. When we achieve this level of mastery over the mind, we will be considered elevated in Yog.

उद्धरेदात्मनात्मानं नात्मानमवसादयेत् ।
आत्मैव ह्यात्मनो बन्धुरात्मैव रिपुरात्मनः ।।5।।

uddhared ātmanātmānaṁ nātmānam avasādayet
ātmaiva hyātmano bandhur ātmaiva ripur ātmanaḥ

uddharet—elevate; *ātmanā*—through the mind; *ātmānam*—the self; *na*—not; *ātmānam*—the self; *avasādayet*—degrade; *ātmā*—the mind; *eva*—certainly; *hi*—indeed; *ātmanaḥ*—of the self; *bandhuḥ*—friend; *ātmā*—the mind; *eva*—certainly; *ripuḥ*—enemy; *ātmanaḥ*—of the self.

Elevate yourself through the power of your mind and not degrade yourself, for the mind can be the friend and also the enemy of the self.

We are responsible for our own elevation or debasement. Nobody can traverse the path of God-realisation for us. Saints and gurus show us the way, but we have to travel it ourselves. There is a saying in Hindi: *ek peḍa do pakṣhī baiṭhe, ek guru ek chelā, apanī karanī guru utare, apanī karanī chelā* 'There are two birds sitting on a tree—one guru and one disciple. The guru will descend by his own work, and the disciple too will only be able to climb down by his own karmas.'

We have had innumerable lifetimes before this one, and God-realised saints have always been present on the earth. At any period of time, if the world is devoid of such saints, then the souls of that period cannot become God-realised. How then can they fulfil the purpose of human life which is God-realisation? For this reason, God ensures that God-realised saints are always present to guide sincere seekers and inspire humanity. So, in infinite past lifetimes, we too must have met God-realised saints many times, and yet we did not become God-realised. This means that the problem was not lack of proper guidance, but either our reluctance in accepting it or working in alignment with it. Before we can move forward, we must first accept responsibility for our present level of spirituality or lack thereof. Only then will we realise that if we have brought ourselves to our present state, we can also elevate ourselves by our own efforts.

When we suffer reversals on the path of spiritual growth, we tend to hold others responsible, and complain that they are our enemies. However, our biggest enemy is our own mind. It is the saboteur that thwarts our aspiration for perfection. Shree Krishna states that, on the one hand, as the greatest benefactor of the soul, the mind has the potential of giving us the most benefit; on the other hand, as our greatest adversary, it also has the potential for causing the maximum harm. A controlled mind can lift us to great heights, whereas an uncontrolled mind can degrade our consciousness with the most ignoble thoughts.

To be able to use our mind as a friend, it is important to understand its nature. Our mind operates at four levels:

Mana (Mind): It creates thoughts, feelings, desires, hankerings, and aversions.

Buddhi (Intellect): Its function is to analyse and decide. It understands, decides, and discriminates i.e., this is good, this is bad.

Chitta (Subconscious mind): It is the repository of impressions and memories. It enables one to get attached to an object or person.

Ahankār (Ego): It is the ego or 'I'ness. It produces the sense of identity with the attributes of the body and creates pride.

These are not four separate entities. They are simply four levels of functioning of the one mind. Hence, we may refer to them all together as the mind, or as the mind-intellect, or as the mind-intellect-ego, or as the mind-intellect-subconscious-ego. They all refer to the same entity.

The use of the word 'ego' here is different from its connotation in Freudian psychology. Sigmund Freud, an Austrian neurologist, propounded the first theory of psychology on how the mind works. According to him, the ego is the 'real self' that bridges the gap between our untamed desires (Id) and the value system that is learned during childhood (Superego).

Various scriptures describe the mind in one of these four ways for the purpose of explaining the concepts presented there. They all refer to the same internal apparatus within us which is together called *antaḥ karaṇ* or the mind. For example:

- The *Pañchadaśhī* refers to all four together as the mind, and states that it is the cause of material bondage.
- In the Bhagavad Gita, Shree Krishna repeatedly talks of the mind and the intellect as two different things and emphasises the need to surrender both to God.
- The *Yog Darshan,* while analysing the various elements of nature, talks of three entities: mind, intellect, and ego.
- Shankaracharya, while explaining the subtle equipment available to the soul, classifies the mind into four—mind, intellect, *chitta,* and ego.

So, when Shree Krishna says that we must use the mind to elevate the self, He means we must use the higher mind to elevate the lower mind. In other words, we must use the intellect to control the mind.

The process of doing this has been explained in detail in verses 2.41–44 and again in verse 3.43.

बन्धुरात्मात्मनस्तस्य येनात्मैवात्मना जितः ।
अनात्मनस्तु शत्रुत्वे वर्तेतात्मैव शत्रुवत् ॥6॥

bandhur ātmātmanas tasya yenātmaivātmanā jitaḥ
anātmanas tu śhatrutve vartetātmaiva śhatru-vat

bandhuḥ—friend; *ātmā*—the mind; *ātmanaḥ*—for the person; *tasya*—of him; *yena*—by whom; *ātmā*—the mind; *eva*—certainly; *ātmanā*—for the person; *jitaḥ*—conquered; *anātmanaḥ*—of those with unconquered mind; *tu*—but; *śhatrutve*—for an enemy; *varteta*—remains; *ātmā*—the mind; *eva*—as; *śhatru-vat*—like an enemy.

For those who have conquered the mind, it is their friend. For those who have failed to do so, the mind works like an enemy.

We dissipate a large portion of our thought power and energy in combating people whom we perceive as enemies and potentially harmful to us. The Vedic scriptures say the biggest enemies—lust, anger, greed, envy, illusion, and other negative emotions—reside in our own mind. These internal enemies are even more pernicious than the outer ones. The external demons may injure us for some time, but the demons sitting within our own mind have the ability to make us live in constant misery. We all know people who had everything favourable in the world but lived miserable lives because their own mind tormented them incessantly through depression, hatred, tension, anxiety, and stress.

The Vedic philosophy lays great emphasis on the ramification of thoughts. Illness is not only caused by viruses and bacteria but also by the negativities we harbour in the mind. If someone accidentally throws a stone at you, it may hurt for a few minutes, but by the next day, you probably would have forgotten about it. However, if someone says something unpleasant, it may continue to agitate your mind for years.

This shows the immense power of thoughts. In the Buddhist scripture, the *Dhammapada* (1.3), the Buddha expressed this truth vividly:

> I have been insulted! I have been hurt! I have been beaten! I have been robbed! Misery does not cease in those who harbour such thoughts.
>
> I have been insulted! I have been hurt! I have been beaten! I have been robbed! Anger ceases in those who do not harbour such thoughts.

When we nourish hatred in our mind, our negative thoughts do more damage to us than the object of our hatred. It has been very sagaciously stated: 'Resentment is like drinking poison and hoping that the other person dies.' The problem is that most people do not even realise that their own uncontrolled mind is causing them so much harm. Hence, Jagadguru Shree Kripaluji Maharaj advises:

mana ko māno śhatru usakī sunahu jani kachhu pyāre

(*Sadhana Bhakti Tattva*)

'Dear spiritual aspirant, look on your uncontrolled mind as your enemy. Do not come under its sway.'

However, the same mind has the potential of becoming our best friend if we bring it under control of the intellect through spiritual practice. The more powerful an entity is, the greater is the danger of its misuse, and also the greater is the scope for its utilisation. Since the mind is such a powerful machine fitted into our bodies, it can work as a two-edged sword. Thus, those who slide to demoniac levels do so because of their own mind while those who attain sublime heights also do so because of their purified minds. Franklin D. Roosevelt, former president of America, expressed this very nicely: 'Men are not prisoners of fate, but only prisoners of their own minds.' In this verse, Shree Krishna enlightens Arjun about the potential harm and benefits our mind can bestow upon us.

In the following three verses, Shree Krishna describes the attributes of one who is yog-ārūḍha (advanced in Yog).

जितात्मनः प्रशान्तस्य परमात्मा समाहितः ।
शीतोष्णसुखदुःखेषु तथा मानापमानयोः ।।7।।

jitātmanaḥ praśhāntasya paramātmā samāhitaḥ
śhītoṣhṇa-sukha-duḥkheṣhu tathā mānāpamānayoḥ

jita-ātmanaḥ—one who has conquered one's mind; *praśhāntasya*—of the peaceful; *parama-ātmā*—God; *samāhitaḥ*—steadfast; *śhīta*—in cold; *uṣhṇa*—heat; *sukha*—happiness; *duḥkheṣhu*—distress; *tathā*—also; *māna*—in honour; *apamānayoḥ*—and dishonour.

The yogis who have conquered the mind rise above the dualities of cold and heat, joy and sorrow, and honour and dishonour. Such yogis remain peaceful and steadfast in their devotion to God.

Shree Krishna explained in verse 2.14 that the contact between the senses and the sense objects gives the mind the experience of heat and cold, joy and sorrow, and other emotions. As long as the mind has not been subdued, a person chases after the sensual perceptions of pleasure and recoils from the perceptions of pain. The yogi who conquers the mind is able to see these fleeting perceptions as the work of the bodily senses, distinct from the immortal soul, and thus, remains unmoved by them. Such an advanced yogi rises above the dualities of heat and cold, joy and sorrow, honour and dishonour, and so on.

There are only two realms in which the mind may dwell—one is the realm of maya and the other is the realm of God. If the mind rises above the sensual dualities of the world, it can easily get absorbed in God. Thus, Shree Krishna has stated that an advanced yogi's mind becomes situated in samadhi (deep meditation) upon God.

ज्ञानविज्ञानतृप्तात्मा कूटस्थो विजितेन्द्रियः ।
युक्त इत्युच्यते योगी समलोष्टाश्मकाञ्चनः ।।8।।

jñāna-vijñāna-tṛiptātmā kūṭa-stho vijitendriyaḥ
yukta ityuchyate yogī sama-loṣhṭāśhma-kāñchanaḥ

jñāna—knowledge; *vijñāna*—realised knowledge, wisdom from within; *tṛipta ātmā*—one fully satisfied; *kūṭa-sthaḥ*—undisturbed; *vijita-indriyaḥ*—one who has conquered the senses; *yuktaḥ*—one who is in constant communion with the Supreme; *iti*—thus; *uchyate*—is said; *yogī*—a yogi; *sama*—looks equally; *loṣhṭra*—pebbles; *aśhma*—stone; *kāñchanaḥ*—gold.

The yogis who are satisfied by knowledge and discrimination, and have conquered their senses, remain undisturbed in all circumstances. They see everything—dirt, stones, and gold—as the same.

Jnana or knowledge is the theoretical understanding obtained by listening to the guru and from the study of the scriptures. Vijnana is the realisation of that knowledge as an internal awakening and wisdom dawning from within. The intellect of the advanced yogi becomes illumined by both jnana and vijnana. Equipped with this wisdom, the yogi sees all material objects as modifications of the material energy. Such a yogi does not differentiate between objects based on their attractiveness to the self. The enlightened yogi sees all things in their relationship with God. Since the material energy belongs to God, all things are meant for His service.

The word *kuṭastha* refers to one who distances the mind from the fluctuating perceptions of senses in contact with the material energy, neither seeking pleasurable situations nor avoiding unpleasurable ones. *Vijitendriya* is one who has subjugated the senses. The word *yukt* means one who is in constant communion with the Supreme. Such a person begins to taste the divine bliss of God, and hence becomes a *tṛiptātmā* or one who is fully satisfied by virtue of realised knowledge.

सुहृन्मित्रार्युदासीनमध्यस्थद्वेष्यबन्धुषु ।
साधुष्वपि च पापेषु समबुद्धिर्विशिष्यते ॥9॥

suhṛin-mitrāryudāsīna-madhyastha-dveṣhya-bandhuṣhu
sādhuṣhvapi cha pāpeṣhu sama-buddhir viśhiṣhyate

su-hṛit—towards the well-wishers; *mitra*—friends; *ari*—enemies; *udāsīna*—neutral persons; *madhya-stha*—mediators; *dveṣhya*—the envious; *bandhuṣhu*—relatives; *sādhuṣhu*—pious; *api*—as well as; *cha*—and; *pāpeṣhu*—the sinners; *sama-buddhiḥ*—of impartial intellect; *viśhiṣhyate*—is distinguished.

The yogis look upon all—well-wishers, friends, foes, the pious, and the sinners—with an impartial intellect. The yogi who is of equal intellect towards friend, companion, and foe, neutral among enemies and relatives, and unbiased between the righteous and sinful, is considered to be distinguished among humans.

It is the nature of the human mind to respond differently to friends and foes. But an elevated yogi's nature is different. Endowed with the realised knowledge of God, elevated yogis see the entire creation in its unity with God. Thus, they are able to see all living beings with equality of vision. This parity of vision is also of various levels:

One level of parity is: 'All living beings are divine souls and hence parts of God.' Thus, they are all equal. Along these lines, Chankaya Pandit said: *ātmavat sarva bhūteṣhu yaḥ paśhyati sa paṇḍitaḥ* 'A true pandit is one who sees everyone as the soul, and hence, similar to oneself.'

Higher is the vision: 'God is seated in everyone, and that is why all are equally respect worthy.'

At the highest level, the yogi develops the vision: 'Everyone is a form of God.' The Vedic scriptures repeatedly state that the whole world is a veritable form of God: *īśhāvāsyam idam sarvaṁ yat kiñcha jagatyāṁ jagat* (*Īśhopaniṣhad* 1) 'The entire universe, with all its living and non-living beings is the manifestation of the Supreme Being, who dwells within it.' *puruṣha evedaṁ sarvaṁ* (*Purush Sūktam*, *Rig Veda*) 'God is everywhere in this world, and everything is His energy.' Hence, the highest yogi sees everyone as a manifestation of God. Endowed with this level of vision, Hanuman says: *sīyā rāma maya saba jaga jānī* (Ramayan) 'I see the face of Sita Ram in everyone.'

These categories have been further detailed in the commentary of verse 6.31. Referring to all three of the above categories, Shree Krishna says that the yogi who can maintain an equal vision towards all persons is even more elevated than the yogi mentioned in the previous verse. *Having described the state of Yog, starting with the next verse, Shree Krishna describes the practice by which we can achieve that state.*

योगी युञ्जीत सततमात्मानं रहसि स्थितः ।
एकाकी यतचित्तात्मा निराशीरपरिग्रहः ।।10।।

yogī yuñjīta satatam ātmānaṁ rahasi sthitaḥ
ekākī yata-chittātmā nirāśhīr aparigrahaḥ

yogī—a yogi; *yuñjīta*—should remain engaged in meditation; *satatam*—constantly; *ātmānam*—self; *rahasi*—in seclusion; *sthitaḥ*—remaining; *ekākī*—alone; *yata-chitta-ātmā*—with a controlled mind and body; *nirāśhīḥ*—free from desires; *aparigrahaḥ*—free from desires for possessions.

Those who seek the state of Yog should reside in seclusion, constantly engaged in meditation with a controlled mind and body, getting rid of desires and possessions for enjoyment.

Having stated the characteristics of one who has attained the state of Yog, Shree Krishna now talks about the self-preparation required for it. Mastery in any field requires daily practice. An Olympic swimming champion is not one who goes to the local neighborhood swimming pool once a week on Saturday evenings. Only one who practises for several hours every day achieves the mastery required to win the Olympics. Practice is essential for spiritual mastery as well. Shree Krishna now explains the process of accomplishing spiritual mastery by recommending the daily practice of meditation. The first point He mentions is the need for a secluded place. All day long, we are usually surrounded by a worldly environment; these material activities, people, and conversations tend to make the mind more worldly. In order to elevate the mind towards God, we need to dedicate some time on a daily basis for secluded sadhana.

The analogy of milk and water can help elucidate this point. If milk is poured into water, it cannot retain its undiluted identity because water naturally mixes with it. However, if the milk is kept separate from water and converted into yogurt, and then the yogurt is churned to extract butter, the butter becomes immiscible. It can now challenge the water, 'I will sit on your head and float; you can do nothing to me because I have become butter.' Our mind is like the milk and the world is like water. In contact with the world, the mind gets affected by it and becomes worldly. However, an environment of seclusion, which offers minimal contact with the objects of the senses, becomes conducive for elevating the mind and focusing it upon God. Once sufficient attachment to God has been achieved, one can challenge the world, 'I will live amidst all the dualities of maya but remain untouched by them.'

This instruction for seclusion has been repeated by Shree Krishna in verse 18.52: *vivikt sevī laghvāśhī* 'Live in a secluded place; control your diet.' There is a beautiful way of practically applying this instruction without disturbing our professional and social activities. In our daily schedule, we can allocate some time for sadhana or spiritual practice, where we isolate ourselves in a room that is free from worldly disturbances. Shutting ourselves out from the world, we should do sadhana to purify the mind and solidify its focus on God. If we practise in this manner for one to two hours every day, we will reap its benefits all through the day even while engaged in worldly activities. In this manner we will be able to retain the elevated state of consciousness that was gathered during the daily sadhana in isolation from the world.

शुचौ देशे प्रतिष्ठाप्य स्थिरमासनमात्मनः ।
नात्युच्छ्रितं नातिनीचं चैलाजिनकुशोत्तरम् ।।11।।

śhuchau deśhe pratiṣhṭhāpya sthiram āsanam ātmanaḥ
nātyuchchhritaṁ nāti-nīchaṁ chailājina-kuśhottaram

śhuchau—in a clean; *deśhe*—place; *pratiṣhṭhāpya*—having established; *sthiram*—steadfast; *āsanam*—seat; *ātmanaḥ*—his own; *na*—not; *ati*—too; *uchchhritam*—high; *na*—not; *ati*—too; *nīcham*—low; *chaila*—cloth; *ajina*—a deerskin; *kuśha*—Kuśh grass; *uttaram*—one over the other.

To practice Yog, one should make an asan (seat) in a sanctified place, by placing Kuśh grass, deer skin, and a cloth, one over the other. The asan should be neither too high nor too low.

In this verse, Shree Krishna explains the external practice for sadhana. *Śhuchau deśhe* means a pure or sanctified place. In the initial stages, the external environment does impact the mind. In later stages of sadhana, one is able to achieve internal purity even in dirty and unclean places. But for neophytes, clean surroundings help in keeping the mind clean as well. A mat of Kuśh grass provides temperature insulation from the ground akin to the yoga mats of today. The deer skin atop it deters poisonous pests like snakes and scorpions from approaching while one is absorbed in meditation. If the asan is too high, there is the risk of falling off; if the asan is too low, there is danger of disturbance from insects on the ground. While some instructions regarding external seating given in this verse may be somewhat anachronous to modern times; the spirit of the instruction is that the mind should be absorbed in loving devotion to God.

तत्रैकाग्रं मनः कृत्वा यतचित्तेन्द्रियक्रियः ।
उपविश्यासने युञ्ज्याद्योगमात्मविशुद्धये ।।12।।

समं कायशिरोग्रीवं धारयन्नचलं स्थिरः ।
सम्प्रेक्ष्य नासिकाग्रं स्वं दिशश्चानवलोकयन् ।।13।।

tatraikāgraṁ manaḥ kṛitvā yata-chittendriya-kriyaḥ
upaviśhyāsane yuñjyād yogam ātma-viśhuddhaye

samaṁ kāya-śhiro-grīvaṁ dhārayann achalaṁ sthiraḥ
samprekṣhya nāsikāgraṁ svaṁ diśhaśh chānavalokayan

tatra—there; *eka-agram*—one-pointed; *manaḥ*—mind; *kṛitvā*—having made; *yata-chitta*—controlling the mind; *indriya*—senses; *kriyaḥ*—activities; *upaviśhya*—being seated; *āsane*—on the seat; *yuñjyāt yogam*—should strive to practise yog; *ātma viśhuddhaye*—for purification of the mind; *samam*—straight; *kāya*—body; *śhiraḥ*—head; *grīvam*—neck; *dhārayan*—holding; *achalam*—

unmoving; *sthiraḥ*—still; *samprekṣhya*—gazing; *nāsika-agram*—at the tip of the nose; *svam*—own; *diśhaḥ*—directions; *cha*—and; *anavalokayan*—not looking.

Seated firmly on it, the yogi should strive to purify the mind by focusing it in meditation with one-pointed concentration, controlling all thoughts and activities. He must hold the body, neck, and head firmly in a straight line, and gaze at the tip of the nose, without allowing the eyes to wander.

Having described the seating for meditation, Shree Krishna next describes the posture of the body that is best for concentrating the mind. In sadhana, there is a tendency to become lazy and doze off. This happens because the material mind does not initially get as much bliss in contemplation of God as it does while relishing sense objects. This creates the possibility for the mind to become languid when focused on God. This is why you do not find people dozing off half-way through their meal, but you do see people falling asleep during meditation and while chanting God's names. To avoid this, Shree Krishna gives the instruction to sit erect. The *Brahma Sutra* also states three aphorisms regarding the posture for meditation:

āsīnaḥ sambhavāt (4.1.7)

'To do sadhana, seat yourself properly.'

achalatvaṁ chāpekṣhya (4.1.9)

'Ensure that you sit erect and still.'

dhyānāchcha (4.1.8)

'Seated in this manner, focus the mind on meditation.'

There are a number of meditative asans described in the *Hath Yoga Pradeepika*, such as *padmasan, ardha padmasan, dhyanveer asan, siddhasan,* and *sukhasan.* We may adopt any asan in which we can comfortably sit, without moving, during the period of the meditation. Maharshi Patanjali states:

sthira sukhamāsanam (*Patanjali Yog Sutra* 2.46)

'To practice meditation, sit motionless in any posture that you are comfortable in.' Some people are unable to sit on the floor due to knee or other health problems. They should not feel discouraged; they can even practise meditation while sitting on a chair, provided they fulfil the condition of sitting motionless and erect.

In this verse, Shree Krishna states that the eyes should be made to focus on the tip of the nose and prevented from wandering. As a variation, the eyes can also be kept closed. Both these techniques will be helpful in blocking out worldly distractions.

The external seat and posture do need to be appropriate, but meditation is truly a journey within us. Through meditation, we can reach deep within and cleanse the mind of endless lifetimes of dross. By learning to hold the mind in concentration, we can work upon it to harness its latent potential. The practice of meditation helps organise our personality, awakens our inner consciousness, and expands our self-awareness. Spiritual benefits of meditation are described later, in the purport on verse 6.15. Some of the additional benefits are:

- It reins in the unbridled mind and harnesses the thought energy to attain difficult goals.
- It helps maintain mental balance in the midst of adverse circumstances.
- It aids in the development of a strong resolve that is necessary for success in life.
- It enables one to eliminate bad *sanskārs* and habits and cultivate good qualities.

The best kind of meditation is one where the mind is focused on God. This is clarified in the next two verses.

प्रशान्तात्मा विगतभीर्ब्रह्मचारिव्रते स्थितः ।
मनः संयम्य मच्चित्तो युक्त आसीत मत्परः ।।14।।

praśhāntātmā vigata-bhīr brahmachāri-vrate sthitaḥ
manaḥ sanyamya mach-chitto yukta āsīta mat-paraḥ

praśhānta—serene; *ātmā*—mind; *vigata-bhīḥ*—fearless; *brahmachāri-vrate*—in the vow of celibacy; *sthitaḥ*—situated;

manaḥ—mind; *sanyamya*—having controlled; *mat-chittaḥ*—meditate on Me (Shree Krishna); *yuktaḥ*—engaged; *āsīta*—should sit; *mat-paraḥ*—having me as the supreme goal.

Thus, with a serene, fearless, and unwavering mind, and staunch in the vow of celibacy, the vigilant yogi should meditate on Me, having Me alone as the supreme goal.

Shree Krishna emphasises the practice of celibacy for success in meditation. Sexual desire facilitates the process of procreation in the animal kingdom, and animals indulge in it primarily for that purpose. In most species, there is a particular mating season; animals do not indulge in sexual activity wantonly. Since humans have a superior intellect and the freedom to indulge at will, the activity of procreation is converted into a means of licentious enjoyment. However, Vedic scriptures lay great emphasis on practising celibacy. Maharshi Patanjali states:

brahmacharya pratiṣhṭhāyāṁ vīrya lābhaḥ (*Yog Sutras* 2.38)

'The practice of celibacy leads to great enhancement of energy.'

Ayurveda, the ancient Indian science of medicine, extolls *brahmacharya* (the practice of celibacy) for its exceptional health benefits. One of the students of Dhanvantari approached his teacher after finishing his full course of Ayurveda and enquired: 'O Sage, now kindly let me know the secret of health.' Dhanvantari replied: 'This seminal energy is verily the atma. The secret of health lies in preservation of this vital force. He who wastes this vital and precious energy cannot have physical, mental, moral, and spiritual development.'

According to Ayurveda, those who waste their semen develop unsteady and agitated pran. They lose their physical and mental energy, and weaken their memory, mind, and intellect. The practice of celibacy leads to a boost of bodily energy, clarity of intellect, gigantic willpower, retentive memory, and a keen spiritual intellect. It creates a sparkle in the eyes and a lustre on the cheeks.

The definition of celibacy is not restricted to mere abstinence from physical indulgence. The *Agni Puran* states that eightfold activities related to sex must be controlled: 1) Thinking about it. 2) Talking about it. 3) Joking about it. 4) Envisioning it. 5) Desiring it. 6) Wooing to get someone interested in it. 7) Enticing someone interested in it. 8) Engaging in it. For one to be considered celibate, all these must be shunned. Thus, celibacy not only requires abstinence from sexual intercourse but also refrainment from masturbation and all other sexual practices.

Further, Shree Krishna states here that the object of meditation should be God alone. *This point is again reiterated in the next verse.*

युञ्जन्नेवं सदात्मानं योगी नियतमानसः ।
शान्तिं निर्वाणपरमां मत्संस्थामधिगच्छति ।।15।।

yuñjann evaṁ sadātmānaṁ yogī niyata-mānasaḥ
śhantiṁ nirvāṇa-paramāṁ mat-sansthām adhigachchhati

yuñjan—keeping the mind absorbed in God; *evam*—thus; *sadā*—constantly; *ātmānam*—the mind; *yogī*—a yogi; *niyata-mānasaḥ*—one with a disciplined mind; *śhāntim*—peace; *nirvāṇa*—liberation from material bondage; *paramām*—supreme; *mat-sansthām*—abides in me; *adhigachchhati*—attains.

Thus, constantly keeping the mind absorbed in Me, the yogi of disciplined mind attains nirvana and abides in Me in supreme peace.

A variety of meditation techniques exist in the world. There are Zen techniques, Buddhist techniques, Tantric techniques, Taoist techniques, Vedic techniques, and so on. Each of these has many sub-branches. Among the followers of Hinduism itself, there are innumerable techniques being practised. The million-dollar question is: which of these should we adopt for our personal practice? Shree Krishna makes this riddle easy to solve. He states that the object of meditation should be God Himself and God alone.

The aim of meditation is not merely to enhance concentration and focus but also to purify the mind. Meditation on the breath, chakras, void, flame, and other items is helpful in developing focus. However, purification of the mind is only possible when we fix it upon an all-pure object, which is God Himself. Verse 14.26 states that God is beyond the three modes of material nature, and when one fixes the mind upon Him, it too rises above the three modes. Thus, while meditating upon the pranas may be called transcendental by its practitioners, true transcendental meditation is upon God alone.

Now, what is the way of to focus the mind on God? We can make all of God's divine attributes—Names, Forms, Virtues, Pastimes, Abodes, and Associates—the objects of meditation. They all are non-different from God and replete with all His energies. Hence, devotees may meditate upon any of these and get the true benefit of meditating upon God. In the various bhakti traditions in India, the name of God is made the basis of contemplation. The Ramayan states:

brahma rām teṅ nāmu baṛa, bara dāyaka bara dāni

'God's name is bigger than God Himself, in terms of its utility to the souls.' Taking His name is a very convenient way of remembering God, since it can be taken anywhere and everywhere—while walking, talking, sitting, eating, and any other activity we do.

However, for most *sādhaks*, His name by itself is not sufficiently attractive for enchanting the mind. Due to *sanskārs* of endless lifetimes, the mind is naturally drawn to forms. Using the form of God as the foundation, meditation becomes natural and easy. This is called *Roop dhyan* meditation.

Once the mind is focused upon the form of God, we can then further enhance it by contemplating on the virtues of God—His compassion, His beauty, His knowledge, His love, His benevolence, His grace, and so on. One can then advance in meditation by serving God in the mind. We can visualise ourselves offering foodstuffs to Him, worshipping Him, singing to Him, massaging Him, fanning Him, bathing Him, cooking for Him, and other services. This is called *mānasī sevā* (serving God in the mind). In this way, we can meditate upon the Names, Forms, Virtues, Pastimes, Abodes, and Associates of God. All these become powerful means of fulfilling Shree Krishna's instruction to Arjun to keep the mind absorbed in Him.

At the end of the verse, Shree Krishna gives the ultimate benefits of meditation, which are liberation from maya and the everlasting beatitude of God-realisation.

नात्यश्नतस्तु योगोऽस्ति न चैकान्तमनश्नतः ।
न चाति स्वप्नशीलस्य जाग्रतो नैव चार्जुन ।।16।।

nātyaśhnatastu yogo 'sti na chaikāntam anaśhnataḥ
na chāti-svapna-śhīlasya jāgrato naiva chārjuna

na—not; *ati*—too much; *aśhnataḥ*—one who eats; *tu*—however; *yogaḥ*—Yog; *asti*—there is; *na*—not; *cha*—and; *ekāntam*—at all; *anaśhnataḥ*—abstaining from eating; *na*—not; *cha*—and; *ati*—too much; *svapna-śhīlasya*—one who sleeps; *jāgrataḥ*—one who does not sleep enough; *na*—not; *eva*—certainly; *cha*—and; *arjuna*—Arjun.

O Arjun, those who eat too much or too little, sleep too much or too little, cannot attain success in Yog.

After describing the object of meditation and the end-goal achieved by it, Shree Krishna shares some regulations to follow. He states that those who break the rules of bodily maintenance cannot be successful in Yog. Often beginners on the path with their incomplete wisdom state: 'You are the soul and not this body. So simply engage in spiritual activity and forget about the maintenance of the body.'

However, such a philosophy cannot get one too far. It is true that we are not the body, yet the body is our carrier as long as we live, and we are obliged to take care of it. The Ayurvedic text, *Charak Samhitā* states: *śharīra mādhyaṁ khalu dharma sādhanam* 'The body is the vehicle for engaging in religious activity.' If the body becomes unwell, then spiritual pursuits get impeded too. The Ramayan states: *tanu binu bhajana veda nahiṅ varanā* 'The Vedas do not recommend that we ignore the body while engaging in spirituality.' On the contrary, they instruct us to take good care of our body with the help of material science. The *Īśhopaniṣhad* states:

andhaṁ tamaḥ praviśhanti ye 'vidyām upāsate
tato bhūya iva te tamo ya u vidyāyām ratāḥ (9)

'Those who cultivate only material science go to hell. But those who cultivate only spiritual science go to an even darker hell.' Material science is necessary for the maintenance of our body while spiritual science is necessary for the manifestation of the internal divinity within us. We must balance both in our life to reach the ultimate goal of God-realisation. Hence, yogasans, pranayam, and the science of proper diet are an essential part of Vedic knowledge.

Each of the four Vedas has its associate Veda for material knowledge. The associate Veda of *Atharva Veda* is Ayurveda, which is the ancient science of medicine and good health. This demonstrates that the Vedas lay emphasis on the maintenance of physical health. Accordingly, Shree Krishna says that overeating or not eating at all, extreme activity or complete inactivity, all are impediments to Yog. Spiritual practitioners should take good care of their body by eating fresh nutritious food, doing daily exercise, and getting the right amount of sleep every night.

युक्ताहारविहारस्य युक्तचेष्टस्य कर्मसु ।
युक्तस्वप्नावबोधस्य योगो भवति दुःखहा ।।17।।

yuktāhāra-vihārasya yukta-cheṣhṭasya karmasu
yukta-svapnāvabodhasya yogo bhavati duḥkha-hā

yukta—moderate; *āhāra*—eating; *vihārasya*—recreation; *yukta cheṣhṭasya karmasu*—balanced in work; *yukta*—regulated; *svapna-avabodhasya*—sleep and wakefulness; *yogaḥ*—Yog; *bhavati*—becomes; *duḥkha-hā*—the slayer of sorrows.

But those who are temperate in eating and recreation, balanced in work, and regulated in sleep, can mitigate all sorrows by practising Yog.

Yog is the union of the soul with God. The opposite of Yog is *bhog* which means engagement in sensual pleasures. Indulgence in *bhog* violates the natural laws of the body and results in *rog* (disease). As stated in the previous verse, if the body becomes diseased, it impedes the practice of

Yog. Thus, in this verse, Shree Krishna states that by being temperate in physical activities and practising Yog, we can become free from the sorrows of the body and mind.

The same instruction was repeated two-and-a-half millennia after Shree Krishna by Gautam Buddha, when He recommended the golden middle path between severe asceticism and sensual indulgence. There is a beautiful story regarding this:

It is said that before gaining enlightenment, Gautam Buddha once gave up eating and drinking, and sat in meditation. However, after a few days of practising in this manner, the lack of nourishment made Him weak and dizzy, and He found it impossible to steady His mind. At that time, some village women happened to be passing by. They were carrying water pots on their heads that they had filled from the nearby river and were singing a song. The words of the song were: 'Tighten the strings of the *tānpurā* (a stringed Indian musical instrument, resembling a guitar). But do not tighten them so much that the strings break.' Their words entered the ears of Gautam Buddha, and He exclaimed, 'These illiterate village women are singing such words of wisdom. They contain a message for us humans. We too should tighten our bodies (practice austerities), but not to the extent that the body is destroyed.'

Benjamin Franklin, a founding father of the United States, is regarded as a self-made man. In an effort to develop his character, starting at the age of twenty, he maintained a diary in which he tracked his performance related to the thirteen activities he wanted to grow in. The first activity was 'Temperance: Eat not to dullness; drink not to elevation.'

यदा विनियतं चित्तमात्मन्येवावतिष्ठते ।
निःस्पृहः सर्वकामेभ्यो युक्त इत्युच्यते तदा ।।18।।

yadā viniyataṁ chittam ātmanyevāvatiṣhṭhate
niḥspṛihaḥ sarva-kāmebhyo yukta ityuchyate tadā

yadā—when; *viniyatam*—fully controlled; *chittam*—the mind; *ātmani*—of the self; *eva*—certainly; *avatiṣhṭhate*—stays; *nispṛihaḥ*—free from cravings: *sarva*—all; *kāmebhyaḥ*—for yearning of the senses; *yuktaḥ*—situated in perfect Yog; *iti*—thus; *uchyate*—is said; *tadā*—then.

With thorough discipline, they learn to withdraw the mind from selfish cravings and rivet it on the unsurpassable good of the self. Such persons are said to be in Yog and are free from all yearning of the senses.

When does a person complete the practice of Yog? The answer is when the controlled *chitta* becomes fixed and focused exclusively on God. It is then simultaneously and automatically weaned away from all cravings of the senses and desires for worldly enjoyment. At that time, one can be considered as *yukt* or having perfect Yog. At the end of this very chapter, in verse 6.47, He also states: 'Of all yogis, those whose minds are always absorbed in Me, and who engage in devotion to Me with great faith, them I consider to be the highest of all.'

यथा दीपो निवातस्थो नेङ्गते सोपमा स्मृता ।
योगिनो यतचित्तस्य युञ्जतो योगमात्मनः ।।19।।

yathā dīpo nivāta-stho neṅgate sopamā smṛitā
yogino yata-chittasya yuñjato yogam ātmanaḥ

yathā—as; *dīpaḥ*—a lamp; *nivāta-sthaḥ*—in a windless place; *na*—does not; *iṅgate*—flickers; *sā*—this; *upamā*—analogy; *smṛitā*—is considered; *yoginaḥ*—of a yogi; *yata-chittasya*—whose mind is disciplined; *yuñjataḥ*—steadily practising; *yogam*—in meditation; *ātmanaḥ*—on the Supreme.

Just as a lamp in a windless place does not flicker, so the disciplined mind of a yogi remains steady in meditation on the Supreme.

In this verse, Shree Krishna gives the simile of the flame of a lamp. In the wind, the flame flickers naturally and is impossible to control. However, in a windless place, the flame becomes as steady as a picture. Similarly, the mind is fickle by nature and very difficult to control. But when the mind of a yogi is in enthralled union with God, it becomes sheltered against the winds of desire. Such a yogi holds the mind steadily under control by the power of devotion.

**यत्रोपरमते चित्तं निरुद्धं योगसेवया ।
यत्र चैवात्मनात्मानं पश्यन्नात्मनि तुष्यति ।।20।।**

*yatroparamate chittaṁ niruddhaṁ yoga-sevayā
yatra chaivātmanātmānaṁ paśhyann ātmani tuṣhyati*

yatra—when; *uparamate*—rejoice inner joy; *chittam*—the mind; *niruddham*—restrained; *yoga-sevayā*—by the practice of yog; *yatra*—when; *cha*—and; *eva*—certainly; *ātmanā*—through the purified mind; *ātmānam*—the soul; *paśhyan*—behold; *ātmani*—in the self; *tuṣhyati*—is satisfied.

When the mind, restrained from material activities, becomes still by the practice of Yog, then the yogi is able to behold the soul through the purified mind, and he rejoices in the inner joy.

After describing the process of meditation and the state of its perfection, Shree Krishna now reveals the results of such effort. When the mind is purified, one is able to perceive the self as distinct from the body, mind, and intellect. For example, if there is muddy water in a glass, we cannot see through it. However, if we put alum in the water, the mud settles down and the water becomes clear. Similarly, when the mind is unclean, it obscures perception of the soul and any acquired scriptural knowledge of the atma is only at the theoretical level. But when the mind becomes pure, the soul is directly perceived through realisation.

**सुखमात्यन्तिकं यत्तद्बुद्धिग्राह्यमतीन्द्रियम् ।
वेत्ति यत्र न चैवायं स्थितश्चलति तत्त्वतः ।।21।।**

*sukham ātyantikaṁ yat tad buddhi-grāhyam atīndriyam
vetti yatra na chaivāyaṁ sthitaśh chalati tattvataḥ*

sukham—happiness; *ātyantikam*—limitless; *yat*—which; *tat*—that; *buddhi*—intellect; *grāhyam*—grasp; *atīndriyam*—transcending the senses; *vetti*—knows; *yatra*—wherein; *na*—never; *cha*—and; *eva*—certainly; *ayam*—he; *sthitaḥ*—situated; *chalati*—deviates; *tattvataḥ*—Eternal Truth.

In that joyous state of Yog, called samadhi, one experiences supreme boundless divine bliss, and thus situated, one never deviates from the Eternal Truth.

The yearning for bliss is the intrinsic nature of the soul. It stems from the fact that we are tiny parts of God, who is an ocean of bliss. Many quotations from the Vedic scriptures establishing this were mentioned in verse 5.21. Here are some more quotations expressing the nature of God as an infinite ocean of bliss:

raso vai saḥ rasaṁ hyevāyaṁ labdhvā nandī bhavati

(*Taittirīya Upanishad* 2.7)

'God is bliss Himself; the individual soul becomes blissful on attaining Him.'

ānandamayo 'bhyāsāt (*Brahma Sutra* 1.1.12)

'God is the veritable form of bliss.'

satya jñānānantānanda mātraika rasa mūrtayaḥ

(Bhagavatam 10.13.54)

'The divine form of God is made of eternity, knowledge, and bliss.'

ānanda sindhu madhya tava vāsā, binu jāne kata marasi piyāsā

(Ramayan)

'God, who is the ocean of bliss, is seated within you. Without knowing Him, how can your thirst for happiness be satiated?'

We have been seeking perfect bliss for eons, and everything we do is in search of that bliss. However, from the objects of gratification, the mind and senses perceive only a shadowy reflection of true bliss. This sensual gratification fails to satisfy the longing of the soul within which yearns for the infinite bliss of God.

When the mind is in union with God, the soul experiences the ineffable and sublime bliss beyond the scope of the senses. This state is called samadhi in the Vedic scriptures. Sage Patanjali states:

samādhisiddhirīśhvara praṇidhānāt

(*Patanjali Yog Darshan* 2.45)

'For success in samadhi, surrender to the Supreme Lord.'

In the state of samadhi, experiencing complete satisfaction and contentment, the soul has nothing left to desire, and thus becomes firmly situated in the Absolute Truth, without deviating from it for even a moment.

यं लब्ध्वा चापरं लाभं मन्यते नाधिकं ततः ।
यस्मिन्स्थितो न दुःखेन गुरुणापि विचाल्यते ।।22।।

yaṁ labdhvā chāparaṁ lābhaṁ manyate nādhikaṁ tataḥ
yasmin sthito na duḥkhena guruṇāpi vichālyate

yam—which; *labdhvā*—having gained; *cha*—and; *aparam*—any other; *lābham*—gain; *manyate*—considers; *na*—not; *adhikam*—greater; *tataḥ*—than that; *yasmin*—in which; *sthitaḥ*—being situated; *na*—never; *duḥkhena*—by sorrow; *guruṇā*—(by) the greatest; *api*—even; *vichālyate*—is shaken.

Having gained that state, one does not consider any attainment to be greater. Being thus established, one is not shaken even in the midst of the greatest calamity.

In the material realm, no extent of attainment satiates a person totally. A poor person strives hard to become rich and feels satisfied if he or she is able to become a millionaire. But when that same millionaire looks at a billionaire, discontentment sets in again. The billionaire is also discontented by looking at an even richer person. No matter what happiness we get, when we perceive a higher state of happiness, the feeling of unfulfilment lingers. But happiness achieved from the state of Yog is the infinite bliss of God. Since there is nothing higher than that, on experiencing that infinite bliss, the soul naturally perceives that it has reached its goal.

God's divine bliss is also eternal, and it can never be snatched away from the yogi who has attained it once. Such a God-realised soul, though residing in the material body, remains in the state of divine consciousness. Sometimes, externally, it may seem that the saint is facing tribulations in the form of illness, antagonistic people, or an oppressive environment, but internally, the saint retains divine consciousness and continues to relish the bliss of God. Thus, even the biggest difficulty cannot shake such a saint. Established in union with God, the saint rises above bodily consciousness and is not affected by physical harm. Such was the internal state of Prahalad when he was tossed in a pit of snakes, tortured with weapons, placed in the fire, and even thrown off a cliff, but none of these difficulties could sever his devotional union with God.

तं विद्याद् दुःखसंयोगवियोगं योगसञ्ज्ञितम् ।
स निश्चयेन योक्तव्यो योगोऽनिर्विण्णचेतसा ।।23।।

taṁ vidyād duḥkha-sanyoga-viyogaṁ yogasañjñitam
sa niśhchayena yoktavyo yogo 'nirviṇṇa-chetasā

tam—that; *vidyāt*—you should know; *duḥkha-sanyoga-viyogam*—state of severance from union with misery; *yoga-sañjñitam*—is known as yog; *saḥ*—that; *niśhchayena*—resolutely; *yoktavyaḥ*—should be practised; *yogaḥ*—yog; *anirviṇṇa-chetasā*—with an undeviating mind.

That state of severance from union with misery is known as Yog. This Yog should be resolutely practised with determination free from pessimism.

The material world is the realm of maya, and it has been termed by Shree Krishna in verse 8.15 as *duḥkhālayam aśhāśhvatam* or temporary and full of misery. The material energy, maya, is compared to darkness. It has put us in the darkness of ignorance and is making us suffer in the world. The darkness of maya naturally gets dispelled when we bring the light of God into our heart. Chaitanya Mahaprabhu states this very beautifully:

kṛiṣhṇa sūrya-sama, māyā haya andhakāra
yāhāñ kṛiṣhṇa, tāhāñ nāhi māyāra adhikāra

(*Chaitanya Charitāmṛit*, *Madhya Leela*, 22.31)

'God is like the light and maya is like darkness. Just as darkness does not have the power to engulf light, similarly, maya can never overcome God.' Now, the nature of God is divine bliss while the consequence of maya is misery. Thus, one who attains the divine bliss of God can never be overcome by the misery of maya again.

Thus, the state of Yog implies both 1) attainment of bliss, and 2) freedom from misery. Shree Krishna emphasises both successively. In the previous verse, the attainment of bliss was highlighted as the result of Yog; in this verse, freedom from misery is being emphasised.

In the second line of this verse, Shree Krishna states that the stage of perfection has to be reached through determined practice. *He then goes on to explain how we must practise meditation.*

सङ्कल्पप्रभवान्कामांस्त्यक्त्वा सर्वानशेषतः ।
मनसैवेन्द्रियग्रामं विनियम्य समन्ततः ।।24।।

शनैः शनैरुपरमेद्बुद्ध्या धृतिगृहीतया ।
आत्मसंस्थं मनः कृत्वा न किञ्चिदपि चिन्तयेत् ।।25।।

saṅkalpa-prabhavān kāmāns tyaktvā sarvān aśheṣhataḥ
manasaivendriya-grāmaṁ viniyamya samantataḥ

śhanaiḥ śhanair uparamed buddhyā dhṛiti-gṛihītayā
ātma-sansthaṁ manaḥ kṛitvā na kiñchid api chintayet

saṅkalpa—a resolve; *prabhavān*—born of; *kāmān*—desires; *tyaktvā*—having abandoned; *sarvān*—all; *aśheṣhataḥ*—completely; *manasā*—through the mind; *eva*—certainly; *indriya-grāmam*—the group of senses; *viniyamya*—restraining; *samantataḥ*—from all sides; *śhanaiḥ*—gradually; *śhanaiḥ*—gradually; *uparamet*—attain peace; *buddhyā*—by intellect; *dhṛiti-gṛihītayā*—achieved through determination of resolve that is in accordance with scriptures; *ātma-sanstham*—fixed in God; *manaḥ*—mind; *kṛitvā*—having made; *na*—not; *kiñchit*—anything; *api*—even; *chintayet*—should think of.

Completely renouncing all desires arising from thoughts of the world, one should restrain the senses from all sides with the mind. Slowly and steadily, with conviction in the intellect, the mind will become fixed in God alone and will think of nothing else.

Meditation requires the dual process of removing the mind from the world and focusing it on God. Here, Shree Krishna begins by describing the first part of the process—taking the mind away from the world.

Thoughts of worldly things, people, events, and other distractions come to the mind when it is attached to the world. Initially, the thoughts are in the form of *sphurṇā* (flashes of feelings and ideas). When we insist on the implementation of *sphurṇā*, it becomes *saṅkalp*. Thus, thoughts lead to *saṅkalp* (pursuit of these objects) and *vikalp* (revulsion from them), depending upon whether the attachment is positive or negative. The seed of pursuit and revulsion grows into the plant of desire, 'This should happen. This should not happen.' Both *saṅkalp* and *vikalp* immediately create impressions on the mind, like the film of a camera exposed to light. In this manner, they directly impede meditation upon God. They also have a natural tendency to flare up, and a desire that is a seed today can become an inferno tomorrow. Consequently, one who desires success in meditation should renounce the affinity for material objects.

Having described the first part of the meditation process—removing the mind from the world—Shree Krishna then talks of the second part. The mind should be made to reside upon God. He says this will not happen automatically, but with determined effort, success will come slowly.

Determination of resolve that is in accordance with the scriptures is called *dhṛiti*. This determination comes with conviction of the intellect.

Many people acquire academic knowledge of the scriptures about the nature of the self and the futility of worldly pursuits. But their daily life is at odds with this knowledge, and they are seen to indulge in sin, sex, and intoxication. This happens because their intellect is not convinced about that knowledge. The power of discrimination comes with the conviction of the intellect about the impermanence of the world and the eternality of one's relationship with God. Thus, utilising the intellect, one must gradually cease sensual indulgence. This is called *pratyāhār* or control of the mind and senses from chasing objects of the senses. Success in *pratyāhār* does not come immediately. It can be achieved through gradual and repeated exercise. *Shree Krishna explains next what that exercise involves.*

यतो यतो निश्चरति मनश्चञ्चलमस्थिरम् ।
ततस्ततो नियम्यैतदात्मन्येव वशं नयेत् ।।26।।

yato yato niśhcharati manaśh chañchalam asthiram
tatas tato niyamyaitad ātmanyeva vaśhaṁ nayet

yataḥ yataḥ—whenever and wherever; *niśhcharati*—wanders; *manaḥ*—the mind; *chañchalam*—restless; *asthiram*—unsteady; *tataḥ tataḥ*—from there; *niyamya*—having restrained; *etat*—this; *ātmani*—on God; *eva*—certainly; *vaśham*—control; *nayet*—should bring.

Whenever and wherever the restless and unsteady mind wanders, one should bring it back and continually focus it on God.

Success in meditation is not achieved in a day; the path to perfection is long and arduous. When we sit for meditation with the resolve to focus our mind on God, we will find that ever so often, it wanders off in worldly *saṅkalp* and *vikalp*. To deal with this, it becomes important to understand the three steps involved in the process of meditation:

- With the intellect's power of discrimination, we decide that the world is not our goal. Hence, we forcefully remove the mind from the world. This requires effort.

- Again, with the power of discrimination, we understand that God alone is ours, and God-realisation is our goal. Hence, we bring the mind to focus upon God. This also requires effort.
- The mind comes away from God and wanders back into the world. This does not require effort; it happens automatically.

When the third step happens by itself, *sādhaks* often become disappointed and lament, 'I tried so hard to focus upon God, but the mind went back into the world.' Shree Krishna advises us not to feel disappointed. He says the mind is fickle and wanders off, despite our best efforts to control it. However, when it does drift away, we should once again repeat steps 1 and 2—take the mind away from the world and bring it back to God. Once again, we will experience that step 3 takes place by itself. We should not lose heart, and instead, again repeat steps 1 and 2.

We will have to do this repeatedly. Then slowly, the mind's attachment towards God will start increasing. And simultaneously, its detachment from the world will also increase. As this happens, it will become easier and easier to meditate. But in the beginning, we must be prepared for the battle involved in disciplining the mind.

प्रशान्तमनसं ह्येनं योगिनं सुखमुत्तमम् ।
उपैति शान्तरजसं ब्रह्मभूतमकल्मषम् ।।27।।

praśhānta-manasaṁ hyenaṁ yoginaṁ sukham uttamam
upaiti śhānta-rajasaṁ brahma-bhūtam akalmaṣham

praśhānta—peaceful; *manasam*—mind; *hi*—certainly; *enam*—this; *yoginam*—yogi; *sukham uttamam*—the highest bliss; *upaiti*—attains; *śhānta-rajasam*—whose passions are subdued; *brahma-bhūtam*—endowed with God-realisation; *akalmaṣham*—without sin.

Great transcendental happiness comes to the yogi whose mind is calm, whose passions are subdued, who is without sin, and who sees everything in connection with God.

As a yogi perfects the practice of withdrawing the mind from sense objects and securing it upon God, passions get subdued, and the mind becomes utterly serene. Earlier, effort was required to focus it on God, but now it naturally runs to Him. At this stage, the elevated meditator sees everything in its connection with God. Sage Narad states:

tat prāpya tad evāvalokayati, tad eva śhṛiṇoti,
tad eva bhāṣhayati, tad eva chintayati

(*Nārad Bhakti Darshan*, Sutra 55)

'The consciousness of the devotee whose mind is united in love with God is always absorbed in Him. Such a devotee always sees Him, hears Him, speaks of Him, and thinks of Him.' When the mind gets absorbed in God in this manner, the soul begins to experience a glimpse of the infinite bliss of God who is seated within.

Sādhaks often ask how they can know that they are progressing. The answer is embedded in this verse. When we find our inner transcendental bliss increasing, we can consider it as a sign that our mind is coming under control and the consciousness is getting spiritually elevated. Here, Shree Krishna says that when we are *śhānta-rajasaṁ* (free from passion) and *akalmaṣham* (sinless), then we will become *brahma-bhūtam* (endowed with God-realisation). At that stage, we will experience *sukham uttamam* (the highest bliss).

युञ्जन्नेवं सदात्मानं योगी विगतकल्मषः ।
सुखेन ब्रह्मसंस्पर्शमत्यन्तं सुखमश्नुते ।।28।।

yuñjann evaṁ sadātmānaṁ yogī vigata-kalmaṣhaḥ
sukhena brahma-sansparśham atyantaṁ sukham aśhnute

yuñjan—uniting (the self with God); *evam*—thus; *sadā*—always; *ātmānam*—the self; *yogī*—a yogi; *vigata*—free from; *kalmaṣhaḥ*—sins; *sukhena*—easily; *brahma-sansparśham*—constantly in touch with the Supreme; *atyantam*—the highest; *sukham*—bliss; *aśhnute*—attains.

The self-controlled yogi, thus uniting the self with God, becomes free from material contamination, and being in constant touch with the Supreme, achieves the highest state of perfect happiness.

Happiness can be classified into four categories:

sāttvikaṁ sukhamātmotthaṁ viṣhayotthaṁ tu rājasam
tāmasaṁ moha dainyotthaṁ nirguṇaṁ madapāśhrayām

(Bhagavatam 11.25.29)

Tamasic happiness: This is the pleasure derived from narcotics, alcohol, cigarettes, meat products, violence, sleep, and so on.

Rajasic happiness: This is the pleasure from the gratification of the five senses and the mind.

Sattvic happiness: This is the pleasure experienced through practising virtues, such as compassion, forgiveness, service to others, cultivation of knowledge, and stilling of the mind. It includes the bliss of self-realisation experienced by the jnanis when they stabilise the mind on the soul.

***Nirguna* happiness:** This is the divine bliss of God which is infinite in extent. Shree Krishna explains that the yogi who becomes free from material contamination and becomes united with God attains this highest state of perfect happiness. He has called this unlimited bliss in verse 5.21 and supreme bliss in verse 6.21.

सर्वभूतस्थमात्मानं सर्वभूतानि चात्मनि ।
ईक्षते योगयुक्तात्मा सर्वत्र समदर्शनः ।।29।।

sarva-bhūta-stham ātmānaṁ sarva-bhūtāni chātmani
īkṣhate yoga-yuktātmā sarvatra sama-darśhanaḥ

sarva-bhūta-stham—situated in all living beings; *ātmānam*—Supreme Soul; *sarva*—all; *bhūtāni*—living beings; *cha*—and; *ātmani*—in God; *īkṣhate*—sees; *yoga-yukta-ātmā*—one united in consciousness with God; *sarvatra*—everywhere; *sama-darśhanaḥ*—equal vision.

The true yogis, uniting their consciousness with God, see with an equal eye, all living beings in God and God in all living beings.

In India, during the festival of Diwali, shops sell sugar candy moulded in various forms, as cars, airplanes, men, women, animals, balls, and caps. Children fight with their parents that they want a car, elephant, and so on. The parents smile at their innocuousness, thinking that they all are made from the same ingredient (sugar) and are equally sweet.

Similarly, the ingredient of everything that exists is God Himself, in the form of His various energies.

eka deśhasthitasyāgnirjyotsnā vistāriṇī yathā
parasya brahmaṇaḥ śhaktistathedamakhilaṁ jagat

(*Nārad Pañcharātra*)

'Just as the sun, while remaining in one place, spreads its light everywhere, similarly the Supreme Lord, by His various energies pervades and sustains everything that exists.' The perfected yogis, in the light of realised knowledge, see everything in its connection with God.

यो मां पश्यति सर्वत्र सर्वं च मयि पश्यति ।
तस्याहं न प्रणश्यामि स च मे न प्रणश्यति ।।30।।

yo māṁ paśhyati sarvatra sarvaṁ cha mayi paśhyati
tasyāhaṁ na praṇaśhyāmi sa cha me na praṇaśhyati

yaḥ—who; *mām*—me; *paśhyati*—see; *sarvatra*—everywhere; *sarvam*—everything; *cha*—and; *mayi*—in me; *paśhyati*—see; *tasya*—for him; *aham*—I; *na*—not; *praṇaśhyāmi*—lost; *saḥ*—that person; *cha*—and; *me*—to me; *na*—nor; *praṇaśhyati*—lost.

For those who see Me everywhere and see all things in Me, I am never lost nor are they ever lost to Me.

To lose God means to let the mind wander away from Him, and to be with Him means to unite the mind with Him. The easy way to unite the mind with God is to learn to see that everything is connected with Him. For example, let us say that someone hurts us. It is the nature of the mind to develop sentiments of resentment and hatred towards such a person. However, if we permit that to happen, then our mind comes away from the divine realm, and the devotional union of our mind with God ceases. Instead, if we see the Supreme Lord seated in that person, we will think, 'God is testing me through this person. He wants me to increase the virtue of tolerance, and that is why He is inspiring this person to behave badly with me. But I will not permit the incident to disturb me.' Thinking in this way, we will be able to prevent the mind from becoming a victim of negative sentiments.

Similarly, the mind separates from God when it gets attached to a friend or relative. Now, if we train the mind to see God in that person, then each time the mind wanders towards him or her, we will think, 'Shree Krishna is seated in this person, and that is why I am feeling this attraction.' In this manner, the mind will continue to retain its devotional absorption in the Supreme.

Sometimes, the mind laments over past incidents. This again separates the mind from the divine realm because lamentation takes the mind into the past and the present contemplation of God and guru ceases. Now if we see that incident in connection with God, we will think, 'The Lord deliberately arranged for me to experience tribulation in the world so that I may develop detachment. He is so concerned about my welfare that He mercifully arranges for the proper circumstances that are beneficial for my spiritual progress.' By thinking thus, we will be able to protect our devotional focus. Sage Narad states:

loka hānau chintā na kāryā niveditātma loka vedatvāt

(*Nārad Bhakti Darshan*, Sutra 61)

'When you suffer a reversal in the world, do not lament or brood over it. See the grace of God in that incident.' Our self-interest lies in somehow or the other keeping the mind in God, and the simple trick to accomplish this is to see God in everything and everyone. That is the practice stage, which slowly leads to the perfection that is mentioned in this verse, where we are never lost to God and He is never lost to us.

सर्वभूतस्थितं यो मां भजत्येकत्वमास्थितः ।
सर्वथा वर्तमानोऽपि स योगी मयि वर्तते ।।31।।

sarva-bhūta-sthitaṁ yo māṁ bhajatyekatvam āsthitaḥ
sarvathā vartamāno 'pi sa yogī mayi vartate

sarva-bhūta-sthitam—situated in all beings; *yaḥ*—who; *mām*—me; *bhajati*—worships; *ekatvam*—in unity; *āsthitaḥ*—established; *sarvathā*—in all kinds of; *varta-mānaḥ*—remain; *api*—although; *saḥ*—he; *yogī*—a yogi; *mayi*—in me; *vartate*—dwells.

The yogi who is established in union with Me and worships Me as the Supreme Soul residing in all beings, dwells only in Me, though engaged in all kinds of activities.

God is all-pervading in the world. He is also seated in everyone's heart as the Supreme Soul. In verse 18.61, Shree Krishna states: 'I am situated in the hearts of all living beings.' Thus, within the body of each living being, there are two personalities—the soul and the Supreme Soul. This leads to primarily four levels of vision based upon the state of people's consciousness:

1. Those in material consciousness see everyone as the body and make distinctions on the basis of caste, creed, gender, age, social status, nationality, and so on.

2. Those in superior consciousness see everyone as the soul. In verse 5.18, Shree Krishna states: 'The truly learned, with the eyes of divine knowledge, see with equal vision a Brahmin, a cow, an elephant, a dog, and a dog-eater.'

3. The elevated yogis in even higher consciousness see God seated as the Supreme Soul in everyone. They also perceive the world, but they are unconcerned about it. They are like the *hansas,* or swans, who can drink the milk and leave out the water from a mixture of milk and water.

4. The most elevated yogis are called *paramahansas*. They only see God and have no perception of the world. This was the level of realisation of Shukadev, son of Ved Vyas, as stated in the Shreemad Bhagavatam:

yaṁ pravrajantam anupetam apeta kṛityaṁ
dvaipāyano viraha-kātara ājuhāva
putreti tan-mayatayā taravo 'bhinedus
taṁ sarva-bhūta-hṛidayaṁ munim ānato 'smi (1.2.2)

The verse states that when Shukadev entered the renounced order of sanyas, walking away from home in his childhood itself, he was at such an elevated level that he had no perception of the world. He did not even notice the beautiful women bathing nude in a lake, while he happened to pass by there. All that he perceived was God; all that he heard was God; all that he thought about was God.

In this verse, Shree Krishna is talking about the perfected yogis who are in the third and fourth stages of the above levels of realisation as listed above.

आत्मौपम्येन सर्वत्र समं पश्यति योऽर्जुन ।
सुखं वा यदि वा दुःखं स योगी परमो मतः ।।32।।

ātmaupamyena sarvatra samaṁ paśhyati yo 'rjuna
sukhaṁ vā yadi vā duḥkhaṁ sa yogī paramo mataḥ

ātma-aupamyena—similar to oneself; *sarvatra*—everywhere; *samam*—equally; *paśhyati*—see; *yaḥ*—who; *arjuna*—Arjun; *sukham*—joy; *vā*—or; *yadi*—if; *vā*—or; *duḥkham*—sorrow; *saḥ*—such; *yogī*—a yogi; *paramaḥ*—highest; *mataḥ*—is considered.

I regard them to be perfect yogis who see the true equality of all living beings and respond to the joys and sorrows of others as if they were their own.

We consider all the limbs of our body as ours and are equally concerned if any of them is damaged. We are incontrovertible in the conviction that the harm done to any of our limbs is harm done to ourselves. Similarly, those who see God in all beings consider the joys and sorrows of others as their own. Therefore, such yogis are always the well-wishers of all souls and they strive for the eternal benefit of all. This is the *sama-darshana* (equality of vision) of perfected yogis.

अर्जुन उवाच ।
योऽयं योगस्त्वया प्रोक्तः साम्येन मधुसूदन ।
एतस्याहं न पश्यामि चञ्चलत्वात्स्थितिं स्थिराम् ।।33।।

arjuna uvācha
yo 'yaṁ yogas tvayā proktaḥ sāmyena madhusūdana
etasyāhaṁ na paśhyāmi chañchalatvāt sthitiṁ sthirām

arjunaḥ uvācha—Arjun said; *yaḥ*—which; *ayam*—this; *yogaḥ*—system of Yog; *tvayā*—by you; *proktaḥ*—described; *sāmyena*—by equanimity; *madhu-sūdana*—Shree Krishna, killer of the demon named Madhu; *etasya*—of this; *aham*—I; *na*—do not; *paśhyāmi*—see; *chañchalatvāt*—due to restlessness; *sthitim*—situation; *sthirām*—steady.

Arjun said: The system of Yog that You have described, O Madhusudan, appears impractical and unattainable to me, due to the restless mind.

Arjun starts this verse with the words *yo yam,* or 'This system of Yog', referring to the process described from verse 6.10 onwards. Shree Krishna has just finished explaining that for perfection in Yog we must:

- Subdue the senses.
- Give up all desires.
- Focus the mind upon God alone.
- Think of Him with an unwavering mind.
- See everyone with equal vision.

Arjun frankly expresses his reservation about what he has heard by saying that it is impractical. None of the above can be accomplished without controlling the mind. If the mind is restless, then all these aspects of Yog become unattainable as well.

चञ्चलं हि मनः कृष्ण प्रमाथि बलवद्दृढम् ।
तस्याहं निग्रहं मन्ये वायोरिव सुदुष्करम् ।।34।।

chañchalaṁ hi manaḥ kṛiṣhṇa pramāthi balavad dṛiḍham
tasyāhaṁ nigrahaṁ manye vāyor iva su-duṣhkaram

chañchalam—restless; *hi*—certainly; *manaḥ*—mind; *kṛiṣhṇa*—Shree Krishna; *pramāthi*—turbulent; *bala-vat*—strong; *dṛiḍham*—obstinate; *tasya*—its; *aham*—I; *nigraham*—control; *manye*—think; *vāyoḥ*—of the wind; *iva*—like; *su-duṣhkaram*—difficult to perform.

The mind is very restless, turbulent, strong, and obstinate, O Krishna. It appears to me that it is more difficult to control than the wind.

Arjun speaks for us all when he describes the troublesome mind. It is restless because it keeps flitting in different directions, from subject to subject. It is turbulent because it creates upheavals in one's consciousness, in the form of hatred, anger, lust, greed, envy, anxiety, fear, attachment, and a host of other negativities. It is strong because it overpowers the intellect with its vigorous currents and destroys the faculty of discrimination. The mind is also obstinate because when it catches a harmful thought, it refuses to let go, and continues to ruminate over it again and again, even to the dismay of the intellect. Thus, enumerating its unwholesome characteristics, Arjun declares that the mind is even more difficult to control than the wind. It is a powerful analogy for no one can ever think of controlling the mighty wind in the sky.

In this verse, Arjun has addressed the Lord as Krishna. The word 'Krishna' means: *karṣhati yogināṁ paramahansānāṁ chetānsi iti kṛiṣhṇaḥ* 'Krishna is He who forcefully attracts the minds of even the most powerfully-minded yogis and *paramahansas*.' With this reference, Arjun is indicating that Krishna should also attract his restless, turbulent, strong, and obstinate mind.

श्रीभगवानुवाच ।
असंशयं महाबाहो मनो दुर्निग्रहं चलम् ।
अभ्यासेन तु कौन्तेय वैराग्येण च गृह्यते ।।35।।

śhrī bhagavān uvācha
asanśhayaṁ mahā-bāho mano durnigrahaṁ chalam
abhyāsena tu kaunteya vairāgyeṇa cha gṛihyate

śhrī-bhagavān uvācha—Lord Krishna said; *asanśhayam*—undoubtedly; *mahā-bāho*—mighty-armed one; *manaḥ*—the mind; *durnigraham*—difficult to restrain; *chalam*—restless; *abhyāsena*—by practice; *tu*—but; *kaunteya*—Arjun, son of Kunti; *vairāgyeṇa*—by detachment; *cha*—and; *gṛihyate*—can be controlled.

Lord Krishna said: O mighty-armed son of Kunti, what you say is correct; the mind is indeed very difficult to restrain. But by practice and detachment, it can be controlled.

Shree Krishna responds to Arjun's comment by calling him *Mahabāho* which means 'mighty armed one'. He implies, 'O Arjun, you defeated the bravest warriors in battle. Can you not defeat the mind?'

Shree Krishna does not deny the problem, by saying, 'Arjun, what nonsense are you speaking? The mind can be controlled very easily.' Rather, He agrees with Arjun's statement that the mind is indeed very difficult to control. However, so many things are difficult to achieve in the world, yet, we remain undaunted and move forward. For example, sailors know that the sea is dangerous, and the possibility of terrible storms exists. However, they have never looked upon those dangers as sufficient reasons for remaining ashore. Here, Shree Krishna assures Arjun that the mind can be controlled by *vairāgya* and *abhyās*.

Vairāgya means detachment. Due to attachments from previous endless lifetimes, the mind has become conditioned to running towards the objects of its attachment. Elimination of attachment eradicates the unnecessary wanderings of the mind.

Abhyās means practise or a concerted and persistent effort to change an old habit or develop a new one. Practice is a very important word for *sādhaks*. In all fields of human endeavour, practice is the key that opens the door to mastery and excellence. Take, for example, a mundane activity such as typing. The first time people begin typing, they are able to type only one word in a minute. But after typing for a year, their fingers fly on the keyboard at the speed of eighty words a minute. This proficiency comes solely through practice. Similarly, the obstinate and turbulent mind has to be made to rest on the lotus feet of the Supreme Lord through *abhyās*. Take the mind away from the world—this is *vairāgya*—and bring the mind to rest on God—this is *abhyās*. Sage Patanjali gives the same instruction:

abhyāsa vairāgyābhyāṁ tannirodhaḥ (*Yog Darshan* 1.12)

'The perturbations of the mind can be controlled by constant practice and detachment.'

असंयतात्मना योगो दुष्प्राप इति मे मतिः ।
वश्यात्मना तु यतता शक्योऽवाप्तुमुपायतः ।।36।।

asaṅyatātmanā yogo duṣhprāpa iti me matiḥ
vaśhyātmanā tu yatatā śhakyo 'vāptum upāyataḥ

asanyata-ātmanā—one whose mind is unbridled; *yogaḥ*—Yog; *duṣhprāpaḥ*—difficult to attain; *iti*—thus; *me*—my; *matiḥ*—opinion; *vaśhya-ātmanā*—by one whose mind is controlled; *tu*—but; *yatatā*—one who strives; *śhakyaḥ*—possible; *avāptum*—to achieve; *upāyataḥ*—by right means.

Yog is difficult to attain for one whose mind is unbridled. However, those who have learnt to control the mind and who strive earnestly by proper means, can attain perfection in Yog. This is My opinion.

The Supreme Divine Personality, Shree Krishna, now gives the link between the control of the mind and success in Yog. He says that those who have not learnt to restrain the mind through *abhyās* and *vairāgya* find great difficulty in the practice of Yog. But those who have brought the mind under their control through persistent effort can achieve success by adopting proper means. The perfect process has already been described by Him from verses 6.10 to 6.32. It was summarized in verse 6.33 as subduing the senses, giving up all desires, focusing the mind upon God alone, thinking of Him with an unwavering mind, and seeing everyone with equal vision.

This statement creates a doubt in Arjun's mind about the sādhak who is unable to control the mind, and he now questions Shree Krishna about it.

अर्जुन उवाच ।
अयतिः श्रद्धयोपेतो योगाच्चलितमानसः ।
अप्राप्य योगसंसिद्धिं कां गतिं कृष्ण गच्छति ।।37।।

arjuna uvācha
ayatiḥ śhraddhayopeto yogāch chalita-mānasaḥ
aprāpya yoga-sansiddhiṁ kāṅ gatiṁ kṛiṣhṇa gachchhati

arjunaḥ uvācha—Arjun said; *ayatiḥ*—lax; *śhraddhayā*—with faith; *upetaḥ*—possessed; *yogāt*—from Yog; *chalita-mānasaḥ*—whose mind becomes deviated; *aprāpya*—failing to attain; *yoga-sansiddhim*—the highest perfection in yog; *kām*—which; *gatim*—destination; *kṛiṣhṇa*—Shree Krishna; *gachchhati*—goes.

Arjun said: What is the fate of the unsuccessful yogi who begins the path with faith, but who does not endeavour sufficiently due to an unsteady mind and is unable to reach the goal of Yog in this life?

The journey towards God-realisation begins with *śhraddhā* (faith). Many sincere souls develop faith in the divine knowledge of the scriptures by virtue of the *sanskārs* of their past lives, or the association of saints, or reversals in the world, or a multitude of other reasons. There are many reasons that create the *śhraddhā* required to begin the journey. However, if these aspirants do not put in the necessary effort and become *ayatiḥ* (lax), then the mind remains *chalit* (restless). Such aspirants are unable to complete the journey in this life. Arjun enquires about the fate of such *sādhaks*.

कच्चिन्नोभयविभ्रष्टश्छिन्नाभ्रमिव नश्यति ।
अप्रतिष्ठो महाबाहो विमूढो ब्रह्मणः पथि ।।38।।

kachchin nobhaya-vibhraṣhṭaśh chhinnābhram iva naśhyati
apratiṣhṭho mahā-bāho vimūḍho brahmaṇaḥ pathi

kachchit—whether; *na*—not; *ubhaya*—both; *vibhraṣhṭaḥ*—deviated from; *chhinna*—broken; *abhram*—cloud; *iva*—like; *naśhyati*—perishes; *apratiṣhṭhaḥ*—without any support; *mahā-bāho*—mighty-armed Krishna; *vimūḍhaḥ*—bewildered; *brahmaṇaḥ*—of God-realisation; *pathi*—one on the path.

Does not such a person who deviates from Yog get deprived of both material and spiritual success, O mighty-armed Krishna, and perish like a broken cloud with no position in either sphere?

The desire to attain success is natural to the *jīva*. It comes from being a part of God, who is all-perfect, and consequently, the soul too wishes to be perfect and successful like its source—God. Success can be attained in two realms—material and spiritual. Those who consider the world to be a source of happiness strive for material advancement. And those who consider spiritual wealth to be the real treasure worthy of possessing, strive for it by rejecting material pursuits. However, if such spiritualists fail in their attempt, they are apparently left with neither spiritual nor material assets. Thinking in this manner, Arjun asks if their position is like that of a broken cloud.

A cloud, which breaks away from a group of clouds, becomes worthless. It neither offers sufficient shade, nor does it increase its weight and become rain-bearing. It merely blows in the wind and perishes like a non-entity in the sky. Arjun questions whether the unsuccessful yogi suffers a similar fate with no position in any sphere.

एतन्मे संशयं कृष्ण छेत्तुमर्हस्यशेषतः ।
त्वदन्यः संशयस्यास्य छेत्ता न ह्युपपद्यते ।।39।।

etan me sanśhayaṁ kṛiṣhṇa chhettum arhasyaśheṣhataḥ
tvad-anyaḥ sanśhayasyāsya chhettā na hyupapadyate

etat—this; *me*—my; *sanśhayam*—doubt; *kṛiṣhṇa*—Krishna; *chhettum*—to dispel; *arhasi*—you can; *aśheṣhataḥ*—completely; *tvat*—than you; *anyaḥ*—other; *sanśhayasya*—of doubt; *asya*—this; *chhettā*—a dispeller; *na*—never; *hi*—certainly; *upapadyate*—is fit.

O Krishna, please dispel this doubt of mine completely for who other than You can do so?

Doubts arise from ignorance, and the power to dispel doubts comes from knowledge. Scholars of the scriptures possess theoretical knowledge, which is not good enough to dispel doubts because the scriptures contain many apparent contradictions that can be reconciled only by realisation. God-realised saints do possess realised knowledge that is limited in extent. They do not become all-knowing. Such realised saints have the power to dispel doubts, but they cannot compete with God, who is all-knowing. God alone is *sarvajña* (omniscient) and *sarva-śhaktimān* (all-powerful), and hence, He is supremely competent in removing all ignorance, just as the sun is competent in repealing darkness.

श्रीभगवानुवाच ।
पार्थ नैवेह नामुत्र विनाशस्तस्य विद्यते ।
न हि कल्याणकृत्कश्चिद् दुर्गतिं तात गच्छति ।।40।।

śhrī bhagavān uvācha
pārtha naiveha nāmutra vināśhas tasya vidyate
na hi kalyāṇa-kṛit kaśhchid durgatiṁ tāta gachchhati

śhrī-bhagavān uvācha—the Supreme Lord said; *pārtha*—Arjun, son of Pritha; *na eva*—never; *iha*—in this world; *na*—never; *amutra*—in the next world; *vināśhaḥ*—destruction; *tasya*—his; *vidyate*—exists; *na*—never; *hi*—certainly; *kalyāṇa-kṛit*—one who strives for God-realisation; *kaśhchit*—anyone; *durgatim*—evil destination; *tāta*—my friend; *gachchhati*—goes.

The Supreme Lord said: O Parth, one who engages on the spiritual path does not meet with destruction either in this world or the world to come. My dear friend, one who strives for God-realisation is never overcome by evil.

The word *tāta* is a word of endearment which literally means 'son'. By addressing Arjun as *tāta* in this verse, Shree Krishna is demonstrating His affection for him. The guru is like a father to his disciple, and sometimes affectionately addresses the disciple as *tāta*. Here, by displaying His affection and grace towards Arjun, Shree Krishna wishes to indicate that God takes care of those who tread on His path. They are dear to God because they engage in the most auspicious kind of activity, and 'the doer of good never comes to grief'. This verse asserts that God preserves the devotee both in this world and the world hereafter. This pronouncement is a great assurance to all spiritual aspirants. *Shree Krishna then goes on to explain how God preserves the efforts of the yogi who does not complete the journey in the present life.*

प्राप्य पुण्यकृतां लोकानुषित्वा शाश्वतीः समाः ।
शुचीनां श्रीमतां गेहे योगभ्रष्टोऽभिजायते ।।41।।

अथवा योगिनामेव कुले भवति धीमताम् ।
एतद्धि दुर्लभतरं लोके जन्म यदीदृशम् ।।42।।

prāpya puṇya-kṛitāṁ lokān uṣhitvā śhāśhvatīḥ samāḥ
śhuchīnāṁ śhrīmatāṁ gehe yoga-bhraṣhṭo 'bhijāyate

atha vā yoginām eva kule bhavati dhīmatām
etad dhi durlabhataraṁ loke janma yad īdṛiśham

prāpya—attain; *puṇya-kṛitām*—of the virtuous; *lokān*—abodes; *uṣhitvā*—after dwelling; *śhāśhvatīḥ*—many; *samāḥ*—ages; *śhuchīnām*—of the pious; *śhrī-matām*—of the prosperous; *gehe*—in the house; *yoga-bhraṣhṭaḥ*—the unsuccessful yogis; *abhijāyate*—take birth; *atha vā*—else; *yoginām*—of those endowed with divine wisdom; *eva*—certainly; *kule*—in the family; *bhavati*—take birth; *dhī-matām*—of the wise; *etat*—this; *hi*—certainly; *durlabha-taram*—very rare; *loke*—in this world; *janma*—birth; *yat*—which; *īdṛiśham*—like this.

The unsuccessful yogis, upon death, go to the abodes of the virtuous. After dwelling there for many ages, they are again reborn in the earth plane, into a family of pious and prosperous people. Else, if they had developed dispassion due to long practice of Yog, they are born into a family endowed with divine wisdom. Such a birth is very difficult to attain in this world.

Residence in the celestial abodes is awarded to those who engage in mundane virtuous deeds and the fruitive *karm-kāṇḍ* activities enjoined in the Vedas. So, why should an unsuccessful yogi go to the celestial abodes? The reason is that the opposite of Yog (union with God) is *bhog* (material enjoyment). One falls from Yog because of the desire for *bhog*. God, like an indulgent father, gives that fallen yogi a chance to engage in *bhog* in the next life and realise that it is an exercise in futility which does not satiate the yearning of the soul for permanent bliss. So, the fallen yogi is sometimes sent to the celestial abodes for a long time, and then again granted birth on earth.

Such souls are then given birth in a family where they have the opportunity to continue their spiritual journey. *Śhuchī* means those who are pious and of good character; *śhree* means those who are wealthy. The unsuccessful yogis are either born in a pious family that will nurture the child's spirituality from childhood, or in a wealthy family where all the material needs are taken care of and one does not need to engage in the struggle for survival. Such a family environment facilitates the opportunity to engage in spiritual pursuits for souls who are so inclined.

The circumstances, situation, and family of our birth have an important bearing upon the course of our life. From our bodily parents, we derive physical hereditary characteristics. This is the genetic process of heredity. However, there is also the process of social heredity. We blindly follow many customs because of the social environment of our upbringing. We do not choose to be Indians, Americans, British, or other nationalities. We identify ourselves with a nationality based upon our birth and even go to the extent of developing enmity with people of other nationalities. Invariably, on the basis of social heredity, we follow the religion of our parents.

Thus, the place and family of our birth has a great impact upon the direction of our life. If the place and family of birth were arbitrarily decided in every life, there would be no justice in the world. However, God has an account of all our thoughts and actions of endless lifetimes. In accordance with the Law of Karma, the spiritual assets earned by the unsuccessful yogi in the previous life bear fruit. Accordingly, those yogis who had traversed quite a distance and developed dispassion are not sent to the celestial abodes. They are given birth in a spiritually evolved family to facilitate the continuance of their journey. Such a birth is a great good fortune because the parents inculcate divine wisdom in the child from the very beginning.

तत्र तं बुद्धिसंयोगं लभते पौर्वदेहिकम् ।
यतते च ततो भूयः संसिद्धौ कुरुनन्दन ।।43।।

tatra taṁ buddhi-sanyogaṁ labhate paurva-dehikam
yatate cha tato bhūyaḥ sansiddhau kuru-nandana

tatra—there; *tam*—that; *buddhi-sanyogam*—reawaken their wisdom; *labhate*—obtains; *paurva-dehikam*—from the previous lives; *yatate*—strives; *cha*—and; *tataḥ*—thereafter; *bhūyaḥ*—again; *sansiddhau*—for perfection; *kuru-nandana*—Arjun, descendant of the Kurus.

On taking such a birth, O descendant of Kurus, they reawaken

the wisdom of their previous lives and strive even harder towards perfection in Yog.

God, who is seated within the heart of every living being, is perfectly just. Whatever spiritual assets we had accumulated in the past life—detachment, wisdom, devotion, faith, tolerance, determination, and other positive qualities—are known to Him. So, at the appropriate time, He gives us the fruits of our past efforts and enhances our spirituality from within, in accordance with our previous attainments. This explains why some people harbouring materialistic views suddenly become deeply spiritual. When their spiritual *sanskārs* awaken, they get the benefit of their sadhana of previous lives.

A traveller may break journey to rest the night in a hotel on the wayside. But when he wakes up, he does not need to again tread the distance already covered. He simply moves ahead to cover the remaining distance. Likewise, by God's grace, the yogi of past lives receives the previous spiritual assets accumulated, to be able to continue the journey where he had left off, like someone who has woken up from sleep. This is why such a yogi never gets lost.

पूर्वाभ्यासेन तेनैव ह्रियते ह्यवशोऽपि सः ।
जिज्ञासुरपि योगस्य शब्दब्रह्मातिवर्तते ।।44।।

pūrvābhyāsena tenaiva hriyate hyavaśho 'pi saḥ
jijñāsur api yogasya śhabda-brahmātivartate

pūrva—past; *abhyāsena*—discipline; *tena*—by that; *eva*—certainly; *hriyate*—is attracted; *hi*—surely; *avaśhaḥ*—helplessly; *api*—although; *saḥ*—that person; *jijñāsuḥ*—inquisitive; *api*—even; *yogasya*—about yog; *śhabda-brahma*—fruitive portion of the Vedas; *ativartate*—transcends.

Indeed, they feel drawn towards God, even against their will, on the strength of their past discipline. Such seekers naturally rise above the ritualistic principles of the scriptures.

Once spiritual sentiments have sprouted, they cannot be wiped out. The soul with devotional *sanskārs* (tendencies and impressions) from present and past lifetimes gets naturally inspired towards spirituality. Such an individual feels drawn towards God; this pull is also referred to as 'the call of God'. Based on past *sanskārs*, the call of God sometimes becomes so strong that it is said, 'The call of God is the strongest call in one's life.' People who experience it reject the entire world and the advice of their friends and family to tread the path that draws their heart. This is how, in history, great princes, noblemen, and wealthy businesspersons renounced the comfort of their worldly position to become ascetics, yogis, sages, mystics, and swamis. And since their hunger was for God alone, they naturally rose above the ritualistic practices prescribed in the Vedas for material advancement.

प्रयत्नाद्यतमानस्तु योगी संशुद्धकिल्बिषः ।
अनेकजन्मसंसिद्धस्ततो याति परां गतिम् ।।45।।

prayatnād yatamānas tu yogī sanśhuddha-kilbiṣhaḥ
aneka-janma-sansiddhas tato yāti parāṁ gatim

prayatnāt—with great effort; *yatamānaḥ*—endeavouring; *tu*—and; *yogī*—a yogi; *sanśhuddha*—purified; *kilbiṣhaḥ*—from material desires; *aneka*—after many, many; *janma*—births; *sansiddhaḥ*—attain perfection; *tataḥ*—then; *yāti*—attains; *parām*—the highest; *gatim*—path.

With the accumulated merits of many past births, when these yogis engage in sincere endeavours to make further progress, they become purified from material desires and attain perfection in this life itself.

The accumulated practice of many past lives becomes the tailwind for spiritual progress. In this breeze, the yogis continuing from past lives, hoist their sail in the form of sincere endeavour in the present life. Shree Krishna uses the words *prayatnād yatamānastu* which means 'striving harder than before'. The word *tu* indicates their present endeavour is deeper than in previous lifetimes when they were unsuccessful in completing the journey.

They are thus able to take advantage of the momentum carried forward from the past and allow the favourable wind to sweep them to the goal. To onlookers, it may seem that they covered the entire distance in the present life, but Shree Krishna says: *aneka janma sansiddhaḥ* 'Perfection in Yog is the result of the accumulated practice of many lives.'

तपस्विभ्योऽधिको योगी ज्ञानिभ्योऽपि मतोऽधिकः ।
कर्मिभ्यश्चाधिको योगी तस्माद्योगी भवार्जुन ।।46।।

tapasvibhyo 'dhiko yogī jñānibhyo 'pi mato 'dhikaḥ
karmibhyaśh chādhiko yogī tasmād yogī bhavārjuna

tapasvibhyaḥ—than the ascetics; *adhikaḥ*—superior; *yogī*—a yogi; *jñānibhyaḥ*—than the persons of learning; *api*—even; *mataḥ*—considered; *adhikaḥ*—superior; *karmibhyaḥ*—than the ritualistic performers; *cha*—and; *adhikaḥ*—superior; *yogī*—a yogi; *tasmāt*—therefore; *yogī*—a yogi; *bhava*—just become; *arjuna*—Arjun.

A yogi is superior to the *tapasvī* (ascetic), superior to the jnani (a person of learning), and even superior to the karmi (ritualistic performer). Therefore, O Arjun, strive to be a yogi.

A *tapasvī* (ascetic) is one who accepts voluntary mortification and lives an extremely austere lifestyle, refraining from sensual pleasures and the accumulation of material wealth, as an aid in the pursuit of salvation. A jnani is a person of learning who actively engages in the cultivation of knowledge. A karmi is one who performs Vedic rituals for attaining material opulence and the celestial abodes. Shree Krishna declares the yogi to be superior to all of them. The reason for this is simple. The goal of the karmi, jnani, and *tapasvī* is worldly attainment; they are still at the bodily platform of existence. The yogi is striving not for the world but for God. As a result, the yogi's accomplishment is at the spiritual platform and is superior to them all.

योगिनामपि सर्वेषां मद्गतेनान्तरात्मना ।
श्रद्धावान्भजते यो मां स मे युक्ततमो मतः ।।47।।

yoginām api sarveṣhāṁ mad-gatenāntar-ātmanā
śhraddhāvān bhajate yo māṁ sa me yuktatamo mataḥ

yoginām—of all yogis; *api*—however; *sarveṣhām*—all types of; *mat-gatena*—absorbed in Me (God); *antaḥ*—inner; *ātmanā*—with the mind; *śhraddhā-vān*—with great faith; *bhajate*—engage in devotion; *yaḥ*—who; *mām*—to me; *saḥ*—he; *me*—by me; *yukta-tamaḥ*—the highest yogi; *mataḥ*—is considered.

Of all yogis, those whose minds are always absorbed in Me, and who engage in devotion to Me with great faith, them I consider to be the highest of all.

Even among yogis, there are karm yogis, bhakti yogis, jnana yogis, ashtang yogis, and others. This verse puts to rest the debate about which form of Yog is the highest. Shree Krishna declares the bhakti yogi to be the highest, superior to even the best ashtang yogi and hatha yogi. That is because bhakti, or devotion, is the highest power of God. It is such a power that binds God and makes Him a slave of His devotee. He states in the Bhagavatam:

ahaṁ bhakta-parādhīno hyasvatantra iva dvija
sādhubhir grasta-hṛidayo bhaktair bhakta-jana-priyaḥ

(9.4.63)

'Although I am supremely independent, yet I become enslaved by My devotees. They conquer My heart. What to speak of My devotees, even the devotees of My devotees are very dear to Me.' The bhakti yogi possesses the power of divine love and is thus most dear to God and considered by Him to be the highest of all.

In this verse, Shree Krishna has used the word *bhajate*. It comes from the root word *bhaj* which means 'to serve'. It is a far more significant word for devotion than 'worship', which means 'to adore'. Here, Shree Krishna is talking about those who, not merely adore Him, but also serve Him with loving devotion. They are thus established in the natural position of the soul as the servant of God. The other kinds of yogis are still incomplete in their realisation; they have connected themselves with God but are not yet situated in the understanding that they are His eternal servants.

muktānām api siddhānāṁ nārāyaṇa-parāyaṇaḥ
su-durlabhaḥ praśhāntātmā koṭiṣhv api mahā-mune

(Bhagavatam 6.14.5)

'Amongst many millions of perfected and liberated saints, the peaceful person who is devoted to the Supreme Lord, Narayan, is very rare.'

Another way of understanding this verse is that bhakti yog provides the closest and most complete realisation of God. This is explained in verse 18.55, where Shree Krishna explains that the bhakti yogi alone understands the true personality of God.

CHAPTER 7

Jnana Vijnana Yog

Yog through the Realisation of Divine Knowledge

This chapter begins by describing the material and spiritual dimensions of God's energies. Shree Krishna explains that all these have emanated from Him, and they rest in Him, as beads strung on a thread. He is the source of the entire creation and into Him, it again dissolves. His material energy, maya, is very difficult to overcome, but those who surrender to Him receive His grace and cross over it easily. Shree Krishna describes the four kinds of people who do not surrender to Him, and the four kinds of people who engage in His devotion. Among His devotees, those who worship Him in knowledge, with mind and intellect merged in Him are considered the dearest to Him. Some, whose intellect has been carried away by material desires, surrender to the celestial gods. But these celestial gods can only bestow temporary material fruits, and even those, by the powers they have received from the Supreme Lord. Thus, the worthiest object of devotion is God Himself. Shree Krishna confirms that He is the highest reality and ultimate attainment, possessing eternal divine attributes, such as omniscience, omnipresence, and omnipotence. However, His personality is hidden by a veil of His divine *Yogmaya* power, and the imperishable nature of His eternal divine form is not known to all. If we take shelter in Him, He bestows upon us knowledge of Himself, and on knowing Him, we also get knowledge of the self and the field of karmic actions.

श्रीभगवानुवाच ।
मय्यासक्तमनाः पार्थ योगं युञ्जन्मदाश्रयः ।
असंशयं समग्रं मां यथा ज्ञास्यसि तच्छृणु ।।1।।

śhrī bhagavān uvācha
mayyāsakta-manāḥ pārtha yogaṁ yuñjan mad-āśhrayaḥ
asanśhayaṁ samagraṁ māṁ yathā jñāsyasi tach chhṛiṇu

śhrī-bhagavān uvācha—the Supreme Lord said; *mayi*—to me; *āsakta-manāḥ*—with the mind attached; *pārtha*—Arjun, son of Pritha; *yogam*—bhakti yog; *yuñjan*—practising; *mad-āśhrayaḥ*—surrendering to me; *asanśhayam*—free from doubt; *samagram*—completely; *mām*—me; *yathā*—how; *jñāsyasi*—you shall know; *tat*—that; *śhṛiṇu*—listen.

The Supreme Lord said: Now listen, O Arjun, how, with the mind attached exclusively to Me, and surrendering to Me through the practice of bhakti yog, you can know Me completely, free from doubt.

At the conclusion of chapter six, Shree Krishna had declared that those who devotedly serve Him, with mind focused exclusively on Him, are the best among all yogis. This statement can lead to some natural questions: What is the way to know the Supreme Lord? How should one meditate upon Him? How should a devotee worship God? Although Arjun did not raise these questions, yet, out of His compassion, the Lord presupposes them, and begins to answer them. He uses the word *śhṛiṇu,* meaning, 'listen', and qualifies it with *mad-āśhrayaḥ*, meaning, 'with your mind focused on Me'.

ज्ञानं तेऽहं सविज्ञानमिदं वक्ष्याम्यशेषतः ।
यज्ज्ञात्वा नेह भूयोऽन्यज्ज्ञातव्यमवशिष्यते ।।2।।

jñānaṁ te 'haṁ sa-vijñānam idaṁ vakṣhyāmyaśheṣhataḥ
yaj jñātvā neha bhūyo 'nyaj jñātavyam-avaśhiṣhyate

jñānam—knowledge; *te*—unto you; *aham*—I; *sa*—with; *vijñānam*—wisdom; *idam*—this; *vakṣhyāmi*—shall reveal; *aśheṣhataḥ*—in full;

yat—which; *jñātvā*—having known; *na*—not; *iha*—in this world; *bhūyaḥ*—further; *anyat*—anything else; *jñātavyam*—to be known; *avaśhiṣhyate*—remains.

I shall now reveal unto you fully this knowledge and wisdom, knowing which nothing else remains to be known in this world.

Knowledge that is acquired through the senses, mind, and intellect is called jnana. Knowledge that comes as insight from within as a consequence of spiritual practice is called vijnana (wisdom). Vijnana is not intellectual knowledge; it is direct experiential realisation. For example, we may keep hearing about the glories of the sweetness of honey kept in a bottle, but it remains theoretical knowledge. However, when we open the the bottle and taste the honey inside, we get experiential realisation of its sweetness. Similarly, the theoretical knowledge we get from the guru and the scriptures is jnana. And when, in accordance with that knowledge, we practise sadhana and purify our mind, then the knowledge that awakens within us as realisation is called vijnana.

When Sage Ved Vyas decided to write the Shreemad Bhagavatam describing the nature, glories, and object of devotion, he was not content to write it on the basis of jnana so, he first engaged in bhakti to get experiential realisation of God:

bhakti-yogena manasi samyak praṇihite 'male
apaśhyat puruṣhaṁ pūrvaṁ māyāṁ cha tad-apāśhrayām

(Bhagavatam 1.7.4)

'Through bhakti yog Ved Vyas fixed his mind upon God without any material sentiments, and thus he attained complete vision and realisation of the Supreme Divine Personality along with His external energy, maya, which was under His control.' Equipped with this realisation, he then wrote the famous scripture.

Shree Krishna declares that He will illumine Arjun with the theoretical knowledge of the Supreme Divine Personality, and also help him gain the inner wisdom about it. On realisation of this knowledge, nothing further will remain to be known.

मनुष्याणां सहस्रेषु कश्चिद्यतति सिद्धये ।
यततामपि सिद्धानां कश्चिन्मां वेत्ति तत्त्वतः ।।3।।

manuṣhyāṇāṁ sahasreṣhu kaśhchid yatati siddhaye
yatatām api siddhānāṁ kaśhchin māṁ vetti tattvataḥ

manuṣhyāṇām—of men; *sahasreṣhu*—out of many thousands; *kaśhchit*—someone; *yatati*—strives; *siddhaye*—for perfection; *yatatām*—of those who strive; *api*—even; *siddhānām*—of those who have achieved perfection; *kaśhchit*—someone; *mām*—me; *vetti*—knows; *tattvataḥ*—in truth.

Among thousands of persons, hardly one strives for perfection; and among those who have achieved perfection, hardly one knows Me in Truth.

In this verse, the word *siddhi* has been used for perfection. This is a word loaded with numerous connotations and meanings. Here are a few meanings of the word *siddhi* from the Sanskrit dictionary: attainment of supernatural power, accomplishment, success, performance, fulfilment, solution of a problem, completion of cooking or a task, healing, hitting the mark, maturing, supreme felicity, beatitude, an unusual skill or faculty, perfection. Shree Krishna uses the word *siddhi* for perfection on the spiritual path, and says, 'Arjun, out of innumerable souls, only a tiny proportion possess the human form. Among those who have attained the human birth, only a few strive for perfection. Even among thousands of perfected souls, those who are aware of My paramount position and divine glories are very rare.'

Why do souls who have achieved perfection in spiritual practices not know God in Truth? This is because it is not possible to know or perceive Him without bhakti (loving devotion to the Lord). Spiritual aspirants who practise karm, jnana, hatha yog, or other techniques, without including devotion alongside, cannot know God. In the Bhagavad Gita itself, Shree Krishna reiterates this fact many times:

> 'Although He is all-pervading and all living beings are situated in Him, yet He can be known only through devotion.' 8.22.

'O Arjun, by unalloyed devotion alone can I be known as I am, standing before you. Thereby, on receiving My divine vision, O scorcher of foes, one can enter into union with Me.' 11.54

'Only by loving devotion to Me does one come to know who I am in Truth. Then, having come to know Me, My devotee enters into full consciousness of Me.' 18.55

Thus, the understanding of those spiritual aspirants who do not include devotion in their sadhana remains restricted to theoretical knowledge of God. They do not get experiential knowledge of the Absolute Truth.

Having said that one in many human beings knows Him in Truth, Shree Krishna now launches into a description of the material and spiritual dimensions of His energies. He first introduces apara prakriti, the field of material energy, which is an inferior energy, and yet, an energy of God.

भूमिरापोऽनलो वायुः खं मनो बुद्धिरेव च ।
अहङ्कार इतीयं मे भिन्ना प्रकृतिरष्टधा ।।4।।

bhūmir-āpo 'nalo vāyuḥ khaṁ mano buddhir eva cha
ahankāra itīyaṁ me bhinnā prakṛitir aṣhṭadhā

bhūmiḥ—earth; *āpaḥ*—water; *analaḥ*—fire; *vāyuḥ*—air; *kham*—space; *manaḥ*—mind; *buddhiḥ*—intellect; *eva*—certainly; *cha*—and; *ahankāraḥ*—ego; *iti*—thus; *iyam*—all these; *me*—my; *bhinnā*—divisions; *prakṛitiḥ*—material energy; *aṣhṭadhā*—eightfold.

Earth, water, fire, air, space, mind, intellect, and ego—these are eight components of My material energy.

The material energy that comprises this world is amazingly complex and fathomless. By classifying and categorising it, we make it slightly comprehensible to our finite intellects. However, each of these categories has further innumerable sub-categories. The system of classification used in modern science looks on matter as the combination of elements. At present, 118 elements have been discovered and are included in the Periodic Table. In the Bhagavad

Gita, and the Vedic philosophy in general, a radically different kind of classification is used. Matter is seen as prakriti, or an energy of God, and eight divisions of this energy are mentioned in this verse. We can now understand how amazingly insightful this is in the light of the trend of modern science in the last century.

In 1905, in his Annus Mirabilis papers, Albert Einstein first propounded the concept of Mass-Energy Equivalence. He stated that matter has the potential of being converted to energy, to the extent that can be numerically determined by the equation $E=mc^2$. This understanding radically transformed the previous Newtonian concept of the universe as consisting of solid matter. Then in the 1920s, Niels Bohr and other scientists proposed the Quantum theory, quantifying the dual particle-wave nature of matter. Since then, scientists have been searching for a Unified Field Theory, which will allow all forces and matter in the universe to be understood in terms of a single field.

What Shree Krishna presented to Arjun five thousand years ago, before the development of modern science, is the perfect Unified Field Theory. He says, 'Arjun, all that exists in the universe is a manifestation of My material energy.' It is just one material energy that has unfolded into myriad shapes, forms, and entities in this world. This is described in detail in the *Taittirīya Upanishad*:

tasmadvā etasmādātmana ākāśhaḥ sambhūtaḥ ākāśhādvāyuḥ vāyoragniḥ agnerāpaḥ adbhyaḥ pṛithivī pṛithivyā oṣhadhayaḥ oṣhadhībhyo 'nnam annātpuruṣhaḥ sa vā eṣha puruṣho 'nnarasamayaḥ (2.1.2)

The primordial form of material energy is prakriti. When God desires to create the world, He glances at it, by which it gets agitated and unfolds into *mahān* (since science has not yet reached to this subtle level of energy, there is no equivalent word for it in the English language). *Mahān* further unfolds, and the next entity to manifest is *ahankār*, which is also subtler than any entity known to science. From *ahankār*, originate the *pañcha tanmātrās*, the five perceptions—taste, touch, smell, sight, and sound. From them come the five gross elements—space, air, fire, water, and earth.

In this verse, Shree Krishna not only includes the five gross elements as different manifestations of His energy, but He also includes the mind, intellect, and ego, as distinctive elements of His energy. Shree Krishna states that all these are simply parts of His material energy, maya. *Beyond these is the soul energy, or the superior energy of God, which He describes in the next verse.*

अपरेयमितस्त्वन्यां प्रकृतिं विद्धि मे पराम् ।
जीवभूतां महाबाहो ययेदं धार्यते जगत् ।।5।।

apareyam itas tvanyāṁ prakṛitiṁ viddhi me parām
jīva-bhūtāṁ mahā-bāho yayedaṁ dhāryate jagat

aparā—inferior; *iyam*—this; *itaḥ*—besides this; *tu*—but; *anyām*—another; *prakṛitim*—energy; *viddhi*—know; *me*—my; *parām*—superior; *jīva-bhūtām*—living beings; *mahā-bāho*—mighty-armed one; *yayā*—by whom; *idam*—this; *dhāryate*—the basis; *jagat*—the material world.

Such is My inferior energy. But beyond it, O mighty-armed Arjun, I have a superior energy. This is the *jīva shakti* (the soul energy) which comprises embodied souls who are the basis of life in this world.

Shree Krishna now goes totally beyond the realm of material science. He explains that the eight-fold prakriti mentioned in the previous verse is His inferior material energy. But it is not all that exists. There is also a superior spiritual energy, which is completely transcendental to insentient matter. This energy is the *jīva shakti* which encapsulates all the souls in this world.

The relationship between the *jīva* (individual soul) and God has been described from various perspectives by India's great philosophers. The non-dualist philosophers state: *jīvo brahmaiva nāparaḥ* 'The soul itself is God.' However, this contention raises a number of unanswerable questions, such as:

- God is all-powerful and maya is His subservient energy. If the soul is God, then how come it has been overpowered by maya? Is maya stronger than God?

- We all know that the soul is suffering from ignorance. Hence, it perceives the need for scriptures like the Bhagavad Gita and the lectures of saints. How can the soul that is subject to ignorance be considered as God, who is all-knowing?
- God is all-pervading in the world. This is repeatedly stated in the Vedas. If the soul is God, then the soul must exist everywhere at the same time; so, where is the question of going to heaven and hell after death?
- The souls are innumerable in quantity, and they all have their individual identity. However, God is one. Now, if the soul itself were God, then God would also have been many.

We thus see that the claim of non-dualistic philosophers of the soul itself being God makes no sense. On the other hand, the dualist philosophers state that the soul is separate from God. This answers some of the questions above, but it is an incomplete understanding compared to what Shree Krishna states in this verse. He says that the soul is a part of the spiritual energy of God.

The Vedic scriptures teach us that God is the one Supreme Energetic, and everything that exists—both spiritual and material—is composed of all His various lower and higher energies.

eka-deśha-sthitasyāgnir jyotsnā vistāriṇī yathā
parasya brahmaṇaḥ śhaktis tathedam akhilaṁ jagat

(*Vishnu Puran* 1.22.53)

'Just as the sun resides in one place, but its sunlight pervades the entire solar system, similarly there is one God, who by His infinite powers pervades the three worlds.' Chaitanya Mahaprabhu said:

jīva-tattva śhakti, kṛiṣhṇa-tattva śhaktimān
gītā-viṣhṇupurāṇādi tāhāte pramāṇa

(*Chaitanya Charitāmṛit*, *Ādi Leela*, 7.117)

'The soul is an energy of God, while He is the Supreme Energetic.'

Once we accept the concept of the soul as a form of His energy, then the non-duality of all creation becomes comprehensible. Any energy is simultaneously one and different from the energetic. For example, a fire and its heat and light can be considered as different entities, but they can also be clubbed together and considered as one. Thus, we can consider the soul and God as one from the point of view of the energy (soul) and the Energetic (God). But we can also consider the soul and God as different, since the energy and Energetic are also distinct entities.

Shree Krishna's statement in verses 7.4 and 7.5 are so perfectly encapsulated by Jagadguru Shree Kripaluji Maharaj in the *Bhakti Śhatak*:

'jīvu' 'māyā', dui śhakti haiñ, śhaktimān bhagavān
śhaktihiñ bheda abheda bhī, śhaktimān te jān (verse 42)

'The soul and maya are both energies of God. Hence, they are both one with God and also different from God.'

From the perspective of unity between the energies and Energetic, the entire world is non-different from God. This is why it is stated that the whole world is the veritable form of God.

sarvaṁ khalvidaṁ brahma (*Chhāndogya Upanishad* 3.14.1)

'All is Brahman.'

īśhāvāsyam idam sarvaṁ (*Īśhopaniṣhad* 1)

'Everything that exists in the world is God.'

puruṣha evedaṁ sarvaṁ (*Śhwetāśhvatar Upanishad* 3.15)

'The Supreme Divine Personality is everything that exists.'

All these Ved Mantras state that there is only one God and nothing else in the world. At the same time, from the perspective of diversity between the energy and the Energetic, we can understand that within that unity, there is also tremendous variety. The soul is different; matter is different; God is different. Matter is insentient while the soul is sentient, and God is the supremely sentient source and basis of both soul and matter. Many Vedic mantras talk of three entities in creation:

kṣharaṁ pradhānamamṛitākṣharaṁ haraḥ
kṣharātmānāvīśhate deva ekaḥ
tasyābhidhyānād yojanāt tattvabhāvad
bhūyaśhchānte viśhwamāyānivṛittiḥ

(*Śhwetāśhvatar Upanishad* 1.10)

'There are three entities in existence: 1) Matter which is perishable. 2) The individual souls who are imperishable. 3) God who is the controller of both matter and the souls. By meditating upon God, uniting with Him, and becoming more like Him, the soul is freed from the world's illusion.'

We see how the Vedas expound both—non-dualistic and dualistic—mantras. Jagadguru Shree Kripaluji Maharaj has upheld the view of simultaneous and inconceivable oneness and difference between the soul and God.

एतद्योनीनि भूतानि सर्वाणीत्युपधारय ।
अहं कृत्स्नस्य जगतः प्रभवः प्रलयस्तथा ।।6।।

etad-yonīni bhūtāni sarvāṇītyupadhāraya
ahaṁ kṛitsnasya jagataḥ prabhavaḥ pralayas tathā

etat yonīni—these two (energies) are the source of; *bhūtāni*—living beings; *sarvāṇi*—all; *iti*—that; *upadhāraya*—know; *aham*—I; *kṛitsnasya*—entire; *jagataḥ*—creation; *prabhavaḥ*—the source; *pralayaḥ*—dissolution; *tathā*—and.

Know that all living beings are manifested by these two energies of Mine. I am the source of the entire creation, and into Me it again dissolves.

All life in the material realm comes into existence by the combination of soul and matter. By itself, matter is insentient; the soul needs a carrier in the form of the body. By the conjugation of these two energies, living beings manifest.

God is the origin of both these energies; the entire creation manifests from Him. When the cycle of creation reaches completion at the end of one hundred years of Brahma, the Lord dissolves the manifestation. The five gross elements merge into the five subtle elements, the five subtle elements merge into *ahankār*; *ahankār* merges into *mahān*; *mahān* into *prakriti*; *prakriti* goes and sits in the body of Maha Vishnu (a form of the Supreme Lord). The souls who did not get liberated in that cycle of creation also reside in God's body in an unmanifest form and wait the next cycle of creation. Once again, when God wishes to create, the cycle begins (as explained in the commentary of verse 7.4), and the world comes into existence. Hence, God alone is the source, support, and final resting ground for all existence.

मत्तः परतरं नान्यत्किञ्चिदस्ति धनञ्जय ।
मयि सर्वमिदं प्रोतं सूत्रे मणिगणा इव ।।7।।

mattaḥ parataraṁ nānyat kiñchid asti dhanañjaya
mayi sarvam idaṁ protaṁ sūtre maṇi-gaṇā iva

mattaḥ—than me; *para-taram*—superior; *na*—not; *anyat kiñchit*—anything else; *asti*—there is; *dhanañjaya*—Arjun, conqueror of wealth; *mayi*—in me; *sarvam*—all; *idam*—which we see; *protam*—is strung; *sūtre*—on a thread; *maṇi-gaṇāḥ*—beads; *iva*—like.

There is nothing higher than Myself, O Arjun. Everything rests in Me as beads strung on a thread.

The Supreme Lord Shree Krishna now speaks of His paramount position over everything and His dominion over all. He is the Creator, Sustainer, and Annihilator of the universe. He is also the Substratum on which everything exists. The analogy used is of beads strung on a thread. Similarly, although individual souls have free will to act as they wish, it is only granted to them by God, who upholds them all, and within whom they all exist. Hence, the *Śhwetāśhvatar Upanishad* states:

na tatsamaśhchābhyadhikaśhcha dṛiśhyate
parāsya śhaktirvividhaiva śhrūyate (6.8)

'There is nothing equal to God, nor is there anything superior to Him.'

This verse of the Bhagavad Gita also dispels the doubt in the mind of many, who believe that Shree Krishna is not the Absolute Truth and speculate that there must be some formless entity that is the ultimate source of even Shree Krishna Himself. However, here He clearly states that in His personal form of Shree Krishna, as He stands before Arjun, He is the ultimate Supreme Truth. The first-born Brahma also prays to Shree Krishna:

īśhwaraḥ paramaḥ kṛiṣhṇaḥ sachchidānanda vigrahaḥ
anādirādir govindaḥ sarva kāraṇa kāraṇam

(*Brahma Samhitā* 5.1)

'Shree Krishna is the Supreme Lord, who is eternal, omniscient, and infinite bliss. He is without beginning and end, the origin of all, and the Cause of all causes.'

रसोऽहमप्सु कौन्तेय प्रभास्मि शशिसूर्ययोः ।
प्रणवः सर्ववेदेषु शब्दः खे पौरुषं नृषु ।।8।।

raso 'ham apsu kaunteya prabhāsmi śhaśhi-sūryayoḥ
praṇavaḥ sarva-vedeṣhu śhabdaḥ khe pauruṣhaṁ nṛiṣhu

rasaḥ—taste; *aham*—I; *apsu*—in water; *kaunteya*—Arjun, son of Kunti; *prabhā*—radiance; *asmi*—I am; *śhaśhi-sūryayoḥ*—of the moon and the sun; *praṇavaḥ*—the sacred syllable Om; *sarva*—in all; *vedeṣhu*—Vedas; *śhabdaḥ*—sound; *khe*—in ether; *pauruṣham*—ability; *nṛiṣhu*—in humans.

I am the taste in water, O son of Kunti, and the radiance of the sun and the moon. I am the sacred syllable 'Om' in the Vedic mantras; I am the sound in ether, and the ability in humans.

Having said that He is the origin and the basis of all that exists, Shree Krishna now explains the truth of His statement in these four verses. When we eat fruits, the sweetness in the taste indicates the presence of sugar in them. Similarly, Shree Krishna reveals His presence in all the modifications of His energies. Thus, He says that He is the taste in water which is its unique intrinsic property. After all, who can separate the taste of water from water? All other forms of material energy—gases, fires, and solids—need liquids to carry their taste. Try putting a solid on your dry tongue, and you will not taste anything. But when solids are dissolved by the saliva in the mouth, then their taste is perceived by the taste buds on the tongue.

Similarly, *ākāśha* (space) functions as the vehicle for sound. Sound modifies itself into various languages, and Shree Krishna explains that He is the basis of it all because the sound in space is His energy. Further, He says that He is the syllable Om which is an important element of Vedic mantras. He is also the energy source of all the abilities that manifest in humans.

पुण्यो गन्धः पृथिव्यां च तेजश्चास्मि विभावसौ ।
जीवनं सर्वभूतेषु तपश्चास्मि तपस्विषु ।।9।।

puṇyo gandhaḥ pṛithivyāṁ cha tejaśh chāsmi vibhāvasau
jīvanaṁ sarva-bhūteṣhu tapaśh chāsmi tapasviṣhu

puṇyaḥ—pure; *gandhaḥ*—fragrance; *pṛithivyām*—of the earth; *cha*—and; *tejaḥ*—brilliance; *cha*—and; *asmi*—I am; *vibhāvasau*—in the fire; *jīvanam*—life force; *sarva*—in all; *bhūteṣhu*—beings; *tapaḥ*—penance; *cha*—and; *asmi*—I am; *tapasviṣhu*—of the ascetics.

I am the pure fragrance of the earth and the brilliance in fire. I am the life force in all beings and the penance of the ascetics.

Shree Krishna continues to describe how He is the essential principle in everything. The specialty of ascetics is their denial of physical pleasures and wilful acceptance of austerities for self-purification. The Lord says He is their capacity for penance. In the earth, He is the fragrance which is its essential quality; and in fire, He is the radiance of the flame.

बीजं मां सर्वभूतानां विद्धि पार्थ सनातनम् ।
बुद्धिर्बुद्धिमतामस्मि तेजस्तेजस्विनामहम् ।।10।।

bījaṁ māṁ sarva-bhūtānāṁ viddhi pārtha sanātanam
buddhir buddhimatām asmi tejas tejasvinām aham

bījam—the seed; *mām*—me; *sarva-bhūtānām*—of all beings; *viddhi*—know; *pārtha*—Arjun, son of Pritha; *sanātanam*—the eternal; *buddhiḥ*—intellect; *buddhi-matām*—of the intelligent; *asmi*—(I) am; *tejaḥ*—splendour; *tejasvinām*—of the splendid; *aham*—I.

O Arjun, know that I am the eternal seed of all beings. I am the intellect of the intelligent and the splendour of the glorious.

The cause is known as the seed of its effect. Hence, the ocean can be considered as the seed of the clouds; the clouds are the seed of the rain. Shree Krishna says that He is the seed from which all beings have been created.

Since everything that exists is an energy of God, the splendid qualities visible in outstanding people are all God's energies manifesting through them. Intelligent people express a greater amount of brilliance in their thoughts and ideas. God says He is that subtle power that makes their thoughts scintillating and analytical.

When someone displays exceptional brilliance that enhances the world in a positive way, it is God's power working through him. William Shakespeare displayed such fascinating brilliance in the field of literature that is still unmatched in modern history. It is possible that God enhanced his intellect so that his works served to nourish the literature of a major language of the world, English. Swami Vivekananda said that the function of the British Empire was to unite the world in one language. Bill Gates displayed such genius in marketing the Windows Operating System that it captured ninety per cent of the market share. If this had not happened and there had been multiple operating systems for computers around the world, there would have been extensive chaos. Possibly, God desired that the world should have one major operating system, to ensure proper interaction, and so He enhanced one person's intellect for the purpose.

The saints, of course, have always attributed the beauty, brilliance, and knowledge of their works to the grace of God. Sage Tulsidas states:

na maiñ kiyā na kari sakauñ, sahiba kartā mor
karata karāvata āpa haiñ, tulasī tulasī śhor

'Neither did I write the Ramayan, nor do I have the ability to write it. The Lord is my Doer. He directs my actions and acts through me, but the world thinks that Tulsidas is doing them.' Here, Shree Krishna clearly states that He is the brilliance of the brilliant and the intellect of the intelligent.

बलं बलवतां चाहं कामरागविवर्जितम् ।
धर्माविरुद्धो भूतेषु कामोऽस्मि भरतर्षभ ।। 11 ।।

balaṁ balavatāṁ chāhaṁ kāma-rāga-vivarjitam
dharmāviruddho bhūteṣhu kāmo 'smi bharatarṣhabha

balam—strength; *bala-vatām*—of the strong; *cha*—and; *aham*—I; *kāma*—desire; *rāga*—passion; *vivarjitam*—devoid of; *dharma-aviruddhaḥ*—not conflicting with dharma; *bhūteṣhu*—in all beings; *kāmaḥ*—sexual activity; *asmi*—(I) am; *bharata-ṛiṣhabha*—Arjun, best of Bharatas.

O best of Bharatas, in strong persons, I am their strength devoid of desire and passion. I am sexual activity not conflicting with virtue or scriptural injunctions.

Passion is an active desire for things unattained. Attachment is a passive mental emotion that incites the thirst for more of a desired object, after already experiencing it. So, when Shree Krishna states *kāma-rāga-vivarjitam*, meaning, 'devoid of passion and attachment', He is explaining the nature of His strength. He is the serene sublime strength that empowers people to perform their duties without deviation or cessation.

Sexual activity, when devoid of regulative principles and carried out for sense enjoyment, is considered animalistic in nature. But as a part of household life, when it is not contrary to virtue and is carried out for the purpose of procreation, it is considered aligned to the scriptural injunctions. Shree Krishna says He is such virtuous, controlled, and well-intended sexual activity within the institution of marriage.

ये चैव सात्त्विका भावा राजसास्तामसाश्च ये ।
मत्त एवेति तान्विद्धि न त्वहं तेषु ते मयि ।।12।।

ye chaiva sāttvikā bhāvā rājasās tāmasāśh cha ye
matta eveti tān viddhi na tvahaṁ teṣhu te mayi

ye—whatever; *cha*—and; *eva*—certainly; *sāttvikāḥ*—in the mode of goodness; *bhāvāḥ*—states of material existence; *rājasāḥ*—in the mode of passion; *tāmasāḥ*—in the mode of ignorance; *cha*—and; *ye*—whatever; *mattaḥ*—from me; *eva*—certainly; *iti*—thus; *tān*—those; *viddhi*—know; *na*—not; *tu*—but; *aham*—I; *teṣhu*—in them; *te*—they; *mayi*—in me.

The three states of material existence—goodness, passion, and ignorance—are manifested by My energy. They are in Me, but I am beyond them.

Having described His glories in the previous four verses, Shree Krishna now sums them up in this verse. He effectively says, 'Arjun, I have explained how I am the essence of all objects. But there is no point in going into details. All good, bad, and ugly objects and states of existence are made possible only by My energy.'

Although all things emanate from God, yet He is independent of them and beyond everything. Alfred Tennyson expressed this in his famous poem *In Memorium*:

Our little systems have their day;
They have their day and cease to be.
They are but broken lights of thee,
And thou, O Lord, art more than they.

त्रिभिर्गुणमयैर्भावैरेभिः सर्वमिदं जगत् ।
मोहितं नाभिजानाति मामेभ्यः परमव्ययम् ।।13।।

tribhir guṇa-mayair bhāvair ebhiḥ sarvam idaṁ jagat
mohitaṁ nābhijānāti māmebhyaḥ param avyayam

tribhiḥ—by three; *guṇa-mayaiḥ*—consisting of the modes of material nature; *bhāvaiḥ*—states; *ebhiḥ*—all these; *sarvam*—whole; *idam*—this; *jagat*—universe; *mohitam*—deluded; *na*—not; *abhijānāti*—know; *mām*—me; *ebhyaḥ*—these; *param*—the supreme; *avyayam*—imperishable.

Deluded by the three modes of maya, people in this world are unable to know Me, the imperishable and eternal.

Having heard the previous verses, Arjun may think, 'O Lord, if such are Your *vibhūtis* (opulences), then why do billions of humans not know You, Lord Krishna, as the Supreme Controller and the Source of creation?' To answer this, Shree Krishna explains that people are deluded by the material modes of ignorance, passion, and goodness. These three modes of maya veil their consciousness, and as a result, they become fascinated by ephemeral allurement of material pleasures.

One of the meanings of the word 'maya' comes from the roots *mā* (not) and *yā* (what is). Thus, maya means 'that which is not what it appears to be'. As an energy of God, maya is also engaged in His service. Its service is to veil the true nature of the Supreme Lord from souls who have not yet attained the eligibility for God-realisation. Maya thus lures and bewilders the souls who are *vimukh* from God (have their backs turned towards Him). At the same time, maya subjects these souls to various difficulties caused by subjugation to the three-fold material miseries. In this way, it tries to bring the souls to the realisation that they can never be happy until they become *sanmukh* towards God (have their face turned towards Him).

दैवी ह्येषा गुणमयी मम माया दुरत्यया ।
मामेव ये प्रपद्यन्ते मायामेतां तरन्ति ते ।।14।।

daivī hyeṣhā guṇa-mayī mama māyā duratyayā
mām eva ye prapadyante māyām etāṁ taranti te

daivī—divine; *hi*—certainly; *eṣhā*—this; *guṇa-mayī*—consisting of the three modes of nature; *mama*—my; *māyā*—God's external energy. *duratyayā*—very difficult to overcome; *mām*—unto me; *eva*—certainly; *ye*—who; *prapadyante*—surrender; *māyām etām*—this maya; *taranti*—cross over; *te*—they.

My divine energy, maya, consisting of the three modes of nature, is very difficult to overcome. But those who surrender unto Me cross over it easily.

Some people declare the material energy to be *mithyā* (non-existent). They say that we perceive maya only because we are in ignorance, but if we become seated in knowledge, then maya will cease to exist. They claim that the illusion will be dispelled, and we will understand that the soul itself is the Ultimate reality. However, this verse of the Bhagavad Gita negates such a theory. Shree Krishna states that maya is not an illusion; it is an energy of God. The *Śhwetāśhvatar Upanishad* too states:

māyāṁ tu prakṛitiṁ vidyānmāyinaṁ tu maheśhvaram (4.10)

'Maya is the energy (prakriti), while God is the Energetic.' The Ramayan states:

so dāsī raghubīra ki samujheṅ mithyā sopi

'Some people think maya is *mithyā* (non-existent), but factually, it is an energy that is engaged in the service of God.'

Here, Shree Krishna says that maya is very difficult to overcome because it is His energy. If anyone conquers maya, it means that person has conquered God Himself. Since no one can defeat God, no one can defeat maya either. And because the mind is made from maya, no yogi, jnani, ascetic, or karmi can successfully control the mind merely by self-effort.

On hearing this, Arjun could ask, 'How then will I overcome maya?' Shree Krishna gives the answer in the second line of the verse. He says, 'Arjun, if you surrender to Me, the Supreme Lord, then by My grace, I will take you across the ocean of material existence. I will indicate to maya that this soul has become Mine. Please leave him.' When the material energy receives this signal from God, it immediately releases such a soul from its bondage. Maya says, 'My work was only this much—to keep troubling the soul until it reaches the feet of God. Since this soul has surrendered to God, my work is done.'

Understand this through an example from everyday life. Let us say that you wish to meet your friend and reach the gate of his house. He has a board on his fence, saying 'Beware of dog.' His pet German Shepherd is standing in the lawn and, as a trained guard dog, growls at you menacingly. You decide to try the back gate and go around the fence. However, the Alsatian comes around too and snarls furiously, conveying the message, 'I dare you to step into this house.' When you have no other option, you call out to your friend. He emerges from his house and sees his dog troubling you. He calls out, 'No, Smokey! Come and sit here.' The dog is immediately pacified and comes and sits by his master's side. Now, you open the gate fearlessly and walk in.

Similarly, the material energy that is troubling us is subservient to God. By our own efforts we cannot overcome it. The way to go across it is to surrender to God. This is emphatically conveyed by Shree Krishna in this verse. *If we can cross over maya simply by surrendering to God, then why do people not surrender to Him? Shree Krishna explains this in the following verse.*

न मां दुष्कृतिनो मूढाः प्रपद्यन्ते नराधमाः ।
माययापहृतज्ञाना आसुरं भावमाश्रिताः ।।15।।

na māṁ duṣhkṛitino mūḍhāḥ prapadyante narādhamāḥ
māyayāpahṛita-jñānā āsuraṁ bhāvam āśhritāḥ

na—not; *mām*—unto me; *duṣhkṛitinaḥ*—the evil doers; *mūḍhāḥ*—the ignorant; *prapadyante*—surrender; *nara-adhamāḥ*—one who lazily follows one's lower nature; *māyayā*—by God's material energy; *apahṛita jñānāḥ*—those with deluded intellect; *āsuram*—demoniac; *bhāvam*—nature; *āśhritāḥ*—surrender.

Four kinds of people do not surrender unto Me—those ignorant of knowledge, those who lazily follow their lower nature though capable of knowing Me, those with deluded intellect, and those with a demoniac nature.

Shree Krishna has given four categories of people who do not surrender to God:

1) **The ignorant.** These are the people who are bereft of spiritual knowledge. They are unaware of their identity as the eternal soul, the goal of life which is God-realisation, and the process of surrendering to the Lord with loving devotion. Their lack of knowledge prevents them from surrendering to God.

2) **Those who lazily follow their lower nature.** These are people who do have basic spiritual knowledge and are aware of what they are supposed to do. However, due to the force of inertia of their lower nature they do not put in the effort to surrender. This laziness in exerting oneself to act according to the religious principles is a big pitfall on the path of spirituality. There is a Sanskrit saying:

ālasya hī manuṣhyāṇāṁ śharīrastho mahān ripuḥ
nāstyudyamasamo bandhuḥ kṛitvā yaṁ nāvasīdati

'Laziness is a big enemy, and it resides in our body itself. Work is a good friend of humans which never leads to downfall.'

3) **Those with deluded intellect.** These are people who are very proud of their intellect. If they hear the teachings of the saints and the scriptures, they are not willing to accept them with faith. However, not all spiritual truths are immediately evident. First, we need to have faith in the process and begin the practice, for only then can we understand the teachings through realisation. Those who refuse to have faith in anything that is not evident to them in the present, refuse to surrender to God, who is beyond sense perception. Shree Krishna puts these people in the third category.

4) **Those with a demoniac nature.** These are the people who know there is a God but work in evil and diametrically opposite ways to

thwart God's purpose in the world. Because of a demoniac nature, they hate the nature of God's revealed personality. They are unable to stand anyone singing His glories or engaging in His devotion. Quite obviously, such people do not surrender to God.

चतुर्विधा भजन्ते मां जनाः सुकृतिनोऽर्जुन ।
आर्तो जिज्ञासुरर्थार्थी ज्ञानी च भरतर्षभ ।।16।।

chatur-vidhā bhajante māṁ janāḥ sukṛitino 'rjuna
ārto jijñāsur arthārthī jñānī cha bharatarṣhabha

chatuḥ-vidhāḥ—four kinds; *bhajante*—worship; *mām*—me; *janāḥ*—people; *su-kṛitinaḥ*—those who are pious; *arjuna*—Arjun; *ārtaḥ*—the distressed; *jijñāsuḥ*—seekers of knowledge; *artha-arthī*—seekers of material gain; *jñānī*—those who are situated in knowledge; *cha*—and; *bharata-ṛiṣhabha*—best amongst Bharatas, Arjun.

O best amongst the Bharatas, four kinds of pious people engage in My devotion—the distressed, the seekers of knowledge, the seekers of worldly possessions, and those who are situated in knowledge.

Having described the kinds of people who do not surrender to Him, Shree Krishna now categorises the kinds of people who do take refuge in Him.

1) **The distressed.** For some people, when the pot of worldly miseries becomes excessive, it leads them to conclude that running after the world is futile, and it is better to take shelter in God. Likewise, when they see that worldly supports are unable to protect them, they then turn to God for protection. Draupadi's surrender to Shree Krishna was an example of this type of surrender. When Draupadi was being disrobed in the assembly of the Kauravas, she first counted upon the protection of her husbands. When they remained silent, she relied upon the pious elders present in the assembly—Dronacharya, Kripacharya, Bheeshma, and Vidur—to help her. When they too failed to offer her protection, she clenched her sari between her teeth. Up to this stage, Shree Krishna did not come to Draupadi's rescue. Finally, when Dushasan pulled her sari with a jerk, it slipped from the grasp of her

teeth. At that point, she no longer had any faith in the protection of others, nor did she rely on her own strength anymore. She surrendered herself totally to Shree Krishna who immediately offered her complete protection; He intervened by extending the length of her sari. No matter how much Dushashan pulled, he was still not able to disrobe Draupadi.

2) **The seekers of knowledge.** Some people take shelter of God out of their curiosity to know. They have heard about others finding beatitude in the spiritual realm and this makes them curious to know what it is all about. So, to satisfy their curiosity, they approach the Lord.

3) **The seekers of worldly possessions.** Another kind of people are very clear about what they want and are convinced that only the Lord can provide it to them, so they go to His shelter. For example, Dhruv began his devotion with the desire to become more powerful than his father, King Uttanapad. But when his devotion matured and God finally gave him darshan, he realised that what he had desired was like broken pieces of glass from One who possessed the priceless jewel of divine love. He then requested the Lord to bestow pure selfless devotion upon him.

4) **Those who are situated in knowledge.** Finally, there are souls who have reached the understanding that they are tiny parts of God and their eternal dharma is to love and serve Him. Shree Krishna says that these are the fourth kind of people who engage in His devotion.

तेषां ज्ञानी नित्ययुक्त एकभक्तिर्विशिष्यते ।
प्रियो हि ज्ञानिनोऽत्यर्थमहं स च मम प्रियः ।।17।।

teṣhāṁ jñānī nitya-yukta eka-bhaktir viśhiṣhyate
priyo hi jñānino 'tyartham ahaṁ sa cha mama priyaḥ

teṣhām—amongst these; *jñānī*—those who are situated in knowledge; *nitya-yuktaḥ*—ever steadfast; *eka*—exclusively; *bhaktiḥ*—devotion; *viśhiṣhyate*—highest; *priyaḥ*—very dear; *hi*—certainly; *jñāninaḥ*—to the person in knowledge; *atyartham*—highly; *aham*—I; *saḥ*—he; *cha*—and; *mama*—to me; *priyaḥ*—very dear.

Amongst these, I consider them to be the highest, who worship Me with knowledge and are steadfastly and exclusively devoted to Me. I am very dear to them, and they are very dear to Me.

Those who approach God in distress, for worldly possessions, or out of curiosity, do not possess selfless devotion as yet. Slowly, by the process of devotion, their heart becomes pure, and they develop knowledge of their eternal relationship with God. Then their devotion becomes exclusive, selfless, and incessant towards God. Since they have gained the knowledge that the world is not theirs and not a source of happiness, they neither thirst for favourable circumstances nor lament over unfavourable circumstances. Thus, they become situated in selfless devotion. In a spirit of total self-surrender, they offer themselves as oblation in the fire of love for their Divine Beloved. Hence, Shree Krishna says that such devotees who are situated in knowledge are the dearest to Him.

उदाराः सर्व एवैते ज्ञानी त्वात्मैव मे मतम् ।
आस्थितः स हि युक्तात्मा मामेवानुत्तमां गतिम् ।।18।।

udārāḥ sarva evaite jñānī tvātmaiva me matam
āsthitaḥ sa hi yuktātmā mām evānuttamāṁ gatim

udārāḥ—noble; *sarve*—all; *eva*—indeed; *ete*—these; *jñānī*—those in knowledge; *tu*—but; *ātmā eva*—my very self; *me*—my; *matam*—opinion; *āsthitaḥ*—situated; *saḥ*—he; *hi*—certainly; *yukta-ātmā*—those who are united; *mām*—in me; *eva*—certainly; *anuttamām*—the supreme; *gatim*—goal.

All those who are devoted to Me are indeed noble. But those in knowledge, who are of steadfast mind, whose intellect is merged in Me, and who have made Me alone as their supreme goal, I consider as My very Self.

Having stated in verse 7.17 that the *jnani bhakt* (devotee situated in knowledge) is the highest, Shree Krishna now clarifies that the other three kinds of devotees are also blessed souls. Whoever engages in devotion for whatever reason is privileged. Still, the devotees who are seated in knowledge do not worship God for material reasons. Consequently, God gets bound by the selfless, unconditional love of such devotees.

Parā bhakti or divine love is vastly different from worldly love. Divine love is imbued with the desire for the happiness of the Divine Beloved; worldly love is motivated by the desire for self-happiness. Divine love is imbued with a giving attitude and sacrifice in service of the Beloved; worldly love is characterised by a receiving attitude where the ultimate goal is to receive something from the other. Chaitanya Mahaprabhu describes:

kāmera tātparya nija-sambhoga kevala
kṛiṣhṇa-sukha-tātparya-mātra prema ta' prabala
ataeva kāma-preme bahuta antara
kāma andha-tamaḥ, prema nirmala bhāskara

(*Chaitanya Charitāmṛit*, *Ādi Leela*, 4.166 & 171)

'Lust (worldly love) exists for self-happiness; divine love is harboured for Shree Krishna's happiness. There is tremendous difference between them—lust is like darkness and ignorance while divine love is pure and illuminating.' Jagadguru Shree Kripaluji Maharaj states this very beautifully:

brahma lok paryanta sukh, aru muktihuñ sukh tyāg,
tabai dharahu paga prema patha, nahiṅ lagi jaiheñ dāg

(*Bhakti Śhatak*, verse 45)

'Give up the desires for worldly pleasures and that of liberation if you wish to walk the path of devotion. Else the pure waters of divine love will get tainted with selfishness.' Sage Narad defined pure devotion in this manner:

tat sukha sukhitvam (*Nārad Bhakti Darshan*, Sutra 24)

'True love is for the happiness of the Beloved.' The materially motivated devotees cannot engage in such devotion but the devotee who is in knowledge rises to this level of selflessness. When one learns to love

God in this manner, He becomes a slave of that devotee. The highest quality of God is *bhakta vatsaltā* (His love for His devotees). The Puranas state:

gītvā cha mama nāmāni vicharenmama sannidhau
iti bravīmi te satyaṁ krītohaṁ tasya chārjuna

(*Ādi Puran* 1.2.231)

Shree Krishna says: 'I become the slave of those devotees of Mine who chant My names and keep Me close to them in their thoughts. This is a fact, O Arjun.' God feels so indebted towards His selfless devotees that in this verse, He goes to the extent of saying He looks upon them as His very Self.

बहूनां जन्मनामन्ते ज्ञानवान्मां प्रपद्यते ।
वासुदेवः सर्वमिति स महात्मा सुदुर्लभः ।।19।।

bahūnāṁ janmanām ante jñānavān māṁ prapadyate
vāsudevaḥ sarvam iti sa mahātmā su-durlabhaḥ

bahūnām—many; *janmanām*—births; *ante*—after; *jñāna-vān*—one who is endowed with knowledge; *mām*—unto me; *prapadyate*—surrenders; *vāsudevaḥ*—Shree Krishna, son of Vasudev; *sarvam*—all; *iti*—that; *saḥ*—that; *mahā-ātmā*—great soul; *su-durlabhaḥ*—very rare.

After many births of spiritual practice, one who is endowed with knowledge surrenders unto Me, knowing Me to be all that is. Such a great soul is indeed very rare.

This verse clears a common misconception. Often people who are intellectually inclined deride bhakti (devotion) as inferior to jnana (knowledge). They maintain a supercilious air about themselves being engaged in the cultivation of knowledge and look down upon those engaged in devotion. However, in this verse, Shree Krishna states the very reverse. He says that after cultivating jnana for many lives, when the jnani's knowledge reaches a ripened state, then he or she finally surrenders to God.

The fact is that true knowledge naturally leads to devotion. Let us say that a person was walking on the beach, and he found a ring on the sand. He picked it up but had no knowledge of its value. He thought it must be artificial jewellery, which so common nowadays, and worth only three hundred rupees.

The next day, he showed the ring to a goldsmith, and asked, 'Can you please value this ring for me?'

The goldsmith checked it, and replied, 'This is 22-carat gold. It must be worth thirty thousand rupees.'

On hearing this, the person's love for the ring increased. Now when he looked at the ring, he got as much pleasure as he would on receiving a gift of thirty thousand rupees.

A few more days went by, and his uncle, who was a jeweller, came from another town. He asked his uncle, 'Could you evaluate this ring and the stone embedded in it?'

His uncle looked at it, and exclaimed, 'Where did you get this from? This is a real diamond. It must be worth one lakh rupees.'

He is overwhelmed. 'Uncle, please do not joke with me.'

'I am not joking, son. If you do not believe me, sell it to me for fifty thousand rupees.'

Now, his knowledge of the true value of the ring was confirmed. Immediately, his love for the ring increased. He felt he had won a jackpot, and his joy knew no bounds.

Notice, how the person's love for the ring kept increasing in proportion to his knowledge? When his knowledge was that the ring was worth three hundred rupees, his love for it was to the same extent. When his knowledge was that the ring is valued at thirty thousand rupees, his love for it increased proportionally, hundred-fold. When his knowledge was validated that the ring is actually worth one lakh rupees, his love for it grew exponentially.

The above example illustrates the direct correlation between knowledge and love. The Ramayan states:

jāneṅ binu na hoi paratītī, binu paratīti hoi nahiṅ prītī

'Without knowledge, there cannot be faith; without faith, love cannot grow.' Thus, true knowledge is naturally accompanied by love. If we claim we possess knowledge of Brahman, but feel no love towards Him, then our knowledge is merely theoretical.

Here, Shree Krishna explains that after many lifetimes of cultivation of knowledge, when that jnani's knowledge matures into true wisdom, he surrenders to the Supreme Lord, knowing Him to be all that is. The verse states that such a noble soul is very rare. He does not say this for jnanis, karmis, hatha yogis, ascetics, or others. He declares it for the devotee and says that the exalted soul who realises 'All is God' and surrenders to Him, is very rare.

कामैस्तैस्तैर्हृतज्ञानाः प्रपद्यन्तेऽन्यदेवताः ।
तं तं नियममास्थाय प्रकृत्या नियताः स्वया ।।20।।

kāmais tais tair hṛita-jñānāḥ prapadyante 'nya-devatāḥ
taṁ taṁ niyamam āsthāya prakṛityā niyatāḥ svayā

kāmaiḥ—by material desires; *taiḥ taiḥ*—by various; *hṛita-jñānāḥ*—whose knowledge has been carried away; *prapadyante*—surrender; *anya*—to other; *devatāḥ*—celestial gods; *tam tam*—various; *niyamam*—rules and regulations; *āsthāya*—following; *prakṛityā*—by nature; *niyatāḥ*—controlled; *svayā*—by their own.

Those whose knowledge has been carried away by material desires surrender to the celestial gods. Following their own nature, they worship the *devatās*, practising rituals meant to propitiate these celestial personalities.

When Shree Krishna (the Supreme Lord) is the basis of all that exists, no celestial god can be independent of Him. Just as the president governs a country with the help of numerous officers, so too, the *devatās* (celestial gods) are all minor officers in God's government. Although souls like us, they are elevated, and as a result of pious deeds in their past lives, they have attained a high post in the administration of the material realm.

They cannot grant anyone liberation from the bondage of maya because they themselves are not liberated. However, they can grant material things within their jurisdiction. Driven by material desires, people worship the *devatās* and observe the guidelines prescribed for their worship. Shree Krishna says that such persons whose knowledge has been clouded by material desires worship the celestial gods.

यो यो यां यां तनुं भक्तः श्रद्धयार्चितुमिच्छति ।
तस्य तस्याचलां श्रद्धां तामेव विदधाम्यहम् ।।21।।

yo yo yāṁ yāṁ tanuṁ bhaktaḥ śhraddhayārchitum ichchhati
tasya tasyāchalāṁ śhraddhāṁ tām eva vidadhāmyaham

yaḥ yaḥ—whoever; *yām yām*—whichever; *tanum*—form; *bhaktaḥ*—devotee; *śhraddhayā*—with faith; *architum*—to worship; *ichchhati*—desires; *tasya tasya*—to him; *achalām*—steady; *śhraddhām*—faith; *tām*—in that; *eva*—certainly; *vidadhāmi*—bestow; *aham*—I.

Whatever celestial form a devotee seeks to worship with faith, I steady the faith of such a devotee in that form.

Faith in the worship of the Supreme Lord is the most beneficial kind of faith which comes with true knowledge. However, if we look around us in the world, we find innumerable devotees of the celestial gods as well, who engage in their devotion with firm and unflinching faith. We may wonder how these people develop such a high level of faith in a lower form of worship.

Shree Krishna provides the answer in this verse. He says that faith in the celestial gods is also strengthened by Him. When He sees people seeking to worship the *devatās* for fulfilment of their material desires, He steadies their faith and helps them in their devotion. The celestial gods themselves do not have the ability to generate faith in their devotees. It is the indwelling Paramatma (Supreme Soul) who inspires *śhraddhā* in them. As Shree Krishna states in verse 15.15, 'I am seated in the hearts of all living beings, and from Me come memory, knowledge, as well as forgetfulness.'

One may ask why the Supreme Lord strengthens faith in the celestial gods when such faith is inappropriately placed. This is just as parents allow their children to shower affection on dolls as if they were real babies. Parents know their child's affection for the doll is out of ignorance, and yet they encourage the child to love and play with dolls. The reason is that the parents know this will help develop qualities of affection, love, and care, which will be beneficial when the child grows up. Similarly, when souls worship the celestial gods for material gains, God steadies their faith, in the expectation that the experience will help evolve the soul upward. Then, one day, the soul will surrender to the Supreme Lord, understanding Him to be the summum bonum of everything.

स तया श्रद्धया युक्तस्तस्याराधनमीहते ।
लभते च ततः कामान्मयैव विहितान्हि तान् ।।22।।

sa tayā śhraddhayā yuktas tasyārādhanam īhate
labhate cha tataḥ kāmān mayaiva vihitān hi tān

saḥ—he; *tayā*—with that; *śhraddhayā*—faith; *yuktaḥ*—endowed with; *tasya*—of that; *ārādhanam*—worship; *īhate*—tries to engage in; *labhate*—obtains; *cha*—and; *tataḥ*—from that; *kāmān*—desires; *mayā*—by me; *eva*—alone; *vihitān*—granted; *hi*—certainly; *tān*—those.

Endowed with faith, the devotee worships a particular celestial god and obtains the objects of desire. But in reality, I alone arrange these benefits.

Labhate means 'they obtain'. Devotees of celestial gods may obtain their desired ends by worshipping the respective celestial gods, but the truth is that it is not the *devatās*, but God, who grants the benefits to be given. This verse clearly means that the celestial gods do not have the right to sanction material benefits; they can only grant them to their devotees when God sanctions it. However, people of mediocre understanding deduce that help comes to them from the gods they worship.

अन्तवत्तु फलं तेषां तद्भवत्यल्पमेधसाम् ।
देवान्देवयजो यान्ति मद्भक्ता यान्ति मामपि ।।23।।

antavat tu phalaṁ teṣhāṁ tad bhavatyalpa-medhasām
devān deva-yajo yānti mad-bhaktā yānti mām api

anta-vat—perishable; *tu*—but; *phalam*—fruit; *teṣhām*—by them; *tat*—that; *bhavati*—is; *alpa-medhasām*—people of little understanding; *devān*—to the celestial gods; *deva-yajaḥ*—worshippers of the celestial gods; *yānti*—go; *mat*—my; *bhaktāḥ*—devotees; *yānti*—go; *mām*—to me; *api*—whereas.

But the fruit gained by these people of little understanding is perishable. Those who worship the celestial gods go to the celestial abodes while My devotees come to Me.

While primary school is necessary, students are expected to outgrow it one day. If a student desires to remain in primary school for longer than necessary, the teacher will discourage it and coach the student to move forward in life. Similarly, for neophyte devotees wishing to worship the celestial gods, Shree Krishna does steady their faith, as stated in verse 7.21. But the Bhagavad Gita is not for primary school students, so He wishes for Arjun to understand the spiritual principle: 'One attains the object of one's worship. Those who worship the *devatās*, go to the planets of the *devatās* after death. Those who worship Me, come to Me.' When the *devatās* are perishable, the fruits of their worship are also perishable. But since God is imperishable, the fruits of His worship are also imperishable. The devotees of God attain His eternal service and His eternal abode.

अव्यक्तं व्यक्तिमापन्नं मन्यन्ते मामबुद्धयः ।
परं भावमजानन्तो ममाव्ययमनुत्तमम् ।।24।।

avyaktaṁ vyaktim āpannaṁ manyante mām abuddhayaḥ
paraṁ bhāvam ajānanto mamāvyayam anuttamam

avyaktam—formless; *vyaktim*—possessing a personality; *āpannam*—to have assumed; *manyante*—think; *mām*—me; *abuddhayaḥ*—less intelligent; *param*—Supreme; *bhāvam*—nature; *ajānantaḥ*—not understanding; *mama*—my; *avyayam*—imperishable; *anuttamam*—excellent.

The less intelligent think that I, the Supreme Lord Shree Krishna, was formless earlier and have now assumed this personality. They do not understand the imperishable exalted nature of My personal form.

Some people emphatically claim that God is only formless while others assert equally vehemently that the Supreme Lord only exists in a personal form. Both these points of view are restricting and incomplete. God is perfect and complete, and therefore, He is both formless and with a form. This has also been discussed in the commentary of verse 4.6.

Among the people who accept both aspects of God's personality, the debate sometimes ensues regarding which of these is the original form. Did the formless manifest from the personal form of God or vice versa? Shree Krishna resolves this debate here by stating that the divine personality is primordial—it did not manifest from the formless Brahman. God exists eternally in His divine form in the spiritual realm. The formless Brahman is the light that emanates from His transcendental body.

The *Padma Puran* states:

yannakhenduruchirbrahma dhyeyaṁ brahmādibhiḥ suraiḥ
guṇatrayamatītaṁ taṁ vande vṛindāvaneśhvaram

(*Pātāl Khaṇḍ* 77.60)

'The light that emanates from the toe-nails of God's personality is worshipped as Brahman by the jnanis.'

Actually, there is no difference between His personal and formless aspects. It is not that one is big and the other is small. In the formless Brahman aspect, all of God's energies and potencies do exist, but they are unmanifest. In His personal aspect, His Names, Forms, Pastimes, Virtues, Abodes, and Associates are all manifest by His divine energy.

Then why do people think of the Lord as an ordinary human? The answer to this question is explained in the next verse.

नाहं प्रकाशः सर्वस्य योगमायासमावृतः ।
मूढोऽयं नाभिजानाति लोको मामजमव्ययम् ।।25।।

nāhaṁ prakāśhaḥ sarvasya yoga-māyā-samāvṛitaḥ
mūḍho 'yaṁ nābhijānāti loko mām ajam avyayam

na—not; *aham*—I; *prakāśhaḥ*—manifest; *sarvasya*—to everyone; *yoga-māyā*—God's supreme (divine) energy; *samāvṛitaḥ*—veiled; *mūḍhaḥ*—deluded; *ayam*—these; *na*—not; *abhijānāti*—know; *lokaḥ*—persons; *mām*—me; *ajam*—unborn; *avyayam*—immutable.

I am not manifest to everyone, being veiled by My divine *Yogmaya* energy. Hence, those without knowledge do not know that I am without birth and changeless.

Having described two of His energies in verses 7.4 and 7.5, Shree Krishna now mentions His third energy—*Yogmaya*. This is His supreme energy. The *Vishnu Puran* states:

viṣhṇu śhaktiḥ parā proktā kṣhetrajñākhyā tathā 'parā
avidyā karma saṁjñānyā tṛitīyā śhaktiriṣhyate (6.7.61)

'The Supreme Lord Shree Vishnu has three main energies—*Yogmaya*, the souls, and maya.' Jagadguru Kripaluji Maharaj states:

śhaktimān kī śhaktiyāñ, aganita yadapi bakhāna
tin mahañ 'māyā', 'jīva', aru 'parā', triśhakti pradhāna

(*Bhakti Śhatak* verse 3)

'The Supreme Energetic Shree Krishna has infinite energies. Among these, *Yogmaya*, the souls, and maya are the main ones.'

The divine power, *Yogmaya*, is God's all-powerful energy. By virtue of it, He manifests His divine pastimes, divine love bliss, and divine abodes. By that *Yogmaya* power, God descends in the world and manifests His divine pastimes on the earth plane as well. By the same *Yogmaya* power, He keeps Himself veiled from us. Although God is seated in our hearts, we do not have any perception of His presence within us. *Yogmaya* keeps His divinity obscured from us until we are eligible for His divine vision. Hence, even if we see the Lord in His personal form at present, we will not be able to recognise Him as God. It is only when the *Yogmaya* power bestows its grace upon us, that we get the divine vision to see and recognise God.

chidānandamaya deha tumhārī, bigata bikāra jāna adhikārī

(Ramayan)

'O God, You have a divine form. Only those whose hearts have been purified can know You by Your grace.'

The *Yogmaya* power is both formless and manifests in the personal form, such as Radha, Sita, Durga, Kali, Lakshmi, and Parvati, and so on. These are all divine forms of the *Yogmaya* energy, and all are revered in Vedic culture as the Mother of the universe. They radiate the motherly qualities of tenderness, compassion, forgiveness, sacrifice, grace, and causeless love. More importantly for us, they bestow divine grace upon the soul and grant it the transcendental knowledge by which it can know God. This is why devotees in Vrindavan sing *Radhe Radhe, Shyam se milā de* 'O Radha, please bestow Your grace and help me meet Shree Krishna.'

Thus, *Yogmaya* performs both functions—it hides God from souls who are not qualified and bestows grace upon surrendered souls so that they may know Him. Those who have their backs turned towards God are covered by maya and bereft of the grace of *Yogmaya*. Those who turn their face towards God are released from maya and come under the shelter of *Yogmaya*.

वेदाहं समतीतानि वर्तमानानि चार्जुन ।
भविष्याणि च भूतानि मां तु वेद न कश्चन ।।26।।

vedāhaṁ samatītāni vartamānāni chārjuna
bhaviṣhyāṇi cha bhūtāni māṁ tu veda na kaśhchana

veda—know; *aham*—I; *samatītāni*—the past; *vartamānāni*—the present; *cha*—and; *arjuna*—Arjun; *bhaviṣhyāṇi*—the future; *cha*—also; *bhūtāni*—all living beings; *mām*—me; *tu*—but; *veda*—knows; *na kaśhchana*—no one.

O Arjun, I know of the past, present, and future, and I also know all living beings, but Me, no one knows.

God is omniscient. He declares here that He is *trikāl-darśhī*—He has knowledge of the past, present, and future. We forget what we ourselves were thinking a few hours ago. But God remembers the thoughts, words, and deeds of each of the infinite souls in the universe, at every moment of their life, in each of their infinite lifetimes. These constitute the *sañchit* karmas (stockpile of karmas of endless lifetimes) for every soul. God has to maintain accounts of this so that He may dispense justice in the form of the Law of Karma. As a result, He says He knows the past, present, and future. The *Muṇḍakopaniṣhad* states:

yaḥ sarvajñaḥ sarvavidyasya jñānamayaṁ tapaḥ (1.1.9)

'God is all-knowing and omniscient. His austerity consists of knowledge.'

In this verse, Shree Krishna says that although He knows everything, nobody knows Him. God is infinite in splendour, glory, energies, qualities, and extent. Since our intellect is finite, there is no way it can comprehend the Almighty God. All the Vedic scriptures state:

naiṣhā tarkeṇa matirāpaneyā (*Kaṭhopaniṣhad* 1.2.9)

'God is beyond the scope of our intellectual logic.'

yato vācho nivartante aprāpya manasā saha

(*Taittirīya Upanishad* 2.9.1)

'God cannot be described in words, nor can our mind comprehend Him.'

rām atarkya buddhi mana bānī, mata hamāra asa sunahi sayānī

(Ramayan)

'God cannot be analysed by arguments or formulated by words, mind, and intellect.'

There is only one personality who knows God and that is God Himself. If He decides to bestow His grace upon some soul, He bestows His intellect upon that fortunate soul. Equipped with God's power, that fortunate soul can then know God. Consequently, the concept of grace is of paramount importance in getting to know God. This point is discussed in detail later in verses 10.11 and 18.56.

इच्छाद्वेषसमुत्थेन द्वन्द्वमोहेन भारत ।
सर्वभूतानि सम्मोहं सर्गे यान्ति परन्तप ॥27॥

ichchhā-dveṣha-samutthena dvandva-mohena bhārata
sarva-bhūtāni sammohaṁ sarge yānti parantapa

ichchhā—desire; *dveṣha*—aversion; *samutthena*—arise from; *dvandva*—of duality; *mohena*—from the illusion; *bhārata*—Arjun, descendant of Bharat; *sarva*—all; *bhūtāni*—living beings; *sammoham*—into delusion; *sarge*—since birth; *yānti*—enter; *parantapa*—Arjun, conqueror of enemies.

O descendent of Bharat, the dualities of desire and aversion arise from illusion. O conqueror of enemies, all living beings in the material realm are deluded by these from birth.

The world is full of dualities—night and day, winter and summer, happiness and distress, pleasure and pain, and so on. The biggest dualities are birth and death. These exist in a pair—the moment birth takes place, death is certain; death, in turn, brings subsequent birth. And between the two ends of birth and death is the arena of life. These dualities are an inseparable part of the experience of anyone who goes through life.

In material consciousness, we desire one and detest the other. This attraction and aversion is not an inherent quality of the dualities; rather, it arises from our ignorance. Our mistaken intellect is convinced that material pleasures will fulfil our self-interest. We are also convinced that pain is harmful to our being. We do not realise that materially pleasurable situations thicken the cover of material illusion on the soul, while adverse situations have the potential to dispel the illusion and elevate the mind. The root cause of this delusion is ignorance. The sign of spiritual wisdom is that a person rises above attraction and aversion, likes and dislikes, and embraces all such dualities as inseparable aspects of God's creation.

येषां त्वन्तगतं पापं जनानां पुण्यकर्मणाम् ।
ते द्वन्द्वमोहनिर्मुक्ता भजन्ते मां दृढव्रताः ।।28।।

yeṣhāṁ tvanta-gataṁ pāpaṁ janānāṁ puṇya-karmaṇām
te dvandva-moha-nirmuktā bhajante māṁ dṛiḍha-vratāḥ

yeṣhām—whose; *tu*—but; *anta-gatam*—completely destroyed; *pāpam*—sins; *janānām*—of persons; *puṇya*—pious; *karmaṇām*—activities; *te*—they; *dvandva*—of dualities; *moha*—illusion; *nirmuktāḥ*—free from; *bhajante*—worship; *mām*—me; *dṛiḍha-vratāḥ*—with determination.

But persons, whose sins have been destroyed by engaging in pious activities, become free from the illusion of dualities. Such persons worship Me with determination.

Shree Krishna stated in verse 2.69 that what the ignorant consider as night, the wise consider as day. Those whose aspiration for God-realisation has been awakened welcome pain as an opportunity for self-abnegation and spiritual growth. They are also wary of pleasure that may cloud their soul. Thus, they neither pine for pleasure nor have aversion for pain. Such souls who have freed their mind from these dualities of desire and hatred are able to worship God with unshakeable determination.

जरामरणमोक्षाय मामाश्रित्य यतन्ति ये ।
ते ब्रह्म तद्विदुः कृत्स्नमध्यात्मं कर्म चाखिलम् ।।29।।

jarā-maraṇa-mokṣhāya mām āśhritya yatanti ye
te brahma tadviduḥ kṛitsnam adhyātmaṁ karma chākhilam

jarā—from old age; *maraṇa*—and death; *mokṣhāya*—for liberation; *mām*—me; *āśhritya*—take shelter in; *yatanti*—strive; *ye*—who; *te*—they; *brahma*—Brahman; *tat*—that; *viduḥ*—know; *kṛitsnam*—everything; *adhyātmam*—the individual self; *karma*—karmic action; *cha*—and; *akhilam*—entire.

Those who take shelter in Me, striving for liberation from old age and death, come to know Brahman, the individual self, and the entire field of karmic action.

As stated in verse 7.26, God cannot be known by the strength of one's intellect. However, those who surrender to Him, become recipients of His grace. Then, by virtue of His grace, they are easily able to know Him. The *Kaṭhopaniṣhad* states:

nāyamātmā pravachanena labhyo
na medhayā na bahunā śhrutena
yamevaiṣha vṛiṇute tena labhya-
stasyaiṣha ātmā vivṛiṇute tanūṁ svām (1.2.23)

'God cannot be known by spiritual discourses, nor through the intellect, nor by hearing various kinds of teachings. Only when He bestows His grace upon someone, does that fortunate soul come to know Him.' And when one acquires knowledge of God, everything else related to Him becomes known as well. The Vedas state: *ekasmin vijñāte sarvamidaṁ vijñātaṁ bhavati* 'If you know God, you will know everything.'

Some spiritual aspirants consider atma jnana (knowledge of the self) as the ultimate goal. However, just as a drop of water is a tiny part of the ocean; atma jnana is only a tiny part of brahma jnana (knowledge of God). Those who have knowledge of the drop do not necessarily know the depth, breadth, and power of the ocean. Similarly, those who know the self do not necessarily know God. However, those who get knowledge of God, automatically obtain knowledge of everything that is a part of Him. Hence, Shree Krishna states that those who take shelter in Him come to know Him, the soul, and the field of karmic action, by His grace.

साधिभूताधिदैवं मां साधियज्ञं च ये विदुः ।
प्रयाणकालेऽपि च मां ते विदुर्युक्तचेतसः ।।30।।

sādhibhūtādhidaivaṁ māṁ sādhiyajñaṁ cha ye viduḥ
prayāṇa-kāle 'pi cha māṁ te vidur yukta-chetasaḥ

sa-adhibhūta—governing principle of the field of matter; *adhidaivam*—governing principle of the celestial gods; *mām*—me; *sa-adhiyajñam*—governing principle of the Lord of all sacrificial performances; *cha*—and; *ye*—who; *viduḥ*—know; *prayāṇa*—of death; *kāle*—at the time; *api*—even; *cha*—and; *mām*—me; *te*—they; *viduḥ*—know; *yukta-chetasaḥ*—in full consciousness of me.

Those who know Me as the governing principle of the *adhibhūta* (field of matter) and the *Adhidaiva* (the celestial gods), and as *Adhiyajna* (the Lord of all sacrificial performances), such enlightened souls are in full consciousness of Me even at the time of death.

In the next chapter, Shree Krishna will state that those elevated souls who remember Him at the time of leaving the body attain His divine abode. However, to remember God at the time of death is exceedingly difficult. The reason is that death is an extremely painful experience. It can be likened to two thousand scorpions biting one at the same time. This is much beyond the capacity of anyone's mind and intellect to tolerate. Even before death comes, the mind and intellect stop working and a person becomes unconscious. How then can one remember God at the time of death?

This is only possible for those who are beyond the pleasure and pain of the body. Such people leave the body with awareness. Shree Krishna states in this verse that those who know Him as the governing principle of *adhibhūta*, *Adhidaiva*, and *Adhiyajna* are in full consciousness of Him even at the time of death. This is because true knowledge leads to complete devotion—the mind becomes fully attached to

God. Consequently, it becomes detached from the hankering and lamentation at the physical platform, and such a soul is no longer in bodily consciousness.

The words *adhibhūta*, *Adhidaiva*, and *Adhiyajna* are explained in the next chapter.

CHAPTER 8

Akṣhar Brahma Yog

The Yog of Eternal God

This chapter briefly explains several important terms and concepts that are presented more fully in the Upanishads. It also describes the factors that determine the destination of the soul after death. If we can remember God at the time of departure from the body, we will certainly attain Him. Therefore, we must practice thinking of Him at all times, while simultaneously doing our daily works. We can remember Him by thinking of His Qualities, Attributes, and Virtues. We must also practise steadfast yogic concentration by chanting His names. When we perfectly absorb our mind in Him through exclusive devotion, we will go beyond this material dimension to the spiritual realm.

The chapter then talks about the various abodes that exist in the material realm. It explains the process by which, in the cycle of creation, these abodes and the multitudes of beings on them come into existence and are then again absorbed back at the time of dissolution. However, transcendental to this manifest and unmanifest creation is the divine abode of God. Those who follow the path of light ultimately reach the divine abode and never return to this mortal world, while those who follow the path of darkness keep transmigrating in the endless cycle of birth, disease, old age, and death.

अर्जुन उवाच ।
किं तद्ब्रह्म किमध्यात्मं किं कर्म पुरुषोत्तम ।
अधिभूतं च किं प्रोक्तमधिदैवं किमुच्यते ।।1।।

अधियज्ञः कथं कोऽत्र देहेऽस्मिन्मधुसूदन ।
प्रयाणकाले च कथं ज्ञेयोऽसि नियतात्मभिः ।।2।।

arjuna uvācha
kiṁ tad brahma kim adhyātmaṁ kiṁ karma puruṣhottama
adhibhūtaṁ cha kiṁ proktam adhidaivaṁ kim uchyate

adhiyajñaḥ kathaṁ ko 'tra dehe 'smin madhusūdana
prayāṇa-kāle cha kathaṁ jñeyo 'si niyatātmabhiḥ

arjunaḥ uvācha—Arjun said; *kim*—what; *tat*—that; *brahma*—Brahman; *kim*—what; *adhyātmam*—the individual soul; *kim*—what; *karma*—the principle of karma; *puruṣha-uttama*—Shree Krishna, the Supreme Divine Personality; *adhibhūtam*—the material manifestation; *cha*—and; *kim*—what; *proktam*—is called; *adhidaivam*—Lord of celestial gods; *kim*—what; *uchyate*—is called; *adhiyajñaḥ*—Lord of all sacrificial performances; *katham*—how; *kaḥ*—who; *atra*—here; *dehe*—in body; *asmin*—this; *madhusūdana*—Shree Krishna, killer of the demon named Madhu; *prayāṇa-kāle*—at the time of death; *cha*—and; *katham*—how; *jñeyaḥ*—to be known; *asi*—are (you); *niyata-ātmabhiḥ*—by those of steadfast mind.

Arjun said: O Supreme Lord, what is Brahman (Absolute Reality), what is *adhyatma* (the individual soul), and what is karma? What is said to be *adhibhūta*, and who is said to be *Adhidaiva*? Who is *Adhiyajna* in the body and how is He the *Adhiyajna*? O Krishna, how are You to be known at the time of death by those of steadfast mind?

At the conclusion of chapter seven, Shree Krishna had introduced terms like Brahman, *adhibhūta*, *adhyatma*, *Adhidaiva*, and *Adhiyajna*. Arjun is curious to learn more about these terms, consequently, he raises seven questions in these two verses. Six of these questions relate to the terms mentioned by Shree Krishna. The seventh question is about the time of death, which Shree Krishna had Himself first mentioned in verse 7.30. Arjun now wishes to know how one can remember God at the moment of death.

श्रीभगवानुवाच ।
अक्षरं ब्रह्म परमं स्वभावोऽध्यात्ममुच्यते ।
भूतभावोद्भवकरो विसर्गः कर्मसञ्ज्ञितः ।।3।।

śhrī bhagavān uvācha
akṣharaṁ brahma paramaṁ svabhāvo 'dhyātmam uchyate
bhūta-bhāvodbhava-karo visargaḥ karma-sanjñitaḥ

śhrī-bhagavān uvācha—the Lord said; *akṣharam*—indestructible; *brahma*—Brahman; *paramam*—the Supreme; *svabhāvaḥ*—nature; *adhyātmam*—one's own self; *uchyate*—is called; *bhūta-bhāva-udbhava-karaḥ*—actions pertaining to the material personality of living beings and its development; *visargaḥ*—creation; *karma*—fruitive activities; *sanjñitaḥ*—are called.

The Lord said: The Supreme Indestructible Entity is called Brahman; one's own self is called *adhyatma*. Actions pertaining to the material personality of living beings and its development are called karma or fruitive activities.

Shree Krishna says that the Supreme Entity is called Brahman (in the Vedas, God is referred to by many names and Brahman is one of them). It is beyond space, time, and the chain of cause and effect. These are the characteristics of the material realm, while Brahman is transcendental to the material plane. It is unaffected by the changes in the universe and is imperishable. Hence, It is described as *akṣharam*. In the *Bṛihadāraṇyak Upanishad* 3.8.8, Brahman has been described in the same manner: 'Learned people speak of Brahman as *akṣhar* (indestructible). It is also designated as *Param* (Supreme) because It possesses qualities beyond those possessed by maya and the souls.'

The path of spirituality is called *adhyatma*, and the science of the soul is also called *adhyatma*. But here the word has been used for one's own self, which includes the soul, body, mind, and intellect.

Karma is actions performed by the self that forge the individual's unique conditions of existence from birth to birth. These karmas keep the soul rotating in samsara (the cycle of material existence).

अधिभूतं क्षरो भावः पुरुषश्चाधिदैवतम् ।
अधियज्ञोऽहमेवात्र देहे देहभृतां वर ।।4।।

adhibhūtaṁ kṣharo bhāvaḥ puruṣhaśh chādhidaivatam
adhiyajño 'ham evātra dehe deha-bhṛitāṁ vara

adhibhūtam—the ever-changing physical manifestation; *kṣharaḥ*—perishable; *bhāvaḥ*—nature; *puruṣhaḥ*—cosmic personality of God encompassing the material creation; *cha*—and; *adhidaivatam*—Lord of the celestial gods; *adhiyajñaḥ*—Lord of all sacrifices; *aham*—I; *eva*—certainly; *atra*—here; *dehe*—in the body; *deha-bhṛitām*—of the embodied; *vara*—O best.

O best of the embodied souls, the physical manifestation that is constantly changing is called *adhibhūta*; the universal form of God which presides over the celestial gods in this creation is called *Adhidaiva*; I, who dwell in the heart of every living being, am called *Adhiyajna* or the Lord of all sacrifices.

The kaleidoscope of the universe, consisting of all manifestations of the five elements—earth, water, fire, air, space—is called *adhibhūta.* The *virāṭ purush*, which is the complete cosmic personality of God encompassing the entire material creation, is called *Adhidaiva* because He has sovereignty over the *devatās* (the celestial gods who oversee the different departments of the universe). The Supreme Divine Personality, Shree Krishna, who dwells in the heart of all living beings as the Paramatma (Supreme Soul) is called *Adhiyajna*. All yajnas (sacrifices) are to be performed for His satisfaction. He is thus the presiding divinity over all the yajnas and the one who bestows rewards for all actions.

This verse and the previous one answer six of Arjun's seven questions which are on terminology. *The next few verses answer the question about the time of death.*

अन्तकाले च मामेव स्मरन्मुक्त्वा कलेवरम् ।
यः प्रयाति स मद्भावं याति नास्त्यत्र संशयः ॥5॥

anta-kāle cha mām eva smaran muktvā kalevaram
yaḥ prayāti sa mad-bhāvaṁ yāti nāstyatra sanśhayaḥ

anta-kāle—at the time of death; *cha*—and; *mām*—me; *eva*—alone; *smaran*—remembering; *muktvā*—relinquish; *kalevaram*—the body; *yaḥ*—who; *prayāti*—goes; *saḥ*—he; *mat-bhāvam*—godlike nature; *yāti*—achieves; *na*—no; *asti*—there is; *atra*—here; *sanśhayaḥ*—doubt.

Those who relinquish the body while remembering Me at the moment of death will come to Me. There is certainly no doubt about this.

In the next verse, Shree Krishna will state the principle that one's next birth is determined by one's state of consciousness at the time of death and the object of one's absorption. So if, at the time of death, one is absorbed in the transcendental Names, Forms, Associates, Virtues, Pastimes, and Abodes of God, one will attain the cherished goal of God-realisation. Shree Krishna uses the words *mad bhāvaṁ,* which mean 'godlike nature'. Thus, if one's consciousness is absorbed in God at the moment of death, one attains Him, and becomes godlike in character.

यं यं वापि स्मरन्भावं त्यजत्यन्ते कलेवरम् ।
तं तमेवैति कौन्तेय सदा तद्भावभावितः ॥6॥

yaṁ yaṁ vāpi smaran bhāvaṁ tyajatyante kalevaram
taṁ tam evaiti kaunteya sadā tad-bhāva-bhāvitaḥ

yam yam—whatever; *vā*—or; *api*—even; *smaran*—remembering; *bhāvam*—remembrance; *tyajati*—gives up; *ante*—in the end; *kalevaram*—the body; *tam*—to that; *tam*—to that; *eva*—certainly; *eti*—gets; *kaunteya*—Arjun, son of Kunti; *sadā*—always; *tat*—that; *bhāva-bhāvitaḥ*—absorbed in contemplation.

Whatever one remembers upon giving up the body at the time of death, O son of Kunti, one attains that state, being always absorbed in such contemplation.

We may succeed in teaching a parrot to say, 'Good morning!' But if we press its throat hard, it will forget what it has artificially learnt and make its natural sound 'Kaw!' Similarly, at the time of death, our mind naturally flows through the channels of thoughts it has created through lifelong habit. The time to decide our travel plans is not when our baggage is already packed; rather, it requires careful planning and execution beforehand. Whatever prominently dominates one's thoughts at the moment of death will determine one's next birth. This is what Shree Krishna states in this verse.

One's final thoughts will naturally be determined by what was constantly contemplated and meditated upon during the span of life, as influenced by one's daily habits and associations. The Puranas relate the story of Maharaj Bharat to drive home this point.

Maharaj Bharat was a powerful king in ancient India, who renounced his kingdom to live in the forest as an ascetic and pursue God-realisation. One day, he saw a pregnant deer jump into the water, on hearing a tiger roar. Out of fear, the pregnant deer delivered a fawn that began floating on the water. Bharat jumped into the water to rescue it. He took it to his hut and began rearing it. With great affection, he would watch its frolicking movements. He would gather grass to feed it and would hug it to keep it warm. Slowly, his mind came away from God and became absorbed in the deer. The absorption became so deep that practically all day long, his thoughts would wander towards the deer. The attachment became so intense that even at the time of death, he called out to the deer in fond remembrance, concerned about what would happen to him.

Consequently, in his next life, Maharaj Bharat became a deer. However, because he had performed spiritual sadhana, he was aware of the mistake in his previous life, so even as a deer, he would reside near the ashrams of saintly persons in the forest. Finally, when he gave up the deer's body, he was again given a human birth. This time, he became the great sage Jadabharat and attained God-realisation by completing his sadhana.

One should not conclude on reading the verse that for the attainment of the ultimate goal, the Supreme Lord is only to be meditated upon at the moment of death. This is well-nigh impossible without a lifetime of preparation. The *Skand Puran* states that at the time of death it is exceedingly difficult to remember God. Death is such a painful experience that the mind naturally gravitates to the thoughts that constitute one's inner nature. For the mind to think of God requires one's inner nature to be united with Him. The inner nature is the consciousness that abides within one's mind and intellect. Only if we contemplate something continuously does it manifest as a part of our inner nature. So, to develop a God-consciousness inner nature, the Lord must be remembered, recollected, and contemplated upon at every moment of our life. *This is what Shree Krishna reiterates in the next verse.*

तस्मात्सर्वेषु कालेषु मामनुस्मर युध्य च ।
मय्यर्पितमनोबुद्धिर्मामेवैष्यस्यसंशयम् ।।7।।

tasmāt sarveṣhu kāleṣhu mām anusmara yudhya cha
mayyarpita-mano-buddhir mām evaiṣhyasyasanśhayam

tasmāt—therefore; *sarveṣhu*—in all; *kāleṣhu*—times; *mām*—me; *anusmara*—remember; *yudhya*—fight; *cha*—and; *mayi*—to me; *arpita*—surrender; *manaḥ*—mind; *buddhiḥ*—intellect; *mām*—to me; *eva*—surely; *eṣhyasi*—you shall attain; *asanśhayaḥ*—without a doubt.

Therefore, always remember Me and also do your duty of fighting the war. With mind and intellect surrendered to Me, you will definitely attain Me; of this, there is no doubt.

The first line of this verse is the essence of the teachings of the Bhagavad Gita. It has the power of making our life divine. It also encapsulates the definition of karm yog. Shree Krishna says, 'Keep your mind attached to Me, and do your worldly duty with your body.' This applies to people in all walks of life—doctors, engineers, lawyers, housewives, students, and everyone else. In Arjun's specific case, he is a warrior, and his duty is to fight. So, he is being instructed to fulfil his duty while keeping his mind on God. Some people neglect their worldly duties on the plea that they have taken to spirituality. Others excuse themselves from spiritual practice on the pretext of worldly engagements. People believe that spiritual and material pursuits are irreconcilable. But God's message is to sanctify one's entire life.

When we practise such karm yog, worldly works will not suffer because the body is actively engaged in them. But since the mind is attached to God, these actions will not bind one in the Law of Karma. Only those activities result in karmic reactions which are performed with attachment. When that attachment does not exist, even worldly law does not hold one culpable. For example, let us say that one man killed another and is brought to court.

The judge asks him, 'Did you kill that man?'

The man replies, 'Yes, your honour, there is no need for any witness. I confess that I killed him.'

'Then you should be punished!'

'No, your honour, you cannot punish me.'

'Why?'

'I had no intention to kill. I was driving the car on the proper side of the road, within speed limits, with my eyes focused ahead. My brakes, steering, everything was perfect. That man suddenly ran in front of my car. What could I do?'

If his attorney can establish that the intention to kill did not exist, the judge will let him off even without the slightest punishment.

From the above example, we see that even in the world we are not culpable for actions performed without attachment. The same principle holds for the Law of Karma as well. That is why, during the Mahabharat war, following Shree Krishna's instructions, Arjun did his duty on the battlefield. By the end of the war, Shree Krishna noted that Arjun did not accrue any bad karma. He would have been entangled in karma if he had been fighting the battle with attachment for worldly gain or fame. However, his mind was attached to Shree Krishna, and so, what he was doing was multiplication in zeros—performing his duty in this world without selfish attachment. Even if you multiply one lakh with zero, the answer will still be zero.

The condition for karm yog has been stated very clearly in this verse: The mind must be constantly engaged in thinking of God. The moment the mind forgets God, it comes under the attack of the big generals of maya's army—lust, anger, greed, envy, hatred, and other negative emotions. Consequently, it is important to always keep it attached to God. Often people claim to be karm yogis because they say they do both—karm and yog. For the major part of the day, they do karm, and for a few minutes, they do yog (meditation on God). But this is not the definition of karm yog that Shree Krishna has given. He states that 1) even while doing work, the mind must be engaged in thinking of God, and 2) the remembrance of God must not be intermittent, but constant throughout the day.

Saint Kabir expresses this in his famous couplet:

sumiran kī sudhi yoṅ karo, jyauṅ gāgar panihāra
bolat dolat surati meṅ, kahe kabīra vichār

'Remember God just as the village woman remembers the water pot on her head. She speaks with others and walks on the path, but her mind keeps holding onto the pot.'

Shree Krishna explains the consequences of practising karm yog in the next verse.

अभ्यासयोगयुक्तेन चेतसा नान्यगामिना ।
परमं पुरुषं दिव्यं याति पार्थानुचिन्तयन् ।।8।।

abhyāsa-yoga-yuktena chetasā nānya-gāminā
paramaṁ puruṣhaṁ divyaṁ yāti pārthānuchintayan

abhyāsa-yoga—by practice of yog; *yuktena*—being constantly engaged in remembrance; *chetasā*—by the mind; *na anya-gāminā*—without deviating; *paramam purușham*—the Supreme Divine Personality; *divyam*—divine; *yāti*—one attains; *pārtha*—Arjun, son of Pritha; *anuchintayan*—constant remembrance.

With practice, O Parth, when you constantly engage the mind in remembering Me, the Supreme Divine Personality, without deviating, you will certainly attain Me.

This instruction to keep the mind always engaged in meditating upon God has been repeated numerous times in the Bhagavad Gita. Here are a few verses:

ananya-chetāḥ satataṁ (8.14)

teṣhāṁ satata-yuktānāṁ (10.10)

mayy eva mana ādhatsva (12.8)

The word *abhyāsa* means practice—the training and conditioning of the mind to meditate upon God. Such practice is to be done, not at fixed times of the day at regular intervals, but continuously, along with all the daily activities of life.

When the mind is attached to God, it will get purified, even while performing worldly duties. It is important to remember that our thoughts fashion our future, not the actions we perform with our body. It is the mind that is to be engaged in devotion, and it is the mind that is to be surrendered to God. And when the absorption of the consciousness in God is complete, one will receive divine grace. By God's grace, one will attain liberation from material bondage, and will receive unlimited divine bliss, divine knowledge, and divine love of God. Such a soul will become God-realised in this body itself, and upon leaving the body, will go to the abode of God.

कविं पुराणमनुशासितार
मणोरणीयांसमनुस्मरेद्यः ।
सर्वस्य धातारमचिन्त्यरूप
मादित्यवर्णं तमसः परस्तात् ।।9।।

प्रयाणकाले मनसाचलेन
भक्त्या युक्तो योगबलेन चैव ।
भ्रुवोर्मध्ये प्राणमावेश्य सम्यक्
स तं परं पुरुषमुपैति दिव्यम् ।।10।।

kaviṁ purāṇam anuśhāsitāram
aṇor aṇīyānsam anusmared yaḥ
sarvasya dhātāram achintya-rūpam
āditya-varṇaṁ tamasaḥ parastāt

prayāṇa-kāle manasāchalena
bhaktyā yukto yoga-balena chaiva
bhruvor madhye prāṇam āveśhya samyak
sa taṁ paraṁ puruṣham upaiti divyam

kavim—poet; *purāṇam*—ancient; *anuśhāsitāram*—Controller; *aṇoḥ*—than the atom; *aṇīyānsam*—smaller; *anusmaret*—always remembers; *yaḥ*—who; *sarvasya*—of everything; *dhātāram*—the support; *achintya*—inconceivable; *rūpam*—divine form; *āditya-varṇam*—effulgent like the sun; *tamasaḥ*—to the darkness of ignorance; *parastāt*—beyond; *prayāṇa-kāle*—at the time of death; *manasā*—mind; *achalena*—steadily; *bhaktyā*—remembering with great devotion; *yuktaḥ*—united; *yoga-balena*—through the power of yog; *cha*—and; *eva*—certainly; *bhruvoḥ*—the two eyebrows; *madhye*—between; *prāṇam*—life airs; *āveśhya*—fixing; *samyak*—completely; *saḥ*—he; *tam*—him; *param puruṣham*—the Supreme Divine Lord; *upaiti*—attains; *divyam*—divine.

God is Omniscient, the most ancient One, the Controller, subtler than the subtlest, the Support of all, and the possessor of an inconceivable divine form; He is brighter than the sun and beyond all darkness of ignorance. One who at the time of death, with unmoving mind attained by the practice of Yog, fixes the pran (life airs) between the eyebrows, and steadily remembers the Divine Lord with great devotion, certainly attains Him.

Meditation upon God can be of a variety of types. One can meditate upon the Names, Forms, Qualities, Pastimes, Abodes, or Associates of God. All these different aspects of the Supreme Divinity are non-different from Him. When we attach our mind to any of these, our mind comes into the divine realm and becomes purified. Hence, any or all of these can be made the object of meditation. Here, eight qualities of the Supreme Lord have been described which can be meditated upon.

Kavi means poet or seer, and by extension, omniscient. As stated in verse 7.26, God knows the past, present, and future.

Puran means without beginning and the most ancient. God is the origin of everything spiritual and material, but there is nothing from which He has originated and nothing that predates Him.

Anuśhāsitāram means the Ruler. God is the Creator of the laws by which the universe runs; He governs its affairs, directly and through His appointed celestial gods. Thus, everything is under His regime.

Aṇoraṇīyān means subtler than the subtlest. Soul is subtler than matter, but God is seated within the soul, and hence, He is subtler than it.

Sarvasya Dhātā means the sustainer of all, just as the ocean is the support of all waves that emanate from it.

Achintya Rūpa means of inconceivable form. Since our mind can only conceive material forms, God is beyond the scope of our material mind. However, if He bestows His grace, then by His *Yogmaya* power He makes our mind divine in nature and becomes conceivable.

Āditya Varna means He is resplendent like the sun.

Tamasaḥ Parastāt means beyond the darkness of ignorance. Just as the sun can never be covered by the clouds, even though it may seem to us that it has been obscured, similarly, God too can never be covered by the material energy even though He may be in contact with it in the world.

In bhakti, the mind is focused upon the divine attributes of God's Forms, Qualities, Pastimes, and so on. When bhakti is performed by itself, it is called *śhuddha bhakti* (pure bhakti). When it is performed alongside with ashtang yog, it is called *yog-miśhra bhakti* (devotion alloyed with ashtang yog sadhana). In this chapter from verses ten to thirteen, Shree Krishna describes *yog-miśhra bhakti*.

One of the beauties of the Bhagavad Gita is that it embraces a variety of sadhanas, thereby bringing people of diverse upbringing, backgrounds, and personalities in its embrace. When western scholars attempt to read the Hindu scriptures without the guidance of a guru, they often become confused by the variety of paths, instructions, and philosophical viewpoints in its various scriptures. However, this variety is actually a blessing. Because of the *sanskārs* (tendencies) of endless lifetimes, we all have different natures and preferences. When four people go to buy clothes for themselves, they end up choosing different colours, styles, and fashions. If the shop kept clothes of only one colour and style, it would be unable to cater to the variety inherent in human nature. Similarly, on the spiritual path too, people have performed various sadhanas in past lifetimes. The Vedic scriptures embrace that variety, while simultaneously stressing bhakti (devotion to God) as the common thread that ties them all together.

In ashtang yog, the life force is raised through the *suṣhumṇā* channel in the spinal column. It is brought between the eyebrows which is the region of the third eye (the inner eye). It is then made to focus on the Supreme Lord with great devotion.

यदक्षरं वेदविदो वदन्ति
विशन्ति यद्यतयो वीतरागाः ।
यदिच्छन्तो ब्रह्मचर्यं चरन्ति
तत्ते पदं संग्रहेण प्रवक्ष्ये ।।11।।

yad akṣharaṁ veda-vido vadanti
viśhanti yad yatayo vīta-rāgāḥ
yad ichchhanto brahmacharyaṁ charanti
tat te padaṁ saṅgraheṇa pravakṣhye

yat—which; *akṣharam*—imperishable; *veda-vidaḥ*—scholars of the Vedas; *vadanti*—describe; *viśhanti*—enter; *yat*—which; *yatayaḥ*—great ascetics; *vīta-rāgāḥ*—free from attachment; *yat*—which;

ichchhantaḥ—desiring; *brahmacharyam*—celibacy; *charanti*—practice; *tat*—that; *te*—to you; *padam*—goal; *saṅgraheṇa*—briefly; *pravakṣhye*—I shall explain.

Scholars of the Vedas describe Him as Imperishable; great ascetics practise the vow of celibacy and renounce worldly pleasures to enter into Him. I shall now explain to you briefly the path to that goal.

God has been referred to by many names in the Vedas. Some of them are: *Sat*, *Avyākṛit*, Pran, Indra, Dev, Brahman, Paramatma, Bhagavan, and Purush. In various places, while referring to the formless aspect of God, He has also been called by the name *Akṣhar*, which means 'imperishable'. The *Bṛihadāraṇyak Upanishad* states:

> *etasya vā akṣharasya praśhāsane gārgi sūryāchandramasau vidhṛitau tiṣhṭhataḥ* (3.8.9)

'Under the mighty control of the Imperishable, the sun and the moon are held on their course.' In this verse, Shree Krishna describes the path of *yog-miśhrā bhakti* to attain the formless aspect of God. The word *sangraheṇa* means 'in brief'. He will describe the path only briefly and not emphasise it, since the path is not suitable for everyone.

On this path, one must perform severe austerities, renounce worldly desires, practise *brahmacharya*, and live a life of rigid continence. *Brahmacharya* is the vow of celibacy. Through it, a person's physical energy gets conserved, and then transformed through sadhana into spiritual energy. An aspirant who practises celibacy enhances memory power and the intellect for comprehending spiritual topics. This has been previously explained in detail in verse 6.14.

सर्वद्वाराणि संयम्य मनो हृदि निरुध्य च ।
मूर्ध्न्याधायात्मनः प्राणमास्थितो योगधारणाम् ।।12।।

sarva-dvārāṇi sanyamya mano hṛidi nirudhya cha
mūrdhnyādhāyātmanaḥ prāṇam āsthito yoga-dhāraṇām

sarva-dvārāṇi—all gates; *sanyamya*—restraining; *manaḥ*—the mind; *hṛidi*—in the heart region; *nirudhya*—confining; *cha*—and;

mūrdhni—in the head; *ādhāya*—establish; *ātmanaḥ*—of the self; *prāṇam*—the life breath; *āsthitaḥ*—situated (in); *yoga-dhāraṇām*—the yogic concentration.

Restraining all the gates of the body and fixing the mind in the heart region and then drawing the life breath to the head, one should get established in steadfast yogic concentration.

The world enters the mind through the senses. We first see, hear, touch, taste, and smell the objects of perception. Then the mind dwells upon these objects. Repeated contemplation creates attachment which automatically creates further repetition of the thoughts in the mind. Restraining the senses is thus an essential aspect of locking the world out of the mind. A practitioner of meditation who neglects this point has to keep grappling with the incessant stream of worldly thoughts that the unrestrained senses create. Hence, Shree Krishna delivers the instruction to guard the gates of the body. The words *sarva-dvārāṇi-sanyamya* mean 'controlling all the passages that enter the body'. This implies restricting the senses from their normal outgoing tendencies. The words *hṛidi nirudhya* mean 'locking the mind in the heart'. This denotes directing devotional feelings from the mind to the *akṣharam* imperishable Supreme Lord enthroned there. The words *yoga-dhāraṇām* mean 'uniting the consciousness with God'. This refers to meditating upon Him with complete attention.

ओमित्येकाक्षरं ब्रह्म व्याहरन्मामनुस्मरन् ।
यः प्रयाति त्यजन्देहं स याति परमां गतिम् ।।13।।

om ityekākṣharaṁ brahma vyāharan mām anusmaran
yaḥ prayāti tyajan dehaṁ sa yāti paramāṁ gatim

om—sacred syllable representing the formless aspect of God; *iti*—thus; *eka-akṣharam*—one-syllabled; *brahma*—the Absolute Truth; *vyāharan*—chanting; *mām*—Me (Shree Krishna); *anusmaran*—remembering; *yaḥ*—who; *prayāti*—departs; *tyajan*—quitting; *deham*—the body; *saḥ*—he; *yāti*—attains; *paramām*—the supreme; *gatim*—goal.

One who departs from the body while remembering Me, the Supreme Personality, and chanting the syllable Om, will attain the supreme goal.

The sacred syllable Om, also called *Praṇav*, represents the sound manifestation of Brahman (the formless aspect of the Supreme Lord without virtues and attributes). Hence, it is considered imperishable like God Himself. Since Shree Krishna is describing here the process of meditation in the context of ashtang yog sadhana, He states that one should chant the syllable Om to bring the mind into focus while practising austerities and maintaining the vow of celibacy. The Vedic scriptures also refer to Om as the *anāhat nād*. It is the sound that pervades creation and can be heard by yogis who tune into it.

The Bible says, 'In the beginning was the Word, and the Word was with God, and the Word was God.' (John 1:1) The Vedic scriptures also state that God first created sound, from sound He created space, and then proceeded further in the process of creation. That original sound was Om. As a result, it is accorded so much of importance in Vedic philosophy. It is called a *maha vākya* or great sound vibration of the Vedas. It is also called the *bīja mantra* because it is often attached to the beginning of the Vedic mantras, just as *hrīṁ, klīṁ*, and others. The vibrations of Om consist of three letters: A ... U ... M. In the proper chanting of Om, one begins by making the sound 'A' from the belly with an open throat and mouth. This is merged into the chanting of the sound 'U' that is created from the middle of the mouth. The sequence ends with chanting 'M' with the mouth closed. The three parts A ... U ... M have many meanings and interpretations. For the devotees, Om is the name for the impersonal aspect of God.

This *Praṇav* sound is the object of meditation in ashtang yog. In the path of bhakti yog, devotees prefer to meditate upon the personal names of the Lord, such as Ram, Krishna, Shiv, etc. because of the greater sweetness of God's bliss in these personal names. The distinction is like the difference between having a baby in the womb and a baby in the lap. The joy of the baby in the lap is far more delightful than the baby in the womb.

The final examination of our meditation is the time of death. Those who are able to fix their consciousness upon God, despite the intense pain of death, pass this exam. Such persons attain the Supreme destination upon leaving their body. This is extremely difficult and requires a lifetime of practice. *In the following verse, Shree Krishna gives an easy way of gaining such mastery.*

अनन्यचेताः सततं यो मां स्मरति नित्यशः ।
तस्याहं सुलभः पार्थ नित्ययुक्तस्य योगिनः ।।14।।

ananya-chetāḥ satataṁ yo māṁ smarati nityaśhaḥ
tasyāhaṁ sulabhaḥ pārtha nitya-yuktasya yoginaḥ

ananya-chetāḥ—without deviation of the mind; *satatam*—always; *yaḥ*—who; *mām*—me; *smarati*—remembers; *nityaśhaḥ*—regularly; *tasya*—to him; *aham*—I; *su-labhaḥ*—easily attainable; *pārtha*—Arjun, son of Pritha; *nitya*—constantly; *yuktasya*—engaged; *yoginaḥ*—of the yogis.

O Parth, for those yogis who always think of Me with exclusive devotion, I am easily attainable because of their constant absorption in Me.

Throughout the Bhagavad Gita, Shree Krishna has repeatedly stressed upon devotion. In the previous verse, Shree Krishna expounded meditation on the formless manifestation of God, devoid of attributes. This is not only dry but also very difficult. So now He gives an easier alternative which is meditation upon His personal form as Krishna, Ram, Shiv, Vishnu, etc. This includes the Names, Forms, Virtues, Pastimes, Abodes, and Associates of His Supreme Divine Form.

In the entire Bhagavad Gita, this is the only verse in which Shree Krishna says that He is easy to attain. However, the condition He states is *ananya-chetāḥ* which means that the mind must be exclusively absorbed in Him and Him alone. The word *ananya* is very important. Etymologically, it means *na anya* or 'no other'. The mind should be attached to no one else but God alone. This condition of exclusivity has often been repeated in the Bhagavad Gita.

ananyāśh chintayanto māṁ (9.22)

tam eva śharaṇaṁ gachchha (18.62)

mām ekaṁ śharaṇaṁ vraja (18.66)

Exclusive devotion has been stressed in the other scriptures too.

mām ekam eva śharaṇam ātmānaṁ sarva-dehinām

(Bhagavatam 11.12.15)

'Surrender to Me alone, who am the Supreme Soul of all living beings.'

eka bharoso eka bala ek āsa visvāsa (Ramayan)

'I have only one support, one strength, one faith, one shelter, and that is Shree Ram.'

anyāśhrayāṇāṁ tyāgo 'nanyatā

(*Nārad Bhakti Darshan*, Sutra 10)

'Reject all other shelters and become exclusive to God.'

Exclusive devotion means that the mind must be attached only to the Names, Forms, Virtues, Pastimes, Abodes, and Associates of God. The logic is very simple. The aim of sadhana is to purify the mind, and this is accomplished only by attaching it to the all-pure God. However, if we cleanse the mind by contemplating upon God, and then again dirty it by dipping it in worldliness, then no matter how long we try, we will never be able to clean it.

This is exactly the mistake that many people make. They love God but they also love and get attached to worldly people and objects. So whatever positive gains they accomplish through sadhana become tarnished by worldly attachment. If you apply soap on a cloth to cleanse it, but simultaneously keep throwing dirt upon it, your effort will be an exercise in futility. Hence, Shree Krishna says that it is not just devotion but exclusive devotion to Him that makes Him easily attainable.

मामुपेत्य पुनर्जन्म दुःखालयमशाश्वतम् ।
नाप्नुवन्ति महात्मानः संसिद्धिं परमां गताः ।।15।।

mām upetya punar janma duḥkhālayam aśhāśhvatam
nāpnuvanti mahātmānaḥ sansiddhiṁ paramāṁ gatāḥ

mām—me; *upetya*—having attained; *punaḥ*—again; *janma*—birth; *duḥkha-ālayam*—place full of miseries; *aśhāśhvatam*—temporary; *na*—never; *āpnuvanti*—attain; *mahā-ātmānaḥ*—the great souls; *sansiddhim*—perfection; *paramām*—highest; *gatāḥ*—having achieved.

Having attained Me, the great souls are no more subject to rebirth in this world, which is transient and full of misery, because they have attained the highest perfection.

What is the result of attaining God? Those who become God-realised get released from the cycle of life and death and reach the divine abode of God. Thus, they do not have to take birth again in this material world which is a place of suffering. We suffer the painful process of birth, crying helplessly. Then as babies, we have needs that we can't express, so we cry. In adolescence, we have to grapple with physical desires that make us suffer mental anguish. In married life, we endure the idiosyncrasies of the spouse. When we reach old age, we suffer from bodily infirmities. All through life, we suffer the miseries from our own body and mind, the behaviour of others, and inclement environment. Finally, we suffer the pain of death.

All this misery is not meaningless; it has a purpose in the grand design of God. It gives us the realisation that the material realm is not our permanent home. It is like the reformatory for souls like us who have turned their backs towards God. If we did not suffer misery here, we would never develop the desire for God. For example, if we put our hand in the fire, two things happen—the skin starts getting burnt, and the neurons create a sensation of pain in the brain. The burning of the skin is a bad thing, but the sensation of pain is a good thing. If we did not experience the pain, we would not extract our hand from the fire, and it would suffer extensive damage. The pain is thus an indication that something is wrong which needs to be corrected. Similarly, the pain we experience in the material realm is God's signal that our consciousness is defective, and we need to progress from material consciousness towards union with God.

Ultimately, we get whatever we have made ourselves worthy of through our chosen efforts. Those who remain with their consciousness turned around from God continue rotating in the wheel of birth and death; and those who achieve exclusive devotion to God attain His divine abode.

आब्रह्मभुवनाल्लोकाः पुनरावर्तिनोऽर्जुन ।
मामुपेत्य तु कौन्तेय पुनर्जन्म न विद्यते ।।16।।

ā-brahma-bhuvanāl lokāḥ punar āvartino 'rjuna
mām upetya tu kaunteya punar janma na vidyate

ā-brahma-bhuvanāt—up to the abode of Brahma; *lokāḥ*—worlds; *punaḥ āvartinaḥ*—subject to rebirth; *arjuna*—Arjun; *mām*—mine; *upetya*—having attained; *tu*—but; *kaunteya*—Arjun, son of Kunti; *punaḥ janma*—rebirth; *na*—never; *vidyate*—is.

In all the worlds of this material creation, up to the highest abode of Brahma, you will be subject to rebirth, O Arjun. But on attaining My abode, O son of Kunti, there is no further rebirth.

The Vedic scriptures describe seven planes of existence lower than the earthly plane—*tal, atal, vital, sutal, talātal, rasātal, pātāl.* These are called *narak* or the hellish abodes. There are also seven planes of existence starting from the earthly plane and above—*bhūḥ, bhuvaḥ, swaḥ, mahaḥ, janaḥ, tapaḥ, satyaḥ.* The ones above are called *swarg* or celestial abodes. Other religious traditions also refer to the seven heavens. In Judaism, seven heavens are named in the *Talmud*, with *Araboth* named as the highest (see also Psalm 68.4). In Islam also, there is mention of seven heavens with the *sātvāñ āsmān* (seventh sky) enumerated as the highest.

The different planes of existence are called the various worlds. There are fourteen worlds in our universe. The highest among them is the abode of Brahma called *Brahma Lok.* All of these *lokas* are within the realm of maya, and the residents of these *lokas* are subject to the cycle of birth and death. Shree Krishna referred to them in the previous verse as *duḥkhālayam* and *aśhāśhvatam* (impermanent and full of misery).

Even Indra, king of the celestial gods, has to die one day. The Puranas relate that once Indra engaged Vishwakarma, the celestial architect, in the construction of a huge palace. Wearied by its construction, which was not ending, Vishwakarma prayed to God for help. God came there, and He asked Indra, 'Such a huge palace! How many Vishwakarmas have been engaged in its making?'

Indra was surprised by the question, and replied, 'I thought there was only one Vishwakarma.'

God smiled and said, 'Like this universe with fourteen worlds, there are unlimited universes. Each has one Indra and one Vishwakarma.'

Then Indra saw lines of ants walking towards him. He was surprised and enquired about the origin of those ants. God said, 'I have brought all those souls here who were Indra once in their past lives and are now in the bodies of ants.' Indra was astonished by their vast number.

Shortly after, Lomash Rishi came to the scene. He was carrying a straw mat on his head; on his chest was a circle of hair. Some hair had fallen from the circle, creating gaps. Indra received the sage, and politely asked him, 'Sir, why do you carry a straw mattress on your head. And what is the meaning of the hair circle on your chest?'

Lomash Rishi replied, 'I have received the boon of *chirāyu* (long life). At the end of one Indra's tenure in this universe, one hair falls of. That explains the gaps in the circle. My disciples wish to build a house for me to stay in, but I think that life is temporary, so why build a residence? I keep this straw mat which protects me from rain and the sun. At night, I spread it on the ground and go to sleep.'

Indra was astonished, thinking, 'This rishi has the lifespan of many Indras, and yet, he says that life is temporary. Then why am I building such a big palace?' His pride squashed, he let Vishwakarma go.

While reading these stories, we must also not fail to marvel at the amazing insight of the Bhagavad Gita on the cosmology of the universe.

As late as in the sixteenth century, Nicholas Copernicus was the first western scientist to propose a proper heliocentric theory stating that the sun was, in fact, the centre of the universe. Until then, the entire Western world believed that the earth was the centre of the universe. Subsequent advances in astronomy revealed that the sun was also not the centre of the universe but revolving around the epicenter of a galaxy called the Milky Way. Further progress enabled scientists to conclude that there are many galaxies like the Milky Way, each of them having innumerable stars, like our Sun.

In contrast, Vedic philosophy states five thousand years ago that the earth is *Bhūr Lok*, which is revolving around *Swar Lok*, and between them is the realm called *Bhuvar Lok*. But *Swar Lok* is also not stationary either; it is fixed in the gravitation of *Jana Lok*, and between them is the realm called *Mahar Lok*. But *Jana Lok* is not stationary either; it is revolving around *Brahma Lok* (*Satya Lok*), and between them is the realm called *Tapa Lok*. This explains the seven higher worlds; similarly, there are seven lower worlds. For an insight given five thousand years ago, this is most amazing!

Shree Krishna says in this verse that all the fourteen worlds in the universe are within the realm of maya, and as a result, their residents are subject to the cycle of birth and death. However, those who attain God-realisation are released from the bondage of the material energy. Upon leaving this material body at death, they attain the divine abode of God. There, they receive divine bodies in which they eternally participate in the divine pastimes of God. Thus, they do not have to take birth in this material world again. Some saints do come back even after liberation from maya. But they do so only to help others get out of bondage as well. These are the great descended Masters and Prophets who engage in the divine welfare of humankind.

सहस्त्रयुगपर्यन्तमहर्यद्ब्रह्मणो विदुः ।
रात्रिं युगसहस्त्रान्तां तेऽहोरात्रविदो जनाः ।।17।।

sahasra-yuga-paryantam ahar yad brahmaṇo viduḥ
rātriṁ yuga-sahasrāntāṁ te 'ho-rātra-vido janāḥ

sahasra—one thousand; *yuga*—age; *paryantam*—until; *ahaḥ*—one day; *yat*—which; *brahmaṇaḥ*—of Brahma; *viduḥ*—know; *rātrim*—night; *yuga-sahasra-antām*—lasts one thousand yugas; *te*—they; *ahaḥ-rātra-vidaḥ*—those who know this day and night; *janāḥ*—people.

One day of Brahma (kalp) lasts a thousand cycles of the four ages (maha yug) and his night also extends for the same span of time. The wise who know this understand the reality about day and night.

The measurements of time in the Vedic cosmological system are also vast and staggering. For example, there are insects that are born in the night—they grow up, procreate, lay eggs, and grow old—all in one night. In the morning, you see them all dead under the streetlights. If these insects were told that their entire lifespan was only one night of human beings, they would find it incredulous.

Similarly, the Vedas state that one day and night of the celestial gods, such as Indra and Varun, corresponds to one year on the earth plane. By this calculation, one year of the celestial gods, consisting of 30 days × 12 months is equal to 360 years on the earth plane. And 12,000 years of the celestial gods correspond to one maha yug (cycle of four yugas) on the earth plane, i.e., 4 million and 320 thousand earth years (12,000 celestial years x 360 earth years).

One thousand such maha yugas comprise one day of Brahma. This is called kalp and is the largest unit of time in the world. Equal to that is Brahma's night. By these calculations, Brahma lives for 100 years. By earth calculations, it is 311 trillion and 40 billion years. Thus, the Vedic calculations of time are as follows:

Kali Yug: 432,000 years.

Dwāpar Yug: 864,000 years.

Tretā Yug: 1,296,000 years.

Satya Yug: 1,728,000 years.

Together, they comprise a maha yug: 4,320,000 years.

One thousand maha yugas comprise one day of Brahma which is a kalp: 4,320,000,000 (4,320,000 x 1,000) earth years. Of equal duration is Brahma's night. Shree Krishna says that those who understand this are the true knowers of day and night.

The entire duration of the universe is equal to Brahma's lifespan of 100 years: 311 trillion and 40 billion earth years. Brahma is also a soul, who attained that position in his present life and is executing his duties for God. Hence, Brahma is also within the cycle of life and death. However, being of extremely elevated consciousness, he is assured that at the end of his life, he will be released from the cycle of life and death and go to the abode of God. Occasionally, when no soul is eligible to perform the duties of Brahma at the time of the creation of the world, God Himself becomes Brahma.

अव्यक्ताद्व्यक्तयः सर्वाः प्रभवन्त्यहरागमे ।
रात्र्यागमे प्रलीयन्ते तत्रैवाव्यक्तसंज्ञके ।।18।।

avyaktād vyaktayaḥ sarvāḥ prabhavantyahar-āgame
rātryāgame pralīyante tatraivāvyakta-sanjñake

avyaktāt—from the unmanifested; *vyaktayaḥ*—the manifested; *sarvāḥ*—all; *prabhavanti*—emanate; *ahaḥ-āgame*—at the advent of Brahma's day; *rātri-āgame*—at the fall of Brahma's night; *pralīyante*—they dissolve; *tatra*—into that; *eva*—certainly; *avyakta-sanjñake*—in that which is called the unmanifest.

At the advent of Brahma's day, all living beings emanate from the unmanifest source. And at the fall of his night, all embodied beings again merge into their unmanifest source.

In the amazing cosmic play of the universe, the various worlds (planes of existence) and their planetary systems undergo repeated cycles of creation, preservation, and dissolution (*sṛiṣhṭi, sthiti,* and pralaya). At the end of Brahma's day, corresponding to one kalp of 4,320,000,000 years, all the planetary systems up to *Mahar Lok* are destroyed. This is called *naimittik pralaya* (partial dissolution). In the Shreemad Bhagavatam, Shukadev tells Parikshit that just as a child makes structures with toys during the day and dismantles them before sleeping, similarly, Brahma creates the planetary systems and their life forms when he wakes up and dismantles them before sleeping.

At the end of Brahma's life of one hundred years, the entire universe is dissolved. At this time, the entire material creation winds up. The *pañcha mahabhūta* merge into the *pañcha tanmātrās*, the *pañcha tanmātrās* merge into *ahankār*, *ahankār* merges into *mahān*, and *mahān* merges into prakriti. Prakriti is the subtle form of the material energy, maya. Maya, in its primordial state, then goes and sits in the body of the Supreme Lord, Maha Vishnu. This is called *prākṛit pralaya* or maha pralaya (great dissolution). Again, when Maha Vishnu wishes to create, He glances at the material energy in the form of prakriti, and by His mere glance, it begins unfolding. From prakriti, *mahān* is created; from *mahān*, *ahankār* is created; from *ahankār*, *pañcha tanmātrās* are created; from *pañcha tanmātrās*, *pañcha mahābhūta* are created. In this way, unlimited universes are created.

Modern-day scientists estimate that there are one hundred billion stars in the Milky Way. Like the Milky Way, there are one billion galaxies in the universe. Thus, by estimation of scientists, there are 10^{20} stars in our universe. According to the Vedas, like our universe, there are innumerable universes of different sizes and features. Every time, Maha Vishnu breathes in, unlimited universes manifest from the pores of His body, and when He breathes out, all the universes dissolve back. Thus, the hundred years of Brahma's life are equal to one breath of Maha Vishnu. Each universe has one Brahma, one Vishnu, and one Shankar. So, there are innumerable Brahmas, Vishnus, and Shankars in innumerable universes. All the Vishnus in all the universes are expansions of Maha Vishnu.

भूतग्रामः स एवायं भूत्वा भूत्वा प्रलीयते ।
रात्र्यागमेऽवशः पार्थ प्रभवत्यहरागमे ।।19।।

bhūta-grāmaḥ sa evāyaṁ bhūtvā bhūtvā pralīyate
rātryāgame 'vaśhaḥ pārtha prabhavatyahar-āgame

bhūta-grāmaḥ—the multitude of beings; *saḥ*—these; *eva*—certainly; *ayam*—this; *bhūtvā bhūtvā*—repeatedly taking birth; *pralīyate*—dissolves; *rātri-āgame*—with the advent of night; *avaśhaḥ*—helpless; *pārtha*—Arjun, son of Pritha; *prabhavati*—become manifest; *ahaḥ-āgame*—with the advent of day.

Multitudes of beings repeatedly take birth with the advent of Brahma's day and are reabsorbed on the arrival of the cosmic night, to manifest again automatically on the advent of the next cosmic day.

The Vedas list four pralayas (dissolutions):

Nitya Pralaya: This is the daily dissolution of our consciousness that takes place when we fall into deep sleep.

Naimittik Pralaya: This is the dissolution of all the abodes up to *Mahar Lok* at the end of Brahma's day. At that time, the souls residing in these abodes become unmanifest. They reside in a state of suspended animation in the body of Vishnu. Again, when Brahma creates these *lokas*, they are given birth according to their past karmas.

Maha Pralaya: This is the dissolution of the entire universe at the end of Brahma's life. At this time, all the souls in the universe go into a state of suspended animation in the body of Maha Vishnu. Their gross (*sthūl*) and subtle (*sūkṣhma*) bodies (*śharīr*) dissolve, but the causal body (*kāraṇ śharīr*) remains. When the next cycle of creation takes place, they are again given birth, according to their *sanskārs* and karmas stored in their causal body.

Ātyantik Pralaya: When the soul finally attains God, it gets released from the cycle of birth and death forever. *Ātyantik Pralaya* is the dissolution of the bonds of maya, which were binding the soul since eternity.

परस्तस्मात्तु भावोऽन्योऽव्यक्तोऽव्यक्तात्सनातनः ।
यः स सर्वेषु भूतेषु नश्यत्सु न विनश्यति ।।20।।

paras tasmāt tu bhāvo 'nyo 'vyakto 'vyaktāt sanātanaḥ
yaḥ sa sarveṣhu bhūteṣhu naśhyatsu na vinaśhyati

paraḥ—transcendental; *tasmāt*—than that; *tu*—but; *bhāvaḥ*—creation; *anyaḥ*—another; *avyaktaḥ*—unmanifest; *avyaktāt*—to the unmanifest; *sanātanaḥ*—eternal; *yaḥ*—who; *saḥ*—that; *sarveṣhu*—all; *bhūteṣhu*—in beings; *naśhyatsu*—cease to exist; *na*—never; *vinaśhyati*—is annihilated.

Transcendental to this manifest and unmanifest creation, there is yet another unmanifest eternal dimension. That realm does not cease even when all others do.

After completing His exposé on the material worlds and their impermanence, Shree Krishna goes on to talk about the spiritual dimension. It is beyond the scope of the material energy and is created by the spiritual *Yogmaya* energy of God. It is not destroyed when all the material worlds are destroyed. Shree Krishna mentions in verse 10.42 that the spiritual dimension is three-fourth of God's entire creation while the material dimension is the remaining one-fourth.

अव्यक्तोऽक्षर इत्युक्तस्तमाहुः परमां गतिम् ।
यं प्राप्य न निवर्तन्ते तद्धाम परमं मम ।।21।।

avyakto 'kṣhara ityuktas tam āhuḥ paramāṁ gatim
yaṁ prāpya na nivartante tad dhāma paramaṁ mama

avyaktaḥ—unmanifest; *akṣharaḥ*—imperishable; *iti*—thus; *uktaḥ*—is said; *tam*—that; *āhuḥ*—is called; *paramām*—the supreme; *gatim*—destination; yam—which; *prāpya*—having reached; *na*—never; *nivartante*—come back; *tat*—that; *dhāma*—abode; *paramam*—the supreme; *mama*—my.

That unmanifest dimension is the supreme goal and upon reaching it, one never returns to this mortal world. That is My supreme abode.

The divine sky of the spiritual realm is called *Paravyom*. It contains the eternal abodes of the different forms of God, such as *Golok* (abode of Shree Krishna), *Saket Lok* (abode of Shree Ram), *Vaikunth Lok* (abode of Narayan), *Shiv Lok* (abode of Sadashiv), *Devi Lok* (abode of Mother Durga), etc. In these *lokas*, the Supreme Lord resides eternally in His divine forms along with His eternal associates. All these forms of God are non-different from each other; they are various forms of the same one God. Whichever form of God one worships, upon God-realisation, one goes to the abode of that form of God. On receiving a divine body in that abode, the soul then participates in the divine activities and pastimes of the Lord for the rest of eternity.

पुरुषः स परः पार्थ भक्त्या लभ्यस्त्वनन्यया ।
यस्यान्तःस्थानि भूतानि येन सर्वमिदं ततम् ।।22।।

puruṣhaḥ sa paraḥ pārtha bhaktyā labhyas tvananyayā
yasyāntaḥ-sthāni bhūtāni yena sarvam idaṁ tatam

puruṣhaḥ—the Supreme Divine Personality; *saḥ*—he; *paraḥ*—greatest; *pārtha*—Arjun, son of Pritha; *bhaktyā*—through devotion; *labhyaḥ*—is attainable; *tu*—indeed; *ananyayā*—without another; *yasya*—of whom; *antaḥ-sthāni*—situated within; *bhūtāni*—beings; *yena*—by whom; *sarvam*—all; *idam*—this; *tatam*—is pervaded.

The Supreme Divine Personality is greater than all that exists. Although He is all-pervading and all living beings are situated in Him, yet He can be known only through devotion.

The same Supreme Lord, who resides in His divine abode in the spiritual sky, is seated in our hearts; He is also all-pervading in every atom of the material world. God is equally present everywhere; we cannot say that the all-pervading God is twenty-five per cent present, while in His personal form, He is a hundred per cent present. He is one hundred per cent everywhere. However, that all-pervading presence of God does not benefit us because we have no perception of it. Sage Shandilya states:

gavāṁ sarpiḥ śharīrasthaṁ na karotyaṅga poṣhaṇam

(*Śhāṇḍilya Bhakti Darshan*)

'Milk resides in the body of the cow, but it does not benefit the health of the cow which is weak and sick.' The same milk is extracted from the body of the cow and converted into yogurt. The yogurt is then fed to the cow with a sprinkling of black pepper, and it cures the cow.

Similarly, the all-pervading presence of God does not have the intimacy to enrich our devotion. First, we need to worship Him in His divine form and develop the purity of our heart. Then we attract God's grace, and by His grace, He imbues our senses, mind, and intellect with His divine *Yogmaya* energy. Our senses then become divine, and we are able to perceive the divinity of the Lord, whether in His personal form or in His all-pervading aspect. Thus, Shree Krishna states that He can be known only through bhakti.

The need for doing bhakti has been repeatedly emphasised by Shree Krishna in the Bhagavad Gita. In verse, 6.47, He stated that He considers one who is engaged in devotion to Him to be the highest of all. Here, He emphatically uses the word *ananyayā* which means 'by no other path' can God be known. Chaitanya Mahaprabhu puts this very nicely:

bhakti mukha nirīkṣhaka karm yoga jñāna

(*Chaitanya Charitāmṛit*, *Madhya Leela*, 22.17)

'Although karm, jnana, and ashtang yog are also pathways to God-realisation, all these require the support of bhakti for their fulfilment.' Jagadguru Shree Kripaluji Maharaj says the same thing:

karm yog aru jñāna saba, sādhana yadapi bakhān
pai binu bhakti sabai janu, mṛitaka deha binu prān

(*Bhakti Śhatak* verse 8)

'Although karm, jnana, and ashtang yog are paths to God-realisation, without blending bhakti in them, they all become like dead bodies without life airs.' Various scriptures also declare:

bhaktyāhamekayā grāhyaḥ śhraddhayātmā priyaḥ satām

(Bhagavatam 11.14.21)

'I am only attained by My devotees who worship Me with faith and love.'

milahiṅ na raghupati binu anurāgā,
kieñ joga tapa gyāna birāgā (Ramayan)

'One may practise ashtang yog, engage in austerities, accumulate knowledge, and develop detachment. Yet, without devotion, one will never attain God.'

यत्र काले त्वनावृत्तिमावृत्तिं चैव योगिनः ।
प्रयाता यान्ति तं कालं वक्ष्यामि भरतर्षभ ।।23।।

अग्निर्ज्योतिरहः शुक्लः षण्मासा उत्तरायणम् ।
तत्र प्रयाता गच्छन्ति ब्रह्म ब्रह्मविदो जनाः ।।24।।

धूमो रात्रिस्तथा कृष्णः षण्मासा दक्षिणायनम् ।
तत्र चान्द्रमसं ज्योतिर्योगी प्राप्य निवर्तते ।।25।।

शुक्लकृष्णे गती ह्येते जगतः शाश्वते मते ।
एकया यात्यनावृत्तिमन्ययावर्तते पुनः ।।26।।

yatra kāle tvanāvṛittim āvṛittiṁ chaiva yoginaḥ
prayātā yānti taṁ kālaṁ vakṣhyāmi bharatarṣhabha

agnir jyotir ahaḥ śhuklaḥ ṣhaṇ-māsā uttarāyaṇam
tatra prayātā gachchhanti brahma brahma-vido janāḥ

dhūmo rātris tathā kṛiṣhṇaḥ ṣhaṇ-māsā dakṣhiṇāyanam
tatra chāndramasaṁ jyotir yogī prāpya nivartate

śhukla-kṛiṣhṇe gatī hyete jagataḥ śhāśhvate mate
ekayā yātyanāvṛittim anyayāvartate punaḥ

yatra—where; *kāle*—time; *tu*—certainly; *anāvṛittim*—no return; *āvṛittim*—return; *cha*—and; *eva*—certainly; *yoginaḥ*—a yogi; *prayātāḥ*—having departed; *yānti*—attain; *tam*—that; *kālam*—time; *vakṣhyāmi*—I shall describe; *bharata-ṛiṣhabha*—Arjun, best of the Bharatas; *agniḥ*—fire; *jyotiḥ*—light; *ahaḥ*—day; *śhuklaḥ*—the bright fortnight of the moon; *ṣhaṭ-māsāḥ*—six months; *uttara-ayanam*—the sun's northern course; *tatra*—there; *prayātāḥ*—departed; *gachchhanti*—go; *brahma*—Brahman; *brahma-vidaḥ*—those who know the Brahman; *janāḥ*—persons; *dhūmaḥ*—smoke; *rātriḥ*—night; *tathā*—and; *kṛiṣhṇaḥ*—the dark fortnight of the moon; *ṣhaṭ-māsāḥ*—six months; *dakṣhiṇa-ayanam*—the sun's southern course; *tatra*—there; *chāndra-masam*—lunar; *jyotiḥ*—light; *yogī*—a yogi; *prāpya*—attain; *nivartate*—comes back; *śhukla*—bright; *kṛiṣhṇe*—dark; *gatī*—paths; *hi*—certainly; *ete*—these; *jagataḥ*—of the material world; *śhāśhvate*—eternal; *mate*—opinion; *ekayā*—by one; *yāti*—goes; *anāvṛittim*—to non return; *anyayā*—by the other; *āvartate*—comes back; *punaḥ*—again.

I shall now describe to you the different paths of passing away from this world, O best of the Bharatas, one of which leads to liberation and the other leads to rebirth. Those who know the Supreme Brahman and who depart from this world, during the six months of the sun's northern course, the bright fortnight of the moon, and the bright part of the day, attain the supreme destination. The practitioners of Vedic rituals, who pass away during the six months of the sun's southern course, the dark fortnight of the moon, the time of smoke, the night, attain the celestial abodes. After enjoying celestial pleasures, they again return to the earth. These two, bright and dark paths, always exist in this world. The way of light leads to liberation and the way of darkness leads to rebirth.

Shree Krishna's statement in these verses still pertains to the question Arjun asked in verse 8.2, 'How can we be united with You at the time of death?' Shree Krishna says that there are two paths—the path of light and the path of darkness. Here, in these somewhat cryptic statements, we may discern a wonderful allegory for expressing spiritual concepts around the themes of light and darkness.

The six months of the northern solstice, the bright fortnight of the moon, and the bright part of the day are all characterised by light. Light symbolises knowledge, while darkness signifies ignorance. The six months of the southern solstice, the dark fortnight of the moon, the night, all these have the commonality of darkness. Those, whose consciousness is established in God and detached from sensual pursuits, depart by the path of light (discrimination and knowledge). Being situated in God-consciousness, they attain the supreme abode of God and are released from the wheel of samsara. But those whose consciousness is attached to the world, depart by the path of darkness (ignorance). Being entangled in the bodily concept of life and the illusion of separation from God, they continue to rotate in the cycle of life and death. If they had performed Vedic ritualistic activities, they are temporarily promoted to the celestial abodes, and then have to return to the earth planet. In this way, all human beings have to take one of the two paths after death. It now depends upon them, according to their karmas, whether they pass along the bright path or the dark path.

नैते सृती पार्थ जानन्योगी मुह्यति कश्चन ।
तस्मात्सर्वेषु कालेषु योगयुक्तो भवार्जुन ।।27।।

naite sṛitī pārtha jānan yogī muhyati kaśhchana
tasmāt sarveṣhu kāleṣhu yoga-yukto bhavārjuna

na—never; *ete*—these two; *sṛitī*—paths; *pārtha*—Arjun, son of Pritha; *jānan*—knowing; *yogī*—a yogi; *muhyati*—bewildered; *kaśhchana*—any; *tasmāt*—therefore; *sarveṣhu kāleṣhu*—always; *yoga-yuktaḥ*—situated in Yog; *bhava*—be; *arjuna*—Arjun.

Yogis who know the secret of these two paths, O Parth, are never bewildered. Therefore, at all times be situated in Yog (union with God).

Yogis are aspirants who are striving to unite their minds with God. Knowing themselves to be tiny fragments of God and the futility of a lascivious life, they attach importance to the enhancement of their love for God rather than the temporary perceptions of sense pleasures. Thus, they are the followers of the path of light. Persons who are deluded by maya, think of this temporary world as permanent, of their body as the self, and of the miseries of the world as sources of pleasure, follow the path of darkness. The results of both paths are diametrically opposite, with one leading to eternal beatitude and the other leading to the continued misery of material existence. Shree Krishna urges Arjun to discriminate between these paths and follow the path of light by becoming a yogi.

He adds a phrase here, 'at all times' which is very important. Many of us follow the path of light for some time, but then regress to the path of darkness. If someone wishes to go north, but keeps going four miles south for every mile north, then that person will end up being south of the starting point, despite endeavoring greatly. Similarly, following the path of light for some time in the day does not ensure our progress. We must constantly move ahead in the right direction and eschew moving in the wrong direction, only then will we go forward. Hence, Shree Krishna says, 'Be a yogi at all times.'

वेदेषु यज्ञेषु तपःसु चैव
दानेषु यत्पुण्यफलं प्रदिष्टम् ।
अत्येति तत्सर्वमिदं विदित्वा
योगी परं स्थानमुपैति चाद्यम् ।।28।।

vedeṣhu yajñeṣhu tapaḥsu chaiva
dāneṣhu yat puṇya-phalaṁ pradiṣhṭam
atyeti tat sarvam idaṁ viditvā
yogī paraṁ sthānam upaiti chādyam

vedeṣhu—in the study of the Vedas; *yajñeṣhu*—in performance of sacrifices; *tapaḥsu*—in austerities; *cha*—and; *eva*—certainly; *dāneṣhu*—in giving charities; *yat*—which; *puṇya-phalam*—fruit of merit; *pradiṣhṭam*—is gained; *atyeti*—surpasses; *tat sarvam*—all; *idam*—this; *viditvā*—having known; *yogī*—a yogi; *param*—supreme; *sthānam*—abode; *upaiti*—achieves; *cha*—and; *ādyam*—original.

The yogis, who know this secret, gain merit far beyond the fruits of Vedic rituals, the study of the Vedas, performance of sacrifices, austerities, and charities. Such yogis reach the supreme abode.

We may perform Vedic sacrifices, accumulate knowledge, perform austerities, and donate to charities, but unless we engage in devotion to God, we are still not on the path of light. All these mundane good deeds result in material rewards while devotion to God leads to liberation from material bondage. The Ramayan states:

nema dharma āchāra tapa gyāna jagya japa dāna,
bheṣhaja puni koṭinha nahiṅ roga jāhiṅ harijāna

'You may engage in good conduct, righteousness, austerities, sacrifices, ashtang yog, chanting of mantras, and charity. But without devotion to God, the mind's disease of material consciousness will not cease.'

The yogis who follow the path of light detach their mind from the world and attach it to God, thereby gaining eternal welfare. As a result, Shree Krishna says they reap fruits beyond those bestowed by all other processes.

CHAPTER 9

Raja Vidyā Yog

Yog through the King of Sciences

In the seventh and eighth chapters, Shree Krishna declared bhakti as the easiest means of attaining Yog and also the highest form of Yog. In the ninth chapter, He speaks of His supreme glories, which inspire awe, reverence and, devotion. He reveals that though He is standing before Arjun in His personal form, He must not be misconstrued to possess a human personality. He explains how He presides over His material energy and creates myriad life-forms at the beginning of creation, absorbs them back at the time of dissolution, and then manifests them again in the next cycle of creation. As the mighty wind blowing everywhere rests always in the sky, likewise, all living beings dwell in Him. And yet, by His divine *Yogmaya* power, He remains a neutral observer, ever aloof and detached from all these activities.

Shree Krishna resolves the apparent confusion of the Hindu pantheon by explaining that the one God is the sole object of worship. He is the goal, the support, the refuge, and the one true friend of all living beings. Those inclined towards the ritualistic ceremonies of the Vedas attain the celestial abodes, and when their pious merits are depleted, they return to the earth again. But those who engage in exclusive devotion towards the Supreme Lord go to His abode. Shree Krishna thus exalts the super-excellence of unalloyed bhakti that is directed towards Him. In such devotion, we must live in complete union with God's will, offering all that we have to Him, and doing everything for Him alone. By such pure devotion, we will be released from the bondage of karmas and attain the goal of mystic union with God.

Further, Shree Krishna asserts that He neither favours nor rejects anyone—He is impartial towards all. Even if vile sinners come to His shelter, He willingly accepts them and quickly makes them virtuous and pure. He makes a promise that His devotees never perish. Seated within them, He provides what they lack and preserves what they already possess. Thus, we should always think of Him, worship Him, dedicate our mind and body to Him, and make Him our supreme goal.

श्रीभगवानुवाच ।
इदं तु ते गुह्यतमं प्रवक्ष्याम्यनसूयवे ।
ज्ञानं विज्ञानसहितं यज्ज्ञात्वा मोक्ष्यसेऽशुभात् ।।1।।

śhrī bhagavān uvācha
idaṁ tu te guhyatamaṁ pravakṣhyāmyanasūyave
jñānaṁ vijñāna-sahitaṁ yaj jñātvā mokṣhyase 'śhubhāt

śhrī-bhagavān uvācha—the Supreme Lord said; *idam*—this; *tu*—but; *te*—to you; *guhya-tamam*—the most confidential; *pravakṣhyāmi*—I shall impart; *anasūyave*—nonenvious; *jñānam*—knowledge; *vijñāna*—realised knowledge; *sahitam*—with; *yat*—which; *jñātvā*—knowing; *mokṣhyase*—you will be released; *aśhubhāt*—miseries of material existence.

The Supreme Lord said: O Arjun, because you are not envious of Me, I shall now impart to you this very confidential knowledge and wisdom, upon knowing which you will be released from the miseries of material existence.

At the very beginning of the topic, Shree Krishna declares the qualification for hearing these teachings. *Anasūyave* means 'non-envious'. He tells Arjun that He is revealing this knowledge because Arjun is non-envious of Him. Lord Krishna clarifies this because God is going to glorify Himself profusely here. *Anasūyave* also has the sense of 'one who does not scorn'. Those listeners who deride Shree Krishna because they believe He is boasting will not benefit from hearing such a message. Rather, they will incur harm, by thinking, 'Look at this egotistic person. He is praising himself.'

Such an attitude is born of arrogance and pride and it robs one of devotional reverence. Envious people cannot grasp the simple fact that God has no need for anything, and therefore, everything He does is for the welfare of the souls. He only praises Himself to enhance devotion of the souls, and not because He has the material flaw of conceit as we do. Since Arjun is magnanimous and free from the fault of envy, he is eminently qualified for the profound knowledge that Shree Krishna is going to reveal in this chapter.

In the second chapter, Shree Krishna explained the knowledge of the atma as a separate and distinct entity from the body. That is *guhya* or secret knowledge. In the seventh and eighth chapters, He explained knowledge of His powers, which is *guhyatar* or more secret. And in the ninth and subsequent chapters, He will reveal knowledge of His pure bhakti, which is *guhyatam* or the most secret.

राजविद्या राजगुह्यं पवित्रमिदमुत्तमम् ।
प्रत्यक्षावगमं धर्म्यं सुसुखं कर्तुमव्ययम् ।।2।।

rāja-vidyā rāja-guhyaṁ pavitram idam uttamam
pratyakṣhāvagamaṁ dharmyaṁ su-sukhaṁ kartum avyayam

rāja-vidyā—the king of sciences; *rāja-guhyam*—the most profound secret; *pavitram*—pure; *idam*—this; *uttamam*—highest; *pratyakṣha*—directly perceptible; *avagamam*—directly realisable; *dharmyam*—virtuous; *su-sukham*—easy; *kartum*—to practise; *avyayam*—everlasting.

This knowledge is the king of sciences and the most profound of all secrets. It purifies those who hear it. It is directly realisable, in accordance with dharma, easy to practise, and everlasting in effect.

Raja means 'king'. Shree Krishna uses the metaphor 'raja' to emphasise the paramount position of the knowledge He is going to reveal.

Vidyā means 'science'. He does not refer to His teachings as creed, religion, dogma, doctrine, or belief. He declares that what He is going to describe to Arjun is the 'king of sciences.'

Guhya means 'secret'. This knowledge is also the supreme secret. Since love is only possible where there is a choice, God deliberately hides Himself from direct perception, thereby providing the soul the freedom to exercise the choice of loving Him or not. A machine cannot love because it is devoid of choices. God wants us to love Him, so He gives us the option to choose between Him and maya. He merely makes us aware of the consequences of what we choose, either way, and then leaves it to us to decide the path we wish to follow.

Pavitram means 'pure'. Knowledge of devotion is supremely pure because it is untainted by petty selfishness. It inspires sacrifice of the self at the altar of divine love for the Supreme Lord. Bhakti also purifies the devotee by destroying *pāp*, *bīja*, and *avidyā*. *Pāp* is the stockpile of past sins of endless lifetimes of the individual soul. Bhakti burns them as a fire burns a bundle of straw. *Bīja* refers to impurities of the heart which are the seeds of sinful activities. If the seeds exist, then destroying the results of past sins will not suffice because the propensity to sin will remain in the heart and one will sin again. Bhakti purifies the heart and destroys the seeds of sin, which are desire, anger, and greed. However, even the destruction of the seeds is not enough. The reason why the heart becomes impure is that there is *avidyā* (ignorance) due to which we identify with the body. Because of this misidentification, we think of the body as the self, and create physical desires thinking they will give happiness to the self. Fulfilment of such material desires further leads to lust, anger, greed, and all the other impurities of the heart. As long as the ignorance remains, even if the heart is cleansed, it will again become impure. Devotion ultimately results in realised knowledge of the soul and God, which in turn, destroys the ignorance of material existence. The benefits of bhakti are described in the *Bhakti Rasāmṛit Sindhu* as follows: *kleśhas tu pāpaṁ tadbījam avidyā cheti te tridhā* (1.1.18) 'Bhakti destroys the three poisons—*pāp* (sins), *bīja* (the seed of sins), *avidyā* (the ignorance in the heart).' Only when the three are completely destroyed, does the heart become truly and permanently pure.

Pratyakṣha means 'directly perceptible'. The practise of the science of bhakti begins with a leap of faith and results in direct perception of God. It is not unlike the methodology of other sciences, where we begin an experiment with a hypothesis and conclude with a verified result.

Dharmyam means 'virtuous'. Devotion performed without desire for material rewards is the most virtuous action. It is continuously nourished by righteous acts such as service to the guru.

Kartum susukham means 'very easy to practise'. God does not need anything from us; He is attained very naturally if we love Him selflessly.

When this is the sovereign science and easy to practice, then why do people not apply themselves to learning it? Shree Krishna explains this next.

अश्रद्दधानाः पुरुषा धर्मस्यास्य परन्तप ।
अप्राप्य मां निवर्तन्ते मृत्युसंसारवर्त्मनि ॥3॥

aśhraddadhānāḥ puruṣhā dharmasyāsya parantapa
aprāpya māṁ nivartante mṛityu-samsāra-vartmani

aśhraddadhānāḥ—people without faith; *puruṣhāḥ*—(such) persons; *dharmasya*—of dharma; *asya*—this; *parantapa*—Arjun, conqueror of enemies; *aprāpya*—without attaining; *mām*—me; *nivartante*—come back; *mṛityu*—death; *samsāra*—material existence; *vartmani*—in the path.

People who have no faith in this dharma are unable to attain Me, O conqueror of enemies. They repeatedly come back to this world in the cycle of birth and death.

In the last two verses, Shree Krishna promised knowledge and then qualified it with eight merits. It is mentioned here as 'this dharma' or the path of loving devotion to God.

No matter how wonderful the knowledge and how effective the path, it remains useless for one who refuses to walk on it. As explained in the previous verse, direct perception of God comes later; initially, a leap of faith is required to begin the process. The *Bhakti Rasāmṛit Sindhu* (1.4.15) states: *ādau śhraddhā tataḥ sādhusaṅgo 'tha bhajanakriyā* 'The first step in the path to God-realisation is to have faith. Then one begins participating in satsang (spiritual programmes). This leads to the personal practice of devotion.'

Often people say that they are only willing to believe in what they can directly perceive, and since there is no immediate perception of God, they do not believe in Him. However, the fact is that we believe in so many things in the world too, without direct perception of them. A judge delivers judgement upon a case concerning an event that took place many years in the past. If the judge adopted the philosophy of believing only what he or she had directly experienced, then the entire legal system would fail. Similarly, a president oversees a country on the basis of reports from all over the country. It is impossible for him to visit and see all the villages and cities within his domain. Now, if he was not willing to believe these reports, on the grounds that he had no direct perception of what was happening, how would he be able to govern the whole country? So, even in material activities, faith is required at every step. The Bible states this very nicely: 'We walk by faith, and not by sight.' (2 Corinthians 5:7)

There is a beautiful story regarding the perception of God:

A king once accosted a sadhu with the statement, 'I do not believe in God because I cannot see Him.' The sadhu asked for a cow to be brought to the king's court. The king obliged and ordered his servants to bring a cow. The sadhu then requested that it be milked. The king again instructed his servants to do as the sadhu wanted.

The sadhu asked, 'O King! Do you believe that this milk, freshly taken out from the cow, contains butter?' The king said he had full faith that it did.

The sadhu said, 'You cannot see the butter in the milk. Then why do you believe it is there?'

The king replied, 'We cannot see it at present because the butter is pervading the milk, but there is a process for seeing it. If we convert the milk into yogurt, and then churn the yogurt, the butter will become visible.'

The sadhu said, 'Like the butter in the milk, God is everywhere. If we cannot immediately perceive Him, we should not jump to the conclusion that there is no God. There is a process for perceiving Him; if we are willing to have faith and follow the process, we will then get direct perception of God and become God-realised.'

Belief in God is not a natural process that we as human beings just follow. We have to exercise our free will and actively make a decision to have faith in God. In the assembly of the Kauravas, when Dushasan endeavoured to disrobe Draupadi, Lord Krishna saved her from shame and embarrassment by lengthening her sari. All the Kauravas present saw this miracle but refused to have faith in the omnipotence of Shree Krishna. The Supreme Lord says in this verse that those who choose not to have faith in the spiritual path remain bereft of divine wisdom and continue to rotate in the cycle of life and death.

मया ततमिदं सर्वं जगदव्यक्तमूर्तिना ।
मत्स्थानि सर्वभूतानि न चाहं तेष्ववस्थितः ।।4।।

mayā tatam idaṁ sarvaṁ jagad avyakta-mūrtinā
mat-sthāni sarva-bhūtāni na chāhaṁ teṣhvavasthitaḥ

mayā—by me; *tatam*—pervaded; *idam*—this; *sarvam*—entire; *jagat*—cosmic manifestation; *avyakta-mūrtinā*—the unmanifested form; *mat-sthāni*—in me; *sarva-bhūtāni*—all living beings; *na*—not; *cha*—and; *aham*—I; *teṣhu*—in them; *avasthitaḥ*—dwell.

This entire cosmic manifestation is pervaded by Me in My unmanifest form. All living beings dwell in Me, but I do not dwell in them.

Vedic philosophy does not accept the concept of God creating the world and then peeping into it from the seventh heaven to check whether His world is running as expected. It repeatedly propounds the theme of God being all-pervading in the world:

eko devaḥ sarvabhūteṣhu gūḍhaḥ sarvavyāpī

(*Śhwetāśhvatar Upanishad* 6.11)

'There is one God; He is seated in everyone's heart; He is also everywhere in the world.'

īśhāvāsyam idam sarvaṁ yat kiñcha jagatyāṁ jagat

(*Īśhopaniṣhad* 1)

'God is everywhere in the world.'

puruṣha evedaṁ sarvaṁ, yad bhūtaṁ yachcha bhavyam

(*Purush Sūktam, Rig Veda*)

'God pervades everything that has existed and all that will exist.'

This concept of God being everywhere is understood subjectively. Some Eastern philosophers claim that the world is a *pariṇām* (transformation) of God. For example, milk is an unadulterated substance. In contact with acid, it transforms to yogurt. Thus, yogurt is a *pariṇām* (effect or product) of milk when it is transformed. Similarly, the protagonists of *pariṇām vāda* state that God has transformed into the world.

Other philosophers claim that the world is *vivarta* (to mistake one object for another). For example, in the darkness a rope may be mistaken for a snake. In the moonlight, a shining oyster may be mistaken for silver. Similarly, they say that there is only God and no world; what we are seeing as the world is actually Brahman.

However, according to verses 7.4 and 7.5, the world is neither *pariṇām* nor *vivarta*. It is created from the material energy of God, called maya shakti. The souls too are the energy of God, but they are His superior energy, called *jīva shakti*. Therefore, the world and all the souls in it are both God's energies and are within His personality.

However, Shree Krishna also says that He does not dwell in living beings, i.e., the infinite is not contained by finite beings. That is because He is far more than the sum total of these two energies. Just as waves are a part of the ocean, but the ocean is greater than the sum total of the waves, similarly too, the souls and maya exist within the personality of God, yet He is beyond them.

न च मत्स्थानि भूतानि पश्य मे योगमैश्वरम् ।
भूतभृन्न च भूतस्थो ममात्मा भूतभावनः ।।5।।

na cha mat-sthāni bhūtāni paśhya me yogam aiśhwaram
bhūta-bhṛin na cha bhūta-stho mamātmā bhūta-bhāvanaḥ

na—never; *cha*—and; *mat-sthāni*—abide in me; *bhūtāni*—all living beings; *paśhya*—behold; *me*—my; *yogam aiśhwaram*—divine energy; *bhūta-bhṛit*—the sustainer of all living beings; *na*—never; *cha*—yet; *bhūta-sthaḥ*—dwelling in; *mama*—my; *ātmā*—Self; *bhūta-bhāvanaḥ*—the Creator of all beings.

And yet, the living beings do not abide in Me. Behold the mystery of My divine energy! Although I am the Creator and Sustainer of all living beings, I am not influenced by them or by material nature.

Beyond the two energies mentioned in the purport to the previous verse—maya shakti and *jīva shakti*—there is a third energy of God. This is called *Yogmaya* shakti, which He refers to in this verse, as divine energy. *Yogmaya* is God's all-powerful energy. It is called *kartum-akartum-samarthaḥ* or 'that which can make the impossible possible' and is responsible for many of the amazing things we attribute to His personality. For example, God is seated in our hearts, yet we have no perception of Him. This is because His divine *Yogmaya* power keeps us aloof from Him.

Similarly, God also keeps Himself aloof from the influence of maya. In the Bhagavatam, the Vedas praise the Lord:

vilajjamānayā yasya sthātumīkṣhā-pathe 'muyā (2.5.13)

'Maya feels embarrassed to even stand before God.' Isn't it a wonder that although God pervades maya, the material energy, yet He is aloof from it? This is again by the mysterious power of *Yogmaya*.

If the world could influence God, then at time of its decay or destruction, His nature and personality will also deteriorate. But despite all modifications in the world, God remains established in His personality. Accordingly, the Vedas call God by the name *Daśhāṅgulī* or 'ten fingers'. He is in the world, and yet ten fingers beyond it, i.e., untouched by it.

यथाकाशस्थितो नित्यं वायुः सर्वत्रगो महान् ।
तथा सर्वाणि भूतानि मत्स्थानीत्युपधारय ।।6।।

yathākāśha-sthito nityaṁ vāyuḥ sarvatra-go mahān
tathā sarvāṇi bhūtāni mat-sthānītyupadhāraya

yathā—as; *ākāśha-sthitaḥ*—rests in the sky; *nityam*—always; *vāyuḥ*—the wind; *sarvatra-gaḥ*—blowing everywhere; *mahān*—mighty; *tathā*—likewise; *sarvāṇi bhūtāni*—all living beings; *mat-sthāni*—rest in me; *iti*—thus; *upadhāraya*—know.

Know that as the mighty wind blowing everywhere always rests in the sky, likewise, all living beings always rest in Me.

Shree Krishna has used the term *mat sthāni* three times, from the fourth verse to the sixth verse. It means 'all living beings rest in Him'. They cannot be separated from Him even though they transmigrate in different bodies and accept affinity with matter.

It may be a little difficult to conceive how the world rests in God. Greek mythology shows a picture of Atlas holding up the globe. In Greek folklore, Atlas fought with the Titans in the war against the deities of Mount Olympus. As punishment, he was condemned to forever bear the earth and the heavens on his back with the great pillar that supposedly separates them on his shoulders. This is not what Shree Krishna means when He says that He is upholding all beings. The entire cosmos exists in space and space is created by God's energy. Thus, all beings can be said to be resting in Him.

The Supreme Lord now gives an analogy to enable Arjun to grasp the concept. The wind has no existence independent from the sky. It moves incessantly and furiously, and yet, it rests within the sky. Likewise, souls have no existence independent of God. They move in time, place, and consciousness, through transitory bodies—sometimes rapidly and sometimes slowly—and yet, they always exist within God.

From another perspective, everything that exists in the cosmos is subordinate to the will of God. It is created, maintained, and annihilated in accordance with His will. In this way also, everything can be said to be resting in Him.

सर्वभूतानि कौन्तेय प्रकृतिं यान्ति मामिकाम् ।
कल्पक्षये पुनस्तानि कल्पादौ विसृजाम्यहम् ।।7।।

प्रकृतिं स्वामवष्टभ्य विसृजामि पुनः पुनः ।
भूतग्राममिमं कृत्स्नमवशं प्रकृतेर्वशात् ।।8।।

sarva-bhūtāni kaunteya prakṛitiṁ yānti māmikām
kalpa-kṣhaye punas tāni kalpādau visṛijāmyaham

prakṛitiṁ svām avaṣhṭabhya visṛijāmi punaḥ punaḥ
bhūta-grāmam imaṁ kṛitsnam avaśhaṁ prakṛiter vaśhāt

sarva-bhūtāni—all living beings; *kaunteya*—Arjun, son of Kunti; *prakṛitim*—primordial material energy; *yānti*—merge; *māmikām*—my; *kalpa-kṣhaye*—at the end of a *kalpa*; *punaḥ*—again; *tāni*—them; *kalpa-ādau*—at the beginning of a *kalpa*; *visṛijāmi*—manifest; *aham*—I; *prakṛitim*—the material energy; *svām*—my own; *avaṣhṭabhya*—presiding over; *visṛijāmi*—generate; *punaḥ punaḥ*—again and again; *bhūta-grāmam*—myriad forms; *imam*—these; *kṛitsnam*—all; *avaśham*—beyond their control; *prakṛiteḥ*—nature; *vaśhāt*—force.

At the end of one kalp, all living beings merge into My primordial material energy. At the beginning of the next creation, O son of Kunti, I manifest them again. Presiding over My material energy, I generate these myriad forms again and again, in accordance with the force of their natures.

Shree Krishna explained in the last few verses that all living beings dwell in Him. This statement may bring up the following question: 'When maha pralaya (the great annihilation) takes place and the entire world is wound up, then where do all the living beings go?' The answer to this question is being given in this verse.

In the previous chapter, verses 8.17–8.19, Shree Krishna explained how creation, maintenance, and annihilation follow a repetitive cycle. Here, the word *kalpa-kṣhaya* means 'the end of Brahma's lifespan'. On the completion of Brahma's life of one hundred years, which is 311 trillion and 40 billion earth years, the entire cosmic manifestation dissolves and goes into an unmanifest state. The *pañcha mahābhūta* merge into the *pañcha tanmātrās*; the *pañcha tanmātrās* merge into *ahankār*; *ahankār* merges into *mahān*; *mahān* merges into prakriti, the primordial form of the material energy; and prakriti goes and rests in the divine body of the Supreme Lord, Maha Vishnu.

At that time, all the souls within the material creation also go and rest in the body of God, in a state of suspended animation. Their gross and subtle bodies merge back into the source, maya. However, the causal body still remains. (The three kinds of bodies have been described in detail in the commentary of verse 2.28) After dissolution, when God creates the world again, the material energy unwinds in the reverse sequence: prakriti—*mahān*—*ahankār*—*pañcha tanmātrā*—*pañcha mahābhūta*. Then, the souls that were lying in a state of suspended animation with only causal bodies are again placed in the world. In accordance with their causal bodies, they again receive subtle and gross bodies, and various life forms are created in the universe. These life forms vary in nature among the different planes of existence. In some planetary systems, fire is the dominant element in the body, just as in the earth plane, the dominant elements of the human body are earth and water. Hence, bodies vary in their subtleness and the functions they can perform. Shree Krishna thus calls them myriad life forms.

न च मां तानि कर्माणि निबध्नन्ति धनञ्जय ।
उदासीनवदासीनमसक्तं तेषु कर्मसु ।।9।।

na cha māṁ tāni karmāṇi nibadhnanti dhanañjaya
udāsīna-vad āsīnam asaktaṁ teṣhu karmasu

na—none; *cha*—as; *mām*—me; *tāni*—those; *karmāṇi*—actions; *nibadhnanti*—bind; *dhanañjaya*—Arjun, conqueror of wealth; *udāsīna-vat*—as neutral; *āsīnam*—situated; *asaktam*—detached; *teṣhu*—those; *karmasu*—actions.

O conqueror of wealth, none of these actions bind Me. I remain like a neutral observer, ever detached from these actions.

The material energy is actually inert and insentient. It is devoid of consciousness which is the source of life. How then, one may wonder, does it perform the wonderful work of creating such an amazing world? The Ramayan explains this well:

jāsu satyatā teṅ jaṛa māyā, bhāsa satya iva moha sahāyā

'The material energy is insentient by itself. But when it receives inspiration from God, it begins to act as if it were sentient.' This is like a pair of tongs in the kitchen. They are lifeless by themselves. But in the hands of a chef, they come to life and do wonderful things, such as lift red-hot bowls. Likewise, by itself, the material energy does not have the power to do anything. When God wishes to create the world, He glances at the material energy and animates it.

The main idea to keep in mind is that although the process of creation goes on by His will and inspiration, He remains unaffected by the work of the material energy. He remains ever-blissful and undisturbed in His personality, by virtue of His *hlāndinī shakti* (bliss-giving power). Hence, the Vedas call Him *ātmārām*, meaning, 'He who rejoices in Himself, without any need for external pleasures.' *Having explained that He is unaffected, God now explains that He is the Non-doer and the Supervisor.*

मयाध्यक्षेण प्रकृतिः सूयते सचराचरम् ।
हेतुनानेन कौन्तेय जगद्विपरिवर्तते ।।10।।

mayādhyakṣheṇa prakṛitiḥ sūyate sa-charācharam
hetunānena kaunteya jagad viparivartate

mayā—by me; *adhyakṣheṇa*—direction; *prakṛitiḥ*—material energy; *sūyate*—brings into being; *sa*—both; *chara-acharam*—animate and inanimate; *hetunā*—reason; *anena*—this; *kaunteya*—Arjun, son of Kunti; *jagat*—material world; *viparivartate*—undergoes the changes.

Working under My direction, this material energy brings into being all animate and inanimate forms, O son of Kunti. For this reason, the material world undergoes the changes (of creation, maintenance, and dissolution).

As explained in the last verse, God does not directly engage in the work of creating life forms. His various energies and souls appointed by Him for this purpose do it under His dominion. For example, the president of a country does not personally do every task of the government. He has various departments under him, and officials appointed to oversee different functions. And yet, the accomplishments and failures of the government are attributed to him. This is because he authorises the government officials to perform tasks under his jurisdiction. Similarly, the first-born Brahma and the material energy accomplish the tasks of creation and manifestation of life forms. Since they work under God's direction, He is also referred to as the Creator.

अवजानन्ति मां मूढा मानुषीं तनुमाश्रितम् ।
परं भावमजानन्तो मम भूतमहेश्वरम् ।।11।।

avajānanti māṁ mūḍhā mānuṣhīṁ tanum āśhritam
paraṁ bhāvam ajānanto mama bhūta-maheśhvaram

avajānanti—disregard; *mām*—me; *mūḍhāḥ*—dim-witted; *mānuṣhīm*—human; *tanum*—form; *āśhritam*—take on; *param*—divine; *bhāvam*—personality; *ajānantaḥ*—not knowing; *mama*—my; *bhūta*—all beings; *mahā-īśhvaram*—the Supreme Lord.

When I descend in My personal form, deluded persons are unable to recognise Me. They do not know the divinity of My personality as the Supreme Lord of all beings.

Good teachers occasionally use strong words to jostle their students out of the complacence of shallow thinking, into a deeper state of thoughtfulness. Here, Shree Krishna uses the word *mūḍha* which means 'dim-witted' to describe those who deny the divinity of His personal form.

Those who say that God is only formless and cannot manifest in a personal form, contradict the definition of God as being all-mighty and all-powerful. The Supreme Lord has created this entire world full of forms, shapes, and colours. If He can do such an amazing feat of creating myriad forms in the world, can He not create a form for Himself? Or is it that God says, 'I do not have the power to manifest in a personal form, and hence I am only formless light.' To say that He cannot possess a personal form makes Him incomplete.

We tiny souls also possess forms. If one holds that God cannot possess a form, then the corollary is that He has even less power than us human beings. For God to be perfect and complete, He must have both attributes to His personality—a personal aspect and a formless aspect. The Vedic scriptures state:

apaśhyaṁ gopāṁ anipadyamānamā

(*Rig Veda* 1.22.164 *sūkta* 31)

'I had the vision of God as a boy who is never annihilated, and who appeared in a family of cowherds.'

dwibhūjaṁ mauna mudrāḍhyaṁ vana mālinamīśhwaram

(*Gopāl Tāpani Upanishad* 1.13)

'The Lord, wearing a garland of forest flowers, plays His flute, enchantingly forming the *mauna mudrā* with His hands.'

gūḍhaṁ paraṁ brahma manuṣhya-liṅgam

(Bhagavatam 7.15.75)

'The deepest knowledge is that God accepts a human-like form.'

yatrāvatīrṇo bhagavān paramātmā narākṛitiḥ

(Bhagavatam 9.23.20)

'At that time, the Supreme Lord, who possesses all opulences, descended in a human-like form.'

īśhwaraḥ paramaḥ kṛiṣhṇaḥ sachchidānanda vigrahaḥ
anādirādir govindaḥ sarvakāraṇa kāraṇam

(*Brahma Samhitā* 5.1)

In this verse, Brahma prays to Shree Krishna, 'I worship Lord Krishna whose form is eternal, all-knowing, and blissful. He is without beginning and end and is the cause of all causes.'

However, regarding the personal form of God, we must keep in mind that it is a divine form which means it is devoid of all the defects found in material forms. The form of God is *sat-chit-anand*—it is eternal, full of knowledge, and constituted of divine bliss.

asyāpi deva vapuṣho mad-anugrahasya
svechchhā-mayasya na tu bhūta-mayasya ko 'pi

(Bhagavatam 10.14.2)

In this verse, Lord Brahma prays to Shree Krishna, 'O Lord, Your body is not made of *pañcha mahābhūta* (the five great elements); it is divine. And You have descended in this form by Your own free will to bestow Your grace upon souls like myself.'

In chapter four of the Bhagavad Gita, Shree Krishna stated: 'Although I am unborn, the Lord of all living entities, and have an imperishable nature, yet I appear in this world by virtue of *Yogmaya*,

My divine power.' (4.6) This means that not only does God possess a form, but He also descends in the world as an Avatar.

Since we souls have been taking birth in the world from time immemorial, it is plausible that we were present in the human form at the same time a previous descension of God was present on the earth. It is even possible that we saw the descension. However, the limitation was that God's form was divine and we possessed material eyes. So, when we saw Him with our eyes, we were unable to recognise the divinity of His personality.

The divine nature of God's form is such that His divinity is perceived by each person only to the extent of his or her spiritual power. When those who are influenced by sattva guna see Him, they think, 'Shree Krishna is a special person. He is very competent but is definitely not God.' When those under the spell of rajo guna see Him, they say, 'There is nothing special in Him. He is very much like us.' When those dominated by tamo guna see Him, they think, 'He is egotistic and characterless, much worse than us.' It is only the God-realised saints who can recognise Him as God since they have received divine vision by His grace. And so, Shree Krishna says that the unaware materially conditioned souls do not know Him when He takes an Avatar in the world.

मोघाशा मोघकर्माणो मोघज्ञाना विचेतसः ।
राक्षसीमासुरीं चैव प्रकृतिं मोहिनीं श्रिताः ।।12।।

moghāśhā mogha-karmāṇo mogha-jñānā vichetasaḥ
rākṣhasīm āsurīṁ chaiva prakṛitiṁ mohinīṁ śhritāḥ

mogha-āśhāḥ—of vain hopes; *mogha-karmāṇaḥ*—of vain actions; *mogha-jñānāḥ*—of baffled knowledge; *vichetasaḥ*—deluded; *rākṣhasīm*—demoniac; *āsurīm*—atheistic; *cha*—and; *eva*—certainly; *prakṛitim*—material energy; *mohinīm*—bewildered; *śhritāḥ*—take shelter.

Bewildered by the material energy, such persons embrace demoniac and atheistic views. In that deluded state, their hopes for welfare are in

vain, their fruitive actions are wasted, and their culture of knowledge is baffled.

There are many strands of atheistic views relating to the personal form of God that are prevalent in the world. Some people declare that God cannot descend in the world in a personal form. Consequently, they say that Shree Krishna was not God; He was merely a yogi. Others say that Shree Krishna is *maya-viśhiṣhṭ brahma*, i.e., a lower grade of the Supreme Divinity due to contact with the material energy. Yet others say that Shree Krishna was a characterless flirt who roamed around with the cowherd maidens of Vrindavan.

According to this verse, all these theories are incorrect, and the intellects of those who subscribe to them are deluded by the material energy. Shree Krishna goes to the extent of saying that those who embrace such ungodly philosophies possess demoniac natures. Since, they do not harbour divine sentiments towards the personal form of the Supreme Lord, they cannot engage in bhakti towards Him. And since devotion to the formless aspect of God is exceedingly difficult, they cannot do that either. As a result, they remain bereft of the path to eternal welfare. Bewildered by the transient attractions of the material energy, their hopes for eternal well-being are in vain.

महात्मानस्तु मां पार्थ दैवीं प्रकृतिमाश्रिताः ।
भजन्त्यनन्यमनसो ज्ञात्वा भूतादिमव्ययम् ।।13।।

mahātmānas tu māṁ pārtha daivīṁ prakṛitim āśhritāḥ
bhajantyananya-manaso jñātvā bhūtādim avyayam

mahā-ātmānaḥ—the great souls; *tu*—but; *mām*—me; *pārtha*—Arjun, son of Pritha; *daivīm prakṛitim*—divine energy; *āśhritāḥ*—take shelter of; *bhajanti*—engage in devotion; *ananya-manasaḥ*—with mind fixed exclusively; *jñātvā*—knowing; *bhūta*—all creation; *ādim*—the origin; *avyayam*—imperishable.

But the great souls, who take shelter of My divine energy, O Parth, know Me, Lord Krishna, as the origin of all creation. They engage in My devotion with their minds fixed exclusively on Me.

Shree Krishna's style of discourse is that He drives the point home by making starkly contrasting comparisons. After describing the ways of the deluded and confused in the previous verse, He now talks about the great souls. Material life is a prolonged dream, which is being experienced by the souls who are sleeping under the sway of the material energy. In contrast, the great souls are those who have woken up from their ignorance and brushed aside material consciousness like a bad dream. Released from the grips of the material energy, maya, they are now under the shelter of the divine *Yogmaya* energy. Such enlightened souls have woken up to the spiritual reality of their eternal relationship with God.

Just as God has both aspects to His personality—the formless and the personal form—His *Yogmaya* energy also possesses both aspects. It is a formless energy, but it also manifests in the personal form as Radha, Sita, Durga, Lakshmi, Kali, and Parvati. All these divine personalities are manifestations of the divine energy of God, and they all are non-different from each other, just as Krishna, Ram, Shiv, and Narayan are non-different forms of the one God.

The *Brahma Vaivarta Puran* states:

yathā tvaṁ rādhikā devī goloke gokule tathā
vaikuṇṭhe cha mahālakṣhmī bhavati cha sarasvatī

kapilasya priyā kāntā bhārate bhāratī satī
dwāravatyāṁ mahālakṣhmī bhavatī rukmiṇī satī

tvaṁ sītā mithilāyāṁ cha tvachchhāyā draupadī satī
rāvaṇena hṛitā tvaṁ cha tvaṁ cha rāmasya kāminī

'O Radha, You are the Divine Goddess of Golok (Shree Krishna's divine abode) and *Gokul* (Shree Krishna's abode in the material realm when He descended on the earth five thousand years ago). You exist in *Vaikunth* (Lord Vishnu's abode) as Mahalakshmi. You are the consort of Lord Kapil (one of the descensions of God). You reside in Dwaraka as Rukmini (the wife of Shree Krishna). You manifested as Sita in the city of Mithila. The wife of the Pandavas, Draupadi, was like a manifestation of Your shadow. It was You who was kidnapped by Ravan in the form of Sita, and You are the wife of Lord Ram.'

In this verse, Shree Krishna mentions that great souls take shelter of the divine energy of God. The reason is that divine grace, knowledge, and love, all are God's divine energies, and subservient to the divine *Yogmaya* energy, which is Radha. Hence, by the grace of *Yogmaya*, one receives the love, knowledge, and grace of God. Great souls, who receive divine grace, become endowed with divine love, and engage in uninterrupted devotion to God.

सततं कीर्तयन्तो मां यतन्तश्च दृढव्रताः ।
नमस्यन्तश्च मां भक्त्या नित्ययुक्ता उपासते ।।14।।

satataṁ kīrtayanto māṁ yatantaśh cha dṛiḍha-vratāḥ
namasyantaśh cha māṁ bhaktyā nitya-yuktā upāsate

satatam—always; *kīrtayantaḥ*—singing divine glories; *mām*—me; *yatantaḥ*—striving; *cha*—and; *dṛiḍha-vratāḥ*—with great determination; *namasyantaḥ*—humbly bowing down; *cha*—and; *mām*—me; *bhaktyā*—loving devotion; *nitya-yuktāḥ*—constantly united; *upāsate*—worship.

Always singing My divine glories, striving with great determination, and humbly bowing down before Me, they constantly worship Me in loving devotion.

Having said that the great souls engage in His devotion, Shree Krishna now explains how they do bhakti. He says that devotees become attached to kirtan as a means of practising their devotion and enhancing it. Chanting of the glories of the Lord is called kirtan which is defined as: *nāma-līlā-guṇadīnām uchchair-bhāṣhā tu kīrtanam* (*Bhakti Rasāmṛit Sindhu* 1.2.145) 'Singing glories of the Names, Forms, Qualities, Pastimes, Abodes, and Associates of God is called kirtan.'

Kirtan is one of the most powerful means of practising bhakti. It involves the three-fold devotion of *śhravaṇa* (hearing), kirtan (chanting), and *smaraṇa* (remembering). The goal is to fix the mind upon God; it becomes easier when done together with hearing and chanting. As stated in chapter six, the mind is as restless as the wind and naturally wanders from thought to thought. Hearing and chanting engage the knowledge senses in the divine realm, which helps in repeatedly bringing back the mind from its wanderings.

Kirtan has many other benefits as well. Often when people practise devotion through *japa* (chanting of mantra or name of God on rosary beads) or plain meditation, they find themselves overwhelmed by sleep. However, kirtan is such an engaging process that it usually drives sleep away. Also, chanting blocks out distracting sounds from the environment. Kirtan can be practised in groups which enables mass participation. In addition, the mind desires variety which it gets through the medium of kirtan in the form of the Names, Virtues, Pastimes, Abodes, etc. of God. And since kirtan involves loud chanting, the divine vibrations of the names of God make the entire environment auspicious and holy.

For all these reasons, kirtan has been the most popular form of devotion among saints in Indian history. All the famous bhakti saints—Soordas, Tulsidas, Meerabai, Guru Nanak, Kabir, Tukaram, Ekanath, Narsi Mehta, Jayadev, Tyagaraja, and others—were great poets. They composed numerous devotional songs, and through them, they engaged in chanting, hearing, and remembering.

The Vedic scriptures particularly extol kirtan as the simplest and most powerful process of devotion in the present age of Kali.

kṛite yad dhyāyato viṣhṇuṁ tretāyāṁ yajato makhaiḥ
dwāpare paricharyāyāṁ kalau tad dhari-kīrtanāt

(Bhagavatam 12.3.52)

'The best process of devotion in the age of Satya was simple meditation upon God. In the age of *Tretā*, it was the performance of sacrifices for the pleasure of God. In the age of *Dwāpar*, worship of the deities was the recommended process. In the present age of Kali, it is kirtan alone.'

avikārī vā vikārī vā sarva doṣhaika bhājanaḥ
parameṣha padaṁ yāti rāma nāmānukīrtanāt

(*Adhyātma Ramayan*)

'Whether you are full of desires or free from them, devoid of defects or full of them, if you engage in kirtan of the names of Lord Ram, you will attain the highest destination.'

sarva dharma bahirbhūtaḥ sarva pāparatasthathā
muchyate nātra sandeho viṣhṇornamānukīrtanāt

(*Vaiśhampāyan Samhitā*)

'Even those who are deeply sinful and bereft of religiosity can be saved by the chanting of the names of Lord Vishnu; of this, there is no doubt.'

kalijuga kevala hari guna gāhā,
gāvata nara pāvahiṅ bhava thāhā (Ramayan)

'In this age of Kali, there is one means of salvation. By engaging in the chanting of the glories of God, one can cross over this material ocean.'

However, one must remember that in the process of kirtan, hearing and chanting are supports. The essence is to remember God. If we leave it out, kirtan will not purify the mind. Thus, Shree Krishna says here that His devotees do kirtan while constantly engaging the mind in thoughts of Him. They practise this with great determination for the purification of the mind.

ज्ञानयज्ञेन चाप्यन्ये यजन्तो मामुपासते ।
एकत्वेन पृथक्त्वेन बहुधा विश्वतोमुखम् ।।15।।

jñāna-yajñena chāpyanye yajanto mām upāsate
ekatvena pṛithaktvena bahudhā viśhwato-mukham

jñāna-yajñena—yajna of cultivating knowledge; *cha*—and; *api*—also; *anye*—others; *yajantaḥ*—worship; *mām*—me; *upāsate*—worship; *ekatvena*—undifferentiated oneness; *pṛithaktvena*—separately; *bahudhā*—various; *viśhwataḥ-mukham*—the cosmic form.

Others, engaging in the yajna of cultivating knowledge, worship Me by many methods. Some see Me as undifferentiated oneness that is non-different from them while others see Me as separate from them. Still others worship Me in the infinite manifestations of My cosmic form.

Sādhaks (spiritual practitioners) follow different paths of spirituality to reach the Absolute Truth. Shree Krishna previously described those who are devotees. Full of devotion, they surrender themselves at the lotus feet of the Supreme Lord, with the attitude of being His eternal parts and servants. He now describes some of the other paths that *sādhaks* follow.

Those who follow the path of jnana yog consider themselves to be non-different from God. They contemplate deeply on sutras such as: *so 'haṁ* (I am That), *śhivo 'haṁ* (I am Shiv), and so on. Their ultimate goal is to attain realisation of the Supreme Entity as the undifferentiated Brahman, which possesses the attributes of eternality, knowledge, and bliss, but is devoid of forms, qualities, virtues, and pastimes. Shree Krishna says that such jnana yogis also worship Him but in His formless all-pervading aspect. In contrast, there are varieties of ashtang yogis and others who see themselves as distinct from God and relate to Him accordingly.

Still others worship the manifest universe as God. In Vedic philosophy, this is called *viśhwaroop upāsanā* (worship of the cosmic form of God). In western philosophy, it is called 'Pantheism' from the Greek words *pan* (all) and *theos* (God). The most famous exponent of this philosophy was Spinoza. Since the world is a part of God, keeping a divine sentiment towards it is correct, but it is incomplete. Such devotees do not have knowledge of the other aspects of the Supreme Divine Entity, such as Brahman (God's undifferentiated all-pervading manifestation), Paramatma (the Supreme Soul seated in everyone's hearts), and Bhagavan (the personal form of God).

How can all these divergent approaches worship the same God? Shree Krishna answers this in the following verses.

अहं क्रतुरहं यज्ञः स्वधाहमहमौषधम् ।
मन्त्रोऽहमहमेवाज्यमहमग्निरहं हुतम् ।।16।।

पिताहमस्य जगतो माता धाता पितामहः ।
वेद्यं पवित्रमोङ्कार ऋक्साम यजुरेव च ।।17।।

ahaṁ kratur ahaṁ yajñaḥ svadhāham aham auṣhadham
mantro 'ham aham evājyam aham agnir ahaṁ hutam

pitāham asya jagato mātā dhātā pitāmahaḥ
vedyaṁ pavitram omkāra ṛik sāma yajur eva cha

aham—I; *kratuḥ*—Vedic ritual; *aham*—I; *yajñaḥ*—sacrifice; *svadhā*—oblation; *aham*—I; *aham*—I; *auṣhadham*—medicinal herb; *mantraḥ*—Vedic mantra; *aham*—I; *aham*—I; *eva*—also; *ājyam*—clarified butter; *aham*—I; *agniḥ*—fire; *aham*—I; *hutam*—the act offering; *pitā*—father; *aham*—I; *asya*—of this; *jagataḥ*—universe; *mātā*—mother; *dhātā*—sustainer; *pitāmahaḥ*—grandsire; *vedyam*—goal of knowledge; *pavitram*—purifier; *om-kāra*—the sacred syllable Om; *ṛik*—*Ṛig Veda*; *sāma*—*Sāma Veda*; *yajuḥ*—*Yajur Veda*; *eva*—also; *cha*—and.

It is I who am the Vedic ritual, I am the sacrifice, and I am the oblation offered to the ancestors. I am the medicinal herb, and I am the Vedic mantra. I am the clarified butter; I am the fire and the act of offering. Of this universe, I am the Father; I am also the Mother, the Sustainer, and the Grandsire. I am the purifier, the goal of knowledge, the sacred syllable Om. I am the *Rig Veda*, *Sama Veda*, and the *Yajur Veda*.

In these verses, Shree Krishna gives a glimpse into the various aspects of His infinite personality. *Kratu* means yajna (sacrifice), such as Agnihotra yajnas mentioned in the Vedas. It also refers to the yajnas, such as Vaiśhva Deva that are described in the Smriti scriptures. *Auṣhadham* refers to the potency in medicinal herbs.

Creation emanates from God, and hence He is its *Pitā* (Father). Before creation, He holds the unmanifested material energy in His womb, so He is also its *Mātā* (Mother). He maintains the universe and nourishes it, and thus He is its *Dhātā* (Sustainer). He is also the Father of Brahma, who is the creator, consequently, He is the Grandfather of this universe.

The Vedas have emanated from God. The Ramayan states: *jākī sahaja svāsa śhruti chārī* 'God manifested the Vedas by His breath.' They are the knowledge potency of God, and therefore, an aspect of His unlimited personality. Shree Krishna states this truth dramatically by saying that He is the Vedas.

गतिर्भर्ता प्रभुः साक्षी निवासः शरणं सुहृत् ।
प्रभवः प्रलयः स्थानं निधानं बीजमव्ययम् ।।18।।

gatir bhartā prabhuḥ sākṣhī nivāsaḥ śharaṇaṁ suhṛit
prabhavaḥ pralayaḥ sthānaṁ nidhānaṁ bījam avyayam

gatiḥ—the supreme goal; *bhartā*—sustainer; *prabhuḥ*—master; *sākṣhī*—witness; *nivāsaḥ*—abode; *śharaṇam*—shelter; *su-hṛit*—friend; *prabhavaḥ*—origin; *pralayaḥ*—dissolution; *sthānam*—repository; *nidhānam*—resting place; *bījam*—seed; *avyayam*—imperishable.

I am the Supreme Goal of all living beings, and I am also their Sustainer, Master, Witness, Abode, Shelter, and Friend. I am the Origin, End, and Resting Place of creation; I am the Repository and Eternal Seed.

Since the soul is a tiny part of God, its every relationship is with Him. However, in bodily consciousness, we look upon the relatives of the body as our father, mother, beloved, child, and friend. We become attached to them and repeatedly bring them to our mind, thereby getting further bound in the material illusion. But none of these material relatives can give us the perfect love that our soul yearns for. This is for two reasons. First, these relationships are temporary, and separation is unavoidable when either they or we depart from the world. Second, even as long as they are alive, the attachment is based on selfishness and so it fluctuates in direct proportion to the extent by which self-interest is satisfied. Thus, the range and intensity of worldly love varies from moment to moment, throughout the day. 'My wife is very nice ... she is not so nice ... she is okay ... she is terrible,' this is the extent of fluctuation of love in the drama of the world. On the other hand, God is such a relative who has accompanied us lifetime after lifetime. Irrespective of the life-form that we received, God accompanied us and remained seated in our heart; He is thus our eternal relative. In addition, He has no self-interest from us; He is perfect and complete in Himself. He loves us selflessly because His only desire is our eternal welfare. Thus, God alone is our perfect relative, who is both eternal and selfless.

To understand this concept from another perspective, consider the analogy of an ocean and the waves that emerge from it. Two neighbouring waves in the ocean flow together for some time and play mirthfully with each other, creating the impression that they have a very deep relationship between them. However, after travelling some distance, one subsides into the ocean, and shortly after, the other does the same. Did they have any relationship between themselves? No, they both were born from the ocean and their relationship was with the ocean itself. Similarly, God is like the ocean, and we are like waves who have emanated from Him. We create attachments among our physical relations, only to leave everyone upon death and journey alone into another birth. The truth is that the souls are not related to each other, but to God, from whom they have emanated.

In this verse, Shree Krishna takes us above material consciousness and its concomitant attachment to worldly relatives. From the platform of the soul, God alone is all our relationships; He is our Friend, Father, Mother, Sister, Brother, and Beloved. This theme is reiterated in all the Vedic scriptures:

divyo deva eko nārāyaṇo mātā pitā bhrātā suhṛit gatiḥ
nivāsaḥ śharaṇaṁ suhṛit gatirnārāyaṇa iti

(*Subāl Śhruti*, mantra 6)

'Lord Narayan alone is the Mother, Father, Beloved, and Destination of the soul.'

more sabai eka tumha swāmī, dīnabhandhu ura antarajāmī

(Ramayan)

'O Lord Ram, You alone are my Master, the Saviour of the destitute, and the Knower of the heart.' Knowing the magnitude of our eternal relationship with God, we must endeavour to attach our mind to Him alone. Then, the mind will be purified, and we will be able to fulfil the condition of *māmekaṁ śharaṇaṁ vraja* or complete surrender which is necessary for receiving God's grace. To achieve this single-mindedness, we must sever all the present attachments of the mind and replace them with attachment to God. Hence, the Ramayan states:

saba kai mamatā tāga baṭorī,
mama pada manahi bāñdha bari ḍorī

'Cut all the strings of worldly attachment of your mind; make a rope of these strings and tie it at the lotus feet of God.' To help us tie our mind to Him, Shree Krishna here explains to Arjun that the soul's every relationship is with God alone.

तपाम्यहमहं वर्षं निगृह्णाम्युत्सृजामि च ।
अमृतं चैव मृत्युश्च सदसच्चाहमर्जुन ।।19।।

tapāmyaham ahaṁ varṣhaṁ nigṛihṇāmyutsṛijāmi cha
amṛitaṁ chaiva mṛityuśh cha sad asach chāham arjuna

tapāmi—radiate heat; *aham*—I; *aham*—I; *varṣham*—rain; *nigṛihṇāmi*—withhold; *utsṛijāmi*—send forth; *cha*—and; *amṛitam*—immortality; *cha*—and; *eva*—also; *mṛityuḥ*—death; *cha*—and; *sat*—eternal spirit; *asat*—temporary matter; *cha*—and; *aham*—I; *arjuna*—Arjun.

I radiate heat as the sun, and I withhold, as well as send forth rain. I am immortality as well as death personified, O Arjun. I am the spirit as well as matter.

The Puranas describe that when God first created the universe, He manifested the first-born Brahma and entrusted him with the work of further creation. Brahma was bewildered by the task of creating the materials and the life-forms in the universe from the subtle material energy. Then God revealed knowledge unto him which is called the

Chatuḥśhlokī Bhāgavat (the four-versed Bhagavatam), on the basis of which Brahma proceeded to create the world. Its first verse states very emphatically:

ahamevāsamevāgre nānyadyatsadasat param
paśhchādahaṁ yadetachcha yo 'vaśhiṣhyeta so 'smyaham

(Bhagavatam 2.9.32)

Shree Krishna tells Brahma: 'I am all that is. Prior to creation, I alone existed. Now that creation has come about, whatever is in the form of the manifested world is My very self. After dissolution, I alone will exist. There is nothing apart from Me.'

The above truth implies that the object with which we worship is also God. When people venerate the holy Ganges, they immerse the lower half of their body in the river. Then they lift water in their palms and pour it into the Ganges. In this way, they use the Ganges water itself to worship it. Similarly, when God is all that exists, then the substance used to worship Him is also non-different from Him. Thus, as previously stated in verses 16 and 17, Shree Krishna reveals that He is the Vedas, the sacrificial fire, the syllable Om, the clarified butter, and the act of offering. No matter what the form and sentiment of our devotion, there is nothing apart from God that we can offer to Him. Nevertheless, it is the sentiment of love that pleases God, not the object being offered.

त्रैविद्या मां सोमपाः पूतपापा
यज्ञैरिष्ट्वा स्वर्गतिं प्रार्थयन्ते ।
ते पुण्यमासाद्य सुरेन्द्रलोक
मश्नन्ति दिव्यान्दिवि देवभोगान् ।।20।।

trai-vidyā māṁ soma-pāḥ pūta-pāpā
yajñair iṣhṭvā svar-gatiṁ prārthayante
te puṇyam āsādya surendra-lokam
aśhnanti divyān divi deva-bhogān

trai-vidyāḥ—the science of *karm kāṇḍ* (Vedic rituals); *mām*—me; *soma-pāḥ*—drinkers of the *Soma* juice; *pūta*—purified; *pāpāḥ*—

sins; *yajñaiḥ*—through sacrifices; *iṣhṭvā*—worship; *svaḥ-gatim*—way to the abode of the king of heaven; *prārthayante*—seek; *te*—they; *puṇyam*—pious; *āsādya*—attain; *sura-indra*—of Indra; *lokam*—abode; *aśhnanti*—enjoy; *divyān*—celestial; *divi*—in heaven; *deva-bhogān*—pleasures of the celestial gods.

Those who are inclined to the fruitive activity described in the Vedas worship Me through ritualistic sacrifices. Being purified from sin by drinking the Soma juice, which is the remnant of the yajnas, they seek to go to heaven. By virtue of their pious deeds, they go to the abode of Indra, the king of heaven, and enjoy the pleasures of the celestial gods.

Previously, in verse 9.12, Shree Krishna described the mentality of the non-believers and the demoniac, who embrace atheistic and ungodly views and the repercussions such people face. Then, He described the nature of great souls who are engaged in loving devotion to Him. Now, in this verse and the next, He mentions those who are not devotees but are not atheistic either. They perform the ritualistic ceremonies of the Vedas. This science of *karm kāṇḍ* (Vedic rituals) is referred to as *trai-vidyā*.

People who are fascinated by the science of *trai-vidyā* worship the celestial gods, such as Indra, through the performance of yajnas (fire sacrifices) and other rituals. They worship the Supreme Lord indirectly because they do not realise that it is He alone who approves the gifts the celestial gods bestow. Ritualistic ceremonies are considered good deeds, but they are not counted as devotion. Performers of ritualistic ceremonies do not get released from the cycle of life and death. They go to the higher planes of existence within the material universe, such as abode of Indra, the king of heaven. There, they enjoy exquisite celestial delights that are thousands of times more pleasurable than the sensual pleasures available on the earth. *In the following verse, Shree Krishna points out the shortcomings of celestial pleasures.*

ते तं भुक्त्वा स्वर्गलोकं विशालं
क्षीणे पुण्ये मर्त्यलोकं विशन्ति ।

एवं त्रयीधर्ममनुप्रपन्ना
गतागतं कामकामा लभन्ते ।।21।।

te taṁ bhuktvā swarga-lokaṁ viśhālaṁ
kṣhīṇe puṇye martya-lokaṁ viśhanti
evaṁ trayī-dharmam anuprapannā
gatāgataṁ kāma-kāmā labhante

te—they; *tam*—that; *bhuktvā*—having enjoyed; *swarga-lokam*—heaven; *viśhālam*—vast; *kṣhīṇe*—at the exhaustion of; *puṇye*—stock of merits; *martya-lokam*—to the earthly plane; *viśhanti*—return; *evam*—thus; *trayī dharmam*—the *karm-kāṇḍ* portion of the three Vedas; *anuprapannāḥ*—follow; *gata-āgatam*—repeated coming and going; *kāma-kāmāḥ*—desiring objects of pleasure; *labhante*—attain.

When they have enjoyed the vast pleasures of heaven, the stock of their merits being exhausted, they return to the earthly plane. Thus, those who follow Vedic rituals, desiring objects of enjoyment, repeatedly come and go in this world.

Shree Krishna explains in this verse that the delights of the celestial abodes are temporary. After people who have been promoted there have fully enjoyed heavenly pleasures and exhausted their stock of merits, they are sent back to the earthly plane. Thus, even attaining a position in the heavenly abodes does not fulfil the eternal quest of the soul. We all have been there many times in endless past lifetimes, and yet the hunger of the soul for infinite Bliss has not yet been satiated. All the Vedic scriptures support this belief:

tāvat pramodate swarge yāvat puṇyaṁ samāpyate
kṣhīṇa puṇyaḥ patatyarvāganichchhan kāla-chālitaḥ

(Bhagavatam 11.10.26)

'Residents of heaven enjoy the celestial delights until their merits have been depleted. Then they are reluctantly forced to fall back to the lower abodes by the passage of time.'

swargahu swalpa anta dukhadāī (Ramayan)

'The attainment of heaven is temporary and is followed by miseries.'

Just as a football gets kicked all over the field, maya is kicking the soul around in forgetfulness of God. Sometimes it goes to the lower abodes, and sometimes to the higher abodes. Among the multitudes of forms it receives across the lower and higher abodes, only the human form offers the facility for God-realisation. Hence, the scriptures state that even the celestial gods pray to be given birth as a human being, so that they may strive for God-realisation.

durlabhaṁ mānuṣhaṁ janma prārthayate tridaśhairapi

(*Nārad Puran*)

'The human form is exceedingly rare. Even the celestial gods pray to attain it.' Lord Ram instructed the residents of Ayodhya:

baṛeñ bhāga mānuṣha tanu pāvā,
sura durlabha saba granthanhi gāvā (Ramayan)

'O people of Ayodhya, you all are extremely fortunate to have been bestowed a human birth, which is exceedingly rare and is desired even by the residents of heaven.' When the celestial beings long for a human birth, then why should we humans seek promotion to the celestial abodes? Rather, we should aim for God-realisation by engaging in devotion to the Supreme Lord.

अनन्याश्चिन्तयन्तो मां ये जनाः पर्युपासते ।
तेषां नित्याभियुक्तानां योगक्षेमं वहाम्यहम् ।।22।।

ananyāśh chintayanto māṁ ye janāḥ paryupāsate
teṣhāṁ nityābhiyuktānāṁ yoga-kṣhemaṁ vahāmyaham

ananyāḥ—always; *chintayantaḥ*—think of; *mām*—me; *ye*—those who; *janāḥ*—persons; *paryupāsate*—worship exclusively; *teṣhām*—of them; *nitya abhiyuktānām*—who are always absorbed; *yoga*—supply spiritual assets; *kṣhemam*—protect spiritual assets; *vahāmi*—carry; *aham*—I.

There are those who always think of Me and engage in exclusive

devotion to Me. To them, whose minds are always absorbed in Me, I provide what they lack and preserve what they already possess.

A mother never thinks of deserting her newborn helpless child who is entirely dependent upon her. The supreme and eternal mother of the soul is God. In this verse, God offers motherly assurance to souls who surrender exclusively to Him. The words used are *vahāmi aham*, meaning, 'I personally carry the burden of maintaining My devotees', just as a married man carries the responsibility of maintaining his wife and children. God promises two things. The first is yog—He bestows His devotees the spiritual assets they do not possess. The second is *kṣhem*—He protects the spiritual assets that His devotees already possess.

However, the condition He has placed for this is exclusive surrender. This can again be understood through the same analogy of the mother and child. A newborn baby is fully dependent upon its mother who takes care of the baby's welfare entirely. The baby simply cries whenever it needs anything; the mother cleans it, feeds it, bathes it, and does other chores to make it comfortable. But when the baby becomes a five-year-old child, it begins doing some actions for itself. To the same extent, the mother reduces her responsibilities. And when the same child becomes a youth and assumes all responsibilities, the mother relinquishes her responsibilities further. Now if the father comes home and enquires about the whereabouts of the son, the mother replies, 'He has not returned home after school. He must have gone for a movie with his friends.' Her attitude is now more neutral towards him. But when the same boy was a five-year-old, and if he had gotten delayed by ten minutes in returning home from school, both the mother and father would begin worrying, saying, 'What has happened? He is a small child. Let's hope he has not met with an accident. Let us call the school and find out.'

In this way, as the child keeps assuming more responsibilities, the mother keeps relinquishing her responsibilities. God's law is exactly the same. When we act from our independent will, thinking that we are the doers of our actions and depend upon our own prowess and abilities,

God does not bestow His grace. He merely notes our karmas and gives the result. When we surrender partially to Him and partially depend upon material crutches, God also partially bestows His grace upon us. And when we offer ourselves exclusively to Him, *māmekaṁ śharaṇaṁ vraja* God bestows His complete grace and takes full responsibility, by preserving what we have and providing what we lack.

येऽप्यन्यदेवता भक्ता यजन्ते श्रद्धयान्विताः ।
तेऽपि मामेव कौन्तेय यजन्त्यविधिपूर्वकम् ।।23।।

ye 'pyanya-devatā-bhaktā yajante śhraddhayānvitāḥ
te 'pi mām eva kaunteya yajantyavidhi-pūrvakam

ye—those who; *api*—although; *anya*—other; *devatā*—celestial gods; *bhaktāḥ*—devotees; *yajante*—worship; *śhraddhayā anvitāḥ*—faithfully; *te*—they; *api*—also; *mām*—me; *eva*—only; *kaunteya*—Arjun, son of Kunti; *yajanti*—worship; *avidhi-pūrvakam*—by the wrong method.

O son of Kunti, even those devotees who faithfully worship other gods also worship Me. But they do so by the wrong method.

Having described the position of those who worship the Supreme Lord, Shree Krishna now explains the situation of those who worship the lower gods for material gains. They are also endowed with faith, and they may have their supplications answered by the celestial gods, but their understanding is incomplete. They do not realise that the celestial beings receive their powers from God Himself. Consequently, they also worship the Supreme Divine Personality, albeit indirectly. For example, if a government officer redresses a complaint by a citizen, he is not credited with being benevolent. He is merely utilising the powers in his jurisdiction that have been bestowed upon him by the government. Similarly, all the powers of the celestial gods come from the Supreme Lord. Thus, those with superior understanding do not go by the indirect route; they worship the source of all powers, which is God Himself. Such worship that is offered to the Supreme Lord automatically satisfies the entire creation:

yathā taror mūla-niṣhechanena
tṛipyanti tatskandhabhujopaśhākhāḥ
prāṇopahārāchcha yathendriyāṇāṁ
tathaiva sarvārhaṇam achyutejyā (Bhagavatam 4.31.14)

'When we water the root of a tree, its trunk, branches, twigs, leaves, and flowers all become nourished. When we put food in our mouth, it nourishes the life airs and the senses automatically. In the same way, by worshipping the Supreme Lord, all His parts, including the *devatās* are also worshipped.' However, if we begin watering the leaves of a tree while neglecting its roots, the tree will perish. Likewise, the worship offered to the celestial gods certainly makes its way to the Supreme Lord, but such devotees do not get spiritual benefits. *This is elaborated in the next verse.*

अहं हि सर्वयज्ञानां भोक्ता च प्रभुरेव च ।
न तु मामभिजानन्ति तत्त्वेनातश्च्यवन्ति ते ।।24।।

ahaṁ hi sarva-yajñānāṁ bhoktā cha prabhureva cha
na tu mām abhijānanti tattvenātaśh chyavanti te

aham—I; *hi*—verily; *sarva*—of all; *yajñānām*—sacrifices; *bhoktā*—the enjoyer; *cha*—and; *prabhuḥ*—the Lord; *eva*—only; *cha*—and; *na*—not; *tu*—but; *mām*—me; *abhijānanti*—realise; *tattvena*—divine nature; *ataḥ*—therefore; *chyavanti*—fall down (wander in samsara); *te*—they.

I am the enjoyer and the only Lord of all sacrifices. But those who fail to realise My divine nature must be reborn.

Shree Krishna now explains the drawback in worshipping the celestial gods. By virtue of the powers bestowed upon them by the Supreme Lord, they do possess the ability to grant material favours, but they cannot liberate their devotees from the cycle of life and death. They can only offer to others what they themselves possess. When the celestial gods themselves are not liberated from samsara, then how can they release their devotees from it? On the other hand, those whose understanding is proper offer their entire veneration at the feet of God

Himself, and when their devotion reaches the stage of perfection, they go beyond the world of mortals to the divine abode.

यान्ति देवव्रता देवान्पितॄन्यान्ति पितृव्रताः ।
भूतानि यान्ति भूतेज्या यान्ति मद्याजिनोऽपि माम् ।।25।।

yānti deva-vratā devān pitṝn yānti pitṛi-vratāḥ
bhūtāni yānti bhūtejyā yānti mad-yājino 'pi mām

yānti—go; *deva-vratāḥ*—worshippers of celestial gods; *devān*—among the celestial gods; *pitṝn*—to the ancestors; *yānti*—go; *pitṛi-vratā*—worshippers of ancestors; *bhūtāni*—to the ghosts; *yānti*—go; *bhūta-ijyāḥ*—worshippers of ghosts; *yānti*—go; *mat*—my; *yājinaḥ*—devotees; *api*—and; *mām*—to me.

Worshippers of the celestial gods take birth amongst the celestial gods, worshippers of the ancestors go to the ancestors, worshippers of ghosts take birth amongst such beings, and My devotees come to Me alone.

Devotees can only be elevated to the level of the entity they worship, just as water in a pipe can only rise to the level of the reservoir to which it is connected. In this verse, Shree Krishna explains the implications of worshipping different entities by revealing the varieties of destinations attained. He gives this knowledge to help us conclude that to reach the highest level of spiritual evolution, we must worship the Supreme.

The worshippers of Indra (the rain god), Kuber (the god of wealth), Agni (the god of fire), and other celestial gods go to the celestial abodes. Then, when their account of good karmas gets depleted, they are sent back from heaven. The *Pitars* are the ancestors. It is good to harbour thoughts of gratefulness towards them, but undue concern about their welfare is detrimental. Those who engage in ancestor worship go to the abodes of their ancestors after death.

Those in the mode of ignorance worship ghosts and spirits. In the Western world, there is witchcraft; in Africa, there is black magic; in India, there are *vām-marg tāntrics* who invoke ghosts and spirits.

Shree Krishna says that persons who indulge in such activities take birth among ghosts and spirits in their next life.

The highest devotees are those who attach their minds to the Supreme Divine Personality. The word *vrata* means 'resolve and undertaking'. Such fortunate souls, who firmly resolve to worship God and engage steadfastly in His devotion, go to His divine abode after death.

पत्रं पुष्पं फलं तोयं यो मे भक्त्या प्रयच्छति ।
तदहं भक्त्युपहृतमश्नामि प्रयतात्मनः ।।26।।

patraṁ puṣhpaṁ phalaṁ toyaṁ yo me bhaktyā prayachchhati
tadahaṁ bhaktyupahṛitam aśhnāmi prayatātmanaḥ

patram—leaf; *puṣhpam*—flower; *phalam*—fruit; *toyam*—water; *yaḥ*—who; *me*—to me; *bhaktyā*—with devotion; *prayachchhati*—offers; *tat*—that; *aham*—I; *bhakti-upahṛitam*—offered with devotion; *aśhnāmi*—partake; *prayata-ātmanaḥ*—one in pure consciousness.

If one offers to Me with devotion a leaf, a flower, a fruit, or even water, I delightfully partake of that item offered with love by My devotee in pure consciousness.

Having established the benefits of worshipping the Supreme, Shree Krishna now explains the ease with which it can be done. In the worship of the *devatās* and the ancestors, there are many rules to propitiate them, all of which must be strictly followed. But God accepts anything that is offered with a loving heart. If you have only a fruit, offer it to God, and He will be pleased. If there is no fruit available, offer Him a flower. If it is not the season for flowers, offer God a mere leaf; even that will suffice, provided it is a gift of love. If leaves are also scarce, make an offering of water, which is available everywhere, but again, ensure that you do it with devotion. The word *bhaktyā* has been used in both the first and second lines of the verse. It is the bhakti of the devotee that is pleasing to God and not the value of the offering.

By making this wonderful statement, Shree Krishna reveals the merciful divine nature of God. He is not concerned with the material value of our offering. On the contrary, He values, above everything else, the love with which we make the offering. The *Hari Bhakti Vilas* states:

tulasī-dala-mātreṇa jalasya chulukena cha
vikrīṇīte svam ātmānaṁ bhaktebhyo bhakta-vatsalaḥ (11.261)

'If you offer God with sincere love, just a Tulsi leaf and as much water as you can hold in your palm, He will offer Himself to you in return because He is endeared by love.' How wonderful it is that the Supreme Master of unlimited universes, whose glorious qualities and virtues are amazing beyond description, and by whose mere thought multitudes of universes come into existence and disappear again, accepts even the most insignificant offerings of His devotees that are given with genuine love and humility. The word used here is *prayatātmanaḥ*, implying, 'I accept the offerings of those whose hearts are pure.'

The Shreemad Bhagavatam contains exactly the same verse as the above verse of the Bhagavad Gita. While eating dry rice at the house of His friend, Sudama, Shree Krishna said:

patraṁ puṣhpaṁ phalaṁ toyaṁ yo me bhaktyā prayachchhati
tadahaṁ bhaktyupahṛitam aśhnāmi prayatātmanaḥ (10.81.4)

'If one offers Me with devotion, a leaf, a flower, a fruit, or even water, I delightfully partake of that article offered with love by My devotee in pure consciousness.'

Whenever God descends upon the earth, He exhibits this quality in His divine pastimes. Before the Mahabharat war, when Shree Krishna went to Hastinapur to explore the possibility of fashioning an agreement between the Kauravas and Pandavas, the evil Duryodhan had proudly prepared for Him a meal of fifty-six different items (*chappan bhog*). However, Shree Krishna rejected his hospitality and instead went to the humble hut of Vidurani, who had been longing deeply for the opportunity to serve her beloved Lord. Vidurani was overjoyed on receiving the Supreme Lord at her home. All she had to offer was bananas, but her intellect was so benumbed with loving sentiments that she did not even realise she was dropping the fruit and putting the banana peels in His mouth. Nevertheless, seeing her devotion, Shree Krishna blissfully ate the peels, as if they were the most delicious food in the world.

यत्करोषि यदश्नासि यज्जुहोषि ददासि यत् ।
यत्तपस्यसि कौन्तेय तत्कुरुष्व मदर्पणम् ।।27।।

yat karoṣhi yad aśhnāsi yaj juhoṣhi dadāsi yat
yat tapasyasi kaunteya tat kuruṣhva mad-arpaṇam

yat—whatever; *karoṣhi*—you do; *yat*—whatever; *aśhnāsi*—you eat; *yat*—whatever; *juhoṣhi*—offer to the sacred fire; *dadāsi*—bestow as a gift; *yat*—whatever; *yat*—whatever; *tapasyasi*—austerities you perform; *kaunteya*—Arjun, son of Kunti; *tat*—them; *kuruṣhva*—do; *mad arpaṇam*—as an offering to me.

Whatever you do, whatever you eat, whatever you offer as oblation to the sacred fire, whatever you bestow as a gift, and whatever austerities you perform, O son of Kunti, do them as an offering to Me.

In the previous verse, Shree Krishna stated that all objects should be offered to Him. Now He says that all actions should also be offered to Him. Whatever social duties one may be engaged in, whatever vegetarian food one may be eating, whatever non-alcoholic beverages one may be drinking, whatever Vedic rites one may perform, whatever vows and austerities one may observe, all should be offered mentally to the Supreme Lord. Very often, people separate devotion from their daily life and look on it as something that is only to be performed inside the temple room. However, devotion is not to be restricted to the periphery of the temple walls; it is to be engaged in at every moment of our life.

Sage Narad defines bhakti in this manner:

nāradastu tadarpitā khilāchāratā tadvismaraṇe
paramavyākulateti (*Nārad Bhakti Darshan*, Sutra 19)

'Devotion means offering your every activity to God and feeling intense separation if ever you lose remembrance of Him.' When our works are dedicated and mentally delivered to God, it is called *arpaṇam*. Doing so metamorphoses the mundane activities of material life into divine service of God. Swami Vivekananda expressed this attitude towards work when he declared: 'No work is secular. Everything is devotion and service.' Saint Kabir stated this in his couplet:

jahañ jahañ chalūñ karūñ parikramā, jo jo karūñ so sevā
jaba sovūñ karūñ daṇḍavat, jānūñ deva na dūjā

'Wherever I walk, I feel I am circumambulating the Lord's temple; whatever I do, I see it as service to God. When I go to sleep, I meditate on the sentiment that I am offering obeisance to God. In this way, I remain ever united with Him.' Without realising its significance, many people recite the following verse in the temple:

kāyena vāchā manasendriyair vā
buddhyātmanā vānusṛita-svabhāvāt
karoti yad yat sakalaṁ parasmai
nārāyaṇāyeti samarpayet tat (Bhagavatam 11.2.36)

'Whatever one does with the body, words, mind, senses, and intellect, in accordance with one's individual nature, should be offered to the Supreme Lord Narayan.' However, this act of offering is not to be done at the end of the work by merely reciting mantras, such as *śhrī kṛiṣhṇāya samarpaṇam astu*, etc., as is done in the Vedic rituals. It is to be done while performing the action itself, by maintaining the consciousness that we are working for the pleasure of the Lord. *Having stated that all works should be offered to Him, Shree Krishna now lists the benefits of doing this.*

शुभाशुभफलैरेवं मोक्ष्यसे कर्मबन्धनैः ।
संन्यासयोगयुक्तात्मा विमुक्तो मामुपैष्यसि ।।28।।

śhubhāśhubha-phalair evaṁ mokṣhyase karma-bandhanaiḥ
sanyāsa-yoga-yuktātmā vimukto mām upaiṣhyasi

śhubha aśhubha phalaiḥ—from good and bad results; *evam*—thus; *mokṣhyase*—you shall be freed; *karma*—work; *bandhanaiḥ*—from bondage; *sanyāsa-yoga*—renunciation of selfishness; *yukta-ātmā*—having the mind attached to me; *vimuktaḥ*—liberated; *mām*—to me; *upaiṣhyasi*—you shall reach.

By dedicating all your works to Me, you will be freed from the bondage of good and bad results. With your mind attached to Me through renunciation, you will be liberated and will reach Me.

Every action has flaws just as fire is covered by smoke. When we walk on the earth, we unknowingly kill millions of tiny living entities. In our occupational duties, no matter how careful we are in the fulfilment of our duties, we still end up harming the environment and hurting others. Even if we eat a cup of yogurt, we still incur the sin of destroying the living entities that reside in it. Some religious sects try to reduce this involuntary killing by wearing a mask to cover their mouth. Even this does not fully eliminate the destruction of living entities in our breath.

When we perform our actions with the intention of fulfilling our self-interest, knowingly or unknowingly, we are culpable for the sins we commit. In accordance with the Law of Karma, we have to reap their karmic reactions. Good actions can also be binding because they oblige the soul to go to the celestial abodes to enjoy their results. Consequently, both bad and good karmas result in the continuity of the cycle of birth and death. However, in this verse, Shree Krishna gives a simple solution for destroying all karmic reactions of work. He uses the word sanyas yog, meaning, renunciation of selfishness. He says that when we dedicate our actions for the pleasure of the Lord, we are freed from the fetters of both good and bad results.

Those who establish themselves in such consciousness are called *yog yuktatma* (united in consciousness with God). Such yogis become *jīvan mukt* (liberated in consciousness) even in this body. And, upon leaving their mortal frame, they receive a divine body and eternal service in the divine abode of God.

समोऽहं सर्वभूतेषु न मे द्वेष्योऽस्ति न प्रियः ।
ये भजन्ति तु मां भक्त्या मयि ते तेषु चाप्यहम् ।।29।।

samo 'haṁ sarva-bhūteṣhu na me dveṣhyo 'sti na priyaḥ
ye bhajanti tu māṁ bhaktyā mayi te teṣhu chāpyaham

samaḥ—equally disposed; *aham*—I; *sarva-bhūteṣhu*—to all living beings; *na*—no one; *me*—to me; *dveṣhyaḥ*—inimical; *asti*—is; *na*—not; *priyaḥ*—dear; *ye*—who; *bhajanti*—worship with love; *tu*—but; *mām*—me; *bhaktyā*—with devotion; *mayi*—reside in me; *te*—such persons; *teṣhu*—in them; *cha*—and; *api*—also; *aham*—I.

I am equally disposed to all living beings; I am neither inimical nor partial to anyone. But the devotees who worship Me with love reside in Me, and I reside in them.

We all intuitively believe that if there is a God, He must be perfectly just; there cannot be an unjust God. People suffering injustice in the world make statements such as, 'Mr Billionaire, you have the power of money on your side. Do what you like. God will settle our dispute. He is watching and will definitely punish you. You cannot escape.' This sort of statement does not indicate that the person making it is a saint possessing absolute faith in God, for even common persons believe that God is perfectly just.

However, the previous verse by Shree Krishna creates the doubt that God is partial towards His devotees, because while everyone is subject to the Law of Karma, God releases His devotees from it. Isn't this symptomatic of the flaw of partiality? Shree Krishna feels it necessary to clarify this point and begins the verse by saying *samo ' ham*, meaning, 'No, no, I am equal to all. But I have a uniform law in accordance with which I bestow My grace.' This law was previously stated in verse 4.11: 'In whatever way people surrender unto Me, I reciprocate accordingly. Everyone follows My path, knowingly or unknowingly, O son of Pritha.'

Rainwater falls equally upon the earth. Yet, the drop that falls on the cornfields gets converted into grain; the drop that falls on the desert bush gets converted into a thorn; the drop that falls in the gutter becomes dirty water; and the drop that falls in the oyster becomes a pearl. There is no partiality on the part of the rain since it is equitable in bestowing its grace upon the land. The raindrops cannot be held responsible for this variation in results which are a consequence of the nature of the recipient. Similarly, God states here that He is equally disposed towards all living beings, and yet, those who do not love Him are bereft of the benefits of His grace because their hearts are unsuitable vessels for receiving it. *So, what can people do whose hearts are impure? Shree Krishna now reveals the purifying power of bhakti.*

अपि चेत्सुदुराचारो भजते मामनन्यभाक् ।
साधुरेव स मन्तव्यः सम्यग्व्यवसितो हि सः ।।30।।

api chet su-durāchāro bhajate mām ananya-bhāk
sādhur eva sa mantavyaḥ samyag vyavasito hi saḥ

api—even; *chet*—if; *su-durāchāraḥ*—the vilest sinners; *bhajate*—worship; *mām*—me; *ananya-bhāk*—exclusive devotion; *sādhuḥ*—righteous; *eva*—certainly; *saḥ*—that person; *mantavyaḥ*—is to be considered; *samyak*—properly; *vyavasitaḥ*—resolve; *hi*—certainly; *saḥ*—that person.

Even if the vilest sinners worship Me with exclusive devotion, they are to be considered righteous because they have made the proper resolve.

Devotion to the Supreme Lord is so potent that it can reform even the most fallen. In the scriptures, the classical examples of this are Ajamil and Valmiki , whose stories are popular in all Indian languages. Valmiki's impious deeds were so overbearing that he was even unable to enunciate 'Ra ... ma', the two syllables in Lord Ram's name. His sins prevented him from taking the divine name. So, his guru thought of a way of engaging him in devotion by making him chant the reverse, 'Ma Ra', with the intention that repetition of Mara Mara Mara Mara ... would automatically create the sound of Rama Rama Rama.... As a result, even such a fallen soul as Valmiki was reformed by the process of *ananya bhakti* (exclusive devotion) and transformed into a legendary saint.

ulaṭā nāmu japata jagu jānā, bālmīki bhae brahma samānā

(Ramayan)

'The whole world is testimony to the fact that Valmiki attained sainthood by chanting the syllables of God's name in the reverse order.' Therefore, sinners are not condemned to eternal damnation. On the strength of the transforming power of bhakti, Shree Krishna declares that even if the vilest sinners begin worshipping God exclusively, they should no longer be designated as sinners. They have made a pure resolve and should thus be considered righteous due to their sublime spiritual intention.

क्षिप्रं भवति धर्मात्मा शश्वच्छान्तिं निगच्छति ।
कौन्तेय प्रतिजानीहि न मे भक्तः प्रणश्यति ।।31।।

kṣhipraṁ bhavati dharmātmā śhaśhvach-chhāntiṁ nigachchhati
kaunteya pratijānīhi na me bhaktaḥ praṇaśhyati

kṣhipram—quickly; *bhavati*—become; *dharma-ātmā*—virtuous; *śhaśhvat-śhāntim*—lasting peace; *nigachchhati*—attain; *kaunteya*—Arjun, son of Kunti; *pratijānīhi*—declare; *na*—never; *me*—my; *bhaktaḥ*—devotee; *praṇaśhyati*—perishes.

Quickly they become virtuous and attain lasting peace. O son of Kunti, declare it boldly that no devotee of Mine is ever lost.

Why should devotees be considered venerable merely for having made the correct resolve? Shree Krishna explains that if they continue the process of exclusive devotion with unflinching faith in God, their hearts will become purified, and they will swiftly develop saintly virtues.

Divine virtues emanate from God Himself. He is perfectly just, truthful, compassionate, loving, merciful, etc. Since we souls are His tiny parts, we are all naturally drawn to these godly qualities. But the process of becoming virtuous remains an elusive mystery. From childhood, we have heard that we must speak the truth, serve others, and be free from anger and other negative emotions, and yet we are unable to put those teachings into practice for the simple reason that our mind is impure. Without purification of the mind, blemishes of character cannot be eradicated fully and permanently. Jagadguru Shree Kripaluji Maharaj declares the irrefutable truth regarding developing divine virtues:

satya ahinsā ādi mana! bina hari bhajana na pāya
jala te ghṛita nikale nahīñ, koṭina kariya upāya

(*Bhakti Śhatak* verse 35)

'No matter how much we try, oil stains on a cloth cannot be removed by water alone. Similarly, truthfulness, non-violence, and other virtuous qualities cannot be acquired without engaging in devotion to God.' These qualities manifest when the mind is purified, which cannot take place without attaching it to the all-pure God.

Further, Shree Krishna asks Arjun to boldly declare that His devotees will never perish. He does not say, 'The jnani (person of knowledge) will not be lost.' Nor does He say, 'The karmi (performer of rituals) shall not perish.' He makes His promise for His bhaktas (devotees), saying that 'they shall never come to ruin.' Thereby, He reiterates what He had stated in verse 9.22 that He personally carries the burden of maintaining those who depend upon Him and engage in exclusive devotion unto Him.

It may seem intriguing why Shree Krishna asks Arjun to make this statement instead of declaring it Himself. The reason is that under special circumstances, the Lord sometimes breaks His word, but He never permits His devotees' word to be broken. For example, Shree Krishna had resolved that He would not lift weapons during the Mahabharat war. But when Grandsire Bheeshma, considered the perfect devotee, resolved that he would either kill Arjun by sunset the next day or make the Lord lift weapons to protect him, Shree Krishna broke His own vow to protect the vow made by Bheeshma. Thus, to reaffirm the strength of His statement, Shree Krishna here says, 'Arjun, you declare that My devotee will never perish, for I shall guarantee that your word will be kept.'

मां हि पार्थ व्यपाश्रित्य येऽपि स्युः पापयोनयः ।
स्त्रियो वैश्यास्तथा शूद्रास्तेऽपि यान्ति परां गतिम् ।।32।।

māṁ hi pārtha vyapāśhritya ye 'pi syuḥ pāpa-yonayaḥ
striyo vaiśhyās tathā śhūdrās te 'pi yānti parāṁ gatim

mām—in me; *hi*—certainly; *pārtha*—Arjun, son of Pritha; *vyapāśhritya*—take refuge; *ye*—who; *api*—even; *syuḥ*—may be; *pāpa yonayaḥ*—of low birth; *striyaḥ*—women; *vaiśhyāḥ*—mercantile people; *tathā*—and; *śhūdrāḥ*—manual workers; *te api*—even they; *yānti*—go; *parām*—the supreme; *gatim*—destination.

All those who take refuge in Me, whatever their birth, race, gender, or caste, even those whom society scorns, will attain the supreme destination.

There are souls who have the good fortune of being born in pious families where they are educated in good values and virtuous living from childhood. This is a consequence of their good deeds in past lives. Then, there are also souls who have the misfortune of being born in families of drunks, criminals, gamblers, and atheists. This is also the result of sins committed in past lives.

Here, Shree Krishna states that irrespective of birth, gender, caste, or race, whoever takes complete shelter in Him will attain the supreme goal. Such is the greatness of the path of devotion that everyone is eligible for it, whereas in other paths, there are strict criteria for eligibility.

For the path of jnana yog, Jagadguru Shankaracharya states the eligibility:

vivekino viraktasya śhamādiguṇa śhalinaḥ
mukukṣhoraiva hi brahma jijñāsā yogyatā matāḥ

'Only those who possess the four qualifications—discrimination, detachment, disciplined mind and senses, and a deep yearning for liberation—are eligible for practising the path of jnana yog.'

In the path of *karm kāṇḍ* (Vedic rituals), there are six conditions to be met:

deśhe kāle upāyena dravyaṁ śhraddhā samanvitam
pātre pradīyate yattat sakalaṁ dharma lakṣhaṇam

'Six criteria must be fulfilled for the fruition of ritualistic activities—the proper place, the correct time, the exact procedure and correct enunciation of mantras, use of pure materials, a qualified Brahmin who performs the yajna, and staunch faith in its efficacy.'

In the path of ashtang yog as well, there are strict regulations:

śhuchau deśhe pratiṣhṭhāpya (Bhagavatam 3.28.8)

'Perform hatha yog in a pure place while seated immovably in the proper asan.'

In contrast, bhakti yog is such that it can be done by anyone, at any time, place, and circumstance, and with any material.

na deśha niyamastasmin na kāla niyamasthathā
(*Padma Puran*)

This verse states that God is not concerned with the time or place where we perform devotion. He only sees the love in our heart. All souls are the children of God, and He is willing to accept everyone with open arms, provided they come to Him with genuine love.

किं पुनर्ब्राह्मणाः पुण्या भक्ता राजर्षयस्तथा ।
अनित्यमसुखं लोकमिमं प्राप्य भजस्व माम् ।।33।।

kiṁ punar brāhmaṇāḥ puṇyā bhaktā rājarṣhayas tathā
anityam asukhaṁ lokam imaṁ prāpya bhajasva mām

kim—what; *punaḥ*—then; *brāhmaṇāḥ*—sages; *puṇyāḥ*—meritorius; *bhaktāḥ*—devotees; *rāja-ṛiṣhayaḥ*—saintly kings; *tathā*—and; *anityam*—transient; *asukham*—joyless; *lokam*—world; *imam*—this; *prāpya*—having achieved; *bhajasva*—engage in devotion; *mām*—unto me.

What then to speak about kings and sages with meritorious deeds? Therefore, having come to this transient and joyless world, engage in devotion unto Me.

When even the most abominable sinners are assured of success on the path of bhakti, then why should more qualified souls have any doubt? Kings and sages should be even more reassured of attaining the supreme destination by engaging in *ananya bhakti* (exclusive devotion). Shree Krishna thus beckons Arjun, 'A saintly king like you should become situated in the knowledge that the world is temporary and a place of misery. Engage yourself in steadfast devotion to Me, the possessor of unlimited eternal happiness. Else the blessing of birth in a kingly and saintly family, good education, and favourable material circumstances will all be wasted.'

मन्मना भव मद्भक्तो मद्याजी मां नमस्कुरु ।
मामेवैष्यसि युक्त्वैवमात्मानं मत्परायणः ।।34।।

man-manā bhava mad-bhakto mad-yājī māṁ namaskuru
mām evaiṣhyasi yuktvaivam ātmānaṁ mat-parāyaṇaḥ

mat-manāḥ—always think of me; *bhava*—be; *mat*—my; *bhaktaḥ*—devotee; *mat*—my; *yājī*—worshipper; *mām*—to me; *namaskuru*—offer obeisances; *mām*—to me; *eva*—certainly; *eṣhyasi*—you will come; *yuktvā*—united with me; *evam*—thus; *ātmānam*—your mind and body; *mat-parāyaṇaḥ*—having dedicated to me.

Always think of Me, be devoted to Me, worship Me, and offer obeisance to Me. Having dedicated your mind and body to Me, you will certainly come to Me.

Having stressed bhakti, the path of devotion, throughout this chapter, Shree Krishna now concludes it by entreating Arjun to become His devotee. He asks Arjun to unite his consciousness with God in true Yog, by worshipping Him, engaging the mind in meditation upon His divine form, and offering obeisance in pure humility to Him.

Namaskuru (the act of humble obeisance) effectively neutralises vestiges of egotism that may arise in the performance of devotion. Thus, free from pride, with the heart immersed in devotion, one should dedicate all one's thoughts and actions to the Supreme. Shree Krishna assures Arjun that such complete communion with Him through bhakti yog will definitely result in the attainment of God-realisation; of this, there should be no doubt.

CHAPTER 10

Vibhūti Yog

Yog through Appreciating the Infinite Opulences of God

This chapter is narrated by Lord Krishna to help Arjun meditate on God by reflecting upon His magnificent and resplendent glories. In chapter nine, Shree Krishna revealed the science of bhakti, or loving devotion, and described some of His opulences. Here, He expounds further on His infinite glories, with the desire to increase Arjun's bhakti. These verses are pleasing to read and enchanting to hear.

Shree Krishna reveals that He is the source of everything that exists. The varieties of human qualities arise from Him. The four great Kumars, the seven great Sages, and the fourteen Manus were born from His mind; and from them all people in the world have descended. Those who know that everything proceeds from Him engage in His devotion with great faith. Such devotees derive great satisfaction in conversing about His glories and enlightening others about Him. Since their minds are united with Him, His dwelling within their hearts gives the divine knowledge by which they can easily attain Him.

Upon hearing Him, Arjun declares that he is completely convinced about Shree Krishna's paramount position and proclaims Him to be the Supreme Divine Personality. He requests the Lord to further describe His divine glories that are like music to his ears. Shree Krishna reveals that since He is the beginning, middle, and end of all things, everything that exists is a manifestation of His powers. He is the infinite reservoir of beauty, glory, power, knowledge, opulence, and renunciation.

Whenever we observe extraordinary splendour anywhere, whatever catches our imagination, sends us in raptures and infuses us with bliss, we should know it to be but a spark of the opulence of God. He is the powerhouse from where all beings and things get their magnificence. For the remaining portion of the chapter, He goes on to describe the objects, personalities, and activities that best display His opulence. Finally, He concludes by saying that the magnitude of His glory cannot be judged by the sum total of what He has described, for He upholds unlimited universes in a fraction of His Being. Therefore, we must make God, who is the source of all glory, the object of our worship.

श्रीभगवानुवाच ।
भूय एव महाबाहो शृणु मे परमं वचः ।
यत्तेऽहं प्रीयमाणाय वक्ष्यामि हितकाम्यया ।।1।।

śhrī bhagavān uvācha
bhūya eva mahā-bāho śhṛiṇu me paramaṁ vachaḥ
yatte 'haṁ prīyamāṇāya vakṣhyāmi hita-kāmyayā

śhrī-bhagavān uvācha—the Lord said; *bhūyaḥ*—again; *eva*—verily; *mahā-bāho*—mighty armed one; *śhṛiṇu*—hear; *me*—my; *paramam*—divine; *vachaḥ*—teachings; *yat*—which; *te*—to you; *aham*—I; *prīyamāṇāya*—you are my beloved confidant; *vakṣhyāmi*—say; *hita-kāmyayā*—desiring your welfare.

The Lord said: Listen again to My divine teachings, O mighty armed one. Desiring your welfare because you are My beloved friend, I shall reveal them to you.

Shree Krishna is delighted with Arjun's keen interest in hearing His glories. Now, to further enhance his joy and fan his enthusiasm for loving devotion, Shree Krishna declares that He will narrate His sublime glories and incomparable attributes. He uses the words *prīyamāṇāya*, implying 'You are My beloved confidant, so I will reveal this very special knowledge to you.'

न मे विदुः सुरगणाः प्रभवं न महर्षयः ।
अहमादिर्हि देवानां महर्षीणां च सर्वशः ।।2।।

na me viduḥ sura-gaṇāḥ prabhavaṁ na maharṣhayaḥ
aham ādir hi devānāṁ maharṣhīṇāṁ cha sarvaśhaḥ

na—neither; *me*—my; *viduḥ*—know; *sura-gaṇāḥ*—the celestial gods; *prabhavam*—origin; *na*—nor; *mahā-ṛiṣhayaḥ*—the great sages; *aham*—I; *ādiḥ*—the source; *hi*—certainly; *devānām*—of the celestial gods; *mahā-ṛiṣhīṇām*—of the great seers; *cha*—also; *sarvaśhaḥ*—in every way.

Neither celestial gods nor the great sages know of My origin. I am the source from which the gods and great seers come.

A father knows about the birth and life of his son because he witnesses it. But the birth and childhood of his father are beyond the ken of the son because they occurred before he was born. Likewise, the *devatās* (celestial gods) and the rishis (sages) cannot comprehend the real nature of the origin of God, who existed before they were even born. The *Rig Veda* states:

ko addhā veda ka iha prāvochat, kuta ā jātā kuta iyaṁ visṛiṣhṭiḥ
arvāgdevā asya visarjanāya, athā ko veda yata ābabhūva

(10.129.6)

'Who in the world can know clearly? Who can proclaim from where this universe was born? Who can state where this creation has come from? The *devatās* came after creation. Therefore, who knows from where the universe arose?' Again, the *Īśhopaniṣhad* states:

nainaddevā āpnuvan pūrvamarṣhat (4)

'God cannot be known by the celestial *devatās* because He existed before them.' Yet, such inaccessible knowledge will now be given by Shree Krishna to nurture the devotion of His dear friend.

यो मामजमनादिं च वेत्ति लोकमहेश्वरम् ।
असम्मूढः स मर्त्येषु सर्वपापैः प्रमुच्यते ।।3।।

yo māmajam anādiṁ cha vetti loka-maheśhvaram
asammūḍhaḥ sa martyeṣhu sarva-pāpaiḥ pramuchyate

yaḥ—who; *mām*—me; *ajam*—unborn; *anādim*—beginningless; *cha*—and; *vetti*—know; *loka*—of the universe; *mahā-īśhvaram*—the Supreme Lord; *asammūḍhaḥ*—undeluded; *saḥ*—they; *martyeṣhu*—among mortals; *sarva-pāpaiḥ*—from all evils; *pramuchyate*—are free from.

Those who know Me as unborn and beginningless and as the Supreme Lord of the universe, they among mortals are free from illusion and released from all evils.

Having said that no one can know Him, Shree Krishna now states that some people do know Him. Is He contradicting Himself? No, He means that by self-effort no one can know God, but if God Himself bestows His grace upon someone, that fortunate soul gets to know Him. Hence, all those who come to know God do so by virtue of His divine grace. As He mentions in verse 10 of this chapter: 'To those whose minds are always united with Me in loving devotion, I give the divine knowledge by which they can attain Me.' Here, Shree Krishna says that those who know Him as the Supreme Lord of all lords are not deluded. Such blessed souls become free from all reactions to their past and present actions and develop loving devotion towards Him.

To make the distinction between the souls and Himself, Shree Krishna declares that He is *loka maheśhwaram* (the great Lord of all the abodes of existence). The same has been declared in the *Śhwetāśhvatar Upanishad*:

tamīśhwarāṇāṁ paramaṁ maheśhwaraṁ
taṁ devatānāṁ paramaṁ cha daivataṁ
patiṁ patīnāṁ paramaṁ parastād
vidāma devaṁ bhuvaneśhamīḍyam (6.7)

'The Supreme Lord is the Controller of all controllers; He is the God of all gods. He is the Beloved of all beloveds; He is the Ruler of the world and beyond the material energy.'

बुद्धिर्ज्ञानमसम्मोहः क्षमा सत्यं दमः शमः ।
सुखं दुःखं भवोऽभावो भयं चाभयमेव च ।।4।।

अहिंसा समता तुष्टिस्तपो दानं यशोऽयशः ।
भवन्ति भावा भूतानां मत्त एव पृथग्विधाः ।।5।।

buddhir jñānam asammohaḥ kṣhamā satyaṁ damaḥ śhamaḥ
sukhaṁ duḥkhaṁ bhavo 'bhāvo bhayaṁ chābhayameva cha

ahinsā samatā tuṣhṭis tapo dānaṁ yaśho 'yaśhaḥ
bhavanti bhāvā bhūtānāṁ matta eva pṛithag-vidhāḥ

buddhiḥ—intellect; *jñānam*—knowledge; *asammohaḥ*—clarity of thought; *kṣhamā*—forgiveness; *satyam*—truthfulness; *damaḥ*—control over the senses; *śhamaḥ*—control of the mind; *sukham*—joy; *duḥkham*—sorrow; *bhavaḥ*—birth; *abhāvaḥ*—death; *bhayam*—fear; *cha*—and; *abhayam*—courage; *eva*—certainly; *cha*—and; *ahinsā*—nonviolence; *samatā*—equanimity; *tuṣhṭiḥ*—contentment; *tapaḥ*—austerity; *dānam*—charity; *yaśhaḥ*—fame; *ayaśhaḥ*—infamy; *bhavanti*—arise; *bhāvāḥ*—qualities; *bhūtānām*—amongst humans; *mattaḥ*—from me; *eva*—alone; *pṛithak-vidhāḥ*—varieties of.

From Me alone arise the varieties of qualities in humans, such as intellect, knowledge, clarity of thought, forgiveness, truthfulness, control over the senses and mind, joy and sorrow, birth and death, fear and courage, non-violence, equanimity, contentment, austerity, charity, fame, and infamy.

In these two verses, Lord Krishna continues to confirm His Supreme Lordship and absolute dominion over all that exists in creation. Here, He mentions twenty emotions that manifest in various of degrees and combinations in different people to form the individual fabric of human nature. He declares that all the varities of moods, temperaments, and dispositions of humankind emanate from Him.

Buddhi is the ability to analyse things in their proper perspective.

Jnana is the ability to discriminate spiritual from material.

Asammoham is the absence of confusion.

Kṣhamā is the ability to forgive those who have harmed us.

Satya is the veracity to declare the truth for the benefit of all.

Dam means restraining the senses from sense objects.

Śham is restraint and control of the mind.

Sukh is the emotion of joy and delight.

Duḥkh is the emotion of sorrow and affliction.

Bhavaḥ is the perception of one's existence, 'I am'.

Abhāvaḥ is the experience of death.

Bhaya is the fear of oncoming difficulties.

Abhaya is freedom from fear.

Ahimsa is abstinence from harming any being through thought, word, or deed.

Samatā is equanimity in good and bad situations.

Tuṣhṭi is feeling content in whatever comes by one's karma.

Tapa is voluntary austerities for spiritual benefit, in accordance with the Vedas.

Dān is giving in charity to one who is worthy.

Yaśh is fame arising from possessing good qualities.

Ayaśh is infamy for possessing bad qualities.

Shree Krishna states that all these qualities manifest in individuals to the extent sanctioned by Him alone. Hence, He is the source of all good and bad natures in living beings. This can be likened to the electric power supplied by the powerhouse. The same electric power passing through different gadgets creates different effects. It creates sound in one, light in the other, and heat in the third. Although the manifestations are different, their source is the same electric supply from the powerhouse. Similarly, the energy of God manifests in us positively or negatively according to our *purushārth* (the actions we perform by exercising our freedom of choice) in the present and past lives.

महर्षयः सप्त पूर्वे चत्वारो मनवस्तथा ।
मद्भावा मानसा जाता येषां लोक इमाः प्रजाः ।।6।।

maharṣhayaḥ sapta pūrve chatvāro manavas tathā
mad-bhāvā mānasā jātā yeṣhāṁ loka imāḥ prajāḥ

mahā-ṛiṣhayaḥ—the great Sages; *sapta*—seven; *pūrve*—before; *chatvāraḥ*—four; *manavaḥ*—*manus*; *tathā*—also; *mat bhāvāḥ*—are born from me; *mānasāḥ*—mind; *jātāḥ*—born; *yeṣhām*—from them; *loke*—in the world; *imāḥ*—all these; *prajāḥ*—people.

The seven great Sages, the four great Saints before them, and the fourteen *manus*, are all born from My mind. From them, all the people in the world have descended.

Here, Shree Krishna continues to explain that He is the source of everything that exists. Previously, He mentioned twenty emotions; now, He mentions twenty-five elevated personalities. These are the four great Kumars, the seven great Sages, and the fourteen *manus*. He also gives a genealogical synopsis of the universe that is born of Him.

Brahma was born from the *Hiraṇyagarbh* energy of Vishnu (the form of God that is responsible for administering material creation). From Brahma were born the four great Saints, who are Sanak, Sanandan, Sanat, and Sanatan. They are also called the four Kumars. In our universe, the four Kumars are the eldest children of Brahma. Since theirs was an asexual birth from the mind of their father alone, they have no mother. Being eternally liberated souls and experts in the science of Yog, they were empowered to help others attain liberation through spiritual sadhana. After the four Kumars, came the seven Sages. They are Mareech, Angira, Atri, Pulastya, Pulaha, Kratu, and Vasishtha. They were empowered with the task of procreation of the human population. Then come the fourteen *manus*—Svayambhuva,

Swarochisha, Uttam, Tamas, Raivat, Chakshusha, Vaivasvat, Savarni, Dakshasavarni, Brahmasavarni, Dharmasavarni, Rudra-putra, Rochya, and Bhautyaka. They were empowered with the administration of humankind from the celestial abodes, and to establish and protect Vedic dharma. We are presently in the era of the seventh *manu* who is called Vaivasvat Manu. This era is thus called Vaivasvat Manvantar. In the present kalp (day of Brahma), there will be seven more *manus.*

In the celestial abodes, there are many *devatās* who oversee the maintenance of the universe. All these personalities are sons and grandsons of Brahma, who was born from Lord Vishnu, who, in turn, is a non-different expansion of Shree Krishna. Therefore, we can say that Shree Krishna is the original Forefather of all forefathers (*prapitāmaha*).

एतां विभूतिं योगं च मम यो वेत्ति तत्त्वतः ।
सोऽविकम्पेन योगेन युज्यते नात्र संशयः ।।7।।

etāṁ vibhūtiṁ yogaṁ cha mama yo vetti tattvataḥ
so 'vikampena yogena yujyate nātra sanśhayaḥ

etām—these; *vibhūtim*—glories; *yogam*—divine powers; *cha*—and; *mama*—my; *yaḥ*—those who; *vetti*—know; *tattvataḥ*—in truth; *saḥ*—they; *avikalpena*—unwavering; *yogena*—in bhakti yog; *yujyate*—becomes united; *na*—never; *atra*—here; *sanśhayaḥ*—doubt.

Those who know in truth My glories and divine powers become united with Me through unwavering bhakti yog. Of this there is no doubt.

The word *vibhūti* refers to the great shaktis (powers) of God that manifest in the universe. The word *yogam* refers to God's connection with these resplendent powers. In this verse, Shree Krishna explains that when we become aware of the magnificence of the Supreme Lord and become convinced about His glory, we naturally become inclined to engage in His devotion.

Knowledge of the greatness of God nourishes the love of the devotees and enhances their devotion. There is a direct relationship between knowledge and love as the following example reveals. Let us say that your friend shows you a black pebble-like stone. You have no knowledge of its importance, and thus, you have no love for it either. Your friend says, 'This is a *śhāligrām*, and a saintly personality gifted it to me.' A *śhāligrām* is a special kind of fossil stone worshipped as a representation of Lord Vishnu. If you are aware of the significance of *śhāligrāms*, when you receive this knowledge that the stone is a *śhāligrām*, your appreciation for it will increase. Let us say your friend further adds, 'Do you know it used to be worshipped five hundred years ago by the great saint, Swami Ramananda?' The moment you hear this piece of knowledge, your respect for the stone will grow. Each time, it is the knowledge that is boosting your reverence for the stone. Similarly, proper knowledge of God enhances our devotion towards Him. Thus, having described God's majestic splendours that manifest in the wondrous workings of unlimited universes, Shree Krishna states that those who become situated in this knowledge naturally become united with Him through unflinching bhakti.

अहं सर्वस्य प्रभवो मत्तः सर्वं प्रवर्तते ।
इति मत्वा भजन्ते मां बुधा भावसमन्विताः ।।8।।

ahaṁ sarvasya prabhavo mattaḥ sarvaṁ pravartate
iti matvā bhajante māṁ budhā bhāva-samanvitāḥ

aham—I; *sarvasya*—of all creation; *prabhavaḥ*—the origin of; *mattaḥ*—from me; *sarvam*—everything; *pravartate*—proceeds; *iti*—thus; *matvā*—having known; *bhajante*—worship; *mām*—me; *budhāḥ*—the wise; *bhāva-samanvitāḥ*—endowed with great faith and devotion.

I am the origin of all creation. Everything proceeds from Me. The wise who know this perfectly worship Me with great faith and devotion.

Shree Krishna begins the verse by saying *ahaṁ sarvasya prabhavo*, meaning, 'I am the Supreme Ultimate Truth and the Cause of all causes'. He has repeated this multiple times in the Bhagavad Gita in verses 7.7, 7.12, 10.2-3, and 15.15. It is also strongly proclaimed in all the other scriptures. The *Rig Veda* states:

> *yaṁ kāmaye taṁ taṁ ugraṁ kṛiṣhṇomi taṁ brahmāṇaṁ taṁ ṛiṣhiṁ taṁ sumedhsam* (10.125.5)

'I make the persons I love exceedingly mighty; I make them men or women; I make them wise sages; I make a soul empowered for the seat of Brahma.' The wise who comprehend this truth develop firm faith and worship Him with loving devotion.

Thus, Shree Krishna is the Supreme Lord of both the material and spiritual creations. However, governing creation is not the primary work of God. Chaitanya Mahaprabhu states:

> *swayaṁ bhagavānera karma nahe bhāra-haraṇa*
>
> (*Chaitanya Charitāmṛit*, *Ādi Leela* 4.8)

'Shree Krishna does not directly involve Himself in the tasks of creating, maintaining, and dissolving the material universes.' Shree Krishna's primary activity is to engage in eternal loving pastimes with liberated souls in *Golok*, His divine abode. For the purpose of material creation, He expands Himself as Karanodakshayi Vishnu, who is also called Maha Vishnu.

Maha Vishnu is thus the form of the Lord that presides over the material realm, consisting of infinite material universes. Maha Vishnu is also known as *Pratham Purush* (first expansion of God in the material realm). He resides in the divine waters of the *kāraṇ* (causal) ocean and manifests innumerable material universes from the pores of His body. He then expands Himself to reside at the bottom of each universe as Garbhodakshayi Vishnu, who is called *Dwitīya Purush* (second expansion of God in the material realm).

From Garbhodakshayi Vishnu, Brahma is born. He guides the process of creation—creating the various gross and subtle elements of the universe, the laws of nature, the galaxies and planetary systems, the forms of life residing in them, and so on. Consequently, Brahma is often referred to as the creator of the universe. However, he is actually the secondary creator.

Garbhodakashayi Vishnu further expands Himself as Kshirodakshayi Vishnu, and resides at the top of each universe, in a place called *Kṣhīra Sāgar*. Kshirodakshayi Vishnu is also known as *Tṛitīya Purush* (third expansion of God in the material realm). He resides at the top of the universe, but He also resides as the Supreme Soul, in the heart of all living beings in the universe, noting their karmas, keeping an account, and giving the results at the appropriate time. He is thus known as the Maintainer of the universe.

All the three forms of Lord Vishnu mentioned here are non-different from Shree Krishna. Thus, in this verse, Shree Krishna states that all spiritual and material creation emanate from Him. Shree Krishna is also called the *Avatārī* (the source of all the Avatars). The Shreemad Bhagavatam states: *ete chāṁśha kalāḥ puṁsaḥ kṛiṣhṇas tu bhagavān svayam* (1.3.28) 'All the forms of God are the expansions, or the expansions of the expansions of Shree Krishna, who is the primordial form of God.' And so, the secondary creator Brahma prays to Shree Krishna:

yasyaikaniśhvasita kālamathāvalambya
jīvanti lomavilajā jagadaṇḍanāthāḥ
viṣhṇurmahān sa ihayasya kalāviśheṣho
govindamādi puruṣhaṁ tamahaṁ bhajāmi

(*Brahma Samhitā* 5.48)

'Infinite universes—each having Shankar, Brahma, and Vishnu—manifest from the pores of Maha Vishnu's body when He breathes in, and again dissolve into Him when He breathes out. I worship Shree Krishna of whom Maha Vishnu is an expansion.' *Shree Krishna now goes on to explain how devotees worship Him.*

मच्चित्ता मद्गतप्राणा बोधयन्तः परस्परम् ।
कथयन्तश्च मां नित्यं तुष्यन्ति च रमन्ति च ।।9।।

mach-chittā mad-gata-prāṇā bodhayantaḥ parasparam
kathayantaśh cha māṁ nityaṁ tuṣhyanti cha ramanti cha

mat-chittāḥ—those with minds fixed on me; *mat-gata-prāṇāḥ*—those who have surrendered their lives to me; *bodhayantaḥ*—enlightening (with divine knowledge of God); *parasparam*—one another; *kathayantaḥ*—speaking; *cha*—and; *mām*—about me; *nityam*—continously; *tuṣhyanti*—satisfaction; *cha*—and; *ramanti*—(they) delight; *cha*—also.

With their minds fixed on Me and their lives surrendered to Me, My devotees remain ever content in Me. They derive great satisfaction and bliss in enlightening one another about Me and in conversing about My glories.

The nature of the mind is to become absorbed in what it likes most. Devotees of the Lord become absorbed in remembering Him because they develop deep adoration for Him. His devotion becomes the basis of their life, from which they derive meaning, purpose, and the strength to live. They feel it as essential to remember God as a fish feels the need to be surrounded by water.

What is most dear to people's hearts can be determined by where they dedicate their mind, body, and wealth. The Bible states: 'For where your treasure is, there your heart will also be.' (Matthew 6:21). You can see where people's hearts are by studying their checkbooks and credit card statements. If they are spending money on fancy cars, that's where their heart is. If they are spending on luxurious holidays, that's what is most dear to them. If they are donating in charity to African children with AIDS, that is what absorbs their attention the most. The love of parents for their children is visible in the fact that they are willing to sacrifice their time and wealth for their welfare. Likewise, the love of the devotees manifests in the dedication of their every word, thought, and deed to God. Shree Krishna says: *mad-gata-prāṇāḥ*, implying, 'My devotees surrender their lives to Me.'

From such surrender, comes contentment. Since devotees offer the results of their activities to their beloved Lord, they see every situation as coming from Him. Hence, they gladly accept both positive and negative circumstances as the will of God and remain equipoised in both.

While the devotees' love for God is displayed in the above sentiments, it also manifests on their lips. They find great relish in conversing about the glories of God, and His Names, Forms, Virtues, Pastimes, Abodes, and Devotees. In this way, by engaging in kirtan (chanting) and *shravaṇa* (hearing) about the glories of God, they savor His sweetness for themselves and share it with others as well. They contribute to one another's progress by enlightening others about divine knowledge of God (*bodhayanti*). Speaking and singing about the glories of God gives the devotees great satisfaction (*tuṣhyanti*) and delight (*ramanti*). In this way, they worship Him through the processes of remembering, hearing, and chanting. This is the threefold bhakti comprising of *shravaṇa*, kirtan, and *smaraṇa*. This has previously been described in the commentary on verse 9.14.

Having described how His devotees worship Him, Shree Krishna now explains His response to their devotional activities.

तेषां सततयुक्तानां भजतां प्रीतिपूर्वकम् ।
ददामि बुद्धियोगं तं येन मामुपयान्ति ते ।।10।।

teṣhāṁ satata-yuktānāṁ bhajatāṁ prīti-pūrvakam
dadāmi buddhi-yogaṁ taṁ yena mām upayānti te

teṣhām—to them; *satata-yuktānām*—ever steadfast; *bhajatām*—who engage in devotion; *prīti-pūrvakam*—with love; *dadāmi*—I give; *buddhi-yogam*—divine knowledge; *tam*—that; *yena*—by which; *mām*—to me; *upayānti*—come; *te*—they.

To those whose minds are always united with Me in loving devotion, I give the divine knowledge by which they can attain Me.

Divine knowledge of God is not attained by the flight of our intellect. No matter how powerful a mental machine we may possess, we have to admit the fact that our intellect is made from maya. Hence, our thoughts, understanding, and wisdom are confined to the material realm; God and His divine realm remain entirely beyond the scope of our corporeal intellect. The Vedas emphatically declare:

yasyā mataṁ tasya mataṁ mataṁ yasya na veda saḥ
avijñātaṁ vijānatāṁ vijñātamavijānatām (*Kenopaniṣhad* 2.3)

'Those who think they can understand God with their intellects have no understanding of God. Only those who think that He is beyond the scope of their comprehension truly understand Him.'

The *Bṛihadāraṇyak Upanishad* states:

sa eṣha neti netyātmā gṛihyoḥ (3.9.26)

'One can never comprehend God by self-effort based upon the intellect.' The Ramayan states:

rāma atarkya buddhi mana bānī, mata hamāra asa sunahi sayānī

'Lord Ram is beyond the scope of our intellect, mind, and words.'

Now, if these statements on the topic of God clearly declare that it is not possible to know Him, how then can God-realisation be possible for anyone? Shree Krishna reveals here how knowledge of God can be gained. He says that it is God who bestows divine knowledge upon the soul, and the fortunate soul who receives His grace is able to know Him. The *Yajur Veda* states: *tasya no rāsva tasya no dhehi* 'Without bathing oneself in the nectar emanating from the lotus feet of God, no one can know Him.' Thus, true knowledge of God is not a result of intellectual gymnastics but a consequence of divine grace. Shree Krishna also mentions in this verse that He does not choose the recipients of His grace in a whimsical manner. Rather, he bestows it on those who unite their minds with Him in devotion. *Next, He talks about the consequences of receiving divine grace.*

तेषामेवानुकम्पार्थमहमज्ञानजं तमः ।
नाशयाम्यात्मभावस्थो ज्ञानदीपेन भास्वता ।।11।।

teṣhām evānukampārtham aham ajñāna-jaṁ tamaḥ
nāśhayāmyātma-bhāva-stho jñāna-dīpena bhāsvatā

teṣhām—for them; *eva*—only; *anukampā-artham*—out of compassion; *aham*—I; *ajñāna-jam*—born of ignorance; *tamaḥ*—darkness; *nāśhayāmi*—destroy; *ātma-bhāva*—within their hearts; *sthaḥ*—dwelling; *jñāna*—of knowledge; *dīpena*—with the lamp; *bhāsvatā*—luminous.

Out of compassion for them, I, who dwell within their hearts, destroy the darkness born of ignorance, with the luminous lamp of knowledge.

In this verse, Shree Krishna further elaborates the concept of grace. Previously, He had explained that He bestows it on those who lovingly absorb their minds in Him and make Him the paramount object of their plans, thoughts, and activities. Now, He reveals what happens when someone receives His grace. He says that He destroys the darkness in their heart with the lamp of wisdom.

Ignorance is often symbolised as darkness, but what is this lamp of wisdom that God is talking about? At present, our senses, mind, and intellect are all material, while God is divine. Hence, we are unable to see Him, hear Him, know Him, or be united with Him. When God bestows His grace, He confers His divine *Yogmaya* energy upon the soul. It is also called *śhuddha sattva* (divine mode of goodness), which is distinct from the sattva guna (mode of goodness) of maya. When we receive that *śhuddha sattva* energy, our senses, mind, and intellect become divine. To put it simply, by His grace, God bestows His divine senses, divine mind, and divine intellect to the soul. Equipped with these divine instruments, the soul is able to see God, hear God, know God, and be united with God. Hence, the *Vedant Darshan* states: *viśheṣhānugrahaśh cha* (3.4.38), 'Only by God's grace does one gain divine knowledge.' In this way, the torchlight that Shree Krishna refers to is His divine power. By the light of God's divine power, the darkness of the material energy is dispelled.

अर्जुन उवाच ।
परं ब्रह्म परं धाम पवित्रं परमं भवान् ।
पुरुषं शाश्वतं दिव्यमादिदेवमजं विभुम् ।।12।।

आहुस्त्वामृषयः सर्वे देवर्षिर्नारदस्तथा ।
असितो देवलो व्यासः स्वयं चैव ब्रवीषि मे ॥13॥

arjuna uvācha
paraṁ brahma paraṁ dhāma pavitraṁ paramaṁ bhavān
puruṣhaṁ śhāśhvataṁ divyam ādi-devam ajaṁ vibhum

āhus tvām ṛiṣhayaḥ sarve devarṣhir nāradas tathā
asito devalo vyāsaḥ svayaṁ chaiva bravīṣhi me

arjunaḥ uvācha—Arjun said; *param*—Supreme; *brahma*—Brahman; *param*—supreme; *dhāma*—abode; *pavitram*—purifier; *paramam*—supreme; *bhavān*—you; *puruṣham*—personality; *śhāśhvatam*—eternal; *divyam*—divine; *ādi-devam*—the primal being; *ajam*—the unborn; *vibhum*—the great; *āhuḥ*—(they) declare; *tvām*—you; *ṛiṣhayaḥ*—sages; *sarve*—all; *deva-ṛiṣhiḥ-nāradaḥ*—*devarṣhi* Narad; *tathā*—also; *asitaḥ*—Asit; *devalaḥ*—Deval; *vyāsaḥ*—Vyās; *svayam*—personally; *cha*—and; *eva*—even; *bravīṣhī*—you are declaring; *me*—to me.

Arjun said: You are the Supreme Divine Personality, the Supreme Abode, the Supreme Purifier, the Eternal God, the Primal Being, the Unborn, and the Greatest. The great sages, like Narad, Asit, Deval, and Vyas proclaimed this, and now You are declaring it to me Yourself.

Commentators on the Vedic scriptures are sometimes fond of saying that Shree Krishna and Shree Ram are not the Supreme Entity. They claim that the Ultimate Reality is formless and without attributes; it takes on forms and manifests as Avatars, and thus these Avatars are a step removed from God. However, Arjun refutes such viewpoints by declaring that Shree Krishna in His personal form is the Supreme Cause of all causes.

Upon hearing the previous four verses, Arjun is totally convinced about the Supreme position of Shree Krishna and emphatically vents the deep conviction that he now feels within himself. When great authorities testify knowledge, its credibility gets established. Great saints are the authorities for spiritual knowledge. Thus, Arjun quotes the saints, such as Narad, Asit, Deval, and Vyas, who have proclaimed Shree Krishna as the Supreme Divine Personality and the Cause of all causes. In the *Bheeshma Parva* of the Mahabharat, there is a poem in which many sages eulogise Shree Krishna.

Sage Narad says: 'Shree Krishna is the Creator of all the worlds and the Knower of all feelings. He is the Lord of the celestial gods, who administer the universe.' (verse 68.2)

Sage Markandeya states: 'Lord Krishna is the goal of all religious sacrifices and the essence of austerities. He is the present, past, and future of everything.' (verse 68.3)

Sage Bhrigu says: 'He is the God of gods and the first original form of Lord Vishnu.' (verse 68.4)

Sage Ved Vyas states: 'O Lord Krishna, You are the Lord of the Vasus. You have conferred power on Indra and the other celestial gods.' (verse 68.5)

Sage Angira says: 'Lord Krishna is the Creator of all beings. All the three worlds exist in His stomach. He is the Supreme Personality of Godhead.' (verse 68.6)

Elsewhere in the Mahabharat, Sages Asit and Deval declare: 'Shree Krishna is the Creator of Brahma, who is the creator of the three worlds.' (Mahabharat *Vana Parva* 12.50)

Quoting these great authorities, Arjun says that now Shree Krishna is Himself reconfirming their statements by declaring that He is the Supreme Cause of all creation.

सर्वमेतदृतं मन्ये यन्मां वदसि केशव ।
न हि ते भगवन्व्यक्तिं विदुर्देवा न दानवाः ।।14।।

sarvam etad ṛitaṁ manye yan māṁ vadasi keśhava
na hi te bhagavan vyaktiṁ vidur devā na dānavāḥ

sarvam—everything; *etat*—this; *ṛitam*—truth; *manye*—I accept; *yat*—which; *mām*—me; *vadasi*—you tell; *keśhava*—Shree Krishna, killer of the demon named Keshi; *na*—neither; *hi*—verily; *te*—your; *bhagavan*—the Supreme Lord; *vyaktim*—personality; *viduḥ*—can understand; *devāḥ*—celestial gods; *na*—nor; *dānavāḥ*—demons.

O Krishna, I totally accept everything You have told me as the truth. O Lord, neither gods nor the demons can understand Your true personality.

Listening attentively to Shree Krishna's divine opulence and unlimited supremacy in brief, Arjun's thirst for hearing more has increased. Wanting Shree Krishna to further describe His glories, he wishes to assure the Lord that he is fully convinced. By using the word *yat*, Arjun means that whatever Shree Krishna has said to him from the seventh to the ninth chapters, he holds as true. He asserts that all Shree Krishna has stated is factual and not any metaphorical description. He addresses Shree Krishna as Bhagavan or the Supreme Lord. The word Bhagavan is defined in the *Devi Bhagavat Puran* in the following manner:

aiśhwaryasya samagrasya dharmasya yaśhasaḥ śhriyaḥ
jñānavairāgyośhchaiva ṣaṇṇāṁ bhagavānniḥ

'Bhagavan is He who possesses these six opulences to the infinite extent—strength, knowledge, beauty, fame, wealth, and renunciation.' The *devatās* (celestial gods), *dānavas* (demons), *mānavas* (human beings) all have finite abilities to understand. They cannot fully comprehend the personality of Bhagavan.

स्वयमेवात्मनात्मानं वेत्थ त्वं पुरुषोत्तम ।
भूतभावन भूतेश देवदेव जगत्पते ।।15।।

swayam evātmanātmānaṁ vettha tvaṁ puruṣhottama
bhūta-bhāvana bhūteśha deva-deva jagat-pate

swayam—yourself; *eva*—indeed; *ātmanā*—by yourself; *ātmānam*—yourself; *vettha*—know; *tvam*—you; *puruṣha-uttama*—Supreme Personality; *bhūta-bhāvana*—Creator of all beings; *bhūta-īśha*—Lord of everything; *deva-deva*—God of gods; *jagat-pate*—Lord of the universe.

Indeed, You alone know Yourself by Your inconceivable energy, O Supreme Personality, the Creator and Lord of all beings, the God of gods, and the Lord of the universe!

Emphasising that Shree Krishna is the Supreme Divine Personality, Arjun refers to Him as:

Bhūta-bhāvana: the Creator of all beings, the Universal Father.

Bhūteśh: the Supreme Controller, the Lord of all beings.

Jagat-pate: the Lord and Master of creation.

Deva-deva: the God of all celestial gods.

The *Śhwetāśhvatar Upanishad* declares the same fact:

yasmāt paraṁ nāparamasti kiñchid (3.9)

'God can never be surpassed; He is beyond everything.'

The previous verse stated that God cannot be known by anyone. This is clearly logical. All souls possess finite intellects while God is infinite, and hence, He is beyond the reach of their intellects. This does not belittle Him; rather, it exalts Him. The Western philosopher F.A. Jacobi stated: 'God whom we could know would be no God.' However, in this verse, Arjun states that there is after all one personality who knows God and that is God Himself. Thus, Shree Krishna alone knows Himself, and if He decides to grant His powers upon a soul, then that fortunate soul comes to know Him as well.

वक्तुमर्हस्यशेषेण दिव्या ह्यात्मविभूतयः ।
याभिर्विभूतिभिर्लोकानिमांस्त्वं व्याप्य तिष्ठसि ।।16।।

कथं विद्यामहं योगिंस्त्वां सदा परिचिन्तयन् ।
केषु केषु च भावेषु चिन्त्योऽसि भगवन्मया ।।17।।

vaktum arhasyaśheṣheṇa divyā hyātma-vibhūtayaḥ
yābhir vibhūtibhir lokān imāṁs tvaṁ vyāpya tiṣhṭhasi

kathaṁ vidyām ahaṁ yogins tvāṁ sadā parichintayan
keṣhu keṣhu cha bhāveṣhu chintyo 'si bhagavan mayā

vaktum—to describe; *arhasi*—please do; *aśheṣheṇa*—completely; *divyāḥ*—divine; *hi*—indeed; *ātma*—your own; *vibhūtayaḥ*—opulences; *yābhiḥ*—by which; *vibhūtibhiḥ*—opulences; *lokān*—all worlds; *imān*—these; *tvam*—you; *vyāpya*—pervade; *tiṣhṭhasi*—reside; *katham*—how; *vidyām aham*—shall I know; *yogin*—Supreme Master of *Yogmaya*; *tvām*—you; *sadā*—always; *parichintayan*—meditating; *keṣhu*—in what; *keṣhu*—in what; *cha*—and; *bhāveṣhu*—forms; *chintyaḥ asi*—to be thought of; *bhagavan*—Supreme Divine Personality; *mayā*—by me.

Please describe to me Your divine opulences, by which You pervade all the worlds and reside in them. O Supreme Master of Yog, how may I know You and think of You? And while meditating, in what forms can I think of You, O Supreme Divine Personality?

Here, 'Yog' refers to *Yogmaya* (God's divine power), and 'yogi' refers to the Master of *Yogmaya*. Arjun has understood that Shree Krishna is Bhagavan. He now wishes to know in what other ways, yet untold, is Shree Krishna's *vibhūti* (transcendental majestic opulence) displayed throughout creation. He wishes to hear about Shree Krishna's eminence and paramount position as the Supreme Controller of all creation. Thus, he implores, 'I am inquisitive to know of Your divine manifestations so that I may be endowed with unfaltering devotion. But the revelation of Your personality is impossible to receive without Your grace. So please be merciful and reveal Your many glories by which I may perceive You.'

विस्तरेणात्मनो योगं विभूतिं च जनार्दन ।
भूयः कथय तृप्तिर्हि शृण्वतो नास्ति मेऽमृतम् ।।18।।

vistareṇātmano yogaṁ vibhūtiṁ cha janārdana
bhūyaḥ kathaya tṛiptir hi śhṛiṇvato nāsti me 'mṛitam

vistareṇa—in detail; *ātmanaḥ*—your; *yogam*—divine glories; *vibhūtim*—opulences; *cha*—also; *janaārdana*—Shree Krishna, He who looks after the public; *bhūyaḥ*—again; *kathaya*—describe; *tṛiptiḥ*—satisfaction; *hi*—because; *śhṛiṇvataḥ*—hearing; *na*—not; *asti*—is; *me*—my; *amṛitam*—nectar.

Tell me again in detail Your divine glories and manifestations, O Janardan. I can never tire of hearing Your nectar.

Arjun says, '... hearing Your nectar,' instead of '... hearing Your words that are like nectar.' He has omitted 'Your words that are like.' This is a literary technique called *atiśhayokti* or hyperbole (statement of extreme expression), in which the subject of comparison is omitted. He also addresses Shree Krishna as Janardan which means 'a benevolent person from whom distressed people ask for relief'.

Descriptions of God's glories are like nectar for those who love Him. He has been drinking Shree Krishna's ambrosial nectar-like words with his ears, and he now cheers Him, by saying *bhūyaḥ kathaya*, 'Once more! My thirst for hearing Your glories is not satiated.' This is the nature of divine nectar. It satiates us while simultaneously increasing the thirst for more. The sages of Naimisharanya made a similar statement while hearing the Shreemad Bhagavatam from Suta Goswami:

vayaṁ tu na vitṛipyāma uttamaśhlokavikrame
yachchhṛiṇvatāṁ rasajñānāṁ svādu svādu pade pade (1.1.19)

'Those who are devoted to Lord Krishna never tire of hearing descriptions of His divine pastimes. The nectar of these pastimes is such that the more it is relished, the more it increases.'

श्रीभगवानुवाच ।
हन्त ते कथयिष्यामि दिव्या ह्यात्मविभूतयः ।
प्राधान्यतः कुरुश्रेष्ठ नास्त्यन्तो विस्तरस्य मे ।।19।।

śhrī bhagavān uvācha
hanta te kathayiṣhyāmi divyā hyātma-vibhūtayaḥ
prādhānyataḥ kuru-śhreṣhṭha nāstyanto vistarasya me

śhrī-bhagavān uvācha—the Lord spoke; *hanta*—yes; *te*—to you; *kathayiṣhyāmi*—I shall describe; *divyāḥ*—divine; *hi*—certainly; *ātma-vibhūtayaḥ*—my divine glories; *prādhānyataḥ*—salient; *kuru-śhreṣhṭha*—best of the Kurus; *na*—not; *asti*—is; *antaḥ*—limit; *vistarasya*—extensive glories; *me*—my.

The Lord spoke: I shall now briefly describe My divine glories to you, O best of the Kurus, for there is no end to their detail.

The *Amar Kosh* (ancient Sanskrit dictionary that is widely respected) defines *vibhūti* as *vibhūtir bhūtir aiśhwaryam* (power and wealth). God's powers and wealth are unlimited. Actually, everything about Him is unlimited. He has unlimited Forms, unlimited Names, unlimited Abodes, unlimited Descensions, unlimited Pastimes, unlimited Devotees, and so on. Hence, the Vedas refer to Him by the name *anant* (unlimited):

anantaśhchātmā viśhwarūpo hyakartā

(*Śhwetāśhvatar Upanishad* 1.9)

'God is infinite and manifests in innumerable forms in the universe. Although He administers the universe, yet, He is the non-doer.' The Ramayan states:

hari ananta hari kathā anantā

'God is unlimited, and the pastimes He enacts in His unlimited Avatars are also unlimited.' Sage Ved Vyas goes to the extent of saying:

yo vā anantasya guṇānanantān
anukramiṣhyan sa tu bāla-buddhiḥ
rajānsi bhūmer gaṇayet kathañchit
kālena naivākhilaśhakti dhāmnaḥ (Bhagavatam 11.4.2)

'Those who think they can count the glories of God have a childish intellect. We may be successful in counting the specks of dust on the crest of the earth, but we can never count the unlimited glories of God.' Therefore, Shree Krishna says here that He will only be describing a small fraction of His *vibhūtis*.

अहमात्मा गुडाकेश सर्वभूताशयस्थितः ।
अहमादिश्च मध्यं च भूतानामन्त एव च ।।20।।

aham ātmā guḍākeśha sarva-bhūtāśhaya-sthitaḥ
aham ādiśh cha madhyaṁ cha bhūtānām anta eva cha

aham—I; *ātmā*—soul; *guḍākeśha*—Arjun, conqueror of sleep; *sarva-bhūta*—of all living entities; *āśhaya-sthitaḥ*—seated in the heart; *aham*—I; *ādiḥ*—the beginning; *cha*—and; *madhyam*—middle; *cha*—and; *bhūtānām*—of all beings; *antaḥ*—end; *eva*—even; *cha*—also.

O Arjun, I am seated in the heart of all living entities. I am the beginning, middle, and end of all beings.

Shree Krishna declares that He is not far from the soul, in fact, He is closer than the closest. The atma or eternal soul is enthroned in the etheric heart of all living beings. The Vedas state: *ya ātmani tiṣhṭhati* 'God is seated within our soul.' Seated inside, He grants the power of consciousness and eternality to the soul. If He were to withdraw His powers, our soul itself would become insentient and perish. We souls are thus eternal and sentient, not by our own power, but because the supremely sentient and eternal God is seated within and is granting us His powers. Hence, Shree Krishna declares that He is situated in the heart of all living beings.

Our soul is the body of God, who is the Soul of our soul. The Bhagavatam states:

harirhi sākṣhādbhagavān śharīriṇā-
mātmā jhaṣhāṇāmiva toyamīpsitam (5.18.13)

'God is the Atma of the atma (Soul of the soul) of all living beings.' Again, in the Bhagavatam, when Shukadev described how the *gopis* used to leave their own children to go and see baby Shree Krishna, Parikshit asked him how this was possible:

brahman parodbhave kṛiṣhṇe iyān premā kathaṁ bhavet

(10.14.49)

'O Brahmin, all mothers are attached to their own children. How did the *gopis* develop such intense attachment to Shree Krishna that they did not even feel towards their own child?' Shukadev replied:

kṛiṣhṇamenamavehi tvamātmānamakhilātmanām

(Bhagavatam 10.14.55)

'Please understand that Lord Krishna is the Supreme Soul of all living beings in the universe. For the benefit of humankind, He has appeared in a human form by His *Yogmaya* power.'

Shree Krishna further states that He is the beginning, middle, and end of all living beings. They have emanated from Him, and so He is their beginning. All life that exists in creation is sustained by His energy, thus, He is the middle. And those who attain liberation go to His divine abode to live eternally with Him. Hence, God is also the end of all living beings. Among the various definitions of God given by the Vedas, one of them is:

yato vā imāni bhūtāni jāyante, yena jātāni jīvanti,
yatprayantyabhisaṁviśhanti (*Taittirīya Upanishad* 3.1.1)

'God is He from whom all living beings have emanated; God is He within whom all living beings are situated; God is He into whom all living beings shall unite.'

आदित्यानामहं विष्णुर्ज्योतिषां रविरंशुमान् ।
मरीचिर्मरुतामस्मि नक्षत्राणामहं शशी ।।21।।

ādityānām ahaṁ viṣhṇur jyotiṣhāṁ ravir anśhumān
marīchir marutām asmi nakṣhatrāṇām ahaṁ śhaśhī

ādityānām—amongst the twelve sons of Aditi; *aham*—I; *viṣhṇuḥ*—Lord Vishnu; *jyotiṣhām*—amongst luminous objects; *raviḥ*—the sun; *anśhu-mān*—radiant; *marīchiḥ*—Marichi; *marutām*—of the *maruts*; *asmi*—(I) am; *nakṣhatrāṇām*—amongst the stars; *aham*—I; *śhaśhī*—the moon.

Among the twelve sons of Aditi, I am Vishnu; among luminous objects, I am the sun. Know Me to be Marichi among the *maruts*, and the moon among the stars in the night sky.

From the Puranas we learn that Sage Kashyap had two wives—Aditi and Diti. From his first wife, Aditi, he fathered twelve celestial personalities—Dhata, Mitra, Aryama, Shakra, Varun, Amsha, Bhaga, Vivasvan, Pusha, Savita, Twashta, and Vaman. Among these, Vaman was the Avatar of the Supreme Lord Vishnu. Thus, Shree Krishna states that among the Adityas (twelve sons of Aditi), Vishnu (in the form of Vaman) manifests His opulence.

Amongst luminous objects, the sun is supreme. The Ramayan states:

rākāpati ṣhoṛasa uahiṅ tārāgana samudāi,
sakala girinha dava lāia binu rabi rāti na jāi

'At night, all the lamps along with all the stars in the sky and the moon as well are together insufficient in removing the darkness of the night. But the moment the sun rises, the night gets dispelled.' That is the power of the sun, which Shree Krishna reveals as His *vibhūti* (magnificence).

Then, He comes to the night sky. There is the well-known saying, 'One moon is better than a thousand stars.' Shree Krishna says that among all the constellations and stars in the night sky, He is the moon because it best reveals His splendour.

The Puranas further relate that Sage Kashyap fathered *daityas* (demons) from his second wife, Diti. In addition to the *daityas,* Diti desired to have a son more powerful than Indra (the king of the celestial gods). So, she kept the baby in her womb for a year. Upon learning of this, Indra used a thunderbolt to destroy her foetus by splitting it into many pieces, but it turned into many foetuses. These became the *maruts,* or the forty-nine kinds of winds that flow in the universe, doing tremendous good. The major ones among them are Avaha, Pravaha, Nivaha, Purvaha, Udvaha, Samvaha, and Parivaha. The chief wind, Parivaha, also bears the name Marichi. Shree Krishna states that His *vibhūti* manifests in the wind called 'Marichi'.

वेदानां सामवेदोऽस्मि देवानामस्मि वासवः ।
इन्द्रियाणां मनश्चास्मि भूतानामस्मि चेतना ।।22।।

vedānāṁ sāma-vedo 'smi devānām asmi vāsavaḥ
indriyāṇāṁ manaśh chāsmi bhūtānām asmi chetanā

vedānām—amongst the Vedas; *sāma-vedaḥ*—the *Sāma Veda*; *asmi*—I am; *devānām*—of all the celestial gods; *asmi*—I am;

vāsavaḥ—Indra; *indriyāṇām*—amongst the senses; *manaḥ*—the mind; *ca*—and; *asmi*—I am; *bhūtānām*—amongst the living beings; *asmi*—I am; *chetanā*—consciousness.

I am the *Sama Veda* amongst the Vedas, and Indra amongst the celestial gods. Amongst the senses, I am the mind; amongst the living beings, I am consciousness.

There are four Vedas—*Rig Veda*, *Yajur Veda*, *Sama Veda*, and *Atharva Veda*. Among these, the *Sama Veda* describes God's glories as they manifest in the celestial gods, who are in charge of administering the universe. The *Sama Veda* is also the most musical and is sung in praise of the Lord. It is enchanting to those who understand it and it evokes devotion amongst its listeners.

Vasava is another name for Indra, chief of the celestial gods. He is unparalleled among souls in fame, power, and rank. Only a soul with many lifetimes of pious deeds is promoted to the position of Indra. Thus, Indra reflects the resplendent glories of God.

The five senses function correctly only if the mind is attentive to them. The senses cannot function properly when the mind drifts away. For example, you hear with your ears what people say, but if your mind wanders while they are speaking, their words are lost to you. In this manner, the mind is the king of the senses. Shree Krishna speaks of it as reflecting His power, and later in the Bhagavad Gita, He mentions it as the sixth and most important sense (verse 15.7).

Consciousness is the quality of the soul that distinguishes it from insentient matter. The difference between a living person and a dead person is the presence of consciousness in the living person's body and its absence in a dead person's body. Consciousness exists in the soul by the divine power of God. Hence, the Vedas state: *chetanaśhchetanānām* (*Kaṭhopaniṣhad* 2.2.13) 'God is the sentience in the sentient.'

रुद्राणां शङ्करश्चास्मि वित्तेशो यक्षरक्षसाम् ।
वसूनां पावकश्चास्मि मेरुः शिखरिणामहम् ।।23।।

rudrāṇāṁ śhaṅkaraśh chāsmi vitteśho yakṣha-rakṣhasām
vasūnāṁ pāvakaśh chāsmi meruḥ śhikhariṇām aham

rudrāṇām—amongst the *rudras*; *śhaṅkaraḥ*—Lord Shiv; *cha*—and; *asmi*—I am; *vitta-īśhaḥ*—the god of wealth and the treasurer of the celestial gods; *yakṣha*—amongst the semi-celestial beings; *rakṣhasām*—amongst the demons; *vasūnām*—amongst the *vasus*; *pāvakaḥ*—Agni (fire); *cha*—and; *asmi*—I am; *meruḥ*—Mount Meru; *śhikhariṇām*—amongst the mountains; *aham*—I am.

Amongst the *rudras*, know Me to be Shankar; amongst the demons, I am Kuber. I am Agni amongst the *vasus* and Meru amongst the mountains.

The *rudras* are the eleven forms of Lord Shiv—Hara, Bahurupa, Tryambaka, Aparajita, Vrisakapi, Shankar, Kapardi, Raivata, Mrigavyadha, Sarva, and Kapali. The Puranas have named them differently in different places. Amongst these, Shankar is the original form of Lord Shiv in the universe.

Yakṣhas (semi-celestial beings) are beings who are very fond of acquiring wealth and hoarding it. Their leader, Kuber, is the god of wealth and the treasurer of the celestial gods. He thus reflects the *vibhūti* of God amongst the demons.

There are eight vasus—land, water, fire, air, space, sun, moon, and stars. They constitute the gross structure of the universe. Amongst these, agni (fire) gives warmth and energy to the rest of the elements. Thus, Shree Krishna mentions it as His special manifestation.

Meru is a mountain in the celestial abodes famed for its rich, natural resources. It is believed to be the axis around which many heavenly bodies rotate. Shree Krishna thus speaks of it as His glory. As wealth distinguishes a wealthy person, these glories reveal the *vibhūtis* of God.

पुरोधसां च मुख्यं मां विद्धि पार्थ बृहस्पतिम् ।
सेनानीनामहं स्कन्दः सरसामस्मि सागरः ।।24।।

purodhasāṁ cha mukhyaṁ māṁ viddhi pārtha bṛihaspatim
senānīnām ahaṁ skandaḥ sarasām asmi sāgaraḥ

purodhasām—amongst priests; *cha*—and; *mukhyam*—the chiefs; *mām*—me; *viddhi*—know; *pārtha*—Arjun, son of Pritha; *bṛihaspatim*—Brihaspati; *senānīnām*—warrior chief; *aham*—I; *skandaḥ*—Kartikeya; *sarasām*—amongst reservoirs of water; *asmi*—I am; *sāgaraḥ*—the ocean.

O Arjun, amongst priests, I am Brihaspati; amongst warrior chiefs, I am Kartikeya; and amongst reservoirs of water, know Me to be the ocean.

A priest executes the function of performing ritualistic worship and ceremonies in temples and homes. Brihaspati is the chief priest in heaven. He is thus the topmost of all priests. Here, Shree Krishna says that amongst priests, He is Brihaspati. However, in the Shreemad Bhagavatam, verse 11.16.22, Shree Krishna states that amongst the priests, He is Vasishtha. Why is He differing in these two places? This implies that we should not attach importance to the item, but to the opulence of God that manifests in that entity. All the objects of glory that Shree Krishna is describing here should also be understood in the same light. It is not the item that is being emphasised, rather, God's splendour that is manifesting in it.

Kartikeya, the son of Lord Shiv, who is also called Skanda, is the commander-in-chief of the celestial gods. He is thus the chief of all military commanders, and best reflects the magnificence of God. Shree Krishna further says that among stagnant bodies of water, He is the grave and mighty ocean.

महर्षीणां भृगुरहं गिरामस्म्येकमक्षरम् ।
यज्ञानां जपयज्ञोऽस्मि स्थावराणां हिमालयः ।।25।।

maharṣhīṇāṁ bhṛigur ahaṁ girām asmyekam akṣharam
yajñānāṁ japa-yajño 'smi sthāvarāṇāṁ himālayaḥ

mahā-ṛiṣhīṇām—amongst the great seers; *bhṛiguḥ*—Bhrigu; *aham*—I; *girām*—amongst chants; *asmi*—I am; *ekam akṣharam*—

the syllable Om; *yajñānām*—of sacrifices; *japa-yajñaḥ*—sacrifice of the devotional repetition of the divine names of God; *asmi*—I am; *sthāvarāṇām*—amongst immovable things; *himālayaḥ*—the Himalayas.

I am Bhrigu amongst the great seers and the transcendental Om amongst sounds. Amongst chants, know Me to be the repetition of the Holy Name; amongst immovable things, I am the Himalayas.

While all fruits and flowers grow from the same land, only the best among them are selected for an exhibition. Similarly, everything that is manifest and unmanifest in the universe is the glory of God, but only the prominent among them are singled out for mention as His opulence.

Amongst the sages in the celestial planes of existence, Bhrigu is special. He possesses wisdom, glory, and devotion. Lord Vishnu holds the mark of his foot on His chest as a consequence of a divine pastime described in the Puranas in which Bhrigu tested the trinity of Brahma, Vishnu, and Shiv. Shree Krishna's glory is best revealed through him.

Worshippers of God in His formless aspect like to meditate on the Om vibration, another *vibhūti* of God. Shree Krishna had declared previously, in verses 7.8 and 8.13, the syllable Om to be a sacred sound. It is the *anāhat nād* (the sound vibration that pervades creation). It is often present in the beginning of Vedic mantras for invoking auspiciousness. It is said that from the monosyllable Om, the Gayatri mantra was revealed, and from the Gayatri mantra, the Vedas were manifested.

The Himalayas are a series of mountain ranges in northern India. Since ages, they have inspired spiritual awe and wonder in billions. Their atmosphere, environment, and solitude are conducive for performing austerities for spiritual progress. Thus, many great sages reside in the Himalayas in their subtle bodies, practising penance for their own advancement and for the benefit of humankind. So, of the multitude of mountain ranges in this world, the Himalayas best display His opulence.

Yajna is the act of dedicating ourselves to the Supreme. The simplest of all yajnas is the chanting of the Holy Names of God. This is called *japa yajna* or the sacrifice of the devotional repetition of the divine names of God. For the successful practice of ritualistic yajnas, a number of rules are applicable, all of which need to be meticulously followed. However, in *japa yajna*, there are no rules. It can be done anywhere, at any time, and is more purifying than the other forms of yajnas. In the present age of Kali, chanting of the names of God has been greatly emphasized in the scriptures.

kalijuga kevala nāma ādhārā, sumiri sumiri nara utarahiṅ pārā

(Ramayan)

'In the age of Kali, the chanting and remembrance of the names of God is the most powerful means of crossing the ocean of material existence.'

अश्वत्थः सर्ववृक्षाणां देवर्षीणां च नारदः ।
गन्धर्वाणां चित्ररथः सिद्धानां कपिलो मुनिः ॥26॥

aśhvatthaḥ sarva-vṛikṣhāṇāṁ devarṣhīṇāṁ cha nāradaḥ
gandharvāṇāṁ chitrarathaḥ siddhānāṁ kapilo muniḥ

aśhvatthaḥ—the peepal tree; *sarva-vṛikṣhāṇām*—amongst all trees; *deva-ṛiṣhīṇām*—amongst celestial sages; *cha*—and; *nāradaḥ*—Narad; *gandharvāṇām*—amongst the *gandharvas*; *chitrarathaḥ*—Chitrarath; *siddhānām*—of all those who are perfected; *kapilaḥ muniḥ*—Sage Kapil.

Amongst trees, I am the peepal tree; of the celestial sages, I am Narad. Amongst the *gandharvas*, I am Chitrath, and amongst the *siddhas*, I am Sage Kapil.

The peepal tree has a very soothing effect on people who sit under it. Since it expands by sending down aerial roots, it is huge and provides cool shade to a large area. The Buddha meditated and attained enlightenment under a peepal tree.

The celestial Sage Narad is the guru of many great personalities such as Ved Vyas, Valmiki, Dhruv, and Prahalad among others. He is always engaged in singing the glories of God and executing divine works throughout the three worlds. He is also famous for deliberately creating quarrels and problems, and people sometimes misunderstand him to be a mischief-maker. However, it is his desire to purify famous personalities *antaḥ karan* that makes him create quarrels which ultimately result in self-introspection and purification.

The Gandharva planet is inhabited by beings who sing beautifully and the best singer among them is Chitrarath. *Siddhas* are yogis who have attained spiritual perfection. Sage Kapil, one of the *siddhas*, revealed the *Sānkhya* system of philosophy and also taught the glories of bhakti yog (described in detail in the third canto of the Shreemad Bhagavatam). He was an Avatar of God and thus Shree Krishna makes special mention of him as a manifestation of His glory.

उच्चैःश्रवसमश्वानां विद्धि माममृतोद्भवम् ।
ऐरावतं गजेन्द्राणां नराणां च नराधिपम् ।।27।।

uchchaiḥśhravasam aśhvānāṁ viddhi mām amṛitodbhavam
airāvataṁ gajendrāṇāṁ narāṇāṁ cha narādhipam

uchchaiḥśhravasam—Uchchaihshrava; *aśhvānām*—amongst horses; *viddhi*—know; *mām*—me; *amṛita-udbhavam*—begotten from the churning of the ocean of nectar; *airāvatam*—Airavata; *gaja-indrāṇām*—amongst all lordly elephants; *narāṇām*—amongst humans; *cha*—and; *nara-adhipam*—the king.

Amongst horses know Me to be Uchchaihshrava, begotten from the churning of the ocean of nectar. I am Airavata amongst all lordly elephants, and the king amongst humans.

Shree Krishna continues naming the most magnificent in each category to reveal His glories to Arjun. Uchchaihshrava is a celestial winged-horse that belongs to Indra, king of the celestial abodes. White in colour, it is the fastest horse in the universe. It emerged during the pastime of the churning of the ocean of nectar by *devatās* (celestial gods) and asuras (demons). Airavata is a white elephant that serves as the vehicle of Indra. It is also called *ardha-mātang* or 'the elephant of the clouds'.

आयुधानामहं वज्रं धेनूनामस्मि कामधुक् ।
प्रजनश्चास्मि कन्दर्पः सर्पाणामस्मि वासुकिः ।।28।।

āyudhānām ahaṁ vajraṁ dhenūnām asmi kāmadhuk
prajanaśh chāsmi kandarpaḥ sarpāṇām asmi vāsukiḥ

āyudhānām—amongst weapons; *aham*—I; *vajram*—the Vajra (thunderbolt); *dhenūnām*—amongst cows; *asmi*—I am; *kāma-dhuk*—Kamdhenu; *prajanaḥ*—amongst causes for procreation; *cha*—and; *asmi*—I am; *kandarpaḥ*—Kaamdev, the god of love; *sarpāṇām*—amongst serpents; *asmi*—I am; *vāsukiḥ*—serpent Vasuki.

I am the Vajra (thunderbolt) amongst weapons and Kamadhenu amongst the cows. I am Kaamdev, the god of love, amongst all causes for procreation; and amongst serpents, I am Vasuki.

The Puranas relate a story of the sacrifice offered by the great Sage Dadhichi which is unparalleled in history.

Indra, the king of heaven, was once driven out of his celestial kingdom by a demon named Vritrasura. The demon had a boon whereby he could not be killed by any weapon known till then. In desperation, Indra approached Lord Shiv for help, who took him to Lord Vishnu. Vishnu revealed to Indra that the only weapon that could kill Vritrasura was a thunderbolt made from the bones of Sage Dadhichi. Indra then beseeched Dadhichi to make the ultimate sacrifice of laying down his life so that his bones could be used for making the thunderbolt. Dadhichi accepted the request but desired to first go on a pilgrimage to all the holy rivers. Indra then brought together the water of all the holy rivers to Naimisharanya, thereby fulfilling the sage's wish immediately. Dadhichi then gave up his body by the practice of yogic techniques. The thunderbolt made from his bones was then used to defeat Vritrasura, allowing Indra to regain his position as the king of the celestial abodes. Shree Krishna deliberately refers to this thunderbolt here as the representation of the glory of God, preferring it above the mace and disc that are always held in the hands of Lord Vishnu.

In this verse, Shree Krishna also reveals that the act of sexual intercourse is not unholy when it is performed for the sole purpose of begetting good children. Kaamdev, the god of love (Cupid), is responsible for the force of attraction between the opposite sexes that facilitates the continuance of humankind through procreation. This sexual urge has its origin in God and should not be mis-utilised for sensual enjoyment; rather, it should be used solely for the purpose of begetting worthy progeny. In verse 7.11 as well, Shree Krishna had declared that He is sexual desire that is not in conflict with virtue and scriptural injunctions.

अनन्तश्चास्मि नागानां वरुणो यादसामहम् ।
पितॄणामर्यमा चास्मि यमः संयमतामहम् ।।29।।

anantaśh chāsmi nāgānāṁ varuṇo yādasām aham
pitṝīṇām aryamā chāsmi yamaḥ sanyamatām aham

anantaḥ—Anant; *cha*—and; *asmi*—I am; *nāgānām*—amongst snakes; *varuṇaḥ*—the celestial god of the ocean; *yādasām*—amongst aquatic creatures; *aham*—I; *pitṝīṇām*—amongst the departed ancestors; *aryamā*—Aryama; *cha*—and; *asmi*—am; *yamaḥ*—the celestial god of death; *sanyamatām*—amongst dispensers of law; *aham*—I.

Amongst the snakes I am Anant; amongst aquatics, I am Varun. Amongst the departed ancestors, I am Aryama; amongst dispensers of law, I am Yamraj, the lord of death.

Anant is the divine serpent on whom Lord Vishnu rests. He possesses ten thousand hoods. It is said that he has been describing the glories of God with each of his hoods since the beginning of creation, but the description is still incomplete.

Varun is the celestial god of the ocean. Aryama is the third son of

Aditi. He is worshipped as the head of the departed ancestors. Yamraj is the celestial god of death. He arranges to take the soul from its mortal frame after death. He dispenses justice on behalf of God based on the soul's actions in this life, granting punishment or reward in the next life. He does not deviate an inch from his duties though they may be gruesome and painful. He reflects the glory of God as the perfect dispenser of justice.

प्रह्लादश्चास्मि दैत्यानां कालः कलयतामहम् ।
मृगाणां च मृगेन्द्रोऽहं वैनतेयश्च पक्षिणाम् ।।30।।

prahlādaśh chāsmi daityānāṁ kālaḥ kalayatām aham
mṛigāṇāṁ cha mṛigendro 'haṁ vainateyaśh cha pakṣhiṇām

prahlādaḥ—Prahalad; *cha*—and; *asmi*—I am; *daityānām*—of the demons; *kālaḥ*—time; *kalayatām*—of all that controls; *aham*—I; *mṛigāṇām*—amongst animals; *cha*—and; *mṛiga-indraḥ*—the lion; *aham*—I; *vainateyaḥ*—Garud; *cha*—and; *pakṣhiṇām*—amongst birds.

I am Prahalad amongst the demons; amongst all that controls, I am time. Know Me to be the lion amongst animals and Garud amongst the birds.

Prahalad was born as the son of the powerful demon king, Hiranyakashipu. However, he turned out to be one of the greatest devotees of Lord Vishnu. Thus, among the demons, Prahalad best reflects God's glory. Time is the great subduer that wears down even the biggest and mightiest entities of the universe.

The majestic lion is the king of the jungle, and among the animals, the power of the Lord indeed reveals itself in the lion. Garud is the divine vehicle of Lord Vishnu and the greatest among birds.

पवनः पवतामस्मि रामः शस्त्रभृतामहम् ।
झषाणां मकरश्चास्मि स्रोतसामस्मि जाह्नवी ।।31।।

pavanaḥ pavatām asmi rāmaḥ śhastra-bhṛitām aham
jhaṣhāṇāṁ makaraśh chāsmi srotasām asmi jāhnavī

pavanaḥ—the wind; *pavatām*—of all that purifies; *asmi*—I am; *rāmaḥ*—Lord Ram; *śhastra-bhṛitām*—of the carriers of weapons; *aham*—I am; *jhaṣhāṇām*—of all acquatics; *makaraḥ*—crocodile; *cha*—also; *asmi*—I am; *srotasām*—of flowing rivers; *asmi*—I am; *jāhnavī*—the Ganges.

Amongst purifiers, I am the wind, and amongst wielders of weapons, I am Ram. Of water creatures, I am the crocodile, and of flowing rivers, I am the Ganges.

In nature, wind performs the work of purification very effectively. It converts impure water into water vapour; it carries away the dirty smells of the earth; it makes fire burn by fuelling it with oxygen. It is thus the great purifier of nature.

Lord Ram was the most powerful warrior on the earth and His bow was the deadliest weapon. Yet, He never once abused His dominant superiority. Every time He used His weapon, it was only for good. He was thus the perfect wielder of weapons. Ram was also an Avatar of God, and thus Shree Krishna identifies with Him.

The Ganges is a holy river that begins from the divine feet of the Lord. It descends on the earth from the celestial abodes. Many great sages have performed austerities on its banks, adding to the holiness of its waters. Unlike normal water, if water from the Ganges is gathered in a vessel, it does not putrefy for years. This phenomenon was very pronounced earlier but has reduced in intensity in modern times because of the millions of gallons of pollutants being poured into it everyday.

सर्गाणामादिरन्तश्च मध्यं चैवाहमर्जुन ।
अध्यात्मविद्या विद्यानां वादः प्रवदतामहम् ।।32।।

sargāṇām ādir antaśh cha madhyaṁ chaivāham arjuna
adhyātma-vidyā vidyānāṁ vādaḥ pravadatām aham

sargāṇām—of all creations; *ādiḥ*—the beginning; *antaḥ*—end; *cha*—and; *madhyam*—middle; *cha*—and; *eva*—indeed; *aham*—I; *arjuna*—Arjun; *adhyātma-vidyā*—science of spirituality; *vidyānām*—amongst sciences; *vādaḥ*—the logical conclusion; *pravadatām*—of debates; *aham*—I.

O Arjun, know Me to be the beginning, middle, and end of all creation. Amongst sciences, I am the science of spirituality, and in debates, I am the logical conclusion.

Earlier in the twentieth verse, Shree Krishna had stated that He is the beginning, middle, and end of all living beings. Now, He states the same for all creation: 'All that is created, such as space, air, fire, water, and earth, is called *sarga*. I am the Creator (*ādi*), Maintainer (*madhya*), and Annihilator (*anta*) of these. Therefore, the processes of creation, maintenance, and dissolution can be meditated upon as My *vibhūtis*.'

Vidyā is the education that a person acquires in relation to subjects of knowledge. The scriptures describe eighteen types of *vidyās*. Amongst them, fourteen are prominent:

aṅgāni vedāśhchatvāro mīmānsā nyāya vistaraḥ
purāṇaṁ dharmaśhāstraṁ cha vidyā hyetāśhchaturdaśha
āyurvedo dhanurvedo gāndharvaśhchaiva te trayaḥ
arthaśhāstraṁ chaturthaṁ tu vidyā hyaṣhṭādaśhaiva tāḥ

(*Vishnu Puran* 3.6.27–28)

'*Śhikśhā, Kalp, Vyākaraṇ, Nirukti, Jyotiṣh, Chhanda*—these are the six types of knowledge known as *Vedāṅg* (limbs of the Vedas). *Rig, Yajur*, Sama, *Atharva*—these are the four branches of Vedic knowledge. Along with Mimansa, Nyaya, Dharma Shastra, and the Puranas, these comprise the fourteen chief *vidyās*.' Practice of these *vidyās* cultivates the intellect, deepens the knowledge, and increases awareness of the path of dharma. In addition to the above benefits, the science of spirituality liberates human beings from material bondage and bestows immortality. As a result, it is superior to the previously mentioned *vidyās*. This is mentioned in the Shreemad Bhagavatam as well: *sā vidyā tanmatiryayā* (verse 4.29.49) 'The best knowledge is that by which the intellect becomes attached to the lotus feet of God.'

In the field of argument and logic, *jalpa* means to find fault with the opponent's statements for the sake of establishing one's own opinion. *Vitaṇḍa* means to avoid proper deliberation on the truth through evasion and frivolous arguments. *Vāda* is the logical conclusion of the discussion. Logic is the basis for communication of ideas and establishment of truths. It is because of a universal sense of logic that knowledge can be easily cultivated, taught, and learnt in human society. The universal principles of logic are a manifestation of the power of God.

अक्षराणामकारोऽस्मि द्वन्द्वः सामासिकस्य च ।
अहमेवाक्षयः कालो धाताहं विश्वतोमुखः ।।33।।

akṣharāṇām a-kāro 'smi dvandvaḥ sāmāsikasya cha
aham evākṣhayaḥ kālo dhātāhaṁ viśhwato-mukhaḥ

akṣharāṇām—amongst all letters; *a-kāraḥ*—the beginning letter 'A'; *asmi*—I am; *dvandvaḥ*—the dual; *sāmāsikasya*—amongst grammatical compounds; *cha*—and; *aham*—I; *eva*—only; *akṣhayaḥ*—endless; *kālaḥ*—time; *dhātā*—amongst the creators; *aham*—I; *viśhwataḥ-mukhaḥ*—Brahma.

I am the beginning 'A' amongst all letters; I am the dual word in grammatical compounds. I am the endless Time, and amongst creators, I am Brahma.

In Sanskrit, all letters are formed by combining a half-letter with 'a'. For example, क् + अ = क (*k* + *a* = *ka*). Hence, the letter 'a' is the most important in the Sanskrit alphabet. 'A' is also the first vowel of the alphabet, and since the vowels are written before the consonants, 'A' comes at the very beginning.

Although Sanskrit is such an ancient language, it is highly refined and sophisticated. A common practice in Sanskrit is to combine words to form compound words. When, in the process of making one compound word, two or more words give up their case endings, it is called *samāsa*, and the resulting word is called *samāsa pada* or compound word. There are primarily six kinds of *samāsa*: 1) *dwandva*, 2) *bahubṛihi*, 3) *karm dhāray*, 4) *tatpuruṣh*, 5) *dwigu*, 6) *avyayī bhāv*. Among these, *dwandva* is the best because both words remain prominent in it, while in the others, either one word becomes more prominent, or both words combine together to give the meaning of a third word. The dual word Radha-Krishna is an example of *dwandva*. Shree Krishna highlights it as His *vibhūti*.

Creation is a magnificent act and awesome to behold. Humankind's most sophisticated and technologically advanced inventions pale in comparison. Therefore, Lord Krishna singles out the first-born Brahma, who made the entire universe, and says that among creators, the creative ability of Brahma best reflects the glory of God.

मृत्युः सर्वहरश्चाहमुद्भवश्च भविष्यताम् ।
कीर्तिः श्रीर्वाक्च नारीणां स्मृतिर्मेधा धृतिः क्षमा ।।34।।

mṛityuḥ sarva-haraśh chāham udbhavaśh cha bhaviṣhyatām
kīrtiḥ śhrīr vāk cha nārīṇāṁ smṛitir medhā dhṛitiḥ kṣhamā

mṛityuḥ—death; *sarva-haraḥ*—all-devouring; *cha*—and; *aham*—I; *udbhavaḥ*—the origin; *cha*—and; *bhaviṣhyatām*—those things that are yet to be; *kīrtiḥ*—fame; *śhrīḥ*—opulence; *vāk*—fine speech; *cha*—and; *nārīṇām*—amongst feminine qualities; *smṛitiḥ*—memory; *medhā*—intelligence; *dhṛitiḥ*—courage; *kṣhamā*—forgiveness.

I am the all-devouring death, and I am the origin of those things that are yet to be. Amongst feminine qualities, I am fame, prosperity, fine speech, memory, intelligence, courage, and forgiveness.

There is a phrase in English: 'as sure as death'. For one who is born, death is certain. All life inevitably ends in death, and thus the phrase, 'dead end'. God is not merely the force of creation; He is also the force of destruction. He devours everything in the form of death. In the cycle of life and death, those who die are born again. Shree Krishna states that He is also the generating principle of all future beings.

Certain qualities are seen as adornments in the personality of women, while other qualities are viewed as especially praiseworthy in men. Ideally, a well-rounded personality is one that possesses both kinds of qualities. Here, Shree Krishna lists fame, prosperity, perfect speech, memory, intelligence, courage, and forgiveness, as virtues that make women glorious. The first three of these qualities manifest on the outside, while the remaining four are internal adornments.

Besides this, the progenitor of humankind Prajapati Daksha had twenty-four daughters. Five of these were considered the best of women—Kirti, Smriti, Medha, Dhriti, and Kshama. Shree was the daughter of Sage Bhrigu. Vak was the daughter of Brahma. In accordance with their respective names, these seven women are the presiding deities of the seven qualities mentioned in this verse. Here, Shree Krishna enlists these qualities as His *vibhūtis*.

बृहत्साम तथा साम्नां गायत्री छन्दसामहम् ।
मासानां मार्गशीर्षोऽहमृतूनां कुसुमाकरः ।।35।।

bṛihat-sāma tathā sāmnāṁ gāyatrī chhandasām aham
māsānāṁ mārga-śhīrṣho 'ham ṛitūnāṁ kusumākaraḥ

bṛihat-sāma—the Brihatsama; *tathā*—also; *sāmnām*—amongst the hymns in the *Sāma Veda*; *gāyatrī*—the Gayatri mantra; *chhandasām*—amongst poetic meters; *aham*—I; *māsānām*—of the twelve months; *mārga-śhīrṣhaḥ*—the months of November-December; *aham*—I; *ṛitūnām*—of all seasons; *kusuma-ākaraḥ*—spring.

Amongst the hymns in the *Sama Veda* know Me to be the *Brihatsama*; amongst poetic meters, I am the Gayatri. Of the twelve months of the Hindu calendar, I am Margsheersh, and of seasons I am spring, which brings forth flowers.

Earlier Shree Krishna had said that of the Vedas, He is the *Sama Veda* which is rich with beautiful devotional songs. Now He says that within the *Sama Veda*, He is the *Brihatsama*, which has an exquisite melody. It is typically sung at midnight.

The Sanskrit language, like other languages, has distinctive systems of rhymes and meters for writing poetry. The poetry of the Vedas is in many meters. Among these, the Gayatri meter is very attractive and melodious. A famous mantra set in this meter is the Gayatri mantra. It is also a deeply meaningful prayer:

bhūrbhuvaḥ swaḥ tatsaviturvareṇyaṁ bhargo devasya dhīmahi
dhiyo yo naḥ prachodayāt (*Rig Veda* 3.62.10)

'We meditate upon the Lord who is illuminating the three worlds and is worthy of our worship. He is the remover of all sins and the destroyer of ignorance. May He illumine our intellects in the proper direction.' The Gayatri mantra is a part of the sacred thread ceremony for young males and is also recited as a part of the daily rituals. The Devi Gayatri, the Rudra Gayatri, the Brahma Gayatri, the Paramhansa Gayatri, and several other Gayatri mantras are also found in the Vedas.

Margsheersh is the ninth month of the Hindu calendar. It falls in November-December. The temperature at that time in India is just right—neither too hot nor too cold. The crops in the field are harvested at this time of the year. For these reasons, it is often the favourite month of most people.

Basant (spring season) is known as *ṛitu raja* or the king of seasons. It is a time when nature seems to be euphorically bursting forth with life. Many festivals are celebrated in spring, epitomising the joy that pervades the atmosphere. Thus, among the seasons, spring manifests God's opulence the most.

द्यूतं छलयतामस्मि तेजस्तेजस्विनामहम् ।
जयोऽस्मि व्यवसायोऽस्मि सत्त्वं सत्त्ववतामहम् ।।36।।

dyūtaṁ chhalayatām asmi tejas tejasvinām aham
jayo 'smi vyavasāyo 'smi sattvaṁ sattvavatām aham

dyūtam—gambling; *chhalayatām*—of all cheats; *asmi*—I am; *tejaḥ*—the splendour; *tejasvinām*—of the splendid; *aham*—I; *jayaḥ*—victory; *asmi*—I am; *vyavasāyaḥ*—firm resolve; *asmi*—I am; *sattvam*—virtue; *sattva-vatām*—of the virtuous; *aham*—I.

I am the gambling of the cheats and the splendour of the splendid. I am the victory of the victorious, the resolve of the resolute, and the virtue of the virtuous.

Shree Krishna mentions not only virtue but also vice as His opulence. Gambling is a dangerous vice that ruins families, businesses, and lives. It was Yudhishthir's weakness for gambling that led to the Mahabharat war. But if gambling is also God's glory, then is there no harm in it, so why is it forbidden?

The answer is that God grants His power to the soul, and along with it, He gives the freedom of choice. If we choose to forget Him, He gives us the power to forget. This is just as electric power can be used both to heat and cool a house. The user is free to choose how to utilise the power. However, the powerhouse that supplies the energy is not responsible for either the use or misuse of the power. Similarly, a gambler too possesses intellect and ability given by God. But if he decides to misuse these God-given gifts, then God is not responsible for the sinful deeds.

Everyone likes victory; it reveals the glory of the Lord. Also, Shree Krishna has laid great emphasis on the quality of determination. It was previously mentioned in verses 2.41, 2.44, and 9.30 as well. The goodness of the virtuous is also a manifestation of God's power. All virtues, achievements, glory, victory, and firm resolve originate from God. Instead of considering these as our own, we should see them as gifts from Him.

वृष्णीनां वासुदेवोऽस्मि पाण्डवानां धनञ्जयः ।
मुनीनामप्यहं व्यासः कवीनामुशना कविः ।।37।।

vṛiṣhṇīnāṁ vāsudevo 'smi pāṇḍavānāṁ dhanañjayaḥ
munīnām apyahaṁ vyāsaḥ kavīnām uśhanā kaviḥ

vṛiṣhṇīnām—amongst the descendants of Vrishni; *vāsudevaḥ*—Krishna, son of Vasudev; *asmi*—I am; *pāṇḍavānām*—amongst the Pandavas; *dhanañjayaḥ*—Arjun, conqueror of wealth; *munīnām*—amongst the sages; *api*—also; *aham*—I; *vyāsaḥ*—Ved Vyas; *kavīnām*—amongst the great thinkers; *uśhanā*—Shukracharya; *kaviḥ*—the thinker.

Amongst the descendants of Vrishni, I am Krishna, and amongst the Pandavas, I am Arjun. Know Me to be Ved Vyas amongst the sages, and Shukracharya amongst the great thinkers.

Lord Krishna took birth on the earth in the Vrishni dynasty as the Son of Vasudev. Since no soul can excel the Lord, He is naturally the most glorious personality of the Vrishni dynasty. The Pandavas were the five sons of Pandu—Yudhishthir, Bheem, Arjun, Nakul, and Sahadev. Among them, Arjun was an archer par-excellence and a very intimate devotee of Shree Krishna. He also looked upon the Lord as his dear Friend.

Ved Vyas is special among the sages. He is also known by the names 'Badarayan' and 'Krishna Dwaipayan'. He revealed Vedic knowledge in various ways and wrote many scriptures for the welfare of the people. In fact, Ved Vyas was an Avatar of Shree Krishna Himself and is mentioned in the list of Avatars in the Shreemad Bhagavatam.

Shukracharya was a very learned sage known for his expertise in the science of ethics. He was compassionate to accept the demons as his disciples and guide their progress. By virtue of his learning, he has been declared as a *vibhūti* of God.

दण्डो दमयतामस्मि नीतिरस्मि जिगीषताम् ।
मौनं चैवास्मि गुह्यानां ज्ञानं ज्ञानवतामहम् ।।38।।

daṇḍo damayatām asmi nītir asmi jigīṣhatām
maunaṁ chaivāsmi guhyānāṁ jñānaṁ jñānavatām aham

daṇḍaḥ—punishment; *damayatām*—amongst means of preventing lawlessness; *asmi*—I am; *nītiḥ*—proper conduct; *asmi*—I am; *jigīṣhatām*—amongst those who seek victory; *maunam*—silence; *cha*—and; *eva*—also; *asmi*—I am; *guhyānām*—amongst secrets; *jñānam*—wisdom; *jñāna-vatām*—in the wise; *aham*—I.

I am just punishment amongst means of preventing lawlessness and proper conduct amongst those who seek victory. Amongst secrets, I am silence, and in the wise, I am their wisdom.

Human nature is such that mere sermons are insufficient to ensure good behaviour. Punishment, when meted out in a timely and just manner, is an important tool for reforming sinful behaviour in people and training them in right conduct. One of its goals is meant to deter those in society that might be inclined to perform wrong actions. Modern management theory describes very nicely how even one minute of proper punishment for wrong actions and one minute of suitable reward for good actions can rectify people's behaviour.

Desire for victory is universal, but those with the strength of character are not willing to sacrifice morals or ethics to achieve it. That victory which is won by the path of righteousness signifies the power of God.

A secret is that which is hidden from public knowledge for a specific purpose. There is a saying in English, 'A secret known to one person is a secret; a secret known to two people is no longer a secret; and a secret known to three people is news shouted out to the rest of the world.' Thus, the greatest secret is that which is hidden in silence.

True wisdom comes to a person with the maturing of spiritual knowledge through the self or God-realisation. A person endowed with it develops the perspective of seeing all events, persons, and objects in the light of their relationship with God. Such wisdom purifies, fulfils, satisfies, and elevates one. It gives direction to life, the strength to cope with its vicissitudes, and determination to persevere till the end is reached. Shree Krishna says that He is such wisdom that manifests in the wise.

यच्चापि सर्वभूतानां बीजं तदहमर्जुन ।
न तदस्ति विना यत्स्यान्मया भूतं चराचरम् ।।39।।

yach chāpi sarva-bhūtānāṁ bījaṁ tad aham arjuna
na tad asti vinā yat syān mayā bhūtaṁ charācharam

yat—which; *cha*—and; *api*—also; *sarva-bhūtānām*—of all living beings; *bījam*—generating seed; *tat*—that; *aham*—I; *arjuna*—Arjun; *na*—not; *tat*—that; *asti*—is; *vinā*—without; *yat*—which; *syāt*—may exist; *mayā*—me; *bhūtam*—creature; *chara-acharam*—moving and nonmoving.

I am the generating seed of all living beings, O Arjun. No creature, moving or non-moving, can exist without Me.

Shree Krishna is both the efficient cause of all creation and also the material cause. Efficient cause means that He is the Creator who performs the work involved in manifesting the world. Material cause means that He is the material from which creation happens. In verses 7.10 and 9.18, Shree Krishna declared Himself as 'the eternal seed'. Again here, He states that He is 'the generating seed'. He is stressing that He is the origin of everything, and nothing can exist without His potency.

Living beings are born in four ways: *Aṇḍaj*—born from eggs, such as birds, snakes, and lizards; *Jarāyuj*—born from the womb, such as humans, cows, dogs, cats, and animals and mammals; *Swedaj*—born from sweat, such as lice, ticks, and so on; *Udbhij*—sprouting from the earth, such as trees, creepers, grass, and corn. There are also other life forms, such as ghosts, evil spirits, manes, etc. and Shree Krishna is the Origin of all of them.

नान्तोऽस्ति मम दिव्यानां विभूतीनां परन्तप ।
एष तूद्देशतः प्रोक्तो विभूतेर्विस्तरो मया ।।40।।

nānto 'sti mama divyānāṁ vibhūtīnāṁ parantapa
eṣha tūddeśhataḥ prokto vibhūter vistaro mayā

na—not; *antaḥ*—end; *asti*—is; *mama*—my; *divyānām*—divine; *vibhūtīnām*—manifestations; *parantapa*—Arjun, conqueror of enemies; *eṣhaḥ*—this; *tu*—but; *uddeśhataḥ*—just one portion; *proktaḥ*—declared; *vibhūteḥ*—of (my) glories; *vistaraḥ*—the breath of the topic; *mayā*—by me.

There is no end to My divine manifestations, O conqueror of enemies. What I have declared to you is a mere sample of My infinite glories.

Shree Krishna is now concluding the topic of His opulences. From verses 20–39, He has described eighty-two of His infinite opulences. He now says that He has spoken only one portion (*uddeśhataḥ*) of the breadth of the topic (*vistāraḥ*).

The question can be asked that if everything is the opulence of God, then what was the need of mentioning these? The answer is that Arjun had asked Shree Krishna how he should think of Him, and these glories have been described in response to Arjun's question. The mind is naturally drawn to specialties, and thus, the Lord has revealed these specialties among His powers. Whenever we see a special splendour manifesting anywhere, if we look on it as God's glory, then our mind will naturally be transported to Him. In the larger scheme of things, however, since God's glories are in all things big and small, one can think of the whole world as providing innumerable examples for us to enhance our devotion. A paint company in India would advertise, 'Whenever you see colours, think of us.' In this case, Shree Krishna's statement is tantamount to saying, 'Wherever you see a manifestation of glory, think of Me.'

यद्यद्विभूतिमत्सत्त्वं श्रीमदूर्जितमेव वा ।
तत्तदेवावगच्छ त्वं मम तेजोंऽशसम्भवम् ।।41।।

yad yad vibhūtimat sattvaṁ śhrīmad ūrjitam eva vā
tat tad evāvagachchha tvaṁ mama tejo 'ṅśha-sambhavam

yat yat—whatever; *vibhūtimat*—opulent; *sattvam*—being; *śhrī-mat*—beautiful; *ūrjitam*—glorious; *eva*—also; *vā*—or; *tat tat*—all that; *eva*—only; *avagachchha*—know; *tvam*—you; *mama*—my; *tejaḥ*—splendour; *anśha*—a part; *sambhavam*—born of.

Whatever you see as beautiful, glorious, or powerful, know it to spring from but a spark of My splendour.

Electricity flowing through a speaker creates sound, but one who does not know the principle behind how it works may think that the sound comes from the speaker itself. Similarly, whenever we observe extraordinary splendour anywhere, and when a phenomenon catches our imagination, sends us in raptures, or infuses us with bliss, we should know it to be but a spark of the glory of God. He is the infinite reservoir of beauty, glory, power, knowledge, and opulence. He is the powerhouse from where all beings and things get their splendour. Thus, we must make God, who is the source of all glory, the object of our worship.

अथवा बहुनैतेन किं ज्ञातेन तवार्जुन ।
विष्टभ्याहमिदं कृत्स्नमेकांशेन स्थितो जगत् ।।42।।

atha vā bahunaitena kiṁ jñātena tavārjuna
viṣhṭabhyāham idaṁ kṛitsnam ekānśhena sthito jagat

athavā—or; *bahunā*—detailed; *etena*—by this; *kim*—what; *jñātena tava*—can be known by you; *arjuna*—Arjun; *viṣhṭabhya*—pervade and support; *aham*—I; *idam*—this; *kṛitsnam*—entire; *eka*—by one; *anśhena*—fraction; *sthitaḥ*—am situated; *jagat*—creation.

What need is there for all this detailed knowledge, O Arjun? Simply know that by one fraction of My being, I pervade and support this entire creation.

Shree Krishna's statement indicates that He has already answered the question. Now, of His own accord, He wants to share something remarkable. Having revealed many amazing aspects of His splendour, He says that the magnitude of His glory cannot be judged even from the sum total of what He has described, for the entire creation of unlimited universes is held within a fraction of His Being.

Why does He make a reference to a fraction of His being here? The reason is that the entire material creation consisting of unlimited universes is only one-fourth of God's entire manifestation; the remaining three-fourths is the spiritual creation.

pādo 'sya viśhwā bhūtāni, tripādasyāmṛitaṁ divi

(*Purush Sūktam*, mantra 3)

'This temporary world made from material energy is but one part of the Supreme Divine Personality. The other three parts are His eternal abodes that are beyond the phenomenon of life and death.'

Interestingly, Shree Krishna is in front of Arjun, within the world, yet He reveals that the entire world is within a fraction of His being. This is like the story of Ganesh and Lord Shiv.

Once, Sage Narad gave Lord Shiv a very special fruit. Lord Shiv's two children, Kartikeya and Ganesh, both began demanding the fruit from Him. Lord Shiv thought that if He would give it to any one of them, the other would think that their father was biased. So, Lord Shiv announced a competition for His two children. Whoever would circumambulate the entire universe and came back to Him first would get the fruit.

On hearing this, Kartikeya immediately started off to go around the universe. He was athletically and powerfully built and decided to take advantage of it. In comparison, Ganesh had a plump body and felt handicapped in competing with His brother. So, Ganesh decided to make up for it by using His intellect. Lord Shiv and Parvati were standing there. Ganesh circumambulated Them thrice, and then announced, 'Father, I have done it. Please give Me the fruit.'

Lord Shiv said, 'But how have You gone around the universe? You have been with Us all the while.'

Ganesh said, 'Father, You are God. The entire universe exists within You. If I have gone around You, I have gone around the entire universe.'

Lord Shiv had to agree that Ganesh was very smart and had indeed won the competition.

Just as Lord Shiv was standing in one place, and yet the entire universe was contained in Him, similarly, Shree Krishna announces to Arjun that the entire creation, consisting of unlimited material universes, is held within a fraction of His Being.

CHAPTER 11

Viśhwaroop Darshan Yog

Yog through Beholding the Cosmic Form of God

In the previous chapter, Shree Krishna described His divine *vibhūtis* (opulences) to nourish and increase Arjun's devotion. At the end, He faintly alluded to His universal cosmic form, by saying that all things beautiful, glorious, and powerful manifest from just a spark of His splendor. In this chapter, Arjun requests to see Shree Krishna's *viśhwaroop*, or the infinite cosmic form of God, which encompasses all the universes. Shree Krishna obliges by granting Him divine vision. Arjun then sees the totality of creation in the body of the God of gods. He observes unlimited faces, eyes, arms, and stomachs in the wonderful and infinite form of the Lord. The form has no beginning or end and extends infinitely in every direction. The splendour of that form is more than a thousand suns blazing forth together in the sky. The vision makes Arjun's hair stand on end. He sees the three worlds trembling in fear of God's laws. He witnesses the celestial gods taking shelter of Him and the great sages extolling Him with profuse hymns and prayers. He observes all the sons of Dhritarashtra along with their allied kings rushing headlong into the mouth of that fearsome form, as moths rushing with great speed into the fire to perish. Arjun then confesses that on beholding the universal form, his heart is trembling with fear, and he has lost his peace of mind. Terrified, he wishes to know the identity of this awesome God, who bears no resemblance now to the Krishna he had known as his Teacher and Friend. Shree Krishna responds by saying that in the form of time, He is the destroyer of the three worlds. He declares that the great Kaurava warriors have already been killed by Him, so being assured of victory, Arjun should get up and fight.

In response, Arjun praises Him as the Lord who possesses infinite valour and power and offers Him repeated salutations. He asks for forgiveness, if during their long friendship he has ever done anything to offend the Lord by mistaking Him for a mere human being. He implores for grace and requests to once again see the pleasing form of God. Shree Krishna grants his desire and first returns to His four-armed form, and then to His gentle and loving two-armed form. He tells Arjun how difficult it is to have a vision of God in the manner that Arjun is seeing Him. His personal form cannot be seen by the study of the Vedas, nor by penance, charity, or fire sacrifices. By unalloyed devotion alone can one know Him as He is, standing before Arjun, and enter into union with Him.

अर्जुन उवाच ।
मदनुग्रहाय परमं गुह्यमध्यात्मसञ्ज्ञितम् ।
यत्त्वयोक्तं वचस्तेन मोहोऽयं विगतो मम ।।1।।

arjuna uvācha
mad-anugrahāya paramaṁ guhyam adhyātma-sanjñitam
yat tvayoktaṁ vachas tena moho 'yaṁ vigato mama

arjunaḥ uvācha—Arjun said; *mat-anugrahāya*—out of compassion to me; *paramam*—the supreme; *guhyam*—confidential; *adhyātma-sanjñitam*—about spiritual knowledge; *yat*—which; *tvayā*—by you; *uktam*—spoken; *vachaḥ*—words; *tena*—by that; *mohaḥ*—illusion; *ayam*—this; *vigataḥ*—is dispelled; *mama*—my.

Arjun said: Having heard the supremely confidential spiritual knowledge, which You have revealed out of compassion for me, my illusion is now dispelled.

Arjun rejoices on hearing about Shree Krishna's *vibhūtis*, as well as knowledge about the Supreme Personality, and believes that his illusion is now dispelled. He has accepted that Shree Krishna is not merely his best Friend, but also the Supreme Divine Personality, who is the source of all opulence in the world. Now in this chapter, he begins by gratefully acknowledging Shree Krishna's compassion in revealing such invaluable knowledge.

भवाप्ययौ हि भूतानां श्रुतौ विस्तरशो मया ।
त्वत्तः कमलपत्राक्ष माहात्म्यमपि चाव्ययम् ।।2।।

bhavāpyayau hi bhūtānāṁ śhrutau vistaraśho mayā
tvattaḥ kamala-patrākṣha māhātmyam api chāvyayam

bhava—appearance; *apyayau*—disappearance; *hi*—indeed; *bhūtānām*—of all living beings; *śhrutau*—have heard; *vistaraśhaḥ*—in detail; *mayā*—by me; *tvattaḥ*—from you; *kamala-patra-akṣha*—lotus-eyed one; *māhātmyam*—greatness; *api*—also; *cha*—and; *avyayam*—eternal.

I have heard from You in detail about the appearance and disappearance of all living beings, O lotus-eyed One, and also about Your eternal magnificence.

Arjun continues to appreciate Lord Krishna's glories by affirming His paramount position as the source of the appearance and disappearance of the entire material manifestation. He addresses Shree Krishna evocatively with the words, *kamala-patrākṣha*, meaning, 'whose eyes are like the lotus flower, which is large, soft, and beautiful, and endowed with the attributes of sweetness and gentleness.'

In this verse, Arjun implies, 'O Shree Krishna, I have heard from You about Your imperishable majestic glories. Although You are present within all, yet You are untainted by their imperfections. Although You are the Supreme Controller, yet You are the Non-doer and are not responsible for our actions. Although You bestow the results of our karmas, yet You are impartial and equal to all. You are the Supreme Witness and the Dispenser of the results of our actions. I thus conclude that You are the object of adoration of all beings.'

एवमेतद्यथात्थ त्वमात्मानं परमेश्वर ।
द्रष्टुमिच्छामि ते रूपमैश्वरं पुरुषोत्तम ।।3।।

evam etad yathāttha tvam ātmānaṁ parameśhvara
draṣhṭum ichchhāmi te rūpam aiśhwaraṁ puruṣhottama

evam—thus; *etat*—this; *yathā*—as; *āttha*—have spoken; *tvam*—you; *ātmānam*—yourself; *parama-īśhvara*—Supreme Lord; *draṣhṭum*—to see; *ichchhāmi*—I desire; *te*—your; *rūpam*—form; *aiśhwaram*—divine; *puruṣha-uttama*—Shree Krishna, the Supreme Divine Personality.

O Supreme Lord, You are precisely what You declare Yourself to be. Now I desire to see Your divine cosmic form, O Greatest of persons.

Arjun addresses Shree Krishna as the 'greatest person' because no other personality is equal to Him. Often scholars, basing their opinion upon dry intellectual analysis, have difficulty in accepting the concept of God as a person. They wish to perceive God as only an impersonal light, without Attributes, Virtues, Qualities, Forms, and Pastimes. However, when we tiny souls possess a personality, then why should we deny a personality to the Supreme Lord? Not only can He have a personality, but He also has the best personality, and, therefore, He is the Supreme Divine Personality. The difference between our personality and God's personality is that He is not only a perfect person, but He also has His impersonal all-pervading aspect, which is devoid of attributes and form.

Arjun declares that He accepts the reality of Shree Krishna's divine personality precisely as has been described to Him. He has complete faith in His personal form, and yet, He desires to see Shree Krishna's *viśhwaroop*, or universal form, replete with all opulences. He wishes to view It with his own eyes.

मन्यसे यदि तच्छक्यं मया द्रष्टुमिति प्रभो ।
योगेश्वर ततो मे त्वं दर्शयात्मानमव्ययम् ।।4।।

manyase yadi tach chhakyaṁ mayā draṣhṭum iti prabho
yogeśhvara tato me tvaṁ darśhayātmānam avyayam

manyase—you think; *yadi*—if; *tat*—that; *śhakyam*—possible; *mayā*—by me; *drashṭum*—to behold; *iti*—thus; *prabho*—Lord; *yoga-īśhvara*—Lord of all mystic powers; *tataḥ*—then; *me*—to me; *tvam*—you; *darśhaya*—reveal; *ātmānam*—yourself; *avyayam*—imperishable.

O Lord of all mystic powers, if You think I am strong enough to behold It, then kindly reveal that imperishable cosmic form to me.

In the previous verse, Arjun desired to see the cosmic form of the Supreme Divine Personality. He now seeks His approval. 'O Yogeshwar, I have expressed my wish. If You consider me worthy of it, then by Your grace, please reveal Your cosmic form to me, and show me Your *Yog-aiśhwarya* (mystic opulence).' Yog is the science of uniting the individual soul with the Supreme Soul, and those who practice this science are called yogis. The word *Yogeśhwar* also means 'Lord of all yogis'. Since the object of attainment for all yogis is the Supreme Lord, Shree Krishna is consequently the Lord of all yogis. Previously, in verse 10.17, Arjun had addressed the Lord as 'Yogi', implying 'Master of yog'. But he has now changed it to 'Yogeshwar' because of his increased respect for Shree Krishna.

श्रीभगवानुवाच ।
पश्य मे पार्थ रूपाणि शतशोऽथ सहस्रशः ।
नानाविधानि दिव्यानि नानावर्णाकृतीनि च ।।5।।

śhrī-bhagavān uvācha
paśhya me pārtha rūpāṇi śhataśho 'tha sahasraśhaḥ
nānā-vidhāni divyāni nānā-varṇākṛitīni cha

śhrī-bhagavān uvācha—the Supreme Lord said; *paśhya*—behold; *me*—my; *pārtha*—Arjun, son of Pritha; *rūpāṇi*—forms; *śhataśhaḥ*—by the hundreds; *atha*—and; *sahasraśhaḥ*—thousands; *nānā-vidhāni*—various; *divyāni*—divine; *nānā*—various; *varṇa*—colours; *ākṛitīni*—shapes; *cha*—and.

The Supreme Lord said: Behold, O Parth, My hundreds and thousands of wonderful forms of various shapes, sizes, and colours.

After listening to Arjun's prayers, Shree Krishna now asks him to have a vision of His *viśhwaroop* or universal form. He uses the word *paśhya*, meaning, 'behold' to indicate that Arjun must pay attention. Although the form is one, it has unlimited features, and contains innumerable personalities of multitude shapes and variegated colours. Shree Krishna uses the phrase *śhataśho 'tha sahasraśhaḥ* to indicate they exist in innumerable fashions and multitude ways.

Having asked Arjun to behold His universal form with infinite shapes and colours, Shree Krishna now asks Arjun to observe the celestial gods and other wonders in that cosmic form.

पश्यादित्यान्वसून्रुद्रानश्विनौ मरुतस्तथा ।
बहून्यदृष्टपूर्वाणि पश्याश्चर्याणि भारत ।।6।।

paśhyādityān vasūn rudrān aśhvinau marutas tathā
bahūny adṛiṣhṭa-pūrvāṇi paśhyāśhcharyāṇi bhārata

paśhya—behold; *ādityān*—the (twelve) sons of Aditi; *vasūn*—the (eight) vasus; *rudrān*—the (eleven) rudras; *aśhvinau*—the (twin) Ashwini Kumars; *marutaḥ*—the (forty-nine) maruts; *tathā*—and; *bahūni*—many; *adṛiṣhṭa*—never revealed; *pūrvāṇi*—before; *paśhya*—behold; *āśhcharyāṇi*—marvels; *bhārata*—Arjun, scion of the Bharatas.

Behold in Me, O scion of the Bharatas, the (twelve) sons of Aditi, the (eight) vasus, the (eleven) rudras, the (twin) Ashwini Kumars, as well as the (forty-nine) maruts and many more marvels never revealed before.

The universal form of the Lord not only contains marvels that exist on earth but also wonders that exist in the higher planetary systems, never before seen together in this manner. He further reveals that the celestial gods are all tiny fragments of His divine form; He shows the twelve *adityas*, eight *vasus*, eleven *rudras*, two Ashwini Kumars, as well as the forty-nine *maruts* within Himself.

The twelve sons of Aditi are: Dhata, Mitra, Aryama, Shakra, Varun, Amsha, Bhaga, Vivasvan, Pusha, Savita, Tvashta, and Vaman. The eight *vasus* are: Dara, Dhruv, Soma, Ahah, Anila, Anala, Pratyush, and Prabhas.

The eleven *rudras* are: Hara, Bahurupa, Tryambaka, Aparajita, Vrisakapi, Shambhu, Kapardi, Raivata, Mrigavyadha, Sarva, and Kapali. The two Ashwini Kumars are the twin-born physicians of the celestials.

The forty-nine *maruts* (wind gods) are: Sattvajyoti, Aditya, Satyajyoti, Tiryagjyoti, Sajyoti, Jyotishman, Harita, Ritajit, Satyajit, Sushena, Senajit, Satyamitra, Abhimitra, Harimitra, Krita, Satya, Dhruv, Dharta, Vidharta, Vidharaya, Dhvanta, Dhuni, Ugra, Bhima, Abhiyu, Sakshipa, Idrik, Anyadrik, Yadrik, Pratikrit, Rik, Samiti, Samrambha, Idriksha, Purusha, Anyadriksha, Chetasa, Samita, Samidriksha, Pratidriksha, Maruti, Sarata, Deva, Disha, Yajuh, Anudrik, Sama, Manusha, and Vish.

इहैकस्थं जगत्कृत्स्नं पश्याद्य सचराचरम् ।
मम देहे गुडाकेश यच्चान्यद्द्रष्टुमिच्छसि ॥7॥

ihaika-sthaṁ jagat kṛitsnaṁ paśhyādya sa-charācharam
mama dehe guḍākeśha yach chānyad draṣhṭum ichchhasi

iha—here; *eka-stham*—assembled together; *jagat*—the universe; *kṛitsnam*—entire; *paśhya*—behold; *adya*—now; *sa*—with; *chara*—the moving; *acharam*—the non-moving; *mama*—my; *dehe*—in this form; *guḍākeśha*—Arjun, conqueror of sleep; *yat*—whatever; *cha*—also; *anyat*—else; *draṣhṭum*—to see; *ichchhasi*—you wish.

Behold now, Arjun, the entire universe, with everything moving and non-moving, assembled together in My universal form. Whatever else you wish to see, observe it all within this universal form.

After hearing Shree Krishna's instructions to behold His form, Arjun wonders where to see it. Shree Krishna states that it is within the body of the Supreme Divine Personality. There, he will see infinite universes with all their moving and non-moving entities. Every entity exists in the universal form, and so do the events of the past and the future. Arjun will thus be able to see the victory of the Pandavas and the defeat of the Kauravas as an event that is a part of the unfoldment of the cosmic plan for the universe.

न तु मां शक्यसे द्रष्टुमनेनैव स्वचक्षुषा ।
दिव्यं ददामि ते चक्षुः पश्य मे योगमैश्वरम् ।।8।।

na tu māṁ śhakyase draṣhṭum anenaiva sva-chakṣhuṣhā
divyaṁ dadāmi te chakṣhuḥ paśhya me yogam aiśhwaram

na—not; *tu*—but; *mām*—me; *śhakyase*—you can; *draṣhṭum*—to see; *anena*—with these; *eva*—even; *sva-chakṣhuṣhā*—with your physical eyes; *divyam*—divine; *dadāmi*—I give; *te*—to you; *chakṣhuḥ*—eyes; *paśhya*—behold; *me*—my; *yogam aiśhwaram*—majestic opulence.

But you cannot see My cosmic form with these physical eyes of yours. Therefore, I grant you divine vision. Behold My majestic opulence!

When the Supreme Lord descends in the world, He has two kinds of forms—one is the material form that can be seen with material eyes, and the other is His divine form that can only be seen with divine vision. Thus, human beings do see Him during His descension upon the earth, but they see only His material form. His divine form is not visible to their material eyes. This is why souls in this material world cannot recognise God when He takes an Avatar on the earth. Shree Krishna mentioned this in chapter 9, verse 11: 'When I descend in My personal form, deluded persons are unable to recognise Me. They do not know the divinity of My personality as the Supreme Lord of all beings.' What people see is only the material form of the divine descension.

The same theory applies to His cosmic form. In the previous two verses, Shree Krishna asked Arjun to see the cosmic form, but Arjun could see nothing because he has material eyes. The physical eyes are insufficient to see that universal form and the ordinary intellect is unequipped to comprehend it. Thus, Shree Krishna now says that He will grant Arjun the divine vision with which it will become possible to behold the universal form in all its glory.

Granting of spiritual vision is an act of grace by the Supreme Lord. By His grace, God adds His divine eyes to the soul's material eyes; He adds His divine mind to the soul's material mind; and His divine intellect to the soul's material intellect. Then, equipped with the divine senses, mind, and intellect of God, the soul can see His divine form, think of it, and comprehend it.

सञ्जय उवाच ।
एवमुक्त्वा ततो राजन्महायोगेश्वरो हरिः ।
दर्शयामास पार्थाय परमं रूपमैश्वरम् ।।9।।

sañjaya uvācha
evam uktvā tato rājan mahā-yogeśhvaro hariḥ
darśhayām āsa pārthāya paramaṁ rūpam aiśhwaram

sañjayaḥ uvācha—Sanjay said; *evam*—thus; *uktvā*—having spoken; *tataḥ*—then; *rājan*—king; *mahā-yoga-īśhvaraḥ*—the Supreme Lord of Yog; *hariḥ*—Shree Krishna; *darśhayām āsa*—displayed; *pārthāya*—to Arjun; *paramam*—divine; *rūpam aiśhwaram*—opulent form.

Sanjay said: O King, having spoken thus, the Supreme Lord of Yog, Shree Krishna, displayed His divine and opulent form to Arjun.

Arjun had referred to Shree Krishna as 'Yogeshwar' in verse 11.4. Now, Sanjay refers to Him as 'Maha-Yogeshwar', adding the superlative 'great' to the address 'Lord of all yogis'. Sanjay was bestowed with the gift of far-sighted vision by his guru, Ved Vyas. As a result, he also beheld the Lord's cosmic form in the same manner as Arjun saw it. In the next four verses, Sanjay describes to Dhritarashtra what Arjun saw. The word *aiśhwarya* means 'opulence'. The cosmic form of God is replete with the manifestation of His opulences, and it invokes fear, awe, and reverence in the beholder.

अनेकवक्त्रनयनमनेकाद्भुतदर्शनम् ।
अनेकदिव्याभरणं दिव्यानेकोद्यतायुधम् ।।10।।

दिव्यमाल्याम्बरधरं दिव्यगन्धानुलेपनम् ।
सर्वाश्चर्यमयं देवमनन्तं विश्वतोमुखम् ।।11।।

aneka-vaktra-nayanam anekādbhuta-darśhanam
aneka-divyābharaṇaṁ divyānekodyatāyudham

divya-mālyāmbara-dharaṁ divya-gandhānulepanam
sarvāśhcharya-mayaṁ devam anantaṁ viśhwato-mukham

aneka—many; *vaktra*—faces; *nayanam*—eyes; *aneka*—many; *adbhuta*—wonderful; *darśhanam*—had a vision of; *aneka*—many; *divya*—divine; *ābharaṇam*—ornaments; *divya*—divine; *aneka*—many; *udyata*—uplifted; *āyudham*—weapons; *divya*—divine; *mālya*—garlands; *āmbara*—garments; *dharam*—wearing; *divya*—divine; *gandha*—fragrances; *anulepanam*—anointed with; *sarva*—all; *āśhcharya-mayam*—wonderful; *devam*—Lord; *anantam*—unlimited; *viśhwataḥ*—all sides; *mukham*—face.

In that cosmic form, Arjun saw unlimited faces and eyes, decorated with many celestial ornaments and wielding many kinds of divine weapons. He wore many garlands on His body and was anointed with many sweet-smelling heavenly fragrances. He revealed Himself as the wonderful and infinite Lord whose face is everywhere.

Sanjay elaborates upon Shree Krishna's divine universal form with the words *aneka* (many) and *anant* (unlimited). The entire creation is the body of God's cosmic form, and therefore it contains countless faces, eyes, mouths, shapes, colours, and forms. The human intellect is conditioned to grasping things within the limited kernel of time, space, and form. The cosmic form of God revealed unusual wonders, marvels, and miracles in all directions, transcending the limitations of space and time. It could be aptly termed as incredible.

दिवि सूर्यसहस्रस्य भवेद्युगपदुत्थिता ।
यदि भाः सदृशी सा स्याद्भासस्तस्य महात्मनः ।।12।।

divi sūrya-sahasrasya bhaved yugapad utthitā
yadi bhāḥ sadṛiśhī sā syād bhāsas tasya mahātmanaḥ

divi—in the sky; *sūrya*—suns; *sahasrasya*—thousand; *bhavet*—were; *yugapat*—simultaneously; *utthitā*—rising; *yadi*—if; *bhāḥ*—splendour; *sadṛiśhī*—like; *sā*—that; *syāt*—would be; *bhāsaḥ*—splendour; *tasya*—of them; *mahā-ātmanaḥ*—the great personality.

If a thousand suns were to blaze forth together in the sky, they would not match the splendour of that great form.

Sanjay now describes the effulgence of the universal form. To give an idea of its dazzling radiance, he compares it to thousands of suns blazing simultaneously in the midday sky. Actually, God's effulgence is unlimited; it cannot be quantified in terms of the effulgence of the sun. However, narrators often describe the unknown by extrapolating from the known. The simile of a thousand suns expressed Sanjay's perception that the splendour of the cosmic form had no parallels.

तत्रैकस्थं जगत्कृत्स्नं प्रविभक्तमनेकधा ।
अपश्यद्देवदेवस्य शरीरे पाण्डवस्तदा ।।13।।

tatraika-sthaṁ jagat kṛitsnaṁ pravibhaktam anekadhā
apaśhyad deva-devasya śharīre pāṇḍavas tadā

tatra—there; *eka-stham*—established in one place; *jagat*—the universe; *kṛitsnam*—entire; *pravibhaktam*—divided; *anekadhā*—many; *apaśhyat*—could see; *deva-devasya*—of the God of gods; *śharīre*—in the body; *pāṇḍavaḥ*—Arjun; *tadā*—at that time.

There, Arjun could see the totality of the entire universe established in one place, in that body of the God of gods.

After describing wondrous spectacles in the cosmic form, Sanjay states that it encompassed the entire universe. Even more amazingly, Arjun saw the totality of existence in the locality of Shree Krishna's body. He beheld the entire creation of infinite universes, with their manifold divisions of galaxies and planetary systems, in a mere fraction of the body of the Supreme Lord.

During His childhood pastimes, Shree Krishna had also revealed the cosmic form to His mother, Yashoda. The Supreme Lord had hidden His mystic opulences and was playing the role of a little child for the pleasure of His devotees. Thinking of Shree Krishna as her son, Yashoda chastised Him severely one day, for eating mud despite her constant admonitions, and asked Him to open His mouth so that she could confirm it for herself. However, to her immense wonder, when Shree Krishna opened His mouth, He revealed within it a vision of His cosmic form by His *Yogmaya* power. Yashoda was bewildered to see such unlimited wonders in the mouth of her little child. She was so overcome by the spectacle that she came on the verge of swooning when Shree Krishna touched her and brought her back to normalcy.

The same cosmic form that the Lord revealed to His mother, Yashoda, He is now revealing to His friend, Arjun. *Now, Sanjay describes Arjun's response to the vision of the cosmic form.*

ततः स विस्मयाविष्टो हृष्टरोमा धनञ्जयः ।
प्रणम्य शिरसा देवं कृताञ्जलिरभाषत ।।14।।

tataḥ sa vismayāviṣhṭo hṛiṣhṭa-romā dhanañjayaḥ
praṇamya śhirasā devaṁ kṛitāñjalir abhāṣhata

tataḥ—then; *saḥ*—he; *vismaya-āviṣhṭaḥ*—full of wonder; *hṛiṣhṭa-romā*—with hair standing on end; *dhanañjayaḥ*—Arjun, conqueror of wealth; *praṇamya*—bow down; *śhirasā*—with (his) head; *devam*—the Lord; *kṛita-añjaliḥ*—with folded hands; *abhāṣhata*—he addressed.

Then, Arjun, full of wonder and with hair standing on end, bowed his head before the Lord, and addressed Him, with folded hands.

Arjun was struck with amazement and deep reverence on seeing that breathtaking spectacle. It struck devotional chords in his heart that evoked paroxysms of delight. The elation experienced through devotional sentiments occasionally finds expression in physical manifestation. The bhakti scriptures describe eight such signs, or the *aṣhṭa sattvic bhav*, which sometimes manifest in devotees when their heart gets thrilled in devotion:

stambha swedo ' tha romāñchaḥ svarabhedo 'tha vepathuḥ
vaivarṇyamaśhru pralaya ityaṣhṭau sātvikāḥ smṛitāḥ

(*Bhakti Rasāmṛit Sindhu*)

'Becoming stupefied, sweating, horripilation, choking of the voice, trembling, complexion becoming ashen, shedding tears, and fainting—these are the physical symptoms by which intense love in the heart sometimes manifests.' That is what Arjun experienced as his hair began standing on end. Bowing down in reverence with folded hands, he uttered the words that follow. *What Arjun said is now described in the next seventeen verses.*

अर्जुन उवाच ।
पश्यामि देवांस्तव देव देहे
सर्वांस्तथा भूतविशेषसङ्घान् ।
ब्रह्माणमीशं कमलासनस्थ-
मृषींश्च सर्वानुरगांश्च दिव्यान् ।।15।।

arjuna uvācha
paśhyāmi devāns tava deva dehe
sarvāns tathā bhūta-viśheṣha-saṅghān
brahmāṇam īśhaṁ kamalāsana-stham
ṛiṣhīnśh cha sarvān uragānśh cha divyān

arjunaḥ uvācha—Arjun said; *paśhyāmi*—I behold; *devān*—all the gods; *tava*—your; *deva*—Lord; *dehe*—within the body; *sarvān*—all; *tathā*—as well as; *bhūta viśheṣha-saṅghān*—hosts of different beings; *brahmāṇam*—Lord Brahma; *īśham*—Shiv; *kamala-āsana-stham*—seated on the lotus flower; *ṛiṣhīn*—sages; *cha*—and; *sarvān*—all; *uragān*—serpents; *cha*—and; *divyān*—divine.

Arjun said: O Shree Krishna, I behold within Your body all the gods and hosts of different beings. I see Brahma seated on the lotus flower; I see Shiv, all the sages, and the celestial serpents.

Arjun exclaimed that he was beholding multitudes of beings from all the three worlds, including the gods of the celestial abodes. The word *kamalāsanasatham* refers to Lord Brahma who sits at the lotus whorl of the universe. Lord Shiv, sages like Vishwamitra, and serpents such as Vasuki were all visible within the cosmic form.

अनेकबाहूदरवक्त्रनेत्रं
पश्यामि त्वां सर्वतोऽनन्तरूपम् ।
नान्तं न मध्यं न पुनस्तवादिं
पश्यामि विश्वेश्वर विश्वरूप ।।16।।

aneka-bāhūdara-vaktra-netraṁ
paśhyāmi tvāṁ sarvato 'nanta-rūpam
nāntaṁ na madhyaṁ na punas tavādiṁ
paśhyāmi viśhweśhwara viśhwa-rūpa

aneka—infinite; *bāhu*—arms; *udara*—stomachs; *vaktra*—faces; *netram*—eyes; *paśhyāmi*—I see; *tvām*—you; *sarvataḥ*—in every direction; *ananta-rūpam*—inifinite forms; *na antam*—without end; *na*—not; *madhyam*—middle; *na*—no; *punaḥ*—again; *tava*—your; *ādim*—beginning; *paśhyāmi*—I see; *viśhwa-īśhwara*—Lord of the universe; *viśhwa-rūpa*—universal form.

I see Your infinite form in every direction, with countless arms, stomachs, faces, and eyes. O Lord of the universe, whose form is the universe itself, I do not see in You any beginning, middle, or end.

Arjun uses two vocatives—*viśhweśhwar*, meaning, 'controller of the universe' and *viśhwaroop*, meaning, 'universal form'. He implies, 'O Shree Krishna, the universe is nothing but Your manifestation, and You are also its Supreme Master.' Further, he expresses the vastness of the form he is experiencing by saying that from whichever angle he looks, he cannot discern any end to the Lord's manifestations. When he searches for the beginning, he is unable to find it; when he tries to see its middle, he again gets no success; and when he searches for the end, he can find no limit to the panorama manifesting before him.

किरीटिनं गदिनं चक्रिणं च
तेजोराशिं सर्वतो दीप्तिमन्तम् ।
पश्यामि त्वां दुर्निरीक्ष्यं समन्ताद्
दीप्तानलार्कद्युतिमप्रमेयम् ।।17।।

kirīṭinaṁ gadinaṁ chakriṇaṁ cha
tejo-rāśhiṁ sarvato dīptimantam
paśhyāmi tvāṁ durnirīkṣhyaṁ samantād
dīptānalārka-dyutim aprameyam

kirīṭinam—adorned with a crown; *gadinam*—with club; *chakriṇam*—with discs; *cha*—and; *tejaḥ-rāśhim*—abode of splendour; *sarvataḥ*—everywhere; *dīpti-mantam*—shining; *paśhyāmi*—I see; *tvām*—you; *durnirīkṣhyam*—difficult to look upon; *samantāt*—in all directions; *dīpta-anala*—blazing fire; *arka*—like the sun; *dyutim*—effulgence; *aprameyam*—immeasurable.

I see Your form, adorned with a crown, and armed with the club and disc, shining everywhere as the abode of splendour. It is hard to look upon You in the blazing fire of Your effulgence which is radiating like the sun in all directions.

Physical eyes get blinded upon seeing something very bright. The cosmic form before Arjun had a brilliance that exceeded thousands of blazing suns. Just as the sun dazzles the eyes, the universal form was simply stunning; the only reason Arjun could behold it was because he had received divine eyes from the Lord.

Within the universal form, Arjun perceived the four-armed Vishnu as another form of the Lord, with the four famous emblems—mace, conch, disc, and lotus flower.

त्वमक्षरं परमं वेदितव्यं
त्वमस्य विश्वस्य परं निधानम् ।
त्वमव्ययः शाश्वतधर्मगोप्ता
सनातनस्त्वं पुरुषो मतो मे ।।18।।

tvam akṣharaṁ paramaṁ veditavyaṁ
tvam asya viśhwasya paraṁ nidhānam
tvam avyayaḥ śhāśhvata-dharma-goptā
sanātanas tvaṁ puruṣho mato me

tvam—you; *akṣharam*—the imperishable; *paramam*—the Supreme Being; *veditavyam*—worthy of being known; *tvam*—you; *asya*—of this; *viśhwasya*—of the creation; *param*—supreme; *nidhānam*—support; *tvam*—you; *avyayaḥ*—eternal; *śhāśhvata-dharma-goptā*—protector of the eternal religion; *sanātanaḥ*—everlasting; *tvam*—you; *puruṣhaḥ*—the Supreme Divine Person; *mataḥ me*—my opinion.

I recognise You as the Supreme Imperishable Being, the Ultimate Truth to be known by the scriptures. You are the support of all creation; You are the eternal protector of *Sanātan Dharma* (the Eternal Religion); and You are the everlasting Supreme Divine Personality.

Arjun announced that he recognised the sovereignty of Shree Krishna's position as the Supreme Lord, who is the support of all creation, and who is to be known through all the scriptures. The *Kaṭhopaniṣhad* states:

sarve vedā yat padamāmananti (1.2.15)

'The aim of all the Vedic mantras is to take us in the direction of God. He is the object of the study of the Vedas.' The Shreemad Bhagavatam states:

vāsudeva-parā vedā vāsudeva-parā makhāḥ (1.2.28)

'The goal of cultivating Vedic knowledge is to reach God. All sacrifices are also meant for pleasing Him.' In his tribute to Shree Krishna, Arjun expressed his realisation that the personal form of the Lord, standing before him, was the same Supreme Absolute Truth that is the object of all Vedic knowledge.

अनादिमध्यान्तमनन्तवीर्य-
मनन्तबाहुं शशिसूर्यनेत्रम् ।

पश्यामि त्वां दीप्तहुताशवक्त्रं-
स्वतेजसा विश्वमिदं तपन्तम् ।।19।।

anādi-madhyāntam ananta-vīryam
ananta-bāhuṁ śhaśhi-sūrya-netram
paśhyāmi tvāṁ dīpta-hutāśha-vaktraṁ
sva-tejasā viśhwam idaṁ tapantam

anādi-madhya-antam—without beginning, middle, or end; *ananta*—infinite; *vīryam*—power; *ananta*—unlimited; *bāhum*—arms; *śhaśhi*—the moon; *sūrya*—the sun; *netram*—eyes; *paśhyāmi*—I see; *tvām*—you; *dīpta*—blazing; *hutāśha*—emanating from; *vaktram*—your mouth; *sva-tejasā*—by your radiance; *viśhwam*—universe; *idam*—this; *tapantam*—warming.

You are without beginning, middle, or end; Your power has no limits. Your arms are infinite; the sun and the moon are like Your eyes; and fire is like Your mouth. I see You warming the entire creation by Your radiance.

In the sixteenth verse, Arjun had said that the form of the Lord is without beginning, middle, or end. He repeats this after just three verses, out of his excitement over what he is seeing. If a statement is uttered repeatedly in amazement, it is taken as an expression of wonder and not considered a literary flaw. For example, on seeing a snake, one may scream, 'Look, a snake! A snake! A snake!' Similarly, Arjun repeats his words in amazement.

God is indeed without a beginning and end. That is because space, time, and causation are within Him. So, He is beyond the measure of their limits. He cannot be encompassed either by space, time, or causation. Further, the sun, moon, and stars receive their energy from the Lord. Thus, it is He who provides warmth to the universe through these entities.

द्यावापृथिव्योरिदमन्तरं हि
व्याप्तं त्वयैकेन दिशश्च सर्वाः ।

दृष्ट्वाद्भुतं रूपमुग्रं तवेदं
लोकत्रयं प्रव्यथितं महात्मन् ।।20।।

dyāv ā-pṛithivyor idam antaraṁ hi
vyāptaṁ tvayaikena diśhaśh cha sarvāḥ
dṛiṣhṭvādbhutaṁ rūpam ugraṁ tavedaṁ
loka-trayaṁ pravyathitaṁ mahātman

dyau-ā-pṛithivyoḥ—between heaven and earth; *idam*—this; *antaram*—space between; *hi*—indeed; *vyāptam*—pervaded; *tvayā*—by you; *ekena*—alone; *diśhaḥ*—directions; *cha*—and; *sarvāḥ*—all; *dṛiṣhṭvā*—seeing; *adbhutam*—wondrous; *rūpam*—form; *ugram*—terrible; *tava*—your; *idam*—this; *loka*—worlds; *trayam*—three; *pravyathitam*—trembling; *mahā-ātman*—greatest of all beings.

The space between heaven and earth and all the directions is pervaded by You alone. Seeing Your wondrous and terrible form, I see the three worlds trembling in fear, O Greatest of all beings.

Arjun says, 'O Omnipresent Lord, You are pervading in all ten directions, the whole earth, the sky above, and the space in-between. All living beings are shuddering in fear of You.' Why should the three worlds shudder before the universal form when they have not even seen it? Arjun implies that everyone is functioning in fear of God's laws. His edicts are in place, and everyone is obliged to submit to them.

karama pradhāna bisva kari rākhā,
jo jasa karai so tasa phala chākhā (Ramayan)

'The world functions according to the Law of Karma. Whatever we do, we will have to reap the karmic results.' Like the Law of Karma, there are innumerable laws in existence. Many scientists make a living out of discovering and theorising the physical laws of nature, but they can never make the laws. God is the Supreme Lawmaker, and everyone is subject to the dominion of His laws.

अमी हि त्वां सुरसङ्घा विशन्ति
केचिद्भीताः प्राञ्जलयो गृणन्ति ।

स्वस्तीत्युक्त्वा महर्षिसिद्धसङ्घाः
स्तुवन्ति त्वां स्तुतिभिः पुष्कलाभिः ।।21।।

amī hi tvāṁ sura-saṅghā viśhanti
kechid bhītāḥ prāñjalayo gṛiṇanti
svastīty uktvā maharṣhi-siddha-saṅghāḥ
stuvanti tvāṁ stutibhiḥ puṣhkalābhiḥ

amī—these; *hi*—indeed; *tvām*—you; *sura-saṅghāḥ*—assembly of celestial gods; *viśhanti*—are entering; *kechit*—some; *bhītāḥ*—in fear; *prāñjalayaḥ*—with folded hands; *gṛiṇanti*—praise; *svasti*—auspicious; *iti*—thus; *uktvā*—reciting; *mahā-ṛiṣhi*—great sages; *siddha-saṅghāḥ*—perfect beings; *stuvanti*—are extolling; *tvām*—you; *stutibhiḥ*—with prayers; *puṣhkalābhiḥ*—hymns.

All the celestial gods are taking Your shelter by entering into You. In awe, some are praising You with folded hands. The great sages and perfected beings are extolling You with auspicious hymns and profuse prayers.

Arjun is seeing here the *kāla roop* of Shree Krishna i.e., His form as all-devouring time. The marching onslaught of time consumes even the greatest of personalities, including the celestial gods. Arjun sees them entering the universal form, with folded hands, in subservience to the *kāla roop* of God. At the same time, he sees the sages and perfected souls extolling the Lord with their thoughts, words, and deeds.

रुद्रादित्या वसवो ये च साध्या
विश्वेऽश्विनौ मरुतश्चोष्मपाश्च ।
गन्धर्वयक्षासुरसिद्धसङ्घा
वीक्षन्ते त्वां विस्मिताश्चैव सर्वे ।।22।।

rudrādityā vasavo ye cha sādhyā
viśhve 'śhvinau marutaśh choṣhmapāśh cha
gandharva-yakṣhāsura-siddha-saṅghā
vīkṣhante tvāṁ vismitāśh chaiva sarve

rudra—a form of Lord Shiv; *ādityāḥ*—the *adityas*; *vasavaḥ*—the *vasus*; *ye*—these; *cha*—and; *sādhyāḥ*—the *sadhyas*; *viśhve*—the *vishvadevas*; *aśhvinau*—the Ashwini Kumars; *marutaḥ*—the *maruts*; *cha*—and; *uṣhma-pāḥ*—the ancestors; *cha*—and; *gandharva*—*gandharvas*; *yakṣha*—the *yakshas*; *asura*—the demons; *siddha*—the perfected beings; *saṅghāḥ*—the assemblies; *vīkṣhante*—are beholding; *tvām*—you; *vismitāḥ*—in wonder; *cha*—and; *eva*—verily; *sarve*—all.

The *rudras, adityas, vasus, sadhyas, vishvadevas,* Ashwini Kumars, *maruts,* ancestors, *gandharvas, yakṣhas,* asuras, and *siddhas* are all beholding You in wonder.

All these personalities receive their positions by the power of God, and they discharge their respective duties in reverence to the Laws of Creation. Thus, they all are mentioned as beholding the cosmic form of God with wonder.

रूपं महत्ते बहुवक्त्रनेत्रं
महाबाहो बहुबाहूरुपादम् ।
बहूदरं बहुदंष्ट्राकरालं
दृष्ट्वा लोकाः प्रव्यथितास्तथाहम् ।।23।।

rūpaṁ mahat te bahu-vaktra-netraṁ
mahā-bāho bahu-bāhūru-pādam
bahūdaraṁ bahu-danṣhṭrā-karālaṁ
dṛiṣhṭvā lokāḥ pravyathitās tathāham

rūpam—form; *mahat*—magnificent; *te*—your; *bahu*—many; *vaktra*—mouths; *netram*—eyes; *mahā-bāho*—mighty-armed Lord; *bahu*—many; *bāhu*—arms; *ūru*—thighs; *pādam*—legs; *bahu-udaram*—many stomachs; *bahu-danṣhṭrā*—many teeth; *karālam*—terrifying; *dṛiṣhṭvā*—seeing; *lokāḥ*—all the worlds; *pravyathitāḥ*—terror-stricken; *tathā*—so also; *aham*—I.

O mighty Lord, in veneration of Your magnificent form with its many mouths, eyes, arms, thighs, legs, stomachs, and terrifying teeth, all the worlds are terror-stricken, and so am I.

The numerous hands, legs, faces, and stomach of God are everywhere. The *Śhwetāśhvatar Upanishad* states:

sahasraśhīrṣhā puruṣhaḥ sahasrākṣhaḥ sahasrapāt
sa bhūmiṁ viśhwato vṛitvātyatiṣhṭhaddaśhāṅgulam (3.14)

'The Supreme Entity has thousands of heads, thousands of eyes, and thousands of feet. He envelopes the universe but is transcendental to it. He resides in all humans, about ten fingers above the navel, in the lotus of the heart.' Those who are beholding and those who are being beheld, the terrified and the terrifying, all are within the universal form of the Lord. Again, the *Kaṭhopaniṣhad* states:

bhayādasyāgnistapati bhayāt tapati sūryaḥ
bhayādindraśhcha vāyuśhcha mṛityurdhāvati pañchamaḥ
(2.3.3)

'It is from the fear of God that the fire burns and the sun shines. It is out of fear of Him that the wind blows, and Indra causes the rain to fall. Even Yamraj, the god of death, trembles before Him.'

नभःस्पृशं दीप्तमनेकवर्णं
व्यात्ताननं दीप्तविशालनेत्रम् ।
दृष्ट्वा हि त्वां प्रव्यथितान्तरात्मा
धृतिं न विन्दामि शमं च विष्णो ।।24।।

nabhaḥ-spṛiśhaṁ dīptam aneka-varṇaṁ
vyāttānanaṁ dīpta-viśhāla-netram
dṛiṣhṭvā hi tvāṁ pravyathitāntar-ātmā
dhṛitiṁ na vindāmi śhamaṁ cha viṣhṇo

nabhaḥ-spṛiśham—touching the sky; *dīptam*—effulgent; *aneka*—many; *varṇam*—colours; *vyātta*—open; *ānanam*—mouths; *dīpta*—blazing; *viśhāla*—enormous; *netram*—eyes; *dṛiṣhṭvā*—seeing; *hi*—indeed; *tvām*—you; *pravyathitāntar-ātmā*—my heart is trembling with fear; *dhṛitim*—firmness; *na*—not; *vindāmi*—I find; *śhamam*—mental peace; *cha*—and; *viṣhṇo*—Lord Vishnu.

O Lord Vishnu, seeing Your form touching the sky, effulgent in many colours, with mouths wide open and enormous blazing eyes, my heart is trembling with fear. I have lost all courage and peace of mind.

Seeing the cosmic form of God changed the nature of Arjun's relationship with Shree Krishna. Earlier, he had looked upon Him as an intimate friend and interacted in a manner befitting a close associate. He was aware at the back of his head that Shree Krishna was God, but the love overflowing in his heart would make him forget the almighty aspect of Shree Krishna's personality. All he would remember was that he loved his Friend Shree Krishna more than anything else in the world.

That is the nature of love. It absorbs the mind so deeply that the devotee forgets the formal position of his Beloved Lord. And if formality is retained, then love is unable to manifest in its fullness. For example, a wife loves her husband deeply. Though he may be the governor of the state, the wife only looks upon him as her husband, and that is how she is able to interact intimately with him. If she keeps this knowledge in her head that her husband is the governor, then each time he comes by, she will be inclined to pay a more ceremonial respect to him. So, the knowledge of the official position of the beloved gets immersed in the loving sentiments. The same phenomenon takes place in devotion to God.

The cowherds of Braj merely viewed Shree Krishna as their bosom buddy. Jagadguru Shree Kripaluji Maharaj describes their pastimes with Shree Krishna very sweetly:

dekho dekho rī, gwāla bālana yārī
rijhavata khela jitāya sakhana ko, ghoṛā bani bani banawārī

(*Prem Ras Madirā*, *Rasiyā Mādhuri*, Pada 7)

'Look at the sweetness of the loving interactions between Shree Krishna and His cowherd friends! They play games together, and when Shree Krishna loses the game, He becomes a horse by sitting on all fours and His friend rides on His back.' If the cowherd friends remembered that Shree Krishna was God, they would never have the gumption to do such a thing. And the Lord too relishes the intimacy of such interactions with His devotees in which they relate to Him as a dear friend.

Shree Krishna enacted the famous Govardhan Leela upon the earth. He lifted the Govardhan Hill on the little finger of His left hand to protect the residents of the land of Braj from the torrential downpour caused by Indra, king of heaven and the celestial god of rain. However, Krishna's little cowherd associates were not impressed. In their eyes, Krishna was merely a loveable friend. They did not believe He could lift the hill. Jagadguru Shree Kripaluji Maharaj states in continuation to the verse above:

nakha dhāryo goverdhana-giri jaba,
sakhana kahyo hama giridhārī

(*Prem Ras Madirā*, *Rasiyā Mādhurī*, Pada 7)

'When Shree Krishna lifted the Govardhan Hill, His cowherd friends applied their sticks to the bottom of the hill, thinking that they were the actual lifters of the hill.' At the end of seven nights and seven days, Indra accepted defeat and came seated on his white elephant. He apologised for having sent the torrential rain, without realising Shree Krishna's supreme position.

Now, when the cowherd boys saw Indra, the king of heaven, coming and offering obeisance to their friend Krishna, they realised that Krishna is God. So, they began looking at Him fearfully from a distance. Seeing their devotional sentiment change from friendship to awe and reverence, Shree Krishna lamented, 'That loving exchange we were enjoying has vanished. They are now thinking I am God.' Then by His *Yogmaya* power, He made them forget the significance of what they had seen, and they again felt that Shree Krishna was nothing more than their friend.

Arjun was also a devotee of Shree Krishna in *sakhya bhav*. He was used to relating to Shree Krishna as his friend. That is why he had agreed to Shree Krishna as his chariot driver. If his devotion had been motivated by the fact that Shree Krishna was the Supreme Lord of all creation, Arjun would never have allowed Him to do such a demeaning service. But now, seeing His infinite splendour and inconceivable opulences, his fraternal sentiment towards Shree Krishna is replaced by fear.

दंष्ट्राकरालानि च ते मुखानि
दृष्ट्वैव कालानलसन्निभानि ।
दिशो न जाने न लभे च शर्म
प्रसीद देवेश जगन्निवास ॥25॥

danṣhṭrā-karālāni cha te mukhāni
dṛiṣhṭvaiva kālānala-sannibhāni
diśho na jāne na labhe cha śharma
prasīda deveśha jagan-nivāsa

danṣhṭrā—teeth; *karālāni*—terrible; *cha*—and; *te*—your; *mukhāni*—mouths; *dṛiṣhṭvā*—having seen; *eva*—indeed; *kāla-anala*—the fire of annihilation; *sannibhāni*—resembling; *diśhaḥ*—the directions; *na*—not; *jāne*—know; *na*—not; *labhe*—I obtain; *cha*—and; *śharma*—peace; *prasīda*—have mercy; *deva-īśha*—Lord of lords; *jagat-nivāsa*—shelter of the universe.

Having seen Your many mouths bearing Your terrible teeth, resembling the raging fire at the time of annihilation, I forget where I am and do not know where to go. O Lord of lords, You are the shelter of the universe; please have mercy on me.

The universal form that Arjun beholds is just another aspect of Shree Krishna's personality and is non-different from Him. And yet, the vision of it has dried up the camaraderie that Arjun previously felt towards Shree Krishna, and he is overcome with fear. Seeing the many wondrous and amazingly frightful manifestations of the Lord, Arjun is now scared, and thinks that Shree Krishna is angry with him. Consequently, he asks for mercy.

अमी च त्वां धृतराष्ट्रस्य पुत्राः
सर्वे सहैवावनिपालसङ्घैः ।

भीष्मो द्रोणः सूतपुत्रस्तथासौ
सहास्मदीयैरपि योधमुख्यैः ।।26।।

वक्त्राणि ते त्वरमाणा विशन्ति
दंष्ट्राकरालानि भयानकानि ।
केचिद्विलग्ना दशनान्तरेषु
सन्दृश्यन्ते चूर्णितैरुत्तमाङ्गैः ।।27।।

amī cha tvāṁ dhṛitarāśhtrasya putrāḥ
sarve sahaivāvani-pāla-saṅghaiḥ
bhīṣhmo droṇaḥ sūta-putras tathāsau
sahāsmadīyair api yodha-mukhyaiḥ

vaktrāṇi te tvaramāṇā viśhanti
danṣhṭrā-karālāni bhayānakāni
kechid vilagnā daśhanāntareṣhu
sandṛiśhyante chūrṇitair uttamāṅgaiḥ

amī—these; *cha*—and; *tvām*—you; *dhṛitarāśhtrasya*—of Dhritarashtra; *putrāḥ*—sons; *sarve*—all; *saha*—with; *eva*—even; *avani-pāla*—their allied kings; *sanghaiḥ*—assembly; *bhīṣhmaḥ*—Bheeshma; *droṇaḥ*—Dronacharya; *sūta-putraḥ*—Karn; *tathā*—and also; *asau*—this; *saha*—with; *asmadīyaiḥ*—from our side; *api*—also; *yodha-mukhyaiḥ*—generals; *vaktrāṇi*—mouths; *te*—your; *tvaramāṇāḥ*—rushing; *viśhanti*—enter; *danṣhṭrā*—teeth; *karālāni*—terrible; *bhayānakāni*—fearsome; *kechit*—some; *vilagnāḥ*—getting stuck; *daśhana-antareṣhu*—between the teeth; *sandṛiśhyante*—are seen; *chūrṇitaiḥ*—getting smashed; *uttama-aṅgaiḥ*—heads.

I see all the sons of Dhritarashtra, along with their allied kings, including Bheeshma, Dronacharya, Karn, and also the generals from our side, rushing headlong into Your fearsome mouths. I see some with their heads smashed between Your terrible teeth.

What are the teeth of God that Arjun is referring to? He mentioned them in the previous verse as well. We use our teeth to grind our food.

God's teeth are His forces of destruction that grind everyone to death with the passage of time. The American poet, H.W. Longfellow wrote:

> Though the mills of God grind slowly,
> Yet they grind exceeding small;
> Though with patience He stands waiting,
> With exactness grinds He all.

Arjun sees the great Kaurava generals—Bheeshma, Dronacharya, and Karn—and also many of the Pandava generals rushing headlong into the mouth of the Lord, to be ground between his teeth. He is beholding the imminent future in the cosmic form of God. Since God is beyond the limits of time, so the past, present, and future are visible within Him in the present.

Bheeshma, the grandsire of the Kauravas and the Pandavas, was the son of Shantanu and Ganga. To facilitate his father's wish for remarriage, Bheeshma renounced his right to the throne, and also took a lifelong vow of celibacy. However, Bheeshma had continued to support Duryodhan, despite knowing very well that he was evil and was usurping the right of the Pandavas. Thus, he was destined to die in this war of goodness versus evil. The Shreemad Bhagavatam describes Bheeshma's prayer to the Lord, when he lay on the bed of arrows at the end of his life:

sapadi sakhi-vacho niśhamya madhye
    nija-parayor balayo rathaṁ niveśhya
sthitavati para-sainikāyur akṣhṇā
    hṛitavati pārtha-sakhe ratir mamāstu (1.9.35)

'Let my mind meditate upon Arjun's dear pal, Shree Krishna, who obeyed His friend's command to drive the chariot to the centre of the two armies, and while there, He shortened the lifespan of the opposing generals by His mere glance.' So, Bheeshma himself was aware that the consequence of fighting against the Supreme Lord Shree Krishna would be death.

Dronacharya was the guru of martial arts for both the Kauravas and the Pandavas. He was so impartial that he taught more about military science to Arjun than even to his son, Ashwatthama. However, he felt obliged to help Duryodhan because he was financially dependent upon him for his maintenance. Thus, Dronacharya too was destined to die in the war. Yet, his heroism can be judged from the fact that when the Pandavas were unable to slay him by any means and approached him for guidance, he gave them a solution.

Karn was a bosom friend of Duryodhan, which is why he supported the Kauravas. He too had heroic qualities. When Shree Krishna disclosed to him that he was the eldest son of Kunti and the Pandavas were actually his brothers, he asked Shree Krishna not to disclose this secret to Yudhishthir, or else he would stop trying to kill Karn and would lose the war. Since Karn had taken the side of Duryodhan in the war, he too was destined to die.

यथा नदीनां बहवोऽम्बुवेगाः
समुद्रमेवाभिमुखा द्रवन्ति ।
तथा तवामी नरलोकवीरा
विशन्ति वक्त्राण्यभिविज्वलन्ति ।।28।।

यथा प्रदीप्तं ज्वलनं पतङ्गा
विशन्ति नाशाय समृद्धवेगाः ।
तथैव नाशाय विशन्ति लोका-
स्तवापि वक्त्राणि समृद्धवेगाः ।।29।।

yathā nadīnāṁ bahavo 'mbu-vegāḥ
samudram evābhimukhā dravanti
tathā tavāmī nara-loka-vīrā
viśhanti vaktrāṇy abhivijvalanti

yathā pradīptaṁ jvalanaṁ pataṅgā
viśhanti nāśhāya samṛiddha-vegāḥ
tathaiva nāśhāya viśhanti lokās
tavāpi vaktrāṇi samṛiddha-vegāḥ

yathā—as; *nadīnām*—of the rivers; *bahavaḥ*—many; *ambu-vegāḥ*—water waves; *samudram*—the ocean; *eva*—indeed; *abhimukhāḥ*—

towards; *dravanti*—flowing rapidly; *tathā*—similarly; *tava*—your; *amī*—these; *nara-loka-vīrāḥ*—kings of human society; *viśhanti*—enter; *vaktrāṇi*—mouths; *abhivijvalanti*—blazing; *yathā*—as; *pradīptam*—burning intensely; *jvalanam*—fire; *pataṅgāḥ*—moths; *viśhanti*—enter; *nāśhāya*—to be perished; *samṛiddha vegāḥ*—with great speed; *tathā eva*—similarly; *nāśhāya*—to be perished; *viśhanti*—enter; *lokāḥ*—these people; *tava*—your; *api*—also; *vaktrāṇi*—mouths; *samṛiddha-vegāḥ*—with great speed.

As many waves of the rivers flowing rapidly into the ocean, so are all these great warriors entering into Your blazing mouths. As moths rush with great speed into the fire to perish, so are all these armies entering with great speed into Your mouths.

There were many noble kings and warriors in the war who fought as their duty and laid down their lives on the battlefield. Arjun compares them to river waves willingly merging into the ocean. There were also many others who fought out of greed and self-interest. Arjun compares them with moths being lured ignorantly into the incinerating fire. But in both cases, they are marching rapidly towards their imminent death.

लेलिह्यसे ग्रसमानः समन्ता-
ल्लोकान्समग्रान्वदनैर्ज्वलद्भिः ।
तेजोभिरापूर्य जगत्समग्रं
भासस्तवोग्राः प्रतपन्ति विष्णो ।।30।।

lelihyase grasamānaḥ samantāl
lokān samagrān vadanair jvaladbhiḥ
tejobhir āpūrya jagat samagraṁ
bhāsas tavogrāḥ pratapanti viṣhṇo

lelihyase—you are licking; *grasamānaḥ*—devouring; *samantāt*—on all sides; *lokān*—worlds; *samagrān*—all; *vadanaiḥ*—with mouths; *jvaladbhiḥ*—blazing; *tejobhiḥ*—by effulgence; *āpūrya*—filled with; *jagat*—the universe; *samagram*—all; *bhāsaḥ*—rays; *tava*—your; *ugrāḥ*—fierce; *pratapanti*—scorching; *viṣhṇo*—Lord Vishnu.

With Your fiery tongues You are licking up the hosts of living beings on all sides and devouring them with Your blazing mouths. O Vishnu, You are scorching the entire universe with the fierce, all-pervading rays of Your effulgence.

The Lord controls the world with grandiose forces of creation, maintenance, and annihilation. At present, He is being perceived by Arjun in this mode as the all-devouring force that is engulfing his friends and allies from all sides. Viewing the apparition of future events in the cosmic form of God, Arjun sees his enemies being wiped out in the imminent battle. He also sees many of his allies in the grip of death. *Petrified by the spectacle he is seeing, Arjun supplicates before Shree Krishna in the next verse.*

आख्याहि मे को भवानुग्ररूपो
नमोऽस्तु ते देववर प्रसीद ।
विज्ञातुमिच्छामि भवन्तमाद्यं
न हि प्रजानामि तव प्रवृत्तिम् ।।31।।

ākhyāhi me ko bhavān ugra-rūpo
namo 'stu te deva-vara prasīda
vijñātum ichchhāmi bhavantam ādyaṁ
na hi prajānāmi tava pravṛittim

ākhyāhi—tell; *me*—me; *kaḥ*—who; *bhavān*—you; *ugra-rūpaḥ*—fierce form; *namaḥ astu*—I bow; *te*—to you; *deva-vara*—God of gods; *prasīda*—be merciful; *vijñātum*—to know; *ichchhāmi*—I wish; *bhavantam*—you; *ādyam*—the primeval; *na*—not; *hi*—because; *prajānāmi*—comprehend; *tava*—your; *pravṛittim*—workings.

Tell me who You are, so fierce of form. O God of gods, I bow before You; please bestow Your mercy on me. You, who existed before all creation, I wish to know who You are, for I do not comprehend Your nature and workings.

Earlier, Arjun had requested to see the universal form. When Shree Krishna exhibited it, Arjun became bewildered and agitated. Having witnessed an almost unbelievable cosmic spectacle, he now wants to know the very heart of God's nature and purpose. Hence, he asks the question, 'Who are You, and what is Your purpose?'

श्रीभगवानुवाच ।
कालोऽस्मि लोकक्षयकृत्प्रवृद्धो
लोकान्समाहर्तुमिह प्रवृत्तः ।
ऋतेऽपि त्वां न भविष्यन्ति सर्वे
येऽवस्थिताः प्रत्यनीकेषु योधाः ।।32।।

śhrī-bhagavān uvācha
kālo 'smi loka-kṣhaya-kṛit pravṛiddho
lokān samāhartum iha pravṛittaḥ
ṛite 'pi tvāṁ na bhaviṣhyanti sarve
ye 'vasthitāḥ pratyanīkeṣhu yodhāḥ

śhrī-bhagavān uvācha—the Supreme Lord said; *kālaḥ*—time; *asmi*—I am; *loka-kṣhaya-kṛit*—the source of destruction of the worlds; *pravṛiddhaḥ*—mighty; *lokān*—the worlds; *samāhartum*—annihilation; *iha*—this world; *pravṛittaḥ*—participation; *ṛite*—without; *api*—even; *tvām*—you; *na bhaviṣhyanti*—shall cease to exist; *sarve*—all; *ye*—who; *avasthitāḥ*—arrayed; *prati-anīkeṣhu*—in the opposing army; *yodhāḥ*—the warriors.

The Supreme Lord said: I am mighty Time, the source of destruction that comes forth to annihilate the worlds. Even without your participation, the warriors arrayed in the opposing army shall cease to exist.

In response to Arjun's question regarding who He is, Shree Krishna reveals His nature as all-powerful Time, destroyer of the universe. The word *kāla* is derived from *kalayati*, which is synonymous with *gaṇayati*, meaning, 'to take count of'. All events in nature get buried in time. When Oppenheimer, who was a part of the first atom bomb project, witnessed the destruction of Hiroshima and Nagasaki, he quoted this verse of Shree Krishna in the following manner: 'Time ... I am the destroyer of all the worlds.' Time counts and controls the lifespan of all beings. It will determine when great personalities like Bheeshma, Dronacharya, and Karn will meet their end. It will destroy the enemy army arrayed on the battlefield even without Arjun participating in the fight because the Lord wants it to happen as a part of His grand plan for the world. *If the warriors are already as good as dead, then why should Arjun fight? Shree Krishna explains this in the next verse.*

तस्मात्त्वमुत्तिष्ठ यशो लभस्व
जित्वा शत्रून्भुङ्क्ष्व राज्यं समृद्धम् ।
मयैवैते निहताः पूर्वमेव
निमित्तमात्रं भव सव्यसाचिन् ।।33।।

tasmāt tvam uttiṣhṭha yaśho labhasva
jitvā śhatrūn bhuṅkṣhva rājyaṁ samṛiddham
mayaivaite nihatāḥ pūrvam eva
nimitta-mātraṁ bhava savya-sāchin

tasmāt—therefore; *tvam*—you; *uttiṣhṭha*—arise; *yaśhaḥ*—honour; *labhasva*—attain; *jitvā*—conquer; *śhatrūn*—foes; *bhuṅkṣhva*—enjoy; *rājyam*—kingdom; *samṛiddham*—prosperous; *mayā*—by me; *eva*—indeed; *ete*—these; *nihatāḥ*—slain; *pūrvam*—already; *eva nimitta-mātram*—only an instrument; *bhava*—become; *savya-sāchin*—Arjun, the one who can shoot arrows with both hands.

Therefore, arise and attain honour! Conquer your foes and enjoy prosperous rulership. These warriors stand already slain by Me, and you will only be an instrument of My work, O expert archer.

Shree Krishna has revealed to Arjun His will that the Kauravas should perish and the kingdom of Hastinapur should be administered by the Pandavas in accordance with rules of dharma. He has already decided the annihilation of the unrighteous and the victory of the righteous as the outcome of the battle. His grand scheme for the welfare of the world cannot be averted by any means. He now informs Arjun that He wishes him to be the *nimitta-mātram* or the instrument of His work. God does not need the help of a human for His work, but humans attain eternal welfare by working to fulfil God's wish. Opportunities that come our way to accomplish something for the pleasure of the Lord are a very special blessing. It is by taking these opportunities that we attract His special grace and achieve our permanent position as the servant of God.

Shree Krishna also encourages Arjun to be His instrument by reminding him of the exceptional skills he has received in the art of archery by His grace. Hence, He addresses him with the evocative *savya-sāchin,* meaning, 'expert archer' since Arjun is admirably ambidextrous and is able to discharge arrows with either hand.

द्रोणं च भीष्मं च जयद्रथं च
कर्णं तथान्यानपि योधवीरान् ।
मया हतांस्त्वं जहि मा व्यथिष्ठा
युध्यस्व जेतासि रणे सपत्नान् ।।34।।

droṇaṁ cha bhīṣhmaṁ cha jayadrathaṁ cha
karṇaṁ tathānyān api yodha-vīrān
mayā hatāṁs tvaṁ jahi mā vyathiṣhṭhā
yudhyasva jetāsi raṇe sapatnān

droṇam—Dronacharya; *cha*—and; *bhīṣhmam*—Bheeshma; *cha*—and; *jayadratham*—Jayadratha; *cha*—and; *karṇam*—Karn; *tathā*—also; *anyān*—others; *api*—also; *yodha-vīrān*—brave warriors; *mayā*—by me; *hatān*—already killed; *tvam*—you; *jahi*—slay; *mā*—not; *vyathiṣhṭhāḥ*—be disturbed; *yudhyasva*—fight; *jetā asi*—you shall be victorious; *raṇe*—in battle; *sapatnān*—enemies.

Dronacharya, Bheeshma, Jayadratha, Karn, and other brave warriors have already been killed by Me. Therefore, slay them without being disturbed. Just fight and you will be victorious over your enemies in battle.

Many of the generals on the side of the Kauravas were heretofore undefeated in combat. Jayadrath had the boon that whoever caused his head to fall on the ground would instantly have his own head burst into pieces. Karn had a special weapon called *Shakti* given to him by Indra, which would slay anyone against whom it was used. But it could only be used once, so Karn had kept it to take vengeance on Arjun. Dronacharya had received knowledge of all weapons and how to neutralise them from Parshuram, who was an Avatar of God. Bheeshma had a boon that he would only die when he chose to do so. And yet, if God wished them to die in the battle, then nothing could save them. There is a saying:

vindhya na īndhana pāiye, sāgara juḍai na nīra
parai upas kuber ghara, jyoṅ vipakṣha raghubīra

'If Lord Ram decides to be against you, then you may live in the Vindhyachal forest, but you will not be able to get firewood to light a fire; you may be by the side of the ocean, but water will be scarce for your usage; and you may live in the house of Kuber, the god of wealth, but you will not have enough to eat.' Thus, even the biggest arrangements for security cannot avert a person's death if God has willed it to happen. Similarly, Shree Krishna says that He has already decided the outcome, but He wishes Arjun to be the medium to accomplish it and receive the glory of the conquest as a reward for his devotion. Just as devotees wish to glorify God, it is God's nature to glorify His devotees. Hence, Shree Krishna does not wish the credit to come to Him; He wishes people to say after the war, 'Arjun fought so valiantly that he secured victory for the Pandavas.'

In spiritual life too, aspirants often become discouraged when they find themselves incapable of removing the defects of anger, greed, envy, lust, pride, and other negative emotions. Their guru then encourages them, 'Do not be dejected. Fight and you will conquer the enemies of your mind because God wants you to succeed. Your effort will be instrumental, while God will fashion your victory by His grace.'

What was Arjun's reaction upon hearing the Lord's call to action? This is stated in the next verse.

सञ्जय उवाच ।
एतच्छ्रुत्वा वचनं केशवस्य
कृताञ्जलिर्वेपमानः किरीटी ।
नमस्कृत्वा भूय एवाह कृष्णं
सगद्गदं भीतभीतः प्रणम्य ।।35।।

sañjaya uvācha
etach chhrutvā vachanaṁ keśhavasya
kṛitāñjalir vepamānaḥ kirīṭī
namaskṛitvā bhūya evāha kṛiṣhṇaṁ
sa-gadgadaṁ bhīta-bhītaḥ praṇamya

sañjayaḥ uvācha—Sanjay said; *etat*—thus; *śhrutvā*—hearing; *vachanam*—words; *keśhavasya*—of Shree Krishna; *kṛita-añjaliḥ*—with joined palms; *vepamānaḥ*—trembling; *kirīṭī*—the crowned one, Arjun; *namaskṛitvā*—with palms joined; *bhūyaḥ*—again; *eva*—indeed; *āha*—spoke; *kṛiṣhṇam*—to Shree Krishna; *sa-gadgadam*—in a faltering voice; *bhīta-bhītaḥ*—overwhelmed with fear; *praṇamya*—bowed down.

Sanjay said: Hearing these words of Keshav, Arjun trembled with dread. With palms joined, he bowed before Shree Krishna and spoke in a faltering voice, overwhelmed with fear.

Here, Arjun is referred to as 'the crowned one'. He had once helped Indra kill two demons. As a token of his pleasure, Indra had placed a dazzling crown on his head. In this verse, Sanjay refers to the crown on Arjun's head. But a crown is also the symbol of monarchy, and Sanjay deliberately uses the word to hint to the old king Dhritarashtra that his sons, the Kauravas, will lose the throne to the Pandavas in the impending war.

अर्जुन उवाच ।
स्थाने हृषीकेश तव प्रकीर्त्या
जगत्प्रहृष्यत्यनुरज्यते च ।

रक्षांसि भीतानि दिशो द्रवन्ति
सर्वे नमस्यन्ति च सिद्धसङ्घाः ।।36।।

arjuna uvācha
sthāne hṛiṣhīkeśha tava prakīrtyā
jagat prahṛiṣhyaty anurajyate cha
rakṣhānsi bhītāni diśho dravanti
sarve namasyanti cha siddha-saṅghāḥ

arjunaḥ uvācha—Arjun said; *sthāne*—it is but apt; *hṛiṣhīka-īśha*—Shree Krishna, master of the senses; *tava*—your; *prakīrtyā*—in praise; *jagat*—universe; *prahṛiṣhyati*—rejoices; *anurajyate*—be enamoured; *cha*—and; *rakṣhānsi*—demons; *bhītāni*—fearfully; *diśhaḥ*—in all directions; *dravanti*—flee; *sarve*—all; *namasyanti*—bow down; *cha*—and; *siddha-saṅghāḥ*—hosts of perfected saints.

Arjun said: O Master of the senses, it is but apt that the universe rejoices in giving You praise and is enamoured by You. Demons flee fearfully from You in all directions and hosts of perfected saints bow to You.

In this verse and the next ten , Arjun eulogises Shree Krishna's glories from various perspectives. He uses the word *sthāne,* meaning, 'it is but apt'. It is but natural that the people of a kingdom who accept the sovereignty of their king delight in glorifying him. It is also natural that those who harbour enmity towards the king fear him and flee from his presence. And it is natural for the king's retinue of ministers to be deeply devoted to him. Arjun draws a parallel to this, saying that it is only appropriate that the world glorifies their Supreme Lord, the demons become frightened of Him, and the saintly personalities offer devotional prayers to Him.

कस्माच्च ते न नमेरन्महात्मन्
गरीयसे ब्रह्मणोऽप्यादिकर्त्रे ।
अनन्त देवेश जगन्निवास
त्वमक्षरं सदसत्तत्परं यत् ।।37।।

kasmāch cha te na nameran mahātman
garīyase brahmaṇo 'py ādi-kartre
ananta deveśha jagan-nivāsa
tvam akṣharaṁ sad-asat tat paraṁ yat

kasmāt—why; *cha*—and; *te*—you; *na nameran*—should they not bow down; *mahā-ātman*—the great One; *garīyase*—who are greater; *brahmaṇaḥ*—than Brahma; *api*—even; *ādi-kartre*—to the original creator; *ananta*—The limitless One; *deva-īśha*—Lord of the *devatās*; *jagat-nivāsa*—Refuge of the universe; *tvam*—you; *akṣharam*—the imperishable; *sat-asat*—manifest and non-manifest; *tat*—that; *param*—beyond; *yat*—which.

O Great One, who are even greater than Brahma, the original creator, why should they not bow to You? O Limitless One, O Lord of the *devatās*, O Refuge of the universe, You are the imperishable reality beyond both the manifest and the non-manifest.

Justifying in four verses why the behaviour mentioned in the previous verse is apt, Arjun uses the words *kasmāchcha tena*, meaning, 'why should they not'. Why shouldn't all living beings offer their humble respects to the Supreme Lord, when the entire creation emanates from Him, is sustained by Him, and shall merge back into Him? He is everything that is manifest in creation because it is all His energy. He is also everything that remains unmanifest because it is His latent energy. And yet He is beyond both the manifest and the unmanifest because He is the Supreme Energetic—the Source and Supreme Master of all the energies. Hence, neither the material energy nor the souls can ever do anything to impact His personality which is transcendental to both.

Arjun specifically mentions that Shree Krishna is greater than the secondary creator Brahma because Brahma is the senior most in the universe. All living beings are either Brahma's progeny or descendants of his progeny. However, Brahma himself was born from a lotus that grew from the navel of Lord Vishnu, who is an expansion of Shree Krishna. Thus, while Brahma is considered the senior most grandsire of the world, Shree Krishna is Brahma's Grandsire. It is thus apt that Brahma should bow to Him.

त्वमादिदेवः पुरुषः पुराणस्-
त्वमस्य विश्वस्य परं निधानम् ।
वेत्तासि वेद्यं च परं च धाम
त्वया ततं विश्वमनन्तरूप ।।38।।

tvam ādi-devaḥ puruṣhaḥ purāṇas
tvam asya viśhwasya paraṁ nidhānam
vettāsi vedyaṁ cha paraṁ cha dhāma
tvayā tataṁ viśhwam ananta-rūpa

tvam—you; *ādi-devaḥ*—the original Divine God; *puruṣhaḥ*—personality; *purāṇaḥ*—primeval; *tvam*—you; *asya*—of (this); *viśhwasya*—universe; *param*—supreme; *nidhānam*—resting place; *vettā*—the knower; *asi*—you are; *vedyam*—the object of knowledge; *cha*—and; *param*—supreme; *cha*—and; *dhāma*—abode; *tvayā*—by you; *tatam*—pervaded; *viśhwam*—universe; *ananta-rūpa*—posessor of infinite forms.

You are the primeval God and the original Divine Personality; You are the sole resting place of this universe. You are both the knower and the object of knowledge; You are the Supreme Abode. O possessor of infinite forms, You alone pervade the entire universe.

Arjun addresses Shree Krishna as the original Divine Person, the Cause of all causes. Every object and every personality has a cause or a source from which it comes into being. Even Lord Vishnu has a cause. Although He is also a form of God, He is an expansion of Shree Krishna. However, Shree Krishna is not the expansion of any personality. He is the causeless first Cause of everything that exists. Hence, Brahma prays to Him:

īśhwaraḥ paramaḥ kṛiṣhaṇaḥ sachchidānanda vigrahaḥ
anādirādi govindaḥ sarva kāraṇa kāraṇam

(*Brahma Samhitā* 5.1)

'Shree Krishna is the original form of the Supreme Lord. His personality is full of knowledge and bliss. He is the origin of all, but He is without origin. He is the Cause of all causes.'

Shree Krishna is omniscient—the knower of everything. Further, He is also the object of all knowledge. The Shreemad Bhagavatam (4.29.49) states: *sā vidyā tanmatir yayā* 'True knowledge is that which helps us know God.' Jagadguru Shree Kripaluji Maharaj states:

jo hari sevā hetu ho, soī karm bakhān
jo hari bhagati baṛhāve, soī samujhiya jñāna

(*Bhakti Śhatak* verse 66)

'Whatever work is done in the service of God, know that truly to be karm. Whatever knowledge enhances our love for God, know that to be true jnana.' Hence, Shree Krishna is both the knower and the object of knowledge.

वायुर्यमोऽग्निर्वरुणः शशाङ्कः
प्रजापतिस्त्वं प्रपितामहश्च ।
नमो नमस्तेऽस्तु सहस्रकृत्वः
पुनश्च भूयोऽपि नमो नमस्ते ।।39।।

vāyur yamo 'gnir varuṇaḥ śhaśhāṅkaḥ
prajāpatis tvaṁ prapitāmahaśh cha
namo namas te 'stu sahasra-kṛitvaḥ
punaśh cha bhūyo 'pi namo namas te

vāyuḥ—god of wind; *yamaḥ*—god of death; *agniḥ*—god of fire; *varuṇaḥ*—god of water; *śhaśha-aṅkaḥ*—moon-God; *prajāpatiḥ*—Brahma; *tvam*—you; *prapitāmahaḥ*—great-grandfather; *cha*—and; *namaḥ*—my salutations; *namaḥ*—my salutations; *te*—unto you; *astu*—let there be; *sahasra-kṛitvaḥ*—a thousand times; *punaḥ cha*—and again; *bhūyaḥ*—again; *api*—also; *namaḥ*—(offering) my salutations; *namaḥ te*—offering my salutations unto you.

You are Vayu (god of wind), Yamraj (god of death), Agni (god of fire), Varun (god of water), and Chandra (moon-god). You are the creator Brahma and the Great-grandfather of all beings. I offer my salutations unto You a thousand times, again and yet again!

Experiencing profuse reverence towards Shree Krishna, Arjun is offering repeated obeisances *sahasra-kṛitvaḥ* (thousands and thousands of times). During Diwali celebrations in India, sugar sweets are made in many shapes—elephant, horse, man, woman, dog, etc. But the ingredient in all of them is the same—sugar. Similarly, the celestial gods have their distinct personalities and unique set of duties to discharge in the administration of the world. However, the same one God sitting in all of them manifests the special powers they possess.

Consider another example. Varieties of ornaments are made from gold. They all have their distinct individuality, and yet they all are gold. So, just as gold is not an ornament, but ornaments are golden, likewise, God is all the *devatās* but the *devatās* are not God. Hence, in this verse, Arjun says that Shree Krishna is also Vayu, Yamraj, Agni, Varun, Chandra, and Brahma.

नमः पुरस्तादथ पृष्ठतस्ते
नमोऽस्तु ते सर्वत एव सर्व ।
अनन्तवीर्यामितविक्रमस्त्वं
सर्वं समाप्नोषि ततोऽसि सर्वः ।।40।।

namaḥ purastād atha pṛiṣhṭhatas te
namo 'stu te sarvata eva sarva
ananta-vīryāmita-vikramas tvaṁ
sarvaṁ samāpnoṣhi tato 'si sarvaḥ

namaḥ—offering salutations; *purastāt*—from the front; *atha*—and; *pṛiṣhṭhataḥ*—the rear; *te*—to you; *namaḥ astu*—I offer my salutations; *te*—to you; *sarvataḥ*—from all sides; *eva*—indeed; *sarva*—all; *ananta-vīrya*—infinite power; *amita-vikramaḥ*—infinite valour and might; *tvam*—you; *sarvam*—everything; *samāpnoṣhi*—pervade; *tataḥ*—thus; *asi*—(you) are; *sarvaḥ*—everything.

O Lord of infinite power, my salutations to You from the front and the rear, indeed from all sides! You possess infinite valour and might and pervade everything, and thus, You are everything.

Arjun continues with his glorification of Shree Krishna by declaring Him as *ananta-vīrya* (possessing infinite strength) and *ananta-vikramaḥ* (immeasurably powerful). Overcome with awe, he offers his salutations to Shree Krishna from all sides, repeatedly exclaiming *Namaḥ! Namaḥ!* (I bow down to You again and again).

सखेति मत्वा प्रसभं यदुक्तं
हे कृष्ण हे यादव हे सखेति ।
अजानता महिमानं तवेदं
मया प्रमादात्प्रणयेन वापि ।।41।।

यच्चावहासार्थमसत्कृतोऽसि
विहारशय्यासनभोजनेषु ।
एकोऽथवाप्यच्युत तत्समक्षं
तत्क्षामये त्वामहमप्रमेयम् ।।42।।

sakheti matvā prasabhaṁ yad uktaṁ
he kṛiṣhṇa he yādava he sakheti
ajānatā mahimānaṁ tavedaṁ
mayā pramādāt praṇayena vāpi

yach chāvahāsārtham asat-kṛito 'si
vihāra-śhayyāsana-bhojaneṣhu
eko 'tha vāpy achyuta tat-samakṣhaṁ
tat kṣhāmaye tvām aham aprameyam

sakhā—friend; *iti*—as; *matvā*—thinking; *prasabham*—presumptuously; *yat*—whatever; *uktam*—addressed; *he kṛiṣhṇa*—O Shree Krishna; *he yādava*—O Shree Krishna, who was born in the Yadu clan; *he sakhe*—O my dear friend; *iti*—thus; *ajānatā*—in ignorance; *mahimānam*—majesty; *tava*—your; *idam*—this; *mayā*—by me; *pramādāt*—out of negligence; *praṇayena*—out of affection; *vā api*—or else; *yat*—whatever; *cha*—also; *avahāsa-artham*—humorously; *asat-kṛitaḥ*—disrespectfully; *asi*—you were; *vihāra*—while at play; *śhayyā*—while resting; *āsana*—while sitting; *bhojaneṣhu*—while eating; *ekaḥ*—(when) alone; *athavā*—or; *api*—

even; *achyuta*—Krishna, the infallible one; *tat-samakṣham*—before others; *tat*—all that; *kṣhāmaye*—beg for forgiveness; *tvām*—from you; *aham*—I; *aprameyam*—immeasurable.

Thinking of You as my friend, I presumptuously addressed You as, 'O Krishna', 'O Yadav', 'O my dear Friend'. I was ignorant of Your majesty, showing negligence and undue affection. And if, jestfully, I treated You with disrespect, while playing, resting, sitting, eating, when alone, or before others—for all that I crave forgiveness.

Declaring the unparalleled supremacy of God, all the scriptures state:

aham evāsam evāgre nānyat kiñchāntaraṁ bahiḥ

(Bhagavatam 6.4.47)

'I, the Supreme Lord, am everything that exists. There is nothing beyond Me and nothing higher than Me.'

tvamomkāraḥ parātparaḥ (Valmiki Ramayan)

'The primordial sound Om is Your manifestation. You are greater than the greatest.'

vāsudevaḥ praḥ prabhuḥ (*Nārad Pañcharātra*)

'Shree Krishna is the ultimate Supreme Lord.'

na devaḥ keśhavāt paraḥ (*Nārad Puran*)

'There is no god higher than Lord Krishna.'

vidyāt taṁ puruṣhaṁ param (*Manu Smriti* 12.122)

'God is the highest and ultimate personality that exists.' However, as was explained previously (commentary of verse 11.24), when love swells immensely, it makes the lover forget the formal position of the beloved. Thus, in his extreme love for Shree Krishna, Arjun had shared many intimate memorable moments with Him, blissfully oblivious of His supreme position.

Having seen the universal form of God, Arjun is now fully aware that Shree Krishna is not merely his friend and comrade-in-arms but is also the Supreme Divine Personality whom even the *devatās*, *gandharvas*, *siddhas*, and all other beings venerate. Thus, he feels regret for the disrespect he thinks he may have shown towards Shree Krishna by audaciously looking upon Him as a mere friend. Those who are venerated are not called by their first names, as a mark of respect towards them. He is worried that due to excessive familiarity, he had put himself on equal status with God and had presumptuously addressed Him with affectionate terms of endearments, such as 'My friend', 'My dear buddy', and 'O Krishna'. So, he implores forgiveness for whatever he may have done in forgetfulness of the divinity of Shree Krishna's personality.

पितासि लोकस्य चराचरस्य
त्वमस्य पूज्यश्च गुरुर्गरीयान् ।
न त्वत्समोऽस्त्यभ्यधिकः कुतोऽन्यो
लोकत्रयेऽप्यप्रतिमप्रभाव ।।43।।

pitāsi lokasya charācharasya
tvam asya pūjyaśh cha gurur garīyān
na tvat-samo 'sty abhyadhikaḥ kuto 'nyo
loka-traye 'py apratima-prabhāva

pitā—father; *asi*—you are; *lokasya*—of the entire universe; *chara*—moving; *acharasya*—nonmoving; *tvam*—you; *asya*—of this; *pūjyaḥ*—worshippable; *cha*—and; *guruḥ*—spiritual master; *garīyān*—glorious; *na*—not; *tvat-samaḥ*—equal to you; *asti*—is; *abhyadhikaḥ*—greater; *kutaḥ*—who is; *anyaḥ*—other; *loka-traye*—in the three worlds; *api*—even; *apratima-prabhāva*—possessor of incomparable power.

You are the Father of the entire universe, of all moving and non-moving beings. You are the most deserving of worship and the Supreme Spiritual Master. When there is none equal to You in all the three worlds, then who can possibly be greater than You, O Possessor of incomparable power?

Arjun says that Shree Krishna is the greatest and the seniormost. The father is always senior to the son. Shree Krishna is the Father of the father ... of all the fathers that exist. Similarly, He is the Spiritual Master of the spiritual master ... of all the spiritual masters that are present. The first spiritual master was the creator Brahma, who passed on the knowledge to his disciple, and the tradition continued thereafter. However, Brahma received the Vedic knowledge from Shree Krishna. The Shreemad Bhagavatam (1.1.1) states: *tene brahma hṛidāya ādi kavaye* 'Shree Krishna imparted Vedic knowledge into the heart of the first-born Brahma.' Thus, He is the Supreme Spiritual Master.

The *Śhwetāśhvatar Upanishad* states:

na tatsamaśhchābhyadhikaśhcha dṛiśhyate (6.8)

'Nobody is equal to God, nor is anyone superior to Him.' Realising Shree Krishna to be that same Supreme Lord of the Vedas, Arjun is declaring His attributes here.

तस्मात्प्रणम्य प्रणिधाय कायं
प्रसादये त्वामहमीशमीड्यम् ।
पितेव पुत्रस्य सखेव सख्युः
प्रियः प्रियायार्हसि देव सोढुम् ।।44।।

tasmāt praṇamya praṇidhāya kāyaṁ
prasādaye tvām aham īśham īḍyam
piteva putrasya sakheva sakhyuḥ
priyaḥ priyāyārhasi deva soḍhum

tasmāt—therefore; *praṇamya*—bowing down; *praṇidhāya*—prostrating; *kāyam*—the body; *prasādaye*—to implore grace; *tvām*—your; *aham*—I; *īśham*—the Supreme Lord; *īḍyam*—adorable; *pitā*—father; *iva*—as; *putrasya*—with a son; *sakhā*—friend; *iva*—as; *sakhyuḥ*—with a friend; *priyaḥ*—a lover; *priyāyāḥ*—with the beloved; *arhasi*—you should; *deva*—Lord; *soḍhum*—forgive.

Therefore, O adorable Lord, bowing deeply and prostrating before You, I implore You for Your grace. As a father tolerates his son, a friend forgives his friend, and a lover pardons the beloved, please forgive me for my offences.

Considering his behaviour as transgressions towards God, Arjun is asking for pardon. While interacting with Shree Krishna—playing, eating, jesting, talking, and resting—he did not show the respect that is appropriate towards the Supreme Almighty. However, no one minds transgressions when they are made because of a high level of intimacy shared with the other person. No government officer has the privilege to joke with the president of a country. Yet, the president's personal friend, teases him, jests with him, and even yells at him. The president does not mind, rather, he values that jest of a close friend more than all the respect he receives from his subordinate officers. Thousands of people salute an army general, but they are not as dear to his heart as his wife who sits intimately by his side. Similarly, Arjun's intimate moments with Shree Krishna were not transgressions; they were expressions of the depth of his loving devotion, nurtured by the sentiment of being a friend. A devotee is humble by nature. Consequently, out of humility, he feels that he may have committed transgressions and is asking for forgiveness.

अदृष्टपूर्वं हृषितोऽस्मि दृष्ट्वा
भयेन च प्रव्यथितं मनो मे ।
तदेव मे दर्शय देवरूपं
प्रसीद देवेश जगन्निवास ।।45।।

adṛiṣhṭa-pūrvaṁ hṛiṣhito 'smi dṛiṣhṭvā
bhayena cha pravyathitaṁ mano me
tad eva me darśhaya deva rūpaṁ
prasīda deveśha jagan-nivāsa

adṛiṣhṭa-pūrvam—that which has not been seen before; *hṛiṣhitaḥ*—great joy; *asmi*—I am; *dṛiṣhṭvā*—having seen; *bhayena*—with fear; *cha*—yet; *pravyathitam*—trembles; *manaḥ*—mind; *me*—my; *tat*—that; *eva*—certainly; *me*—to me; *darśhaya*—show; *deva*—Lord; *rūpam*—form; *prasīda*—please have mercy; *deva-īśha*—God of gods; *jagat-nivāsa*—abode of the universe.

Having seen Your universal form that I had never seen before, I feel great joy. And yet, my mind trembles with fear. Please have mercy on me and again show me Your pleasing form, O God of gods, O Abode of the universe.

There are two kinds of bhakti—*aiśhwarya* bhakti and *mādhurya* bhakti. *Aiśhwarya* bhakti is that where the devotee is motivated to engage in devotion by contemplating upon the almighty aspect of God. The dominant sentiment in *aiśhwarya* bhakti is of awe and reverence. In such devotion, the feeling of remoteness from God and the need for maintaining propriety of conduct is always perceived. Examples of *aiśhwarya* bhakti are the residents of Dwaraka and Ayodhya who worshipped Shree Krishna and Lord Ram, respectively, as their kings. Ordinary citizens are highly respectful and obedient towards their king, although they never feel intimate with him.

Mādhurya bhakti is that where the devotee feels an intimate personal relationship with God. The dominant sentiment in such devotion is 'Shree Krishna is mine and I am His'. Examples of *mādhurya* bhakti are the cowherd boys of Vrindavan who loved Krishna as their friend, Yashoda and Nand baba, who loved Krishna as their child, and the gopis who loved Him as their beloved. *Mādhurya* bhakti is infinitely sweeter than *aiśhwarya* bhakti. Hence, Jagadguru Shree Kripaluji Maharaj states:

sabai sarasa rasa dwārikā
mathurā aru braja māhiñ
madhura, madhuratara, madhuratama
rasa brajarasa sama nāhiñ (*Bhakti Śhatak*, verse 70)

'The divine bliss of God is immensely sweet in all His forms. Yet, there is a gradation in it—the bliss of His Dwaraka pastimes is sweet, the bliss of His Mathura pastimes is sweeter, and the bliss of His Braj pastimes is the sweetest.'

In *Mādhurya* bhakti, forgetting the almightiness of God, devotees establish four kinds of relationships with Shree Krishna:

Dāsya bhav—Shree Krishna is my Master, and I am His servant. The devotion of Shree Krishna's personal servants, such as Raktak, Patrak, and others was in *dāsya* bhav. The sentiment that God is my Father or Mother is a variation of *dāsya* bhav and is included in it.

Sakhya bhav—Shree Krishna is my Friend, and I am His intimate companion. The devotion of the cowherd boys of Vrindavan, such as Shreedama, Madhumangal, Dhansukh, Mansukh, and others was in *sakhya* bhav.

Vātsalya bhav—Shree Krishna is my Child, and I am His parent. The devotion of Yashoda and Nand baba was in *vātsalya* bhav.

Mādhurya bhav—Shree Krishna is our Beloved, and I am His lover. The devotion of the *gopis* of Vrindavan was in *mādhurya* bhav.

Arjun is a *sakhya* bhav devotee and relishes a fraternal relationship with the Lord. On seeing the universal form of God, Arjun experienced tremendous awe and reverence, and yet he longed for the sweetness of *sakhya* bhav that he was used to savouring. Hence, he prays to Shree Krishna to hide the almighty form that he is now seeing and again show His human form.

किरीटिनं गदिनं चक्रहस्त-
मिच्छामि त्वां द्रष्टुमहं तथैव ।
तेनैव रूपेण चतुर्भुजेन
सहस्रबाहो भव विश्वमूर्ते ।।46।।

kirīṭinaṁ gadinaṁ chakra-hastam
ichchhāmi tvāṁ draṣhṭum ahaṁ tathaiva
tenaiva rūpeṇa chatur-bhujena
sahasra-bāho bhava viśhwa-mūrte

kirīṭinam—wearing the crown; *gadinam*—carrying the mace; *chakra-hastam*—disc in hand; *ichchhāmi*—I wish; *tvām*—you; *draṣhṭum*—to see; *aham*—I; *tathā eva*—similarly; *tena eva*—in that; *rūpeṇa*—form; *chatuḥ-bhujena*—four-armed; *sahasra-bāho*—thousand-armed one; *bhava*—be; *viśhwa-mūrte*—universal form.

O Thousand-armed One, though You are the embodiment of all creation, I wish to see You in Your four-armed form, carrying the mace and disc, and wearing the crown.

By special grace, Arjun has been shown the cosmic form that is not easily seen by anyone. Arjun has realised that Shree Krishna is much more than merely his friend. His divine personality encompasses unlimited universes. Yet, he is not attracted by the infinite opulences and is not interested in doing *aiśhwarya* bhakti of God Almighty. Rather, he prefers seeing that Almighty Lord in the human form, so that he can relate to Him as before, like a friend. Addressing Lord Krishna as *sahasra-bāho*, meaning, 'thousand-armed one', Arjuna is now specifically requesting to see the *chatur-bhuj roop* or four-armed form of Lord Krishna.

In the four-armed form, Shree Krishna appeared before Arjun on another occasion as well. When Arjun tied Ashwatthama, the killer of the five sons of Draupadi and brought him before her, at that time Shree Krishna had revealed Himself in his four-armed form.

niśhamya bhīma-gaditaṁ draupadyāśh cha chatur-bhujaḥ
ālokya vadanaṁ sakhyur idam āha hasanniva

(Shreemad Bhagavatam 1.7.52)

'The four-armed Shree Krishna heard the statements of Bheem, Draupadi, and others. Then He looked towards His dear friend Arjun and began smiling.' By requesting Shree Krishna to manifest in His four-armed form, Arjun is also confirming that the four-armed form of the Lord is non-different from His two-armed form.

श्रीभगवानुवाच ।
मया प्रसन्नेन तवार्जुनेदं
रूपं परं दर्शितमात्मयोगात् ।
तेजोमयं विश्वमनन्तमाद्यं
यन्मे त्वदन्येन न दृष्टपूर्वम् ।।47।।

śhrī-bhagavān uvācha
mayā prasannena tavārjunedaṁ
rūpaṁ paraṁ darśhitam ātma-yogāt
tejo-mayaṁ viśhwam anantam ādyaṁ
yan me tvad anyena na dṛiṣhṭa-pūrvam

śhrī-bhagavān uvācha—the Lord said; *mayā*—by me; *prasannena*—being pleased; *tava*—with you; *arjuna*—Arjun; *idam*—this; *rūpam*—form; *param*—divine; *darśhitam*—shown; *ātma-yogāt*—by my *Yogmaya* power; *tejaḥ-mayam*—resplendent; *viśhwam*—cosmic; *anantam*—unlimited; *ādyam*—primeval; *yat*—which; *me*—my; *tvat anyena*—other than you; *na dṛiṣhṭa-pūrvam*—no one has ever seen.

The Lord said: Arjun, being pleased with you, by My *Yogmaya* power, I gave you a vision of My resplendent, unlimited, and primeval cosmic form. No one before you has ever seen it.

Since Arjun had become fearful and beseeched that the cosmic form be hidden, Shree Krishna now pacifies him by explaining that there is no need to be scared. He had bestowed a vision of His universal form by His grace, not as a form of punishment, but because He was very pleased with Arjun. He uses hyperbole as a figure of speech to stress how rare it is to see the universal form by saying that Arjun is the first one to see it. Although Duryodhan and Yashoda were also given a glimpse of the universal form, it was not of this intensity, depth, and magnitude.

Shree Krishna bestowed this divine vision upon Arjun with the help of His *Yogmaya* energy. This is the divine all-powerful energy of God. He has referred to it in many places, such as in verses 4.6 and 7.25. It is by virtue of this *Yogmaya* energy that God is *kartumakartum anyathā karatum samarthaḥ* 'He can do the possible, the impossible, and the contradictory at the same time.' This divine power of God also manifests in the personal form and is worshipped in the Hindu tradition as the Divine Mother of the universe, in the form of Radha, Durga, Lakshmi, Kali, Sita, Parvati, and so on.

न वेदयज्ञाध्ययनैर्न दानैर्-
न च क्रियाभिर्न तपोभिरुग्रैः ।
एवंरूपः शक्य अहं नृलोके
द्रष्टुं त्वदन्येन कुरुप्रवीर ॥ 48 ॥

na veda-yajñādhyayanair na dānair
na cha kriyābhir na tapobhir ugraiḥ
evaṁ-rūpaḥ śhakya ahaṁ nṛi-loke
drașhṭuṁ tvad anyena kuru-pravīra

na—not; *veda-yajña*—by performance of sacrifice; *adhyayanaiḥ*—by study of the Vedas; *na*—nor; *dānaiḥ*—by charity; *na*—nor; *cha*—and; *kriyābhiḥ*—by rituals; *na*—not; *tapobhiḥ*—by austerities; *ugraiḥ*—severe; *evam-rūpaḥ*—in this form; *śhakyaḥ*—possible; *aham*—I; *nṛi-loke*—in the world of mortals; *drașhṭum*—to be seen; *tvat*—than you; *anyena*—by another; *kuru-pravīra*—best of the Kuru warriors.

Not by study of the Vedas, nor by the performance of sacrifice, rituals, or charity, nor even by practising severe austerities, has any mortal ever seen what you have seen, O best of the Kuru warriors.

Shree Krishna declares that no amount of self-effort—the study of the Vedic texts, performance of ritualistic ceremonies, undertaking of severe austerities, abstinence from food, or generous acts of charity—is sufficient to bestow a vision of the cosmic form of God. This is only possible by His divine grace. This has been repeatedly stated in the Vedas as well:

tasya no rāsva tasya no dhehi (*Yajur Veda*)

'Without being anointed by the nectar of the grace of the Supreme Lord, nobody can see Him.'

The logic behind this is very straightforward. Our physical eyes are made from matter, and hence all that we can see is also material. The Supreme Lord is non-material—He is divine. Thus it logically follows that we need divine eyes to have a vision of His divine form. When God bestows His grace upon the soul, He adds His divine power to our material eyes, and only then can we see Him.

One may ask how Sanjay was also able to see that cosmic form which Arjun saw by divine grace. The Mahabharat states that Sanjay also received divine vision by the grace of his guru, Ved Vyas, who was an Avatar of God. Before the war, Ved Vyas offered his student Sanjay divine vision so that he may be able to communicate the details of the war to Dhritarashtra. Hence, he was able to see the same cosmic form that Arjun saw. But later, when Duryodhan died, Sanjay was overwhelmed with grief and lost his divine vision.

मा ते व्यथा मा च विमूढभावो
दृष्ट्वा रूपं घोरमीदृङ्ममेदम् ।
व्यपेतभीः प्रीतमनाः पुनस्त्वं
तदेव मे रूपमिदं प्रपश्य ।।49।।

mā te vyathā mā cha vimūḍha-bhāvo
dṛiṣhṭvā rūpaṁ ghoram īdṛiṅ mamedam
vyapeta-bhīḥ prīta-manāḥ punas tvaṁ
tad eva me rūpam idaṁ prapaśhya

mā te—you should not be; *vyathā*—afraid; *mā*—not; *cha*—and; *vimūḍha-bhāvaḥ*—bewildered state; *dṛiṣhṭvā*—on seeing; *rūpam*—form; *ghoram*—terrible; *īdṛik*—such; *mama*—of mine; *idam*—this; *vyapeta-bhīḥ*—free from fear; *prīta-manāḥ*—cheerful mind; *punaḥ*—again; *tvam*—you; *tat eva*—that very; *me*—my; *rūpam*—form; *idam*—this; *prapaśhya*—behold.

Be neither afraid nor bewildered on seeing this terrible form of Mine. Be free from fear and with a cheerful heart, behold Me once again in My personal form.

Shree Krishna continues to pacify Arjun, telling him that rather than being scared, he should feel privileged to be blessed with a vision of the cosmic form. Further, He tells Arjun to behold His personal form again and shed his fear.

सञ्जय उवाच ।
इत्यर्जुनं वासुदेवस्तथोक्त्वा
स्वकं रूपं दर्शयामास भूयः ।
आश्वासयामास च भीतमेनं
भूत्वा पुनः सौम्यवपुर्महात्मा ।।50।।

sañjaya uvācha
ity arjunaṁ vāsudevas tathoktvā
svakaṁ rūpaṁ darśhayām āsa bhūyaḥ
āśhvāsayām āsa cha bhītam enaṁ
bhūtvā punaḥ saumya-vapur mahātmā

sañjayaḥ uvācha—Sanjay said; *iti*—thus; *arjunam*—to Arjun; *vāsudevaḥ*—Krishna, son of Vasudev; *tathā*—in that way; *uktvā*—having spoken; *svakam*—his personal; *rūpam*—form; *darśhayām āsa*—displayed; *bhūyaḥ*—again; *āśhvāsayām āsa*—consoled; *cha*—and; *bhītam*—frightened; *enam*—him; *bhūtvā*—becoming; *punaḥ*—again; *saumya-vapuḥ*—the gentle (two-armed) form; *mahā-ātmā*—the compassionate.

Sanjay said: Having spoken thus, the compassionate son of Vasudev displayed His personal (four-armed) form again. Then, He further consoled the frightened Arjun by assuming His gentle (two-armed) form.

Shree Krishna hid the vision of His cosmic form and manifested before Arjun in His four-armed form, which is adorned with a golden diadem, disc, mace, and lotus flower. It is the repository of all divine opulences such as majesty, omniscience, omnipotence, etc. The four-armed form of Shree Krishna evokes the sentiments of awe and reverence, much like the sentiments of the citizens of a kingdom towards their king. However, Arjun was a *sakhā* (friend) of Shree Krishna, and devotion dominated by the sentiments of awe and reverence would never satisfy him. He had played with Shree Krishna, eaten with Him, confided his secrets to Him, and shared loving personal moments with Him. Such blissful devotion of *sakhya bhav* (devotion where God is seen as a personal friend) is infinitely sweeter than *aiśhwarya* bhakti (devotion where God is revered as the distant and almighty Lord). Hence, to conform to Arjun's sentiment of devotion, Shree Krishna finally hid even His four-armed form and transformed into His original two-armed form.

Once in the forest of Vrindavan, Shree Krishna was engaging in loving pastimes with the *gopis*, when He suddenly disappeared from their midst. The *gopis* prayed for Him to come back. Hearing their supplications, He manifested again but in His four-armed form. The *gopis* thought Him to be the Supreme Lord Vishnu, and accordingly they paid their obeisance. But they moved on, not being attracted to spend any further time with Him. They had been habituated to seeing the Supreme Lord Shree Krishna as their soul-beloved, and this form of His as Lord Vishnu held no attraction for them. However, when Radha Rani came onto the scene, Shree Krishna became overwhelmed with love for Her and was unable maintain His four-armed form. His two arms automatically disappeared, and He resumed His two-armed form. In this verse too, Shree Krishna returned to His most attractive two-armed form.

अर्जुन उवाच ।
दृष्ट्वेदं मानुषं रूपं तव सौम्यं जनार्दन ।
इदानीमस्मि संवृत्तः सचेताः प्रकृतिं गतः ।।51।।

arjuna uvācha
dṛiṣhṭvedaṁ mānuṣhaṁ rūpaṁ tava saumyaṁ janārdana
idānīm asmi saṁvṛittaḥ sa-chetāḥ prakṛitiṁ gataḥ

arjunaḥ uvācha—Arjun said; *dṛiṣhṭvā*—seeing; *idam*—this; *mānuṣham*—human; *rūpam*—form; *tava*—your; *saumyam*—gentle; *janārdana*—He who looks after the public, Krishna; *idānīm*—now;

asmi—I am; *saṁvṛittaḥ*—composed; *sa-chetāḥ*—in my mind; *prakṛitim*—to normality; *gataḥ*—have become.

Arjun said: O Shree Krishna, seeing Your gentle human form (two-armed), I have regained my composure and my mind is restored to normal.

Seeing Shree Krishna in His beautiful two-armed form reconfirmed and strengthened Arjun's sentiment of *sakhya bhav*. Thus, Arjun says he has regained his composure and is back to normal. Seeing Shree Krishna's pastimes with the Pandavas, the celestial sage Narad had earlier told Arjun's elder brother, King Yudhishthir: *gūḍhaṁ paraṁ brahma manuṣhya liṅgam* (Bhagavatam 7.15.75) 'Shree Krishna resides in your house and lives with you just like your brother.' Thus, Arjun was habituated to having the privilege of interacting with the Lord as a brother and friend.

श्रीभगवानुवाच ।
सुदुर्दर्शमिदं रूपं दृष्टवानसि यन्मम ।
देवा अप्यस्य रूपस्य नित्यं दर्शनकाङ्क्षिणः ।।52।।

नाहं वेदैर्न तपसा न दानेन न चेज्यया ।
शक्य एवंविधो द्रष्टुं दृष्टवानसि मां यथा ।।53।।

śhrī-bhagavān uvācha
su-durdarśham idaṁ rūpaṁ dṛiṣhṭavān asi yan mama
devā apy asya rūpasya nityaṁ darśhana-kāṅkṣhiṇaḥ

nāhaṁ vedair na tapasā na dānena na chejyayā
śhakya evaṁ-vidho draṣhṭuṁ dṛiṣhṭavān asi māṁ yathā

śhrī-bhagavān uvācha—the Supreme Lord said; *su-durdarśham*—exceedingly difficult to behold; *idam*—this; *rūpam*—form; *dṛiṣhṭavān asi*—that you are seeing; *yat*—which; *mama*—of mine; *devāḥ*—celestial gods; *api*—even; *asya*—this; *rūpasya*—form; *nityam*—eternally; *darśhana-kāṅkṣhiṇaḥ*—aspiring to see; *na*—never; *aham*—I; *vedaiḥ*—by study of the Vedas; *na*—never; *tapasā*—by serious penances; *na*—never; *dānena*—by charity;

na—never; *cha*—also; *ijyayā*—by worship; *śhakyaḥ*—it is possible; *evam-vidhaḥ*—like this; *draṣhṭum*—to see; *dṛiṣhṭavān*—seeing; *asi*—you are; *mām*—me; *yathā*—as.

The Supreme Lord said: This form of Mine that you are seeing is exceedingly difficult to behold. Even the celestial gods are eager to see it. Neither by the study of the Vedas, nor by penance, charity, or fire sacrifices, can I be seen as you have seen Me.

After showing Arjun His cosmic form and praising it for being manifest exclusively to him, Sree Krishna wants to ensure that Arjun's love for the personal form of God is firm and strong. Hence, Shree Krishna says that the way in which Arjun sees God is exceedingly rare. He emphasises that even the celestial gods yearn to realise God in His two-armed personal form as He is standing before Arjun. This is not possible by any amount of Vedic studies, austerities, or fire sacrifices. The basic spiritual principle is that God cannot be known by the strength of one's efforts. However, those who engage in devotion to Him become recipients of His grace. Then, by virtue of His grace, they are easily able to know Him. The *Muṇḍakopaniṣhad* states:

nāyamātmā pravachanena labhyo
na medhayā na bahunā śhrutena (3.2.3)

'God cannot be known either by spiritual discourses or through the intellect; nor can He be known by hearing various kinds of teachings.'

If none of these means can help realise God in His personal form, then how can He be seen in this manner? Shree Krishna now reveals the secret.

भक्त्या त्वनन्यया शक्य अहमेवंविधोऽर्जुन ।
ज्ञातुं द्रष्टुं च तत्त्वेन प्रवेष्टुं च परन्तप ।।54।।

bhaktyā tvananyayā śhakya aham evaṁ-vidho 'rjuna
jñātuṁ draṣhṭuṁ cha tattvena praveṣhṭuṁ cha parantapa

bhaktyā—by devotion; *tu*—alone; *ananyayā*—unalloyed; *śhakyaḥ*—possible; *aham*—I; *evam-vidhaḥ*—like this; *arjuna*—Arjun; *jñātum*—to be known; *draṣhṭum*—to be seen; *cha*—and;

tattvena—truly; *praveṣhṭum*—to enter into (union with me); *cha*—and; *parantapa*—scorcher of foes.

O Arjun, by unalloyed devotion alone can I be known as I am, standing before you. Thereby, on receiving My divine vision, O scorcher of foes, one can enter into union with Me.

In this verse, Shree Krishna emphasises bhakti as the means for attaining Him. Earlier, in verse 11.48, He had stated that His universal form can be seen only by devotion. Now, in this verse, Shree Krishna emphatically declares that His two-armed form as He is standing before Arjun can only be realised through bhakti. This has been repeatedly stated in the Vedic scriptures:

bhaktirevainaṁ nayati bhaktirevainaṁ paśhyati bhaktirevainaṁ
darśhayati bhakti vaśhaḥ puruṣho bhaktireva garīyasī

(*Māṭhar Śhruti*)

'Devotion alone will unite us with God; devotion alone will help us see Him; devotion alone will help us attain Him; God is enslaved by true devotion, which is the best of all paths.'

na sādhayati māṁ yogo na sānkhyaṁ dharma uddhava
na svādhyāyas tapas tyāgo yathā bhaktir mamorjitā

(Bhagavatam 11.14.20)

'Uddhav, I come under the control of My devotees and am won over by them. But those who do not engage in devotion can never attain Me by practising ashtang yog, studying *Sānkhya* and other philosophies, performing pious acts and austerities, or cultivating renunciation.'

bhaktyāham ekayā grāhyaḥ śhraddhayātmā priyaḥ satām

(Bhagavatam 11.14.21)

'I am only attained through bhakti. Those who engage in My bhakti with faith are very dear to Me.'

milahiṅ na raghupati binu anurāgā,
kieñ joga tapa gyāna birāgā (Ramayan)

'Without devotion, one can never attain God, no matter how much one endeavours through the practice of ashtang yog, austerities, knowledge, and detachment.' *In the next verse, Shree Krishna describes the nature of bhakti.*

मत्कर्मकृन्मत्परमो मद्भक्तः सङ्गवर्जितः ।
निर्वैरः सर्वभूतेषु यः स मामेति पाण्डव ।।55।।

mat-karma-kṛin mat-paramo mad-bhaktaḥ saṅga-varjitaḥ
nirvairaḥ sarva-bhūteṣhu yaḥ sa mām eti pāṇḍava

mat-karma-kṛit—perform duties for my sake; *mat-paramaḥ*—considering me the Supreme; *mat-bhaktaḥ*—devoted to me; *saṅga-varjitaḥ*—free from attachment; *nirvairaḥ*—without malice; *sarva-bhūteṣhu*—towards all entities; *yaḥ*—who; *saḥ*—he; *mām*—to me; *eti*—comes; *pāṇḍava*—Arjun, son of Pandu.

Those who perform all their duties for My sake, who depend upon Me and are devoted to Me, who are free from attachment and are without malice towards all beings, such devotees certainly come to Me.

At the end of the ninth chapter, Shree Krishna had told Arjun to fix his mind upon Him and be devoted to Him. To enhance that devotion, He further revealed secrets about Himself in the tenth and eleventh chapters. In the previous verse, He again emphasised the supremacy of the path of devotion. Now, He concludes this chapter by highlighting five characteristics of those who engage in exclusive devotion:

They perform all their duties for My sake: Accomplished devotees do not divide their works into material and spiritual. They perform every work for the pleasure of God, thus consecrating every act of theirs to Him. Saint Kabir states:

jahañ jahañ chalūñ karūñ parikramā, jo jo karūñ so sevā
jaba sovūñ karūñ daṇḍavat, jānūñ deva na dūjā

'When I walk, I think I am circumambulating the Lord; when I work, I think I am serving the Lord; and when I sleep, I think I am offering Him obeisance. In this manner, I perform no activity other than that which is offered to Him.'

They depend upon Me: Those who rely upon their spiritual practices to reach God are not exclusively dependent upon Him. That is because He is attained by His grace and not by spiritual practice. His exclusive devotees do not even rely upon their devotion as a means of attaining Him. Rather, they place their entire faith in His grace alone and see their devotion as merely a way of attracting divine grace.

They are devoted to Me: The devotees do not feel the need for performing any other spiritual practices, such as cultivation of the knowledge of *Sānkhya*, practice of ashtang yog, performance of fire sacrifices, etc. In this way, they feel that their relationship is with God alone. They behold only their Beloved Lord pervading all objects and personalities.

They are free of attachment: Devotion requires the engagement of the mind. This is only possible if the mind is detached from the world. So exclusive devotees are free from all worldly attachments and repose their mind in God alone.

They are without malice towards all beings: If the heart fills up with malice, it will again not remain exclusive towards God. Thus, exclusive devotees do not harbour any malice, even towards those who have harmed them. Instead, thinking that God resides in the heart of all beings, they see all actions as stemming from Him and so they forgive even their wrongdoers.

CHAPTER 12

Bhakti Yog

The Yog of Devotion

This short chapter stresses the super-excellence of the path of loving devotion over all other types of spiritual practices. It begins with Arjun asking Shree Krishna whom He considers more perfect in Yog—those who are devoted to the personal form of God or those who worship the formless Brahman. Shree Krishna responds by declaring that both paths lead to God-realisation. However, He regards the devotees of His personal form as the best yogis. He explains that meditation on the impersonal unmanifest aspect of God is full of tribulations and exceedingly difficult for embodied beings. But devotees of the personal form, with their consciousness merged in Him and all their actions dedicated to Him, are swiftly delivered from the cycle of life and death. Shree Krishna thus asks Arjun to surrender his intellect to Him and fix his mind in exclusive loving devotion on Him alone.

However, such love is often not forthcoming for the struggling soul. So, Shree Krishna gives other options, and says that if Arjun cannot immediately reach the stage of complete absorption of the mind in God, he should strive to reach that stage of perfection by constant practice. Devotion is not a mysterious gift and can be cultivated by regular effort. If Arjun cannot do even this much, he should still not admit defeat; rather, he should work in devotion for the pleasure of Shree Krishna. If this is also not possible, then he should merely renounce the fruits of his works and be situated in the self. He then explains that higher than mechanical practice is the cultivation of knowledge; higher than the cultivation of knowledge is meditation; and higher than meditation is the renunciation of fruits of actions, which immediately leads to great peace. The remaining verses of the chapter describe the wonderful qualities of God's loving devotees who are very dear to Him.

अर्जुन उवाच ।
एवं सततयुक्ता ये भक्तास्त्वां पर्युपासते ।
ये चाप्यक्षरमव्यक्तं तेषां के योगवित्तमाः ।।1।।

arjuna uvācha
evaṁ satata-yuktā ye bhaktās tvāṁ paryupāsate
ye chāpy akṣharam avyaktaṁ teṣhāṁ ke yoga-vittamāḥ

arjunaḥ uvācha—Arjun said; *evam*—thus; *satata*—steadfastly; *yuktāḥ*—devoted; *ye*—those; *bhaktāḥ*—devotees; *tvām*—you; *paryupāsate*—worship; *ye*—those; *cha*—and; *api*—also; *akṣharam*—the imperishable; *avyaktam*—the formless Brahman; *teṣhām*—of them; *ke*—who; *yoga-vit-tamāḥ*—more perfect in Yog.

Arjun enquired: Between those who are steadfastly devoted to Your personal form and those who worship the formless Brahman, whom do You consider to be more perfect in Yog?

In the last chapter, Arjun saw the cosmic form of the Lord, which encompasses the entire universe. Having seen it, he preferred to behold God in His personal form, with Attributes, Qualities, Pastimes, and Associates. So, he is now curious about who is more perfect—the devotee who worships the personal form of God or the one who worships the impersonal Brahman.

Arjun's question once again confirms that God has both aspects—the all-pervading formless Brahman and the personal form. Those who say that God cannot possess a personal form limit Him, and those who say that God only exists in a personal form also limit Him. God is perfect and complete, and so He is both formless and with form. We individual souls too have both aspects to our personality. The soul is formless, and yet it has taken on a body, not once, but innumerable times, in countless past lifetimes. If we tiny souls have the ability to possess a form, can the all-powerful God not possess a form whenever He wishes? Even the great proponent of the path of jnana yog, Jagadguru Shankaracharya, stated:

mūrtaṁ chaivāmūrtaṁ dwe eva brahmaṇo rūpe,
ityupaniṣhat tayorvā dwau
bhaktau bhagavadupadiṣhṭau,
kleṣhādakleśhādwā muktisyāderatayormadhye

'The Supreme entity is both personal and impersonal. Practitioners of the spiritual path are also of two kinds—devotees of the formless Brahman, and devotees of the personal form. But the path of worshipping the formless is very difficult.'

श्रीभगवानुवाच ।
मय्यावेश्य मनो ये मां नित्ययुक्ता उपासते ।
श्रद्धया परयोपेतास्ते मे युक्ततमा मताः ।।2।।

śhrī-bhagavān uvācha
mayy āveśhya mano ye māṁ nitya-yuktā upāsate
śhraddhayā parayopetās te me yuktatamā matāḥ

śhrī-bhagavān uvācha—the Lord said; *mayi*—on me; *āveśhya*—fix; *manaḥ*—the mind; *ye*—those; *mām*—me; *nitya yuktāḥ*—always engaged; *upāsate*—worship; *śhraddhayā*—with faith; *parayā*—best; *upetāḥ*—endowed; *te*—they; *me*—by me; *yukta-tamāḥ*—situated highest in Yog; *matāḥ*—I consider.

The Lord said: Those who fix their minds on Me and always engage in My devotion with steadfast faith, I consider them to be the best yogis.

God can be realised in varying degrees of closeness. Let us understand this through an example. Suppose say you are standing by the railway tracks. A train is coming from afar with its headlight shining. It seems to you as if a light is approaching. When the train comes closer, you can see a shimmering form along with the light. Finally, when it comes and parks on the platform in front, you realise, 'Oh! It's a train. I can see all these people sitting inside the compartments and peeping out of the windows.' The same train seemed like a light from far. As it came closer, it appeared to have a shimmering form along with the light. When it drew even nearer, you realised that it was a train. The train was the same, but on being closer to it, your understanding of its different attributes such as shape, colour, passengers, compartments, doors, and windows grew.

Similarly, God is perfect and complete, and the possessor of unlimited energies. His personality is replete with divine Names, Forms, Pastimes, Virtues, Associates, and Abodes. However, He is realised in varying levels of closeness, as the Brahman (formless all-pervading manifestation of God), the Paramatma (the Supreme Soul seated in the heart of all living beings, distinct from the individual soul), and Bhagavan (the personal manifestation of God that descends upon the earth). The Bhagavatam states:

vadanti tat tattva vidastattvaṁ yaj-jñānamadvayam
brahmeti paramātmeti bhagavān iti śhabdyate (1.2.11)

'The knowers of the Truth have stated that there is only one Supreme Entity that manifests in three ways in the world—Brahman, Paramatma, and Bhagavan.' They are not three different Gods; rather, They are three manifestations of the one Almighty God. However, Their qualities are different. This is just as water, steam, and ice are all made from the same substance—hydrogen dioxide molecules—but their physical qualities are different. If a thirsty person asks for water, and we give ice, it will not quench the thirst. Ice and water are both the same substance, but their physical properties are different. Similarly, Brahman, Paramatma, and Bhagavan are manifestations of the one Supreme Lord, but Their qualities are different.

Brahman is the all-pervading form of God which is everywhere. The *Śhwetāśhvatar Upanishad* states:

eko devaḥ sarvabhūteṣhu gūḍhaḥ sarvavyāpī
sarvabhūtāntarātmā (6.11)

'There is only one Supreme Entity. He is seated in everything and in everyone.' This all-pervading aspect of the Lord is called Brahman. It is full of eternality, knowledge, and bliss. However, in this aspect, God does not manifest His infinite qualities, enchanting personal beauty, and sweet pastimes. He is like a divine light that is *nirguna* (without qualities), *nirvivśeṣh* (without attributes), *nirākār* (without form).

Those who follow the path of jnana yog worship this aspect of God. This is a distant realisation of God as a formless light, just as the train from far appeared like light.

Paramatma is the aspect of God that is seated in everyone's hearts. In verse 18.61, Shree Krishna states: 'The Supreme Lord dwells in the heart of all living beings, O Arjun. According to their karmas, He directs the wanderings of the souls who are seated on a machine made of material energy.' Residing within, God notes all our thoughts and actions, keeps an account of them, and gives the results at the appropriate time. We may forget what we have done, but God does not. He remembers our every thought, word, and deed since we were born. And not only in this life! In endless lifetimes, wherever we went, God went along with us. He is such a Friend who never leaves us for even a moment. This aspect of God dwelling within is the Paramatma.

The path of ashtang yog, as revealed by Patanjali in the *Yog Darshan*, strives to realise God seated inside and leads to the Paramatma realisation of God. Just as the train, which appeared as light from far, was seen as a shimmering form when it came closer, similarly, the realisation of the Supreme Entity as Paramatma is a closer realisation than Brahman.

Bhagavan is the aspect of God that manifests with a personal form. The Shreemad Bhagavatam states:

kṛiṣhṇam enam avehi tvam ātmānam akhilātmanām
jagad-dhitāya so 'pyatra dehīvābhāti māyayā (10.14.55)

'The Supreme Lord Who is the Soul of all souls, has descended upon the earth in His personal form, as Shree Krishna, for the welfare of the world.' In this Bhagavan aspect, God manifests all the sweetness of His Names, Forms, Qualities, Abodes, Pastimes, and Associates. These attributes exist in Brahman and Paramatma as well, but they remain latent, just as fire is latent in a matchstick, and only manifests when struck against the igniting strip of the matchbox. Similarly, as Bhagavan, all the powers and aspects of God's personality, which are latent in other forms, are revealed.

The path of bhakti or devotion leads to the realisation of the Supreme Entity in His Bhagavan aspect. This is the closest realisation of God, just as the details of a train become visible when it comes and stops in front of the observer. Hence, in verse 18.55, Shree Krishna states: 'Only by loving devotion to Me does one come to know who I am in Truth.' Thus, Shree Krishna answers Arjun's question by clarifying that He considers the devotee of His personal form to be the highest yogi.

ये त्वक्षरमनिर्देश्यमव्यक्तं पर्युपासते ।
सर्वत्रगमचिन्त्यञ्च कूटस्थमचलन्ध्रुवम् ।।3।।

सन्नियम्येन्द्रियग्रामं सर्वत्र समबुद्धयः ।
ते प्राप्नुवन्ति मामेव सर्वभूतहिते रताः ।।4।।

ye tv akṣharam anirdeśhyam avyaktaṁ paryupāsate
sarvatra-gam achintyañcha kūṭa-stham achalandhruvam

sanniyamyendriya-grāmaṁ sarvatra sama-buddhayaḥ
te prāpnuvanti mām eva sarva-bhūta-hite ratāḥ

ye—who; *tu*—but; *akṣharam*—the imperishable; *anirdeśhyam*—the indefinable; *avyaktam*—the unmanifest; *paryupāsate*—worship; *sarvatra-gam*—the all-pervading; *achintyam*—the unthinkable; *cha*—and; *kūṭa-stham*—the unchanging; *achalam*—the immovable; *dhruvam*—the eternal; *sanniyamya*—restraining; *indriya-grāmam*—the senses; *sarvatra*—everywhere; *sama-buddhayaḥ*—even-minded; *te*—they; *prāpnuvanti*—attain; *mām*—me; *eva*—also; *sarva-bhūta-hite*—in the welfare of all beings; *ratāḥ*—engaged.

But those who worship the formless aspect of the Absolute Truth—the imperishable, the indefinable, the unmanifest, the all-pervading, the

unthinkable, the unchanging, the eternal, and the immoveable—by restraining their senses and being even-minded everywhere, such persons, engaged in the welfare of all beings, also attain Me.

Having said that worship of the personal form is the best, Shree Krishna clarifies that in no way does He reject the worship of the formless. Those who devote themselves to the all-pervading, indefinable, unmanifest, inconceivable, immovable, eternal Brahman, also attain God.

Living beings are of an infinite variety of natures. The Supreme Lord who has created this variety also possesses an infinite variety of aspects to His personality. For the sake of our finite comprehension, we classify the infinite manifestations of God into categories. Accordingly, Ved Vyas has classified God's various manifestations into three types, Brahman, Paramatma, and Bhagavan, as mentioned in the commentary of the previous verse. One may worship either of these categories, but one should never claim that one's own conception of God is the only correct one while that of others is erroneous.

In verse 4.11, Shree Krishna had stated: 'In whatever way people surrender unto Me, I reciprocate accordingly. Everyone follows My path, knowingly or unknowingly, O son of Pritha.' Here, Shree Krishna confirms that the worshippers of the formless also reach Him. Since their choice is to unite with the attributeless manifestation of the Supreme Absolute Truth, God meets them as the unmanifest, all-pervading Brahman.

क्लेशोऽधिकतरस्तेषामव्यक्तासक्तचेतसाम् ।।
अव्यक्ता हि गतिर्दुःखं देहवद्भिरवाप्यते ।।5।।

kleśho 'dhikataras teṣhām avyaktāsakta-chetasām
avyaktā hi gatir duḥkhaṁ dehavadbhir avāpyate

kleśhaḥ—tribulations; *adhika-taraḥ*—full of; *teṣhām*—of those; *avyakta*—to the unmanifest; *āsakta*—attached; *chetasām*—whose minds; *avyaktā*—the unmanifest; *hi*—indeed; *gatiḥ*—path; *duḥkham*—exceedingly difficult; *deha-vadbhiḥ*—for the embodied; *avāpyate*—is reached.

For those whose minds are attached to the unmanifest, the path of realisation is full of tribulations. Worship of the unmanifest is exceedingly difficult for embodied beings.

Having embraced worshippers of all His various manifestations into the fold, Shree Krishna again reiterates His preference for the worship of the personal form. He surmises the worship of the impersonal Brahman by saying that it is an exceedingly challenging path that is full of tribulations.

Why is the worship of the formless Brahman so difficult? The first and foremost reason for this is that we humans possess a form ourselves and we have been habituated to interacting with forms in endless lifetimes. Thus, while striving to love God as well, if our mind has an enchanting form to meditate upon, it can easily focus on it and increase its attachment to the Lord. However, in the case of the formless, the intellect cannot conceive of it, and the mind and senses have no tangible object to relate to. So, both the endeavours of meditating on God and increasing the mind's attachment to Him become difficult.

Worship of Brahman is also difficult in comparison to that of Bhagavan for another reason. The difference in paths can be understood through the *markaṭ-kiśhore nyāya* (the logic of the baby monkey) and *mārjār-kiśhore nyāya* (the logic of the baby kitten). The baby monkey is responsible for holding onto the mother's stomach; it is not helped by its mother. When the mother monkey jumps from one branch to another, the onus of clinging tightly onto the mother is upon the baby, and if it is unable to do so, it falls. In contrast, a kitten is very small and delicate, but the mother takes the responsibility of carrying it from one place to another by holding the kitten from behind the neck and lifting it up.

In the analogy, the devotees of the formless can be compared to the baby monkey and the devotees of the personal form can be compared to the baby kitten. Those who worship the formless Brahman have the onus of progressing on the path by themselves because Brahman cannot bestow grace upon them. Brahman is not only formless; It is also without attributes. It has been described as *nirguna* (without qualities), *nirviśheṣh* (without attributes), and *nirākār* (without form). From this, it follows that Brahman does not manifest the quality of grace. The jnanis who worship God as *nirguna, nirviśheṣh,* and *nirākār,* have to rely entirely on self-effort for progress. On the other hand, the personal form of God is an ocean of compassion and mercy. Hence, devotees of the personal form receive the help of divine support in their sadhana. On the basis of the protection that God bestows upon His devotees, Shree Krishna stated in verse 9.31: 'O son of Kunti, declare it boldly that My devotee never perishes.' *He confirms the same statement in the next two verses.*

ये तु सर्वाणि कर्माणि मयि संन्यस्य मत्परः ।
अनन्येनैव योगेन मां ध्यायन्त उपासते ।।6।।

तेषामहं समुद्धर्ता मृत्युसंसारसागरात् ।
भवामि नचिरात्पार्थ मय्यावेशितचेतसाम् ।।7।।

ye tu sarvāṇi karmāṇi mayi sannyasya mat-paraḥ
ananyenaiva yogena māṁ dhyāyanta upāsate

teṣhām ahaṁ samuddhartā mṛityu-saṁsāra-sāgarāt
bhavāmi na chirāt pārtha mayy āveśhita-chetasām

ye—who; *tu*—but; *sarvāṇi*—all; *karmāṇi*—actions; *mayi*—to me; *sannyasya*—dedicating; *mat-paraḥ*—regarding me as the supreme goal; *ananyena*—exclusively; *eva*—certainly; *yogena*—with devotion; *mām*—me; *dhyāyantaḥ*—meditating; *upāsate*—worship; *teṣhām*—of those; *aham*—I; *samuddhartā*—the deliverer; *mṛityu-saṁsāra-sāgarāt*—from the ocean of birth and death; *bhavāmi*—(I) become; *na*—not; *chirāt*—after a long time; *pārtha*—Arjun, son of Pritha; *mayi*—with me; *āveśhita chetasām*—of those whose consciousness is united.

But those who dedicate all their actions to Me, regarding Me as the Supreme goal, worshiping Me and meditating on Me with exclusive devotion, O Parth, I swiftly deliver them from the ocean of birth and death, for their consciousness is united with Me.

Shree Krishna reiterates that His devotees reach Him quickly. First, with the personal form of God as the object of their devotion, they can easily focus their mind and senses on Him. They engage their tongue and ears in chanting and hearing the divine names of God, their eyes in seeing the image of His divine form, their body in performing actions for His pleasure, their mind in thinking of His wonderful pastimes and virtues, and their intellect in contemplating upon His glories. In this way, they quickly unite their consciousness with God.

Second, since such devotees continuously offer their hearts in uninterrupted bhakti, God quickly bestows His grace upon them and removes any obstacles on their path. For those who are in communion with Him, He dispels their ignorance with the lamp of knowledge. In this way, God Himself becomes the Saviour of His devotees and delivers them from *mṛityu saṁsāra sāgarāt* (the ocean of life and death).

मय्येव मन आधत्स्व मयि बुद्धिं निवेशय ।
निवसिष्यसि मय्येव अत ऊर्ध्वं न संशयः ।।8।।

mayy eva mana ādhatsva mayi buddhiṁ niveśhaya
nivasiṣhyasi mayy eva ata ūrdhvaṁ na sanśhayaḥ

mayi—on me; *eva*—alone; *manaḥ*—mind; *ādhatsva*—fix; *mayi*—on me; *buddhim*—intellect; *niveśhaya*—surrender; *nivasiṣhyasi*—you shall always live; *mayi*—in me; *eva*—alone; *ataḥ ūrdhvam*—thereafter; *na*—not; *sanśhayaḥ*—doubt.

Fix your mind on Me alone and surrender your intellect to Me. Thereupon, you will always live in Me. Of this, there is no doubt.

Having explained that worship of the personal form is better, Shree Krishna now begins to explain how to worship Him. He asks Arjun to do two things—fix the mind on God and also surrender the intellect to Him. The function of the mind is to create desires, attractions, and aversions. The function of the intellect is to think, analyse, and discriminate.

The importance of the mind has been repeatedly stated in the Vedic scriptures:

chetaḥ khalvasya bandhāya muktaye chātmano matam
guṇeṣhu saktaṁ bandhāya rataṁ vā puṁsi muktaye

(Bhagavatam 3.25.15)

'Captivity in maya and liberation from it is determined by the mind. If it is attached to the world, one is in bondage, and if the mind is detached from the world, one gets liberated.'

mana eva manuṣhyāṇāṁ kāraṇaṁ bandha mokṣhayoḥ

(*Pañchadaśhī*)

'Bondage and liberation are decided by the state of the mind.' Mere physical devotion is not sufficient; we must absorb the mind in thinking of God. The reason is that without the engagement of the mind, mere sensory activity is of no value. For example, we hear a sermon with our ears, but if the mind wanders off, we will not know what was said. The words will fall on the ears, but they will not register. This shows that without engaging the mind, the work of the senses does not count. On the other hand, the mind is such an instrument that all the senses reside in the subtle form within it. Thus, even without the actual sensory activity, the mind experiences the perceptions of sight, smell, taste, touch, and sound. For example, at night when we sleep our senses are inactive. Yet while dreaming, our mind experiences the objects of all the senses. This proves that the mind has the capacity to experience all perceptions even without the gross senses. Therefore, while noting our karmas, God gives importance to the mental works and not the physical works of the senses.

Even beyond the mind is the intellect. We can only fix the mind upon God when we surrender our intellect to Him. In material pursuits as well, when we face situations beyond the capability of our intellect, we take guidance from a person with superior intellect. For example, we visit a doctor when we are sick. Since we have no knowledge of medical science ourselves, we follow the advice of a qualified medical doctor. The doctor checks our symptoms, looks at our medical reports, makes a diagnosis, and then prescribes the medicines. We surrender our intellect and take the medicines according to the doctor's prescription. Similarly, if we are involved in a legal case, we take the help of a lawyer. The lawyer instructs us how to handle the interrogation by the opposing lawyer. Having no knowledge of law ourselves, we surrender our intellect and simply do as the lawyer says.

In the same way, at present our intellect is subject to many defects. Akrur, who went to get Shree Krishna from Vrindavan to Mathura, described these imperfections of the intellect in the Bhagavatam (10.40.25): *anityānātma duḥkheṣhu viparyaya matirhyaham* Akrur said: 'Our intellect is strapped with wrong knowledge. Though we are eternal souls, we think of ourselves to be the perishable body. Although all the objects of the world are perishable, we think they will always remain with us, and hence, we busily accumulate them day and night. And though the pursuit of sensual pleasures only results in misery in the long run, we still chase them in the hope that we will find happiness.'

The above three defects of the intellect are called *viparyaya* or reversals of knowledge under material illusion. The gravity of our problem is further aggravated because our intellect is conditioned to this kind of faulty thinking from innumerable past lifetimes. If we run our life in accordance with the directions of our intellect, we will definitely not make much progress on the divine path. Thus, if we wish to achieve spiritual success by attaching the mind to God, we must surrender our intellect to Him and follow His directions. Surrendering the intellect means to think in accordance with the knowledge received from God via the medium of the scriptures and the bonafide guru. The characteristics of a surrendered intellect are described in verse 18.62.

अथ चित्तं समाधातुं न शक्नोषि मयि स्थिरम् ।
अभ्यासयोगेन ततो मामिच्छाप्तुं धनञ्जय ।।9।।

atha chittaṁ samādhātuṁ na śhaknoṣhi mayi sthiram
abhyāsa-yogena tato mām ichchhāptuṁ dhanañjaya

atha—if; *chittam*—mind; *samādhātum*—to fix; *na śhaknoṣhi*—

(you) are unable; *mayi*—on me; *sthiram*—steadily; *abhyāsa-yogena*—by uniting with God through repeated practice; *tataḥ*—then; *mām*—me; *ichchhā*—desire; *āptum*—to attain; *dhanañjaya*—Arjun, conqueror of wealth.

If you are unable to fix your mind steadily on Me, O Arjun, then practice remembering Me with devotion while constantly restraining the mind from worldly affairs.

By fixing the mind on Shree Krishna, we can perfect our sadhana (spiritual practice). But we cannot expect to become perfect as soon as we begin treading this path. So, what should those people who cannot perfectly fix their mind on God do? Shree Krishna states here that they should endeavour to remember Him with devotion. As the saying goes, 'Practice makes perfect.' This is called *abhyāsa yog* or 'union with God through repeated practice.' Each time the mind wanders towards other objects and ideas, the devotee must strive to bring it back to God through remembrance of His Names, Forms, Virtues, Pastimes, Abodes, and Associates.

Jagadguru Shree Kripaluji Maharaj emphasises this repeated practice in his instructions for *sādhaks*:

jagata te mana ko haṭā kara, lagā hari meñ pyāre
isī kā abhyāsa puni puni, karu nirantara pyāre

(*Sadhana Karu Pyāre*)

'O dear one, remove the mind from the world and fix it on God. Practice this constantly, again and again!'

अभ्यासेऽप्यसमर्थोऽसि मत्कर्मपरमो भव ।
मदर्थमपि कर्माणि कुर्वन्सिद्धिमवाप्स्यसि ।।10।।

abhyāse 'py asamartho 'si mat-karma-paramo bhava
mad-artham api karmāṇi kurvan siddhim avāpsyasi

abhyāse—in practice; *api*—if; *asamarthaḥ*—unable; *asi*—you; *mat-karma paramaḥ*—devotedly work for me; *bhava*—be; *mat-*

artham—for my sake; *api*—also; *karmāṇi*—work; *kurvan*—performing; *siddhim*—perfection; *avāpsyasi*—you shall achieve.

If you cannot practise remembering Me with devotion, then just try to work for Me. Thus, performing devotional service to Me, you shall achieve the stage of perfection.

The instruction to practise to remember God is also often easier said than done. The mind is made from the material energy, and it naturally runs towards the material objects of the world, while taking it towards God requires conscious and determined effort. We may hear the instruction that we should think of God, and we may desire to implement it, but when we get absorbed in our work, God slips out of the mind. So, what should those people do who find it difficult to practice the remembrance of God at all times of the day? Shree Krishna answers this question in this verse.

Those who cannot constantly remember God should practise to simply work for Him. In every work they perform, they should cultivate the intention that they are doing it for the pleasure of the Lord, as stated previously in verses 9.27 and 9.28. In household life, a major portion of one's time goes in the maintenance of the family. One should keep doing the same work but change the internal consciousness. Rather than doing it out of worldly attachment for them, one should develop the consciousness that the family members are all children of God, and one has a responsibility to take care of them for His pleasure. One has to continue earning one's living, but again, a modification can be done in the consciousness with which one works. Instead of thinking that it is for the purpose of earning money for material enjoyment, one can think, 'I wish to maintain my family and myself with the earnings to enable us all to engage in devotion. And whatever I can save, I will donate in the service of God.' Similarly, the physical activities of eating, sleeping, bathing, etc. cannot be given up. But here again, we can develop divine consciousness, 'I need to keep my body healthy so that I can serve God with it. That is why I will carefully do the tasks required for its maintenance.'

When we practise working for the pleasure of God, we will naturally stop engaging in selfish activities and move towards those that are more in the nature of devotional service. In this way, by performing all actions for the exclusive satisfaction of the Supreme Lord Krishna, our mind will become steady, and we will soon be able to focus upon Him. Then, gradually love for God will manifest within the heart, and we will succeed in constantly thinking of Him.

अथैतदप्यशक्तोऽसि कर्तुं मद्योगमाश्रितः ।
सर्वकर्मफलत्यागं ततः कुरु यतात्मवान् ।।11।।

athaitad apy aśhakto 'si kartuṁ mad-yogam āśhritaḥ
sarva-karma-phala-tyāgaṁ tataḥ kuru yatātmavān

atha—if; *etat*—this; *api*—even; *aśhaktaḥ*—unable; *asi*—you are; *kartum*—to work; *mad-yogam*—with devotion to me; *āśhritaḥ*—taking refuge; *sarva-karma*—of all actions; *phala-tyāgam*—to renounce the fruits; *tataḥ*—then; *kuru*—do; *yata-ātma-vān*—be situated in the self.

If you are unable to even work for Me in devotion, then try to renounce the fruits of your actions and be situated in the self.

Beginning with verse 12.8, Shree Krishna gave three ways for Arjun's welfare. In the third, He asked Arjun to work for Him. However, that also requires a purified and resolute intellect. Those who are not yet convinced about their relationship with God and have not yet made God-realisation the goal of their lives, may find it impossible to work for His pleasure. Therefore, Shree Krishna now gives the fourth alternative for welfare. He says, 'Arjun keep doing your works as before, but become detached from the fruits of your actions'. Such detachment will purify our mind from the modes of ignorance (tamas) and passion (rajas) and raise it to the mode of goodness (sattva). In this way, renouncing the fruits of our efforts will help remove worldliness from our mind and strengthen the intellect. Then, the purified intellect will more easily be able to comprehend transcendental knowledge and be able to move to the higher levels of sadhana.

श्रेयो हि ज्ञानमभ्यासाज्ज्ञानाद्ध्यानं विशिष्यते ।
ध्यानात्कर्मफलत्यागस्त्यागाच्छान्तिरनन्तरम् ।।12।।

śhreyo hi jñānam abhyāsāj jñānād dhyānaṁ viśhiṣhyate
dhyānāt karma-phala-tyāgas tyāgāch chhāntir anantaram

śhreyaḥ—better; *hi*—for; *jñānam*—knowledge; *abhyāsāt*—than (mechanical) practice; *jñānāt*—than knowledge; *dhyānam*—meditation; *viśhiṣhyate*—better; *dhyānāt*—than meditation; *karma-phala-tyāgaḥ*—renunciation of the fruits of actions; *tyāgāt*—renunciation; *śhāntiḥ*—peace; *anantaram*—immediately.

Better than mechanical practice is knowledge; better than knowledge is meditation. Better than meditation is renunciation of the fruits of actions, for peace immediately follows such renunciation.

Many people are at the level of mechanical practice. They perform the rituals enjoined by their religious creed, but do not engage their mind in God. When they purchase a new house or a new car, they call the pandit to perform the puja (worship) ceremony. And while the pandit performs the puja, they sit and talk in the other room or sip a cup of tea. For them, devotion is nothing more than performing an empty ritual. It is often performed as a ceremonial habit passed on from parents and elders. Performing rituals mechanically is not a bad thing because something is better than nothing; at least such people are externally engaging in devotion.

However, Shree Krishna says that higher than mechanical practice is the cultivation of spiritual knowledge. Knowledge bestows the understanding that the goal of life is God-realisation and not material progress. One who is well-versed in knowledge goes beyond empty rituals and develops the desire to purify the mind. But mere knowledge by itself cannot cleanse the heart. This is why Shree Krishna says that higher than the cultivation of knowledge is the process of engaging the mind in meditation. By practically controlling the mind through meditation, we begin to develop detachment from worldly pleasures. When the mind develops some measure of the quality of detachment, we can practice the next step, which is renunciation of the fruits of actions. As explained in the previous verse, this will help remove worldliness from the mind and strengthen the intellect for subsequent higher stages.

अद्वेष्टा सर्वभूतानां मैत्रः करुण एव च ।
निर्ममो निरहङ्कारः समदुःखसुखः क्षमी ।।13।।

सन्तुष्टः सततं योगी यतात्मा दृढनिश्चयः ।
मय्यर्पितमनोबुद्धिर्यो मद्भक्तः स मे प्रियः ।।14।।

adveṣhṭā sarva-bhūtānāṁ maitraḥ karuṇa eva cha
nirmamo nirahankāraḥ sama-duḥkha-sukhaḥ kṣhamī

santuṣhṭaḥ satataṁ yogī yatātmā dṛiḍha-niśhchayaḥ
mayy arpita-mano-buddhir yo mad-bhaktaḥ sa me priyaḥ

adveṣhṭā—free from malice; *sarva-bhūtānām*—towards all living beings; *maitraḥ*—friendly; *karuṇaḥ*—compassionate; *eva*—indeed; *cha*—and; *nirmamaḥ*—free from attachment to possession; *nirahankāraḥ*—free from egoism; *sama*—equipoised; *duḥkha*—distress; *sukhaḥ*—happiness; *kṣhamī*—forgiving; *santuṣhṭaḥ*—content; *satatam*—steadily; *yogī*—united in devotion; *yata-ātmā*—self-controlled; *dṛiḍha-niśhchayaḥ*—firm resolve; *mayi*—to me; *arpita*—dedicated; *manaḥ*—mind; *buddhiḥ*—intellect; *yaḥ*—who; *mat-bhaktaḥ*—my devotees; *saḥ*—they; *me*—to me; *priyaḥ*—very dear.

Those devotees are very dear to Me who are free from malice towards all living beings, who are friendly and compassionate. They are free from attachment to possessions and egotism, equipoised in happiness and distress, and ever-forgiving. They are ever-content, steadily united with Me in devotion, self-controlled, of firm resolve, and dedicated to Me in mind and intellect.

Affirming that devotion to His personal form is the best, Shree Krishna now goes on to explain the qualities of His loving devotees in verses 13 to 19.

Free from malice towards all living beings: The devotees realise that all living beings are tiny parts of God. If they harbour envy towards others, it is tantamount to harbouring envy towards God Himself. So, the devotees should be free from malice even to those who are inimical towards them.

Friendly and compassionate: Devotion engenders the feeling of unity among all living beings by virtue of their being children of the one God. The notion of seeing others as alien to oneself is wiped out. This leads to the growth of affability in the devotees and sympathy towards the sufferings of others.

Free from attachment to possessions and egotism: The biggest enemy of devotion is pride. One can only progress on the spiritual path if one practises self-effacement. Proficient devotees naturally become humble and eliminate pride and proprietorship from their personality, as well as the false identification of being the body.

Equipoised in happiness and distress: Devotees have faith that only efforts are in their hands while the results are in the hands of God. So whatever results come their way, they see them as the will of God and accept them with equanimity.

Ever-forgiving: Devotees never think of punishing wrongdoers for their emotional satisfaction. Harbouring such negative thoughts towards others ruins one's own devotion. So, accomplished devotees refuse to harbour unforgiving thoughts in all circumstances and leave the task of punishing wrongdoers to God.

Ever-content: Contentment comes not from increasing our possessions but by decreasing our wants. Devotees no longer look upon material objects as the source of pleasure and are content with whatever they get.

Steadily united with Me in devotion: As explained previously, 'Yog' means union. Devotees are yogis because their consciousness is absorbed in God. This absorption is not occasional or intermittent, but steady and constant because they are established in their relationship with God.

Self-controlled: Devotees attach their mind to God in loving devotion. It is thus detached from the world, and this gives them mastery over their mind and senses.

Of firm resolve: The quality of determination comes from possessing a resolute intellect. Since devotees tie their intellect to the knowledge of the scriptures and the instructions of the guru, it becomes so resolute that even if the whole world tries to convince them otherwise, they do not budge an inch from their position.

Dedicated to Me in mind and intellect: The soul is a servant of God by its inherent nature, and as we become enlightened with this knowledge, we naturally dedicate ourselves to the Supreme Lord. In this surrender, the mind and intellect are of primary importance. When they are devoted to God, the rest of our personality—body, working senses, knowledge senses, worldly possessions, and soul—naturally get dedicated in His service.

Shree Krishna says that devotees who exhibit these qualities are very dear to Him.

यस्मान्नोद्विजते लोको लोकान्नोद्विजते च यः ।
हर्षामर्षभयोद्वेगैर्मुक्तो यः स च मे प्रियः ।।15।।

yasmān nodvijate loko lokān nodvijate cha yaḥ
harṣhāmarṣha-bhayodvegair mukto yaḥ sa cha me priyaḥ

yasmāt—by whom; *na*—not; *udvijate*—are agitated; *lokaḥ*—people; *lokāt*—from people; *na*—not; *udvijate*—are disturbed; *cha*—and; *yaḥ*—who; *harṣha*—pleasure; *amarṣha*—pain; *bhaya*—fear; *udvegaiḥ*—anxiety; *muktaḥ*—free; *yaḥ*—who; *saḥ*—they; *cha*—and; *me*—to me; *priyaḥ*—very dear.

Those who are not a source of annoyance to anyone and who in turn are not agitated by anyone, who are equal in pleasure and pain, and free from fear and anxiety, such devotees of Mine are very dear to Me.

The soul is by nature pure and uncontaminated; the problem is that it is presently covered by the impure mind. Once these impurities are removed, the glorious qualities of the soul naturally shine forth. The Shreemad Bhagavatam states:

yasyāsti bhaktir bhagavatyakiñchanā
sarvair guṇais tatra samāsate surāḥ
harāvabhaktasya kuto mahad-guṇā
manorathenāsati dhāvato bahiḥ (5.18.12)

'All the wonderful qualities of the celestial gods manifest in those who devote themselves to the Supreme Lord. But those who do not engage in devotion only keep running on the chariot of their mind (no matter how many self-transformational techniques they may practise).' Here, Shree Krishna describes some more qualities that develop in His devotees.

Not a source of annoyance to anyone: Devotion melts and softens the heart. As a result, the devotees naturally become gentle in their dealings with everyone. Besides, they behold God seated in everyone and see all as His tiny fragments. Therefore, they can never think of harming anyone.

Not agitated by anyone: Though devotees never hurt others, it does not mean that others do not try to hurt them. The history of saints around the world reveals that during their lifetime, those who felt threatened by their welfare work and principles often oppressed them. However, the saints always maintained a compassionate attitude even towards the inimical. Thus, we see how Jesus of Nazareth prayed on the cross, 'Father, forgive them for they know not what they do.' (Luke 23.34)

Equal in pleasure and pain: Devotees are equipped with the wisdom of the scriptures, and hence, they are aware that pleasure and pain are both inevitable with the flow of life, just like the passing summer and winter seasons. With their inexhaustible positive attitude, they see the grace of God in both, and leverage all situations to enhance their devotion.

Free from fear and anxiety: The cause of fear and anxiety is attachment. It makes us yearn for the object of attachment and fear separation from it. The moment we become detached from material objects, we become fearless. Devotees are not only free from attachment; they also are in harmony with the will of God. As a result, they experience neither fear nor anxiety.

अनपेक्षः शुचिर्दक्ष उदासीनो गतव्यथः ।
सर्वारम्भपरित्यागी यो मद्भक्तः स मे प्रियः ।।16।।

anapekṣhaḥ śhuchir dakṣha udāsīno gata-vyathaḥ
sarvārambha-parityāgī yo mad-bhaktaḥ sa me priyaḥ

anapekṣhaḥ—indifferent to worldly gain; *śhuchiḥ*—pure; *dakṣhaḥ*—skilful; *udāsīnaḥ*—without cares; *gata-vyathaḥ*—untroubled; *sarva-ārambha*—of all undertakings; *parityāgī*—renouncer; *saḥ*—who; *mad-bhaktaḥ*—my devotee; *saḥ*—he; *me*—to me; *priyaḥ*—very dear.

Those who are indifferent to worldly gains, externally and internally pure, skilful, without cares, untroubled, and free from selfishness in all undertakings, such devotees of Mine are very dear to Me.

Indifferent to worldly gains: To a penurious person, the loss or gain of Rs 1,000 would be an important matter, but a multi-billionaire would consider it insignificant and not give any further thought to it. Devotees are rich in divine love for God, and they consider it to be the highest treasure worthy of possessing. They also give the highest priority to the loving service of the Lord. Hence, they become unconcerned about worldly gains.

Externally and internally pure: Since their minds are constantly absorbed in the all-pure Lord, devotees become internally cleansed from the defects of lust, anger, greed, envy, ego, and other negativities. In this state of mind, they naturally prefer to keep the external body and environment pure as well. Thus, in accordance with the old saying, 'Cleanliness is next to Godliness', they are also externally pure.

Skilful: Devotees look on all their tasks as opportunities to serve God. Consequently, they perform their work with great care and attention. This naturally makes them skilful.

Without cares: Having faith that God is always protecting them, they become without care.

Untroubled: Since devotees are surrendered to the will of God, they simply put in their best effort in all endeavours and leave the results in the hands of the Supreme. Thus, whatever the outcome, they remain untroubled, subjugating their will to the divine will.

Free from selfishness in all undertakings: Their attitude of service makes them rise above petty selfishness.

यो न हृष्यति न द्वेष्टि न शोचति न काङ्क्षति ।
शुभाशुभपरित्यागी भक्तिमान्यः स मे प्रियः ।।17।।

yo na hṛiṣhyati na dveṣhṭi na śhochati na kāṅkṣhati
śhubhāśhubha-parityāgī bhaktimān yaḥ sa me priyaḥ

yaḥ—who; *na*—neither; *hṛiṣhyati*—rejoice; *na*—nor; *dveṣhṭi*—despair; *na*—neither; *śhochati*—lament; *na*—nor; *kāṅkṣhati*—hanker for gain; *śhubha-aśhubha-parityāgī*—who renounce both good and evil deeds; *bhakti-mān*—full of devotion; *yaḥ*—who; *saḥ*—that person; *me*—to me; *priyaḥ*—very dear.

Those who neither rejoice in mundane pleasures nor despair in worldly sorrows, who neither lament for any loss nor hanker for any gain, who renounce both good and evil deeds, such persons who are full of devotion are very dear to Me.

They neither rejoice in mundane pleasures nor despair in worldly sorrows: If we are in the dark and someone offers help by showing a lamp, we naturally rejoice. Then, if someone blows out the flame, we feel annoyed. But if we are standing under the noonday sun, we feel indifferent whether someone shows us a lamp or blows it out. Similarly, devotees of the Lord, blessed with the divine love of God, rise above pleasure and despair.

Neither lament for any loss nor hanker for any gain: Such devotees neither hanker after pleasant worldly situations nor grieve in unpleasant ones. The *Nārad Bhakti Darshan* states:

yatprāpya na kiñchidvāñchhati, na śhochati, na dveṣhṭi, na ramate, notsāhi bhavati (Sutra 5)

'On attaining divine love for God, the devotee neither yearns for pleasant things nor grieves on losing them. They are not hateful to those who harm them. They have no liking for worldly enjoyments. They are not anxious for the enhancement of their worldly position.' Devotees relish the bliss of God, so the bliss of all material objects seems insignificant in comparison.

Renounce both good and evil actions: Devotees obviously renounce evil actions (*vikarm*), for they are against their nature and displeasing to God. The good actions Shree Krishna refers to are prescribed ritualistic duties (karm) mentioned in the scriptures. All actions performed by the devotees become *akarm* (inaction) because they are not performed with any selfish motive and are dedicated to God. The concept of *akarm* has been explained in great detail in verses 4.17–20.

Full of devotion: *Bhaktimān* means 'filled with devotion'. The nature of divine love is such that it keeps increasing for eternity. Bhakti poets have said: *prem meñ pūrṇimā nahīñ* 'Unlike the moon which waxes to a limit and then wanes, divine love keeps growing without limit.' So, the heart of the devotee contains an ocean of love for God. Shree Krishna says that such devotees are very dear to Him.

समः शत्रौ च मित्रे च तथा मानापमानयोः ।
शीतोष्णसुखदुःखेषु समः सङ्गविवर्जितः ।।18।।

तुल्यनिन्दास्तुतिर्मौनी सन्तुष्टो येन केनचित् ।
अनिकेतः स्थिरमतिर्भक्तिमान्मे प्रियो नरः ।।19।।

samaḥ śhatrau cha mitre cha tathā mānāpamānayoḥ
śhītoṣhṇa-sukha-duḥkheṣhu samaḥ saṅga-vivarjitaḥ

tulya-nindā-stutir maunī santuṣhṭo yena kenachit
aniketaḥ sthira-matir bhaktimān me priyo naraḥ

samaḥ—alike; *śhatrau*—to a foe; *cha*—and; *mitre*—to a friend; *cha tathā*—as well as; *māna-apamānayoḥ*—in honour and dishonour; *śhīta-uṣhṇa*—in cold and heat; *sukha-duḥkheṣhu*—in joy and sorrow; *samaḥ*—equipoised; *saṅga-vivarjitaḥ*—free from all unfavourable association; *tulya*—alike; *nindā-stutiḥ*—reproach and praise; *maunī*—silent contemplation; *santuṣhṭaḥ*—content; *yena kenachit*—with anything; *aniketaḥ*—without attachment to the place of residence; *sthira*—firmly fixed; *matiḥ*—intellect; *bhakti-mān*—full of devotion; *me*—to me; *priyaḥ*—very dear; *naraḥ*—a person.

Those, who are alike to friend and foe, equipoised in honour and dishonour, cold and heat, joy and sorrow, and are free from all unfavourable association; those who take praise and reproach alike, who are given to silent contemplation, content with what comes their way, without attachment to the place of residence, whose intellect is firmly fixed in Me, and who are full of devotion to Me, such persons are very dear to Me.

Shree Krishna describes ten more qualities here.

Alike to friend and foe: Devotees are positively disposed towards all and are not swayed by the sentiments of enmity and friendship. There is a beautiful story about Prahalad on this:

Once, his son, Virochan, got into an argument with his guru's son Sudhanva. Virochan said, 'I am superior to you because I am the son of a king.'

Sudhanva claimed, 'I am superior because I am the son of a rishi.' They were both young, and in their impetuousness, laid bets. Both agreed, 'Whoever is proved superior will live while the other will have to die.' Now, who would be the judge? Sudhanva said to Virochan, 'Your father, Prahalad, will be the judge.'

Virochan exclaimed, 'Really! But then you will complain that he has been partial.'

'No, my father, Rishi Angira, has said that your father Prahalad is perfectly just and will never differentiate between friend and foe.'

The two boys went to Prahalad. Virochan asked, 'Father, am I superior or Sudhanva?'

Prahalad asked, 'Why did this question arise?'

Virochan replied, 'Father, we have laid bets that whoever is proved superior will remain alive while the other will have to die.'

Prahalad smiled and said, 'Your friend, Sudhanva, is superior since he is the son of your father's guru.' Prahalad ordered his servants, 'Take my son to the gallows and hang him.'

At that moment, Sudhanva intervened. 'Wait!' he said to Prahalad, 'I have a second question. Am I superior or you?'

Prahalad replied, 'I have been born in a family of demons, while you are the son of a rishi, who is also my guru. Hence, you are superior.'

Sudhanva again asked, 'In that case, will you obey my instruction?'

'Yes, of course,' responded Prahalad.

'Ok, then leave Virochan,' said Sudhanva.

Prahalad instructed his servants, 'Leave him,' in the same manner as he had said, 'Take him to the gallows.'

The celestial gods showered flowers onto his court and hailed the quality of justice that Prahalad displayed. This attitude of justice came naturally to Prahalad because by virtue of being a perfect devotee of the Lord he was equal to friend, foe, relative, kith, kin, and outsider.

Equipoised in honour and dishonour: Shree Krishna further mentions that devotees pay no heed to honour and dishonour. This is just like when a person begins engaging in an illicit relationship, he or she is mindful of what others will say, but when the relationship becomes deep, then the person no longer cares about the disrepute it will bring. Similarly, in the heart of the devotee the flame of divine love burns so brightly that worldly honour and dishonour no longer carry any importance.

Alike in cold and heat, joy and sorrow: The devotees are equipoised in favourable and unfavourable circumstances. They know that none of these are permanent. They come and go like the day and the night, and so they do not consider it worth their while to take their thoughts off God and focus on either of them.

An incident from the life of Ramakrishna Paramahansa illustrates the nature of saints. He was diagnosed with throat cancer in his old age. People asked him to pray to Mother Kali for a cure. He said, 'My mind is absorbed in love for Mother Kali. Why should I take it off from Her and apply it to this dirty bodily cancer? Whatever God has willed, let it happen.'

Free from unfavourable association: Associating with persons or objects is called *saṅg*. There are two kinds of *saṅg*. Association that takes our mind to the world is *kusaṅg* (unfavourable association) and that which takes our mind away from the world and towards God is called satsang (favourable association). Since devotees do not relish worldly thoughts, they naturally avoid *kusaṅg* and engage in satsang.

Take praise and reproach alike: For those who are externally motivated, the appreciation and rejection by others is all-important. However, devotees are internally motivated by the principles they value within themselves. Hence, neither commendation nor denunciation by others makes any difference to them.

Given to silent contemplation: Crows and swans have diametrically opposite proclivities. While crows are drawn to garbage piles, the majestic swans are attracted by tranquil lakes. Similarly, the minds of worldly people find great relish in conversing about materialistic topics. But saintly devotees possess pure minds, and thus worldly talks seem as attractive to them as a pile of garbage. This does not mean that they do not converse. Like the swan drawn to the lakes, their minds are drawn towards topics such as the Names, Forms, Pastimes, Virtues, Abodes, Associates, and Glories of God.

Content with whatever comes their way: The needs of the devotees shrink to the bare necessities for maintaining the body. Saint Kabir expresses this in his famous couplet:

mālik itanā dījiye, jāme kuṭumba samāya
maiṅ bhī bhūkhā na rahūñ, sādhu na bhūkhā jāya

'O Lord, give me just enough for the bare maintenance of my family's physical needs and for giving alms to the sadhu who comes to my door.'

Without attachment to the place of residence: No earthly home can be a permanent residence for the soul, for it must necessarily be left behind at the time of death. When the Mogul Emperor, Akbar, built his capital, Fatehpur Sikri, he put the following inscription on the main entrance gate: 'The world is a bridge; cross over it but build no house on it.' In the same vein, Jagadguru Shree Kripaluji Maharaj states:

jaga meñ raho aise govinda radhey,
dharmaśhālā meñ yātrī raheñ jyoñ batā de

(*Radha Govind Geet*)

'Live in this world as a traveller lives in a wayside inn (aware that it is to be vacated the next morning).' Realising the truth of this statement, devotees look on their home as only a temporary dwelling place.

Intellect is firmly fixed in Me: Devotees have deep conviction in the supremacy of God's position in creation and in their eternal relationship with Him. They are also firm in their faith that if they surrender to Him lovingly, by God's grace they will achieve the highest realisation. Hence, they neither wander from attraction-to-attraction or from path-to-path.

Shree Krishna declares such resolute devotees to be very dear to Him.

ये तु धर्म्यामृतमिदं यथोक्तं पर्युपासते ।
श्रद्दधाना मत्परमा भक्तास्तेऽतीव मे प्रियाः ।।20।।

ye tu dharmyāmṛitam idaṁ yathoktaṁ paryupāsate
śhraddadhānā mat-paramā bhaktās te 'tīva me priyāḥ

ye—who; *tu*—indeed; *dharma*—of wisdom; *amṛitam*—nectar; *idam*—this; *yathā*—as; *uktam*—declared; *paryupāsate*—exclusive devotion; *śhraddadhānāḥ*—with faith; *mat-paramāḥ*—intent on me as the supreme goal; *bhaktāḥ*—devotees; *te*—they; *atīva*—exceedingly; *me*—to me; *priyāḥ*—dear.

Those who honour this nectar of wisdom declared here, have faith in Me, and are devoted and intent on Me as the supreme goal, they are exceedingly dear to Me.

Shree Krishna concludes the chapter by summing up His answer to Arjun's question. At the beginning of the chapter, Arjun had asked Him whom He considered superior—those who are devoted to His personal form through bhakti yog or those who worship the formless Brahman through jnana yog. Shree Krishna responded in the second verse that He considers them to be the highest yogis who steadfastly engage in devotion upon His personal form. He then continued on the topic of bhakti by first explaining the means of performing devotion and then the qualities of His devotees. He now ends with the affirmation that the supreme path of spirituality is bhakti. Those who make the Supreme Lord as their goal and cultivate devotion with great faith, imbued with the virtues mentioned in the previous verses, such devotees are exceedingly dear to God.

CHAPTER 13

Kṣhetra Kṣhetrajña Vibhāg Yog

Yog through Distinguishing the Field and the Knower of the Field

The Bhagavad Gita consists of three sections, each of which has six chapters, for a total of eighteen chapters. The first set of six chapters describes karm yog. The second set describes the glories of bhakti, and for the nourishment of bhakti, it also dwells upon the opulences of God. The third set of six chapters expounds upon *tattva jnana* (knowledge scriptural terms and principles). The present chapter is the first of the third section. It introduces two terms—*kṣhetra* (the 'field') and *kṣhetrajña* (the 'knower of the field'). We may think of the field as the body and the knower of the field as the soul that resides within. But this is a simplification; the field is actually much more—it includes the mind, intellect, and ego, and all other components of the material energy that comprise our personality. In this wider sense, the field of the body encompasses all aspects of our personality, except for the soul who is the 'knower the field'.

As a farmer sows seeds in a field and reaps the harvest from it, we sow the field of our body with good or bad thoughts and actions and reap the consequent destiny. The Buddha had explained: 'All that we are is the result of what we have thought; it is founded on our thoughts; and it is made of our thoughts.' Therefore, as we think, that is what we become. The great American thinker, Ralph Waldo Emerson, said: 'The ancestor of every action is thought.' Thus, we must learn the art of cultivating the field of our body with appropriate thoughts and actions. This requires knowledge of the distinction between the field and the knower of the field. In the present chapter, Shree Krishna goes into a detailed analysis of this distinction. He enumerates the elements of material nature that compose the field of the body. He describes the modifications that arise in the field, in the form of emotions, sentiments, and feelings. He also mentions the virtues and qualities that purify the field and illumine it with the light of knowledge. Such knowledge helps us gain realisation of the soul who is the knower of the field. The chapter then describes God, who is the Supreme Knower of the fields of all living beings. That Supreme Lord holds contradictory attributes i.e., He possesses opposite qualities at the same time. So, He is all-pervading in creation and yet seated in the hearts of all living beings. He is thus the Supreme Soul of all living beings.

Having described the soul, the Supreme Soul, and material nature, Shree Krishna then explains which of these is responsible for actions by living beings, and which is responsible for cause and effect in the world at large. Those, who can perceive these distinctions and properly pinpoint the causes of action, are the ones who actually see; they are the ones who are situated in knowledge. They observe the Supreme Soul present in all living beings and do not degrade themselves by their mind. They can see the variety of living beings situated in the same material nature. And when they see the common spiritual substratum pervading all existence, they attain the realisation of Brahman.

अर्जुन उवाच ।
प्रकृतिं पुरुषं चैव क्षेत्रं क्षेत्रज्ञमेव च ।
एतद्वेदितुमिच्छामि ज्ञानं ज्ञेयं च केशव ।।1।।[1]

arjuna uvācha
prakṛitiṁ puruṣhaṁ chaiva kṣhetraṁ kṣhetra-jñam eva cha
etad veditum ichchhāmi jñānaṁ jñeyaṁ cha keśhava[1]

arjunaḥ uvācha—Arjun said; *prakṛitim*—material nature; *puruṣham*—the enjoyer; *cha*—and; *eva*—indeed; *kṣhetram*—the

1 In some editions of the Bhagavad Gita, this verse has been omitted, and the next verse figures as the first verse of the thirteenth chapter.

field of activities; *kṣhetra-jñam*—the knower of the field; *eva*—even; *cha*—also; *etat*—this; *veditum*—to know; *ichchhāmi*—I wish; *jñānam*—knowledge; *jñeyam*—the goal of knowledge; *cha*—and; *keśhava*—Krishna, killer of the demon named Keshi.

Arjun said, 'O Keshav, I wish to understand what are prakriti and purush, and what are *kṣhetra* and *kṣhetrajña*? I also wish to know what is true knowledge, and what is the goal of this knowledge?

श्रीभगवानुवाच ।
इदं शरीरं कौन्तेय क्षेत्रमित्यभिधीयते ।
एतद्यो वेत्ति तं प्राहुः क्षेत्रज्ञ इति तद्विदः ।।2।।

śhrī-bhagavān uvācha
idaṁ śharīraṁ kaunteya kṣhetram ity abhidhīyate
etad yo vetti taṁ prāhuḥ kṣhetra-jña iti tad-vidaḥ

śhrī-bhagavān uvācha—the Supreme Divine Lord said; *idam*—this; *śharīram*—body; *kaunteya*—Arjun, son of Kunti; *kṣhetram*—the field of activities; *iti*—thus; *abhidhīyate*—is termed as; *etat*—this; *yaḥ*—one who; *vetti*—knows; *tam*—that person; *prāhuḥ*—is called; *kṣhetra-jñaḥ*—the knower of the field; *iti*—thus; *tat-vidaḥ*—those who discern the truth.

The Supreme Divine Lord said: O Arjun, this body is termed as *kṣhetra* (the field of activities), and the one who knows this body is called *kṣhetrajña* (the knower of the field) by the sages who discern the truth about both.

Here, Shree Krishna begins explaining the topic of distinction between the body and spirit. The soul is divine, and can neither eat, see, smell, hear, taste, nor touch. It vicariously does all these works through the body-mind-intellect mechanism, which is thus termed as the field of activities. In modern science, we have terms like 'field of energy'. A magnet has a magnetic field around it which creates electricity on rapid movement. An electric charge has a force field around it. Here, the body is the receptacle for the activities of the individual. Hence, it is termed as *kṣhetra* (the field of activities).

The soul is distinct from the body-mind-intellect mechanism, but forgetful of its divine nature, it identifies with these material entities. Yet, because it has knowledge of the body, it is called *kṣhetrajña* (knower of the field of the body). This terminology has been given by self-realised sages, who were transcendentally situated at the platform of the soul and perceived their distinct identity as separate from the body.

क्षेत्रज्ञं चापि मां विद्धि सर्वक्षेत्रेषु भारत ।
क्षेत्रक्षेत्रज्ञयोर्ज्ञानं यत्तज्ज्ञानं मतं मम ।।3।।

kṣhetra-jñaṁ chāpi māṁ viddhi sarva-kṣhetreṣhu bhārata
kṣhetra-kṣhetrajñayor jñānaṁ yat taj jñānaṁ mataṁ mama

kṣhetra-jñam—knower of the field; *cha*—also; *api*—only; *mām*—me; *viddhi*—know; *sarva*—all; *kṣhetreṣhu*—in individual fields of activities; *bhārata*—scion of Bharat; *kṣhetra*—the field of activities; *kṣhetra-jñayoḥ*—of the knower of the field; *jñānam*—understanding of; *yat*—which; *tat*—that; *jñānam*—knowledge; *matam*—opinion; *mama*—my.

O scion of Bharat, I am also the knower of all the individual fields of activity. The understanding of the body as the field of activities, and the soul and God as the knowers of the field, this I hold to be true knowledge.

The soul is only the knower of the individual field of its own body. Even in this limited context, the soul's knowledge of its field is incomplete. God, as the Supreme Soul in the heart of all living beings, is the knower of the fields of all souls. Further, God's knowledge of each *kṣhetra* is perfect and complete. By explaining these distinctions, Shree Krishna establishes the position of the three entities vis-à-vis each other—the material body, the soul, and the Supreme Soul.

In the second part of the above verse, He gives His definition of knowledge. 'True knowledge is understanding not only of the self, the Supreme Lord, and the physical body, but also the distinction amongst them.' In this light, persons with PhDs and DLitts may consider themselves to be erudite, but if they do not understand the distinction between their body, the soul, and God, then according to Shree Krishna's definition, they are really not knowledgeable.

तत्क्षेत्रं यच्च यादृक्च यद्विकारि यतश्च यत् ।
स च यो यत्प्रभावश्च तत्समासेन मे शृणु ।।4।।

tat kṣhetraṁ yach cha yādṛik cha yad-vikāri yataśh cha yat
sa cha yo yat-prabhāvaśh cha tat samāsena me śhṛiṇu

tat—that; *kṣhetram*—field of activities; *yat*—what; *cha*—and; *yādṛik*—its nature; *cha*—and; *yat-vikāri*—how change takes place in it; *yataḥ*—from what; *cha*—also; *yat*—what; *saḥ*—he; *cha*—also; *yaḥ*—who; *yat-prabhāvaḥ*—what his powers are; *cha*—and; *tat*—that; *samāsena*—in summary; *me*—from me; *śhṛiṇu*—listen.

Listen and I will explain to you what that field is and what its nature is. I will also explain how change takes place within it, from what it was created, who the knower of the field of activities is, and what his powers are.

Shree Krishna now poses many questions Himself and tells Arjun to listen carefully to their answers.

ऋषिभिर्बहुधा गीतं छन्दोभिर्विविधैः पृथक् ।
ब्रह्मसूत्रपदैश्चैव हेतुमद्भिर्विनिश्चितैः ।।5।।

ṛiṣhibhir bahudhā gītaṁ chhandobhir vividhaiḥ pṛithak
brahma-sūtra-padaiśh chaiva hetumadbhir viniśhchitaiḥ

ṛiṣhibhiḥ—by great sages; *bahudhā*—in manifold ways; *gītam*—sung; *chhandobhiḥ*—in Vedic hymns; *vividhaiḥ*—various; *pṛithak*—various; *brahma-sūtra*—the *Brahma Sūtra*; *padaiḥ*—by the hymns; *cha*—and; *eva*—especially; *hetu-madbhiḥ*—with logic; *viniśhchitaiḥ*—conclusive evidence.

Great sages have sung the truth about the field and the knower of the field in manifold ways. It has been stated in various Vedic hymns,

and especially revealed in the *Brahma Sutra* with sound logic and conclusive evidence.

Knowledge is appealing to the intellect when it is expressed with precision and clarity and is substantiated with sound logic. Further, for it to be accepted as infallible, it must be confirmed on the basis of infallible authority. The reference for validating spiritual knowledge is the Vedas.

Vedas: These are not just the name of some books; they are the eternal knowledge of God. Whenever God creates the world, He manifests the Vedas for the benefit of the souls. The *Bṛihadāraṇyak Upanishad* (4.5.11) states: *niḥśhvasitamasya vedāḥ* 'The Vedas manifested from the breath of God.' They were first revealed in the heart of the first-born Brahma. From there, they came down through the oral tradition, and hence, another name for them is *Śhruti* or 'knowledge received through the ear'. At the beginning of the age of Kali, Ved Vyas, who was himself a descension of God, documented the Vedas in the form of a book, and divided the one body of knowledge into four—*Rig Veda*, *Yajur Veda*, *Sama Veda*, and *Atharva Veda*. This is why he received the name *Ved Vyās* or 'one who divided the Vedas'. The distinction must be borne in mind that Ved Vyas is never referred to as the composer of the Vedas but merely the one who divided them. Hence, the Vedas are also called *apauruṣheya* which means 'not created by any person'. They are respected as the infallible authority for spiritual knowledge.

bhūtaṁ bhavyaṁ bhaviṣhyaṁ cha sarvaṁ vedāt prasidhyati

(*Manu Smriti* 12.97)

'Any spiritual principle must be validated on the authority of the Vedas.' To elaborate this knowledge of the Vedas, many sages wrote texts and these traditionally became included in the gamut of the Vedic scriptures because they conform to the authority of the Vedas. Some of the important Vedic scriptures are listed below.

Itihās: These are historical texts and are two in number, the Ramayan and the Mahabharat. They describe the history related to two important descensions of God. The Ramayan was written by Sage Valmiki and describes the leelas or divine pastimes of Lord Ram. Amazingly, it was written by Valmiki before Shree Ram actually displayed His leelas. The great poet sage was empowered with divine vision by which he could see the pastimes Lord Ram would enact upon descending into the world. He thus put them down in twenty-four thousand most beautifully composed Sanskrit verses of the Ramayan. These verses also contain lessons on ideal behaviour in various social roles, such as son, brother, wife, king, and married couples. The Ramayan has also been written in many regional languages of India, thereby increasing its popularity among the people. The most famous among these is the Hindi Ramayan, Ramcharitmanas, written by a great devotee of Lord Ram, Saint Tulsidas.

The Mahabharat was written by Sage Ved Vyas. It contains one hundred thousand verses and is considered the longest poem in the world. The divine leelas of Lord Krishna are the central theme of the Mahabharat. It is full of wisdom and guidance related to duties in all stages of human life and devotion to God.

The Bhagavad Gita is a portion of the Mahabharat. It is the most popular Hindu scripture since it contains the essence of spiritual knowledge, so beautifully described by Lord Krishna Himself. It has been translated in many different languages of the world. Innumerable commentaries have been written on the Bhagavad Gita.

Puranas: There are eighteen Puranas written by Sage Ved Vyas. Together, they contain four hundred thousand verses. These describe the divine pastimes of the various forms of God and His devotees. The Puranas are also full of philosophic knowledge. They discuss the creation of the universe, its annihilation and recreation, the history of humankind, the genealogy of the celestial gods and the holy sages. The most important among them is the *Bhāgavat Puran* or the Shreemad Bhagavatam. It was the last scripture written by Sage Ved Vyas. In it, he mentions that in this scripture, he is going to reveal the highest dharma of pure selfless love for God. Philosophically, the Shreemad Bhagavatam begins where the Bhagavad Gita ends.

Ṣhaḍ-darshan: These come next in importance among the Vedic scriptures. Six sages wrote six scriptures highlighting different aspects of Hindu philosophy. These became known as the *Ṣhaḍ-darshan* or six philosophic works. They are:

- ***Mimansa***: Written by Maharishi (Sage) Jaimini, it describes ritualistic duties and ceremonies.
- ***Vedant Darshan:*** Written by Maharishi Ved Vyas, it discusses the nature of the Absolute Truth.
- ***Nyaya Darshan:*** Written by Maharishi Gautam, it develops a system of logic for understanding life and the Absolute Truth.
- ***Vaiśheṣhik Darshan:*** Written by Maharishi Kanad, it analyses cosmology and creation from the perspective of its various elements.
- ***Yog Darshan:*** Written by Maharishi Patanjali, it describes an eightfold path to union with God, beginning with physical postures.
- ***Sānkhya Darshan:*** Written by Maharishi Kapil, it describes the evolution of the universe from prakriti, the primordial form of the material energy.

Apart from these, there are hundreds of other scriptures in the Hindu tradition. It would be impossible to describe them all here. Suffice it to say that the Vedic scriptures are a vast treasure house of divine knowledge revealed by God and the saints for the eternal welfare of all humankind.

Amongst these scriptural texts, the *Brahma Sutra* (*Vedant Darshan*) is considered as the last word on the topic of the distinction between the soul, the material body, and God. Hence, Shree Krishna particularly mentions it in the above verse. 'Ved' refers to the Vedas, and 'ant' means 'the conclusion'. Consequently, 'Vedant' means 'the conclusion of Vedic knowledge.'

Although, the *Vedant Darshan* was written by Sage Ved Vyas, many great scholars accepted it as the reference authority for philosophical dissertation and wrote commentaries on it to establish their unique philosophic viewpoint regarding the soul and God. Jagadguru Shankaracharya's commentary on the *Vedant Darshan* is called *Śhārīrak*

Bhāṣhya which lays the foundation for the *advait-vād* tradition of philosophy. Many of his followers, such as Vachaspati and Padmapada, have elaborated upon his commentary. Jagadguru Nimbarkarcharya wrote the *Vedānt Pārijāta Saurabh* which explains the *dwait-advait-vād* school of thought. Jagadguru Ramanujacharya's commentary is called *Śhrī Bhāṣhya* which lays the basis for the *viśhiṣhṭ-advait-vād* system of philosophy. Jagadguru Madhvacharya's commentary is called *Brahma Sutra Bhāṣhyam* which is the foundation for the *dwait-vād* school of thought. Mahaprabhu Vallabhacharya wrote *Aṇu Bhāṣhya* in which he established the *śhuddhadvait-vād* system of philosophy. Apart from these, some of the other well-known commentators have been Bhat Bhaskar, Yadav Prakash, Keshav, Nilakanth, Vijnanabhikshu, and Baladev Vidyabhushan.

Chaitanya Mahaprabhu, a Vedic scholar par excellence, did not write any commentary on the *Vedant Darshan*. He took the view that the writer of the *Vedant*, Sage Ved Vyas himself, declared that his final scripture, the Shreemad Bhagavatam is its perfect commentary:

arthoyaṁ brahmasūtrāṇaṁ sarvopaniṣhadāmapi

'The Shreemad Bhagavatam reveals the meaning and the essence of the *Vedant Darshan* and all the Upanishads.' Hence, out of respect for Ved Vyas, Chaitanya Mahaprabhu did not deem it fit to write another commentary on the scripture.

महाभूतान्यङ्कारो बुद्धिरव्यक्त मेव च ।
इन्द्रियाणि दशैकं च पञ्च चेन्द्रियगोचराः ।।6।।

mahā-bhūtāny ahankāro buddhir avyaktam eva cha
indriyāṇi daśhaikaṁ cha pañcha chendriya-gocharāḥ

mahā-bhūtāni—the (five) great elements; *ahankāraḥ*—the ego; *buddhiḥ*—the intellect; *avyaktam*—the unmanifested primordial matter; *eva*—indeed; *cha*—and; *indriyāṇi*—the senses; *daśha-ekam*—eleven; *cha*—and; *pañcha*—five; *cha*—and; *indriya-go-charāḥ*—the (five) objects of the senses.

The field of activities is composed of the five great elements, the ego, the intellect, the unmanifest primordial matter, the eleven senses (five knowledge senses, five working senses, and mind), and the five objects of the senses.

The twenty-four elements that constitute the field of activities are: *pañcha mahābhūta* (the five gross elements—earth, water, fire, air, and space), the *pañcha tanmātrās* (five sense objects—taste, touch, smell, sight, and sound), the five working senses (voice, hands, legs, genitals, and anus), the five knowledge senses (ears, eyes, tongue, skin, and nose), mind, intellect, ego, and prakriti (the primordial form of the material energy). Shree Krishna uses the word *daśhaikaṁ* (ten plus one) to indicate the eleven senses. In these, He includes the mind along with the five knowledge senses and the five working senses. Previously, in verse 10.22, He had mentioned that He is the mind among the senses.

One may wonder why the five sense objects have been included in the field of activities when they exist outside the body. The reason is that the mind contemplates upon the sense objects, and these five sense objects reside in a subtle form in the mind. That is why, while sleeping, when we dream with our mind, in our dream state we see, hear, feel, taste, and smell, even though our gross senses are resting on the bed. This illustrates that the gross objects of the senses also exist mentally in the subtle form. Shree Krishna has included them here because He is referring to the entire field of activity for the soul. Some other scriptures exclude the five sense objects while describing the body. Instead, they include the five pranas (life airs). This is merely a matter of classification and not a philosophical difference.

The same knowledge is also explained in terms of sheaths. The field of the body has five *kośhas* (sheaths) that cover the soul that is ensconced within:

Annamaya kośh: It is the gross sheath consisting of the five gross elements (earth, water, fire, air, and space).

Pranamaya kośh: It is the life airs sheath consisting of the five life airs (*pran*, *apān*, *vyān*, *samān*, and *udān*).

Manomaya kośh: It is the mental sheath consisting of the mind and the five working senses (voice, hands, legs, genitals, and anus).

Vijnanamaya kośh: It is the intellectual sheath consisting of the intellect and the five knowledge senses (ears, eyes, tongue, skin, and nose).

Anandmaya kośh: It is the bliss sheath which consists of the ego that makes us identify with the tiny bliss of the body-mind-intellect mechanism.

इच्छा द्वेषः सुखं दुःखं सङ्घातश्चेतना धृतिः ।
एतत्क्षेत्रं समासेन सविकारमुदाहृतम् ।।7।।

ichchhā dveṣhaḥ sukhaṁ duḥkhaṁ saṅghātaśh chetanā dhṛitiḥ
etat kṣhetraṁ samāsena sa-vikāram udāhṛitam

ichchhā—desire; *dveṣhaḥ*—aversion; *sukham*—happiness; *duḥkham*—misery; *saṅghātaḥ*—the aggregate; *chetanā*—the consciousness; *dhṛitiḥ*—the will; *etat*—all these; *kṣhetram*—the field of activities; *samāsena*—comprise of; *sa-vikāram*—with modifications; *udāhṛitam*—are said.

Desire and aversion, happiness and misery, the body, consciousness, and the will—all these comprise the field and its modifications.

Shree Krishna now elucidates the attributes of the *kṣhetra* (field) and its modifications thereof:

Body: The field of activities includes the body but is much more than that. The body undergoes six transformations until death—*asti* (coming into existence), *jāyate* (birth), *vardhate* (growth), *viparinamate* (reproduction), *apakṣhīyate* (withering with age), *vinaśhyati* (death). The body supports the soul in its quest for happiness in the world or in God, as the soul guides it.

Consciousness: It is the life force that exists in the soul, which it also imparts to the body while present in it. This is just as fire has the ability to heat, and if we put an iron rod into it, the rod too becomes red hot with the heat it receives from the fire. Similarly, the soul makes the body seem lifelike by imparting the quality of consciousness in it. Shree Krishna thus includes consciousness as a trait of the field of activities.

Will: This is the determination that keeps the constituent elements of the body active and focused in a particular direction. It is the will that enables the soul to achieve goals through the field of activities. The will is a quality of the intellect which is energised by the soul. Variations in the will due to the influence of sattva guna, rajo guna, and tamo guna are described in verses 18.33–18.35.

Desire: This is a function of the mind and the intellect which creates a longing for the acquisition of an object, a situation, a person, or something else. In discussing the body, we would probably take desire for granted, but imagine how different the nature of life would have been if there were no desires! So, the Supreme Lord, who designed the field of activities and included desire as a part of it, naturally makes special mention of it. The intellect analyses the desirability of an object, and the mind harbours its desire. When one becomes self-realised, all material desires are extinguished, and now the purified mind harbours the desire for God. While material desires are the cause of bondage, spiritual desires lead to liberation.

Aversion: It is a state of the mind and intellect that creates revulsion for objects, persons, and situations that are disagreeable to it and seeks to avoid them.

Happiness: This is a feeling of pleasure that is experienced in the mind through agreeable circumstances and fulfilment of desires. The mind perceives the sensations of happiness, and the soul does so along with it because it identifies with the mind. However, material happiness never satiates the hunger of the soul which remains discontent until it experiences the infinite divine bliss of God.

Misery: It is the pain experienced in the mind through disagreeable circumstances.

Now Shree Krishna goes on to describe the virtues and attributes that will enable one to cultivate knowledge, and thereby fulfil the purpose of the field of activities, which is the human form.

अमानित्वमदम्भित्वमहिंसा क्षान्तिरार्जवम् ।
आचार्योपासनं शौचं स्थैर्यमात्मविनिग्रहः ।।8।।

इन्द्रियार्थेषु वैराग्यमनहङ्कार एव च ।
जन्ममृत्युजराव्याधिदुःखदोषानुदर्शनम् ।।9।।

असक्तिरनभिष्वङ्गः पुत्रदारगृहादिषु ।
नित्यं च समचित्तत्वमिष्टानिष्टोपपत्तिषु ।।10।।

मयि चानन्ययोगेन भक्तिरव्यभिचारिणी ।
विविक्तदेशसेवित्वमरतिर्जनसंसदि ।।11।।

अध्यात्मज्ञाननित्यत्वं तत्त्वज्ञानार्थदर्शनम् ।
एतज्ज्ञानमिति प्रोक्तमज्ञानं यदतोऽन्यथा ।।12।।

amānitvam adambhitvam ahinsā kṣhāntir ārjavam
āchāryopāsanaṁ śhauchaṁ sthairyam ātma-vinigrahaḥ

indriyārtheṣhu vairāgyam anahankāra eva cha
janma-mṛityu-jarā-vyādhi-duḥkha-doṣhānudarśhanam

asaktir anabhiṣhvaṅgaḥ putra-dāra-gṛihādiṣhu
nityaṁ cha sama-chittatvam iṣhṭāniṣhṭopapattiṣhu

mayi chānanya-yogena bhaktir avyabhichāriṇī
vivikta-deśha-sevitvam aratir jana-sansadi

adhyātma-jñāna-nityatvaṁ tattva-jñānārtha-darśhanam
etaj jñānam iti proktam ajñānaṁ yad ato 'nyathā

amānitvam—humbleness; *adambhitvam*—freedom from hypocrisy; *ahinsā*—non-violence; *kṣhāntiḥ*—forgiveness; *ārjavam*—simplicity; *āchārya-upāsanam*—service of the guru; *śhaucham*—cleanliness of body and mind; *sthairyam*—steadfastness; *ātma-vinigrahaḥ*—self-control; *indriya-artheṣhu*—towards objects of the senses; *vairāgyam*—dispassion; *anahankāraḥ*—absence of egotism; *eva cha*—and also; *janma*—of birth; *mṛityu*—death; *jarā*—old age; *vyādhi*—disease; *duḥkha*—evils; *doṣha*—faults; *anudarśhanam*—perception; *asaktiḥ*—non-attachment; *anabhiṣhvaṅgaḥ*—absence of craving; *putra*—children; *dāra*—spouse; *gṛiha-ādiṣhu*—home, etc.; *nityam*—constant; *cha*—and; *sama-chittatvam*—even-mindedness; *iṣhṭa*—desirable; *aniṣhṭa*—undesirable; *upapattiṣhu*—having obtained; *mayi*—towards me; *cha*—also; *ananya-yogena*—exclusively united; *bhaktiḥ*—devotion; *avyabhichāriṇī*—constant; *vivikta*—solitary; *deśha*—places; *sevitvam*—inclination for; *aratiḥ*—aversion; *jana-sansadi*—for mundane society; *adhyātma*—spiritual; *jñāna*—knowledge; *nityatvam*—constancy; *tattva-jñāna*—knowledge of spiritual principles; *artha*—for; *darśhanam*—philosophy; *etat*—all this; *jñānam*—knowledge; *iti*—thus; *proktam*—declared; *ajñānam*—ignorance; *yat*—what; *ataḥ*—to this; *anyathā*—contrary.

Humility; freedom from hypocrisy; non-violence; forgiveness; simplicity; service of the guru; cleanliness of body and mind; steadfastness; self-control; dispassion towards the objects of the senses; absence of egotism; keeping in mind the evils of birth, disease, old age, and death; non-attachment; absence of clinging to spouse, children, home, and so on; even-mindedness amidst desired and undesired events in life; constant and exclusive devotion towards Me; an inclination for solitary places and an aversion for mundane society; constancy in spiritual knowledge; and philosophical pursuit of the Absolute Truth—all these I declare to be knowledge, and what is contrary to it, I call ignorance.

To gain knowledge of the *kṣhetra* and *kṣhetrajña* is not merely an intellectual exercise. Unlike bookish knowledge that can be cultivated without a change in one's character, the spiritual knowledge that Shree Krishna is talking about requires purification of the heart. (Here, heart does not refer to the physical organ. The inner apparatus of mind and intellect is also sometimes referred to as the heart.) These five verses describe the virtues, habits, behaviours, and attitudes that purify one's life and illuminate it with the light of knowledge.

Humbleness: When we become proud of the attributes of our individual field, such as beauty, intellect, talent, strength, etc. we forget that God has given all these attributes to us. Pride thus results in distancing our consciousness from God. It is a big obstacle on the path of self-realisation since it contaminates the entire field by affecting the qualities of the mind and intellect.

Freedom from hypocrisy: The hypocrite develops an artificial external personality. A person is defective from inside but creates a facade of virtuosity on the outside. Unfortunately, the external display of virtues is skin-deep and hollow.

Non-violence: Cultivation of knowledge requires respect for all living beings. This requires the practice of non-violence. Hence the scriptures state: *ātmanaḥ pratikūlāni pareśhāṁ na samācharet* 'If you dislike a certain behaviour from others, do not behave with them in that manner yourself.' The Bible states the same: 'Do unto others as you would have them do unto you.' (Matthew 7:12)

Forgiveness: It is freedom from ill will even towards those who have harmed one. Actually, harbouring ill will harms oneself more than the other. By practising forgiveness, a person of discrimination releases the negativities in the mind and purifies it.

Simplicity: It is straightforwardness in thought, speech, and action. Straightforwardness in thought includes absence of deceit, envy, crookedness, and other negative thoughts. Straightforwardness in speech includes absence of taunt, censure, gossip, and ornamentation. Straightforwardness in action includes simple living, forthrightness in behaviour, etc.

Service of the guru: Spiritual knowledge is received from the guru. This imparting of divine knowledge requires the disciple to have an attitude of dedication and devotion towards the guru. By serving the guru, the disciple develops humility and commitment that enables the guru to impart knowledge. Shree Krishna explained to Arjun in verse 4.34: 'Learn the Truth by approaching a spiritual master. Enquire from him with reverence and render service unto him. Such an enlightened saint can impart knowledge unto you because he has seen the Truth.'

Cleanliness of body and mind: Purity should be both internal and external. The *Śhāṇḍilya Upanishad* states: *śhauchaṁ nāma dwividhaṁ-bāhyamāntaraṁ cheti* (1.1) 'There are two types of cleanliness—internal and external.' External cleanliness is helpful in maintaining good health, developing discipline, and uncluttering the mind. But mental cleanliness is even more important and is achieved by focusing the mind on the all-pure God. Jagadguru Shree Kripaluji Maharaj states:

māyādhīn malīn mana, hai anādi kālīn,
hari virahānala dhoya jala, karu nirmala bani dīn

(*Bhakti Śhatak* verse 79)

'The material mind is dirty since endless lifetimes. Purify it in the fire of longing for God while practising utmost humility.'

Steadfastness: Self-knowledge and God-realisation are not goals that are attainable in a day. Steadfastness is the persistence to remain on the path until the goal is reached. The scriptures state: *charaivaite charaivate, charan vai madhu vindati* 'Keep moving forward. Keep moving forward. Those who do not give up will get the honey at the end.'

Self-control: It is the restraint of the mind and the senses from running after mundane pleasures that dirty the mind and intellect. Self-control prevents the dissipation of the one's life force through indulgence.

Dispassion towards the objects of the senses: It is a stage higher than the self-control mentioned above in which we restrain ourselves by force. Dispassion means a lack of taste for sense pleasures that are obstacles on the path of God-realisation.

Absence of egotism: Egotism is the conscious awareness of 'I', 'me', and 'mine'. This is classified as nescience because it is at the bodily level, arising out of the identification of the self with the body. It is also called the *aham chetanā* (pride arising out of the sense of self). All mystics emphatically declare that to invite God into our hearts, we must get rid of the pride of the self.

jaba maiṅ thā taba hari nathīṅ, ab hari hai, maiṅ nāhīṅ
prem galī ati sankarī, yā meṅ dwe na samāhīṅ

(Saint Kabir)

'When 'I' existed, God was not there; now God exists and 'I' do not. The path of divine love is very narrow; it cannot accommodate both 'I' and God.'

In the path of jnana yog and ashtang yog, there are elaborate sadhanas for getting rid of the *aham chetanā*. But in the path of bhakti yog, it gets eliminated very simply. We add *dās* (servant) in front of *aham* (the sense of self), making it *dāsoham* (I am the servant of God). Now the 'I' no longer remains harmful, and self-consciousness is replaced by God-consciousness.

Keeping in mind the evils of birth, disease, old age, and death: If the intellect is undecided about what is more important—material enhancement or spiritual wealth—then it becomes difficult to develop the strong will required for acquiring knowledge of the self. But when the intellect is convinced about the unattractiveness of the world, it becomes firm in its resolve. To get this firmness, we should constantly contemplate about the miseries that are an inseparable part of life in the material world. This is what set the Buddha on the spiritual path. He saw a sick person, and thought, 'O there is sickness in the world. I will also fall sick one day.' Then He saw an old person, and thought, 'There is also old age. This means that I will also become old one day.' After that, He saw a dead person, and realised, 'This is also a part of existence. It means that I too will have to die one day.' The Buddha's intellect was so perceptive that one exposure to these facts of life made Him renounce worldly existence. Since we do not have such decisive intellects, we must repeatedly contemplate on these facts to allow the unattractiveness of the world to sink in.

Non-attachment: It means dispassion towards the world. We have only one mind and if we wish to engage it in pursuing spiritual goals, we have to detach it from material objects and persons. The *sādhak* replaces worldly attachment with love and attachment for God.

Absence of clinging to spouse, children, home, and so on: These are areas where the mind easily becomes attached. In worldly thinking, one spontaneously identifies with the family and home as 'mine'. Thus, they linger upon the mind more often and attachment to them shackles the mind to material consciousness. Attachment causes expectations of the kind of behaviour we want from family members, and when these expectations are not met, it leads to mental anguish. Also inevitably, there is separation from the family, either temporarily, if they go to another place, or permanently, if they die. All these experiences and their apprehensions begin to weigh heavily upon the mind and drag it away from God. Hence, if we seek immortal bliss, we must practise prudence while interacting with the spouse, child, and home, to prevent the mind from becoming entangled. We must do our duty towards them, without attachment, just as a nurse does her duty in the hospital, or as a teacher does her duty towards her students in the school.

Even-mindedness amidst desired and undesired events in life: Pleasurable and painful events come without invitation, just as night and day. That is life. To rise above these dualities, we must learn to enhance our spiritual strength through detachment towards the world. We must develop the ability to remain unperturbed by life's reversals and also not get carried away with the euphoria of success.

Constant and exclusive devotion towards Me: Mere detachment means that the mind is not going in a negative direction. But life is more than merely preventing the undesirable. Life is about engaging in the desirable. The desirable goal of life is to consecrate it at the lotus feet of God. Therefore, Shree Krishna has highlighted it here.

Inclination for solitary places: Unlike worldly people, devotees are not driven by the need for company to overcome feelings of loneliness. They prefer solitude that enables them to engage their mind in communion with God. Hence, they are naturally inclined to choosing solitary places where they are able to absorb themselves in devotional thoughts.

Aversion for mundane society: The sign of a materialistic mind is that it finds pleasure in talks about worldly people and worldly affairs. One who is cultivating divine consciousness develops a natural distaste for these activities, and thus avoids mundane society. At the same time, if it is necessary to participate in it for the sake of service to God, the devotee accepts it and develops the strength to remain mentally unaffected by it.

Constancy in spiritual knowledge: To theoretically know something is not enough. One may know that anger is a bad thing but may still give vent to it repeatedly. We have to learn to practically implement spiritual knowledge in our life. This does not happen by hearing profound truths just once. After hearing them, we must repeatedly contemplate upon them. Such mulling over the divine truths is the constancy in spiritual knowledge that Shree Krishna is talking about.

Philosophical pursuit of the Absolute Truth: Even animals engage in the physical activities of eating, sleeping, mating, and defending. However, God has especially blessed the human form with the faculty of knowledge. This is not to enable us to engage in material activities in a deluxe way, but for us to contemplate on the questions: 'Who am I? Why am I here? What is my goal in life? How was this world created? What is my connection with the Creator? How will I fulfil my purpose in life?' This philosophic pursuit of the Truth sublimates our thinking above the animalistic level and leads us to hear and read about the divine science of God-realisation.

All the virtues, habits, behaviours, and attitudes described above result in growth of wisdom and knowledge. The opposite of these are vanity, hypocrisy, violence, vengeance, duplicity, disrespect for the guru, uncleanliness of body and mind, unsteadiness, lack of self-control, longing for sense objects, conceit, entanglement with spouse, children, home, etc. Such dispositions cripple the development of self-knowledge. Thus, Shree Krishna calls them ignorance and darkness.

ज्ञेयं यत्तत्प्रवक्ष्यामि यज्ज्ञात्वामृतमश्नुते ।
अनादिमत्परं ब्रह्म न सत्तन्नासदुच्यते ।।13।।

jñeyaṁ yat tat pravakṣhyāmi yaj jñātvāmṛitam aśhnute
anādi mat-paraṁ brahma na sat tan nāsad uchyate

jñeyam—ought to be known; *yat*—which; *tat*—that; *pravakṣhyāmi*—I shall now reveal; *yat*—which; *jñātvā*—knowing; *amṛitam*—immortality; *aśhnute*—one achieves; *anādi*—beginningless; *mat-param*—subordinate to me; *brahma*—Brahman; *na*—not; *sat*—existent; *tat*—that; *na*—not; *asat*—non-existent; *uchyate*—is called.

I shall now reveal to you that which ought to be known, and by knowing which, one attains immortality. It is the beginningless Brahman, which lies beyond existence and non-existence.

Day and night are like two sides of the same coin, for one cannot exist without the other. We can only say it is day in some place if night too falls in that place. But if there is no night, then there is no day either; there is only perpetual light. Similarly, in the case of Brahman, the word 'existence' is not descriptive enough. Shree Krishna says that Brahman is beyond the relative terms of existence and non-existence.

Brahman, in Its formless and attributeless aspect, is the object of worship of the jnanis. In Its personal form, as Bhagavan, It is the object of worship of the bhaktas. Residing within the body, It is known as Paramatma. All these are three manifestations of the same Supreme Reality. Later, in verse 14.27, Shree Krishna states: *brahmaṇo hi pratiṣhṭhāham* 'I am the basis of the formless Brahman'. Thus, the formless Brahman and the personal form of God are both two aspects of the Supreme Entity. *Both exist everywhere, and hence They both can be called all-pervading. Referring to These, Shree Krishna reveals the contradictory qualities that manifest in God.*

सर्वतः पाणिपादं तत्सर्वतोऽक्षिशिरोमुखम् ।
सर्वतः श्रुतिमल्लोके सर्वमावृत्य तिष्ठति ।।14।।

sarvataḥ pāṇi-pādaṁ tat sarvato 'kṣhi-śhiro-mukham
sarvataḥ śhrutimal loke sarvam āvṛitya tiṣhṭhati

sarvataḥ—everywhere; *pāṇi*—hands; *pādam*—feet; *tat*—that; *sarvataḥ*—everywhere; *akṣhi*—eyes; *śhiraḥ*—heads; *mukham*—

faces; *sarvataḥ*—everywhere; *śhruti-mat*—having ears; *loke*—in the universe; *sarvam*—everything; *āvṛitya*—pervades; *tiṣhṭhati*—exists.

Everywhere are His hands and feet, eyes, heads, and faces. His ears too are in all places, for He pervades everything in the universe.

Often people argue that God cannot have hands, feet, eyes, ears, and other body parts. But Shree Krishna says that God has all these and to an innumerable extent. We should never fall into the trap of circumscribing God within our limited understanding. He is *kartumakartuṁ anyathā karatuṁ samarthaḥ* 'He can do the possible, the impossible, and the reverse of the possible.' To say that the all-powerful God cannot have hands and feet, is placing a constraint upon Him.

Keep in mind that God's limbs and senses are divine while ours are material. The difference between the material and the transcendental is that while we are limited to one set of senses, God possesses unlimited hands, legs, eyes, and ears. While our senses exist in one place, God's senses are everywhere. Thus, God sees everything that happens in the world and hears everything that is ever said. This is possible because just as He is all-pervading in creation, His eyes and ears are also ubiquitous. The *Chhāndogya Upanishad* states: *sarvaṁ khalvidaṁ brahma* (3.14.1) 'Everywhere is Brahman.' Hence, He accepts food offerings made to Him anywhere in the universe; He hears the prayers of His devotees wherever they may be; and He is the Witness of all that occurs in the three worlds. If millions of devotees venerate Him at the same time, He has no problem accepting the prayers of all of them.

सर्वेन्द्रियगुणाभासं सर्वेन्द्रियविवर्जितम् ।
असक्तं सर्वभृच्चैव निर्गुणं गुणभोक्तृ च ।।15।।

sarvendriya-guṇābhāsaṁ sarvendriya-vivarjitam
asaktaṁ sarva-bhṛich chaiva nirguṇaṁ guṇa-bhoktṛi cha

sarva—all; *indriya*—senses; *guṇa*—sense-objects; *ābhāsam*—the perceiver; *sarva*—all; *indriya*—senses; *vivarjitam*—devoid of;

asaktam—unattached; *sarva-bhṛit*—the sustainer of all; *cha*—yet; *eva*—indeed; *nirguṇam*—beyond the three modes of material nature; *guṇa-bhoktṛi*—the enjoyer of the three modes of material nature; *cha*—although.

Though He perceives all sense-objects, yet He is devoid of the senses. He is unattached to anything, and yet He is the sustainer of all. Although He is without attributes, yet He is the enjoyer of the three modes of material nature.

Having stated that God's senses are everywhere, Shree Krishna now states the exact opposite that He does not possess any senses. If we try to understand this through mundane logic, we will find this contradictory. We will enquire, 'How can God have both infinite senses and also be without senses?' However, mundane logic does not apply to Him who is beyond the reach of the intellect. God possesses infinite contradictory attributes at the same time. The *Brahma Vaivarta Puran* states:

viruddha dharmo rūposā vaiśhvaryāt puruṣhottamāh

'The Supreme Lord is the reservoir of innumerable contradictory attributes.' In this verse, Shree Krishna mentions a few of the infinite contradictory attributes that exist in the personality of God.

He is devoid of mundane senses like ours, and hence it is correct to say that He does not have senses. *Sarvendriya vivarjitam* means 'He is without material senses.' However, He possesses divine senses that are everywhere, consequently, it is also correct to say that the senses of God are in all places. *Sarvendriya guṇābhāsaṁ* means 'He manifests the functions of the senses and grasps the sense objects.' Referring to both these attributes, the *Śhwetāśhvatar Upanishad* states:

apāṇipādo javano grahītā
paśhyatyachakṣhuḥ sa śhṛiṇotyakarṇaḥ (3.19)

'God does not possess material hands, feet, eyes, and ears. Yet He grasps, walks, sees, and hears.'

Further, Shree Krishna states that He is the Sustainer of creation, and yet detached from it. In His form as Lord Vishnu, God maintains the entire creation. He sits in the hearts of all living beings, notes their karmas, and gives the results. Under Lord Vishnu's dominion, Brahma manipulates the laws of material science to ensure that the universe functions stably. Also, under Lord Vishnu's dominion, the celestial gods arrange to provide the air, earth, water, rain, and other elements that are necessary for our survival. Hence, God is the Sustainer of all. Yet, He is complete in Himself and is, thus, detached from everyone. The Vedas mention Him as *ātmārām*, meaning, 'one who rejoices in the self and has no need of anything external.'

The material energy is subservient to God, and it works for His pleasure by serving Him. He is thus the enjoyer of the three gunas (modes of material nature). At the same time, He is also *nirguna* (beyond the three gunas) because these gunas are material while God is divine.

बहिरन्तश्च भूतानामचरं चरमेव च ।
सूक्ष्मत्वात्तदविज्ञेयं दूरस्थं चान्तिके च तत् ।। 16 ।।

bahir antaśh cha bhūtānām acharaṁ charam eva cha
sūkṣhmatvāt tad avijñeyaṁ dūra-sthaṁ chāntike cha tat

bahiḥ—outside; *antaḥ*—inside; *cha*—and; *bhūtānām*—all living beings; *acharam*—not moving; *charam*—moving; *eva*—indeed; *cha*—and; *sūkṣhmatvāt*—due to subtlety; *tat*—he; *avijñeyam*—incomprehensible; *dūra-stham*—very far away; *cha*—and; *antike*—very near; *cha*—also; *tat*—he.

He exists outside and inside all living beings, those that are moving and not moving. He is subtle, and hence, He is incomprehensible. He is very far, but He is also very near.

There is a Vedic mantra that describes God in practically the same manner as Shree Krishna has described here:

tad ejati tan naijati taddūre tadvantike
tad antar asya sarvasya tadusarvasyāsya bāhyataḥ

(*Īśhopaniṣhad* mantra 5)

'The Supreme Brahman does not walk, and yet He walks; He is far, but He is also near. He exists inside everything, but He is also outside everything.'

Previously in verse 13.3, Shree Krishna said that to know God is true knowledge. However, here He states that the Supreme Entity is incomprehensible. This again seems to be a contradiction, but what He means is that God is not knowable by the senses, mind, and intellect. The intellect is made from material energy, so it cannot reach God who is Divine. However, if God Himself bestows His grace upon someone, then that fortunate soul can come to know Him.

अविभक्तं च भूतेषु विभक्तमिव च स्थितम् ।
भूतभर्तृ च तज्ज्ञेयं ग्रसिष्णु प्रभविष्णु च ।। 17 ।।

avibhaktaṁ cha bhūteṣhu vibhaktam iva cha sthitam
bhūta-bhartṛi cha taj jñeyaṁ grasiṣhṇu prabhaviṣhṇu cha

avibhaktam—indivisible; *cha*—although; *bhūteṣhu*—amongst living beings; *vibhaktam*—divided; *iva*—apparently; *cha*—yet; *sthitam*—situated; *bhūta-bhartṛi*—sustainer of all beings; *cha*—also; *tat*—that; *jñeyam*—to be known; *grasiṣhṇu*—annihilator; *prabhaviṣhṇu*—creator; *cha*—and.

He is indivisible, yet He appears to be divided amongst living beings. Know the Supreme Entity to be the Creator, Sustainer, and Annihilator of all beings.

God's personality includes His various energies. All manifest and unmanifest objects are but expansions of His energy. Thus, we can say He is all that exists. Accordingly, Shreemad Bhagavatam states:

dravyaṁ karma cha kālaśh cha svabhāvo jīva eva cha
vāsudevāt paro brahman na chānyo 'rtho 'sti tattvataḥ (2.5.14)

'The various aspects of creation—time, karma, the nature of individual living beings, and the material ingredients of creation—are all part of the Supreme Lord Shree Krishna Himself. There is nothing in existence apart from Him.'

God may appear to be divided among the objects of His creation, but since He is all that exists, He remains undivided as well. For example, space may seem to be divided among the objects that it contains. Yet, all objects are within the one entity called space, which manifested at the beginning of creation. Again, the reflection of the sun in puddles of water makes it appear as if it is divided, yet the sun remains indivisible.

Just as the ocean throws up waves and then absorbs them back into itself, similarly God creates the world, maintains it, and then absorbs it back into Himself. Therefore, He may be equally seen as the Creator, the Maintainer, and the Destroyer of everything.

ज्योतिषामपि तज्ज्योतिस्तमसः परमुच्यते ।
ज्ञानं ज्ञेयं ज्ञानगम्यं हृदि सर्वस्य विष्ठितम् ।।18।।

jyotiṣhām api taj jyotis tamasaḥ param uchyate
jñānaṁ jñeyaṁ jñāna-gamyaṁ hṛidi sarvasya viṣhṭhitam

jyotiṣhām—in all luminaries; *api*—and; *tat*—that; *jyotiḥ*—the source of light; *tamasaḥ*—the darkness; *param*—beyond; *uchyate*—is said (to be); *jñānam*—knowledge; *jñeyam*—the object of knowledge; *jñāna-gamyam*—the goal of knowledge; *hṛidi*—within the heart; *sarvasya*—of all living beings; *viṣhṭhitam*—dwells.

He is the source of light in all luminaries and is entirely beyond the darkness of ignorance. He is knowledge, the object of knowledge, and the goal of knowledge. He dwells within the hearts of all living beings.

Here, Shree Krishna establishes the supremacy of God in different ways. There are various illuminating objects, such as the sun, moon, stars, fire, and jewels. Left alone, none of these have any power to illuminate. When God imparts the power to them, only then can they illumine anything. The *Kaṭhopaniṣhad* says:

tameva bhāntamanubhāti sarvaṁ
tasya bhāsā saravamidaṁ vibhāti (2.2.15)

'God makes all things luminous. It is by His luminosity that all luminous objects give light.' The Vedas further state:

sūryastapati tejasendraḥ

'By His radiance, the sun and moon become luminous.' In other words, the luminosity of the sun and the moon is borrowed from God. They may lose their luminosity someday, but God can never lose His.

God has three unique names: *Veda-kṛit*, *Veda-vit*, and *Veda-vedya*. He is *Veda-kṛit* which means 'One who manifested the Vedas'. He is *Veda-vit* which means 'One who knows the Vedas'. He is also *Veda-vedya* which means 'One who is to be known through the Vedas'. In the same manner, Shree Krishna describes the Supreme Entity as the *jneya* (the object worthy of knowing), *jnana-gamya* (the goal of all knowledge), and jnana (true knowledge).

इति क्षेत्रं तथा ज्ञानं ज्ञेयं चोक्तं समासतः ।
मद्भक्त एतद्विज्ञाय मद्भावायोपपद्यते ।।19।।

iti kṣhetraṁ tathā jñānaṁ jñeyaṁ choktaṁ samāsataḥ
mad-bhakta etad vijñāya mad-bhāvāyopapadyate

iti—thus; *kṣhetram*—the nature of the field; *tathā*—and; *jñānam*—the meaning of knowledge; *jñeyam*—the object of knowledge; *cha*—and; *uktam*—revealed; *samāsataḥ*—in summary; *mat-bhaktaḥ*—my devotee; *etat*—this; *vijñāya*—having understood; *mat-bhāvāya*—my divine nature; *upapadyate*—attain.

I have thus revealed to you the nature of the field, the meaning of knowledge, and the object of knowledge. Only My devotees can understand this in reality, and by doing so, they attain My divine nature.

Shree Krishna now concludes His description of the field and the object of knowledge, by mentioning the fruit of knowing this topic. However, once again, He deems it fit to bring in devotion and says that only the bhaktas (devotees) can truly understand this knowledge. Those who practice karm, jnana, ashtang, etc. but are still devoid of bhakti cannot truly understand the import of the Bhagavad Gita, even though they themselves may think that they do. Bhakti is the essential ingredient in all paths leading to knowledge of God.

Jagadguru Shree Kripaluji Maharaj puts this very nicely:

jo hari sevā hetu ho, soī karm bakhāna
jo hari bhagati baṛhāve, soī samujhiya jñāna

(*Bhakti Śhatak*, verse 66)

'That work which is done in devotion to God is the real karm; and that knowledge which increases love for God is real knowledge.'

Devotion not only helps us to know God; it also makes the devotee godlike, and hence, Shree Krishna states that devotees attain His nature. This has been repeatedly emphasised in the Vedic scriptures. The Vedas state:

bhaktirevainaṁ nayati bhaktirevainaṁ paśhyati bhaktirevainaṁ
darśhayati bhakti vaśhaḥ puruṣho bhaktireva bhūyasī

(*Māṭhar Śhruti*)

'Bhakti alone can lead us to God. Bhakti alone can make us see God. Bhakti alone can bring us in the presence of God. God is under the control of bhakti. Hence, do bhakti exclusively.' The *Muṇḍakopaniṣhad* states:

upāsate puruṣhaṁ ye hyakāmā-ste śhukrametadativartanti dhīrāḥ

(3.2.1)

'Those who engage in bhakti towards the Supreme Divine Personality, giving up all material desires, escape the cycle of life and death.' The *Śhwetāśhvatar Upanishad* also states:

yasya deve parā bhaktiryathā deve tathā gurau
tasyaite kathitā hyarthā prakāśhante mahātmanaḥ (6.23)

'Those who have unflinching bhakti towards God and identical bhakti towards the guru, in the hearts of such saintly persons, by the grace of God the imports of the Vedic scriptures are automatically revealed.' The other Vedic scriptures also reiterate this emphatically:

na sādhayati māṁ yogo na sāṅkhyaṁ dharma uddhava
na svādhyāyas tapas tyāgo yathā bhaktir mamorjitā

(Bhagavatam 11.14.20)

Shree Krishna states: 'Uddhav, I am not attained by ashtang yog, by the study of *Sānkhya*, cultivation of scriptural knowledge, austerities, nor by renunciation. It is by bhakti alone that I am won over.' In the Bhagavad Gita, Shree Krishna repeatedly states this in verses 8.22 and 11.54, among others. In verse 18.55, He says: 'Only by loving devotion does one come to know who I am in Truth. Then, having come to know Me, My devotee enters into full consciousness of Me.' The Ramayan also says:

rāmahi kevala premu piārā, jāni leu jo jānanihārā

'The Supreme Lord Ram is only attained through love. Let this truth be known by all who care to know.'

This principle is emphasised in the other religious traditions as well. In the Jewish Torah it is written: 'You shall love the Lord your God with all your heart, and with all your soul, and with all your might.' (Deuteronomy 6.5). Jesus of Nazareth repeats this commandment in the Christian New Testament as one of the first and foremost commandments to follow (Mark 12.30). The Guru Granth Sahib states:

hari sama jaga mahañ vastu nahiṅ, prem panth soñ pantha
sadguru sama sajjan nahīñ, gītā sama nahiñ grantha

'There is no personality like God; there is no path equal to the path of devotion; there is no human equal to the guru; and there is no scripture that can compare with the Gita.'

प्रकृतिं पुरुषं चैव विद्ध्यनादी उभावपि ।
विकारांश्च गुणांश्चैव विद्धि प्रकृतिसम्भवान् ।।20।।

prakṛitiṁ puruṣhaṁ chaiva viddhy anādī ubhāv api
vikārānśh cha guṇānśh chaiva viddhi prakṛiti-sambhavān

prakṛitim—material nature; *puruṣham*—the individual souls; *cha*—and; *eva*—indeed; *viddhi*—know; *anādī*—beginningless; *ubhau*—both; *api*—and; *vikārān*—transformations (of the body); *cha*—also; *guṇān*—the three modes of nature; *cha*—and; *eva*—indeed; *viddhi*—know; *prakṛiti*—material energy; *sambhavān*—produced by.

Know that prakriti (material nature) and purush (individual souls) are both beginningless. Also know that all transformations of the body and the three modes of nature are produced by material energy.

The material nature is called maya or prakriti. As an energy of God, it has existed ever since He has existed; in other words, it is eternal. The soul is also eternal, and here it is called purush (the living entity), while God Himself is called Param Purush (the Supreme Living Entity).

The soul is also an expansion of the energy of God *śhaktitvenaivāṁśhatvaṁ vyañjayanti* (*Paramatma Sandarbh* 39.1) 'The soul is a fragment of the *jīva shakti* (soul energy) of God.' While material nature is an insentient energy, the *jīva shakti* is a sentient energy. It is divine and intransmutable. It remains unchanged through different lifetimes, and the different stages of each lifetime. The six stages through which the body passes in one lifetime are *asti* (existence in the womb), *jāyate* (birth), *vardhate* (growth), *vipariṇamate* (procreation), *apakṣhīyate* (diminution), *vinaśhyati* (death). These changes in the body are brought about by the material energy, prakriti or maya. It creates the three modes of nature—sattva, rajas, and tamas—and their countless varieties of combinations.

कार्यकारणकर्तृत्वे हेतुः प्रकृतिरुच्यते ।
पुरुषः सुखदुःखानां भोक्तृत्वे हेतुरुच्यते ।।21।।

kārya-kāraṇa-kartṛitve hetuḥ prakṛitir uchyate
puruṣhaḥ sukha-duḥkhānāṁ bhoktṛitve hetur uchyate

kārya—effect; *kāraṇa*—cause; *kartṛitve*—in the matter of creation; *hetuḥ*—the medium; *prakṛitiḥ*—the material energy; *uchyate*—is said to be; *puruṣhaḥ*—the individual soul; *sukha-duḥkhānām*—of happiness and distress; *bhoktṛitve*—in experiencing; *hetuḥ*—is responsible; *uchyate*—is said to be.

In the matter of creation, the material energy is responsible for cause and effect; in the matter of experiencing happiness and distress, the individual soul is declared responsible.

The material energy, under the direction of Brahma, creates myriad elements and forms of life that compose creation. Brahma makes the master plan, and the material energy executes it. The Vedas state that there are 8.4 million species of life in the material world. All these forms are transformations of the material energy. Hence, material nature is responsible for all the cause and effect in the world.

The soul gets a body (field of activity) according to its past karmas, and it identifies itself with the body, mind, and intellect. Thus, it seeks the pleasure of the bodily senses. When the senses come in contact with the sense objects, the mind experiences a pleasurable sensation. Since the soul identifies with the mind, it vicariously enjoys that pleasurable sensation. In this way, the soul perceives the sensations of both pleasure and pain, through the medium of the senses, mind, and intellect. This can be compared to a dream state:

ehi bidhi jaga hari āśhrita rahaī, jadapi asatya deta duḥkha ahaī

(Ramayan)

jauṅ sapaneṅ sira kāṭai koī, binu jāgeṅ na dūri dukh hoī

(Ramayan)

'The world is sustained by God. It creates an illusion, which, although unreal, gives misery to the soul. This is just like if someone's head gets cut in a dream, the misery will continue until the person wakes up and stops dreaming.' In this dream state of identifying with the body, the soul experiences pleasure and pain based on its own past and present karmas. As a result, it is said to be responsible for both kinds of experiences.

पुरुषः प्रकृतिस्थो हि भुङ्क्ते प्रकृतिजान्गुणान् ।
कारणं गुणसङ्गोऽस्य सदसद्योनिजन्मसु ।।22।।

puruṣhaḥ prakṛiti-stho hi bhuṅkte prakṛiti-jān guṇān
kāraṇaṁ guṇa-saṅgo 'sya sad-asad-yoni-janmasu

puruṣhaḥ—the individual soul; *prakṛiti-sthaḥ*—seated in the material energy; *hi*—indeed; *bhuṅkte*—desires to enjoy; *prakṛiti-*

jān—produced by the material energy; *guṇān*—the three modes of nature; *kāraṇam*—the cause; *guṇa-saṅgaḥ*—the attachment (to three gunas); *asya*—of its; *sat-asat-yoni*—in superior and inferior wombs; *janmasu*—of birth.

When the purush (individual soul) seated in prakriti (material energy) desires to enjoy the three gunas, attachment to them becomes the cause of its birth in superior and inferior wombs.

In the previous verse, Shree Krishna explained that the purush (soul) is responsible for the experience of pleasure and pain. Now, He explains how this is so. Considering the body to be the self, the soul energises it into activity that is directed at enjoying bodily pleasures. Since the body is made of maya, it seeks to enjoy the material energy that is made of the three modes (gunas)—mode of goodness, mode of passion, and mode of ignorance.

Due to the ego, the soul identifies itself as the doer and the enjoyer of the body. The body, mind, and intellect perform all the activities, but the soul is held responsible for them, just as the driver, and not the wheels or the steering, is held answerable for an accident to a bus. Similarly, the senses, mind, and intellect are energised by the soul and they work under its dominion. Hence, the soul accumulates the karmas for all activities performed by the body. This inventory of karmas, accumulated from innumerable past lives, causes its repeated birth in superior and inferior wombs.

उपद्रष्टानुमन्ता च भर्ता भोक्ता महेश्वरः ।
परमात्मेति चाप्युक्तो देहेऽस्मिन्पुरुषः परः ।।23।।

upadraṣhṭānumantā cha bhartā bhoktā maheśhvaraḥ
paramātmeti chāpy ukto dehe 'smin puruṣhaḥ paraḥ

upadraṣhṭā—the witness; *anumantā*—the permitter; *cha*—and; *bhartā*—the supporter; *bhoktā*—the transcendental enjoyer; *mahā-īśhvaraḥ*—the ultimate controller; *parama-ātmā*—Supreme Soul; *iti*—that; *cha api*—and also; *uktaḥ*—is said; *dehe*—within the body; *asmin*—this; *puruṣhaḥ paraḥ*—the Supreme Lord.

Within the body also resides the Supreme Lord. He is said to be the Witness, the Permitter, the Supporter, Transcendental Enjoyer, the ultimate Controller, and the Paramatma (Supreme Soul).

Shree Krishna has explained the status of the jivatma (individual soul) within the body. Now in this verse, He explains the position of the Paramatma who also resides within the body. He previously mentioned the Paramatma in verse 13.3 as well, when He stated that the individual soul is the knower of the individual body, while the Supreme Soul is the knower of all the infinite bodies.

The Supreme Soul, who is located within everyone, also manifests in the personal form as Lord Vishnu. The Supreme Lord in His form as Vishnu is responsible for maintaining this creation. He resides in the *Kṣhīr Sāgar* (the ocean of milk) at the top of the universe in His personal form. He also expands Himself to reside in the hearts of all living beings as the Paramatma. Seated within, He notes their actions, keeps an account of their karmas, and bestows the results at the proper time. He accompanies the jivatma (individual soul) to whatever body it receives in each lifetime. He does not hesitate to reside in the body of a snake, a pig, or insect. The *Muṇḍakopaniṣhad* states:

dvā suparṇā sayujā sakhāyā
samānaṁ vṛikṣhaṁ pariṣhasvajāte
tayoranyaḥ pippalaṁ svādvattya-
naśhnannanyo abhichākaśhīti

samāne vṛikṣhe puruṣho nimagno-
'nīśhayā śhochati muhyamānaḥ
juṣhtaṁ yadā paśhyatyanyamīśha-
masya mahimānamiti vītaśhokaḥ (3.1.1–2)

'Two birds are seated in the nest (heart) of the tree (body) of the living form. They are the jivatma and Paramatma. The jivatma has its back towards the Paramatma and is busy enjoying the fruits of the tree (results of the karmas it receives while residing in the body). When a sweet fruit comes, it becomes happy; when a bitter fruit comes, it becomes sad. The Paramatma is a friend of the jivatma, but He does not interfere; He simply sits and watches. If the jivatma can only turn around to the Paramatma, all its miseries will come to an end.' The jivatma has been bestowed with free will i.e., the freedom to turn away or towards God. By the improper use of that free will, the jivatma is in bondage; by learning its proper usage, it can attain the eternal service of God and experience infinite bliss.

य एवं वेत्ति पुरुषं प्रकृतिं च गुणैः सह ।
सर्वथा वर्तमानोऽपि न स भूयोऽभिजायते ।।24।।

ya evaṁ vetti puruṣhaṁ prakṛitiṁ cha guṇaiḥ saha
sarvathā vartamāno 'pi na sa bhūyo 'bhijāyate

yaḥ—who; *evam*—thus; *vetti*—understand; *puruṣham*—Purush; *prakṛitim*—the material nature; *cha*—and; *guṇaiḥ*—the three modes of nature; *saha*—with; *sarvathā*—in every way; *vartamānaḥ*—situated; *api*—although; *na*—not; *saḥ*—they; *bhūyaḥ*—again; *abhijāyate*—take birth.

Those who understand the truth about the Supreme Soul, the individual soul, material nature, and the interaction of the three modes of nature will not take birth here again. They will be liberated regardless of their present condition.

Ignorance has led the soul into its present predicament. Having forgotten its spiritual identity as a tiny fragment of God, it has fallen into material consciousness. Therefore, knowledge is vital for resurrecting itself from its present position. The *Śhwetāśhvatar Upanishad* states exactly the same thing:

sanyuktametat kṣharam akṣharaṁ cha
vyaktāvyaktaṁ bharate viśhwam īśhaḥ
anīśhaśh chātmā badhyate bhoktṛibhāvā-
jjñātvā devaṁ muchyate sarvapāśhaiḥ (1.8)

'There are three entities in creation—the ever-changing material nature, the unchangeable souls, and the Master of both, who is the

Supreme Lord. Ignorance of these entities is the cause of bondage of the soul while knowledge of them helps it cut asunder the fetters of maya.'

The knowledge that Shree Krishna is talking about is not just bookish information but realised wisdom. Realisation of knowledge is achieved when we first acquire theoretical knowledge of the three entities from the guru and the scriptures, and then engage in spiritual practice in alignment with that knowledge. *Shree Krishna now talks about some of these spiritual practices in the next verse.*

ध्यानेनात्मनि पश्यन्ति केचिदात्मानमात्मना ।
अन्ये साङ्ख्येन योगेन कर्मयोगेन चापरे ।।25।।

dhyānenātmani paśhyanti kechid ātmānam ātmanā
anye sānkhyena yogena karma-yogena chāpare

dhyānena—through meditation; *ātmani*—within one's heart; *paśhyanti*—perceive; *kechit*—some; *ātmānam*—the Supreme Soul; *ātmanā*—by the mind; *anye*—others; *sānkhyena*—through cultivation of knowledge; *yogena*—the yog system; *karma-yogena*—union with God through path of action; *cha*—and; *apare*—others.

Some try to perceive the Supreme Soul within their hearts through meditation, and others try to do so through the cultivation of knowledge, while still others strive to attain that realisation by the path of action.

Variety is a universal characteristic of God's creation. No two leaves of a tree are alike; no two human beings have exactly the same fingerprints; no two human societies have the same features. Similarly, all souls are unique; they have their distinctive traits that have been acquired in their unique journey through the cycle of life and death. So, in the realm of spiritual practice as well, not all are attracted to the same kind of practice. The beauty of the Bhagavad Gita and the Vedic scriptures is that they realise this inherent variety among human beings and account for it in their instructions.

Here, Shree Krishna explains that some *sādhaks* (spiritual aspirants) find great joy in grappling with their mind and bringing it under control. They are attracted to meditating upon God seated within their hearts. They relish the spiritual bliss that they experience when their mind comes to rest upon the Lord within them.

Others find satisfaction in exercising their intellect. The idea of the distinction of the soul and the body, mind, intellect, and ego excites them greatly. They relish cultivating knowledge about the three entities—soul, God, and maya—through the processes of *śhravaṇa, manan, nididhyāsan* (hearing, contemplating, and internalising with firm faith).

Yet others find their spirits soaring when they can engage in meaningful action. They strive to engage their God-given abilities in working for Him. Nothing satisfies them more than using the last drop of their energy in service of God. In this way, all kinds of *sādhaks* use their individual propensities to realise the Supreme. The fulfilment of any endeavour involving knowledge, action, or love is when it is combined with devotion for the pleasure of God. The Shreemad Bhagavatam states:

sā vidyā tanmatir yayā (4.29.49)

'True knowledge is that which helps us develop love for God. The fulfilment of karma occurs when it is done for the pleasure of the Lord.'

अन्ये त्वेवमजानन्तः श्रुत्वान्येभ्य उपासते ।
तेऽपि चातितरन्त्येव मृत्युं श्रुतिपरायणाः ।।26।।

anye tv evam ajānantaḥ śhrutvānyebhya upāsate
te 'pi chātitaranty eva mṛityuṁ śhruti-parāyaṇāḥ

anye—others; *tu*—still; *evam*—thus; *ajānantaḥ*—those who are unaware (of spiritual paths); *śhrutvā*—by hearing; *anyebhyaḥ*—from others; *upāsate*—begin to worship; *te*—they; *api*—also; *cha*—and; *atitaranti*—cross over; *eva*—even; *mṛityum*—death; *śhruti-parāyaṇāḥ*—devotion to hearing (from saints).

There are still others who are unaware of these spiritual paths, but they hear from others and begin worshipping the Supreme Lord. By such devotion to hearing from saints, they too can gradually cross over the ocean of birth and death.

There are those who are unaware of the methods of sadhana. But somehow, they acquire the knowledge through others and get drawn to the spiritual path. In fact, this is usually the case with most people who come to spirituality. They do not have any formal education in spiritual knowledge, but somehow or the other they get the opportunity to hear or read about it. Then their interest in devotion to the Lord develops, and they begin their journey.

In the Vedic tradition, hearing from the saints has been highly emphasised as a powerful tool for spiritual elevation. In the Shreemad Bhagavatam, King Parikshit asked Shukadev the question: 'How can we purify the undesirable entities in our heart, such as lust, anger, greed, envy, and hatred?' Shukadev replied:

śhṛiṇvatāṁ sva-kathāṁ kṛiṣhṇaḥ puṇya-śhravaṇa-kīrtanaḥ
hṛidy antaḥ stho hy abhadrāṇi vidhunoti suhṛit satām

(Bhagavatam 1.2.17)

'Parikshit! Simply hear the descriptions of the divine Names, Forms, Pastimes, Virtues, Abodes, and Associates of God from a saint. This will naturally cleanse the heart of the unwanted dirt of endless lifetimes.'

When we hear from the proper source, we develop authentic knowledge of spirituality. Besides this, the deep faith of the saint from whom we hear begins to flow into us. Hearing from the saints is the easiest way of building our faith in spiritual truths. Further, the enthusiasm of the saint for spiritual activity also brushes onto us. Enthusiasm for devotion provides the force that enables the *sādhak* to shrug aside the inertia of material consciousness and cut through the obstacles on the path of sadhana. Enthusiasm and faith in the heart are the foundation stones on which the palace of devotion stands.

यावत्सञ्जायते किञ्चित्सत्त्वं स्थावरजङ्गमम् ।
क्षेत्रक्षेत्रज्ञसंयोगात्तद्विद्धि भरतर्षभ ।।27।।

yāvat sañjāyate kiñchit sattvaṁ sthāvara-jaṅgamam
kṣhetra-kṣhetrajña-sanyogāt tad viddhi bharatarṣhabha

yāvat—whatever; *sañjāyate*—manifesting; *kiñchit*—anything; *sattvam*—being; *sthāvara*—unmoving; *jaṅgamam*—moving; *kṣhetra*—field of activities; *kṣhetra-jña*—knower of the field; *sanyogāt*—combination of; *tat*—that; *viddhi*—know; *bharata-ṛiṣhabha*—best of the Bharatas.

O best of the Bharatas, whatever moving or unmoving being you see in existence, know it to be a combination of the field of activities and the knower of the field.

Shree Krishna uses the words *yāvat kiñchit*, meaning, 'whatsoever form of life that exists' regardless of how enormous or infinitesimal it may be, is all born of the union of the *kṣhetrajña* (knower of the field) and the *kṣhetra* (field of activities). The Abrahamic traditions accept the existence of the soul in humans, but do not accept that other forms of life also have souls. This concept condones violence towards the other life forms. However, Vedic philosophy stresses that wherever consciousness exists, there must be the presence of the soul. Without it, there can be no consciousness.

In the early twentieth century, Sir J.C. Bose established through experiments that even plants, which are non-moving life forms, can feel and respond to emotions. His experiments proved that soothing music can enhance the growth of plants. When a hunter shoots a bird sitting on a tree, the vibrations of the tree seem to indicate that it weeps for the bird. And when a loving gardener enters the garden, the trees feel joyous. The changes in the vibrations of the tree reveal that it also possesses consciousness and can experience semblances of emotions. These observations corroborate Shree Krishna's statement here that all life forms possess consciousness; they are the combination of the eternal soul, which is the source of consciousness, and the body, which is made of the insentient material energy.

**समं सर्वेषु भूतेषु तिष्ठन्तं परमेश्वरम् ।
विनश्यत्स्वविनश्यन्तं यः पश्यति स पश्यति ।।28।।**

*samaṁ sarveṣhu bhūteṣhu tiṣhṭhantaṁ parameśhvaram
vinaśhyatsv avinaśhyantaṁ yaḥ paśhyati sa paśhyati*

samam—equally; *sarveṣhu*—in all; *bhūteṣhu*—beings; *tiṣhṭhantam*—accompanying; *parama-īśhvaram*—Supreme Soul; *vinaśhyatsu*—amongst the perishable; *avinaśhyantam*—the imperishable; *yaḥ*—who; *paśhyati*—see; *saḥ*—they; *paśhyati*—perceive.

They alone truly see, who perceive the Paramatma (Supreme Soul) accompanying the soul in all beings, and who understand both to be imperishable in this perishable body.

Shree Krishna had earlier used the expression *yaḥ paśhyati sa paśhyati* (they alone truly see, who see that...) in verse 5.5. Now He uses it again to state that it is not enough to see the presence of the soul within the body. We must also appreciate that God, the Supreme Soul, is seated within all bodies. His presence in the heart of all living beings was previously stated in verse 13.23 in this chapter. It is also mentioned in verses 10.20 and 18.61 of the Bhagavad Gita, and in other Vedic scriptures as well:

> *eko devaḥ sarvabhūteṣhu gūḍhaḥ sarvavyāpī*
> *sarvabhūtāntarātmā* (*Śhwetāśhvatar Upanishad* 6.11)

'God is one. He resides in the hearts of all living beings. He is omnipresent. He is the Supreme Soul of all souls.'

> *bhavān hi sarva-bhūtānām ātmā sākṣhī sva-dṛig vibho*

(Bhagavatam 10.86.31)

'God is seated inside all living beings as the Witness and the Master.'

> *rām brahma chinamaya abināsī, sarba rahit saba ura pura bāsī*

(Ramayan)

'The Supreme Lord Ram is eternal and beyond everything. He resides in the hearts of all living entities.'

The Supreme Soul accompanies the individual soul as it journeys from body to body in the cycle of life and death. *Shree Krishna now explains how realising the presence of God in everyone changes the life of the sādhak.*

समं पश्यन्हि सर्वत्र समवस्थितमीश्वरम् ।
न हिनस्त्यात्मनात्मानं ततो याति परां गतिम् ।।29।।

samaṁ paśhyan hi sarvatra samavasthitam īśhvaram
na hinasty ātmanātmānaṁ tato yāti parāṁ gatim

samam—equally; *paśhyan*—see; *hi*—indeed; *sarvatra*—everywhere; *samavasthitam*—equally present; *īśhvaram*—God as the Supreme Soul; *na*—do not; *hinasti*—degrade; *ātmanā*—by one's mind; *ātmānam*—the self; *tataḥ*—thereby; *yāti*—reach; *parām*—the supreme; *gatim*—destination.

Those who see God as the Supreme Soul equally present everywhere and in all living beings, do not degrade themselves by their mind. Thereby, they reach the supreme destination.

The mind is pleasure seeking by nature, and as a product of the material energy, it is spontaneously inclined towards material pleasures. If we follow the inclinations of our mind, we become degraded into deeper and deeper material consciousness. The way to prevent this downslide is to keep the mind in check with the help of the intellect. For this, the intellect needs to be empowered with true knowledge.

Those who learn to see God as the Supreme Soul present in all beings begin to live by this knowledge. They no longer seek personal gain and enjoyment in their relationships with others. They neither get attached to others for the good done by them, nor hate them for any harm caused by them. Rather, seeing everyone as a part of God, they maintain a healthy attitude of respect and service towards others. They naturally refrain from mistreating, cheating, or insulting others, when they perceive in them the presence of God. In addition, the man-made distinctions of nationality, creed, caste, gender, status, and colour become irrelevant. In this manner, they elevate their mind by seeing God in all living beings and finally reach the supreme goal.

प्रकृत्यैव च कर्माणि क्रियमाणानि सर्वशः ।
यः पश्यति तथात्मानमकर्तारं स पश्यति ।।30।।

prakṛityaiva cha karmāṇi kriyamāṇāni sarvaśhaḥ
yaḥ paśhyati tathātmānam akartāraṁ sa paśhyati

prakṛityā—by material nature; *eva*—truly; *cha*—also; *karmāṇi*—actions; *kriyamāṇāni*—are performed; *sarvaśhaḥ*—all; *yaḥ*—who; *paśhyati*—see; *tathā*—also; *ātmānam*—(embodied) soul; *akartāram*—actionless; *saḥ*—they; *paśhyati*—see.

They alone truly see who understand that all actions (of the body) are performed by material nature, while the embodied soul actually does nothing.

The *Tantra Bhagavat* states: *ahankārāt tu samsāro bhavet jīvasya na svataḥ* 'The ego of being the body and the pride of being the doer trap the soul in the samsara of life and death.' In material consciousness, the ego makes us identify with the body, and thus we attribute the actions of the body to the soul, and think, 'I am doing this ... I am doing that.' But the enlightened soul perceives that while eating, drinking, talking, walking, and during all other activities it is only the body that acts. Yet, it cannot shrug the responsibility of the actions performed by the body. Just as the president is responsible for the decision of the country to go to war, although he does not fight in it himself, so too, the soul is responsible for the actions of a living entity, even though they are performed by the body, mind, and intellect. This is why a spiritual aspirant must keep both sides in mind. Maharishi Vasishth instructed Ram: *kartā bahirkartāntarloke vihara rāghava* (*Yog Vāsiṣhṭh*) 'Ram, while working, externally exert Yourself as if the results depend upon You; but internally, realise Yourself to be the non-doer.'

**यदा भूतपृथग्भावमेकस्थमनुपश्यति ।
तत एव च विस्तारं ब्रह्म सम्पद्यते तदा ।।31।।**

yadā bhūta-pṛithag-bhāvam eka-stham anupaśhyati
tata eva cha vistāraṁ brahma sampadyate tadā

yadā—when; *bhūta*—living entities; *pṛithak-bhāvam*—diverse variety; *eka-stham*—situated in the same place; *anupaśhyati*—see; *tataḥ*—thereafter; *eva*—indeed; *cha*—and; *vistāram*—born from; *brahma*—Brahman; *sampadyate*—(they) attain; *tadā*—then.

When they see the diverse variety of living beings situated in the same material nature and understand all of them to be born from it, they attain the realisation of Brahman.

The ocean modifies itself in many forms, such as the wave, froth, tide, and ripples. One who is shown all these individually for the first time may conclude that they are all different. But one who has knowledge of the ocean sees the inherent unity in all this variety. Similarly, there are numerous forms of life in existence, from the tiniest amoeba to the most powerful celestial gods. All of them are rooted in the same reality—the soul, which is a part of God, seated in a body, which is made from the material energy. The distinctions among the forms are not due to the soul, but due to the different bodies manifested by the material energy. Upon birth, the bodies of all living beings are created from the material energy, and at death, their bodies again merge into it. When we see the variety of living beings all rooted in the same material nature, we realise the unity behind the diversity. And since material nature is the energy of God, such an understanding makes us see the same spiritual substratum pervading all existence. This leads to the Brahman realisation.

**अनादित्वान्निर्गुणत्वात्परमात्मायमव्ययः ।
शरीरस्थोऽपि कौन्तेय न करोति न लिप्यते ।।32।।**

anāditvān nirguṇatvāt paramātmāyam avyayaḥ
śharīra-stho 'pi kaunteya na karoti na lipyate

anāditvāt—being without beginning; *nirguṇatvāt*—being devoid of any material qualities; *parama*—the Supreme; *ātmā*—soul; *ayam*—this; *avyayaḥ*—imperishable; *śharīra-sthaḥ*—dwelling in the body; *api*—although; *kaunteya*—Arjun, son of Kunti; *na*—neither; *karoti*—acts; *na*—nor; *lipyate*—is tainted.

The Supreme Soul is imperishable, without beginning, and devoid of any material qualities, O son of Kunti. Although situated within the body, It neither acts, nor is It tainted by material energy.

God, situated within the heart of the living being as the Supreme Soul, never identifies with the body, nor is affected by its states of existence. His presence in the material body does not make Him material in any way, nor is He subject to the Law of Karma and the cycle of birth and death, though these are experienced by the soul.

यथा सर्वगतं सौक्ष्म्यादाकाशं नोपलिप्यते ।
सर्वत्रावस्थितो देहे तथात्मा नोपलिप्यते ।।33।।

yathā sarva-gataṁ saukṣhmyād ākāśhaṁ nopalipyate
sarvatrāvasthito dehe tathātmā nopalipyate

yathā—as; *sarva-gatam*—all-pervading; *saukṣhmyāt*—due to subtlety; *ākāśham*—the space; *na*—not; *upalipyate*—is contaminated; *sarvatra*—everywhere; *avasthitaḥ*—situated; *dehe*—the body; *tathā*—similarly; *ātmā*—the soul; *na*—not; *upalipyate*—is contaminated.

Space holds everything within it, but being subtle, does not get contaminated by what it holds. Similarly, though its consciousness pervades the body, the soul is not affected by the attributes of the body.

The soul experiences sleep, waking, tiredness, refreshment, and other states, due to the ego that makes it identify with the body. One may ask why changes in the body in which it resides do not taint the soul. Shree Krishna explains it with the example of space. It holds everything, yet remains unaffected, because it is subtler than the gross objects it holds. Similarly, the soul is a subtler energy compared to the body; it retains its divinity even while identifying with the material body.

यथा प्रकाशयत्येकः कृत्स्नं लोकमिमं रविः ।
क्षेत्रं क्षेत्री तथा कृत्स्नं प्रकाशयति भारत ।।34।।

yathā prakāśhayaty ekaḥ kṛitsnaṁ lokam imaṁ raviḥ
kṣhetraṁ kṣhetrī tathā kṛitsnaṁ prakāśhayati bhārata

yathā—as; *prakāśhayati*—illumines; *ekaḥ*—one; *kṛitsnam*—entire; *lokam*—solar system; *imam*—this; *raviḥ*—sun; *kṣhetram*—the body; *kṣhetrī*—the soul; *tathā*—so; *kṛitsnam*—entire; *prakāśhayati*—illumine; *bhārata*—Arjun, son of Bharat.

Just as one sun illumines the entire solar system, so does the individual soul illumine the entire body (with consciousness).

Although the soul energises the entire body in which it is present with consciousness, yet by itself, it is exceedingly small. *eṣho 'ṇurātmā* (*Muṇḍakopaniṣhad* 3.1.9) 'The soul is very tiny in size.' The *Śhwetāśhvatar Upanishad* states:

bālāgraśhatabhāgasya śhatadhā kalpitasya cha
bhāgo jīvaḥ sa vijñeyaḥ sa chānantyāya kalpate (5.9)

'If we divide the tip of a hair into a hundred parts, and then divide each part into further hundred parts, we will get the size of the soul. These souls are innumerable in number.' This is a manner of expressing the minuteness of the soul.

How can such an infinitesimal soul energise the body which is huge in comparison? Shree Krishna explains this with the analogy of the sun. Although situated in one place, the sun illumines the entire solar system with its light. Likewise, the *Vedant Darshan* states:

guṇādvā lokavat (2.3.25)

'The soul, although seated in the heart spreads its consciousness throughout the field of the body.'

क्षेत्रक्षेत्रज्ञयोरेवमन्तरं ज्ञानचक्षुषा ।
भूतप्रकृतिमोक्षं च ये विदुर्यान्ति ते परम् ।।35।।

kṣhetra-kṣhetrajñayor evam antaraṁ jñāna-chakṣhuṣhā
bhūta-prakṛiti-mokṣhaṁ cha ye vidur yānti te param

kṣhetra—the body; *kṣhetra-jñayoḥ*—of the knower of the body; *evam*—thus; *antaram*—the difference; *jñāna-chakṣhuṣhā*—with the eyes of knowledge; *bhūta*—the living entity; *prakṛiti-mokṣham*—release from material nature; *cha*—and; *ye*—who; *viduḥ*—know; *yānti*—approach; *te*—they; *param*—the Supreme.

Those who perceive with the eyes of knowledge the difference between the body and the knower of the body, and the process of release from material nature, attain the supreme destination.

In His customary style, Shree Krishna now winds up the topic of the field and the knower of the field by summing up all that He has said. True knowledge is to know the distinction between the material *kṣhetra* (field of activity) and the spiritual *kṣhetrajña* (knower of the field). Those possessing such discriminative knowledge do not look upon themselves as the material body. They identify with their spiritual nature as souls and tiny parts of God. Hence, they seek the path of spiritual elevation and release from material nature. Then, by treading on the path of spiritual enlightenment, such persons of wisdom attain their ultimate goal of God-realisation.

CHAPTER 14

Guna Traya Vibhāg Yog

Yog through Understanding the Three Modes of Material Nature

The previous chapter explained in detail the distinction between the soul and the material body. This chapter describes the nature of the material energy, which is the source of the body and its elements and is thus the origin of both mind and matter. Shree Krishna explains that material nature is constituted of three modes (gunas)—goodness, passion, and ignorance. The body, mind, and intellect that are made from the material energy also possess these three modes, and the combination of the modes in our being determines the colour of our personality. The mode of goodness is characterised by peacefulness, well-being, virtue, and serenity; the mode of passion gives rise to endless desires and insatiable ambitions for worldly enhancement; and the mode of ignorance is the cause for delusion, laziness, intoxication, and sleep. Until the soul attains illumination, it must learn to deal with these three powerful forces of material nature. Liberation lies in transcending all the three modes.

Shree Krishna reveals a simple solution for breaking out of the bondage of these gunas. The Supreme Lord is transcendental to the three modes, and if we attach ourselves to Him, then our mind will also rise to the divine platform. At this point, Arjun enquires about the characteristics of those who have gone beyond the three gunas. Shree Krishna then systematically explains the traits of such liberated souls. He expounds that illumined persons remain ever equipoised; they are not disturbed when they see the gunas functioning in the world and their effects manifesting in persons, objects, and situations. They see everything as a manifestation of God's energies which are ultimately in His hands. Thus, worldly situations neither make them jubilant nor miserable, and without wavering, they remain established in the self. The chapter ends with Shree Krishna again reminding us of the power of devotion and its ability to make us transcend the three gunas.

श्रीभगवानुवाच ।
परं भूयः प्रवक्ष्यामि ज्ञानानां ज्ञानमुत्तमम् ।
यज्ज्ञात्वा मुनयः सर्वे परां सिद्धिमितो गताः ॥1॥

śhrī-bhagavān uvācha
paraṁ bhūyaḥ pravakṣhyāmi jñānānāṁ jñānam uttamam
yaj jñātvā munayaḥ sarve parāṁ siddhim ito gatāḥ

śhrī-bhagavān uvācha—the Divine Lord said; *param*—supreme; *bhūyaḥ*—again; *pravakṣhyāmi*—I shall explain; *jñānānām*—of all knowledge; *jñānam uttamam*—the supreme wisdom; *yat*—which; *jñātvā*—knowing; *munayaḥ*—saints; *sarve*—all; *parām*—highest; *siddhim*—perfection; *itaḥ*—through this; *gatāḥ*—attained.

The Divine Lord said: I shall once again explain to you the supreme wisdom, the best of all knowledge, by knowing which, all the great saints attained the highest perfection.

In the previous chapter, Shree Krishna had explained that all life forms are a combination of soul and matter. He had also elucidated that prakriti (material nature) is responsible for creating the field of activities for the purush (soul). He added that this does not happen independently, but under the direction of the Supreme Lord, who is also seated within the body of the living being. In this chapter, He goes on to elaborate in detail about the three-fold qualities of material nature (the gunas). By gaining this knowledge and imbibing it into our consciousness as realised wisdom, we can ascend to the highest perfection.

इदं ज्ञानमुपाश्रित्य मम साधर्म्यमागताः ।
सर्गेऽपि नोपजायन्ते प्रलये न व्यथन्ति च ।।2।।

idaṁ jñānam upāśhritya mama sādharmyam āgatāḥ
sarge 'pi nopajāyante pralaye na vyathanti cha

idam—this; *jñānam*—wisdom; *upāśhritya*—take refuge in; *mama*—mine; *sādharmyam*—of similar nature; *āgatāḥ*—having attained; *sarge*—at the time of creation; *api*—even; *na*—not; *upajāyante*—are born; *pralaye*—at the time of dissolution; *na-vyathanti*—they will not experience misery; *cha*—and.

Those who take refuge in this wisdom will be united with Me. They will not be reborn at the time of creation nor destroyed at the time of dissolution.

Shree Krishna assures Arjun that those who equip themselves with the knowledge He is about to bestow will no longer have to accept repeated confinement in a mother's womb. They will also not be obliged to stay in a state of suspended animation in the womb of God at the time of the universal dissolution or be reborn along with the next creation. The three gunas (modes of material nature) are indeed the cause of bondage, and knowledge of them will illumine the path to freedom.

To bring His student to rapt attention Shree Krishna repeatedly uses the strategy of proclaiming the results of what He is about to teach. The words *na vyathanti* mean 'they will not experience misery.' The word *sādharmyam* means they will acquire 'a similar divine nature' as God Himself. When the soul is released from the bondage of the material energy, it comes under the dominion of God's divine *Yogmaya* energy. This divine energy equips it with God's divine knowledge, love, and bliss. As a result, the soul acquires the nature of God—and takes on divine godlike qualities.

मम योनिर्महद्ब्रह्म तस्मिन्गर्भं दधाम्यहम् ।
सम्भवः सर्वभूतानां ततो भवति भारत ।।3।।

सर्वयोनिषु कौन्तेय मूर्तयः सम्भवन्ति याः ।
तासां ब्रह्म महद्योनिरहं बीजप्रदः पिता ।।4।।

mama yonir mahad brahma tasmin garbhaṁ dadhāmy aham
sambhavaḥ sarva-bhūtānāṁ tato bhavati bhārata

sarva-yoniṣhu kaunteya mūrtayaḥ sambhavanti yāḥ
tāsāṁ brahma mahad yonir ahaṁ bīja-pradaḥ pitā

mama—my; *yoniḥ*—womb; *mahat brahma*—the total material substance, prakriti; *tasmin*—in that; *garbham*—womb; *dadhāmi*—impregnate; *aham*—I; *sambhavaḥ*—birth; *sarva-bhūtānām*—of all living beings; *tataḥ*—thereby; *bhavati*—becomes; *bhārata*—Arjun, son of Bharat; *sarva*—all; *yoniṣhu*—species of life; *kaunteya*—Arjun, son of Kunti; *mūrtayaḥ*—forms; *sambhavanti*—are produced; *yāḥ*—which; *tāsām*—of all of them; *brahma-mahat*—great material nature; *yoniḥ*—womb; *aham*—I; *bīja-pradaḥ*—seed-giving; *pitā*—Father.

The total material substance, prakriti, is the womb. I impregnate it with individual souls, and thus all living beings are born. O son of Kunti, for all species of life that are produced, the material nature is the womb, and I am the seed-giving Father.

As explained in chapters 7 and 8, material creation follows the cycle of creation, maintenance, and dissolution. During dissolution, souls who are *vimukh* (have their backs) towards God remain in a state of suspended animation within the body of Maha Vishnu. The material energy, prakriti, also lies unmanifest in God's *mahodar* (big stomach). When He desires to activate the process of creation, He glances at prakriti. It then begins to unwind, and sequentially, the entities *mahān*, *ahankār*, *pañcha tanmātrās*, and *pañcha mahābhūta* are created. Also, with the help of the secondary creator, Brahma, the material energy creates various life forms; God determines the appropriate physical form for each soul based on accumulated past karmas of endless past lifetimes. Thus, Shree Krishna states that prakriti is like the womb and the souls are like the sperms. He places the souls in the womb of Mother Nature to give birth to multitudes of living beings. Sage Ved Vyas also describes it in the same fashion in the Shreemad Bhagavatam:

daivāt kṣhubhita-dharmiṇyāṁ svasyāṁ yonau paraḥ pumān
ādhatta vīryaṁ sāsūta mahat-tattvaṁ hiraṇmayam (3.26.19)

'The Supreme Lord impregnates the womb of material nature with the souls. Then, inspired by the karmas of the individual souls, material nature gets to work to create suitable life forms for them.' He does not cast all souls into the material world; rather, only those who are *vimukh*.

सत्त्वं रजस्तम इति गुणाः प्रकृतिसम्भवाः ।
निबध्नन्ति महाबाहो देहे देहिनमव्ययम् ।।5।।

sattvaṁ rajas tama iti guṇāḥ prakṛiti-sambhavāḥ
nibadhnanti mahā-bāho dehe dehinam avyayam

sattvam—mode of goodness; *rajaḥ*—mode of passion; *tamaḥ*—mode of ignorance; *iti*—thus; *guṇāḥ*—modes; *prakṛiti*—material nature; *sambhavāḥ*—consists of; *nibadhnanti*—bind; *mahā-bāho*—mighty-armed one; *dehe*—in the body; *dehinam*—the embodied soul; *avyayam*—eternal.

O mighty-armed Arjun, material energy consists of three gunas (modes)—sattva (goodness), rajas (passion), and tamas (ignorance). These modes bind the eternal soul to the perishable body.

Having explained that all life forms are born from purush and prakriti, Shree Krishna now explains in the next fourteen verses how prakriti binds the soul. Although the soul is divine, its identification with the body ties it to material nature. Material energy possesses three gunas—goodness, passion, and ignorance. Hence the body, mind, and intellect that are made from prakriti also possess these three modes.

Consider the example of three-colour printing. If any one of the colours is released in excess, then the picture acquires a hue of that colour. Similarly, prakriti has the ink of the three colours. Based on one's internal thoughts, external circumstances, past *sanskārs*, and other factors, one or the other of these modes becomes dominant in that person. And the mode that predominates creates its corresponding shade upon that person's personality. Hence, the soul is swayed by the influence of these dominating modes. Shree Krishna now describes the impact of these modes upon the living being.

तत्र सत्त्वं निर्मलत्वात्प्रकाशकमनामयम् ।
सुखसङ्गेन बध्नाति ज्ञानसङ्गेन चानघ ।।6।।

tatra sattvaṁ nirmalatvāt prakāśhakam anāmayam
sukha-saṅgena badhnāti jñāna-saṅgena chānagha

tatra—amongst these; *sattvam*—mode of goodness; *nirmalatvāt*—being purest; *prakāśhakam*—illuminating; *anāmayam*—healthy and full of well-being; *sukha*—happiness; *saṅgena*—attachment; *badhnāti*—binds; *jñāna*—knowledge; *saṅgena*—attachment; *cha*—also; *anagha*—Arjun, the sinless one.

Amongst these, sattva guna, the mode of goodness, being purer than the others, is illuminating and full of well-being. O sinless one, it binds the soul by creating attachment for a sense of happiness and knowledge.

The word *prakāśhakam* means 'illuminating.' The word *anāmayam* means 'healthy and full of well-being.' By extension, it also means 'of peaceful quality' devoid of any inherent cause for pain, discomfort, or misery. The mode of goodness is serene and illuminating. Thus, sattva guna engenders virtues in one's personality and illuminates the intellect with knowledge. It makes a person calm, satisfied, charitable, compassionate, helpful, serene, and tranquil. It also nurtures good health and freedom from sickness. While the mode of goodness creates an effect of serenity and happiness, attachment to them itself binds the soul to material nature.

Let us understand this through an example. A traveller was passing through a forest when three robbers attacked him. The first said, 'Let us kill him and steal all his wealth.' The second said, 'No, let us not kill him. We will simply bind him and take away his possessions.' Following the advice of the second robber, they tied him up in ropes and stole his wealth. When they had gone some distance away, the third robber returned. He opened the ropes of the traveller and took him to the edge of the forest. He showed the way out, and said, 'I cannot go out myself, but if you follow this path, you will be able to get out of the forest.'

In this example, the first robber was tamo guna, the mode of ignorance, which literally wants to kill the soul by degrading it into sloth, languor, and nescience. The second robber was rajo guna, the mode of passion, which excites the passions of the living being and binds the soul in innumerable worldly desires. The third robber was sattva guna, the mode of goodness, which reduces the vices of the living being, eases material discomfort, and puts the soul on the path of virtue. Yet even sattva guna is within the realm of material nature. We must not get attached to it; instead, we must use it to step up to the transcendental platform.

Beyond these three is *śhuddha sattva*, the transcendental mode of goodness. It is the mode of the divine energy of God that is beyond material nature. When the soul becomes God-realised, by His grace, God bestows *śhuddha sattva* upon the soul, making the senses, mind, and intellect divine.

रजो रागात्मकं विद्धि तृष्णासङ्गसमुद्भवम् ।
तन्निबध्नाति कौन्तेय कर्मसङ्गेन देहिनम् ।।7।।

rajo rāgātmakaṁ viddhi tṛiṣhṇā-saṅga-samudbhavam
tan nibadhnāti kaunteya karma-saṅgena dehinam

rajaḥ—mode of passion; *rāga-ātmakam*—of the nature of passion; *viddhi*—know; *tṛiṣhṇā*—desires; *saṅga*—association; *samudbhavam*—arises from; *tat*—that; *nibadhnāti*—binds; *kaunteya*—Arjun, son of Kunti; *karma-saṅgena*—through attachment to fruitive actions; *dehinam*—the embodied soul.

O Arjun, rajo guna is of the nature of passion. It arises from worldly desires and affections and binds the soul through attachment to fruitive actions.

Shree Krishna now explains the working of rajo guna and the process by which it binds the soul to material existence. The *Patanjali Yog*

Darshan describes material activity as the primary manifestation of rajo guna. Here, Shree Krishna describes its principal manifestation as attachment and desire.

The mode of passion fuels lust for sensual enjoyment. It inflames desires for mental and physical pleasures. It also promotes attachment to worldly things. Persons influenced by rajo guna get engrossed in worldly pursuits of status, prestige, career, family, and home. They look on these as sources of pleasure and are motivated to undertake intense activity for the sake of these. In this way, the mode of passion increases desires, and these desires further fuel an increase of the mode of passion. They both nourish each other and trap the soul in worldly life.

The way to break out of this is to engage in karm yog i.e., to begin offering the results of one's activities to God. This creates detachment from the world and pacifies the effect of rajo guna.

तमस्त्वज्ञानजं विद्धि मोहनं सर्वदेहिनाम् ।
प्रमादालस्यनिद्राभिस्तन्निबध्नाति भारत ।।8।।

tamas tv ajñāna-jaṁ viddhi mohanaṁ sarva-dehinām
pramādālasya-nidrābhis tan nibadhnāti bhārata

tamaḥ—mode of ignorance; *tu*—but; *ajñāna-jam*—born of ignorance; *viddhi*—know; *mohanam*—illusion; *sarva-dehinām*—for all the embodied souls; *pramāda*—negligence; *ālasya*—laziness; *nidrābhiḥ*—sleep; *tat*—that; *nibadhnāti*—binds; *bhārata*—Arjun, son of Bharat.

O Arjun, tamo guna, which is born of ignorance, is the cause of illusion for the embodied souls. It deludes all living beings through negligence, laziness, and sleep.

Tamo guna is the antithesis of sattva guna. Persons influenced by it get pleasure through sleep, laziness, intoxication, violence, and gambling. They lose their discrimination of what is right and what is wrong, and do not hesitate in resorting to immoral behaviour for fulfilling their self-will. Doing their duty becomes burdensome to them and they neglect it, becoming more inclined to sloth and sleep. In this way, the mode of ignorance leads the soul deeper into the darkness of ignorance. It becomes totally oblivious of its spiritual identity, its goal in life, and the opportunity for progress that the human form provides.

सत्त्वं सुखे सञ्जयति रजः कर्मणि भारत ।
ज्ञानमावृत्य तु तमः प्रमादे सञ्जयत्युत ।।9।।

sattvaṁ sukhe sañjayati rajaḥ karmaṇi bhārata
jñānam āvṛitya tu tamaḥ pramāde sañjayaty uta

sattvam—mode of goodness; *sukhe*—to happiness; *sañjayati*—binds; *rajaḥ*—mode of passion; *karmaṇi*—towards actions; *bhārata*—Arjun, son of Bharat; *jñānam*—wisdom; *āvṛitya*—clouds; tu—but; *tamaḥ*—mode of ignorance; *pramāde*—to delusion; *sañjayati*—binds; *uta*—indeed.

Sattva binds one to material happiness; rajas conditions the soul towards actions; and tamas clouds wisdom and binds one to delusion.

In the mode of goodness, the miseries of material existence reduce, and worldly desires become subdued. This gives rise to a feeling of contentment with one's present state. This is a good thing, but it can have a negative side too. For instance, those who experience pain in the world and are disturbed by the desires in their mind feel impelled to look for a solution to their problems, and this impetus sometimes brings them to the spiritual path. However, those in goodness can easily become complacent and feel no urge to progress to the transcendental platform. Also, sattva guna illumines the intellect with knowledge. If this is not accompanied by spiritual wisdom, then knowledge results in pride and that pride comes in the way of devotion to God. This is often seen in the case of scientists, academicians, scholars, and others of similar profession. The mode of goodness usually predominates in them since they spend their time and energy cultivating knowledge. And yet, the knowledge they possess often makes them proud, and they begin to feel that there can be no truth beyond the grasp of their intellect. Thus, they find it difficult to develop faith towards either the scriptures or the God-realised saints.

In the mode of passion, the souls are impelled towards intense activity. Their attachment to the world and preference for pleasure, prestige, wealth, and physical comforts, propels them to work hard in the world for achieving these goals, which they consider to be the most important in life. Rajo guna increases the attraction between man and woman and generates *kām* (lust). To satiate that lust, man and woman enter into the relationship of marriage and have a home. The upkeep of the home creates the need for wealth, so they begin to work hard for economic development. They engage in intense activity, but each action creates karmas which further bind them in material existence.

The mode of ignorance clouds the intellect of the living being. The desire for happiness now manifests in perverse manners. For example, everyone knows that cigarette smoking is injurious to health. Every cigarette pack carries a warning to that extent issued by government authorities. Cigarette smokers read this, and yet do not refrain from smoking. This happens because the intellect loses its discriminative power and does not hesitate to inflict self-injury to get the pleasure of smoking. As someone jokingly said, 'A cigarette is a pipe with a fire at one end and a fool at the other.' That is the influence of tamo guna which binds the soul in the darkness of ignorance.

रजस्तमश्चाभिभूय सत्त्वं भवति भारत ।
रजः सत्त्वं तमश्चैव तमः सत्त्वं रजस्तथा ।।10।।

rajas tamaśh chābhibhūya sattvaṁ bhavati bhārata
rajaḥ sattvaṁ tamaśh chaiva tamaḥ sattvaṁ rajas tathā

rajaḥ—mode of passion; *tamaḥ*—mode of ignorance; *cha*—and; *abhibhūya*—prevails; *sattvam*—mode of goodness; *bhavati*—becomes; *bhārata*—Arjun, son of Bharat; *rajaḥ*—mode of passion; *sattvam*—mode of goodness; *tamaḥ*—mode of ignorance; *cha*—and; *eva*—indeed; *tamaḥ*—mode of ignorance; *sattvam*—mode of goodness; *rajaḥ*—mode of passion; *tathā*—also.

Sometimes goodness (sattva) prevails over passion (rajas) and ignorance (tamas), O scion of Bharat. Sometimes passion (rajas) dominates goodness (sattva) and ignorance (tamas), and at other times ignorance (tamas) overcomes goodness (sattva) and passion (rajas).

Shree Krishna now explains that the same individual's temperament oscillates among the three gunas. These three gunas are present in the material energy, and our mind is made from the same energy. Hence, all the three gunas are present in our mind as well. They can be compared to three wrestlers competing with each other. Each keeps throwing the others down, and so, sometimes the first is on top, sometimes the second, and sometimes the third. In the same manner, the three gunas keep gaining dominance over the individual's temperament which oscillates amongst the three modes. Depending upon the external environment, the internal contemplation, and the *sanskārs* (tendencies) of past lives, one or the other guna begins to dominate. There is no rule for how long it stays—one guna may dominate the mind and intellect for as short as a moment or for as long as an hour.

If sattva guna dominates, one becomes peaceful, content, generous, kind, helpful, serene, and tranquil. When rajo guna gains prominence, one becomes passionate, agitated, ambitious, envious of others' success, and develops a gusto for sense pleasures. When tamo guna becomes prominent, one is overcome by sleep, laziness, hatred, anger, resentment, violence, and doubt.

For example, let us suppose you are studying in your library. There is no worldly disturbance, and your mind has become sattvic. After finishing your study, you sit in your living room and switch on the television. Seeing all the images makes your mind rajasic and increases your hankering for sense pleasures. While you are watching your favourite channel, your family member comes and changes the channel. This disturbance causes tamo guna to increase in your mind, and you are filled with anger. In this way, the mind sways among the three gunas and adopts their qualities.

सर्वद्वारेषु देहेऽस्मिन्प्रकाश उपजायते ।
ज्ञानं यदा तदा विद्याद्विवृद्धं सत्त्वमित्युत ।।11।।

लोभः प्रवृत्तिरारम्भः कर्मणामशमः स्पृहा ।
रजस्येतानि जायन्ते विवृद्धे भरतर्षभ ।।12।।

अप्रकाशोऽप्रवृत्तिश्च प्रमादो मोह एव च ।
तमस्येतानि जायन्ते विवृद्धे कुरुनन्दन ।।13।।

sarva-dvāreṣhu dehe 'smin prakāśha upajāyate
jñānaṁ yadā tadā vidyād vivṛiddhaṁ sattvam ity uta

lobhaḥ pravṛittir ārambhaḥ karmaṇām aśhamaḥ spṛihā
rajasy etāni jāyante vivṛiddhe bharatarṣhabha

aprakāśho 'pravṛittiśh cha pramādo moha eva cha
tamasy etāni jāyante vivṛiddhe kuru-nandana

sarva—all; *dvāreṣhu*—through the gates; *dehe*—body; *asmin*—in this; *prakāśhaḥ*—illumination; *upajāyate*—manifest; *jñānam*—knowledge; *yadā*—when; *tadā*—then; *vidyāt*—know; *vivṛiddham*—predominates; *sattvam*—mode of goodness; *iti*—thus; *uta*—certainly; *lobhaḥ*—greed; *pravṛittiḥ*—activity; *ārambhaḥ*—exertion; *karmaṇām*—for fruitive actions; *aśhamaḥ*—restlessness; *spṛihā*—craving; *rajasi*—of the mode of passion; *etāni*—these; *jāyante*—develop; *vivṛiddhe*—when predominates; *bharata-ṛiṣhabha*—best of the Bharatas, Arjun; *aprakāśhaḥ*—nescience; *apravṛittiḥ*—inertia; *cha*—and; *pramādaḥ*—negligence; *mohaḥ*—delusion; *eva*—indeed; *cha*—also; *tamasi*—mode of ignorance; *etāni*—these; *jāyante*—manifest; *vivṛiddhe*—when dominates; *kuru-nandana*—joy of the Kurus, Arjun.

When all the gates of the body are illumined by knowledge, know it to be a manifestation of the mode of goodness. When the mode of passion predominates, O Arjun, the symptoms of greed, exertion for worldly gain, restlessness, and craving develop. O Arjun, nescience, inertia, negligence, and delusion—these are the dominant signs of the mode of ignorance.

Shree Krishna once again repeats how the three modes influence one's thinking. Sattva guna leads to the development of virtues and the illumination of knowledge. Rajo guna leads to greed, inordinate activity for worldly attainments, and restlessness of the mind. Tamo guna results in delusion of the intellect, laziness, and inclination towards intoxication and violence.

In fact, these modes even influence our attitudes towards God and the spiritual path. To give an example, when the mode of goodness becomes prominent in the mind, we may start thinking, 'I have received so much grace from my guru. I should endeavour to progress rapidly in my sadhana since the human form is precious and should not be wasted in mundane pursuits.' When the mode of passion becomes prominent, we may think, 'I must surely progress on the spiritual path, but what is the hurry? At present, I have many responsibilities to discharge, and they are more important.' When the mode of ignorance dominates, we could think, 'I am not really sure if there is any God or not, for no one has ever seen Him. So why waste time in sadhana?' Notice how the same person's thoughts oscillated from such heights to the depths of devotion.

For the mind to fluctuate due to the three gunas is very natural. However, we are not to be dejected by this state of affairs; rather, we should understand why it happens and work to rise above it. Sadhana means to fight with the flow of the three gunas in the mind and force it to maintain the devotional feelings towards God and guru. If our consciousness remained at the highest consciousness all day, there would be no need for sadhana. Though the mind's natural sentiments may be inclined towards the world, yet with the intellect, we have to force it into the spiritual realm. Initially, this may seem difficult, but with practice it becomes easy. This is just as driving a car is difficult initially, but with practice, it becomes natural.

Shree Krishna now begins to explain the destinations bestowed by the three gunas, and the need for making it our goal to transcend them.

यदा सत्त्वे प्रवृद्धे तु प्रलयं याति देहभृत् ।
तदोत्तमविदां लोकानमलान्प्रतिपद्यते ॥14॥

रजसि प्रलयं गत्वा कर्मसङ्गिषु जायते ।
तथा प्रलीनस्तमसि मूढयोनिषु जायते ॥15॥

yadā sattve pravṛiddhe tu pralayaṁ yāti deha-bhṛit
tadottama-vidāṁ lokān amalān pratipadyate

rajasi pralayaṁ gatvā karma-saṅgiṣhu jāyate
tathā pralīnas tamasi mūḍha-yoniṣhu jāyate

yadā—when; *sattve*—in the mode of goodness; *pravṛiddhe*—when premodinates; *tu*—indeed; *pralayam*—death; *yāti*—reach; *deha-bhṛit*—the embodied; *tadā*—then; *uttama-vidām*—of the learned; *lokān*—abodes; *amalān*—pure; *pratipadyate*—attains; *rajasi*—in the mode of passion; *pralayam*—death; *gatvā*—attaining; *karma-saṅgiṣhu*—among people driven by work; *jāyate*—are born; *tathā*—likewise; *pralīnaḥ*—dying; *tamasi*—in the mode of ignorance; *mūḍha-yoniṣhu*—in the animal kingdom; *jāyate*—takes birth.

Those who die with predominance of sattva reach the pure abodes (which are free from rajas and tamas) of the learned. Those who die with prevalence of the mode of passion are born among people driven by work, while those dying in the mode of ignorance take birth in the animal kingdom.

Shree Krishna explains that the destiny awaiting the souls is based on the gunas of their personalities. We get what we deserve is God's law, the Law of Karma. Those who cultivated virtues, knowledge, and a service attitude towards others are born in families of pious people, scholars, and social workers. Or else, they go to the higher celestial abodes. Those who permitted themselves to be overcome by greed, avarice, and worldly ambitions are born in families focused on intense material activity, very often the business class. Those who were inclined to intoxication, violence, laziness, and dereliction of duty are born among families of drunks and illiterate people. Otherwise, they are made to descend down the evolutionary ladder and are born into the animal species.

Many people wonder whether having once attained the human form, it is possible to slip back into the lower species. This verse reveals that the human form does not remain permanently reserved for the soul. Those who do not put it to good use are subject to the terrible danger of moving down into the animal forms again. Thus, all the paths are open at all times. The soul can climb up in its spiritual evolution, remain at the same level, or even slide down, based upon the intensity and frequency of the gunas it adopts.

कर्मणः सुकृतस्याहुः सात्त्विकं निर्मलं फलम् ।
रजसस्तु फलं दुःखमज्ञानं तमसः फलम् ।।16।।

karmaṇaḥ sukṛitasyāhuḥ sāttvikaṁ nirmalaṁ phalam
rajasas tu phalaṁ duḥkham ajñānaṁ tamasaḥ phalam

karmaṇaḥ—of action; *su-kṛitasya*—pure; *āhuḥ*—is said; *sāttvikam*—mode of goodness; *nirmalam*—pure; *phalam*—result; *rajasaḥ*—mode of passion; *tu*—indeed; *phalam*—result; *duḥkham*—pain; *ajñānam*—ignorance; *tamasaḥ*—mode of ignorance; *phalam*—result.

It is said the fruit of actions performed in the mode of goodness bestow pure results. Actions done in the mode of passion result in pain, while those performed in the mode of ignorance result in darkness.

Those influenced by sattva are equipped with a measure of purity, virtue, knowledge, and selflessness. Hence, their actions are performed with a relatively pure intention and the results are uplifting and satisfying. Those influenced by rajas are agitated by the desires of their senses and mind. The intention behind their works is primarily self-aggrandisement and sense-gratification for themselves and their dependents. Thus, their work leads to the enjoyment of sense pleasures which further fuels their sensual desires. Those who are predominated by tamas have no respect for scriptural injunctions and codes of conduct. They commit sinful deeds to relish perverse pleasures which further immerses them in delusion.

सत्त्वात्सञ्जायते ज्ञानं रजसो लोभ एव च ।
प्रमादमोहौ तमसो भवतोऽज्ञानमेव च ।।17।।

sattvāt sañjāyate jñānaṁ rajaso lobha eva cha
pramāda-mohau tamaso bhavato 'jñānam eva cha

sattvāt—from the mode of goodness; *sañjāyate*—arises; *jñānam*—knowledge; *rajasaḥ*—from the mode of passion; *lobhaḥ*—greed; *eva*—indeed; *cha*—and; *pramāda*—negligence; *mohau*—delusion; *tamasaḥ*—from the mode of ignorance; *bhavataḥ*—arise; *ajñānam*—ignorance; *eva*—indeed; *cha*—and.

From the mode of goodness arises knowledge, from the mode of passion arises greed, and from the mode of ignorance arise negligence and delusion.

Having mentioned the variation in the results that accrue from the three gunas, Shree Krishna now gives the reason for this. Sattva guna gives rise to wisdom which confers the ability to discriminate between right and wrong. It also pacifies the desires of the senses for gratification and creates a concurrent feeling of happiness and contentment. People influenced by it are inclined towards intellectual pursuits and virtuous ideas. Thus, the mode of goodness promotes wise actions. Rajo guna inflames the senses and puts the mind out of control, sending it into a spin of ambitious desires. The living being is trapped by it and hankers for wealth and pleasures that are meaningless from the perspective of the soul. Tamo guna covers the living being with inertia and nescience. Shrouded in ignorance, a person performs wicked and impious deeds and faces the karmic results for one's actions.

ऊर्ध्वं गच्छन्ति सत्त्वस्था मध्ये तिष्ठन्ति राजसाः ।
जघन्यगुणवृत्तिस्था अधो गच्छन्ति तामसाः ।।18।।

ūrdhvaṁ gachchhanti sattva-sthā madhye tiṣhṭhanti rājasāḥ
jaghanya-guṇa-vṛitti-sthā adho gachchhanti tāmasāḥ

ūrdhvam—upward; *gachchhanti*—rise; *sattva-sthāḥ*—those situated in the mode of goodness; *madhye*—in the middle; *tiṣhṭhanti*—stay; *rājasāḥ*—those in the mode of passion; *jaghanya*—abominable; *guṇa*—quality; *vṛitti-sthāḥ*—engaged in activities; *adhaḥ*—down; *gachchhanti*—go; *tāmasāḥ*—those in the mode of ignorance.

Those situated in the mode of goodness rise upward; those in the mode of passion stay in the middle; those in the mode of ignorance go downward.

Shree Krishna explains that the reincarnation of the souls in their next birth is linked to the guna that predominates their personality. On completion of their sojourn in the present life, souls reach the kind of place that corresponds to their gunas. This can be compared to students applying for college admission after completing high school. Those students with good qualifying criteria at the school level gain admission in the best colleges, while those with poor grades and other scores are admitted to the worst ones. Likewise, the Bhagavatam says:

sattve pralīnāḥ svar yānti nara-lokaṁ rajo-layāḥ
tamo-layās tu nirayaṁ yānti mām eva nirguṇāḥ (11.25.22)

'Those in sattva guna reach the higher celestial abodes; those in rajo guna return to the earth planet; those in tamo guna go to the nether worlds; and those who are transcendental to three modes attain Me.'

नान्यं गुणेभ्यः कर्तारं यदा द्रष्टानुपश्यति ।
गुणेभ्यश्च परं वेत्ति मद्भावं सोऽधिगच्छति ।।19।।

nānyaṁ guṇebhyaḥ kartāraṁ yadā draṣhṭānupaśhyati
guṇebhyaśh cha paraṁ vetti mad-bhāvaṁ so 'dhigachchhati

na—no; *anyam*—other; *guṇebhyaḥ*—of the guṇas; *kartāram*—agents of action; *yadā*—when; *draṣhṭā*—the seer; *anupaśhyati*—see; *guṇebhyaḥ*—to the modes of nature; *cha*—and; *param*—

transcendental; *vetti*—know; *mad-bhāvam*—my divine nature; *saḥ*—they; *adhigachchhati*—attain.

When wise persons see that in all work there is no agent of action other than the three gunas, and they know Me to be transcendental to these gunas, they attain My divine nature.

Having revealed the complex workings of the three gunas, Shree Krishna now shows a simple solution for breaking out of their bondage. As all living entities are under the grip of the three gunas, the gunas are active agents in all work being done in the world. But the Supreme Lord is beyond them. Therefore, He is called *triguṇātīt* (transcendental to the modes of material nature). Similarly, all the Attributes of God—His Names, Forms, Virtues, Pastimes, Abodes, and Associates—are also *triguṇātīt*.

If we attach our mind to any personality or object within the realm of the three gunas, it results in increasing their corresponding influence on our mind and intellect. However, if we attach our mind to the divine realm, it transcends the gunas and becomes divine. Those who understand this principle start loosening their relationship with worldly objects and people, and instead, strengthen their equation with God and the Guru through bhakti. This enables them to transcend the three gunas and attain the divine nature of God. This is further elaborated in verse 14.26.

गुणानेतानतीत्य त्रीन्देही देहसमुद्भवान् ।
जन्ममृत्युजरादुःखैर्विमुक्तोऽमृतमश्नुते ।।20।।

guṇān etān atītya trīn dehī deha-samudbhavān
janma-mṛityu-jarā-duḥkhair vimukto 'mṛitam aśhnute

guṇān—the three modes of material nature; *etān*—these; *atītya*—transcending; *trīn*—three; *dehī*—the embodied; *deha*—body; *samudbhavān*—produced of; *janma*—birth; *mṛityu*—death; *jarā*—old age; *duḥkhaiḥ*—misery; *vimuktaḥ*—free from; *amṛitam*—immortality; *aśhnute*—attains.

By transcending the three modes of material nature associated with the body, one becomes free from birth, death, old age, and misery, and attains immortality.

If we drink water from a dirty well, we are bound to get a stomach upset. Similarly, if we are influenced by the three modes, we are bound to experience their consequences, which are repeated births within the material realm, disease, old age, and death. These four consequences are the primary miseries of material life. It was by seeing these that the Buddha first realised that the world is a place of misery, and then searched for the way out of misery.

The Vedas prescribe a number of codes of conduct, social duties, rituals, and regulations for human beings. These prescribed duties and codes of conduct are together called karm dharma or varnashram dharma or *śhārīrik dharma*. They help elevate us from tamo guna and rajo guna to sattva guna. However, to reach sattva guna is not enough; it is also a form of bondage. The mode of goodness can be equated to being fettered with chains of gold. Our goal lies even beyond it—to get out of the prison of material existence.

Shree Krishna explains that when we transcend the three modes, then maya no longer binds the living being. Thus, the soul gets released from the cycle of life and death and attains immortality. Factually, the soul is always immortal. However, its identification with the material body makes it suffer the illusion of birth and death. This illusory experience is against the eternal nature of the soul which seeks release from it. Hence, the material illusion is naturally discomforting to our inner being and, from within, we all seek the taste of immortality.

अर्जुन उवाच ।
कैर्लिङ्गैस्त्रीन्गुणानेतानतीतो भवति प्रभो ।
किमाचारः कथं चैतांस्त्रीन्गुणानतिवर्तते ।।21।।

arjuna uvācha
kair liṅgais trīn guṇān etān atīto bhavati prabho
kim āchāraḥ kathaṁ chaitāns trīn guṇān ativartate

arjunaḥ uvācha—Arjun enquired; *kaiḥ*—by what; *liṅgaiḥ*—symptoms; *trīn*—three; *guṇān*—modes of material nature; *etān*—these; *atītaḥ*—having transcended; *bhavati*—is; *prabho*—Lord; *kim*—what; *āchāraḥ*—conduct; *katham*—how; *cha*—and; *etān*—these; *trīn*—three; *guṇān*—modes of material nature; *ativartate*—transcend.

Arjun enquired: What are the characteristics of those who have gone beyond the three gunas, O Lord? How do they act? How do they go beyond the bondage of the gunas?

Arjun heard from Shree Krishna about transcending the three gunas. So, now he asks three questions in relation to them. The word *liṅgais* means 'symptoms'. His first question is: 'What are the symptoms of those who have transcended the three gunas?' The word *āchāraḥ* means 'conduct'. Arjun's second question is: 'In what manner do such transcendentalists conduct themselves?' The word *ativartate* means 'transcend'. The third question he asks is: 'How does one transcend the three gunas?' *Shree Krishna answers his questions systematically.*

श्रीभगवानुवाच ।
प्रकाशं च प्रवृत्तिं च मोहमेव च पाण्डव ।
न द्वेष्टि सम्प्रवृत्तानि न निवृत्तानि काङ्क्षति ।।22।।

उदासीनवदासीनो गुणैर्यो न विचाल्यते ।
गुणा वर्तन्त इत्येवं योऽवतिष्ठति नेङ्गते ।।23।।

śhrī-bhagavān uvācha
prakāśhaṁ cha pravṛittiṁ cha moham eva cha pāṇḍava
na dveṣhṭi sampravṛittāni na nivṛittāni kāṅkṣhati

udāsīna-vad āsīno guṇair yo na vichālyate
guṇā vartanta ity evaṁ yo 'vatiṣhṭhati neṅgate

śhrī-bhagavān uvācha—the Supreme Divine Personality said; *prakāśham*—illumination; *cha*—and; *pravṛittim*—activity; *cha*—and; *moham*—delusion; *eva*—even; *cha*—and; *pāṇḍava*—Arjun, son of Pandu; *na dveṣhṭi*—do not hate; *sampravṛittāni*—when present; *na*—nor; *nivṛittāni*—when absent; *kāṅkṣhati*—longs; *udāsīna-vat*—neutral; *āsīnaḥ*—situated; *guṇaiḥ*—to the modes of material nature; *yaḥ*—who; *na*—not; *vichālyate*—are disturbed; *guṇāḥ*—modes of material nature; *vartante*—act; *iti-evam*—knowing it in this way; *yaḥ*—who; *avatiṣhṭhati*—established in the self; *na*—not; *iṅgate*—wavering.

The Supreme Divine Personality said: O Arjun, the persons who are transcendental to the three gunas neither hate illumination (which is born of sattva), nor activity (which is born of rajas), nor even delusion (which is born of tamas), when these are abundantly present, nor do they long for them when they are absent. They remain neutral to the modes of nature and are not disturbed by them. Knowing it is only the gunas that act, they stay established in the self, without wavering.

Shree Krishna now clarifies the traits of those who have transcended the three gunas. They are not disturbed when they see the gunas functioning in the world and their effects manifesting in persons, objects, and situations around them. Illumined persons do not hate ignorance when they see it, nor get implicated in it. Worldly-minded become overly concerned with the condition of the world. They spend their time and energy brooding about the state of things in the world. The enlightened souls also strive for human welfare, but they do so because it is their nature to help others. At the same time, they realise that the world is ultimately in the hands of God. They simply have to do their duty to the best of their ability and leave the rest in the hands of God. Having come into God's world, our first duty is to purify ourselves. Then, with a pure mind, we will naturally do good and beneficial works in the world without allowing worldly situations to bear too heavily upon us. As Mahatma Gandhi said: 'Be the change that you wish to see in the world.'

Shree Krishna explains that persons of illumination, who know themselves to be transcendental to the functioning of the modes, are neither miserable nor jubilant when the modes of nature perform their natural functions. In fact, even when they perceive these gunas in their mind, they do not feel disturbed. The mind is made from the material energy, and thus contains the three modes of maya. So, it is natural for the mind to be subjected to the influence of the gunas and their corresponding thoughts. The problem is that in bodily consciousness we do not see the mind as different from ourselves. And so, when the mind presents a disturbing thought, we feel, 'Oh! I am thinking in this negative manner.' We begin to associate with the poisonous thoughts, allowing them to reside in us and damage us spiritually. To the extent that even if the mind presents a thought against God and guru, we accept the thought as ours. If, at that time, we could see the mind as separate from us, we would be able to dissociate ourselves from negative thoughts. We would then reject the thoughts of the mind, 'I will have nothing to do with any thought that is not conducive to my devotion.' Persons on the transcendental platform have mastered the art of distancing themselves from all negative thoughts arising in the mind from the flow of the gunas.

समदुःखसुखः स्वस्थः समलोष्टाश्मकाञ्चनः ।
तुल्यप्रियाप्रियो धीरस्तुल्यनिन्दात्मसंस्तुतिः ।।24।।

मानापमानयोस्तुल्यस्तुल्यो मित्रारिपक्षयोः ।
सर्वारम्भपरित्यागी गुणातीतः स उच्यते ।।25।।

sama-duḥkha-sukhaḥ sva-sthaḥ sama-loṣhṭāśhma-kāñchanaḥ
tulya-priyāpriyo dhīras tulya-nindātma-sanstutiḥ

mānāpamānayos tulyas tulyo mitrāri-pakṣhayoḥ
sarvārambha-parityāgī guṇātītaḥ sa uchyate

sama—alike; *duḥkha*—distress; *sukhaḥ*—happiness; *sva-sthaḥ*—established in the self; *sama*—equally; *loṣhṭa*—a clod; *aśhma*—stone; *kāñchanaḥ*—gold; *tulya*—of equal value; *priya*—pleasant; *apriyaḥ*—unpleasant; *dhīraḥ*—steady; *tulya*—the same; *nindā*—blame; *ātma-sanstutiḥ*—praise; *māna*—honour; *apamānayoḥ*—dishonour; *tulyaḥ*—equal; *tulyaḥ*—equal; *mitra*—friend; *ari*—foe; *pakṣhayoḥ*—to the parties; *sarva*—all; *ārambha*—enterprises; *parityāgī*—renouncer; *guṇa-atītaḥ*—risen above the three modes of material nature; *saḥ*—they; *uchyate*—are said to have.

Those who are alike in happiness and distress; who are established in the self; who look upon a clod, a stone, and a piece of gold as of equal value; who remain the same amidst pleasant and unpleasant events; who are intelligent; who accept both blame and praise with equanimity; who remain the same in honour and dishonour; who treat both friend and foe alike; and who have abandoned all enterprises—they are said to have risen above the three gunas.

Like God, the soul too is beyond the three gunas. In bodily consciousness, we identify with the pain and pleasures of the body, and consequently vacillate between the emotions of elation and dejection. But those who are established on the transcendental platform of the self do not identify either with the happiness or the distress of the body. Such self-realised mystics do perceive the dualities of the world but remain unaffected by them. Thus, they become *nirguna* (beyond the influence of the gunas). This gives them an equal vision with which they see a lump of earth, a piece of stone, gold, favourable and unfavourable situations, and criticisms and glory as all the same.

मां च योऽव्यभिचारेण भक्तियोगेन सेवते ।
स गुणान्समतीत्यैतान्ब्रह्मभूयाय कल्पते ।।26।।

māṁ cha yo 'vyabhichāreṇa bhakti-yogena sevate
sa guṇān samatītyaitān brahma-bhūyāya kalpate

mām—me; *cha*—only; *yaḥ*—who; *avyabhichāreṇa*—unalloyed; *bhakti-yogena*—through devotion; *sevate*—serve; *saḥ*—they; *guṇān*—the three modes of material nature; *samatītya*—rise above; *etān*—these; *brahma-bhūyāya*—level of Brahman; *kalpate*—comes to.

Those who serve Me with unalloyed devotion rise above the three modes of material nature and come to the level of Brahman.

Having explained the traits of those who are situated beyond the three gunas, Shree Krishna now reveals the one and only method of transcending these modes of material nature. The above verse indicates that mere knowledge of the self and its distinction with the body is not enough. With the help of bhakti yog, the mind has to be fixed on the Supreme Lord, Shree Krishna. Then alone will the mind become *nirguna* (untouched by the three modes), just as Shree Krishna is *nirguna.*

Many people are of the view that if the mind is fixed upon the personal form of God, it will not rise to the transcendental platform. Only when it is attached to the formless Brahman, will the mind become transcendental to the modes of material nature. However, this verse refutes such a view. Although the personal form of God possesses infinite gunas (qualities), these are all divine and beyond the modes of material nature. Hence, the personal form of God is also *nirguna* (beyond the three material modes). Sage Ved Vyas explains this in the *Padma Puran*:

yastu nirguṇa ityuktaḥ śhāstreṣhu jagadīśhvaraḥ
prākṛitairheya sanyuktairguṇairhīnatvamuchyate

'Wherever the scriptures refer to God as *nirguna* (without attributes), they mean that He is without material attributes. Nevertheless, His divine personality is not devoid of qualities—He possesses infinite divine attributes.'

This verse also reveals the proper object of meditation. Transcendental meditation does not mean to meditate upon nothingness. The entity transcendental to the three modes of material nature is God. So, only when the object of our meditation is God can it truly be called transcendental meditation.

ब्रह्मणो हि प्रतिष्ठाहममृतस्याव्ययस्य च ।
शाश्वतस्य च धर्मस्य सुखस्यैकान्तिकस्य च ।।27।।

brahmaṇo hi pratiṣhṭhāham amṛitasyāvyayasya cha
śhāśhvatasya cha dharmasya sukhasyaikāntikasya cha

brahmaṇaḥ—of Brahman; *hi*—only; *pratiṣhṭhā*—the basis; *aham*—I; *amṛitasya*—of the immortal; *avyayasya*—of the imperishable; *cha*—and; *śhāśhvatasya*—of the eternal; *cha*—and; *dharmasya*—of the dharma; *sukhasya*—of bliss; *aikāntikasya*—unending; *cha*—and.

I am the basis of the formless Brahman, the immortal and imperishable, of eternal dharma, and of unending divine bliss.

The previous verse may give rise to the question about the relationship between Shree Krishna and the formless Brahman. It was previously stated that the all-powerful God has both aspects to His personality—the formless and the personal form. Here, Shree Krishna reveals that the Brahman which the jnanis worship is the light from the personal form of God. The *Padma Puran* states:

yannakhenduruchirbrahma dhyeyaṁ brahmādibhiḥ suraiḥ
guṇatrayamatītaṁ taṁ vande vṛindāvaneśhvaram

(*Pātāl Khaṇḍ* 77.60)

'The light that emanates from the toe-nails of the feet of the Lord of Vrindavan, Shree Krishna, is the transcendental Brahman that the jnanis and even the celestial gods meditate upon.' Similarly, Chaitanya Mahaprabhu said:

tāñhāra aṅgera śhuddha kiraṇa-maṇḍala
upaniṣhat kahe tāñre brahma sunirmala

(*Chaitanya Charitāmṛit*, *Ādi Leela* 2.12)

'The effulgence emanating from the divine body of God is described by the Upanishads as Brahman.' Thus, in this verse, Shree Krishna unequivocally confirms that the panacea for the disease of the three gunas is to engage in unwavering devotion to the personal form of the Supreme Lord.

CHAPTER 15

Purushottam Yog

The Yog of the Supreme Divine Personality

In the previous chapter, Shree Krishna explained that by transcending the three modes of material nature, one attains the divine goal. He also revealed that the best means for going beyond the gunas is by engaging in exclusive devotion. To engage in such devotion, we must detach the mind from the world and attach it to God alone. Thus, it is necessary to understand the nature of the world.

In this chapter, Shree Krishna explains this material world in a graphic manner, to help Arjun develop detachment from it. He compares the material world to an upside down *aśhvatth* tree (sacred fig). The embodied soul wanders up and down the branches of the tree, from lifetime to lifetime, without comprehending from where it originated, how long it has existed, and how it keeps growing. The roots of the tree are above, as it has its source in God. The fruitive activities described in the Vedas are like its leaves. The tree is irrigated by the three modes of material nature. These modes create sense objects that are like the buds on the tree. The buds sprout aerial roots that engender further growth of the tree. The chapter describes this symbolism in detail, to convey the idea that the embodied soul in ignorance of the nature of this tree of material existence only keeps perpetuating its bondage here. Shree Krishna explains that the axe of detachment must be used to cut down the tree. Then, we must search for the base of the tree, which is the Supreme Lord Himself. Finding the source, we must surrender to Him in the manner described in this chapter. When we do so, we will attain the divine abode of God, from where we will not return to the material world again.

Shree Krishna then describes that all souls, being His eternal fragmental parts, are divine. But bound by material nature, they struggle with the six senses including the mind. He explains how the embodied soul, though divine, savours material objects of the senses. He also describes how the soul transmigrates to a new body at the time of death, carrying with it the mind and senses from the present life. The ignorant neither realise the presence of the soul in the body when alive, nor when it departs from the body upon death. But yogis perceive it with the eyes of knowledge and by the purity of their mind. In the same way, God is also present in His creation, but He needs to be perceived with the eyes of knowledge. Shree Krishna reveals that we can cognise the existence of God in this world through His glories that shine forth everywhere. The chapter ends with explanations of the terms: *kṣhar*, *akṣhar*, and *Purushottam*. *Kṣhar* are the perishable beings of the material realm. *Akṣhar* are the liberated beings in the abode of God. *Purushottam* is the Supreme Divine Personality, who is the unchanging Controller and Sustainer of the world. He is transcendental to both perishable and imperishable beings. He must be worshipped with all our heart.

श्रीभगवानुवाच ।
ऊर्ध्वमूलमधःशाखमश्वत्थं प्राहुरव्ययम् ।
छन्दांसि यस्य पर्णानि यस्तं वेद स वेदवित् ।।1।।

śhrī-bhagavān uvācha
ūrdhva-mūlam adhaḥ-śhākham aśhvatthaṁ prāhur avyayam
chhandānsi yasya parṇāni yas taṁ veda sa veda-vit

śhrī-bhagavān uvācha—the Supreme Divine Personality said; *ūrdhva-mūlam*—with roots above; *adhaḥ*—downward; *śhākham*—branches; *aśhvattham*—the sacred fig tree; *prāhuḥ*—they speak; *avyayam*—eternal; *chhandānsi*—Vedic mantras; *yasya*—of which; *parṇāni*—leaves; *yaḥ*—who; *tam*—that; *veda*—knows; *saḥ*—he; *veda-vit*—the knower of the Vedas.

The Supreme Divine Personality said: They speak of an eternal *aśhvatth* tree with its roots above and branches below. Its leaves are the Vedic hymns, and one who knows the secret of this tree is the knower of the Vedas.

The word *aśhvatth* means that which will not remain the same until even the next day. This world is also *aśhvatth* because it is constantly changing. The Sanskrit dictionary defines the world in the following manner: *sansaratīti sansāraḥ* 'That which is constantly shifting is *Sansar* (a Sanskrit word for world).' *Gachchhatīti jagat* 'That which is always moving is *Jagat* (another Sanskrit word for world).' Not only is the world always changing, but it will also be annihilated and absorbed back into God one day. Thus, everything in it is temporary or *aśhvatth.*

Aśhvatth also has another meaning. It is the peepal tree (sacred fig) of the banyan tree family. Shree Krishna explains that for the soul, this material world is like a huge *aśhvatth* tree. Generally, trees have their roots below and branches above. But this tree has its roots above (*ūrdhva-mūlam*) i.e., it originated from God, is based in Him, and is supported by Him. Its trunk and branches extend downward (*adhaḥ-śhākham*), encompassing all life-forms in all the abodes of the material realm.

The leaves of the tree are those Vedic mantras (*chhandānsi*) that deal with ritualistic ceremonies and their rewards. They provide the juice for nourishing the tree of material existence. By engaging in the fruitive ritualistic yajnas described in these Vedic mantras, the soul goes to the heavenly abodes to enjoy celestial pleasures, only to descend back to earth when the meritorious deeds are depleted. Thus, the leaves of the tree nourish it by perpetuating the cycle of life and death. This tree in the form of the world is called eternal (*avyayam*) because its flow is continuous, and its beginning and end are not experienced by the souls. Just as the water of the sea evaporates to form clouds, then rains down on earth and merges into the sea again in a continuous process, similarly the cycle of life and death is perpetual.

The Vedas also mention this tree:

ūrdhvamūlo 'vākśhākha eṣho 'śhvatthaḥ sanātanaḥ

(*Kaṭhopaniṣhad* 2.3.1)

'The *aśhvatth* tree, with its roots upward and branches downward is eternal.'

ūrdhvamūlaṁ arvākśhākhaṁ vṛikṣhaṁ yo samprati
na sa jātu janaḥ śhraddhayātmṛityutyurmā mārayaditi

(*Taittirīya Āraṇyak* 1.11.5)

'Those who know this tree with its roots upward and branches downward will not believe that death can finish them.'

The Vedas describe this tree with the intention that we should endeavour to chop it down. Thus, Shree Krishna says that one who knows the secret of cutting down this tree of samsara is the knower of the Vedas (*Veda-vit*).

अधश्चोर्ध्वं प्रसृतास्तस्य शाखा
गुणप्रवृद्धा विषयप्रवालाः ।
अधश्च मूलान्यनुसन्ततानि
कर्मानुबन्धीनि मनुष्यलोके ।।2।।

adhaśh chordhvaṁ prasṛitās tasya śhākhā
guṇa-pravṛiddhā viṣhaya-pravālāḥ
adhaśh cha mūlāny anusantatāni
karmānubandhīni manuṣhya-loke

adhaḥ—downward; *cha*—and; *ūrdhvam*—upward; *prasṛitāḥ*—extended; *tasya*—its; *śhākhāḥ*—branches; *guṇa*—modes of material nature; *pravṛiddhāḥ*—nourished; *viṣhaya*—objects of the senses; *pravālāḥ*—buds; *adhaḥ*—downward; *cha*—and; *mūlāni*—roots; *anusantatāni*—keep growing; *karma*—actions; *anubandhīni*—bound; *manuṣhya-loke*—in the world of humans.

The branches of the tree extend upward and downward, nourished by the three gunas, with the objects of the senses as tender buds. The roots of the tree hang downward, causing the flow of karma in the

human form. Below, its roots branch out causing (karmic) actions in the world of humans.

Shree Krishna continues comparing the material creation with the *aśhvatth* tree. The main trunk of the tree is the human form in which the soul performs karmas. The branches (*śhākhās*) of the tree extend both downward (*adhaḥ*) and upward (*ūrddhva*). If the soul commits sinful activities, it is reborn either in the animal species or in the nether regions. These are the downward branches. If the soul performs virtuous acts, it is reborn in the celestial abodes as a *gandharva*, *devatā*, or another being in those abodes. These are the upward branches.

As a tree is irrigated by water, this tree of material existence is irrigated by the three modes of material nature. These three modes generate sense objects that are like the buds on the tree (*viṣhaya-pravālāḥ*). The function of buds is to sprout and cause further growth. The buds on this *aśhvatth* tree sprout and create material desires that are like the aerial roots of the tree. The specialty of banyan trees is that they send down aerial roots from the branches to the ground. Hence, the aerial roots become secondary trunks enabling banyan trees to grow to vast sizes. The biggest known banyan tree is 'The Great Banyan' in the Botanical Garden of Kolkata. The area occupied by the tree is more than four acres. The crown of the tree has a circumference of about 485 meters, and there are about 3,700 aerial roots reaching down to the ground. Similarly, in the analogy of the *aśhvatth* tree, in the material world, the sense objects are like the buds on the tree. They sprout and evoke desires for sensual enjoyment in the individual. These desires are compared to the aerial roots of the tree. They provide nutrients for the tree to keep growing. Impelled by desires for material enjoyment, the living being engages in karma. But sensual desires are never fulfilled; rather, they only multiply as we try to satiate them. Thus, the aerial roots of this metaphorical tree keep expanding in size and growing unlimitedly. In this way, they entangle the soul further in material consciousness.

न रूपमस्येह तथोपलभ्यते
नान्तो न चादिर्न च सम्प्रतिष्ठा ।
अश्वत्थमेनं सुविरूढमूल
मसङ्गशस्त्रेण दृढेन छित्त्वा ।।3।।

ततः पदं तत्परिमार्गितव्यं
यस्मिन्गता न निवर्तन्ति भूयः ।
तमेव चाद्यं पुरुषं प्रपद्ये
यतः प्रवृत्तिः प्रसृता पुराणी ।।4।।

na rūpam asyeha tathopalabhyate
nānto na chādir na cha sampratiṣhṭhā
aśhvattham enaṁ su-virūḍha-mūlam
asaṅga-śhastreṇa dṛiḍhena chhittvā

tataḥ padaṁ tat parimārgitavyaṁ
yasmin gatā na nivartanti bhūyaḥ
tam eva chādyaṁ puruṣhaṁ prapadye
yataḥ pravṛittiḥ prasṛitā purāṇī

na—not; *rūpam*—form; *asya*—of this; *iha*—in this world; *tathā*—as such; *upalabhyate*—is perceived; *na*—neither; *antaḥ*—end; *na*—nor; *cha*—also; *ādiḥ*—beginning; *na*—never; *cha*—also; *sampratiṣhṭhā*—the basis; *aśhvattham*—sacred fig tree; *enam*—this; *su-virūḍha-mūlam*—deep-rooted; *asaṅga-śhastreṇa*—by the axe of detachment; *dṛiḍhena*—strong; *chhittvā*—having cut down; *tataḥ*—then; *padam*—place; *tat*—that; *parimārgitavyam*—one must search out; *yasmin*—where; *gatāḥ*—having gone; *na*—not; *nivartanti*—return; *bhūyaḥ*—again; *tam*—to him; *eva*—certainly; *cha*—and; *ādyam*—original; *puruṣham*—the Supreme Lord; *prapadye*—take refuge; *yataḥ*—whence; *pravṛittiḥ*—the activity; *prasṛitā*—streamed forth; *purāṇi*—very old.

The real form of this tree is not perceived in this world, neither its beginning, nor end, nor its continued existence. But this deep-rooted *aśhvatth* tree must be cut down with a strong axe of detachment. Then one must search out the base of the tree, which is the Supreme Lord,

from whom streamed forth the activity of the universe a long time ago. Upon taking refuge in Him, one will not return to this world again.

The embodied souls immersed in samsara, or the perpetual cycle of life and death, are unable to comprehend the nature of this *aśhvatth* tree. They find the buds of the tree to be very attractive i.e., they are lured by the objects of the senses and develop desires for them. To fulfil these desires, they undertake great endeavours without realising that their efforts only nourish the tree to grow even further. When desires are satiated, they come back with redoubled intensity in the form of greed. When they are obstructed, they give rise to anger, which bewilders the intellect and deepens the ignorance.

Shree Krishna explains that this riddle of the *aśhvatth* tree is understood only by a few. All that the soul understands is 'I am Ramprasad, son of Hariprasad, and so on. I am living in this town of this country. I want to maximise my happiness. So, I act according to my bodily identification, but happiness eludes me, and I become confused.' Not comprehending the origin and nature of the tree, the living being engages in worthless actions. To satiate one's materialistic desires, a human being sometimes commits sins and goes downward into the lower species and the nether regions of the material world. Sometimes, the propensity for material enjoyment attracts one to the leaves of the tree, which are the ritualistic ceremonies of the Vedas. By engaging in these activities, one goes upward to the celestial abodes, only to come back again when the pious merits are depleted. This is why, Chaitanya Mahaprabhu said:

kṛiṣhṇa bhuli 'sei jīva anādi-bahirmukha
ataeva māyā tāre deya samsāra-duḥkha
kabhu swarge uṭhāya, kabhu narake ḍubāya
daṇḍya-jane rājā yena nadīte chubāya

(*Chaitanya Charitāmṛit, Madhya Leela* 20.117–118)

'Since the soul is forgetful of God since eternity, the material energy is subjecting it to worldly miseries. Sometimes, it lifts the soul to the celestial abodes, and other times it drops it down to the hellish regions.

This is akin to the torture meted out by kings in olden times.' As a form of torture, ancient kings would have a person's head ducked into the water until he was close to suffocation, and then release him for a few gasps, only to duck him in again. The situation of the soul is similar to this. It finds temporary relief in the celestial abodes, only to be dropped back on earth again.

In this manner, endless lifetimes have passed. All the endeavours of the soul for material enjoyment only result in expanding the tree further by sending more roots to the ground. Shree Krishna says that the axe to cut this tree is dispassion. The word *asaṅg* means detachment, and it is the remedy for the soul's endless miseries. Desires fuelled by the three modes of material nature will have to be destroyed by the axe of detachment. This axe should be made from knowledge of the self: 'I am an eternal spiritual being and not this material body. The eternal divine bliss that I seek will never be attained from material things. The material desires that I harbour while thinking that I am the body only perpetuate my existence in the samsara of life and death. There is no satiation or respite in this direction.' When one develops detachment, further growth of the tree stops, and it starts withering.

We must then search for the base of this tree, which is situated above the roots and is higher than everything else. That base is the Supreme Lord, as Shree Krishna previously stated: 'I am the origin of all creation. Everything proceeds from Me. The wise who know this perfectly worship Me with great faith and devotion.' (verse 10.8) Thus, finding the original source of the tree, we must surrender to it in the manner described in this verse: 'I submit unto Him from Whom the universe came into being a long time ago.'

In this manner, the tree that was previously unfathomable and difficult to comprehend can be overcome. Shree Krishna had also previously stated: 'My divine energy, maya, consisting of the three modes of nature, is very difficult to overcome. But those who surrender unto Me cross over it easily.' (verse 7.14) Hence, on taking refuge of the Supreme Lord, the *aśhvatth* tree will be cut down. We will not have to return to this world again and will go to His divine abode after death. *Shree Krishna discloses in the following verse what the process of surrender entails.*

निर्मानमोहा जितसङ्गदोषा
अध्यात्मनित्या विनिवृत्तकामाः ।
द्वन्द्वैर्विमुक्ताः सुखदुःखसंज्ञै
गच्छन्त्यमूढाः पदमव्ययं तत् ।।5।।

nirmāna-mohā jita-saṅga-doṣhā
adhyātma-nityā vinivṛitta-kāmāḥ
dvandvair vimuktāḥ sukha-duḥkha-sanjñair
gachchhanty amūḍhāḥ padam avyayaṁ tat

niḥ—free from; *māna*—vanity; *mohāḥ*—delusion; *jita*—having overcome; *saṅga*—attachment; *doṣhāḥ*—evils; *adhyātma-nityāḥ*—dwelling constantly on the self and on God; *vinivṛitta*—free from; *kāmāḥ*—desire to enjoy senses; *dvandvaiḥ*—from the dualities; *vimuktāḥ*—liberated; *sukha-duḥkha*—pleasure and pain; *saṁjñaiḥ*—known as; *gachchhanti*—attain; *amūḍhāḥ*—unbewildered; *padam*—abode; *avyayam*—eternal; *tat*—that.

Those who are free from vanity and delusion, who have overcome the evil of attachment, who dwell constantly on the self and on God, who are free from the desire to enjoy the senses and are beyond the dualities of pleasure and pain, such liberated personalities attain My eternal abode.

Shree Krishna now explains how to surrender to the base of the tree that is the Supreme Lord. He says that first of all one must give up pride that is born of ignorance. The embodied soul, in illusion, presently thinks, 'I am the lord of all that I have, and in future, I shall possess even more. All this is for my enjoyment and happiness.' As long as we remain intoxicated by pride, we think of ourselves as the enjoyer of material nature. In such a state, we disregard the Lord and have no desire to surrender to His will.

This false notion of being the enjoyer must be removed with the help of knowledge. We must realise that material energy belongs to

God and is meant for His service. The soul too is a servant of God, and so, the present attitude of seeking enjoyment must be transformed into an attitude of service. For this, we must eliminate material attachments that pull the mind towards the world and away from God. Instead, we must attach the mind to God in an attitude of selfless service, understanding the true nature of the self as an eternal servant of God. The *Padma Puran* states:

dāsa bhūtamidaṁ tasya jagatsthāvara jangamam
śhrīmannārāyaṇa swāmī jagatāṁprabhurīśhwaraḥ

'The Supreme Lord Narayan is the Controller and the Lord of the world. All moving and non-moving beings and entities in this creation are His servants.' Hence, the more we develop the desire to serve God, the more the illusion of being the enjoyer of prakriti will be dispelled and the heart will become cleansed. Jagadguru Shree Kripaluji Maharaj emphasised this point above everything else, as the most powerful means for purifying the heart:

sau bātana kī bāta ika, dharu muralīdhara dhyāna,
baṛhavahu sevā-vāsanā, yaha sau jñānana jñāna

(*Bhakti Śhatak*, verse 74)

'Out of a hundred advices for purification, the most important is this: Let your mind be absorbed in the divine flute-player, Shree Krishna, and keep increasing your desire to serve Him. This counsel is more important than a hundred such gems of knowledge.'

Once we succeed in cleansing our etheric hearts and become perfectly situated in loving service of God, then what happens? Shree Krishna explains in this verse that such perfected souls go to the spiritual realm for the rest of eternity. When the state of God-consciousness is achieved, the material realm serves no further purpose. The soul is then qualified to reside in God's divine abode along with other God-realised souls. Just as a prison occupies only a small part of a city, so too is the material realm. It is only one-fourth of God's entire creation, while the spiritual realm is three-fourths. The Vedas state:

pādo 'sya viśhwā bhūtāni, tripādasya amṛitam divi

(*Purush Sūktam*, mantra 3)

'This temporary world made from the material energy is but one part of creation. The other three parts is the eternal abode of God that is beyond the phenomenon of life and death.' *Shree Krishna explains the nature of that eternal abode in the following verse.*

न तद्भासयते सूर्यो न शशाङ्को न पावकः ।
यद्गत्वा न निवर्तन्ते तद्धाम परमं मम ।।6।।

na tad bhāsayate sūryo na śhaśhāṅko na pāvakaḥ
yad gatvā na nivartante tad dhāma paramaṁ mama

na—neither; *tat*—that; *bhāsayate*—illumine; *sūryaḥ*—the sun; *na*—nor; *śhaśhāṅkaḥ*—the moon; *na*—nor; *pāvakaḥ*—fire; *yat*—where; *gatvā*—having gone; *na*—never; *nivartante*—they return; *tat*—that; *dhāma*—abode; *paramam*—supreme; *mama*—mine.

Neither the sun nor the moon, nor fire can illumine that supreme abode of Mine. Having gone There, one does not return to this material world again.

Here, Shree Krishna gives a brief idea of the nature of the divine realm. The sun, moon, and fire are not required to illuminate this spiritual abode as it is naturally self-luminous. While the material realm is made from the material energy, maya, the divine realm is made from the spiritual energy, *Yogmaya*. It is transcendental to the dualities and defects of material nature and is perfect in every way. It is *sat-chit-anand* i.e., full of eternality, knowledge, and bliss.

That divine realm consists of a spiritual sky, called *Paravyom*, which contains numerous abodes full of godly opulence and splendours. All the eternal forms of God, such as Krishna, Ram, Narayan, and others have Their own abodes in that spiritual sky, where They reside eternally with Their devotees and engage in divine pastimes (leelas). Brahma states in his prayers to Shree Krishna:

goloka-nāmni nija-dhāmni tale cha tasya
devī maheśha-hari-dhāmasu teṣhu teṣhu
te te prabhāva-nichayā vihitāśh cha yena
govindam ādi-puruṣhaṁ tam ahaṁ bhajāmi

(*Brahma Samhitā* verse 43)

'In the spiritual sky is *Golok*, the personal abode of Shree Krishna. That spiritual sky also contains the abodes of Narayan, Shiv, Durga, etc. I adore Supreme Divine Personality Lord Krishna, by the majesty of whose opulence, this is possible.' About *Golok*, the divine abode of Shree Krishna, Brahma further says:

ānanda-chinmaya-rasa-pratibhāvitābhis
tābhir ya eva nija-rūpatayā kalābhiḥ
goloka eva nivasaty akhilātma-bhūto
govindam ādi-puruṣhaṁ tam ahaṁ bhajāmi

(*Brahma Samhitā* verse 37)

'I worship Govind, the Supreme Lord, who resides in *Golok* with the expansion of His own form, Radha. Their eternal associates are the *sakhis*, who are enlivened by the ever-blissful spiritual energy and are the embodiments of sixty-four artistic abilities.' The devotees who attain God and go to His supreme abode participate in His divine pastimes that are imbued with the perfection of the spiritual energy. Shree Krishna assures Arjun that those souls who go there cross the samsara of birth and death.

ममैवांशो जीवलोके जीवभूतः सनातनः ।
मनःषष्ठानीन्द्रियाणि प्रकृतिस्थानि कर्षति ।।7।।

mamaivānśho jīva-loke jīva-bhūtaḥ sanātanaḥ
manaḥ-ṣhaṣhṭhānīndriyāṇi prakṛiti-sthāni karṣhati

mama—My; *eva*—only; *anśhaḥ*—fragmental part; *jīva-loke*—in the material world; *jīva-bhūtaḥ*—the embodied souls; *sanātanaḥ*—eternal; *manaḥ*—with the mind; *ṣhaṣhṭhāni*—the six; *indriyāṇi*—senses; *prakṛiti-sthāni*—bound by material nature; *karṣhati*—struggling.

The embodied souls in this material world are My eternal fragmental parts. But bound by material nature, they are struggling with the six senses including the mind.

Shree Krishna previously explained that the souls who go to His abode do not come back. Now He speaks about the souls who remain in the material realm. First, He reassures that they are also His fragmental parts.

So, let us understand the kinds of parts that God has. They are of two kinds:

Swānśh: These are all the Avatars of God, such as Ram, Nrisingh, and Varaha. They are non-different from Shree Krishna, and thus They are called *swānśh* which means integrated parts.

Vibhinnānśh: These are the differentiated parts of God. They are not direct fragments of God, rather, they are parts of His soul energy (*jīva shakti*). In this category come all the souls in existence. This was stated by Shree Krishna in verse 7.5: 'But beyond the material energy, O mighty-armed Arjun, there is another superior energy of Mine. This is the embodied souls who are the basis of life in this world.'

Further, the *vibhinnānśh* souls are of three kinds:

Nitya siddha: These are the souls who were always liberated and have therefore resided in the divine realm of God since eternity, participating in His divine pastimes.

Sādhan siddha: These are the souls who were previously in the material realm, like us, but they practised sadhana and attained the Supreme Lord. Now they reside in the divine realm for the rest of eternity and participate in God's pastimes.

Nitya baddha: These are the souls who have been in the material realm since eternity. They are embodied with five senses and the mind, and consequently, are struggling.

The *Kaṭhopaniṣhad* states:

parāñchi khāni vyatṛiṇatsvayambhūḥ (2.1.1)

'The creator, Brahma, has made the senses such that they are turned outward towards the world.' For these *vibhinnānśh nitya baddha* parts, Shree Krishna states that they are struggling to satiate the mind and senses and experiencing misery in the process. *He now explains, in the following verse, what happens to the mind and senses as the soul moves into another body upon death.*

शरीरं यदवाप्नोति यच्चाप्युत्क्रामतीश्वरः ।
गृहीत्वैतानि संयाति वायुर्गन्धानिवाशयात् ।।8।।

śharīraṁ yad avāpnoti yach chāpy utkrāmatīśhvaraḥ
gṛihītvaitāni sanyāti vāyur gandhān ivāśhayāt

śharīram—the body; *yat*—as; *avāpnoti*—carries; *yat*—as; *cha api*—also; *utkrāmati*—leaves; *īśhvaraḥ*—lord of the material body, the embodied soul; *gṛihītvā*—taking; *etāni*—these; *sanyāti*—goes away; *vāyuḥ*—the air; *gandhān*—fragrance; *iva*—like; *āśhayāt*—from seats.

As the air carries fragrance from place to place, so does the embodied soul carry the mind and senses with it, when it leaves an old body and enters a new one.

The phenomenon of transmigration of the soul is explained here. The example given is of the breeze transporting the fragrance of flowers from one place to another. Likewise, when the soul departs at the time of death, it discards the gross body. But it carries with it the subtle and causal bodies, which include the mind and senses. (The three kinds of bodies were previously described in detail in verse 2.28.)

While the soul gets a new body in every life, the mind continues journeying with it from past lifetimes. This explains why even people who are blind from birth can see dreams. Usually, dreams are a result of the distortion of our visions and thoughts during the waking state that get disjointed and connected while asleep. For example, let us say that someone sees a bird flying and thinks, 'How nice it would be if I were a bird!' In the dream, he finds himself flying in the human body itself.

This is because the thoughts and visions of the waking state became distorted and linked in the dream state. However, a person who is blind from birth has never seen any forms and shapes, and yet that person can see dreams because impressions of the waking state are stored in the subconscious of the mind from endless past lifetimes. *Having explained that the soul takes the mind and senses with it when it departs from the body, Shree Krishna next explains what it does with these.*

श्रोत्रं चक्षुः स्पर्शनं च रसनं घ्राणमेव च ।
अधिष्ठाय मनश्चायं विषयानुपसेवते ।।9।।

śhrotraṁ chakṣhuḥ sparśhanaṁ cha rasanaṁ ghrāṇam eva cha
adhiṣhṭhāya manaśh chāyaṁ viṣhayān upasevate

śhrotram—ears; *chakṣhuḥ*—eyes; *sparśhanam*—the sense of touch; *cha*—and; *rasanam*—tongue; *ghrāṇam*—nose; *eva*—also; *cha*—and; *adhiṣhṭhāya*—grouped around; *manaḥ*—mind; *cha*—also; *ayam*—they; *viṣhayān*—sense objects; *upasevate*—savours.

Using the sense perceptions of the ears, eyes, skin, tongue, and nose, which are grouped around the mind, the embodied soul savours the objects of the senses.

Since the soul, being divine, cannot directly taste, touch, feel, smell, or hear, then how does it savour these perceptions? The answer is that the senses and the mind help it to do so. The senses and mind are actually insentient, but they are energised by consciousness of the soul and become lifelike. Hence, they perceive pleasure and pain from objects, situations, thoughts, and persons. Due to the ego, the soul identifies with the mind and senses, and vicariously perceives the same pleasures.

The problem is that while the soul itself is divine, the happiness it perceives in this manner is material. Thus, no matter how much pleasure the senses and mind bring to the soul, it remains dissatisfied. The feeling that it has still not reached its goal persists, and the search continues for perfect happiness that would truly satisfy it. The American philosopher, Ralph Waldo Emerson put this very beautifully:

'We grant that human life is mean. But how did we find out that it is mean? What is the ground of this uneasiness, of this old discontent? What is this universal sense of want and ignorance, but the fine innuendo by which the soul makes its enormous claim?'

Another famous philosopher, Meister Eckhart writes: 'There is something in the soul, which is above the living being, divine and simple. This light is only satisfied with the supra essential essence.'

The infinite, eternal, and divine bliss that the soul seeks can only be attained from God. When one realises this, the same senses and mind that were the cause of bondage can be turned in the direction of God and utilised as instruments of devotion. A wonderful example of this was Saint Tulsidas, who wrote the Hindi Ramayan.

In his youth, he was deeply attached to his wife. Once, she had gone to stay at her parents' home for a few days, when Tulsidas became eager to meet her. He set off on foot to his father-in-law's house, but there was a stream on the way and no boatman was willing to take him across, since it was raining heavily. A dead body came floating by. Absorbed in the longing to meet his wife, Tulsidas thought it was a piece of log. He clung to it and went across.

His desire to meet his wife, who was living on the second floor of the house, was overpowering him. A snake was hanging from the wall. Tulsidas did not see it carefully and thought it to be a rope. So, rather than waste time by knocking at the main door, he grabbed the snake and climbed up. When he came in through the window, his wife was astonished. She enquired how he crossed the river and climbed up the wall. He pointed outside to what he had mistaken to be the log of wood and the rope. She was shocked to see the dead body and the snake. She exclaimed, 'You have such desire for this body made of blood and flesh. If only you had desired God so intensely you would never have to take birth in this world again!'

His wife's words hit him so hard that he realised his folly and became detached. He renounced his household and went to engage in devotion. He practiced hard and the desires of his same mind and senses that had troubled him in the past were now redirected towards God. Thus, by the process of devotion, he purified himself and became the great poet Saint Tulsidas. Later, he wrote:

kāmihi nāri piāri jimi lobhihi priya jimi dāma,
timi raghunātha nirantara priya lāgahu mohi rāma (Ramayan)

'As a lustful man desires a beautiful woman, and as an avaricious person desires wealth, may my mind and senses constantly desire Lord Ram.'

उत्क्रामन्तं स्थितं वापि भुञ्जानं वा गुणान्वितम् ।
विमूढा नानुपश्यन्ति पश्यन्ति ज्ञानचक्षुषः ।।10।।

utkrāmantaṁ sthitaṁ vāpi bhuñjānaṁ vā guṇānvitam
vimūḍhā nānupaśhyanti paśhyanti jñāna-chakṣhuṣhaḥ

utkrāmantam—departing; *sthitam*—residing; *vā api*—or even; *bhuñjānam*—enjoys; *vā*—or; *guṇa-anvitam*—under the spell of the modes of material nature; *vimūḍhāḥ*—the ignorant; *na*—not; *anupaśhyanti*—perceive; *paśhyanti*—behold; *jñāna-chakṣhuṣhaḥ*—those who possess the eyes of knowledge.

The ignorant do not perceive the soul as it resides in the body and as it enjoys sense objects; nor do they perceive it when it departs. But those who possess the eyes of knowledge can behold it.

Although the soul is seated within the body and savours the perceptions of the mind and senses, not everyone cognises this. The reason is that the soul is non-material and cannot be seen or touched by the material senses. Scientists cannot detect it in laboratories with their instruments, so they mistakenly conclude that the body is the self. This is like a mechanic trying to figure out how a car moves. He traces the movement of the wheels backwards and reaches the accelerator, the ignition switch, and the steering wheel. He labels these as the car's causes of motion without realising that it is a driver who operates these. Similarly, without knowledge of the existence of the soul, physiologists conclude that the physical parts together are the source of life within the body.

However, those who have walked the path of spirituality see with eyes of knowledge that the soul energises these bodily parts. When it departs, even though all the different organs of the material body such as the heart, brain, lungs, and so on are all there, consciousness ceases to exist. Consciousness is a symptom of the soul; it is present in the body as long as the soul is present and leaves when the soul leaves. Only those who possess the eyes of knowledge (*jnana chakṣhu*) can see this. Shree Krishna says here that the ignorant (*vimūḍha*), unaware of their own divine identity, presume the corporeal body to be the self.

यतन्तो योगिनश्चैनं पश्यन्त्यात्मन्यवस्थितम् ।
यतन्तोऽप्यकृतात्मानो नैनं पश्यन्त्यचेतसः ।।11।।

yatanto yoginaśh chainaṁ paśhyanty ātmany avasthitam
yatanto 'py akṛitātmāno nainaṁ paśhyanty achetasaḥ

yatantaḥ—striving; *yoginaḥ*—yogis; *cha*—too; *enam*—this (the soul); *paśhyanti*—see; *ātmani*—in the body; *avasthitam*—enshrined; *yatantaḥ*—strive; *api*—even though; *akṛita-ātmānaḥ*—those whose minds are not purified; *na*—not; *enam*—this; *paśhyanti*—cognize; *achetasaḥ*—unaware.

Striving yogis too are able to realise the soul enshrined in the body. However, those whose minds are not purified cannot cognize it, even though they strive to do so.

To strive for knowledge is not enough; our endeavour must also be properly directed. Humans make the mistake that they seek to know divine entities by the same means as they have gotten to know the world. They take the perception of their senses and the power of their intellect as the basis for deciding the rightness and wrongness of all knowledge. They presume that if their senses cannot perceive something and their intellect cannot comprehend it, then that entity cannot exist. And because the soul cannot be perceived by their senses, they conclude that there is no such entity. Describing this phenomenon, Alexis Carrel states in his book, *Man the Unknown*:

Our mind has a natural tendency to reject the things that do not fit into the frame of scientific or philosophical beliefs of our time. After all, scientists are only human. They are saturated with the prejudices of their environment and epoch. They willingly believe that facts which cannot be explained by current theories do not exist. At present times, scientists still look upon telepathy and other metaphysical phenomena as illusions. Evident facts having an unorthodox appearance are suppressed.

The *Nyaya Darshan* calls this kind of thinking as *kūpa-maṇḍūka-nyāya* (the logic of the frog in the well).

A frog lived in a well and was very familiar with the dimensions of its own dwelling. One day, a Rana Cancrivora (a species of frogs that lives in the ocean) jumped into the well. They began chatting with each other. The frog of the well asked the ocean frog, 'How big is this ocean from where you have come?'

The Rana Cancrivora replied, 'It is very big.'

'Is it five times the size of the well?'

'No, much bigger.'

'Is it ten times the size of the well?'

'No, even bigger.'

'Hundred times?'

'No, that is nothing. It is far bigger.'

'You are lying,' the frog of the well said, 'How can anything be more than hundred times the size of my well?'

Its intellect had been conditioned by the lifelong experience of the well. As a result, it could not conceive of the vast ocean. Similarly, limited by the experience of their tiny intellects, materialistic people refuse to accept the possibility of the existence of the non-material soul. However, those who pursue the spiritual path realise that there can be knowledge beyond the purview of their material intellects. With humility and faith, they begin treading the spiritual path and aim to purify their hearts. When the mind becomes cleansed, the presence of the soul is naturally perceived. Then the truth of the scriptures is experienced through realisation.

Just as the senses cannot initially cognize the soul, God too, is not under their purview and has to be perceived through the eyes of knowledge. In the following verses, Shree Krishna shares the method for perceiving the existence of God.

यदादित्यगतं तेजो जगद्भासयतेऽखिलम् ।
यच्चन्द्रमसि यच्चाग्नौ तत्तेजो विद्धि मामकम् ।।12।।

yad āditya-gataṁ tejo jagad bhāsayate 'khilam
yach chandramasi yach chāgnau tat tejo viddhi māmakam

yat—which; *āditya-gatam*—in the sun; *tejaḥ*—brilliance; *jagat*—solar system; *bhāsayate*—illuminates; *akhilam*—entire; *yat*—which; *chandramasi*—in the moon; *yat*—which; *cha*—also; *agnau*—in the fire; *tat*—that; *tejaḥ*—brightness; *viddhi*—know; *māmakam*—mine.

Know that I am like the brilliance of the sun that illuminates the entire solar system. The radiance of the moon and the brightness of the fire also come from Me.

Our human nature is such that we are attracted towards what we feel is significant. By regarding the body, spouse, children, and wealth as significant, we become attracted to them. In these verses, Shree Krishna reveals that it is His energy which manifests in all significant things in creation. He says He is responsible for the effulgence of the sun. Scientists estimate that the sun emits as much energy as millions of nuclear power plants every second. It has been doing so since billions of years, and yet, it has neither been depleted, nor has anything gone wrong in its processes. To think that such an amazing celestial body as the sun came into being by random probability, as a result of a big bang, is naive. The sun is what it is by the glory of God.

Similarly, the moon performs an amazing function by lighting up the night sky. Through mundane intellect, we may conclude scientifically that the moonshine just happens to exist because of the reflection of the sun's light. However, this amazing arrangement has been brought into place by God's opulence, and the moon is one of the many manifestations of God's *vibhūtis* (opulences).

In this context, there is a story in the *Kenopaniṣhad*:

It relates that there was a prolonged war between the *devatās* (celestial gods) and the *daityas* (demons residing in the nether regions), in which the *devatās* finally won. However, their victory led to pride, and they began thinking they had secured it by their own prowess. To destroy their pride, God manifested as a *yakṣha* (a semi-celestial being) and situated Himself in the celestial sky. His form was exceedingly effulgent.

Indra, the king of heaven, first spotted Him and was astonished to see a mere *yakṣha* was more effulgent than him. He sent Agni, the fire god to enquire about Him. Agni went to the *yakṣha* and said, 'I am the fire god, and I possess the power to burn the entire universe to ashes in a moment. Now please reveal who You are.'

God, in the form of the *yakṣha*, put a blade of straw in front and said, 'Please burn this.'

Seeing it, Agni began laughing, 'Will this puny blade of grass be any test for my unlimited power?' However, when Agni lunged forward to burn it, God switched off his power source from inside him. Poor Agni himself began shivering with cold, so where was the question of burning anything else? He returned to Indra, embarrassed at his failure in the assigned task.

Indra then sent Vayu, the wind god to enquire into the personality of the *yakṣha*. Vayu went and announced, 'I am the wind god and, if I wish, in a moment I can turn the whole world upside down. Now You please reveal who You are.'

Again, God, in the form of the *yakṣha*, put the piece of straw in front of him and requested, 'Please turn this over.'

Seeing the straw, Vayu chuckled. He moved ahead with great speed, but in the meantime, God switched off his energy source too. Poor Vayu found it extremely difficult even to drag even his own feet, so where was the question of turning anything else over?

Finally, Indra himself went to determine who the *yakṣha* was. However, when Indra came, God disappeared, and in His place, His divine *Yogmaya* power, Uma, was seated. When Indra enquired from Her about the *yakṣha*, Uma replied, 'He was your Supreme Father, from Whom all of you celestial gods derive your strength. He had come to destroy your pride.'

गामाविश्य च भूतानि धारयाम्यहमोजसा ।
पुष्णामि चौषधीः सर्वाः सोमो भूत्वा रसात्मकः ।।13।।

gām āviśhya cha bhūtāni dhārayāmy aham ojasā
puṣhṇāmi chauṣhadhīḥ sarvāḥ somo bhūtvā rasātmakaḥ

gām—earth; *āviśhya*—permeating; *cha*—and; *bhūtāni*—living beings; *dhārayāmi*—sustain; *aham*—I; *ojasā*—energy; *puṣhṇāmi*—nourish; *cha*—and; *auṣhadhīḥ*—plants; *sarvāḥ*—all; *somaḥ*—the moon; *bhūtvā*—becoming; *rasa-ātmakaḥ*—supplying the juice of life.

Permeating the earth, I nourish all living beings with My energy. Becoming the moon, I nourish all plants with the juice of life.

The word *gām* means 'earth' and the word *ojasā* means 'energy'. The earth is a mass of matter, but by the power of God, it is made inhabitable, and it sustains various species of movable and non-movable living beings. For example, as children we wondered why the ocean water is salty. The fact is that if it were not salty, it would have bred disease in abundance and become uninhabitable. So, whatever the physical phenomena associated with it, ocean water is salty by the will of God. George Wald, a Nobel Prize winning scientist states in his book, *A Universe that Breeds Life*: 'If any one of the considerable number of the physical properties of our universe were other than they are, then life, that now appears to be so prevalent, would be impossible, here or anywhere.' From Shree Krishna's statement, we understand that it is God's energy which has brought about the appropriate physical properties for life to exist on the planet earth.

Further, the moonlight, which has the quality of ambrosial nectar, nourishes all plant life, such as herbs, vegetables, fruits, and grains. Shree Krishna states that it is He who imparts this nourishing characteristic to the moonlight.

अहं वैश्वानरो भूत्वा प्राणिनां देहमाश्रितः ।
प्राणापानसमायुक्तः पचाम्यन्नं चतुर्विधम् ।।14।।

ahaṁ vaiśhvānaro bhūtvā prāṇināṁ deham āśhritaḥ
prāṇāpāna-samāyuktaḥ pachāmy annaṁ chatur-vidham

aham—I; *vaiśhvānaraḥ*—fire of digestion; *bhūtvā*—becoming; *prāṇinām*—of all living beings; *deham*—the body; *āśhritaḥ*—situated; *prāṇa-apāna*—outgoing and incoming breath; *samāyuktaḥ*—keeping in balance; *pachāmi*—I digest; *annam*—foods; *chatuḥ-vidham*—the four kinds.

It is I who take the form of the fire of digestion in the stomachs of all living beings, and combine with the incoming and outgoing breaths, to digest and assimilate the four kinds of foods.

Scientists would attribute the forces of digestion to the gastric juices secreted by the gall bladder, pancreas, liver, and other organs involved in the process. However, this verse reveals that such thinking is again simplistic. Behind all these gastric juices is God's energy that works to make the process of digestion possible. The *vaiśhvānara*, meaning, 'fire of digestion' is ignited by the power of God. The *Bṛihadāraṇyak Upanishad* also states:

ayam agnir vaiśhvānaro yo 'yam antaḥ puruṣhe
yenedam annaṁ pachyate (5.9.1)

'God is the fire inside the stomach that enables living beings to digest food.'

The four kinds of food (*chaturvidham*) alluded to in this verse are: 1. *Bhojya*: These include foods that are chewed with the teeth, such as bread, chapatti, and others. 2. *Peya*: These are foods that are swallowed, such as milk, juice, etc. 3. *Kośhya*: These are foods that are sucked, such as sugarcane. 4. *Lehya*: These include foods that are licked, such as honey, ice cream cone, etc.

In verses 12 to 14, Shree Krishna explained that God makes all aspects of life possible. He energises the earth to make it inhabitable. He energises the moon to nourish all vegetation, and He becomes the gastric fire to digest the four kinds of food. He now concludes this topic in the next verse by stating that He alone is the goal of all knowledge.

सर्वस्य चाहं हृदि सन्निविष्टो
मत्तः स्मृतिर्ज्ञानमपोहनं च ।
वेदैश्च सर्वैरहमेव वेद्यो
वेदान्तकृद्वेदविदेव चाहम् ।।15।।

sarvasya chāhaṁ hṛidi sanniviṣhṭo
mattaḥ smṛitir jñānam apohanaṁ cha
vedaiśh cha sarvair aham eva vedyo
vedānta-kṛid veda-vid eva chāham

sarvasya—of all living beings; *cha*—and; *aham*—I; *hṛidi*—in the hearts; *sanniviṣhṭaḥ*—seated; *mattaḥ*—from me; *smṛitiḥ*—memory; *jñānam*—knowledge; *apohanam*—forgetfulness; *cha*—as well as; *vedaiḥ*—by the Vedas; *cha*—and; *sarvaiḥ*—all; *aham*—I; *eva*—alone; *vedyaḥ*—to be known; *vedānta-kṛit*—the author of the Vedant; *veda-vit*—the knower of the meaning of the Vedas; *eva*—alone; *cha*—and; *aham*—I.

I am seated in the hearts of all living beings, and from Me come memory, knowledge, as well as forgetfulness. I alone am to be known by all the Vedas, am the author of the *Vedant*, and the knower of the meaning of the Vedas.

God has created within us an amazing mechanism equipped with the faculties of knowledge and memory. The brain is its hardware, and the mind and intellect are like its software. We often take this mechanism for granted. Surgeons perform a brain transplant and become proud of their feat, but they do not stop to ponder how this amazing mechanism of the brain was created. There are still many areas where, despite all the progress in technology, computers cannot compare with the functioning of the human brain. For example, software engineers are still working on perfecting face-recognition technology, while humans can easily recognise people even after their looks change. This is why, we hear remarks such as, 'Dear friend, it is so nice to see you after such a long time. You have changed so much since we last met!' This demonstrates that the human brain can identify faces even though they change over the years, while computers cannot even perfectly recognise unchanged faces. At present, engineers are still struggling with scanner software that reads handwritten material flawlessly. In contrast, humans can perfectly understand even sketchy handwritings of others. Shree Krishna states that the amazing faculties of memory and knowledge come from Him.

Further, He also attributes the power of forgetfulness to Him. As unwanted records are destroyed, the living being does away with purposeless retention of memory, without which it would have been clogged with information. In the Shreemad Bhagavatam, Uddhav tells Shree Krishna:

tvatto jñānaṁ hi jīvānāṁ pramoṣhas te 'tra śhaktitaḥ

(11.22.28)

'From You alone the knowledge of the living being arises, and by Your potency that knowledge is stolen away.'

Apart from this internal faculty of knowledge that we possess, the external source of knowledge is the scriptures, and Shree Krishna reveals His glories in that context as well. It is He who manifested the Vedas at the beginning of creation. However, as God is divine and beyond the purview of the intellect, these Vedas are also divine. Hence, He alone knows their true meaning, and if He bestows His grace upon someone, then that fortunate soul also becomes a knower of the Vedas. Ved Vyas, who was an Avatar of God, wrote the *Vedant Darshan*. Thus, Shree Krishna states that He is the author of the *Vedant* as well.

Finally, He says that although the Vedas contain innumerable material and spiritual instructions, the object of all Vedic knowledge is to know Him. The fruitive ritualistic ceremonies are also there for a purpose. They lure people who are deeply attached to the material world, and provide them with an intermediate step, before directing them to God. The *Kaṭhopaniṣhad* (1.2.15) states: *sarve vedā yat padamāmananti* 'All the Vedic mantras are actually pointing towards God.' We may memorise all the Vedic mantras, learn to recite them in proper meter, master all the rites and rituals, engage in meditation, and even awaken the kundalini power, but if we do not know God, then we do not really understand the true objective of the Vedas. On the other hand, those who develop love for God automatically comprehend the purpose of all the Vedic scriptures. Jagadguru Shree Kripaluji Maharaj states:

sarva śhāstra sāra yaha govind rādhe,
āṭhoṅ yām mana hari guru meṅ lagā de

(*Radha Govind Geet*)

'The essence of all the scriptures is to engage your mind day and night in loving devotion to God and guru.'

In this chapter, Shree Krishna explained the tree of creation. Now while concluding the topic, He describes the terms kṣhar, akṣhar, and Purushottam in the next two verses, to put that knowledge in proper perspective.

द्वाविमौ पुरुषौ लोके क्षरश्चाक्षर एव च ।
क्षरः सर्वाणि भूतानि कूटस्थोऽक्षर उच्यते ।।16।।

dvāv imau puruṣhau loke kṣharaśh chākṣhara eva cha
kṣharaḥ sarvāṇi bhūtāni kūṭa-stho 'kṣhara uchyate

dvau—two; *imau*—these; *puruṣhau*—beings; *loke*—in creation; *kṣharaḥ*—the perishable; *cha*—and; *akṣharaḥ*—the imperishable; *eva*—even; *cha*—and; *kṣharaḥ*—the perishable; *sarvāṇi*—all; *bhūtāni*—beings; *kūṭa-sthaḥ*—the liberated; *akṣharaḥ*—the imperishable; *uchyate*—is said.

There are two kinds of beings in creation, the *kṣhar* (perishable) and

the *akṣhar* (imperishable). The perishable are all beings in the material realm. The imperishable are the liberated beings.

In the material realm, maya binds the individual soul to the material body. Although the soul itself is eternal, it repeatedly experiences the phenomenon of birth and death of the body. Thus, Shree Krishna calls the embodied living entities in the material world as *kṣhar* (perishable). This includes all the beings from the tiniest insect to the highest celestial gods.

Apart from these are the souls in the divine realm, the abode of God. These souls possess an immortal body in which they do not have to experience the phenomenon of death, and hence they are categorised as *akṣhar* (imperishable).

उत्तमः पुरुषस्त्वन्यः परमात्मेत्युदाहृतः ।
यो लोकत्रयमाविश्य बिभर्त्यव्यय ईश्वरः ।।17।।

uttamaḥ puruṣhas tv anyaḥ paramātmety udāhṛitaḥ
yo loka-trayam āviśhya bibharty avyaya īśhvaraḥ

uttamaḥ—the Supreme; *puruṣhaḥ*—Divine Personality; *tu*—but; *anyaḥ*—besides; *parama-ātmā*—the Supreme Soul; *iti*—thus; *udāhṛitaḥ*—is said; yaḥ—who; *loka trayam*—the three worlds; *āviśhya*—enters; *bibharti*—supports; *avyayaḥ*—indestructible; *īśhvaraḥ*—the controller.

Besides these, is the Supreme Divine Personality, who is the indestructible Supreme Soul. He enters the three worlds as the unchanging Controller and supports all living beings.

Having spoken about the world and the souls, Shree Krishna now speaks of God, who is transcendental to both worlds and to perishable and imperishable living beings. In the scriptures, He is also designated as Paramatma, meaning, 'Supreme Soul'. The epithet of *Param* highlights that Paramatma is different from the atma, or the individual soul. This verse clearly disproves the claim of the non-dualistic philosophers who state that the individual soul itself is the Supreme Soul.

The individual soul is tiny and only pervades the body that it resides in. However, the Supreme Soul resides in the hearts of all living beings. He notes their karmas, keeps an account of them, and gives the results at the appropriate moment. He accompanies the soul from lifetime to lifetime into whatever body it receives. If the soul is given a dog's body in a particular lifetime, the Supreme Soul accompanies it there as well, and bestows the results of past karmas. Thus, there is such a difference between the fortunes of dogs. Some are stray dogs living wretched lives in the streets of India, while others are pet dogs living in luxury in the United States. This stark difference takes place as a result of their stock of karmas, and it is the Supreme Soul who hands out the consequences of karmas.

The Supreme Soul who resides in the heart of all living beings also exists in the personal form as the four-armed Kshirodakshayi Vishnu (more commonly known as 'Vishnu'). There is a popular saying in Hindi: *mārane vāle ke do hāth, bachāne vāle ke chār hāth* 'The person coming to kill has two arms, but the Protector sitting within has four arms.' This four-armed personality being referred to is the Paramatma or the Supreme Soul.

यस्मात्क्षरमतीतोऽहमक्षरादपि चोत्तमः ।
अतोऽस्मि लोके वेदे च प्रथितः पुरुषोत्तमः ।।18।।

yasmāt kṣharam atīto 'ham akṣharād api chottamaḥ
ato 'smi loke vede cha prathitaḥ puruṣhottamaḥ

yasmāt—hence; *kṣharam*—to the perishable; *atītaḥ*—transcendental; *aham*—I; *akṣharāt*—to the imperishable; *api*—even; *cha*—and; *uttamaḥ*—transcendental; *ataḥ*—therefore; *asmi*—I am; *loke*—in the world; *vede*—in the Vedas; *cha*—and; *prathitaḥ*—celebrated; *puruṣha-uttamaḥ*—as the Supreme Divine Personality.

I am transcendental to the perishable world of matter and even to the imperishable soul; hence I am celebrated, both in the Vedas and the Smritis, as the Supreme Divine Personality.

In the last few verses, Shree Krishna described in detail that the glorious things of nature are all manifestations of His opulence. However, He does not exhaust Himself in creating the visible universe. His transcendental personality is beyond both material nature and the divine souls. Here, He calls His divine personality as *Purushottam* (Supreme Person).

One may doubt whether Lord Krishna and the Supreme Being He is referring to are the same. To remove any such vestiges of misunderstanding, Shree Krishna phrases this verse so as to refer to Himself in the first person singular. Further, He says that the Vedas too proclaim Him in this manner:

kṛiṣhṇa eva paro devas taṁ dhyāyet taṁ rasayet taṁ yajet taṁ bhajed (*Gopāl Tāpani Upanishad*)

'Lord Krishna is the Supreme Lord. Meditate upon Him, relish the bliss of His devotion, and worship Him.' Again:

yo 'sau paraṁ brahma gopālaḥ (*Gopāl Tāpani Upanishad*)

'Gopal (Lord Krishna) is the Supreme Being.' One may then ask about the position of Lord Vishnu, Lord Ram, Lord Shiv, and others. They are all different forms of the same Supreme Being, and They are non-different from each other. As a result, They all are manifestations of Bhagavan or the Supreme Divine Personality.

यो मामेवमसम्मूढो जानाति पुरुषोत्तमम् ।
स सर्वविद्भजति मां सर्वभावेन भारत ।।19।।

yo mām evam asammūḍho jānāti puruṣhottamam
sa sarva-vid bhajati māṁ sarva-bhāvena bhārata

yaḥ—who; *mām*—me; *evam*—thus; *asammūḍhaḥ*—without a doubt; *jānāti*—know; *puruṣha-uttamam*—the Supreme Divine Personality; *saḥ*—they; *sarva-vit*—those with complete knowledge; *bhajati*—worship; *mām*—me; *sarva-bhāvena*—with one's whole being; *bhārata*—Arjun, son of Bharat.

Those who know Me without doubt as the Supreme Divine Personality truly have complete knowledge. O Arjun, they worship Me with their whole being.

The Shreemad Bhagavatam states that God can be realised in three ways:

> *vadanti tat tattva-vidas tattvaṁ yaj jñānam advayam*
> *brahmeti paramātmeti bhagavān iti śhabdyate* (1.2.11)

'The knowers of the Truth have stated that there is only one Supreme Entity that manifests in three ways in the world—Brahman, Paramatma, and Bhagavan.' These are not three different entities, but merely three manifestations of the same Supreme Entity. For example, water, ice, and steam may appear to be distinct entities, but they are actually three forms of the same substance. Similarly, Brahman is the aspect of God that is formless and all-pervading. Those who follow the path of jnana yog worship the Brahman aspect of God. Paramatma is the aspect of the Supreme Entity that resides in the hearts of all living beings as the Supreme Soul. The path of ashtang yog leads to the Paramatma realisation of God. Bhagavan is the aspect of the Lord that manifests in a personal form and performs sweet leelas (pastimes). The path of bhakti, or devotion, leads to the realisation of God in His Bhagavan aspect. This was also explained previously in verse 12.2.

In this chapter, from verse 12 onwards, Shree Krishna described all these three aspects of God. Verses 12 to 14 referred to the all-pervading Brahman manifestation, verse 17 mentioned the Paramatma aspect, and verse 18 talked about Bhagavan. Now, which of these realisations is the highest and most complete? He answers this question here by saying that those who know Him through bhakti as Bhagavan, the Supreme Divine Personality, truly have complete knowledge of Him. A detailed explanation of why the Bhagavan realisation is the highest is given by Jagadguru Shree Kripaluji Maharaj in his composition, *Bhakti Śhatak*. He begins by quoting the above-stated verse of the Shreemad Bhagavatam:

tīna rūp śhrī kṛiṣhṇa ko, vedavyās batāya,
brahma aura paramātmā, aru bhagavān kahāya

(*Bhakti Śhatak* verse 21)

'Ved Vyas has declared that the Supreme Lord manifests in three ways—Brahman, Paramatma, and Bhagavan.' Then he goes on to describe these three manifestations of the Absolute Truth.

sarvaśhakti sampann ho, śhakti vikāsa na hoya,
sat chit ānand rūp jo, brahma kahāve soya

(*Bhakti Śhatak* verse 22)

'As Brahman, the infinite energies of God are all latent. He merely displays eternal knowledge and bliss.'

sarvaśhakti sanyukta ho, nāma rūp guṇa hoya,
līlā parikara rahit ho, paramātmā hai soya

(*Bhakti Śhatak* verse 23)

'As Paramatma, God displays His Form, Name, and Virtues. But He does not engage in Leelas, nor does He have Associates.'

sarvaśhakti prākaṭya ho, līlā vividha prakāra,
viharata parikara sang jo, tehi bhagavān pukāra

(*Bhakti Śhatak* verse 24)

'The aspect of God in which He manifests all His energies and engages in various loving pastimes with His devotees is called Bhagavan.' These verses by Jagadguru Shree Kripaluji Maharaj clarify that in the Brahman and Paramatma manifestations, God does not reveal all His powers. The complete realisation of the Supreme Entity is as Bhagavan, in which He manifests all His Names, Forms, Virtues, Pastimes, Abodes, and Associates. (This has also been explained in verse 12.2 with the help of the example of a train.) Thus, those who know Him as Bhagavan, the Supreme Divine Personality, truly have complete knowledge.

इति गुह्यतमं शास्त्रमिदमुक्तं मयानघ ।
एतद्बुद्ध्वा बुद्धिमान्स्यात्कृतकृत्यश्च भारत ।।20।।

iti guhyatamaṁ śhāstram idam uktaṁ mayānagha
etad buddhvā buddhimān syāt kṛita-kṛityaśh cha bhārata

iti—these; *guhya-tamam*—most secret; *śhāstram*—Vedic scriptures; *idam*—this; *uktam*—spoken; *mayā*—by me; *anagha*—Arjun, the sinless one; *etat*—this; *buddhvā*—understanding; *buddhi-mān*—enlightened; *syāt*—one becomes; *kṛita-kṛityaḥ*—who fulfils all that is to be accomplished; *cha*—and; *bhārata*—Arjun, son of Bharat.

I have shared this most secret principle of the Vedic scriptures with you, O sinless Arjun. By understanding this, a person becomes enlightened and fulfils all that is to be accomplished.

The final verse of this chapter begins with the word *iti*, meaning, 'these'. Shree Krishna implies: 'In these twenty verses, I have summarised the import of all the Vedic scriptures. I have taken you from the description of the nature of the world, to the distinction between matter and spirit, and finally to the highest realisation of Absolute Truth as the Supreme Divine Personality. Now I give you My assurance that whoever embraces this knowledge will become truly enlightened. Such a soul will accomplish the goal of all works and duties, which is God-realisation.'

CHAPTER 16

Daivāsura Sampad Vibhāg Yog

Yog through Discerning the Divine and Demoniac Natures

In this chapter, Shree Krishna describes the two kinds of natures amongst human beings—the saintly and the demoniac. The saintly nature develops by following the instructions of the scriptures, cultivating the mode of goodness, and purifying the mind through spiritual practices. It leads to the enhancement of *daivī sampatti* (godly qualities), eventually culminating in God-realisation. In contrast, there is also the demoniac nature that develops from associating with the modes of passion and ignorance and embracing materialistic views. It breeds unwholesome traits in one's personality, and eventually throws the soul into hellish kinds of existence.

The chapter begins by describing the saintly virtues of those endowed with a divine nature. It then goes on to describe the demoniac qualities that must be scrupulously shunned because they drag the soul further into ignorance and the samsara of life and death. Shree Krishna concludes the chapter by saying that the scriptures should be our authority in determining right and wrong behaviour. We must understand these scriptural injunctions and then behave accordingly in this world.

श्रीभगवानुवाच ।
अभयं सत्त्वसंशुद्धिर्ज्ञानयोगव्यवस्थितिः ।
दानं दमश्च यज्ञश्च स्वाध्यायस्तप आर्जवम् ॥1॥

अहिंसा सत्यमक्रोधस्त्यागः शान्तिरपैशुनम् ।
दया भूतेष्वलोलुप्त्वं मार्दवं ह्रीरचापलम् ।।2।।

तेजः क्षमा धृतिः शौचमद्रोहोनातिमानिता ।
भवन्ति सम्पदं दैवीमभिजातस्य भारत ।।3।।

śhrī-bhagavān uvācha
abhayaṁ sattva-sanśhuddhir jñāna-yoga-vyavasthitiḥ
dānaṁ damaśh cha yajñaśh cha svādhyāyas tapa ārjavam

ahinsā satyam akrodhas tyāgaḥ śhāntir apaiśhunam
dayā bhūteṣhv aloluptvaṁ mārdavaṁ hrīr achāpalam

tejaḥ kṣhamā dhṛitiḥ śhaucham adroho nāti-mānitā
bhavanti sampadaṁ daivīm abhijātasya bhārata

śhrī-bhagavān uvācha—the Supreme Divine Personality said; *abhayam*—fearlessness; *sattva-sanśhuddhiḥ*—purity of mind; *jñāna*—knowledge; *yoga*—spiritual; *vyavasthitiḥ*—steadfastness; *dānam*—charity; *damaḥ*—control of the senses; *cha*—and; *yajñaḥ*—sacrifice; *cha*—and; *svādhyāyaḥ*—study of sacred books; *tapaḥ*—austerity; *ārjavam*—straightforwardness; *ahinsā*—non-violence; *satyam*—truthfulness; *akrodhaḥ*—absence of anger; *tyāgaḥ*—renunciation; *śhāntiḥ*—peacefulness; *apaiśhunam*—restraint from fault-finding; *dayā*—compassion; *bhūteṣhu*—towards all living beings; *aloluptvam*—absence of covetousness; *mārdavam*—gentleness; *hrīḥ*—modesty; *achāpalam*—lack of fickleness; *tejaḥ*—vigour; *kṣhamā*—forgiveness; *dhṛitiḥ*—fortitude; *śhaucham*—cleanliness; *adrohaḥ*—bearing enmity towards none; *na*—not; *ati-mānitā*—absence of vanity; *bhavanti*—are; *sampadam*—qualities; *daivīm*—godly; *abhijātasya*—of those endowed with; *bhārata*—scion of Bharat.

The Supreme Divine Personality said: O scion of Bharat, these are the saintly virtues of those endowed with a divine nature—fearlessness, purity of mind, steadfastness in spiritual knowledge, charity, control of the senses, sacrifice, study of the sacred books, austerity, and straightforwardness; non-violence, truthfulness, absence of anger,

renunciation, peacefulness, restraint from fault-finding, compassion towards all living beings, absence of covetousness, gentleness, modesty, and lack of fickleness; vigour, forgiveness, fortitude, cleanliness, bearing enmity towards none, and absence of vanity.

Here, Shree Krishna describes twenty-six virtues of a saintly nature. These should be cultivated as a part of our spiritual practice for elevating ourselves to the supreme goal.

Fearlessness: It is the state of freedom from concern for present and future miseries. Inordinate attachment of any kind causes fear. Attachment to wealth leads to dread of impoverishment, attachment to social prestige causes fear of infamy, attachment to vice leads to anxiety about the consequences of sin, attachment to bodily comfort causes the fear of ill health, and so on. Detachment and surrender to God vanquish all fear from the heart.

Purity of mind: This is the state of inner cleanliness. The mind generates and harbours thoughts, sentiments, feelings, and emotions. When these are ethical, wholesome, positive, and uplifting, the mind is considered pure, and when they are unethical and degrading, the mind is considered impure. Attachment to objects in the modes of passion and ignorance contaminate the mind, while attachment to God purifies it.

Steadfastness in spiritual knowledge: It is said: *tattva vismaraṇāt bhekivat* 'When human beings forget what is right and wrong, they become like animals.' Thus, the path of virtue is forged by remaining steadfast in the awareness of spiritual principles.

Charity: It refers to the giving away of one's possessions for a good cause or to needy persons. True charity is that which is done, not with a feeling of superiority, but with a sense of gratefulness to God for the opportunity to be of service. Material charity, done for the welfare of the body, benefits others temporarily. Spiritual charity, done at the platform of the soul, helps eliminate the cause of all suffering, which is separation from God. Consequently, it is considered higher than material charity.

Control of the senses: The senses are notorious in their ability to drag the mind deeper into material illusion. They tempt the living being to seek immediate gratification. However, walking the path of virtue requires forsaking the lower sensual pleasures for achieving the higher goal. Thus, restraint of the senses is an essential virtue for treading the path to God.

Sacrifice: It means executing one's Vedic duties and social obligations, even though they may not be enjoyable. Sacrifice is considered perfect when it is done for the pleasure of God.

Study of the sacred books: An important aspect of cultivating divine nature is to feed the intellect with uplifting knowledge from the scriptures. When the intellect is illumined with proper knowledge, one's actions naturally become sublime.

Austerity: The body-mind-senses are such that, if we pamper them, they become pleasure-seeking, but if we restrain them, they become disciplined. Thus, austerity is the voluntary acceptance of hardships for purifying the body, mind, and intellect.

Straightforwardness: Simplicity in speech and conduct unclutters the mind and engenders the sprouting of noble thoughts. The English phrase 'simple living, high thinking' aptly expresses the benefits of the virtue of straightforwardness.

Non-violence: It means not impeding the progressive life of other living beings through thought, word, or deed.

Truthfulness: It means restraining oneself from distorting facts to suit one's purpose. God is the Absolute Truth, and hence the practice of truthfulness takes us towards Him; on the other hand, falsehood, while convenient, takes us away from God.

Absence of anger: Manifestation of anger is a defect of the material mind. It takes place when the desires for happiness are obstructed and things do not turn out how one envisaged. One overcomes anger by developing detachment and surrendering to the will of God.

Renunciation: The entire material energy belongs to God and is for His pleasure. Hence, the opulences of the world are not for one's enjoyment, but to be utilised in the service of God. To be fixed in this understanding is renunciation.

Peacefulness: The cultivation of virtues requires mental poise. Peacefulness is the ability to retain inner equilibrium despite disturbing external situations.

Restraint from fault-finding: The whole world and everything in it is a mixture of good and bad qualities. Focusing upon defects in others dirties our mind, while focusing upon their virtues purifies it. The nature of a saintly person is to see his or her own defects and observe the virtues of others.

Compassion towards all living beings: As individuals evolve spiritually, they naturally rise above self-centredness and develop empathy for all living beings. Compassion is the deep sympathy that arises upon seeing the sufferings of others.w

Absence of covetousness: Greed is the desire to accumulate more than what one legitimately needs for the maintenance of the body. Under its sway, people acquire huge amounts of wealth and possessions, though they know that at the time of death, everything will be left behind. Freedom from such covetousness leads to contentment and inner peace.

Gentleness: The disposition of behaving roughly with others arises from insensitivity to their feelings. But as one grows in spiritual stature, one naturally stops crude behaviour. Gentleness is a sign of spiritual refinement.

Modesty: *Hrīḥ* means 'sense of guilt in performing actions contrary to the injunctions of scriptures and society.' The saintly nature is imbued with a ruthless inner conscience that gives one a sense of guilt while committing sinful acts.

Lack of fickleness: We may begin with good intentions, but if we get distracted by temptations and hardships, we cannot complete the journey. Success on the path of virtue comes by unwaveringly pursuing the goal despite all diversions on the way.

Vigour: From purity of mind comes a deep inner drive to act according to one's values and beliefs. Hence, saintly personalities bring immense power and vigour to the tasks they pursue.

Forgiveness or forbearance: This is the ability to tolerate the offences of others without feeling the need to retaliate. Through forgiveness, one heals the emotional wounds caused by others that would otherwise fester and disturb the mind.

Fortitude: It is the inner strength and determination to pursue a goal, even when the mind and senses are wearied due to unfavourable circumstances. Most of the important things in the world have been accomplished by people who kept on trying when there seemed to be no hope at all. Sri Aurobindo put this very eloquently: 'You have to be more persistent than the difficulty; there is no other way.'

Cleanliness: It refers to both internal and external purity. Virtuous people believe in maintaining external cleanliness because it is conducive to internal purity. George Bernard Shaw said, 'Better keep yourself clean and bright; you are the window through which you must see the world.'

Bearing enmity towards none: Bearing enmity towards others poisons our own mind, and this becomes an impediment in the path of spiritual progress. The quality of freedom from hatred towards others is developed by realising that they are also like us, and God resides in all.

Absence of vanity: Self-praise, boastfulness, and ostentation—all stem from pride. Saintly personalities see nothing in themselves to be proud about, but instead, feel gratitude to God for the good qualities they possess. Thus, they refrain from self-aggrandisement.

दम्भो दर्पोऽभिमानश्च क्रोधः पारुष्यमेव च ।
अज्ञानं चाभिजातस्य पार्थ सम्पदमासुरीम् ।।4।।

dambho darpo 'bhimānaśh cha krodhaḥ pāruṣhyam eva cha
ajñānaṁ chābhijātasya pārtha sampadam āsurīm

dambhaḥ—hypocrisy; *darpaḥ*—arrogance; *abhimānaḥ*—conceit; *cha*—and; *krodhaḥ*—anger; *pārushyam*—harshness; *eva*—certainly; *cha*—and; *ajñānam*—ignorance; *cha*—and; *abhijātasya*—of those who possess; *pārtha*—Arjun, son of Pritha; *sampadam*—qualities; *āsurīm*—demoniac.

O Parth, the qualities of those who possess a demoniac nature are hypocrisy, arrogance, conceit, anger, harshness, and ignorance.

Shree Krishna now expounds upon the six traits of those who possess a demoniac nature. They are hypocrites, meaning, they make an external show of virtuous behaviour for impressing others without possessing the matching internal traits. This creates an artificial Jekyll and Hyde personality, which is impure internally but has the external appearance of being pure.

The behaviour of demoniac-natured people is arrogant and disrespectful to others. They are proud and conceited about their material possessions and designations, such as wealth, education, beauty, position, and other tangibles and intangibles. They become angry when, due to lack of control of the mind, their lust and greed are frustrated. They are cruel and harsh, and devoid of sensitivity for others' sufferings in their interactions with them. They have no understanding of the spiritual principles and hold unrighteousness to be righteousness.

दैवी सम्पद्विमोक्षाय निबन्धायासुरी मता ।
मा शुचः सम्पदं दैवीमभिजातोऽसि पाण्डव ।।5।।

daivī sampad vimokṣhāya nibandhāyāsurī matā
mā śhuchaḥ sampadaṁ daivīm abhijāto 'si pāṇḍava

daivī—divine; *sampat*—qualities; *vimokṣhāya*—towards liberation; *nibandhāya*—to bondage; *āsurī*—demoniac qualities; *matā*—are considered; *mā*—do not; *śhuchaḥ*—grieve; *sampadam*—virtues; *daivīm*—saintly; *abhijātaḥ*—born; *asi*—you are; *pāṇḍava*—Arjun, son of Pandu.

The divine qualities lead to liberation, while the demoniac qualities are the cause for a continuing destiny of bondage. Grieve not, O Arjun, as you were born with saintly virtues.

Having described the two kinds of natures, Shree Krishna now declares the consequences of both. He says that the demoniac qualities keep one fettered to the samsara of life and death, while the cultivation of saintly virtues helps one break through the bondage of maya.

To tread the spiritual path successfully and pursue it till the end, a *sādhak* (aspirant) needs to watch out for many things. If even one of the demoniac qualities, such as arrogance, hypocrisy, etc. remains in the personality, it can become the cause of failure. Simultaneously, divine virtues need to be developed, for without saintly qualities, our spiritual progress can again become crippled. For example, without fortitude, we will give up the journey when the going becomes difficult; without forgiveness, the mind will be tied down to hatred, unable to stay absorbed in God. But if we possess the saintly virtues that Shree Krishna mentions, then our ability to progress rapidly and cope with obstacles on the path increases. Thus, developing good qualities and eliminating bad ones is an integral part of spiritual practice. A useful technique that helps us work on removing our weaknesses and developing virtues is the maintenance of a personal diary. Many successful people kept memoirs and diaries to help them develop the virtues they felt were necessary for success. Mahatma Gandhi and Benjamin Franklin both mention having used such techniques in their autobiographies.

Some may argue that if we develop devotion to God, we will naturally, over time, acquire the saintly virtues described by Shree Krishna. That is indeed true, but it is unlikely that we will start out on the path full of devotion from the outset itself, and free from all the negative traits, any one of which can dramatically interfere with devotional progress. Most people need to slowly develop bhakti through practice. Success in practice comes by developing saintly qualities and eliminating demoniac ones. Hence, as a part of our efforts in devotion, we must also keep working on ourselves to develop the divine qualities that Shree Krishna has mentioned in this chapter and shed any demoniac ones.

द्वौ भूतसर्गौ लोकेऽस्मिन्दैव आसुर एव च ।
दैवो विस्तरशः प्रोक्त आसुरं पार्थ मे शृणु ।।6।।

dvau bhūta-sargau loke 'smin daiva āsura eva cha
daivo vistaraśhaḥ prokta āsuraṁ pārtha me śhṛiṇu

dvau—two; *bhūta-sargau*—of created living beings; *loke*—in the world; *asmin*—this; *daivaḥ*—divine; *āsuraḥ*—demoniac; *eva*—certainly; *cha*—and; *daivaḥ*—the divine; *vistaraśhaḥ*—at great length; *proktaḥ*—said; *āsuram*—the demoniac; *pārtha*—Arjun, son of Pritha; *me*—from me; *śhṛiṇu*—hear.

There are two kinds of beings in this world—those endowed with a divine nature and those possessing a demoniac nature. I have described the divine qualities in detail, O Arjun. Now hear from Me about the demoniac nature.

All souls carry their natures with them from past lives. Accordingly, those who cultivated virtuous qualities and performed meritorious deeds in their past lives were born with divine natures, while those who indulged in sin and defiled their minds in previous lives carry the same tendencies into the present one. This explains the varieties of natures of living beings in the world. The divine and demoniac natures are the two extremes of this spectrum.

The living beings in the celestial abodes possess more virtuous qualities while the demoniac traits dominate in the lower abodes. Humans possess a mixture of both divine and demoniac traits. Even in the cruelest butcher, we sometimes find the quality of kindness existing in personal life. And even in elevated spiritual aspirants we find defects of virtue. It is said that in Satya Yug, the gods and demons lived on different planets (i.e., separate planes of existence); in *Tretā Yug*, they resided on the same planet; during *Dwāpar Yug*, they lived in the same family; and in Kali Yug, godly and demoniac natures coexist in the same person's heart. That is the dilemma of human existence, where the higher self pulls it upward towards God, while the lower self pulls it downward. *Having described the saintly qualities, Shree Krishna now goes into an extended description of the lower nature, to help us identify and avoid it.*

प्रवृत्तिं च निवृत्तिं च जना न विदुरासुराः ।
न शौचं नापि चाचारो न सत्यं तेषु विद्यते ।।7।।

pravṛittiṁ cha nivṛittiṁ cha janā na vidur āsurāḥ
na śhauchaṁ nāpi chāchāro na satyaṁ teṣhu vidyate

pravṛittim—proper actions; *cha*—and; *nivṛittim*—improper actions; *cha*—and; *janāḥ*—persons; *na*—not; *viduḥ*—comprehend; *āsurāḥ*—those possessing demoniac nature; *na*—neither; *śhaucham*—purity; *na*—nor; *api*—even; *cha*—and; *āchāraḥ*—conduct; *na*—nor; *satyam*—truthfulness; *teṣhu*—in them; *vidyate*—exist.

Those possessing a demoniac nature do not comprehend which actions are proper and which are improper. Hence, they possess neither purity, nor good conduct, nor even truthfulness.

Dharma consists of codes of conduct that are conducive to one's purification and the general welfare of all living beings. *Adharma* consists of prohibited actions that lead to degradation and cause harm to society. The demoniac nature is devoid of faith in the knowledge and wisdom of the scriptures. Hence, those under its sway are confused about what is right and wrong.

A typical example of this is the present trend in western philosophy. Having evolved through various schools of thought after the Renaissance, such as the Ages of Enlightenment, Humanism, Empiricism, Communism, Existentialism, and Scepticism, the present era in western philosophy is labeled as 'Postmodernism'. The prevalent view of Postmodernist thought is that there is no Absolute Truth. Multitudes have rejected the possibility that such a thing as Absolute Truth could exist. 'All is relative' has become the slogan of the Postmodernist era of philosophy. We often hear phrases like

'That may be true for you, but it's not true for me.' Truth is seen as a personal preference or perception that cannot extend beyond a person's individual boundaries. This viewpoint has a big bearing on the subject of ethics which deals with the question of right and wrong behaviour. If there is no such thing as Absolute Truth, then there is no ultimate moral rightness or wrongness about anything. Then, people are justified in saying, 'It may be right for you but that does not mean it is right for me.'

Such an idea is very appealing to many, but if taken to its logical extreme, it proves absurd and disastrous. For example, what if it is right for someone to ignore traffic lights even when they are red? That person will put the life of others at risk by doing what he believes is right. What if it is considered right by someone to go on a suicide-bombing mission in a heavily populated civilian area against people he perceives as enemies? He may be fully convinced that what he is doing is correct. But does that make it right in any sense of the word? If there is no such thing as Absolute Truth, then no one can really say 'he should do that' or 'she shouldn't do that.' All one can say is, 'A lot of people do not feel good about this action.' According to the Relativist viewpoint, one might respond, 'That may be true for you, but it is certainly not true for us.' There can be the ruinous ethical consequences of disregarding the belief of an Absolute Truth.

Shree Krishna states that the demoniac nature is confused about what is right and what is wrong, and thus, neither purity, nor truth, nor right conduct is found in them. *In the following verse, He goes on to describe the predominant views of such people.*

असत्यमप्रतिष्ठं ते जगदाहुरनीश्वरम् ।
अपरस्परसम्भूतं किमन्यत्कामहैतुकम् ।।8।।

asatyam apratiṣhṭhaṁ te jagad āhur anīśhvaram
aparaspara-sambhūtaṁ kim anyat kāma-haitukam

asatyam—without Absolute Truth; *apratiṣhṭham*—without any basis; *te*—they; *jagat*—the world; *āhuḥ*—say; *anīśhvaram*—without a God; *aparaspara*—without cause; *sambhūtam*—

created; *kim*—what; *anyat*—other; *kāma-haitukam*—for sexual gratification only.

They say, 'The world is without Absolute Truth, without any basis (for moral order), and without a God (who has created or is controlling it). It is created from the combination of the two sexes and has no purpose other than sexual gratification.'

There are two ways of refraining from immoral behaviour. The first is to refrain from unrighteousness through the exercise of willpower. The second way is to abstain from sin due to fear of God. People who have the ability to abstain from sinning merely by willpower are very few. The majority desist from doing wrong due to the fear of punishment. For example, it is observed on highways that the moment a police car is spotted, people immediately slow down to the permissible speed limit, but when they perceive there is no danger of being caught, they do not hesitate in exceeding the speed limit. Thus, if we believe in God, out of fear of Him, we will refrain from immoral behaviour. On the other hand, if we do not believe in God, all His laws will still apply to us, and we will suffer the consequences of wrong behaviour.

Those with demoniac natures do not wish to accept this imposition of authority and regulation of behaviour that is a necessary corollary of belief in God. Instead, they prefer to subscribe to the view that there is no God, and the world has no basis for moral order. They propagate ideas such as the 'Big Bang Theory', which postulates that the world was created by an accidental explosion that took place at time zero of creation, and thus there is no God who sustains the world. Such theories permit them to engage in sensual gratification without scruples or fear of consequences.

Among the various forms of sensual gratification, sexual indulgence is the most intense. This is because the material realm is like a distorted reflection of the spiritual realm. In the spiritual realm, divine love is the basis of the activities of liberated souls and their interactions with God. In the material realm, its distorted reflection, lust, dominates the consciousness of materially conditioned souls, particularly those under the mode of passion. Thus, the demoniac-minded see engagement in lustful activities as the purpose of human life.

एतां दृष्टिमवष्टभ्य नष्टात्मानोऽल्पबुद्धयः ।
प्रभवन्त्युग्रकर्माणः क्षयाय जगतोऽहिताः ।।9।।

etāṁ dṛiṣhṭim avaṣhṭabhya naṣhṭātmāno 'lpa-buddhayaḥ
prabhavanty ugra-karmāṇaḥ kṣhayāya jagato 'hitāḥ

etām—such; *dṛiṣhṭim*—views; *avaṣhṭabhya*—holding; *naṣhṭa*—misdirected; *ātmānaḥ*—souls; *alpa-buddhayaḥ*—of small intellect; *prabhavanti*—arise; *ugra*—cruel; *karmāṇaḥ*—actions; *kṣhayāya*—destruction; *jagataḥ*—of the world; *ahitāḥ*—enemies.

Holding fast to such views, these misdirected souls, with small intellect and cruel actions, arise as enemies of the world threatening its destruction.

Bereft of true self-knowledge, the demoniac-minded fabricate distorted views of the truth with their impure intellects. An example of this is the theory proposed by Charvak, a well-known materialistic philosopher in Indian history. He said:

yāvajjīveta sukaṁ jīvet, ṛiṇaṁ kṛitvā ghṛitaṁ pivet
bhasmī bhūtasya dehasya punarāgamanaṁ kutaḥ

'As long as you live, enjoy yourself. If drinking ghee gives you pleasure, then do so even if you have to take on a debt for the purpose. When the body is cremated, you will cease to exist, and will not come back in the world again (so do not worry of any karmic consequences of your actions).'

In this fashion, the demoniac-minded reject the eternality of the soul and the possibility of karmic reactions, so that they may engage in self-serving and even cruel deeds without any qualms. If they happen to possess power over other humans, they impose their misleading materialistic views upon them as well. They do not hesitate to aggressively pursue their self-centred goals, even if it results in grief to others and destruction to the world. In history, humankind has repeatedly witnessed megalomaniac dictators and emperors, such as Hitler, Mussolini, and Stalin who were motivated by their perverse views of the Truth and brought about untold suffering and devastation to the world.

काममाश्रित्य दुष्पूरं दम्भमानमदान्विताः ।
मोहाद्गृहीत्वासद्ग्राहान्प्रवर्तन्तेऽशुचिव्रताः ।।10।।

kāmam āśhritya duṣhpūraṁ dambha-māna-madānvitāḥ
mohād-gṛihītvāsad-grāhān pravartante-'śhuchi-vratāḥ

kāmam—lust; *āśhritya*—harbouring; *duṣhpūram*—insatiable; *dambha*—hypocrisy; *māna*—arrogance; *mada-anvitāḥ*—clinging to false tenets; *mohāt*—the illusioned; *gṛihītvā*—being attracted to; *asat*—impermanent; *grāhān*—things; *pravartante*—they flourish; *aśhuchi-vratāḥ*—with impure resolve.

Harbouring insatiable lust, full of hypocrisy, pride, and arrogance, the demoniac cling to their false tenets. Thus illusioned, they are attracted to the impermanent and work with impure resolve.

By giving vent to insatiable lustful desires, the demoniac-minded develop terribly impure etheric hearts. They become full of hypocrisy and pretend to be what they are not. Their deluded intellect embraces wrong ideas, and their pride makes them believe that nobody is more intelligent than them. Attracted to the fleeting pleasures of sense objects, their intellect becomes mean, selfish, and arrogant. Thus, they disregard the injunctions of the scriptures and act contrary to what is proper and truthful.

चिन्तामपरिमेयां च प्रलयान्तामुपाश्रिताः ।
कामोपभोगपरमा एतावदिति निश्चिताः ।।11।।

chintām aparimeyāṁ cha pralayāntām upāśhritāḥ
kāmopabhoga-paramā etāvad iti niśhchitāḥ

chintām—anxieties; *aparimeyām*—endless; *cha*—and; *pralaya-antām*—until death; *upāśhritāḥ*—taking refuge; *kāma-upabhoga*—gratification of desires; *paramāḥ*—the purpose of life; *etāvat*—still; *iti*—thus; *niśhchitāḥ*—with complete assurance.

They are obsessed with endless anxieties that end only with death. Still, they maintain with complete assurance that gratification of desires and accumulation of wealth is the highest purpose of life.

Materially inclined people often reject the spiritual path on the grounds that it is too burdensome and laborious, and the final goal is too distant. They prefer to pursue the way of the world that promises to provide immediate gratification, but they end up struggling even more in the worldly direction. Their desires for material attainments torment them, and they undertake enormous schemes to fulfil their aspirations. When a cherished object is attained, for a moment they experience relief, but then new anguish begins. They are worried about the object being snatched away and they labour to retain it. Finally, when the inevitable separation from the object of attachment takes place, there is only misery. Thus, it is said:

yā chintā bhuvi putra pautra bharaṇavyāpāra sambhāṣhaṇe
yā chintā dhana dhānya yaśhasāṁ lābhe sadā jāyate
sā chintā yadi nandanandan padadvandvāra vindekṣhaṇam
kā chintā yamarāja bhīma sadandvāraprayāṇe vibho

(*Sukti Sudhakar*)

'People experience untold worries and stress in worldly endeavours—bringing up children and grandchildren, engaging in business, accumulating wealth and treasures, and acquiring fame. If they show the same level of attachment and concern for developing love for Shree Krishna's lotus feet, they will never again have to worry about Yamraj, the god of death (for they will cross over the cycle of life and death).' But the demoniac-minded refuse to accept this blatant fact because their intellects are convinced that worldly pleasures are the highest experience of joy. They cannot even see that death is patiently waiting to carry them off to miserable destinies and more suffering in future lives.

आशापाशशतैर्बद्धाः कामक्रोधपरायणाः ।
ईहन्ते कामभोगार्थमन्यायेनार्थसञ्चयान् ।।12।।

āśhā-pāśha-śhatair baddhāḥ kāma-krodha-parāyaṇāḥ
īhante kāma-bhogārtham anyāyenārtha-sañchayān

āśhā-pāśha—bondage of desires; *śhataiḥ*—by hundreds; *baddhāḥ*—bound; *kāma*—lust; *krodha*—anger; *parāyaṇāḥ*—dedicated to; *īhante*—strive; *kāma*—lust; *bhoga*—gratification of the senses; *artham*—for; *anyāyena*—by unjust means; *artha*—wealth; *sañchayān*—to accumulate.

Held in bondage by hundreds of desires and driven by lust and anger, they strive to accumulate wealth by unjust means, all for the gratification of their senses.

Money is the means for enjoying the world. This is why materialistic people who are driven by insatiable desires accord such priority to accumulating it in their lives. They do not even hesitate to adopt unlawful means for earning wealth. Therefore, double punishment awaits them for their unethical conduct. The Bhagavatam states:

yāvad bhriyeta jaṭharaṁ tāvat svatvaṁ hi dehinām
adhikaṁ yo 'bhimanyeta sa steno daṇḍam arhati (7.14.8)

'One is entitled to keep only as much wealth as is necessary for one's maintenance (the rest must be given away in charity). If one accumulates more than one's need, one is a thief in the eyes of God and will be punished for it.' What is the punishment? First, at the time of death, the wealth one earned will not go along—it will be snatched away. Second, according to the Law of Karma, one will be punished for the sins committed in earning that wealth. This is just as, when a smuggler is caught, not only are his goods confiscated, but he is also punished for breaking the law.

इदमद्य मयालब्धमिमं प्राप्स्ये मनोरथम् ।
इदमस्तीदमपि मे भविष्यति पुनर्धनम् ।।13।।

असौ मया हतः शत्रुर्हनिष्ये चापरानपि ।
ईश्वरोऽहमहं भोगी सिद्धोऽहं बलवान्सुखी ।।14।।

आढ्योऽभिजनवानस्मि कोऽन्योऽस्ति सदृशो मया ।
यक्ष्ये दास्यामि मोदिष्य इत्यज्ञानविमोहिताः ।।15।।

idam adya mayā labdham imaṁ prāpsye manoratham
idam astīdam api me bhavişhyati punar dhanam

asau mayā hataḥ śhatrur hanişhye chāparān api
īśhvaro 'ham ahaṁ bhogī siddho 'haṁ balavān sukhī

āḍhyo 'bhijanavān asmi ko 'nyo 'sti sadṛiśho mayā
yakṣhye dāsyāmi modiṣhya ity ajñāna-vimohitāḥ

idam—this; *adya*—today; *mayā*—by me; *labdham*—gained; *imam*—this; *prāpsye*—I shall acquire; *manaḥ-ratham*—desire; *idam*—this; *asti*—is; *idam*—this; *api*—also; *me*—mine; *bhavişhyati*—in future; *punaḥ*—again; *dhanam*—wealth; *asau*—that; *mayā*—by me; *hataḥ*—has been destroyed; *śhatruḥ*—enemy; *hanişhye*—I shall destroy; *cha*—and; *aparān*—others; *api*—also; *īśhvaraḥ*—God; *aham*—I; *aham*—I; *bhogī*—the enjoyer; *siddhaḥ*—perfect; *aham*—I; *bala-vān*—powerful; *sukhī*—happy; *āḍhyaḥ*—wealthy; *abhijana-vān*—having highly placed relatives; *asmi*—me; *kaḥ*—who; *anyaḥ*—else; *asti*—is; *sadṛiśhaḥ*—like; *mayā*—to me; *yakṣhye*—I shall perform sacrifices; *dāsyāmi*—I shall give alms; *modiṣhye*—I shall rejoice; *iti*—thus; *ajñāna*—ignorance; *vimohitāḥ*—deluded.

The demoniac persons think, 'I have gained so much wealth today, and I shall now fulfil this desire of mine. This is mine, and tomorrow I shall have even more. That enemy has been destroyed by me, and I shall destroy the others too! I am like God Himself, I am the enjoyer, I am perfect, I am powerful, and I am happy. I am wealthy and I have highly placed relatives. Who else is equal to me? I shall perform sacrifices (to the celestial gods); I shall give alms; I shall rejoice.' In this way, they are deluded by ignorance.

Ignoring all morality, the demoniac presume they have a right to enjoy whatever they find pleasurable. They make concerted efforts to orchestrate events to fulfil their ambitions. Realising that the ritualistic practices of the Vedas will help them become materially affluent, they even perform these ceremonies to accrue abundance and fame from them. However, like the vulture that flies high but keeps its sight fixed low, the demoniac sometimes rise in social status, but their actions remain mean and lowly. Such people respect power and believe in the principle of 'might is right'. Hence, for the fulfilment of their desires, they do not hesitate to eliminate obstacles even if this means harming or injuring others. The *Sukti Sudhakar* states that there are four kinds of people:

eke satpuruṣāḥ parārthaghaṭakāḥ swārthān parityajya ye
sāmānyāstu parārthamudyamabhṛitaḥ swārthā virodhena ye
te 'mī mānav rākṣasāḥ parahitaṁ swārthāya nighnanti ye
ye tughnanti nirarthakaṁ parahitaṃ te ke na jānīmahe

'The first kind of people are the saintly personalities who sacrifice their self-interest for the welfare of others. The second kind are common people who believe in engaging in the welfare of others, provided it does not harm them. The third kind are the demoniac who do not mind harming others, if it helps fulfil their self-interest. There is also a fourth kind of people who harm others, for no reason (except sadistic delight). There is no suitable name for them.' Shree Krishna vividly describes the degraded nature of the demoniac-mentality. Blinded by pride, they think along these lines: 'I was born in a wealthy and aristocratic family. I am rich and powerful, and I do what I like. There is no need for me to bow down before God because I am like God myself.'

In most cases, when people say 'I', it is their ego speaking, not them. The ego contains personal identifications with opinions, external appearances, resentments, etc. This ego builds a personality of its own, and under its sway, people identify with thoughts, emotions, and bundles of memories, which they see as integral parts of themselves. The ego identifies with owning, but the satisfaction of having is usually short-lived. Concealed within it is a deep-rooted dissatisfaction of 'not enough'. This unfulfilled want results in unease, restlessness, boredom, anxiety, and dissatisfaction. Consequently, a much-distorted perception of reality is created, which further alienates their perception of 'I' from the real self.

The ego creates the biggest untruth in our lives and makes us believe what we are not. Thus, for progress along the saintly path, all the religious traditions and saints urge us to dismantle our egotistic thought patterns. The *Tao Te Ching* teaches: 'Instead of trying to be the mountain, be the valley of the Universe.' (Chapter 6) Jesus of Nazareth also stated: 'When you are invited, go and sit in the lowest place so that when the host comes, he may say to you, friend, move up higher. For everyone who exalts himself will be humbled, and everyone who humbles himself will be exalted.' (Luke 14:10–11). Saint Kabir put this very nicely:

ūñche pānī na ṭike, nīche hī ṭhaharāye
nīchā hoya so bhari pī, ūñchā pyāsā jāya

'Water does not remain above; it naturally flows down. Those who are low and unassuming drink (God's grace) to their heart's content, while those who are high and pompous remain thirsty.'

अनेकचित्तविभ्रान्ता मोहजालसमावृताः ।
प्रसक्ताः कामभोगेषु पतन्ति नरकेऽशुचौ ।।16।।

aneka-chitta-vibhrāntā moha-jāla-samāvṛitāḥ
prasaktāḥ kāma-bhogeṣhu patanti narake 'śhuchau

aneka—many; *chitta*—imaginings; *vibhrāntāḥ*—led astray; *moha*—delusion; *jāla*—mesh; *samāvṛitāḥ*—enveloped; *prasaktāḥ*—addicted; *kāma-bhogeṣhu*—gratification of sensuous pleasures; *patanti*—descend; *narake*—to hell; *aśhuchau*—murky.

Possessed and led astray by such imaginings, enveloped in a mesh of delusion, and addicted to the gratification of sensuous pleasures, they descend to the murkiest hell.

Under the sway of the ego, people identify with their mind and become confined by its dysfunctional and repetitive thought patterns. They practically become possessed by their own mind, which goes on and on like a broken record, and they live in the reality their thoughts create for them. One such favourite thought pattern of the impure mind is complaining. It loves to whine and feel resentful not only about people but also about situations. The implication is, 'This should not be happening,' 'I do not want to be here,' 'I am being treated unfairly,' and so on. Every complaint is a little story that the mind fabricates, and the individual completely believes it. The voice in the head tells sad, anxious, or angry stories about one's life. And the poor individual, under the sway of the ego, accepts what the voice says. When complaining aggravates, it turns into resentment. Resentment means feeling bitter, indignant, aggrieved, or offended. When the resentment becomes longstanding, it is called a grievance. A grievance is a strong negative emotion connected to an event in the past that is being kept alive by compulsive thinking, by retelling the story in the head of 'what someone did to me.' In this verse, Shree Krishna says that the demoniac who choose to live in the mesh of delusion created by the ego become bewildered by numerous thoughts of the poorest quality. Consequently, they obscure their own destiny.

Humans are free to perform karmas by their choice, but they are not free to determine the results of their actions. The results are bestowed by God in accordance with the Law of Karma. The Ramayan states:

karama pradhāna bisva kari rākhā,
jo jasa karai so tasa phala chākhā

'Actions are important in this world. Whatever actions people perform, they taste the corresponding fruits.'

Consequently, everyone has to face the karmic consequences of their actions. The Bible also states: 'Be sure your sin will find you out.' (Numbers 32.23)

In their next life, God casts those who choose to cultivate demoniac qualities into inferior states of existence. The principle is very simple:

ūrdhvaṁ gachchhanti sattvasthā madhye tiṣhṭhanti rājasāḥ
jaghanya guṇa vṛittisthā adho tiṣhṭhanti tāmasāḥ

(*Garuḍ Puran*)

'Those who act out of sattvic mentalities rise to the higher levels of existence; those who act out of rajasic mentalities remain in the middle regions; and those who act out of a tamasic mentality and are inclined towards sin descend to the lower levels of existence.'

आत्मसम्भाविताः स्तब्धा धनमानमदान्विताः ।
यजन्ते नामयज्ञैस्ते दम्भेनाविधिपूर्वकम् ।।17।।

ātma-sambhāvitāḥ stabdhā dhana-māna-madānvitāḥ
yajante nāma-yajñais te dambhenāvidhi-pūrvakam

ātma-sambhāvitāḥ—self-conceited; *stabdhāḥ*—stubborn; *dhana*—wealth; *māna*—pride; *mada*—arrogance; *anvitāḥ*—full of; *yajante*—perform sacrifice; *nāma*—in name only; *yajñaiḥ*—sacrifices; *te*—they; *dambhena*—ostentatiously; *avidhi-pūrvakam*—with no regards to the rules of the scriptures.

Such self-conceited and stubborn people, full of pride and arrogant in their wealth, perform ostentatious sacrifices in name only, with no regard to the rules of the scriptures.

Virtuous people perform sacrifices to purify the self and to please God. The travesty is that demoniac people also perform sacrifices but with an impure intent. They conduct grandiose ritualistic ceremonies to look pious in the eyes of society. But they do not adhere to the injunctions of the scriptures, and instead, perform sacrifices for personal advertisement and pretentious display. However, the injunction of the scriptures is: *gūhitasya bhaved vṛiddhiḥ kīrtitasya bhavet kṣhayaḥ* (Mahabharat) 'If we advertise a good deed we have done, its merit decreases; if we keep it secret, its merit multiplies.' In this verse, Shree Krishna dismisses the ritualistic ceremonies of the demoniac by saying that they are incorrectly performed.

अहङ्कारं बलं दर्पं कामं क्रोधं च संश्रिताः ।
मामात्मपरदेहेषु प्रद्विषन्तोऽभ्यसूयकाः ।।18।।

ahankāraṁ balaṁ darpaṁ kāmaṁ krodhaṁ cha sanśhritāḥ
mām-ātma-para-deheṣhu pradviṣhanto-'bhyasūyakāḥ

ahankāram—egotism; *balam*—strength; *darpam*—arrogance; *kāmam*—desire; *krodham*—anger; *cha*—and; *sanśhritāḥ*—covered by; *mām*—me; *ātma-para-deheṣhu*—within one's own and bodies of others; *pradviṣhantaḥ*—abuse; *abhyasūyakāḥ*—the demoniac.

Blinded by egotism, strength, arrogance, desire, and anger, the demoniac abuse Me, who am present in their own body and in the bodies of others.

Here, Shree Krishna describes more telltale signs of people possessing a demoniac nature. They are vile, malicious, cruel, belligerent, and insolent. Although they do not possess righteous qualities themselves, they enjoy finding fault in everyone else. They consider themselves all-important, and as a consequence of this nature of self-aggrandisement, they are envious of others' success. If ever they are opposed in their plans, they become enraged and cause agony to others as well as to their own selves. As a result, they disregard and disrespect the Supreme Soul who is seated within their own hearts and in the hearts of others.

तानहं द्विषतः क्रूरान्संसारेषु नराधमान् ।
क्षिपाम्यजस्रमशुभानासुरीष्वेव योनिषु ।।19।।

आसुरीं योनिमापन्ना मूढा जन्मनि जन्मनि ।
मामप्राप्यैव कौन्तेय ततो यान्त्यधमां गतिम् ।।20।।

tān ahaṁ dviṣhataḥ krūrān sansāreṣhu narādhamān
kṣhipāmy-ajasram-aśhubhān-āsurīṣhv-eva yoniṣhu

āsurīṁ yonim āpannā mūḍhā janmani janmani
mām-aprāpyaiva kaunteya tato yānty-adhamāṁ gatim

tān—these; *aham*—I; *dviṣhataḥ*—hateful; *krūrān*—cruel; *sansāreṣhu*—in the material world; *nara-adhamān*—the vile and vicious of humankind; *kṣhipāmi*—I hurl; *ajasram*—again and again; *aśhubhān*—inauspicious; *āsurīṣhu*—demoniac; *eva*—indeed; *yoniṣhu*—into the wombs; *āsurīm*—demoniac; *yonim*—wombs; *āpannāḥ*—gaining; *mūḍhāḥ*—the ignorant; *janmani janmani*—in birth after birth; *mām*—me; *aprāpya*—failing to reach; *eva*—even; *kaunteya*—Arjun, son of Kunti; *tataḥ*—thereafter; *yānti*—go; *adhamām*—abominable; *gatim*—destination.

These cruel and hateful persons, the vile and vicious of humankind, I constantly hurl into the wombs of those with similar demoniac natures in the cycle of rebirth in the material world. These ignorant souls take birth again and again in demoniac wombs. Failing to reach Me, O Arjun, they gradually sink to the most abominable type of existence.

Shree Krishna once again describes the repercussions of the demoniac mentality. He says that in their next lives, He gives them birth in families with similar consciousness, where they get a suitable demoniac environment to exercise their free will and heartily vent their degraded nature. From this verse, we can also infer that it is not in the soul's hands to choose the species, abode, and environment of its next birth. God makes this decision according to the nature and karma of the individual. Thus, the demoniac are sent into lower and degraded wombs, even to the level of snakes, lizards, and scorpions, which are receptacles for the evil-minded.

त्रिविधं नरकस्येदं द्वारं नाशनमात्मनः ।
कामः क्रोधस्तथा लोभस्तस्मादेतत्त्रयं त्यजेत् ।।21।।

tri-vidhaṁ narakasyedaṁ dvāraṁ nāśhanam ātmanaḥ
kāmaḥ krodhas-tathā lobhas-tasmād-etat-trayaṁ tyajet

tri-vidham—three types of; *narakasya*—to the hell; *idam*—this; *dvāram*—gates; *nāśhanam*—destruction; *ātmanaḥ*—self; *kāmaḥ*—lust; *krodhaḥ*—anger; *tathā*—and; *lobhaḥ*—greed; *tasmāt*—therefore; *etat*—these; *trayam*—three; *tyajet*—should abandon.

There are three gates leading to the hell of self-destruction for the soul—lust, anger, and greed. Therefore, one should abandon all three.

Shree Krishna now describes the origin of the demoniac disposition, and pinpoints lust, anger, and greed as the three causes for it. Previously, in verse 3.36, Arjun had asked Him why people are impelled to commit sin, even unwillingly, as if by force. Shree Krishna had answered that it is lust, which later transforms into anger, and is the all-devouring enemy of the world. Greed is also a transformation of lust, as explained in detail in the commentary of verse 2.62. Together, lust, anger, and greed are the foundations from which demoniac vices develop. They fester in the mind and make it a suitable ground for all other vices to take root. Consequently, Shree Krishna labels them as gateways to hell and strongly advices to shun them to avoid self-destruction. Those desirous of welfare should learn to dread these three and carefully avoid their presence in their own personality.

एतैर्विमुक्तः कौन्तेय तमोद्वारैस्त्रिभिर्नरः ।
आचरत्यात्मनः श्रेयस्ततो याति परां गतिम् ।।22।।

etair vimuktaḥ kaunteya tamo-dvārais tribhir naraḥ
ācharaty ātmanaḥ śhreyas tato yāti parāṁ gatim

etaiḥ—from this; *vimuktaḥ*—free; *kaunteya*—Arjun, son of Kunti; *tamaḥ-dvāraiḥ*—gates to darkness; *tribhiḥ*—three; *naraḥ*—a person; *ācharati*—endeavour; *ātmanaḥ*—soul; *śhreyaḥ*—welfare; *tataḥ*—thereby; *yāti*—attain; *parām*—supreme; *gatim*—goal.

Those who are free from the three gates to darkness endeavour for the welfare of their soul, and thereby attain the supreme goal.

In this verse, Shree Krishna gives the result of renouncing lust, anger, and greed. As long as these are present, one is attracted towards *preya*, or happiness that seems sweet in the present but becomes bitter in the end. But when materialistic yearnings diminish, the intellect, free from the material mode of passion, is able to perceive the shortsightedness of pursuing the path of *preya*. Then one gets drawn towards *śhreya*, or happiness that is unpleasant in the present but becomes sweet in the end. And for those attracted to *śhreya*, the path of enlightenment opens up. They begin endeavouring for the eternal welfare of their soul, thereby moving towards the supreme goal.

यः शास्त्रविधिमुत्सृज्य वर्तते कामकारतः ।
न स सिद्धिमवाप्नोति न सुखं न परां गतिम् ।।23।।

yaḥ śhāstra-vidhim-utsṛijya vartate kāma-kārataḥ
na sa siddhim-avāpnoti na sukhaṁ na parāṁ gatim

yaḥ—who; *śhāstra-vidhim*—scriptural injunctions; *utsṛijya*—discarding; *vartate*—act; *kāma-kārataḥ*—under the impulse of desire; *na*—neither; *saḥ*—they; *siddhim*—perfection; *avāpnoti*—attain; *na*—nor; *sukham*—happiness; *na*—nor; *parām*—the supreme; *gatim*—goal.

Those who act under the impulse of desire, discarding the injunctions of the scriptures, attain neither perfection, nor happiness, nor the supreme goal in life.

Scriptures are the guide maps given to humans on the journey towards enlightenment. They provide us with knowledge and understanding. They also give us instructions on what to do and what not to do. These instructions are of two kinds—*vidhi* and *niṣhedh*. The directives to perform certain activities are called *vidhi*. The directives not to perform certain activities are called *niṣhedh*. By faithfully following both these kinds of injunctions, human beings can proceed towards perfection. But the ways of the demoniac are the reverse of the teachings of the scriptures. They engage in prohibited acts and refrain from recommended ones. Referring to such people, Shree Krishna declares that those who renounce the authorised path and act according to their whims, impelled by the impulses of their desires, achieve neither true knowledge, nor the perfection of happiness, nor liberation from material bondage.

तस्माच्छास्त्रं प्रमाणं ते कार्याकार्यव्यवस्थितौ ।
ज्ञात्वा शास्त्रविधानोक्तं कर्म कर्तुमिहार्हसि ।।24।।

tasmāch-chhāstraṁ pramāṇaṁ te kāryākārya-vyavasthitau
jñātvā śhāstra-vidhānoktaṁ karma kartum ihārhasi

tasmāt—therefore; *śhāstram*—scriptures; *pramāṇam*—authority; *te*—your; *kārya*—duty; *akārya*—forbidden action; *vyavasthitau*—in determining; *jñātvā*—having understood; *śhāstra*—scriptures; *vidhāna*—injunctions; *uktam*—as revealed; *karma*—actions; *kartum*—perform; *iha*—in this world; *arhasi*—you should.

Therefore, let the scriptures be your authority in determining what should be done and what should not be done. Understand the scriptural injunctions and teachings, and then perform your actions in this world accordingly.

Shree Krishna now gives the final conclusion of the teachings in this chapter. By comparing and differentiating between divine and demoniac natures, He highlighted how the demoniac nature leads to hellish existence. Thus, He established that nothing is to be gained by discarding the injunctions of the scriptures. Now He drives home the point by stating that the absolute authority in ascertaining the propriety of any activity, or lack of it, are the Vedic scriptures.

Sometimes, even well-intentioned people say, 'I do not care for rules. I follow my heart and do my own thing.' It is all very well to follow the heart, but how can they be sure that their heart is not misleading them? As the saying goes, 'The road to hell is paved with good intentions.' This is why, it is always best to check with the scriptures whether our heart is truly guiding us in the proper direction. The *Manu Smriti* states:

bhūtaṁ bhavyaṁ bhaviṣhyaṁ cha sarvaṁ vedāt prasidhyati

(12.97)

'The authenticity of any spiritual principle of the past, present, or future, must be established on the basis of the Vedas.' Hence, Shree Krishna concludes by instructing Arjun to comprehend the teachings of the scriptures and act according to them.

CHAPTER 17

Śhraddhā Traya Vibhāg Yog

Yog through Discerning the Three Divisions of Faith

In the fourteenth chapter, Shree Krishna had explained the three modes of material nature and the manner in which they hold sway over humans. In this seventeenth chapter, He goes into greater detail about the influence of the gunas. First, He discusses the topic of faith and explains that nobody is devoid of faith, for it is an inseparable aspect of human nature. But depending upon the nature of their mind, people's faith takes on a corresponding colour—sattvic, rajasic, or tamasic. The nature of their faith determines the quality of their life. People also prefer food according to their dispositions. Shree Krishna classifies food into three categories and discusses the impact of each of these upon us. He then moves on to the topic of sacrifice (yajna) and explains that sacrifice takes different forms in each of the three modes of nature. The chapter moves on to the subject of austerity (*tapaḥ*) and explains austerities of the body, speech, and mind. Each of these kinds of austerity takes on a different form as influenced by the mode of goodness, passion, or ignorance. The topic of charity (*dān*) is then discussed, and its three-fold divisions are described.

Finally, Shree Krishna goes beyond the three gunas and explains the relevance and import of the words 'Om Tat Sat' which symbolise different aspects of the Absolute Truth. The syllable 'Om' is a symbolic representation of the impersonal aspect of God; the syllable 'Tat' is uttered for consecrating activities and ceremonies to the Supreme Lord; the syllable 'Sat' means eternal goodness and virtue. Taken together, they usher the concept of transcendence. The chapter concludes by emphasising the futility of acts of sacrifice, austerity, and charity, which are done without regard to the injunctions of the scriptures.

अर्जुन उवाच ।
ये शास्त्रविधिमुत्सृज्य यजन्ते श्रद्धयान्विताः ।
तेषां निष्ठा तु का कृष्ण सत्त्वमाहो रजस्तमः ।।1।।

arjuna uvācha
ye śhāstra-vidhim-utsṛijya yajante śhraddhayānvitāḥ
teṣhāṁ niṣhṭhā tu kā kṛiṣhṇa sattvam āho rajas tamaḥ

arjunaḥ uvācha—Arjun said; *ye*—who; *śhāstra-vidhim*—scriptural injunctions; *utsṛijya*—disregard; *yajante*—worship; *śhraddhayā-anvitāḥ*—with faith; *teṣhām*—their; *niṣhṭhā*—faith; *tu*—indeed; *kā*—what; *kṛiṣhṇa*—Krishna; *sattvam*—mode of goodness; *āho*—or; *rajaḥ*—mode of passion; *tamaḥ*—mode of ignorance.

Arjun said: O Krishna, where do they stand who disregard the injunctions of the scriptures, but still worship with faith? Is their faith in the mode of goodness, passion, or ignorance?

In the preceding chapter, Shree Krishna spoke of the differences between divine and demoniac natures, to help Arjun understand the virtues that should be cultivated and personality traits that should be eradicated. At the end of the chapter, He stated that one who disregards the injunctions of the scriptures, and instead foolishly follows the impulses of the body and the whims of the mind, will not achieve perfection, happiness, or freedom from the cycle of life and death. He thus recommended that people follow the guidance of the scriptures and act accordingly. This instruction led to the present question. Arjun desires to know the nature of faith of those who worship without reference to Vedic scriptures. In particular, he wishes to understand the answer in terms of the three modes of material nature.

श्रीभगवानुवाच ।
त्रिविधा भवति श्रद्धा देहिनां सा स्वभावजा ।
सात्त्विकी राजसी चैव तामसी चेति तां शृणु ।।2।।

śhrī-bhagavān uvācha
tri-vidhā bhavati śhraddhā dehināṁ sā svabhāva-jā
sāttvikī rājasī chaiva tāmasī cheti tāṁ śhṛiṇu

śhrī-bhagavān uvācha—the Supreme Personality said; *tri-vidhā*—of three kinds; *bhavati*—is; *śhraddhā*—faith; *dehinām*—embodied beings; *sā*—which; *sva-bhāva-jā*—born of one's innate nature; *sāttvikī*—of the mode of goodness; *rājasī*—of the mode of passion; *cha*—and; *eva*—certainly; *tāmasī*—of the mode of ignorance; *cha*—and; *iti*—thus; *tām*—about this; *śhṛiṇu*—hear.

The Supreme Divine Personality said: Every human being is born with innate faith which can be of three kinds—sattvic, rajasic, or tamasic. Now hear about this from Me.

Nobody can be without faith, for it is an inseparable aspect of the human personality. Those who do not believe in the scriptures are also not bereft of faith. Their faith is reposed elsewhere. It could be on the logical ability of their intellect, or the perceptions of their senses, or the theories they have decided to believe in. For example, when people say, 'I do not believe in God because I cannot see Him,' they do not have faith in God, but they have faith in their eyes. Hence, they assume that if their eyes cannot see something, it probably does not exist. This is also a kind of faith. Others say, 'I do not believe in the authenticity of the ancient scriptures. Instead, I accept the theories of modern science.' This is also a kind of faith, for we have seen in the last few centuries how theories of science keep getting amended and overthrown. It is possible that the present scientific theories we believe to be true may also be proven incorrect in the future. Accepting them as truths is also a leap of faith. Prof. Charles H. Townes, Nobel Prize winner in physics, expressed this very nicely:

'Science itself requires faith. We don't know if our logic is correct. I don't know if you are there. You don't know if I am here. We may just be imagining all this. I have faith that the world is what it seems like, and thus I believe you are there. I can't prove it from any fundamental point of view.... Yet I have to accept a certain framework in which to operate. The idea that "religion is faith" and "science is knowledge," I think, is quite wrong. We scientists believe in the existence of the external world and the validity of our own logic. We feel quite comfortable about it. Nevertheless, these are acts of faith. We can't prove them.'

Whether one is a material scientist, a social scientist, or a spiritual scientist, one cannot avoid the leap of faith required to accept knowledge. *Shree Krishna now explains the reason why different people choose to place their faith in different places.*

सत्त्वानुरूपा सर्वस्य श्रद्धा भवति भारत ।
श्रद्धामयोऽयं पुरुषो यो यच्छ्रद्धः स एव सः ।।3।।

sattvānurūpā sarvasya śhraddhā bhavati bhārata
śhraddhā-mayo 'yaṁ puruṣho yo yach-chhraddhaḥ sa eva saḥ

sattva-anurūpā—conforming to the nature of one's mind; *sarvasya*—all; *śhraddhā*—faith; *bhavati*—is; *bhārata*—Arjun, scion of Bharat; *śhraddhāmayaḥ*—possessing faith; *ayam*—that; *puruṣhaḥ*—human being; *yaḥ*—who; *yat-śhraddhaḥ*—whatever the nature of their faith; *saḥ*—their; *eva*—verily; *saḥ*—they.

The faith of all humans conforms to the nature of their mind. All people possess faith, and whatever the nature of their faith, that is verily what they are.

In the previous verse, it was explained that we all repose our faith somewhere or the other. Where we decide to place our faith and what we choose to believe in practically shapes the direction of our life. Those who develop the conviction that money is of paramount importance in the world spend their entire life accumulating it. Those who believe that fame counts more than anything else dedicate their time and energy in chasing political positions and social designations. Those who believe in noble values sacrifice everything to uphold them. Mahatma Gandhi had faith in the incomparable importance of satya (truth) and ahinsa (non-violence), and by the strength of his convictions he launched a non-violent movement that succeeded in evicting the most powerful empire in the world from India. Those who develop deep faith in the overriding importance of God-realisation renounce their material life in search of Him. Thus, Shree Krishna states that the quality of our faith decides the direction of our life. In turn, the quality of our faith is decided by the nature of our mind. *And so, in response to Arjun's question, Shree Krishna begins expounding on the kinds of faith that exist.*

यजन्ते सात्त्विका देवान्यक्षरक्षांसि राजसाः ।
प्रेतान्भूतगणांश्चान्ये यजन्ते तामसा जनाः ।।4।।

yajante sāttvikā devān yakṣha-rakṣhānsi rājasāḥ
pretān bhūta-gaṇānśh chānye yajante tāmasā janāḥ

yajante—worship; *sāttvikāḥ*—those in the mode of goodness; *devān*—celestial gods; *yakṣha*—semi-celestial beings who exude power and wealth; *rakṣhānsi*—powerful beings who embody sensual enjoyment, revenge, and wrath; *rājasāḥ*—those in the mode of passion; *pretān-bhūta-gaṇān*—ghosts and spirits; *cha*—and; *anye*—others; *yajante*—worship; *tāmasāḥ*—those in the mode of ignorance; *janāḥ*—persons.

Those in the mode of goodness worship the celestial gods; those in the mode of passion worship the *yakṣhas* and rakshasas; those in the mode of ignorance worship ghosts and spirits.

It is said that the good are drawn to the good and the bad to the bad. Those in tamo guna are drawn towards ghosts and spirits, despite the evil and cruel nature of such beings. Those who are rajasic get drawn to the *yakṣhas* (semi-celestial beings who exude power and wealth) and rakshasas (powerful beings who embody sensual enjoyment, revenge, and wrath). They even offer the blood of animals to appease these lower beings, with faith in the propriety of such lowly worship. Those who are imbued with sattva guna become attracted to the worship of celestial gods in whom they perceive the qualities of goodness. True worship is perfectly directed when it is offered to God.

अशास्त्रविहितं घोरं तप्यन्ते ये तपो जनाः ।
दम्भाहङ्कारसंयुक्ताः कामरागबलान्विताः ।।5।।

कर्षयन्तः शरीरस्थं भूतग्राममचेतसः ।
मां चैवान्तःशरीरस्थं तान्विद्ध्यासुरनिश्चयान् ।।6।।

aśhāstra-vihitaṁ ghoraṁ tapyante ye tapo janāḥ
dambhāhankāra-sanyuktāḥ kāma-rāga-balānvitāḥ

karṣhayantaḥ śharīra-sthaṁ bhūta-grāmam achetasaḥ
māṁ chaivāntaḥ śharīra-sthaṁ tān viddhy āsura-niśhchayān

aśhāstra-vihitam—not enjoined by the scriptures; *ghoram*—stern; *tapyante*—perform; *ye*—who; *tapaḥ*—austerities; *janāḥ*—people; *dambha*—hypocrisy; *ahankāra*—egotism; *sanyuktāḥ*—possessed of; *kāma*—desire; *rāga*—attachment; *bala*—force; *anvitāḥ*—impelled by; *karṣhayantaḥ*—torment; *śharīra-stham*—within the body; *bhūta-grāmam*—elements of the body; *achetasaḥ*—senseless; *mām*—me; *cha*—and; *eva*—even; *antaḥ*—within; *śharīra-stham*—dwelling in the body; *tān*—them; *viddhi*—know; *āsura-niśhchayān*—of demoniacal resolves.

Some people perform stern austerities that are not enjoined by the scriptures, but rather motivated by hypocrisy and egotism. Impelled by desire and attachment, they torment not only the elements of their body, but also I who dwell within them as the Supreme Soul. Know these senseless people to be of demoniacal resolves.

In the name of spirituality, people perform senseless austerities. Some lie on beds of thorns or drive spikes through their bodies as a part of macabre rituals for dominion over material existence. Others keep one hand raised for years as a procedure they believe will help them gain mystic abilities. Some gaze constantly at the sun unmindful of the harm it does to their eyes. Others undertake long fasts withering away their body for imagined material gains. Shree Krishna says: 'O Arjun, you asked Me about the status of those who disregard the injunctions of the scriptures and yet worship with faith. I am telling you that faith is visible even in people who perform severe austerities, but it is bereft of a proper basis of knowledge. Such people do possess deep conviction in the efficacy of their practices, but their faith is in the mode of ignorance. Those who abuse and torture their own physical body disrespect the Supreme Soul who resides within. All these are contrary to the recommended path of the scriptures.'

Having described the three categories of faith, Shree Krishna now explains, corresponding to each of these, the categories of food, activities, sacrifice, charity, and so forth.

आहारस्त्वपि सर्वस्य त्रिविधो भवति प्रियः ।
यज्ञस्तपस्तथा दानं तेषां भेदमिमं शृणु ।।7।।

āhāras tv api sarvasya tri-vidho bhavati priyaḥ
yajñas tapas tathā dānaṁ teṣhāṁ bhedam imaṁ śhṛiṇu

āhāraḥ—food; *tu*—indeed; *api*—even; *sarvasya*—of all; *tri-vidhaḥ*—of three kinds; *bhavati*—is; *priyaḥ*—dear; *yajñaḥ*—sacrifice; *tapaḥ*—austerity; *tathā*—and; *dānam*—charity; *teṣhām*—of them; *bhedam*—distinctions; *imam*—this; *śhṛiṇu*—hear.

The food that people prefer is according to their dispositions. The same is true for the sacrifice, austerity, and charity they are inclined (or predisposed) towards. Now hear of the distinctions from Me.

The mind and body impact each other. Thus, the food people eat influences their nature and vice versa. The *Chhāndogya Upanishad* explains that the coarsest part of the food we eat passes out as faeces; the subtler part becomes flesh; and the subtlest part becomes the mind (6.5.1). Again, it states: *āhāra śhuddhau sattva śhuddhiḥ* (7.26.2) 'By eating pure food, the mind becomes pure.' *The reverse is also true—people with pure minds prefer pure foods.*

आयुःसत्त्वबलारोग्यसुखप्रीतिविवर्धनाः ।
रस्याः स्निग्धाः स्थिरा हृद्या आहाराः सात्त्विकप्रियाः ।।8।।

āyuḥ-sattva-balārogya-sukha-prīti-vivardhanāḥ
rasyāḥ snigdhāḥ sthirā hṛidyā āhārāḥ sāttvika-priyāḥ

āyuḥ sattva—which promote longevity; *bala*—strength; *ārogya*—health; *sukha*—happiness; *prīti*—satisfaction; *vivardhanāḥ*—increase; *rasyāḥ*—juicy; *snigdhāḥ*—succulent; *sthirāḥ*—nourishing; *hṛidyāḥ*—pleasing to the heart; *āhārāḥ*—food; *sāttvika-priyāḥ*—dear to those in the mode of goodness.

Persons in the mode of goodness prefer foods that promote life span, and increase virtue, strength, health, happiness, and satisfaction. Such foods are juicy, succulent, nourishing, and naturally tasteful.

In Chapter 14, verse 6, Shree Krishna had explained that the mode of goodness is pure, illuminating, and serene, and creates a sense of happiness and satisfaction. Foods in the mode of goodness have the same effect. In the above verse, these foods are described with the words *āyuḥ sattva*, meaning, 'which promote longevity'. They bestow good health, virtue, happiness, and satisfaction. Such foods are juicy, naturally tasteful, mild, and beneficial. These include grains, pulses, beans, fruits, vegetables, milk, and other vegetarian food.

Hence, a vegetarian diet is beneficial for cultivating the qualities of the mode of goodness that is conducive for spiritual life. Numerous sattvic (influenced by the mode of goodness) thinkers and philosophers in history have echoed this sentiment:

> Is it not a reproach that man is a carnivorous animal? True, he can and does live, in a great measure, by preying on other animals; but this is a miserable way... I have no doubt that it is a part of the destiny of the human race, in its gradual improvement, to leave off eating animals, as surely as the savage tribes have left off eating each other when they came in contact with the more civilized.
>
> —*Henry David Thoreau* in *Walden*

My refusing to eat flesh occasioned an inconveniency, and I was frequently chided for my singularity, but, with this lighter repast, I made the greater progress, for greater clearness of head and quicker comprehension. Flesh-eating is an unprovoked murder.

—Benjamin Franklin

It is necessary to correct the error that vegetarianism has made us weak in mind, or passive, or inert in action. I do not regard flesh-food as necessary at any stage.

—Mahatma Gandhi

O my fellow men, do not defile your bodies with sinful foods. We have corn and we have apples bending down the branches with their weight. There are vegetables that can be cooked and softened over the fire. The earth affords a lavish supply of riches, of innocent foods, and offers you banquets that involve no bloodshed or slaughter; only beasts satisfy their hunger with flesh, and not even all of those, because horses, cattle, and sheep live on grass.

—Pythagoras

I do not want to make my stomach a graveyard of dead animals.

—George Bernard Shaw

Even among violence against animals, killing of the cow is particularly heinous. The cow provides milk for human consumption, so it is like a mother to human beings. To kill the mother cow when it is no longer capable of giving milk is an insensitive, uncultured, and ungrateful act.

कट्वम्ललवणात्युष्णतीक्ष्णरूक्षविदाहिनः ।
आहारा राजसस्येष्टा दुःखशोकामयप्रदाः ।।9।।

kaṭv-amla-lavaṇāty-ushṇa-tīkṣhṇa-rūkṣha-vidāhinaḥ
āhārā rājasasyeṣhṭā duḥkha-śhokāmaya-pradāḥ

kaṭu—bitter; *amla*—sour; *lavaṇa*—salty; *ati-uṣhṇa*—very hot; *tīkṣhṇa*—pungent; *rūkṣha*—dry; *vidāhinaḥ*—full of chillies; *āhārāḥ*—food; *rājasasya*—to persons in the mode of passion;

iṣhṭāḥ—dear; *duḥkha*—pain; *śhoka*—grief; *āmaya*—disease; *pradāḥ*—produce.

Foods that are too bitter, too sour, salty, very hot, pungent, dry, and full of chillies, are dear to persons in the mode of passion. Such foods produce pain, grief, and disease.

When vegetarian foods are cooked with excessive chillies, sugar, salt, and other condiments they become rajasic. While describing them, the word 'very' can be added to all the adjectives used. Thus, rajasic foods are very bitter, very sour, very salty, very hot, very pungent, very dry, very chilliful, and so on. They tend to result in ill-health, agitation, and despair. Persons in the mode of passion find such foods attractive, but those in the mode of goodness find them disgusting. The purpose of eating is not to relish bliss through the palate, but to keep the body healthy and strong. As the old adage states: 'Eat to live; do not live to eat.' Thus, the wise partake of foods that are conducive to good health and have a peaceable impact upon the mind i.e., sattvic foods.

यातयामं गतरसं पूति पर्युषितं च यत् ।
उच्छिष्टमपि चामेध्यं भोजनं तामसप्रियम् ।।10।।

yāta-yāmaṁ gata-rasaṁ pūti paryuṣhitaṁ cha yat
uchchhiṣhṭam api chāmedhyaṁ bhojanaṁ tāmasa-priyam

yāta-yāmam—stale foods; *gata-rasam*—tasteless; *pūti*—putrid; *paryuṣhitam*—polluted; *cha*—and; *yat*—which; *uchchhiṣhṭam*—left over; *api*—also; *cha*—and; *amedhyam*—impure; *bhojanam*—foods; *tāmasa*—to persons in the mode of ignorance; *priyam*—dear.

Foods that are overcooked, stale, putrid, polluted, and impure are dear to persons in the mode of ignorance.

Cooked foods that have remained for more than one *yām* (three hours) are classified in the mode of ignorance. Foods that are impure, have bad taste, or possess foul smells come in the same category. Impure foods also include all kinds of meat products. Nature has designed the human body to be vegetarian. Human beings do not have long canine teeth as carnivorous animals do or a wide jaw suitable for tearing flesh. Carnivores have short bowels to allow minimal transit time for the unstable and dead animal food which putrefies and decays faster. On the contrary, humans have a longer digestive tract for the slow and better absorption of plant food. The stomach of carnivores is more acidic than human beings, which enables them to digest raw meat. Interestingly, carnivorous animals do not sweat through their pores. Rather, they regulate body temperature through their tongue. On the other hand, herbivorous animals and humans control body temperature by sweating through their skin. While drinking, carnivores lap up water rather than suck it. In contrast, herbivores do not lap up water; they suck it. Humans too suck water while drinking; they do not lap it up. All these physical characteristics of the human body reveal that God has not created us as carnivorous creatures, and consequently, meat is considered impure food for humans.

Meat-eating also creates bad karma. The *Manu Smriti* states:

māṁ sa bhakṣhayitā 'mutra yasya māṁsam ihādmy aham
etan māṁsasya māṁsatvaṁ pravadanti manīṣhiṇaḥ (5.55)

'The word *mānsa* (meat) means "that whom I am eating here will eat me in my next life." For this reason, the learned say that meat is called *mānsa* (a repeated act: I eat him, he eats me).'

अफलाकाङ्क्षिभिर्यज्ञो विधिदृष्टो य इज्यते ।
यष्टव्यमेवेति मनः समाधाय स सात्त्विकः ।।11।।

aphalākāṅkṣhibhir yajño vidhi-driṣhṭo ya ijyate
yaṣhṭavyam eveti manaḥ samādhāya sa sāttvikaḥ

aphala-ākāṅkṣhibhiḥ—without expectation of any reward; *yajñaḥ*—sacrifice; *vidhi-driṣhṭaḥ*—that is in accordance with the scriptural injunctions; *yaḥ*—which; *ijyate*—is performed; *yaṣhṭavyam-eva-iti*—ought to be offered; *manaḥ*—mind; *samādhāya*—with conviction; *saḥ*—that; *sāttvikaḥ*—of the nature of goodness.

Sacrifice that is performed according to scriptural injunctions without expectation of rewards, with the firm conviction of the mind that it is a matter of duty, is of the nature of goodness.

The nature of yajna also corresponds to the three gunas. Shree Krishna begins by explaining the type of sacrifice in the mode of goodness. *Aphala-ākāṅkṣhibhiḥ* means that the sacrifice should be performed without expectation of any reward. *Vidhi drişhṭaḥ* means that it must be done according to injunctions of Vedic scriptures. *Yaṣhṭavyam evaiti* means that it must be performed only for the sake of worship of the Lord, as required by the scriptures. When yajna is performed in this manner, it is classified in the mode of goodness.

अभिसन्धाय तु फलं दम्भार्थमपि चैव यत् ।
इज्यते भरतश्रेष्ठ तं यज्ञं विद्धि राजसम् ।।12।।

abhisandhāya tu phalaṁ dambhārtham api chaiva yat
ijyate bharata-śhreṣhṭha taṁ yajñaṁ viddhi rājasam

abhisandhāya—motivated by; *tu*—but; *phalam*—result; *dambha*—pride; *artham*—for the sake of; *api*—also; *cha*—and; *eva*—certainly; *yat*—that which; *ijyate*—is performed; *bharata-śhreṣhṭha*—Arjun, best of the Bharatas; *tam*—that; *yajñam*—sacrifice; *viddhi*—know; *rājasam*—in the mode of passion.

O best of the Bharatas, know that sacrifice performed for material benefit, or with a hypocritical aim, is in the mode of passion.

Sacrifice becomes a form of business with God if it is performed with great pomp and show, but the spirit behind it is one of selfishness i.e., 'What will I get in return?' Pure devotion is that where one seeks nothing in return. Shree Krishna says that sacrifice may be done with great ceremony, but if it is for the sake of rewards in the form of prestige, aggrandisement, and the like, it is rajasic in nature.

विधिहीनमसृष्टान्नं मन्त्रहीनमदक्षिणम् ।
श्रद्धाविरहितं यज्ञं तामसं परिचक्षते ।।13।।

vidhi-hīnam asṛiṣhṭānnaṁ mantra-hīnam adakṣhiṇam
śhraddhā-virahitaṁ yajñaṁ tāmasaṁ parichakṣhate

vidhi-hīnam—without scriptural direction; *asṛiṣhṭa-annam*—without distribution of prasad; *mantra-hīnam*—with no chanting of the Vedic hymns; *adakṣhiṇam*—with no remunerations to the priests; *śhraddhā*—faith; *virahitam*—without; *yajñam*—sacrifice; *tāmasam*—in the mode of ignorance; *parichakṣhate*—is to be considered.

Sacrifice devoid of faith and contrary to the injunctions of the scriptures, in which no food is offered, no mantras chanted, and no donation made, is to be considered in the mode of ignorance.

At every moment in life, individuals have the freedom to choose their actions. There are proper actions that are beneficial for society and for us. At the same time, there are inappropriate actions that are harmful for others and us. However, who is to decide what is beneficial and what is harmful? And in case a dispute arises, what is the basis for resolving it? If everyone makes their own decisions, pandemonium will prevail. So, the injunctions of the scriptures serve as guide maps and wherever a doubt arises, we consult these scriptures to ascertain the propriety of any action. However, those in the mode of ignorance do not have faith in the scriptures. They carry out religious ceremonies but disregard the ordinances of the scriptures.

In India, specific gods and goddess associated with each festival are worshipped with great pomp and splendour. Often the motive behind the external grandeur of the ceremony—gaudy decorations, dazzling illumination, and blaring music—is to collect contributions from the neighbourhood. Further, the Vedic injunction of offering a donation to the priests performing a religious ceremony, as a mark of gratitude and respect, is not followed. Sacrifice in which such injunctions of the scriptures are ignored and a self-determined process is followed due to laziness, indifference, or belligerence, is in the mode of ignorance. Such faith is actually a form of faithlessness in God and the scriptures.

देवद्विजगुरुप्राज्ञपूजनं शौचमार्जवम् ।
ब्रह्मचर्यमहिंसा च शारीरं तप उच्यते ।।14।।

deva-dwija-guru-prājña-pūjanaṁ śhaucham ārjavam
brahmacharyam ahinsā cha śhārīraṁ tapa uchyate

deva—the Supreme Lord; *dwija*—the Brahmins; *guru*—the spiritual master; *prājña*—the wise and the elders; *pūjanam*—worship; *śhaucham*—cleanliness; *ārjavam*—simplicity; *brahmacharyam*—celibacy; *ahinsā*—non-violence; *cha*—and; *śhārīram*—of the body; *tapa*—austerity; *uchyate*—is declared as.

When worship of the Supreme Lord, the Brahmins, the spiritual master, the wise, and the elders is done with the observance of cleanliness, simplicity, celibacy, and non-violence, then this worship is declared as the austerity of the body.

The word *tapa* means 'to heat up' e.g., by placing on fire. In the process of purification, metals are heated and melted, so that impurities may rise to the top and be removed. When gold is placed in the fire, its impurities get burnt and its lustre increases. Similarly, the *Rig Veda* states:

atapta tanurnatadā mośhnute (9.83.1)

'Without purifying the body through austerity, one cannot reach the final state of yog.' By sincerely practising austerity, human beings can uplift and transform their life from the mundane to the divine. Such austerity should be performed without show, with pure intent, in a peaceful manner, and in conformance with the guidance of the spiritual master and the scriptures.

Shree Krishna now classifies such austerity into three categories—of the body, speech, and mind. In this verse, He talks of the austerity of the body. When the body is dedicated to the service of the pure and saintly, and all sense indulgence in general, and sexual indulgence in particular, is eschewed, it is acclaimed as austerity of the body. Such austerity should be done with cleanliness, simplicity, and without hurting others. Here, 'Brahmins' does not refer to those who consider themselves Brahmins by birth, but to those endowed with sattvic qualities, as described in verse 18.42.

अनुद्वेगकरं वाक्यं सत्यं प्रियहितं च यत् ।
स्वाध्यायाभ्यसनं चैव वाङ्मयं तप उच्यते ।।15।।

anudvega-karaṁ vākyaṁ satyaṁ priya-hitaṁ cha yat
svādhyāyābhyasanaṁ chaiva vāṅ-mayaṁ tapa uchyate

anudvega-karam—not causing distress; *vākyam*—words; *satyam*—truthful; *priya-hitam*—beneficial; *cha*—and; *yat*—which; *svādhyāya-abhyasanam*—recitation of the Vedic scriptures; *cha eva*—as well as; *vāṅ-mayam*—of speech; *tapa*—austerity; *uchyate*—are declared as.

Words that do not cause distress, are truthful, inoffensive, and beneficial, as well as regular recitation of the Vedic scriptures—these are declared as austerity of speech.

Austerity of speech is speaking words that are truthful, unoffending, pleasing, and beneficial for the listener. The practice of the recitation of Vedic mantras is also included in austerities of speech. The progenitor, Manu, wrote:

satyaṁ brūyāt priyaṁ brūyān na brūyāt satyam apriyam
priyaṁ cha nānṛitaṁ brūyād eṣha dharmaḥ sanātanaḥ

(*Manu Smriti* 4.138)

'Speak the truth in such a way that it is pleasing to others. Do not speak the truth in a manner injurious to others. Never speak untruth, even though it may be pleasant. This is the eternal path of morality and dharma.'

मनः प्रसादः सौम्यत्वं मौनमात्मविनिग्रहः ।
भावसंशुद्धिरित्येतत्तपो मानसमुच्यते ।।16।।

manaḥ-prasādaḥ saumyatvaṁ maunam ātma-vinigrahaḥ
bhāva-sanśhuddhir-ity-etat-tapo mānasam uchyate

manaḥ-prasādaḥ—serenity of thought; *saumyatvam*—gentleness; *maunam*—silence; *ātma-vinigrahaḥ*—self-control; *bhāva-sanśhuddhiḥ*—purity of purpose; *iti*—thus; *etat*—these; *tapaḥ*—austerity; *mānasam*—of the mind; *uchyate*—are declared as.

Serenity of thought, gentleness, silence, self-control, and purity of purpose—all these are declared as austerity of the mind.

Austerity of the mind is higher than the austerity of body and speech, for if we learn to master the mind, the body and speech automatically get mastered, while the reverse is not necessarily true. Factually, the state of the mind determines the state of an individual's consciousness. Shree Krishna had stated in verse 6.5, 'Elevate yourself through the power of your mind and not degrade yourself, for the mind can be the friend and also the enemy of the self.'

The mind may be likened to a garden, which can either be intelligently cultivated or allowed to run wild. Gardeners cultivate their plot, growing fruits, flowers, and vegetables in it. At the same time, they also ensure that it remains free from weeds. Similarly, we must cultivate our own mind with rich and noble thoughts, while weeding out negative and debilitating thoughts. If we allow resentful, hateful, blaming, unforgiving, critical, and condemning thoughts to reside in our mind, they will have a debilitating effect on our personality. We can never get a fair amount of constructive action out of the mind until we have learned to control it and keep it from becoming stimulated by anger, hatred, dislike, and other negative emotions. These are the weeds that choke out the manifestation of divine grace within our hearts.

People imagine that their thoughts are secret and have no external consequences because they dwell within the mind, away from the sight of others. They do not realise that thoughts not only forge their inner character but also their external personality. That is why we look upon someone and say, 'He seems like a very simple and trustworthy person.' For another person, we say, 'She seems to be very cunning and deceitful. Stay away from her.' In each case, it was the thoughts people harboured that sculpted their appearance. Ralph Waldo Emerson said:

There is full confession in the glances of our eyes, in our smiles, in salutations, in the grasp of the hands. Our sin bedaubs us, mars all the good impressions. Men do not know why they do not trust us. The vice glasses the eyes, demeans the cheek, pinches the nose, and writes, "O fool, fool!" on the forehead of a king.

Another powerful saying linking thoughts to character states:

Watch your thoughts, for they become words.
Watch your words, for they become actions.
Watch your actions, for they become habits.
Watch your habits, for they become character.
Watch your character, for it becomes your destiny.

It is important to realise that we harm ourselves with every negative thought that we harbour in our mind. At the same time, we uplift ourselves with every positive thought that we dwell upon. Henry Van Dyke expressed this very vividly, in his poem *Thoughts are things*:

I hold it true that thoughts are things;
They're endowed with bodies and breath and wings
That which we call our secret thought
Speeds forth to earth's remotest spot,
Leaving its blessings or its woes,
Like tracks behind as it goes.
We build our future, thought by thought.
For good or ill, yet know it not,
Choose, then, thy destiny and wait,
For love brings love, and hate brings hate.

Each thought we dwell upon has consequences, and thought-by-thought, we forge our destiny. For this reason, to veer the mind from negative emotions and make it dwell upon positive sentiments is considered austerity of the mind.

श्रद्धया परया तप्तं तपस्तत्त्रिविधं नरैः ।
अफलाकाङ्क्षिभिर्युक्तैः सात्त्विकं परिचक्षते ।।17।।

śhraddhayā parayā taptaṁ tapas tat tri-vidhaṁ naraiḥ
aphalākāṅkṣhibhir yuktaiḥ sāttvikaṁ parichakṣhate

śhraddhayā—with faith; *parayā*—transcendental; *taptam*—practised; *tapaḥ*—austerity; *tat*—that; *tri-vidham*—three-fold; *naraiḥ*—by persons; *aphala-ākāṅkṣhibhiḥ*—without yearning for material rewards; *yuktaiḥ*—steadfast; *sāttvikam*—in the mode of goodness; *parichakṣhate*—are designated.

When devout persons with ardent faith practise these three-fold austerities without yearning for material rewards, they are designated as austerities in the mode of goodness.

Having delineated the austerities of the body, speech, and mind, Shree Krishna now mentions their characteristics when they are performed in the mode of goodness. He says that an austerity loses its sanctity when material benefits are sought from its performance. It must be performed in a selfless manner, without attachment to rewards. Also, our faith in the value of the austerity should remain steadfast in both success and failure, and its practice should not be suspended because of laziness or inconvenience.

सत्कारमानपूजार्थं तपो दम्भेन चैव यत् ।
क्रियते तदिह प्रोक्तं राजसं चलमध्रुवम् ।।18।।

satkāra-māna-pūjārthaṁ tapo dambhena chaiva yat
kriyate tad iha proktaṁ rājasaṁ chalam adhruvam

sat-kāra—respect; *māna*—honour; *pūjā*—adoration; *artham*—for the sake of; *tapaḥ*—austerity; *dambhena*—with ostentation; *cha*—also; *eva*—certainly; *yat*—which; *kriyate*—is performed; *tat*—that; *iha*—in this world; *proktam*—is said; *rājasam*—in the mode of passion; *chalam*—flickering; *adhruvam*—temporary.

Austerity that is performed with ostentation for the sake of gaining honour, respect, and adoration is in the mode of passion. Its benefits are unstable and transitory.

Although austerity is a powerful tool for the purification of the self, not everyone practises it with pure intention. A politician labours rigorously to give many lectures a day, which is also a form of austerity, but the purpose is to gain position and prestige. Similarly, if one engages in spiritual activities to achieve honour and adulation, then the motive is equally material though the means is different. An austerity is classified in the mode of passion if it is performed for the sake of gaining respect, power, or other material rewards.

मूढग्राहेणात्मनो यत्पीडया क्रियते तपः ।
परस्योत्सादनार्थं वा तत्तामसमुदाहृतम् ।।19।।

mūḍha-grāheṇātmano yat pīḍayā kriyate tapaḥ
parasyotsādanārthaṁ vā tat tāmasam udāhṛitam

mūḍha—those with confused notions; *grāheṇa*—with endeavour; *ātmanaḥ*—one's own self; *yat*—which; *pīḍayā*—torturing; *kriyate*—is performed; *tapaḥ*—austerity; *parasya*—of others; *utsādana-artham*—for harming; *vā*—or; *tat*—that; *tāmasam*—in the mode of ignorance; *udāhṛitam*—is described to be.

Austerity that is performed by those with confused notions, and which involves torturing the self or harming others, is described to be in the mode of ignorance.

Mūḍha grāheṇāt refers to people with confused notions or ideas, who in the name of austerity, heedlessly torture themselves or even injure others without any respect for the teachings of the scriptures or the limits of the body. Such austerities accomplish nothing positive. They are performed in bodily consciousness and only serve to propagate the grossness of the personality.

दातव्यमिति यद्दानं दीयतेऽनुपकारिणे ।
देशे काले च पात्रे च तद्दानं सात्त्विकं स्मृतम् ।।20।।

dātavyam iti yad dānaṁ dīyate 'nupakāriṇe
deśhe kāle cha pātre cha tad dānaṁ sāttvikaṁ smṛitam

dātavyam—worthy of charity; *iti*—thus; *yat*—which; *dānam*—charity; *dīyate*—is given; *anupakāriṇe*—to one who cannot give in return; *deshe*—in the proper place; *kāle*—at the proper time; *cha*—and; *pātre*—to a worthy person; *cha*—and; *tat*—that; *dānam*—charity; *sāttvikam*—in the mode of goodness; *smṛitam*—is stated to be.

Charity given to a worthy person simply because it is right to give, without consideration of anything in return, at the proper time and in the proper place, is stated to be in the mode of goodness.

The three-fold divisions of *dān* or charity are now being described. It is an act of duty to give according to one's capacity. The *Bhaviṣhya Puran* states: *dānamekaṁ kalau yuge* 'In the age of Kali, giving in charity is the means for purification.' The Ramayan states this too:

pragaṭa chāri pada dharma ke kali mahuñ ek pradhāna
jena kena bidhi dīnheṅ dāna karai kalyāna

'Dharma has four basic tenets, one amongst which is the most important in the age of Kali—give in charity by whatever means possible.' The act of charity bestows many benefits. It reduces the attachment of the giver towards material objects; it develops the attitude of service; it expands the heart and fosters the sentiment of compassion for others. This is why most religious traditions follow the injunction of giving away one-tenth of one's earnings in charity. The *Skand Puran* states:

nyāyopārjita vittasya daśhamānśhena dhīmataḥ
kartavyo viniyogaśhcha īśhvaraprityarthameva cha

'From the wealth you have earned by rightful means, take out one-tenth, and as a matter of duty, give it away in charity. Dedicate your charity for the pleasure of God.' Charity is classified as proper or improper, superior or inferior, according to the factors mentioned by Shree Krishna in this verse. When it is offered freely from the heart to worthy recipients, at the proper time, and at the appropriate place, it is bequeathed to be in the mode of goodness.

यत्तु प्रत्युपकारार्थं फलमुद्दिश्य वा पुनः ।
दीयते च परिक्लिष्टं तद्दानं राजसं स्मृतम् ।।21।।

yat tu pratyupakārārthaṁ phalam uddiśhya vā punaḥ
dīyate cha parikliṣhṭaṁ tad dānaṁ rājasaṁ smṛitam

yat—which; *tu*—but; *prati-upakāra-artham*—with the hope of a return; *phalam*—reward; *uddiśhya*—expectation; *vā*—or; *punaḥ*—again; *dīyate*—is given; *cha*—and; *parikliṣhṭam*—reluctantly; *tat*—that; *dānam*—charity; *rājasam*—in the mode of passion; *smṛitam*—is said to be.

But charity given with reluctance, with the hope of a return or in expectation of a reward, is said to be in the mode of passion.

The best attitude of charity is to give without even being asked to do so. The second-best attitude is to give happily upon being requested for it. The third-best sentiment of charity is to give begrudgingly, when asked for a donation, or to regret later, asking oneself, 'Why did I give so much? I could have gotten away with a smaller amount.' Shree Krishna classifies this kind of charity in the mode of passion.

अदेशकाले यद्दानमपात्रेभ्यश्च दीयते ।
असत्कृतमवज्ञातं तत्तामसमुदाहृतम् ।।22।।

adeśha-kāle yad dānam apātrebhyaśh cha dīyate
asat-kṛitam avajñātaṁ tat tāmasam udāhṛitam

adeśha—at the wrong place; *kāle*—at the wrong time; *yat*—which; *dānam*—charity; *apātrebhyaḥ*—to unworthy persons; *cha*—and; *dīyate*—is given; *asat-kṛitam*—without respect; *avajñātam*—with contempt; *tat*—that; *tāmasam*—of the nature of nescience; *udāhṛitam*—is held to be.

And that charity, which is given at the wrong place and wrong time to unworthy persons, without showing respect, or with contempt, is held to be of the nature of nescience.

Charity in the mode of ignorance is done without consideration of proper place, person, attitude, or time. No beneficial purpose is served by it. For example, if money is offered to an alcoholic, who uses it to get inebriated and then ends up committing a murder, the murderer will definitely be punished according to the Law of Karma, but the person who gave the charity will also be morally culpable for the offence. This is an example of charity in the mode of ignorance that is given to an undeserving person.

ॐ तत्सदिति निर्देशो ब्रह्मणस्त्रिविधः स्मृतः ।
ब्राह्मणास्तेन वेदाश्च यज्ञाश्च विहिताः पुरा ।।23।।

om tat sad iti nirdeśho brahmaṇas-tri-vidhaḥ smṛitaḥ
brāhmaṇās-tena vedāśh-cha yajñāśh-cha vihitāḥ purā

om tat sat—syllables representing aspects of transcendence; *iti*—thus; *nirdeśhaḥ*—symbolic representatives; *brahmaṇaḥ*—the Supreme Absolute Truth; *tri-vidhaḥ*—of three kinds; *smṛitaḥ*—have been declared; *brāhmaṇāḥ*—the priests; *tena*—from them; *vedāḥ*—scriptures; *cha*—and; *yajñāḥ*—sacrifice; *cha*—and; *vihitāḥ*—came about; *purā*—from the beginning of creation.

The words 'Om Tat Sat' have been declared as symbolic representations of the Supreme Absolute Truth from the beginning of creation. From them came the priests, scriptures, and sacrifice.

In this chapter, Shree Krishna explained the categories of yajna (sacrifice), *tapa* (austerity), and *dān* (charity), according to the three modes of material nature. Among these three modes, the mode of ignorance degrades the soul into nescience, languor, and sloth. The mode of passion excites the living being and binds it in innumerable desires. The mode of goodness is serene and illuminating and engenders the development of virtues. Yet, the mode of goodness is also within the realm of maya. We must not get attached to it; instead, we must use the mode of goodness as a stepping-stone to reach the transcendental platform. In this verse, Shree Krishna goes beyond the three gunas and discusses the words 'Om Tat Sat', which symbolise different aspects of the Absolute Truth. *In the following verses, He explains the significance of these three words.*

तस्माद् ॐ इत्युदाहृत्य यज्ञदानतपःक्रियाः ।
प्रवर्तन्ते विधानोक्ताः सततं ब्रह्मवादिनाम् ।।24।।

tasmād om ity udāhṛitya yajña-dāna-tapaḥ-kriyāḥ
pravartante vidhānoktāḥ satataṁ brahma-vādinām

tasmāt—therefore; *om*—sacred syllable 'Om'; *iti*—thus; *udāhṛitya*—by uttering; *yajña*—sacrifice; *dāna*—charity; *tapaḥ*—penance; *kriyāḥ*—performing; *pravartante*—begin; *vidhāna-uktāḥ*—according to the prescriptions of Vedic injunctions; *satatam*—always; *brahma-vādinām*—expounders of the Vedas.

Therefore, when performing acts of sacrifice, offering charity, or undertaking penance, expounders of the Vedas always begin by uttering 'Om' according to the prescriptions of Vedic injunctions.

The syllable Om is a symbolic representation of the impersonal aspect of God. It is also considered as the name for the formless Brahman. It is also the primordial sound that pervades creation. Its proper pronunciation is: 'Aaa' with the mouth open, 'Ooh' with the lips puckered, and 'Mmm' with the lips pursed. It is placed in the beginning of many Vedic mantras as a *bīja* (seed) mantra to invoke auspiciousness.

तदित्यनभिसन्धाय फलं यज्ञतपःक्रियाः ।
दानक्रियाश्च विविधाः क्रियन्ते मोक्षकाङ्क्षिभिः ।।25।।

tad-ity-anabhisandhāya phalaṁ yajña-tapaḥ-kriyāḥ
dāna-kriyāśh-cha vividhāḥ kriyante mokṣha-kāṅkṣhibhiḥ

tat—the syllable 'Tat'; *iti*—thus; *anabhisandhāya*—without desiring; *phalam*—fruitive rewards; *yajña*—sacrifice; *tapaḥ*—austerity; *kriyāḥ*—acts; *dāna*—charity; *kriyāḥ*—acts; *cha*—and; *vividhāḥ*—various; *kriyante*—are done; *mokṣha-kāṅkṣhibhiḥ*—by seekers of freedom from material entanglements.

Persons who do not desire fruitive rewards, but seek to be free from material entanglements, utter the word 'Tat' along with acts of austerity, sacrifice, and charity.

The fruits of all actions belong to God, and hence, any yajna (sacrifice), *tapa* (austerity), and *dān* (charity), must be consecrated by offering it for the pleasure of the Supreme Lord. Now, Shree Krishna glorifies the sound vibration Tat which refers to Brahman. Chanting Tat along with austerity, sacrifice, and charity symbolises that they are not to be performed for material rewards, but for the eternal welfare of the soul through God-realisation.

सद्भावे साधुभावे च सदित्येतत्प्रयुज्यते ।
प्रशस्ते कर्मणि तथा सच्छब्दः पार्थ युज्यते ।।26।।

यज्ञे तपसि दाने च स्थितिः सदिति चोच्यते ।
कर्म चैव तदर्थीयं सदित्येवाभिधीयते ।।27।।

sad-bhāve sādhu-bhāve cha sad ity etat prayujyate
praśhaste karmaṇi tathā sach-chhabdaḥ pārtha yujyate

yajñe tapasi dāne cha sthitiḥ sad iti chochyate
karma chaiva tad-arthīyaṁ sad ity evābhidhīyate

sat-bhāve—with the intention of eternal existence and goodness; *sādhu-bhāve*—with auspicious intention; *cha*—also; *sat*—the syllable 'Sat'; *iti*—thus; *etat*—this; *prayujyate*—is used; *praśhaste*—auspicious; *karmaṇi*—action; *tathā*—also; *sat-śhabdaḥ*—the word 'Sat'; *pārtha*—Arjun, son of Pritha; *yujyate*—is used; *yajñe*—in sacrifice; *tapasi*—in penance; *dāne*—in charity; *cha*—and; *sthitiḥ*—established in steadiness; *sat*—the syllable 'Sat'; *iti*—thus; *cha*—and; *uchyate*—is pronounced; *karma*—action; *cha*—and; *eva*—indeed; *tat-arthīyam*—for such purposes; *sat*—the syllable 'Sat'; *iti*—thus; *eva*—indeed; *abhidhīyate*—is described.

The word 'Sat' means eternal existence and goodness. O Arjun, it is also used to describe an auspicious action. Being established in the performance of sacrifice, penance, and charity, is also described by the word, Sat. And so, any act for such purposes is named Sat.

Now the auspiciousness of the word 'Sat' is being glorified by Shree Krishna. The word Sat has many connotations, and the above two verses describe some of these. Sat is used to mean perpetual goodness and virtue. In addition, auspicious performance of sacrifice, austerity, and charity is also described as Sat. Sat also means that which always exists i.e., it is an eternal truth. The Shreemad Bhagavatam states:

satya-vrataṁ satya-paraṁ tri-satyaṁ
satyasya yoniṁ nihitaṁ cha satye
satyasya satyam ṛita-satya-netraṁ
satyātmakaṁ tvāṁ śharaṇaṁ prapannāḥ (10.2.26)

'O Lord, Your vow is true, for not only are You the Supreme Truth, but You are also the truth in the three phases of the cosmic manifestation—creation, maintenance, and dissolution. You are the origin of all that is true, and You are also its end. You are the essence of all truth, and You are also the eyes by which the truth is seen. Therefore, we surrender unto You, the Sat i.e., Supreme Absolute Truth. Please protect us.'

अश्रद्धया हुतं दत्तं तपस्तप्तं कृतं च यत् ।
असदित्युच्यते पार्थ न च तत्प्रेत्य नो इह ।।28।।

aśhraddhayā hutaṁ dattaṁ tapas taptaṁ kṛitaṁ cha yat
asad ity uchyate pārtha na cha tat pretya no iha

aśhraddhayā—without faith; *hutam*—sacrifice; *dattam*—charity; *tapaḥ*—penance; *taptam*—practised; *kṛitam*—done; *cha*—and; *yat*—which; *asat*—perishable; *iti*—thus; *uchyate*—are termed as; *pārtha*—Arjun, son of Pritha; *na*—not; *cha*—and; *tat*—that; *pretya*—in the next world; *no*—not; *iha*—in this world.

O son of Pritha, whatever acts of sacrifice, charity, or penance are done without faith, are termed as Asat. They are useless both in this world and the next.

In order to firmly establish that all Vedic activities should be performed with faith, Shree Krishna now emphasises the futility of Vedic activities done without it. He says that those who act without faith in the scriptures do not get good fruits in this life because their actions are not perfectly executed. And since they do not fulfil the conditions of the

Vedic scriptures, they do not receive good fruits in the next life either. Thus, one's faith should not be based upon one's own impressions of the mind and intellect. Instead, it should be based upon the infallible authority of the Vedic scriptures and the guru. This is the essence of the seventeenth chapter.

CHAPTER 18

Moksha Sanyas Yog

Yog through the Perfection of Renunciation and Surrender

The final chapter of the Bhagavad Gita is the longest and covers many subjects. Arjun initiates the topic of renunciation with a question about two commonly used Sanskrit words, sanyas (renunciation of actions) and *tyāg* (renunciation of desires). Both words come from roots words meaning, 'to abandon'. A sanyasi (monk) is one who does not participate in family life and withdraws from society to practice sadhana (spiritual discipline). A *tyāgī* is one who engages in activities but gives up selfish desire for enjoying the rewards of actions (this is the connotation of the word in the Gita). Shree Krishna recommends the second kind of renunciation. He advises that sacrifice, charity, penance, and other acts of duty should never be renounced, for they purify even the wise. Rather, they should be performed as a matter of duty simply because they ought to be done, without any attachment to the fruits of these actions.

Then, Shree Krishna goes into a detailed analysis of the three factors that motivate action, the three components of action, and the five factors that contribute to the result of action. He describes each of these in terms of the three gunas. He establishes that those with deficient understanding see themselves as the only cause of their works. But the enlightened souls, with purified intellect, neither consider themselves as the doer nor the enjoyer of their actions. Ever detached from the fruits of what they do, they are not bound in karmic reactions. The chapter then explains why people differ in their motives and activities.

According to the three modes of material nature, it describes the kinds of knowledge, the types of actions, and the categories of performers. It then offers the same analysis for the intellect, resolve, and happiness. The chapter then goes on to paint a picture of those who have attained perfection in spiritual life and are situated in Brahman-realisation. It adds that even such perfected yogis find completion in their realisation by engaging in bhakti. Thus, the secret of the Supreme Divine Personality can only be known through loving devotion.

Shree Krishna then reminds Arjun that God dwells in the hearts of all living beings and directs their wanderings according to their karmas. If we remember Him and dedicate all our activities to Him, taking shelter of Him and making Him our supreme goal, then by His grace we will overcome all obstacles and difficulties. But if, motivated by pride, we act according to our whims, we will not attain success. Finally, Shree Krishna reveals that the most confidential knowledge is to abandon all varieties of religiosity and simply surrender to God. However, this knowledge should not be given to those who are not austere or devoted, for they will misinterpret it and misuse it to irresponsibly abandon actions. But if we explain this confidential knowledge to qualified souls, it is the greatest act of love and is very pleasing to God.

Arjun then informs Shree Krishna that his illusion is dispelled, and he is ready to act as instructed. In the end, Sanjay, who has been narrating the dialogue to the blind king Dhritarashtra remarks how amazed and astounded he is on hearing the divine conversation. His hair stands on end in ecstasy as he recalls the sacred dialogue and remembers the stupendous cosmic form of God. He concludes with a profound pronouncement that victory will always be on the side of God and His pure devotee and so will goodness, supremacy, and opulence, for the darkness of falsehood will always be vanquished by the light of the Absolute Truth.

अर्जुन उवाच ।
सन्न्यासस्य महाबाहो तत्त्वमिच्छामि वेदितुम् ।
त्यागस्य च हृषीकेश पृथक्केशिनिषूदन ।।1।।

arjuna uvācha
sanyāsasya mahā-bāho tattvam ichchhāmi veditum
tyāgasya cha hṛiṣhīkeśha pṛithak keśhi-niṣhūdana

arjunaḥ uvācha—Arjun said; *sanyāsasya*—of renunciation of actions; *mahā-bāho*—mighty-armed one; *tattvam*—the truth; *ichchhāmi*—I wish; *veditum*—to understand; *tyāgasya*—of renunciation of desires for enjoying the fruits of actions; *cha*—and; *hṛiṣhīkeśha*—Krishna, Lord of the senses; *pṛithak*—difference; *keśhī-niṣhūdana*—Krishna, killer of the Keshi demon.

Arjun said: O mighty-armed Krishna, I wish to understand the nature of sanyas (renunciation of actions) and *tyāg* (renunciation of desire for the fruits of actions). O Hrishikesh, I also wish to know the distinction between the two, O Keshinisudan.

Arjun addresses Shree Krishna as 'Keshi-nisudan', meaning, 'killer of the Keshi demon'. In His divine pastimes on the earth, Lord Krishna had killed a furious and violent demon called Keshi who had taken the form of a mad horse and created havoc in the land of Braj. Doubt is also like an untamed horse that runs wild in the mind and destroys the garden of devotion. Arjun supplicates, 'Just as You slayed the Keshi demon, please slay the demon of doubt in my mind.' His question is penetrating and poignant. He wishes to know the nature of sanyas which means 'renunciation of actions'. He also wishes to know the nature of *tyāg* which means 'renunciation of desires for enjoying the fruits of actions'. Further, he uses the word *pṛithak*, meaning, difference; he wishes to understand the distinction between the two terms. Arjun also refers to Shree Krishna as Hrishikesh, meaning, 'master of the senses'. Arjun's goal is to accomplish the greatest of conquests which is to subdue the mind and the senses. It is this conquest that can bestow perfect peace. And the Supreme Lord Shree Krishna, as the Master of the senses, Himself embodies this state of perfection.

This topic had been explained in the previous chapters as well. Shree Krishna had talked about sanyas in verses 5.13 and 9.28 and about *tyāg* in verses 4.20 and 12.11, but He explains it here from another angle. The same truth permits itself to be presented from a variety of perspectives, and each perspective provides its own unique appeal. For example, various sections of a garden leave differing impressions on the viewer's mind while the entire garden creates yet another impression. The Bhagavad Gita is very much like this. Each chapter is designated as a particular Yog while the eighteenth chapter is considered the synopsis. In this chapter, Shree Krishna briefly summarises the perennial principles and eternal truths that were presented in the previous seventeen chapters and establishes the collective conclusion of all of them. After discussing the topics of renunciation and detachment, He goes on to explain the natures of the three gunas and how they affect people's natural propensities for work. He reiterates that the mode of goodness is the only mode worthy of cultivation. He then concludes that bhakti or exclusive loving devotion to the Supreme Lord is the paramount duty, and its attainment is the goal of human life.

श्रीभगवानुवाच ।
काम्यानां कर्मणां न्यासं सन्न्यासं कवयो विदुः ।
सर्वकर्मफलत्यागं प्राहुस्त्यागं विचक्षणाः ।।2।।

śhrī-bhagavān uvācha
kāmyānāṁ karmaṇāṁ nyāsaṁ sanyāsaṁ kavayo viduḥ
sarva-karma-phala-tyāgaṁ prāhus tyāgaṁ vichakṣhaṇāḥ

śhrī-bhagavān uvācha—the Supreme Divine Personality said; *kāmyānām*—desireful; *karmaṇām*—of actions; *nyāsam*—giving up; *sanyāsam*—renunciation of actions; *kavayaḥ*—the learned; *viduḥ*—to understand; *sarva*—all; *karma-phala*—fruits of actions; *tyāgam*—renunciation of desires for enjoying the fruits of actions; *prāhuḥ*—declare; *tyāgam*—renunciation of desires for enjoying the fruits of actions; *vichakṣhaṇāḥ*—the wise.

The Supreme Divine Personality said: Giving up actions motivated by desire is what the wise understand as sanyas. Relinquishing the fruits of all actions is what the learned declare to be *tyāg*.

Kavayaḥ are the learned. Shree Krishna states that learned people consider sanyas as the renunciation of work. Those who renounce work for material enjoyment and enter the renounced order are called karm sanyasis. They continue to do some of the *nitya karm* (daily work for the maintenance of the body), but they renounce *kāmya karm* (work related to acquisition of wealth, progeny, prestige, status, power, and so on). Such works bind the soul further in the wheel of karma and lead to repeated rebirths in the samsara of birth and death.

Vichakṣhaṇāḥ are the wise. Shree Krishna states that wise people lay emphasis on *tyāg*, meaning, 'internal renunciation'. This implies not relinquishing the prescribed Vedic duties, rather, renouncing the desires for enjoying their fruits. Thus, the attitude of giving up attachment to the rewards of action is *tyāg*, while the attitude of giving up work is sanyas. Both sanyas and *tyāg* seem plausible and reasonable options to pursue for enlightenment. Of these two courses of action, which one does Shree Krishna recommend? He provides more clarity on this topic in the subsequent verses.

त्याज्यं दोषवदित्येके कर्म प्राहुर्मनीषिणः ।
यज्ञदानतपःकर्म न त्याज्यमिति चापरे ।।3।।

tyājyaṁ doṣha-vad-ity eke karma prāhur manīṣhiṇaḥ
yajña-dāna-tapaḥ-karma na tyājyam iti chāpare

tyājyam—should be given up; *doṣha-vat*—as evil; *iti*—thus; *eke*—some; *karma*—actions; *prāhuḥ*—declare; *manīṣhiṇaḥ*—the learned; *yajña*—sacrifice; *dāna*—charity; *tapaḥ*—penance; *karma*—acts; *na*—never; *tyājyam*—should be abandoned; *iti*—thus; *cha*—and; *apare*—others.

Some learned people declare that all kinds of action should be given up as evil, while others maintain that acts of sacrifice, charity, and penance should never be abandoned.

Some philosophers, such as those of the *Sānkhya* school of thought, are in favour of discarding mundane life as quickly as possible. They opine that all actions should be abandoned because they are motivated by desire which promotes further transmigration in the cycle of life and death. They contend that all works are subject to inherent defects, such as indirect violence. For example, if one lights a fire, there is always the possibility of insects getting involuntarily burned in it. Hence, they recommend the path of cessation of all actions except those for the sustenance of the body.

Other learned philosophers, such as those of the Mimansa school of thought, declare that prescribed Vedic activities should never be given up. They contend that wherever there are two contradictory injunctions of the Vedas, if a specific one is more prominent, it annuls the general one. For example, the Vedas instruct us: *mā hinsyāt sarvā bhūtāni* 'Do not commit violence towards any living entity.' This is a general instruction. The same Vedas also instruct us to perform fire sacrifice. This is a specific instruction. It is possible that in performing a fire sacrifice, some creatures may get killed in the fire unintentionally. But the *Mimansakas* (followers of the Mimansa philosophy) contend that the specific instruction for performing the sacrifice prevails, and it must be followed even though it conflicts with the general instruction for not committing violence. Keeping this in mind, the *Mimansakas* say we must never give up beneficial activities, such as sacrifice, charity, and penance.

निश्चयं शृणु मे तत्र त्यागे भरतसत्तम ।
त्यागो हि पुरुषव्याघ्र त्रिविधः सम्प्रकीर्तितः ।।4।।

niśhchayaṁ śhṛiṇu me tatra tyāge bharata-sattama
tyāgo hi puruṣha-vyāghra tri-vidhaḥ samprakīrtitaḥ

niśhchayam—conclusion; *śhṛiṇu*—hear; *me*—my; *tatra*—there; *tyāge*—about renunciation of desires for enjoying the fruits of actions; *bharata-sat-tama*—best of the Bharatas; *tyāgaḥ*—renunciation of desires for enjoying the fruits of actions; *hi*—indeed; *puruṣha-vyāghra*—tiger amongst men; *tri-vidhaḥ*—of three kinds; *samprakīrtitaḥ*—declared.

Now hear My conclusion on the subject of renunciation, O tiger amongst men, for renunciation has been declared to be of three kinds.

Renunciation is important because it is the basis for higher life. It is only by giving up lower desires that we can cultivate higher aspirations. Likewise, it is by giving up lower actions that we can dedicate ourselves to higher duties and activities and walk the path of enlightenment. However, in the previous verse, Shree Krishna revealed that there are differing views on the true understanding of what renunciation actually entails. Having mentioned the two primary opposing views in the previous verse, Shree Krishna now reveals His opinion, which is the final verdict on the subject. He says that He will expound upon the subject by dividing renunciation into three categories (described in verses 7 to 9). He addresses Arjun as *vyāghra,* meaning, 'tiger amongst men' because renunciation is for the brave-hearted. Saint Kabir said:

tīra talavār se jo laṛai, so śhūravīra nahīṅ hoya
māyā taji bhakti kare, śhūra kahāvai soya

'One is not brave by virtue of fighting with arrows and swords; that person is truly brave who renounces maya and engages in bhakti.'

यज्ञदानतपःकर्म न त्याज्यं कार्यमेव तत् ।
यज्ञो दानं तपश्चैव पावनानि मनीषिणाम् ।।5।।

yajña-dāna-tapaḥ-karma na tyājyaṁ kāryam-eva tat
yajño dānaṁ tapaśh chaiva pāvanāni manīṣhiṇām

yajña—sacrifice; *dāna*—charity; *tapaḥ*—penance; *karma*—actions; *na*—never; *tyājyam*—should be abandoned; *kāryam eva*—must certainly be performed; *tat*—that; *yajñaḥ*—sacrifice; *dānam*—charity; *tapaḥ*—penance; *cha*—and; *eva*—indeed; *pāvanāni*—purifying; *manīṣhiṇām*—for the wise.

Actions based upon sacrifice, charity, and penance should never be abandoned; they must certainly be performed. Indeed, acts of sacrifice, charity, and penance are purifying even for those who are wise.

Here, Shree Krishna pronounces His verdict that we should never renounce actions which elevate us and are beneficial for humankind. Such actions, if performed in proper consciousness, do not bind us; instead, they help us grow spiritually. Consider, for example, a caterpillar. In order to transform itself, it weaves a cocoon for its evolution and encages itself in it. Once it becomes a butterfly, it breaks open the cocoon and soars into the sky. Our position in the world is similar to this. Like the ugly caterpillar, we are presently attached to the world and bereft of noble qualities. As a part of our self-preparation and self-education, we need to perform actions that bring about the inner transformation we desire. Yajna (sacrifice), *dān* (charity), and *tapa* (penance) are acts that help our spiritual evolution and growth. At times, it may seem that they are binding too, but they are like the caterpillar's cocoon. They melt our impurities, beautify us from within, and effectually help us break through the shackles of material life. Hence, Shree Krishna instructs in this verse that such auspicious activities must never be abandoned. *He now qualifies His statement by revealing the proper attitude with which they must be performed.*

एतान्यपि तु कर्माणि सङ्गं त्यक्त्वा फलानि च ।
कर्तव्यानीति मे पार्थ निश्चितं मतमुत्तमम् ।।6।।

etāny api tu karmāṇi saṅgaṁ tyaktvā phalāni cha
kartavyānīti me pārtha niśhchitaṁ matam uttamam

etāni—these; *api tu*—must certainly be; *karmāṇi*—activities; *saṅgam*—attachment; *tyaktvā*—giving up; *phalāni*—rewards; *cha*—and; *kartavyāni*—should be done as duty; *iti*—such; *me*—my; *pārtha*— Arjun, son of Pritha; *niśhchitam*—definite; *matam*—opinion; *uttamam*—supreme.

These activities must be performed without attachment and expectation of rewards. This is My definite and supreme verdict, O Arjun.

Acts of sacrifice, charity, and penance should be done with the sentiment of devotion to the Supreme Lord. If that consciousness has not been attained, then they should verily be performed as a matter of duty, without desire for reward. A mother abandons her selfish joys to perform her duty to her offspring. She offers the milk in her breast to her baby and nourishes the baby. She does not lose by giving to the child, rather, she fulfils her motherhood. Similarly, a cow grazes grass in the meadow all day long but yields the milk in her udder to her calf. The cow does not become any less by performing its duty; on the other hand, people hold it in greater respect. These activities are viewed as sacred because they are performed selflessly. Shree Krishna states in this verse that the wise should perform auspicious and beneficial acts in the same attitude of selflessness. *He now explains the three kinds of renunciation in the following three verses.*

नियतस्य तु सन्न्यासः कर्मणो नोपपद्यते ।
मोहात्तस्य परित्यागस्तामसः परिकीर्तितः ।।7।।

niyatasya tu sanyāsaḥ karmaṇo nopapadyate
mohāt tasya parityāgas tāmasaḥ parikīrtitaḥ

niyatasya—of prescribed duties; *tu*—but; *sanyāsaḥ*—renunciation; *karmaṇaḥ*—actions; *na*—never; *upapadyate*—to be performed; *mohāt*—deluded; *tasya*—of that; *parityāgaḥ*—renunciation; *tāmasaḥ*—in the mode of ignorance; *parikīrtitaḥ*—has been declared.

Prescribed duties should never be renounced. Such deluded renunciation is said to be in the mode of ignorance.

Renouncing prohibited actions and unrighteous actions is proper; renouncing desire for the rewards of actions is also proper; but renouncing prescribed duties is never proper. Prescribed duties help purify the mind and elevate it from tamo guna to rajo guna to sattva guna. Abandoning them is an erroneous display of foolishness. Shree Krishna states that giving up prescribed duties in the name of renunciation is said to be in the mode of ignorance.

Having come in this world, we all have obligatory duties. Fulfilling them helps develop many qualities in an individual, such as responsibility, discipline of the mind and senses, and tolerance of pain and hardships. Abandoning them, out of ignorance, leads to the degradation of the soul. These obligatory duties vary according to one's level of consciousness. For an ordinary person, acts such as earning wealth, taking care of the family, bathing, eating, and other daily activities are prescribed duties. As one gets elevated, these obligatory duties change. For an elevated soul, sacrifice, charity, and penance are the duties.

दुःखमित्येव यत्कर्म कायक्लेशभयात्त्यजेत् ।
स कृत्वा राजसं त्यागं नैव त्यागफलं लभेत् ।।8।।

duḥkham ity eva yat karma kāya-kleśha-bhayāt-tyajet
sa kṛitvā rājasaṁ tyāgaṁ naiva tyāga-phalaṁ labhet

duḥkham—troublesome; *iti*—as; *eva*—indeed; *yat*—which; *karma*—duties; *kāya*—bodily; *kleśha*—discomfort; *bhayāt*—out of fear; *tyajet*—giving up; *saḥ*—they; *kṛitvā*—having done; *rājasam*—in the mode of passion; *tyāgam*—renunciation of desires for enjoying the fruits of actions; *na*—never; *eva*—certainly; *tyāga*—renunciation of desires for enjoying the fruits of actions; *phalam*—result; *labhet*—attain.

To give up prescribed duties because they are troublesome or cause bodily discomfort is renunciation in the mode of passion. Such renunciation is never beneficial or elevating.

To advance in life does not mean abandoning our responsibilities, instead, it entails increasing them. Novice spiritualists often do not understand this truth. Wishing to avoid pain and taking an escapist attitude, they make spiritual aspiration a pretext for relinquishing their obligatory duties. However, life is never meant to be without burdens. Advanced *sādhaks* are not those who are undisturbed because they do nothing; on the contrary, they retain their peace despite upholding a huge burden placed upon their shoulders. Shree Krishna declares in this verse that giving up duties because they are troublesome is renunciation in the mode of passion.

From the very beginning, the Bhagavad Gita is a call for action. Arjun finds his duty unpleasant and bothersome and, as a result, wishes to run away from the battlefield. Shree Krishna calls this ignorance and weakness. He encourages Arjun to continue doing his duty, even though it may be unpleasant, while simultaneously bringing about an internal transformation from within. For this purpose, He enlightens Arjun with spiritual knowledge and helps him develop the eyes of wisdom. Having heard the Bhagavad Gita, Arjun does not change his profession, but changes the consciousness he brings to bear upon his activities. Previously, the motive behind his work was to secure the kingdom of Hastinapur for his comfort and glory. Later, he continues to do his work, but as an act of devotion to God.

कार्यमित्येव यत्कर्म नियतं क्रियतेऽर्जुन ।
सङ्गं त्यक्त्वा फलं चैव स त्यागः सात्त्विको मतः ॥९॥

kāryam ity eva yat karma niyataṁ kriyate 'rjuna
saṅgaṁ tyaktvā phalaṁ chaiva sa tyāgaḥ sāttviko mataḥ

kāryam—as a duty; *iti*—as; *eva*—indeed; *yat*—which; *karma niyatam*—obligatory actions; *kriyate*—are performed; *arjuna*—Arjun; *saṅgam*—attachment; *tyaktvā*—relinquishing; *phalam*—reward; *cha*—and; *eva*—certainly; *saḥ*—such; *tyāgaḥ*—renunciation of desires for enjoying the fruits of actions; *sāttvikaḥ*—in the mode of goodness; *mataḥ*—considered.

When actions are undertaken in response to duty, and one relinquishes attachment to any reward, O Arjun, it is considered renunciation in the nature of goodness.

Shree Krishna now describes the superior kind of renunciation where we continue to perform our obligatory duties but give up attachment to the fruit of actions. He describes this as the highest kind of renunciation which is situated in the mode of goodness (sattvic).

Renunciation is definitely necessary for spiritual attainment. But the problem is that people's understanding of renunciation is very shallow, and they look upon it as only the external abandonment of works. Such renunciation leads to hypocrisy, in which, while externally donning the robes of a renunciant, one internally contemplates upon the objects of the senses. There are many sadhus in India who come in this category. They left the world with the noble intention of God-realisation, but because the mind was not yet detached from the objects of the senses, their renunciation did not bestow the desired fruits. Consequently, they found their actions did not lead them to a higher spiritual life at all. The defect was in their sequence—they strove first for external renunciation and later for internal detachment. The instruction of this verse is to reverse the sequence—first develop internal detachment and then renounce externally.

न द्वेष्ट्यकुशलं कर्म कुशले नानुषज्जते ।
त्यागी सत्त्वसमाविष्टो मेधावी छिन्नसंशयः ॥10॥

na dveṣhṭy akuśhalaṁ karma kuśhale nānuṣhajjate
tyāgī sattva-samāviṣhṭo medhāvī chhinna-sanśhayaḥ

na—neither; *dveṣhṭi*—hate; *akuśhalam*—disagreeable; *karma*—work; *kuśhale*—to an agreeable; *na*—nor; *anuṣhajjate*—seek; *tyāgī*—one who renounces desires for enjoying the fruits of actions; *sattva*—in the mode of goodness; *samāviṣhṭaḥ*—endowed with; *medhāvī*—intelligent; *chhinna-sanśhayaḥ*—those who have no doubts.

Those who neither avoid disagreeable work nor seek work because it is agreeable are persons of true renunciation. They are endowed with the quality of the mode of goodness and have no doubts (about the nature of work).

People who are situated in sattvic renunciation are not miserable in disagreeable circumstances; nor do they get attached to situations that are agreeable to them. They simply do their duty under all conditions, without feeling elated when the going is good or feeling dejected when life becomes tough. They are not like a dry leaf that is tossed hither and thither by every passing breeze. On the contrary, they are like the reeds in the sea, gently negotiating every rising and falling wave. While retaining their equanimity and without succumbing to anger, greed, envy, or attachment, they watch the waves of events rising and falling around them.

Bal Gangadhar Tilak was a scholar of the Bhagavad Gita and a famous karm yogi. Before Mahatma Gandhi came on the scene, he was at the forefront of the freedom struggle of India. He was asked what position he would choose if India became independent—prime minister or foreign minister? He replied, 'I always desired to write a book on differential calculus. I will fulfil it.'

Once, the police arrested him for creating unrest. He asked his friend to find out the provisions under which he was arrested and to inform him in prison. When the friend reached him after an hour, Tilak was fast asleep in the jail.

Another time, he was working in his office, and his clerk brought him the news that his elder son was seriously ill. Instead of getting emotionally wrought, he asked the clerk to get a doctor and continued working. Half an hour later, his friend came and conveyed the same news. He said, 'I have called for the doctor to see him. What else can I do?' These instances reveal how he retained his composure despite being in the midst of tumultuous situations. He was able to continue performing his actions because of the internal emotional composure; had he been emotionally distressed, he would have been unable to sleep in the prison cell or concentrate on his work at the office.

न हि देहभृता शक्यं त्यक्तुं कर्माण्यशेषतः ।
यस्तु कर्मफलत्यागी स त्यागीत्यभिधीयते ।।11।।

na hi deha-bhṛitā śhakyaṁ tyaktuṁ karmāṇy aśheṣhataḥ
yas tu karma-phala-tyāgī sa tyāgīty abhidhīyate

na—not; *hi*—indeed; *deha-bhṛitā*—for the embodied being; *śhakyam*—possible; *tyaktum*—to give up; *karmāṇi*—activities; *aśheṣhataḥ*—entirely; *yaḥ*—who; *tu*—but; *karma-phala*—fruits of actions; *tyāgī*—one who renounces all desires for enjoying the fruits of actions; *saḥ*—they; *tyāgī*—one who renounces all desires for enjoying the fruits of actions; *iti*—as; *abhidhīyate*—are said.

For the embodied being, it is impossible to give up activities entirely. But those who relinquish the fruits of their actions are said to be truly renounced.

It may be contended that better than renunciation of the fruits of actions is to simply renounce all actions, for then there will be no distraction from meditation and contemplation. Shree Krishna rejects this as a possible option by stating that the state of complete inactivity is impossible for the embodied being. The basic functions for the maintenance of the body, such as eating, sleeping, bathing, and other daily tasks have to be performed by everyone. Besides, standing, sitting, thinking, walking, talking, and so on are also activities that cannot be avoided. If we understand renunciation to be the external abandonment of work, then no one can ever be truly renounced. However, Shree Krishna states here that if one can give up attachment to the fruits of actions, it is considered perfect renunciation.

अनिष्टमिष्टं मिश्रं च त्रिविधं कर्मणः फलम् ।
भवत्यत्यागिनां प्रेत्य न तु सन्न्यासिनां क्वचित् ।।12।।

anishṭam ishṭaṁ miśhraṁ cha tri-vidhaṁ karmaṇaḥ phalam
bhavaty atyāgināṁ pretya na tu sanyāsināṁ kvachit

anishṭam—unpleasant; *ishṭam*—pleasant; *miśhram*—mixed; *cha*—and; *tri-vidham*—three-fold; *karmaṇaḥ phalam*—fruits of actions; *bhavati*—accrue; *atyāginām*—to those who are attached to personal reward; *pretya*—after death; *na*—not; *tu*—but; *sanyāsinām*—for the renouncers of actions; *kvachit*—ever.

The three-fold fruits of actions—pleasant, unpleasant, and mixed—accrue even after death to those who are attached to personal reward. But, for those who renounce the fruits of their actions, there are no such results in the here or hereafter.

The three kinds of rewards that the soul reaps after death are: 1) *ishṭam* or pleasant experiences in the celestial abodes, 2) *anishṭam* or unpleasant experiences in the hellish abodes, and 3) *miśhram* or mixed experiences in the human form on the earth planet. Those who perform virtuous actions are awarded the celestial realms; those who perform unrighteous actions are given birth in the nether realms; and those who perform a mixture of both come back to the human realm.

But this applies only when the actions are performed with a desire for rewards. When such fruitive desire is renounced and work is done merely as a duty to God, then no such results accrue from actions.

A similar rule exists in the world as well. When one person kills another it is considered murder which is a crime that can even result in the death sentence. However, if the government declares that someone is a notorious murderer or thief who is wanted dead or alive, then killing such a person is not considered an offence in the eyes of the law. Instead, it is rewarded by the government, and the killer is even respected as a national hero. Similarly, when we give up personal motive in our actions, then the three-fold fruits of actions do not accrue.

पञ्चैतानि महाबाहो कारणानि निबोध मे ।
साङ्ख्ये कृतान्ते प्रोक्तानि सिद्धये सर्वकर्मणाम् ।।13।।

pañchaitāni mahā-bāho kāraṇāni nibodha me
sānkhye kṛitānte proktāni siddhaye sarva-karmaṇām

pañcha—five; *etāni*—these; *mahā-bāho*—mighty-armed one; *kāraṇāni*—causes; *nibodha*—listen; *me*—from me; *sānkhye*—of *Sānkhya*; *kṛita-ante*—stop reactions of karmas; *proktāni*—explains; *siddhaye*—for the accomplishment; *sarva*—all; *karmaṇām*—of karmas.

O Arjun, now learn from Me about the five factors that have been mentioned for the accomplishment of all actions in the doctrine of *Sānkhya*, which explains how to stop the reactions of karmas.

On knowing that work can be performed without attachment to the fruits, a natural question arises: 'What constitutes action?' Shree Krishna announces to Arjun that He is going to address this question now, as this knowledge will help develop detachment from the results of actions. Simultaneously, He clarifies that the description of the five limbs of action is not a new analysis, but what has previously been described in the *Sānkhya* philosophy as well. *Sānkhya* refers to the system of philosophy established by Maharishi Kapil, who was a descension of God and appeared on the earth as the child of Kardam Muni and Devahuti. The *Sānkhya* philosophy he propounded is based upon a system of analytical rationality. It develops knowledge of the self through an analysis of the elements within the body and in the world. It also ascertains the nature of cause and effect by an analysis of the elements of action.

अधिष्ठानं तथा कर्ता करणं च पृथग्विधम् ।
विविधाश्च पृथक्चेष्टा दैवं चैवात्र पञ्चमम् ।।14।।

adhiṣhṭhānaṁ tathā kartā karaṇaṁ cha pṛithag-vidham
vividhāśh cha pṛithak cheṣhṭā daivaṁ chaivātra pañchamam

adhiṣhṭhānam—the body; *tathā*—also; *kartā*—the doer (soul); *karaṇam*—senses; *cha*—and; *pṛithak-vidham*—various kinds; *vividhāḥ*—many; *cha*—and; *pṛithak*—distinct; *cheṣhṭāḥ*—efforts; *daivam*—Divine Providence; *cha eva atra*—these certainly are (causes); *pañchamam*—the fifth.

The body, the doer (soul), the various senses, the many kinds of efforts, and Divine Providence—these are the five factors of action.

In this verse, *adhiṣhṭhānam* means 'place of residence' and refers to the body, since karmas can only be performed when the soul is situated in the body. *Kartā* means 'the doer' and refers to the soul. Although the soul itself does not perform actions, it inspires the body-mind-intellect mechanism with the life force to act. Further, due to the influence of the ego, it identifies with their actions. Therefore, it is responsible for the actions performed by the body and is called both the knower and the doer. The *Praśhna Upanishad* states:

eṣha hi draṣhṭā spraṣhṭā śhrotā ghrātā rasayitā mantā boddhā
kartā vijñānātmā puruṣhaḥ sa pare 'kṣhara ātmani sampratiṣhṭhate

(4.9)

'It is the soul that sees, touches, hears, feels, tastes, thinks, and comprehends. Thus, the soul is to be considered both—the knower and the doer of actions.' The *Brahma Sutra* also states: *jño 'ta eva* (2.3.18) 'It is truly the soul that is the knower.' Again, the *Brahma Sutra* states: *kartā śhāstrārthavattvāt* (2.3.33) 'The soul is the doer of actions, and this is confirmed by the scriptures.' From the above quotations, it is clear that the soul is also a factor in accomplishing actions.

The senses are instruments used for performing actions. Without the senses, the soul could not have experienced the sensations of taste, touch, sight, smell, or sound. Alongside are the five working senses—hands, legs, voice, genitals, and anus. It is with their help that the soul accomplishes various kinds of work. Thus, the senses are also listed as factors in accomplishing actions.

Despite all the instruments of action, if one does not put in the effort, nothing is ever done. In fact, effort is so important that Chanakya Pandit states in his *Neeti Sutras*: *utsāhavatāṁ śhatravopi vaśhībhavanti* 'With sufficient effort, even poor destiny can be transformed into good fortune.' *Nirutvāhād daivaṁ patita* 'Without proper effort, even good destiny can be converted into misfortune.' Therefore, *cheṣhṭhā* (effort) is another ingredient of action.

God is seated within the body of the living being as the Witness. Based upon their past karmas, He also bestows different abilities to different people to perform actions. One may call this Divine Providence. For example, some people possess the acumen for earning huge amounts of wealth. Their acquaintances become astonished by their brilliant financial analysis of complex situations. They also seem to be lucky with the risks they take. This special intellect is granted to them by God. Similarly, others seem to have God-given talents in fields such as sports, music, art, literature, and so on. It is God who bestows people these special abilities in accordance with their past karmas. He also grants the results of the present karmas. Hence, He is listed as one of the factors responsible for action.

शरीरवाङ्मनोभिर्यत्कर्म प्रारभते नरः ।
न्याय्यं वा विपरीतं वा पञ्चैते तस्य हेतवः ।।15।।

तत्रैवं सति कर्तारमात्मानं केवलं तु यः ।
पश्यत्यकृतबुद्धित्वान्न स पश्यति दुर्मतिः ।।16।।

śharīra-vāṅ-manobhir yat karma prārabhate naraḥ
nyāyyaṁ vā viparītaṁ vā pañchaite tasya hetavaḥ

tatraivaṁ sati kartāram ātmānaṁ kevalaṁ tu yaḥ
paśhyaty akṛita-buddhitvān na sa paśhyati durmatiḥ

śharīra-vāk-manobhiḥ—with body, speech, or mind; *yat*—which; *karma*—action; *prārabhate*—performs; *naraḥ*—a person; *nyāyyam*—proper; *vā*—or; *viparītam*—improper; *vā*—or; *pañcha*—five; *ete*—these; *tasya*—their; *hetavaḥ*—factors; *tatra*—there; *evam sati*—in spite of this; *kartāram*—the doer; *ātmānam*—the soul; *kevalam*—only; *tu*—but; *yaḥ*—who; *paśhyati*—see; *akṛita-buddhitvāt*—with impure intellect; *na*—not; *saḥ*—they; *paśhyati*—see; *durmatiḥ*—foolish.

These five are the contributory factors for whatever action is performed, whether proper or improper, with body, speech, or mind. Those who do not understand this regard the soul as the only doer. With their impure intellects, they cannot see things as they are.

The three kinds of actions are—*kāyik* (those performed with the body), *vāchik* (those performed by speech), and *mānasik* (those performed by the mind). In each of these categories, whether we do virtuous or sinful acts, the five causes mentioned in the previous verse are responsible. Due to the ego, we think of ourselves as the doers of our actions. 'I achieved this.' 'I accomplished that.' 'I will do this.' These are statements we make under the illusion of being the doer. Shree Krishna's purpose in revealing this knowledge is to annihilate the soul's pride of doership. Thus, He states that those who see the soul as the only contributory factor for action do not see things as they truly are. If the soul were not granted a body by God, it could not have done anything at all. Further, if the body were not energised by God, it could still not have done anything. The *Kenopaniṣhad* states:

yadvāchānabhyuditaṁ yena vāgabhyudyate (1.4)

'Brahman cannot be described by the voice. By Its inspiration, the voice gets the power to speak.'

yanmanasā na manute yenāhurmano matam (1.5)

'Brahman cannot be understood by the mind and intellect. By Its power, the mind and intellect work.'

yachchakṣhuṣhā na paśhyati yena chakṣhūṁṣhi paśhyati (1.6)

'Brahman cannot be seen with the eyes. By Its inspiration, the eyes see.'

yachchhrotreṇa na śhṛiṇoti yena śhrotramidaṁ śhrutam (1.7)

'Brahman cannot be heard with the ears. By Its power, the ears hear.'

yat prāṇena na prāṇiti yena prāṇaḥ praṇīyate (1.8)

'Brahman cannot be energised by the life airs. By Its inspiration, the life airs function.'

This does not mean that the soul has no role in performing karmas. It is like the driver in the car who controls the steering wheel of the car and decides where to turn it and at what speed to drive. Similarly, the soul too governs the actions of the body, mind, and intellect, but it should not claim credit for any action(s) for itself. If we see ourselves to be the sole cause of action, then we want to be the enjoyers of our actions as well. But when we free ourselves from the pride of doership and ascribe the credit of our efforts to the grace of God and the tools provided by Him, then we also realise that we are not the enjoyers of our actions, and all actions are meant for His pleasure. *As explained in the next verse, this understanding helps us to dedicate every act of sacrifice, charity, and penance to Him and perform them with devotion.*

यस्य नाहङ्कृतो भावो बुद्धिर्यस्य न लिप्यते ।
हत्वाऽपि स इमाँल्लोकान्न हन्ति न निबध्यते ।।17।।

yasya nāhankṛito bhāvo buddhir yasya na lipyate
hatvā 'pi sa imāñl lokān na hanti na nibadhyate

yasya—whose; *na ahankṛitaḥ*—free from the ego of being the doer; *bhāvaḥ*—nature; *buddhiḥ*—intellect; *yasya*—whose; *na lipyate*—unattached; *hatvā*—slay; *api*—even; *saḥ*—they; *imān*—this; *lokān*—living beings; *na*—neither; *hanti*—kill; *na*—nor; *nibadhyate*—get bound.

Those who are free from the ego of being the doer and whose intellect is unattached, though they may slay living beings, they neither kill nor are they bound by actions.

Having described the obtuse intellect in the previous verse, Shree Krishna now describes the pure intellect. He says that those with purified intellect are free from the false pride of being the doer. They also do not seek to enjoy the fruits of their actions. Thus, they are not bound in the karmic reactions of what they do. Previously in verse 5.10 as well, He had stated that those who are detached from results are never tainted by sin. From a material perspective, they may appear to be working, but from a spiritual perspective, they are free from selfish motivations, and therefore they do not become bound by the results of karma.

Rahim Khankhana was a famous poet-saint during the Mughal period in Indian history. Although a Muslim by birth, he was a great devotee of Lord Krishna. When he would give alms in charity, he would lower his eyes. An endearing incident is related about this habit of his. It is said that Saint Tulsidas heard of Rahim's style of giving alms and asked him:

aisī denī dena jyuñ, kita sīkhe ho saina
jyoṅ jyoṅ kara ūñchyo karo, tyoṅ tyoṅ niche naina

'Sir, where did you learn to give alms like this? Your hands are as high as your eyes are low.' Rahim replied beautifully and in all humility:

denahāra koī aur hai, bhejata hai dina raina
loga bharama hama para kareṅ, yāte niche naina

'The giver is someone else, giving day and night. But the world gives me the credit, so I lower my eyes.'

Understanding that we are not the sole cause responsible for our accomplishments frees us from the egoistic pride of doership.

ज्ञानं ज्ञेयं परिज्ञाता त्रिविधा कर्मचोदना ।
करणं कर्म कर्तेति त्रिविधः कर्मसंग्रहः ।।18।।

jñānaṁ jñeyaṁ parijñātā tri-vidhā karma-chodanā
karaṇaṁ karma karteti tri-vidhaḥ karma-saṅgrahaḥ

jñānam—knowledge; *jñeyam*—the object of knowledge; *parijñātā*—the knower; *tri-vidhā*—three factors; *karma-chodanā*—factors that induce action; *karaṇam*—the instrumens of action; *karma*—the act; *kartā*—the doer; *iti*—thus; *tri-vidhaḥ*—threefold; *karma-saṅgrahaḥ*—constituents of action.

Knowledge, the object of knowledge, and the knower—these are the three factors that induce action. The instrument of action, the act itself, and the doer—these are the three constituents of action.

In His systematic treatment of the science of action, Shree Krishna explained its limbs. He also explained the karmic reactions of actions and the process of becoming free from them. Now, He discusses the three-fold factors that propel actions. These are *jnana* (knowledge), *jneya* (the object of knowledge), and *jnata* (the knower). Together, the three are called the *jnana tripuṭī* (triad of knowledge).

'Knowledge' is a primary impetus for action; it provides understanding to the 'knower' about the 'object of knowledge'. This triad jointly induces action. For example, knowledge of the remuneration to be paid by the employer motivates employees to work; information of the discovery of gold in various parts of the world led to the gold rushes involving feverish migration by workers; awareness of the importance of winning a medal in the Olympics motivates sportspersons to practice for years. Knowledge also has a correlation to the quality of work. For instance, a degree from a top college carries weight in the job market. Corporations realise that people with higher quality knowledge can perform work more proficiently. That's why good corporations invest in the development of their people, such as sponsoring employees for developmental seminars to further advance their skill sets.

The second set named is the *karm tripuṭī* (triad of action). It includes the *kartā* (doer), *kāraṇ* (the instrument of action), and *karm* (the act itself). This triad of work jointly constitutes the content of action. The 'doer' utilises the 'instruments of action' to perform 'the action'. *Having analysed the constituents of action, Shree Krishna now relates them to the three modes of material nature to explain why people differ from each other in their motives and actions.*

ज्ञानं कर्म च कर्ता च त्रिधैव गुणभेदतः ।
प्रोच्यते गुणसङ्ख्याने यथावच्छृणु तान्यपि ।।19।।

jñānaṁ karma cha kartā cha tridhaiva guṇa-bhedataḥ
prochyate guṇa-saṅkhyāne yathāvach chhṛiṇu tāny api

jñānam—knowledge; *karma*—action; *cha*—and; *kartā*—doer; *cha*—also; *tridhā*—of three kinds; *eva*—certainly; *guṇa-bhedataḥ*—distinguished according to the three modes of material nature; *prochyate*—are declared; *guṇa-saṅkhyāne*—*Sāṅkhya* philosophy, which describes the modes of material nature; *yathā-vat*—as they are; *śhṛiṇu*—listen; *tāni*—them; *api*—also.

Knowledge, action, and the doer are declared to be of three kinds in *Sāṅkhya* philosophy, distinguished according to the three modes of material nature. Listen, and I will explain their distinctions to you.

Shree Krishna once again refers to the three modes of nature. In chapter 14, He had given an introduction about these modes, and described how they bind the soul to the samsara of life and death. Then in chapter 17, He went into great detail about how these three modes influence the kinds of faith people develop and also their choice of foods. He also explained the three categories of sacrifice, charity, and penance. Here, according to the three gunas, the Lord will explain the three types of knowledge, action, and doers.

Among the six systems of thought in Indian philosophy, the *Sāṅkhya* philosophy (also called *Purush Prakriti Vāda*) is recognised as the authority in the analysis of material nature. It considers the soul as the purush (lord), and thus recognises many purushas. Prakriti is the material nature and includes all things made from it. *Sānkhya* states the cause for misery is the desire of the purush to enjoy prakriti. When this enjoying propensity subsides, then the purush is released from the bondage of material nature and attains eternal beatitude. The *Sānkhya* system does not acknowledge the existence of the Param Purush or the Supreme Lord, hence it is insufficient for knowing the Absolute Truth. However, in the matter of knowledge about prakriti (material nature), Shree Krishna refers to it as the authority.

सर्वभूतेषु येनैकं भावमव्ययमीक्षते ।
अविभक्तं विभक्तेषु तज्ज्ञानं विद्धि सात्त्विकम् ।।20।।

sarva-bhūteṣhu yenaikaṁ bhāvam avyayam īkṣhate
avibhaktaṁ vibhakteṣhu taj jñānaṁ viddhi sāttvikam

sarva-bhūteṣhu—within all living beings; *yena*—by which; *ekam*—one; *bhāvam*—nature; *avyayam*—imperishable; *īkṣhate*—one sees; *avibhaktam*—undivided; *vibhakteṣhu*—in diversity; *tat*—that; *jñānam*—knowledge; *viddhi*—understand; *sāttvikam*—in the mode of goodness.

Understand that knowledge to be in the mode of goodness by which a person sees one undivided imperishable reality within all diverse living beings.

Creation gives the appearance of a panorama of diverse living beings and material entities. But the substratum of this apparent diversity is the Supreme Lord. Those who possess this vision of knowledge see the unity that exists behind the variety of creation, just as an electrical engineer sees the same electricity flowing through different gadgets, and a goldsmith sees the same gold cast into different ornaments. The Shreemad Bhagavatam states:

vadanti tat tattva-vidas tattvaṁ yaj jñānam advayam (1.2.11)

'Knowers of the truth have stated that there is only one entity in existence, without a second.' Chaitanya Mahaprabhu referred to God, in His form as Shree Krishna, as *advaya jnana tattva* (one without a second, the only thing and everything that exists in creation), on the basis of the following four criteria:

1. ***Sajātīya Bhed Śhūnya*** (He is one with all similar entities): Shree Krishna is one with the various other forms of God, such as Ram, Shiv, and Vishnu, since these are different manifestations of the one God.

   Shree Krishna is also one with the souls, who are His tiny fragmental parts. A fragment is one with its whole, just as flames are one with the fire of which they are tiny parts.

2. ***Vijātīya Bhed Śhūnya*** (He is one with all dissimilar entities): Dissimilar to God is maya, which is insentient, while God is sentient. However, maya is an energy of God, and energy is one with its energetic, just as the energies of fire—heat and light—are non-different from it.

3. ***Swagat Bhed Śhūnya*** (The various parts of His body are non-different from Him): The amazing thing about God's body is that all the parts perform the functions of all the other parts. The *Brahma Samhitā* states:

   aṅgāni yasya sakalendriya-vṛitti-manti
   paśhyanti pānti kalayanti chiraṁ jaganti (5.32)

   'With every limb of his body, God can see, hear, talk, smell, eat, and think.' Hence, all the limbs of God's body are non-different from Him.

4. ***Swayam Siddha*** (He needs the support of no other entity): Maya and the soul are both dependent upon God for their existence. If He did not energise them, they would cease to exist. On the other hand, God is supremely independent and does not need the support of any other entity for His existence.

The Supreme Lord Shree Krishna satisfies all the four points listed above, and thus He is the *advaya jnana tattva*; in other words, He is everything that exists in creation. With this understanding, when we see the entire creation in its unity with God, it is considered sattvic knowledge. And love based upon such knowledge is not racial or national, rather, it is universal.

पृथक्त्वेन तु यज्ज्ञानं नानाभावान्पृथग्विधान् ।
वेत्ति सर्वेषु भूतेषु तज्ज्ञानं विद्धि राजसम् ।।21।।

pṛithaktvena tu yaj jñānaṁ nānā-bhāvān pṛithag-vidhān
vetti sarveṣhu bhūteṣhu taj jñānaṁ viddhi rājasam

pṛithaktvena—unconnected; *tu*—however; *yat*—which; *jñānam*—knowledge; *nānā-bhāvān*—manifold entities; *pṛithak-vidhān*—of diversity; *vetti*—consider; *sarveṣhu*—in all; *bhūteṣhu*—living entities; *tat*—that; *jñānam*—knowledge; *viddhi*—know; *rājasam*—in the mode of passion.

That knowledge is to be considered in the mode of passion by which one sees manifold living entities in diverse bodies as individual and unconnected.

Shree Krishna now explains rajasic knowledge. That knowledge is said to be in the mode of passion where the world is not seen in its connection with God, and thus the living beings are perceived in their plurality, with distinctions of race, class, creed, sect, nationality, and so on. Such knowledge divides the one human society along innumerable lines. When knowledge unites, it is in the mode of goodness, and when knowledge divides, it is in the mode of passion.

यत्तु कृत्स्नवदेकस्मिन्कार्ये सक्तमहैतुकम् ।
अतत्त्वार्थवदल्पं च तत्तामसमुदाहृतम् ।।22।।

yat-tu kṛitsna-vad ekasmin kārye saktam ahaitukam
atattvārtha-vad alpaṁ cha tat tāmasam udāhṛitam

yat—which; *tu*—but; *kṛitsna-vat*—as if it encompasses the whole; *ekasmin*—in single; *kārye*—action; *saktam*—engrossed; *ahaitukam*—without a reason; *atattva-artha-vat*—not based on truth; *alpam*—fragmental; *cha*—and; *tat*—that; *tāmasam*—in the mode of ignorance; *udāhṛitam*—is said to be.

Knowledge is said to be in the mode of ignorance where one is engrossed in a fragmental concept as if it encompasses the whole and is neither grounded in reason nor based on the truth.

When the intellect is dulled under the effect of tamo guna, it clings to a fragmental concept as if it were the complete truth. People with such views often become fanatic about what they perceive to be the Absolute Truth. Their understanding is usually not even rational, nor grounded in the scriptures or in reality, and yet they zealously desire to impose their beliefs on others. The history of humankind has repeatedly seen religious zealots who imagine themselves as self-appointed champions of God and defenders of faith. They fanatically proselytize and find a few followers with the same kind of intellect, creating the phenomenon of the blind leading the blind. However, in the name of serving God and religion, they create disruption in society and obstruct its harmonious growth.

नियतं सङ्गरहितमरागद्वेषतः कृतम् ।
अफलप्रेप्सुना कर्म यत्तत्सात्त्विकमुच्यते ।।23।।

niyataṁ saṅga-rahitam arāga-dveṣhataḥ kṛitam
aphala-prepsunā karma yat tat sāttvikam uchyate

niyatam—in accordance with scriptures; *saṅga-rahitam*—free from attachment; *arāga-dveṣhataḥ*—free from attachment and aversion; *kṛitam*—done; *aphala-prepsunā*—without desire for rewards; *karma*—action; *yat*—which; *tat*—that; *sāttvikam*—in the mode of goodness; *uchyate*—is called.

Action that is in accordance with the scriptures, free from attachment and aversion, and done without desire for rewards, is in the mode of goodness.

Having explained the three kinds of knowledge, Shree Krishna now describes the three kinds of action. In the passage of history, many social scientists and philosophers have given their opinion regarding what is proper action. A few of the important ones and their philosophies are mentioned here.

The Epicureans of Greece (third century BC) believed that to 'eat, drink, and be merry' was the right action.

More refined was the philosophy of Hobbs of England (1588–1679) and Helvetius of France (1715–1771). They said that if everyone becomes selfish and does not think of others, there will be chaos in the world. So, they recommended that along with personal sense gratification, we should also care for others. For example, if the husband is sick, the wife should take care of him; and if the wife is sick, the husband should take care of her. In the case where helping others conflicts with self-interest, they advised that self-interest should be given priority.

Joseph Butler's (1692–1752) philosophy went beyond this. He said that the idea of service to others after catering to our own self-interest was wrong. Helping others is a natural human virtue. Even a lioness feeds her cubs while remaining hungry herself. So, service to others must always take priority. However, Butler's concept of service was limited to the alleviation of material suffering; for example, if a person is hungry, he should be fed. But this does not really solve problems because after six hours, the person is hungry again.

After Butler came Jeremy Bentham (1748–1832) and John Stuart Mill (1806–1873). They recommended the utilitarian principle of doing what is best for the majority. They suggested following majority opinion for determining proper behaviour. But if the majority is wrong or misguided, then this philosophy falls through, for even a thousand ignorant people together cannot match the quality of thought of one learned person.

Other philosophers recommended following the dictates of the conscience. They suggested that it is the best guide in determining proper behaviour. However, the problem is that everyone's conscience is different. Even in one family, two children have different moral values and conscience. Besides, even the same person's conscience changes over time. If a murderer is asked whether he feels bad on killing people, he replies, 'Initially I would feel bad, but later it became as trivial as killing mosquitoes. I feel no remorse.'

Regarding proper action, the Mahabharat states:

ātmanaḥ pratikūlāni pareśhāṁ na samācharet
śhrutiḥ smṛitiḥ sadāchāraḥ svasya cha priyamātmanaḥ

(5.15.17)

'If you do not like it when others behave with you in a certain way, then do not behave with them in that way, either. But always verify that your behaviour is in accordance with the scriptures.' Conduct yourself with others as you desire them to behave with you. The Bible also says, 'Do to others as you would have them do to you.' (Luke 6:31) Here, Shree Krishna declares, in a similar way that action in the mode of goodness is doing one's duty in accordance with the scriptures. He further adds that such work should be without attachment or aversion and without the desire to enjoy its results.

यत्तु कामेप्सुना कर्म साहङ्कारेण वा पुनः ।
क्रियते बहुलायासं तद्राजसमुदाहृतम् ।।24।।

yat tu kāmepsunā karma sāhankārena vā punaḥ
kriyate bahulāyāsaṁ tad rājasam udāhṛitam

yat—which; *tu*—but; *kāma-īpsunā*—prompted by selfish desire; *karma*—action; *sa-ahaṅkārena*—with pride; *vā*—or; *punaḥ*—again; *kriyate*—enacted; *bahula-āyāsam*—stressfully; *tat*—that; *rājasam*—in the nature of passion; *udāhṛitam*—is said to be.

Action that is prompted by selfish desire, enacted with pride, and full of stress, is in the nature of passion.

The nature of rajo guna is that it creates intense desires for materialistic enhancement and sensual enjoyment. So, action in the mode of passion is motivated by huge ambition and characterised by intense effort. It entails heavy toil and great physical and mental fatigue. An example of rajasic action is the corporate world. Management executives regularly complain of stress. This is because their actions are usually motivated by pride and an inordinate ambition for power, prestige, and wealth. The efforts of political leaders, over-anxious parents, and businesspeople are also often typical examples of actions in the mode of passion.

अनुबन्धं क्षयं हिंसामनपेक्ष्य च पौरुषम् ।
मोहादारभ्यते कर्म यत्तत्तामसमुच्यते ।।25।।

anubandhaṁ kṣhayaṁ hinsām anapekṣhya cha pauruṣham
mohād ārabhyate karma yat tat tāmasam uchyate

anubandham—consequences; *kṣhayam*—loss; *hinsām*—injury; *anapekṣhya*—by disregarding; *cha*—and; *pauruṣham*—one's own ability; *mohāt*—out of delusion; *ārabhyate*—is begun; *karma*—action; *yat*—which; *tat*—that; *tāmasam*—in the mode of ignorance; *uchyate*—is declared to be.

That action is declared to be in the mode of ignorance, which is begun out of delusion, without thought to one's own ability, and disregarding consequences, loss, and injury to others.

The intellects of those in tamo guna are covered by the fog of ignorance. They are oblivious to or unconcerned with what is right and what is wrong and are only interested in themselves and their self-interest. They pay no heed to money or resources at hand, or even to the hardships incurred by others. Such work brings harm to them and to others. Shree Krishna uses the word *kṣhaya* meaning, 'decay'. Tamasic action causes decay of one's health and vitality. It is a waste of effort, a waste of time, and a waste of resources. Typical examples of this are gambling, stealing, corruption, drinking, and other vices.

मुक्तसङ्गोऽनहंवादी धृत्युत्साहसमन्वितः ।
सिद्ध्यसिद्ध्योर्निर्विकारः कर्ता सात्त्विक उच्यते ।।26।।

mukta-saṅgo 'nahaṁ-vādī dhṛity-utsāha-samanvitaḥ
siddhy-asiddhyor nirvikāraḥ kartā sāttvika uchyate

mukta-saṅgaḥ—free from worldly attachment; *anaham-vādī*—free from ego; *dhṛiti*—strong resolve; *utsāha*—zeal; *samanvitaḥ*—endowed with; *siddhi-asiddhyoḥ*—in success and failure; *nirvikāraḥ*—unaffected; *kartā*—worker; *sāttvikaḥ*—in the mode of goodness; *uchyate*—is said to be.

The performer is said to be in the mode of goodness when he or she is free from egotism and attachment, endowed with enthusiasm and determination, and equipoised in success and failure.

Shree Krishna had earlier mentioned knowledge, action, and the doer are of three kinds. Having described the categories of two of them—knowledge and actions—He now moves on to the three kinds of performers of actions. He clarifies that those situated in the mode of goodness are not inactive; rather, they work with enthusiasm and determination. The difference is that their work is performed in proper consciousness. Sattvic doers are *mukta sangaḥ* i.e., they do not try to cling to things in worldly attachment, nor do they believe that worldly things can bestow satisfaction to the soul. Hence, they work with noble motives. And since their intentions are pure, they are filled with *utsāha* (zeal) and *dhṛiti* (strong resolve) in their endeavours. Their mental attitude results in the least dissipation of energies while working. Thus, they are able to work tirelessly to fulfil their sublime motives. Though they may accomplish great things, they are *anaham vādī* (free from egotism), and they give all credit for their success to God.

रागी कर्मफलप्रेप्सुर्लुब्धो हिंसात्मकोऽशुचिः ।
हर्षशोकान्वितः कर्ता राजसः परिकीर्तितः ।।27।।

rāgī karma-phala-prepsur lubdho hinsātmako 'śhuchiḥ
harṣha-śhokānvitaḥ kartā rājasaḥ parikīrtitaḥ

rāgī—craving; *karma-phala*—fruit of work; *prepsuḥ*—covet; *lubdhaḥ*—greedy; *hinsā-ātmakaḥ*—violent-natured; *aśhuchiḥ*—impure; *harṣha-śhoka-anvitaḥ*—moved by joy and sorrow; *kartā*—performer; *rājasaḥ*—in the mode of passion; *parikīrtitaḥ*—is declared.

The performer is considered in the mode of passion when he or she craves the fruits of the work, is covetous, violent-natured, impure, and moved by joy and sorrow.

Rajasic workers are being described here. While sattvic workers are motivated by the desire for spiritual growth, rajasic workers are deeply ambitious for materialistic enhancement. They do not realise that everything here is temporary and will have to be left behind one day. Agitated with immoderate *rāg* (attachment of the mind and senses), they lack the purity of intention. They are convinced that the pleasure they seek is present in worldly things. Hence, never satisfied by what comes their way, they are *lubdhaḥ* (greedy for more). When they see others succeeding or enjoying more than them, they become *hinsātmakaḥ* (enviously bent on injury). To fulfil their ends, they sometimes sacrifice morality, and hence become *aśhuchiḥ* (impure). When their desires are fulfilled, they become elated, and when they are unsuccessful, they get dejected. In this way, their lives become *harṣha śhoka anvitaḥ* (a mixture of delight and sorrow).

अयुक्तः प्राकृतः स्तब्धः शठो नैष्कृतिकोऽलसः ।
विषादी दीर्घसूत्री च कर्ता तामस उच्यते ।।28।।

ayuktaḥ prākṛitaḥ stabdhaḥ śhaṭho naiṣhkṛitiko 'lasaḥ
viṣhādī dīrgha-sūtrī cha kartā tāmasa uchyate

ayuktaḥ—undisciplined; *prākṛitaḥ*—vulgar; *stabdhaḥ*—obstinate; *śhaṭhaḥ*—cunning; *naiṣhkṛitikaḥ*—dishonest or vile; *alasaḥ*—slothful; *viṣhādī*—unhappy and morose; *dīrgha-sūtrī*—procrastinator; *cha*—and; *kartā*—performer; *tāmasaḥ*—in the mode of ignorance; *uchyate*—is said to be.

A performer in the mode of ignorance is one who is undisciplined, vulgar, stubborn, deceitful, slothful, despondent, and a procrastinator.

Shree Krishna now gives a description of tamasic workers. Their mind is blotted with negative obsessions and thus they are *ayuktaḥ* (undisciplined). The scriptures give injunctions regarding what is proper and improper behaviour. But workers in the mode of ignorance are *stabdhaḥ* (obstinate in their views), for they have closed their ears and mind to reason. Thus, they are often *śhaṭhaḥ* (cunning) and *naiṣhkṛitikaḥ* (dishonest or vile) in their ways. They are *prākṛitaḥ* (vulgar) because they do not believe in controlling their animal instincts. Though they may have duties to perform, they see effort as laborious and painful, and so they are *alasaḥ* (lazy) and *dīrgha-sūtrī* (procrastinators). Their ignoble and base thoughts impact them more than anyone else, making them *viṣhādī* (unhappy and morose).

The Shreemad Bhagavatam also describes types of performers of actions:

sāttvikaḥ kārako 'saṅgī rāgāndho rājasaḥ smṛitaḥ
tāmasaḥ smṛiti-vibhraṣhṭo nirguṇo mad-apāśhrayaḥ

(11.25.26)

'The worker who is detached is sattvic in nature; the one who is excessively attached to action and its results is rajasic; one who is devoid of discrimination is tamasic. But the worker who is surrendered to Me is transcendental to the three modes.'

बुद्धेर्भेदं धृतेश्चैव गुणतस्त्रिविधं शृणु ।
प्रोच्यमानमशेषेण पृथक्त्वेन धनञ्जय ।।29।।

buddher bhedaṁ dhṛiteśh chaiva guṇatas-tri-vidhaṁ śhṛiṇu
prochyamānam aśheṣheṇa pṛithaktvena dhanañjaya

buddheḥ—of intellect; *bhedam*—the distinctions; *dhṛiteḥ*—of determination; *cha*—and; *eva*—certainly; *guṇataḥ tri-vidham*—according to the three modes of material nature; *śhṛiṇu*—hear; *prochyamānam*—described; *aśheṣheṇa*—in detail; *pṛithaktvena*—distinctly; *dhanañjaya*—conqueror of wealth, Arjun.

Hear now, O Arjun, of the distinctions of intellect and determination, according to the three modes of material nature, as I describe them in detail.

In the previous nine verses, Shree Krishna explained the constituents of work and showed that each of three constituents falls in three categories. Now He explains the two factors that impact the quality and quantity of work. They not only propel action but also control and direct it. These are the intellect and determination. *Buddhi* is the faculty of discrimination that distinguishes between right and wrong. *Dhṛiti* is the inner determination to persist in accomplishing the work undertaken, despite hardships and obstacles on the way. Both are of three kinds in accordance with the modes of nature. Shree Krishna now discusses both these faculties and their three-fold classifications.

प्रवृत्तिं च निवृत्तिं च कार्याकार्ये भयाभये ।
बन्धं मोक्षं च या वेत्ति बुद्धिः सा पार्थ सात्त्विकी ।।30।।

pravṛittiṁ cha nivṛittiṁ cha kāryākārye bhayābhaye
bandhaṁ mokṣhaṁ cha yā vetti buddhiḥ sā pārtha sāttvikī

pravṛittim—activities; *cha*—and; *nivṛittim*—renuncation from action; *cha*—and; *kārya*—proper action; *akārye*—improper action; *bhaya*—fear; *abhaye*—without fear; *bandham*—what is binding; *mokṣham*—what is liberating; *cha*—and; *yā*—which; *vetti*—understands; *buddhiḥ*—intellect; *sā*—that; *pārtha*—son of Pritha; *sāttvikī*—in the nature of goodness.

The intellect is said to be in the nature of goodness, O Parth, when it understands what is proper and improper action, what is duty and non-duty, what is to be feared and what is not to be feared, what is binding and what is liberating.

We constantly exercise our free will to make choices, and our cumulative choices determine where we reach in life. Robert Frost vividly describes this in his poem, *The Road Not Taken*:

I shall be telling this with a sigh
Somewhere ages and ages hence;
Two roads diverged in a wood, and I,
I took the one less traveled by,
And that has made all the difference.

To make right choices, we need a developed faculty of discrimination. The Bhagavad Gita itself was spoken to Arjun to equip him with the power of discrimination. At the outset, Arjun was confused about his duty. His inordinate attachment to his relatives had clouded his judgement regarding proper and improper action. Feeling weak and fearful, and in utter confusion, he had surrendered to the Lord and requested Him to enlighten him about his duty. Through the divine song of wisdom, Lord Krishna helped Arjun develop his power of discrimination, until He finally concluded: 'I have explained to you the knowledge that is more secret than all secrets. Ponder over it deeply, and then do as you wish.' (verse 18.63)

The mode of goodness illumines the intellect with the light of knowledge thereby refining its ability to discriminate between the right and wrong of things, actions, and sentiments. The sattvic intellect enables us to know which actions are proper and which are to be avoided; it lets us know what tofear and what to ignore. It explains to us the reasons for the shortcomings in our personality and reveals the solutions for them.

यया धर्ममधर्मं च कार्यं चाकार्यमेव च ।
अयथावत्प्रजानाति बुद्धिः सा पार्थ राजसी ।।31।।

yayā dharmam adharmaṁ cha kāryaṁ chākāryam eva cha
ayathāvat prajānāti buddhiḥ sā pārtha rājasī

yayā—by which; *dharmam*—righteousness; *adharmam*—unrighteousness; *cha*—and; *kāryam*—right conduct; *cha*—and; *akāryam*—wrong conduct; *eva*—certainly; *cha*—and; *ayathā-vat*—confused; *prajānāti*—distinguish; *buddhiḥ*—intellect; *sā*—that; *pārtha*—Arjun, son of Pritha; *rājasī*—in the mode of passion.

The intellect is considered in the mode of passion when it is confused between righteousness and unrighteousness and cannot distinguish between right and wrong conduct, O Parth.

The rajasic intellect becomes mixed due to personal attachments. At times it sees clearly, but when self-interest comes into play, it becomes tainted and confused. For example, there are people who are very competent in their profession, but childish in familial relationships. They succeed on the career front but fail miserably on the home front because their attachment prevents them from proper perception and conduct. The rajasic intellect, coloured by attachments and aversions, likes and dislikes, is unable to discern the proper course of action.

It becomes confused between the important and the trivial, the permanent and the transient, the valuable and the worthless.

अधर्मं धर्ममिति या मन्यते तमसावृता ।
सर्वार्थान्विपरीतांश्च बुद्धिः सा पार्थ तामसी ।।32।।

adharmaṁ dharmam iti yā manyate tamasāvṛitā
sarvārthān viparītānśh cha buddhiḥ sā pārtha tāmasī

adharmam—irreligion; *dharmam*—religion; *iti*—thus; *yā*—which; *manyate*—imagines; *tamasa-āvṛitā*—shrouded in darkness; *sarva-arthān*—all things; *viparītān*—opposite; *cha*—and; *buddhiḥ*—intellect; *sā*—that; *pārtha*—Arjun, son of Pritha; *tāmasī*—of the nature of ignorance.

That intellect which is shrouded in darkness, imagining irreligion to be religion and perceiving untruth to be the truth, is of the nature of ignorance, O Parth.

The tamasic intellect is without the illumination of sublime knowledge. Hence, it misconstrues *adharma* to be dharma. For example, a drunk is attached to the intoxication that alcohol provides. Hence, his poor intellect, covered with the fog of darkness, cannot even perceive the sheer ruin that he brings onto himself, so much so that he does not even mind selling his property to get his next bottle. In the tamasic intellect, the faculty of judgement and the ability for logical reasoning are lost.

धृत्या यया धारयते मनःप्राणेन्द्रियक्रियाः ।
योगेनाव्यभिचारिण्या धृतिः सा पार्थ सात्त्विकी ।।33।।

dhṛityā yayā dhārayate manaḥ-prāṇendriya-kriyāḥ
yogenāvyabhichāriṇyā dhṛitiḥ sā pārtha sāttvikī

dhṛityā—by determining; *yayā*—which; *dhārayate*—sustains; *manaḥ*—of the mind; *prāṇa*—life airs; *indriya*—senses; *kriyāḥ*—activities; *yogena*—through Yog; *avyabhichāriṇyā*—with steadfastness; *dhṛitiḥ*—determination; *sā*—that; *pārtha*—Arjun, son of Pritha; *sāttvikī*—in the mode of goodness.

The steadfast willpower that is developed through Yog, and which sustains the activities of the mind, the life airs, and the senses, O Parth, is said to be determination in the mode of goodness.

Dhṛiti (determination) is the inner strength of our mind and intellect to persevere on our path despite difficulties and obstacles. *Dhṛiti* is what keeps our vision focused towards the goal and mobilises the latent powers of the body, mind, and intellect to overcome apparently insurmountable impasses on the journey.

Shree Krishna now moves on to describe the three kinds of determination. Through the practice of Yog, the mind becomes disciplined and develops the capacity to rule over the senses and the body. The steadfast willpower that develops when one learns to subdue the senses, discipline the life airs, and control the mind is sattvic *dhṛiti* (determination in the mode of goodness).

यया तु धर्मकामार्थान्धृत्या धारयतेऽर्जुन ।
प्रसङ्गेन फलाकाङ्क्षी धृतिः सा पार्थ राजसी ।।34।।

yayā tu dharma-kāmārthān dhṛityā dhārayate 'rjuna
prasaṅgena phalākāṅkṣhī dhṛitiḥ sā pārtha rājasī

yayā—by which; *tu*—but; *dharma-kāma-arthān*—duty, pleasures, and wealth; *dhṛityā*—through steadfast will; *dhārayate*—holds; *arjuna*—Arjun; *prasaṅgena*—due of attachment; *phala-ākāṅkṣhī*—desire for rewards; *dhṛitiḥ*—determination; *sā*—that; *pārtha*—Arjun, son of Pritha; *rājasī*—in the mode of passion.

The steadfast willpower by which one holds on to duty, pleasures, and wealth, out of attachment and desire for rewards, O Arjun, is determination in the mode of passion.

Determination is not found exclusively in yogis. Worldly-minded people are also staunchly determined in their pursuits. However, their determination is fanned by their desire to delight in the fruits of their efforts. They are focused on enjoying sensual pleasures, acquiring wealth, and accumulating other materialistic rewards. And since money is the means for acquiring these, such people cling to money for their very life. Shree Krishna says that determination fuelled by the desire for enjoying rewards is in the mode of passion.

यया स्वप्नं भयं शोकं विषादं मदमेव च ।
न विमुञ्चति दुर्मेधा धृतिः सा पार्थ तामसी ।।35।।

yayā svapnaṁ bhayaṁ śhokaṁ viṣhādaṁ madam eva cha
na vimuñchati durmedhā dhṛitiḥ sā pārtha tāmasī

yayā—in which; *svapnam*—dreaming; *bhayam*—fearing; *śhokam*—grieving; *viṣhādam*—despair; *madam*—conceit; *eva*—indeed; *cha*—and; *na*—not; *vimuñchati*—give up; *durmedhā*—unintelligent; *dhṛitiḥ*—resolve; *sā*—that; *pārtha*—Arjun, son of Pritha; *tāmasī*—in the mode of ignorance.

That unintelligent resolve is said to be determination in the mode of ignorance, O Arjun, in which one does not give up dreaming, fearing, grieving, despair, and conceit.

Determination is seen in the unintelligent and ignorant too. But it is the obstinacy that arises from fear, despair, and pride. For instance, some people are victims of a fear-complex, and it is interesting to note how they hold on to it with great tenacity, as if it is an inseparable part of their personality. There are others who make their life a living hell because they cling to some past disappointment and refuse to let go of it, despite observing its ruinous impact upon them. Some insist upon quarrelling with all who hurt their ego and its imagined conception of themselves. Shree Krishna states that determination based upon such stubborn clinging to unproductive thoughts is in the mode of ignorance.

सुखं त्विदानीं त्रिविधं शृणु मे भरतर्षभ ।
अभ्यासाद्रमते यत्र दुःखान्तं च निगच्छति ।।36।।

sukhaṁ tv idānīṁ tri-vidhaṁ śhṛiṇu me bharatarṣhabha
abhyāsād ramate yatra duḥkhāntaṁ cha nigachchhati

sukham—happiness; *tu*—but; *idānīm*—now; tri-*vidham*—of three kinds; *śhṛiṇu*—hear; *me*—from me; *bharata-ṛiṣhabha*—Arjun, best of the Bharatas; *abhyāsāt*—by practice; *ramate*—rejoices; *yatra*—in which; *duḥkha-antam*—end of all suffering; *cha*—and; *nigachchhati*—reaches.

Now hear from Me, O Arjun, of the three kinds of happiness in which the embodied soul rejoices and can even reach the end of all suffering.

In the previous verses, Shree Krishna discussed the constituents of action. Then He described the factors that motivate and control action. Now, He moves on to the goal of action. The ultimate motive behind people's actions is the search for happiness. Everyone desires to be happy, and through their actions, they seek fulfilment, peace, and satisfaction. But since everyone's actions differ in their constituent factors, the kind of happiness they derive out of their work is also different. Shree Krishna now goes on to explain the three categories of happiness.

यत्तदग्रे विषमिव परिणामेऽमृतोपमम् ।
तत्सुखं सात्त्विकं प्रोक्तमात्मबुद्धिप्रसादजम् ।।37।।

yat tad agre viṣham iva pariṇāme 'mṛitopamam
tat sukhaṁ sāttvikaṁ proktam ātma-buddhi-prasāda-jam

yat—which; *tat*—that; *agre*—at first; *viṣham iva*—like poison; *pariṇāme*—in the end; *amṛita-upamam*—like nectar; *tat*—that; *sukham*—happiness; *sāttvikam*—in the mode of goodness; *proktam*—is said to be; *ātma-buddhi*—situated in self-knowledge; *prasāda-jam*—generated by the pure intellect.

That which seems like poison at first, but tastes like nectar in the end, is said to be happiness in the mode of goodness. It is generated by the pure intellect that is situated in self-knowledge.

The Indian gooseberry (*āmlā*) is one of those super-foods that are very beneficial for health. It has the vitamin C of more than ten oranges. But children dislike it because of its bitter taste. Parents in North India encourage children to eat it, saying: *āmle kā khāyā aur baḍoṅ kā kahā, bād meṅ patā chalatā hai* 'The benefits of both these—eating of *āmlā* and the advice of the elders—are experienced in the future.' Interestingly, after eating *āmlā,* in just a couple of minutes, the bitterness disappears, and it tastes sweet. And the long-term benefits of consuming natural vitamin C are undoubtedly numerous. In the above verse, Shree Krishna says that happiness in the mode of goodness is of the same nature; it seems bitter in the short-term but tastes like nectar in the end.

The Vedas refer to happiness in the mode of goodness as *śhreya,* which is unpleasant in the present but ultimately beneficial. In contrast to this is *preya,* which is pleasant in the beginning but ultimately harmful. On *śhreya* and *preya,* the *Kaṭhopaniṣhad* states:

anyachchhreyo 'nyadutaiva preya-ste
ubhe nānārthe puruṣhaṁ sinītaḥ
tayoḥ śhreya ādadānasya sādhu bhavati
hīyate 'rthādya u preyo vṛiṇīte

śhreyaśhcha preyaśhcha manuṣhyameta-stau
samparītya vivinakti dhīraḥ
śhreyo hi dhīro 'bhi preyaso vṛiṇīte
preyo mando yogakṣhemād vṛinīte (1.2.1–2)

'There are two paths—one is the "beneficial" and the other is the "pleasant". These two lead humans to very different ends. The pleasant is enjoyable in the beginning but ends in pain. The ignorant are ensnared to the pleasant and perish. But the wise are not deceived by its attractions; they choose the beneficial, and finally attain happiness.'

विषयेन्द्रियसंयोगाद्यत्तदग्रेऽमृतोपमम् ।
परिणामे विषमिव तत्सुखं राजसं स्मृतम् ।।38।।

viṣhayendriya-sanyogād yat tad agre 'mṛitopamam
pariṇāme viṣham iva tat sukhaṁ rājasaṁ smṛitam

viṣhaya—with the sense objects; *indriya*—the senses; *sanyogāt*—from the contact; *yat*—which; *tat*—that; *agre*—at first; *amṛita-upamam*—like nectar; *pariṇāme*—at the end; *viṣham iva*—like poison; *tat*—that; *sukham*—happiness; *rājasam*—in the mode of passion; *smṛitam*—is said to be.

Happiness is said to be in the mode of passion when it is derived from the contact of the senses with their objects. Such happiness is like nectar at first but poison at the end.

Rajasic happiness is experienced as a thrill that arises from the contact between the senses and their objects, but the joy is as short-lived as the contact itself; it leaves in its wake, greed, anxiety, guilt, and a thickening of the material illusion. Even in the material realm, for meaningful accomplishment, it is necessary to reject rajasic happiness. As a reminder to steer him away from immediate but misleading joys, India's first prime minister, Jawaharlal Nehru, used to keep these lines from the poem, *Stopping by Woods on a Snowy Evening*, on his desk:

The woods are lovely, dark, and deep,
But I have promises to keep,
And miles to go before I sleep,
And miles to go before I sleep.

The path to lasting and divine bliss lies not in indulgence but in renunciation, austerities, and discipline.

यदग्रे चानुबन्धे च सुखं मोहनमात्मनः ।
निद्रालस्यप्रमादोत्थं तत्तामसमुदाहृतम् ।।39।।

yad agre chānubandhe cha sukhaṁ mohanam ātmanaḥ
nidrālasya-pramādotthaṁ tat tāmasam udāhṛitam

yat—which; *agre*—from beginning; *cha*—and; *anubandhe*—to end; *cha*—and; *sukham*—happiness; *mohanam*—illusory; *ātmanaḥ*—of the self; *nidrā*—sleep; *ālasya*—indolence; *pramāda*—negligence;

uttham—derived from; *tat*—that; *tāmasam*—in the mode of ignorance; *udāhṛitam*—is said to be.

That happiness which covers the nature of the self from beginning to end, and which is derived from sleep, indolence, and negligence, is said to be in the mode of ignorance.

Tamasic happiness is of the lowest kind and is foolishness from beginning to end. It throws the soul into the darkness of ignorance. And yet, since there is a tiny experience of pleasure in it, people get addicted to it. That is why cigarette smokers find it difficult to break their habit, even while knowing fully well it is harming them. They are unable to reject the happiness they get from the addiction. Shree Krishna states that such pleasures—derived from sleep, laziness, and negligence—are in the mode of ignorance.

न तदस्ति पृथिव्यां वा दिवि देवेषु वा पुनः ।
सत्त्वं प्रकृतिजैर्मुक्तं यदेभिः स्यात्त्रिभिर्गुणैः ।।40।।

na tad asti pṛithivyāṁ vā divi deveṣhu vā punaḥ
sattvaṁ prakṛiti-jair muktaṁ yad ebhiḥ syāt tribhir guṇaiḥ

na—no; *tat*—that; *asti*—exists; *pṛithivyām*—on earth; *vā*—or; *divi*—the higher celestial abodes; *deveṣhu*—amongst the celestial gods; *vā*—or; *punaḥ*—again; *sattvam*—existence; *prakṛiti-jaiḥ*—born of material nature; *muktam*—liberated; *yat*—that; *ebhiḥ*—from the influence of these; *syāt*—is; *tribhiḥ*—three; *guṇaiḥ*—modes of material nature.

No living being on earth or the higher celestial abodes of this material realm is free from the influence of these three modes of nature.

The *Śhwetāśhvatar Upanishad* states that the material energy, maya, is tri-coloured:

ajāmekāṁ lohita-śhukla-kṛiṣhṇāṁ
bahvīḥ prajāḥ sṛijamānāṁ sa-rūpāḥ
ajo hy eko juṣhamāṇo 'nuśhete
jahāty enāṁ bhukta-bhogām ajo 'nyaḥ (4.5)

'Material nature has three colours—white, red, and black i.e., it has three modes—goodness, passion, and ignorance. It is the mother-like womb of the innumerable living beings within the universe. It is brought into existence and supported by the one unborn Lord who is full of knowledge. God, however, does not consort with His material energy. He independently enjoys the pleasure of His transcendental pastimes. But the living entity enjoys her and thus becomes bound.'

Maya's domain extends from the nether regions to the celestial abode of Brahma. Since the three modes of nature—sattva, rajas, and tamas—are inherent attributes of maya, they exist in all the material abodes of existence. Hence all living beings in these abodes, whether humans or the celestial gods, are under the sway of these three modes. The difference is only in the relative proportions of the three gunas. The residents of the nether regions have a predominance of tamas; the residents of the earth planet have a predominance of rajas; and the residents of the celestial abodes have a predominance of sattva. *Now, using these three variables, Shree Krishna explains why human beings possess differing natures.*

ब्राह्मणक्षत्रियविशां शूद्राणां च परन्तप ।
कर्माणि प्रविभक्तानि स्वभावप्रभवैर्गुणैः ।।41।।

brāhmaṇa-kṣhatriya-viśhāṁ śhūdrāṇāṁ cha parantapa
karmāṇi pravibhaktāni svabhāva-prabhavair guṇaiḥ

brāhmaṇa—of the priestly class; *kṣhatriya*—the warrior and administrative class; *viśhām*—the mercantile and farming class; *śhūdrāṇām*—of the worker class; *cha*—and; *parantapa*—Arjun, subduer of enemies; *karmāṇi*—duties; *pravibhaktāni*—distributed; *svabhāva-prabhavaiḥ-guṇaiḥ*—work based on one's nature and guṇas.

The duties of the Brahmins, Kshatriyas, Vaishyas, and Shudras—are distributed according to their qualities, in accordance with their gunas (and not by birth).

Someone said very appropriately that to find the perfect profession is like finding a perfect life-partner. But how do we discover the perfect profession for ourselves? Here, Shree Krishna explains that people have different natures, according to the gunas that constitute their personality, and thus different professional duties are suitable for them. The system of varnashram dharma was a scientific organisation of society according to *svabhāva-prabhavair guṇaiḥ* (work based on one's nature and gunas). In this system of categorisation, there were four ashrams (stages of life) and four varnas (occupational categories). The stages in life were:

1. *Brahmacharya ashram* (student life) which lasted from birth till the age of twenty-five.
2. *Gṛihastha ashram* (household life) which was regular married life from the age of twenty-five to fifty.
3. *Vānaprastha ashram* (semi-renounced life) which was from the age of fifty to seventy-five. In this stage, one continued to live with the family but practised renunciation.
4. *Sanyas ashram* (renounced order) which was from the age of seventy-five onwards, where one gave up all household duties and resided in a holy place, absorbing the mind in God.

The four varnas were Brahmin (priestly class), Kshatriya (warrior and administrative class), Vaishya (mercantile and farming class), and Shudra (worker class). The varnas were not considered higher or lower among themselves. Since the centre of society was God, everyone worked according to their intrinsic qualities to sustain themselves and society and make their life a success by progressing towards God-realisation. Thus, in the varnashram system, there was unity in diversity. Diversity is inherent in nature and can never be removed. We have various limbs in our body, and they all perform different functions. Expecting all limbs to perform the same functions is futile. Seeing them all as different is not a sign of ignorance but factual knowledge of their utilities. Similarly, the variety amidst human beings cannot be ignored. Even in communist countries where equality is the foremost principle, there are party leaders who formulate ideologies; there is the military that wields guns and protects the nation; there are farmers who cultivate the land; and there are industrial workers who do mechanical jobs. The four classes of occupations exist there as well, despite all attempts to equalize. The varnashram system recognised the diversity in human nature and scientifically prescribed duties and occupations matching people's natures.

However, with the passage of time, the varnashram system deteriorated, and the basis of the varnas changed from one's nature to one's birth. The children of Brahmins started calling themselves as Brahmins irrespective of whether they possessed the corresponding qualities or not. Also, the concept of upper and lower castes got propagated and the upper castes began looking down upon the lower castes. When the system grew rigid and birth-based, it became dysfunctional. This was a social defect that crept in with time and was not the original intention of the varnashram system. *In the next few verses, according to the original categorisation of the system, Shree Krishna maps the gunas of people with their natural qualities of work.*

शमो दमस्तपः शौचं क्षान्तिरार्जवमेव च ।
ज्ञानं विज्ञानमास्तिक्यं ब्रह्मकर्म स्वभावजम् ।।42।।

śhamo damas tapaḥ śhauchaṁ kṣhāntir ārjavam eva cha
jñānaṁ vijñānam āstikyaṁ brahma-karma svabhāva-jam

śhamaḥ—tranquillity; *damaḥ*—restraint; *tapaḥ*—austerity; *śhaucham*—purity; *kṣhāntiḥ*—patience; *ārjavam*—integrity; *eva*—certainly; *cha*—and; *jñānam*—knowledge; *vijñānam*—wisdom; *āstikyam*—belief in a hereafter; *brahma*—of the priestly class; *karma*—work; *svabhāva-jam*—born of one's intrinsic qualities.

Tranquillity, restraint, austerity, purity, patience, integrity, knowledge, wisdom, and belief in a hereafter—these are the intrinsic qualities of work for Brahmins.

Those who possessed predominantly sattvic natures were the Brahmins. Their primary duties were to undertake austerities, practise purity of mind, do devotion, and inspire others by their examples. Thus, they were expected to be tolerant, humble, and spiritually minded. They were expected to perform Vedic rituals for themselves and for the other classes. Their nature inclined them towards love for knowledge. So, the profession of teaching—cultivating knowledge and sharing it with others—was also suitable for them. Although they did not participate in the government administration themselves, they guided the executives. And because they possessed wisdom of the scriptures, their views on social and political matters were greatly valued.

शौर्यं तेजो धृतिर्दाक्ष्यं युद्धे चाप्यपलायनम् ।
दानमीश्वरभावश्च क्षात्रं कर्म स्वभावजम् ।।43।।

śhauryaṁ tejo dhṛitir dākṣhyaṁ yuddhe chāpy apalāyanam
dānam īśhvara-bhāvaśh cha kṣhātraṁ karma svabhāva-jam

śhauryam—valour; *tejaḥ*—strength; *dhṛitiḥ*—fortitude; *dākṣhyam yuddhe*—skill in weaponry; *cha*—and; *api*—also; *apalāyanam*—not fleeing; *dānam*—large-heartedness; *īśhvara*—leadership; *bhāvaḥ*—qualities; *cha*—and; *kṣhātram*—of the warrior and administrative class; *karma*—work; *svabhāva-jam*—born of one's intrinsic qualities.

Valour, strength, fortitude, skill in weaponry, resolve never to retreat from battle, large-heartedness in charity, and leadership abilities, these are the natural qualities of work for Kshatriyas.

The Kshatriyas were those whose natures were predominantly rajasic with a mix of sattva guna. This made them royal, heroic, daring, commanding, and charitable. Their qualities were suitable for martial and leadership works, and they formed the administrative class that governed the country. Yet, they realised that they were not as learned and pure as the Brahmins. Hence, they respected the Brahmins and took advice from them on ideological, spiritual, and policy matters.

कृषिगौरक्ष्यवाणिज्यं वैश्यकर्म स्वभावजम् ।
परिचर्यात्मकं कर्म शूद्रस्यापि स्वभावजम् ।।44।।

kṛiṣhi-gau-rakṣhya-vāṇijyaṁ vaiśhya-karma svabhāva-jam
paricharyātmakaṁ karma śhūdrasyāpi svabhāva-jam

kṛiṣhi—agriculture; *gau-rakṣhya*—dairy farming; *vāṇijyam*—commerce; *vaiśhya*—of the mercantile and farming class; *karma*—work; *svabhāva-jam*—born of one's intrinsic qualities; *paricharyā*—serving through work; *ātmakam*—natural; *karma*—duty; *śhūdrasya*—of the worker class; *api*—and; *svabhāva-jam*—born of one's intrinsic qualities.

Agriculture, dairy farming, and commerce are the natural works for those with the qualities of Vaishyas. Serving through work is the natural duty for those with the qualities of Shudras.

The Vaishyas were those whose natures were predominantly rajasic with a mix of tamo guna. They were thus inclined towards producing and possessing economic wealth through business and agriculture. They sustained the economy of the nation and created jobs for the other classes. They were also expected to undertake charitable projects to share their wealth with the deprived sections of society.

The Shudras were those who possessed tamasic natures. They were not inclined towards scholarship, administration, or commercial enterprise. The best way for their progress was to serve society according to their calling. Artisans, technicians, job-workers, tailors, craftsmen, barbers, and other similar professions were included in this class.

स्वे स्वे कर्मण्यभिरतः संसिद्धिं लभते नरः ।
स्वकर्मनिरतः सिद्धिं यथा विन्दति तच्छृणु ।।45।।

sve sve karmaṇy abhirataḥ sansiddhiṁ labhate naraḥ
sva-karma-nirataḥ siddhiṁ yathā vindati tach chhṛiṇu

sve sve—respectively; *karmaṇi*—work; *abhirataḥ*—fulfilling; *sansiddhim*—perfection; *labhate*—achieve; *naraḥ*—a person; *sva-karma*—to one's own prescribed duty; *nirataḥ*—engaged; *siddhim*—perfection; *yathā*—as; *vindati*—attains; *tat*—that; *śhṛiṇu*—hear.

By fulfilling their duties, born of their innate qualities, human beings can attain perfection. Now hear from Me how one can become perfect by discharging one's prescribed duties.

Swa-dharma is the prescribed duties based upon our gunas and station in life. Performing them ensures that we use the potential abilities of our body and mind in a constructive and beneficial manner. This leads to purification and growth; it is also auspicious for the self and society. And since prescribed duties are in accordance with our innate qualities, we feel comfortable and stable in discharging them. Then, as we enhance our competence, the *swa-dharma* also changes, and we step into the next higher class. In this manner, we keep advancing by dutifully executing our responsibilities.

यतः प्रवृत्तिर्भूतानां येन सर्वमिदं ततम् ।
स्वकर्मणा तमभ्यर्च्य सिद्धिं विन्दति मानवः ।।46।।

yataḥ pravṛittir bhūtānāṁ yena sarvam idaṁ tatam
sva-karmaṇā tam abhyarchya siddhiṁ vindati mānavaḥ

yataḥ—from whom; *pravṛittiḥ*—have come into being; *bhūtānām*—of all living entities; *yena*—by whom; *sarvam*—all; *idam*—this; *tatam*—pervaded; *sva-karmaṇā*—by one's natural occupation; *tam*—him; *abhyarchya*—by worshipping; *siddhim*—perfection; *vindati*—attains; *mānavaḥ*—a person.

By performing one's natural occupation, one worships the Creator from whom all living entities have come into being and by whom the whole universe is pervaded. By such performance of work, a person easily attains perfection.

No soul is superfluous in God's creation. His divine plan is for the gradual perfection of all living beings. We all fit into His scheme like tiny cogs in a giant wheel. And He does not expect more from us than the competence He has given to us. Therefore, if we can simply perform our *swa-dharma* in accordance with our nature and position in life, we will participate in His divine plan for our purification. When done in devotional consciousness, our work itself becomes a form of worship.

A powerful story illustrating that no duty is ugly or impure, and it is only the consciousness with which we do it that determines its worth, was told to Yudhishthir by Sage Markandeya, in the *Vana Parva* of the Mahabharat:

The story goes that a young sanyasi went into the forest where he meditated and performed austerities for a long time. A few years went by, and one day a crow's droppings fell upon him from the tree above. He looked angrily at the bird, and it fell dead on the ground. The sanyasi realised he had developed mystical powers as a result of his austerities. He became filled with pride.

Shortly thereafter, he went to a house to beg for alms. The housewife came to the door and requested him to wait a while since she was nursing her sick husband. This angered the monk and he glanced angrily at her, thinking, 'You wretched woman, how dare you make me wait! You do not know my powers.' Reading his mind, the woman replied, 'Do not look at me with such anger. I am not a crow to be burned by your glance.' The monk was shocked and asked how she knew about the incident. The housewife said she did not practice any austerities but did her duties with devotion and dedication. By virtue of it, she had been illumined and was able to read his mind. She then asked him to meet a righteous butcher who lived in the town of Mithila and said that he would answer his questions on dharma.

The sanyasi overcame his initial hesitation of speaking to a lowly butcher and went to Mithila. The righteous butcher then explained to him that we all have our respective *swa-dharma* based upon our past karmas and competence. But if we discharge our natural duty, while renouncing the desire for personal gain and rising above the fleeting happiness and misery coming our way, we will purify ourselves and graduate to the next class of dharma. In this manner, by doing the prescribed duties and not running away from them, the soul gradually evolves from its present gross consciousness to divine consciousness. The lecture the butcher delivered is known as the *Vyadha Gita* of the Mahabharat.

This message is particularly applicable to Arjun because he wanted to run away from his dharma, thinking it to be painful and miserable. In this verse, Shree Krishna instructs him that by doing his prescribed duty in proper consciousness, he will be worshipping the Supreme and will easily attain perfection.

श्रेयान्स्वधर्मो विगुणः परधर्मात्स्वनुष्ठितात् ।
स्वभावनियतं कर्म कुर्वन्नाप्नोति किल्बिषम् ।।47।।

śhreyān swa-dharmo viguṇaḥ para-dharmāt-sv-anuṣhṭhitāt
svabhāva-niyataṁ karma kurvan nāpnoti kilbiṣham

śhreyān—better; *swa-dharmaḥ*—one's own prescribed occupational duty; *viguṇaḥ*—imperfectly done; *para-dharmāt*—than another's dharma; *su-anuṣhṭhitāt*—perfectly done; *svabhāva-niyatam*—according to one's innate nature; *karma*—duty; *kurvan*—by performing; *na āpnoti*—does not incur; *kilbiṣham*—sin.

It is better to do one's own dharma, even though imperfectly, than to do another's dharma, even though perfectly. By doing one's innate duties, a person does not incur sin.

When we do our *swa-dharma* (prescribed occupational duties), there is a two-fold advantage. It is aligned with our disposition and is hence, as natural to our personality as flying is to a bird and swimming is to a fish. Second, since it is comfortable for the mind, it can almost be done involuntarily, and the consciousness becomes free to be engaged in devotion.

On the other hand, if we abandon our duties thinking them to be burdensome and take up another's duties unsuitable for our nature, we struggle against the innate inclination of our personality. This was exactly Arjun's situation. His Kshatriya nature was inclined to military and administrative activities. Events drove him to a situation where it was necessary to participate in a war of righteousness. If he were to shirk from his duty and withdraw from the battlefield to practice austerities in the forest, it would not help him spiritually, for even in the forest, he would not be able to get away from his inherent nature. In all likelihood, he would gather the tribal people in the jungle and become their king. Instead, it would be better for him to continue doing his duty born of his nature and worship God by offering the fruits of his works to Him.

When one becomes spiritually accomplished, the *swa-dharma* changes. It no longer remains at the bodily platform; rather, it becomes the dharma of the soul which is devotion to God. At that stage, one is justified in giving up occupational duties and engaging wholeheartedly in devotion because that is now the *swa-dharma* of one's nature. For people with that eligibility, Shree Krishna will give the final conclusion in the end of the Bhagavad Gita: 'Give up all varieties of dharmas and simply surrender unto Me.' (18.66) However, until that stage is reached, the instruction given in this verse applies. Thus, the Shreemad Bhagavatam states:

tāvat karmāṇi kurvīta na nirvidyeta yāvatā
mat-kathā-śhravaṇādau vā śhraddhā yāvan na jāyate (11.20.9)

'We must keep doing our prescribed occupational duties as long as the taste for devotion through hearing, chanting, and meditating on the leelas of God has not developed.'

सहजं कर्म कौन्तेय सदोषमपि न त्यजेत् ।
सर्वारम्भा हि दोषेण धूमेनाग्निरिवावृताः ।।48।।

saha-jaṁ karma kaunteya sa-doṣham api na tyajet
sarvārambhā hi doṣheṇa dhūmenāgnir ivāvṛitāḥ

saha-jam—born of one's nature; *karma*—duty; *kaunteya*—Arjun, son of Kunti; *sa-doṣham*—with defects; *api*—even if; *na tyajet*—one should not abandon; *sarva-ārambhāḥ*—all endeavours; *hi*—indeed; *doṣheṇa*—with evil; *dhūmena*—with smoke; *agniḥ*—fire; *iva*—as; *āvṛitāḥ*—veiled.

One should not abandon duties born of one's nature, even if one sees defects in them, O son of Kunti. Indeed, all endeavours are veiled by some evil, as fire is by smoke.

People sometimes recoil from their duty because they see a defect in it. Here, Shree Krishna states that no work is free from fault, just as fire naturally has smoke on top of it. For example, we cannot breathe without killing millions of microbes. If we cultivate the land, we destroy innumerable microorganisms. If we succeed against competition in business, we deprive others of wealth. When we eat, we deprive another of food. Since *swa-dharma* entails activity, it cannot be devoid of defects.

But the benefits of *swa-dharma* far outweigh its defects. And the foremost benefit is that it provides a comfortable and natural path for one's purification and elevation. In his book, *Making a Life, Making a Living,* Mark Albion, who was a professor at the Harvard Business School, cites a study in which the careers of 1,500 business school graduates were tracked from 1960 to 1980. From the beginning, graduates were grouped into two categories. In category A were those who said they wanted to make money first, so that they could do what they really wanted to do later, after they had taken care of their financial concerns. Eighty-three per cent fell in category A. In category B were those who pursued their interests first, sure that money would eventually follow. Seventeen per cent came in category B. After twenty years, there were 101 millionaires. One person was from category A (who wanted to make money first), and one hundred from category B (who pursued their interest first). The overwhelming majority of the people who became wealthy did so thanks to their work which they found profoundly absorbing. Mark Albion concludes that for most people there is a difference between work and play. But if they do what they love, then work becomes play, and they never have to work for another day in their life. That is what Shree Krishna is asking Arjun to do—not to abandon the work that is best suited to his nature, even if it has defects in it, rather, to work according to his natural propensity.

But for work to be elevating, it must be done in the proper consciousness, as described in the next verse.

असक्तबुद्धिः सर्वत्र जितात्मा विगतस्पृहः ।
नैष्कर्म्यसिद्धिं परमां सन्न्यासेनाधिगच्छति ।।49।।

asakta-buddhiḥ sarvatra jitātmā vigata-spṛihaḥ
naiṣhkarmya-siddhiṁ paramāṁ sanyāsenādhigachchhati

asakta-buddhiḥ—those whose intellect is unattached; *sarvatra*—everywhere; *jita-ātmā*—who have mastered their mind; *vigata-spṛihaḥ*—free from desires; *naiṣhkarmya-siddhim*—state of actionlessness; *paramām*—highest; *sanyāsena*—by the practice of renunciation; *adhigachchhati*—attain.

Those whose intellect is unattached everywhere, who have mastered the mind, and are free from desires by the practice of renunciation, attain the highest perfection of freedom from action.

In this last chapter, Shree Krishna repeats many of the principles He has already explained. At the beginning of this chapter, He explained to Arjun that merely running away from the responsibilities of life is not sanyas, nor is it renunciation. Now He describes the state of actionlessness or *naiṣhkarmya-siddhi*. This state can be reached even amidst the flow of the world by detaching ourselves from events and outcomes and by simply focusing on doing our duty. This is just as water flowing under a bridge enters from one side and flows out from the other. The bridge is neither the recipient of the water, nor its distributor; it remains unaffected by its flow. Likewise, karm yogis do their duty but keep the mind unaffected by the stream of events. They do not neglect putting in their best efforts in doing their duty, as an act of worship to God, but they leave the final outcome in His hands and are thus contented and undisturbed with whatever happens. Here's a simple story to illustrate this point:

A man had two daughters. The first was married to a farmer and the second was married to a brick kiln owner. One day, the father rang up the first daughter and enquired about her well-being. She replied, 'Father, we are going through economic hardships. Please pray to God for us that we may have plentiful rains in the coming months.' He then called the second daughter, and she requested, 'Father, we are low on funds. Please request God not to send rains this year, so that we may have lots of sunshine and a good production of bricks.' The father heard the opposite requests of his daughters, and thought, 'God alone knows what is best. Let Him do what He thinks is right.' Such acceptance of the will of God brings detachment from outcomes despite being immersed in the incessant stream of events in the world.

सिद्धिं प्राप्तो यथा ब्रह्म तथाप्नोति निबोध मे ।
समासेनैव कौन्तेय निष्ठा ज्ञानस्य या परा ।।50।।

siddhiṁ prāpto yathā brahma tathāpnoti nibodha me
samāsenaiva kaunteya niṣhṭhā jñānasya yā parā

siddhim—perfection; *prāptaḥ*—attained; *yathā*—how; *brahma*—Brahman; *tathā*—also; *āpnoti*—attain; *nibodha*—hear; *me*—from me; *samāsena*—briefly; *eva*—indeed; *kaunteya*—Arjun, son of Kunti; *niṣhṭhā*—firmly fixed; *jñānasya*—of knowledge; *yā*—which; *parā*—transcendental.

Hear from Me briefly, O Arjun, and I shall explain how one, who has attained perfection (of cessation of actions), can also attain Brahman by being firmly fixed in transcendental knowledge.

It is one matter to read theoretical knowledge, but it is a different matter to realise it practically. It is said that good ideas are a dime a dozen, but they are not worth a nickel if you don't act on them. The theoretical pundits may have knowledge of all the scriptures in their head but still be bereft of realisation. On the other hand, karm yogis get opportunities day and night to practice the truths of the scriptures. Thus, the consistent performance of karm yog results in the realisation of spiritual knowledge. And when one attains the perfection of *naiṣhkarmya-siddhi*, or actionlessness while performing work, transcendental knowledge becomes available through experience. Fixed in that knowledge, the karm yogi attains the highest perfection of God-realisation. *Shree Krishna explains how this happens in the next few verses.*

बुद्ध्या विशुद्धया युक्तो धृत्यात्मानं नियम्य च ।
शब्दादीन्विषयांस्त्यक्त्वा रागद्वेषौ व्युदस्य च ।।51।।

विविक्तसेवी लघ्वाशी यतवाक्कायमानसः ।
ध्यानयोगपरो नित्यं वैराग्यं समुपाश्रितः ।।52।।

अहङ्कारं बलं दर्पं कामं क्रोधं परिग्रहम् ।
विमुच्य निर्ममः शान्तो ब्रह्मभूयाय कल्पते ।।53।।

buddhyā viśhuddhayā yukto dhṛityātmānaṁ niyamya cha
śhabdādīn viṣhayāns tyaktvā rāga-dveṣhau vyudasya cha

vivikta-sevī laghv-āśhī yata-vāk-kāya-mānasaḥ
dhyāna-yoga-paro nityaṁ vairāgyaṁ samupāśhritaḥ

ahankāraṁ balaṁ darpaṁ kāmaṁ krodhaṁ parigraham
vimuchya nirmamaḥ śhānto brahma-bhūyāya kalpate

buddhyā—intellect; *viśhuddhayā*—purified; *yuktaḥ*—endowed with; *dhṛityā*—by determination; *ātmānam*—the self; *niyamya*—restraining; *cha*—and; *śhabda-ādīn viṣhayān*—sound and other objects of the senses; *tyaktvā*—abandoning; *rāga-dveṣhau*—attachment and aversion; *vyudasya*—casting aside; *cha*—and; *vivikta-sevī*—relishing solitude; *laghu-āśhī*—eating light; *yata*—controls; *vāk*—speech; *kāya*—body; *mānasaḥ*—and mind; *dhyāna-yoga-paraḥ*—engaged in meditation; *nityam*—always; *vairāgyam*—dispassion; *samupāśhritaḥ*—having taken shelter of; *ahankāram*—egotism; *balam*—violence; *darpam*—arrogance; *kāmam*—desire; *krodham*—anger; *parigraham*—selfishness; *vimuchya*—being freed from; *nirmamaḥ*—without possessiveness of property; *śhāntaḥ*—peaceful; *brahma-bhūyāya*—union with Brahman; *kalpate*—is fit.

One becomes fit to attain Brahman when he or she possesses a purified intellect and firmly restrains the senses, abandoning sound and other

objects of the senses, casting aside attraction and aversion. Such a person relishes solitude, eats lightly, controls body, mind, and speech, is ever engaged in meditation, and practices dispassion. Free from egotism, violence, arrogance, desire, possessiveness of property, and selfishness, such a person, situated in tranquillity, is fit for union with Brahman (i.e., realisation of the Absolute Truth as Brahman).

Shree Krishna has been explaining how, by performing our duties in proper consciousness, we can attain perfection. He now describes the excellence that is required for the perfection of Brahman-realisation. He says in that state of perfection, we develop a purified intellect that is established in transcendental knowledge. The mind is controlled due to not indulging in likes and dislikes. The senses are restrained, and the impulses of the body and speech are tenaciously disciplined. Activities for maintenance of the body, such as eating and sleeping, are wisely held in balance. Such a yogi is deeply contemplative, and hence prefers solitude. The ego and its lust for power and prestige are dissolved. Constantly engaging the mind in transcendence, the yogi is tranquil and free from the bonds of desire, anger, and greed. Such a yogi attains realisation of the Absolute Truth as Brahman.

ब्रह्मभूतः प्रसन्नात्मा न शोचति न काङ्क्षति ।
समः सर्वेषु भूतेषु मद्भक्तिं लभते पराम् ।।54।।

brahma-bhūtaḥ prasannātmā na śhochati na kāṅkṣhati
samaḥ sarveṣhu bhūteṣhu mad-bhaktiṁ labhate parām

brahma-bhūtaḥ—one situated in Brahman; *prasanna-ātmā*—mentally serene; *na*—neither; *śhochati*—grieving; *na*—nor; *kāṅkṣhati*—desiring; *samaḥ*—equitably disposed; *sarveṣhu*—towards all; *bhūteṣhu*—living beings; *mat-bhaktim*—devotion to me; *labhate*—attains; *parām*—supreme.

One situated in the transcendental Brahman realisation becomes mentally serene, neither grieving nor desiring. Being equitably disposed towards all living beings, such a yogi attains supreme devotion unto Me.

Shree Krishna concludes His description of the stage of perfection. The words *Brahma-bhūtaḥ* mean the state of Brahman realisation. Situated in It, one is *prasannātmā*, meaning, serene and unaffected by turbid and painful experiences. *Na śhochati* means one does not grieve nor feel any incompleteness. *Na kāṅkṣhati* means one does not crave for anything material to make one happy. Such a yogi sees all living beings with equal vision, realising the substratum of Brahman in all of them. In such a state, one is situated on the platform of realised knowledge. However, Shree Krishna concludes the verse with a twist. He says that in such a realised state of knowledge, one then attains *parā bhakti* (divine love) for God.

The jnanis are often fond of saying that bhakti is only to be done as an intermediate step towards Brahman realisation. They claim that bhakti is for the purpose of purifying the heart, and only jnana remains at the end of the journey. Thus, they recommend that those who possess a strong intellect can ignore devotion and simply cultivate knowledge. But this verse negates such a viewpoint. Shree Krishna states that after attaining the highest realisation of jnana, one develops *parā bhakti*. Ved Vyas declared the same in the Shreemad Bhagavatam:

ātmārāmāśh cha munayo nirgranthā apy urukrame
kurvanty ahaitukīṁ bhaktim ittham-bhūta-guṇo hariḥ (1.7.10)

'Even those who are *ātmārām* (rejoicing in the self), established in self-knowledge, and liberated from material bonds, such perfected souls desire to possess bhakti towards God. The super-excellent qualities of God are such that they attract even liberated souls.' There are many examples of renowned jnanis who had attained self-knowledge and were situated in the realisation of the formless Brahman. However, when they got a glimpse of the transcendental divine qualities of God, they naturally got drawn towards bhakti. Instances of such jnanis from each of the four yugas are given here.

The greatest jnanis in Satya Yug were the four sons of Brahma—Sanat Kumar, Sanatan Kumar, Sanak Kumar, and Sanandan Kumar. They were self-realised from birth, and their minds were always absorbed in the formless Brahman. These four brothers once visited *Vaikunth*, the divine abode of Lord Vishnu. There, the fragrance from the Tulsi (holy basil) leaves at the lotus feet of the Lord entered their nostrils, causing a thrill of ecstasy in their hearts. Immediately, their meditation on the attributeless Brahman ended, and they were immersed in the bliss of divine love for Lord Vishnu. They beseeched Him for a boon:

kāmaṁ bhavaḥ sva-vṛijinair nirayeṣhu naḥ stā-
chcheto 'livad yadi nu te padayo rameta

(Bhagavatam 3.15.49)

'O Lord, we do not even mind if You send us to hell, so long as our mind gets the opportunity to drink the divine love bliss that emanates from Your lotus feet.' Just imagine, even after having realised the formless Brahman, these foremost jnanis were willing to reside in hell for the sake of relishing the bliss of the personal form of God.

Let us now move on to *Tretā Yug*. The topmost jnani in this age was King Janak. He was the father of Sita, the eternal consort of Lord Ram. He was also known as Videha, one who was beyond all perceptions of the body. His mind would remain ever absorbed in the formless Brahman. One day, however, Sage Vishwamitra came to meet him along with Lord Ram and Lakshman. What took place then is described in the Ramayan:

inhani bilokata ati anurāgā, barabasa brahmasukhahi mana tyāgā

'On seeing Lord Ram, King Janak became detached from the bliss of the formless Brahman and deeply attached to the personal form of the Supreme Lord.' In this manner, the greatest jnani of the age of *Tretā* came to the path of bhakti.

The topmost jnani in the age of *Dwāpar* was Shukadev, son of Sage Ved Vyas. The Puranas describe him as being so elevated that he remained in his mother's womb for twelve years, thinking that if he came into the world, the material energy, maya, would overpower him. Finally, Sage Narad came and spoke to him through his mother's ear, reassuring him that nothing would happen, and he should emerge from the womb. Then, he emerged, and by his yogic power, expanded his body to that of a twelve-year old and renounced home to live in the forest. There, he soon reached the highest state of samadhi.

Years went by, and one day Ved Vyas's students were cutting wood in the forest, when they saw him in samadhi. They went back and told the sage about it. He told them to recite a verse in Shukadev's ears, describing the beauty of the personal form of Lord Krishna:

barhāpīḍaṁ naṭa-vara-vapuḥ karṇayoḥ karṇikāraṁ
bibhrad vāsaḥ kanaka-kapiśhaṁ vaijayantīṁ cha mālām
randhrān veṇor adhara-sudhayāpūrayan gopa-vṛindair
vṛindāraṇyaṁ sva-pada-ramaṇaṁ prāviśhad gīta-kīrtiḥ

(Bhagavatam 10.21.5)

'Shree Krishna is adorned with a peacock feathered crown upon His head and exhibits His form as the greatest Dancer. His ears are decorated with blue *karṇikā* flowers. His shawl is the colour of brilliant gold. He wears a garland made of *vaijayantī* beads. He fills the holes of His flute with the nectar from His lips. His praises are sung as He enters Vrindavan, surrounded by His cowherd friends, and the marks of His footprints beautify the earth.' Shukadev was absorbed in the formless Brahman when the verse entered his ears. Suddenly, the object of his meditation transformed into the enchanting form of Lord Krishna. He felt so deeply attracted to the bliss of the personal form of God that he left his samadhi and went back to his father, Ved Vyas. From him, he heard the Shreemad Bhagavatam which is full of the sweetness of bhakti. Later, on the banks of the Ganges, he related it to King Parikshit, grandson of Arjun. In this manner, the greatest jnani of the age of *Dwāpar* got drawn to the path of bhakti.

Finally, we come to Kali Yug. Jagadguru Shankaracharya is widely considered the greatest jnani of this age. He is widely acclaimed as the propagator of *advaita vāda* (non-dualism), wherein he stated that there is only one entity in existence, which is the *nirguna* (without qualities), *nirviśheṣh* (attributeless), *nirākār* (formless) Brahman. However, many people are unaware that from the age of twenty until he left his body at the age of thirty-two, he wrote hundreds of verses in praise of Lord Krishna, Lord Ram, Lord Shiv, and Mother Durga. He also visited the four *dhāms* (centers of spirituality in the four corners of India) and worshipped deities of the personal forms of God in all of them. In *Prabodh Sudhākar*, he writes:

kāmyopāsanayārthayantyanudinaṁ kiñchitphalaṁ swepsitam
kechit swargamathāpavargamapare yogādiyajñādibhiḥ
asmākaṁ yadunandanāṅghriyugaladhyānāvadhānārthinām
kiṁ lokena damena kiṁ nṛipatinā swargāpavargaiśhcha kim

(verse 250)

'Those who perform righteous actions for the attainment of celestial abodes may do so. Those who desire liberation via the path of jnana or ashtang yog may pursue that goal. As for me, I want nothing of these two paths. I wish only to engross myself in the nectar of Shree Krishna's lotus feet. I do not desire either worldly or heavenly pleasures, nor do I desire liberation. I am a *rasik* who relishes the bliss of divine love.'

The fact is that Shankaracharya was a great devotee of Lord Krishna. What he taught in his *bhāṣhyas* (commentaries) was the need of the times. When he appeared on earth, Buddhism prevailed all over India. In such an environment, to re-establish the faith of the Buddhists in the Vedas, he sidelined devotion while writing his *bhāṣhyas*. But later, in the numerous *stutis* (praises) he wrote for the personal forms of God, he revealed his inner devotion. Shankaracharya was thus an example in the age of Kali, of someone, who had reached the highest realisation of jnana, and who then did devotion.

भक्त्या मामभिजानाति यावान्यश्चास्मि तत्त्वतः ।
ततो मां तत्त्वतो ज्ञात्वा विशते तदनन्तरम् ।।55।।

bhaktyā mām abhijānāti yāvān yaśh chāsmi tattvataḥ
tato māṁ tattvato jñātvā viśhate tad-anantaram

bhaktyā—by loving devotion; *mām*—me; *abhijānāti*—one comes to know; *yāvān*—as much as; *yaḥ cha asmi*—as I am; *tattvataḥ*—in truth; *tataḥ*—then; *mām*—me; *tattvataḥ*—in truth; *jñātvā*—having known; *viśhate*—enters; *tat-anantaram*—thereafter.

Only by loving devotion to Me does one come to know who I am in Truth. Then, having come to know Me, My devotee enters into full consciousness of Me.

Shree Krishna stated in the previous verse that one develops devotion on becoming situated in transcendental knowledge. Now He says that only through devotion can one come to know God's personality. Previously, the jnani had realised God as the *nirguna* (qualityless), *nirviśheṣh* (attributeless), *nirākār* (formless) Brahman. But the jnani had no realisation of the personal form of God. The secret of that personal form cannot be known through karm, jnana, ashtang yog, or any other means. It is love that opens the door to the impossible and makes way for the inaccessible. Shree Krishna states here that the mystery of God's Names, Forms, Virtues, Pastimes, Abodes, and Associates can only be comprehended through unalloyed devotion. The devotees understand God because they possess the eyes of love.

The *Padma Puran* mentions a beautiful incident illustrating the above truth.

A rishi by the name of Jabali saw a very effulgent and peaceful maiden meditating in the forest. He requested her to reveal her identity and purpose of meditation. She replied:

brahmavidyāhamatulā yogiṁdrairyā cha mṛigyate
sāhaṁ hari padāmbhoja kāmyayā suchiraṁ tapaḥ
charāmyasmin vane ghore dhyāyantī puruṣhottamam
brahmānandena pūrṇāhaṁ tenānandena tṛiptadhīḥ
tathāpi śhūnyamātmānaṁ manye kṛiṣhṇaratiṁ vinā

'I am *brahma vidyā* (the science of knowing the self, which ultimately leads to the Brahman realisation of God). Great yogis and mystics perform austerities to know me. However, I am myself performing severe austerities to develop love at the lotus feet of the personal form of God. I am replete and satiated with the bliss of Brahman. Yet, without loving attachment to Lord Krishna, I feel empty and void.'

Thus, mere knowledge is insufficient for relishing the bliss of the personal form of God. It is through bhakti that one enters into this secret and achieves full God-consciousness.

सर्वकर्माण्यपि सदा कुर्वाणो मद्व्यपाश्रयः ।
मत्प्रसादादवाप्नोति शाश्वतं पदमव्ययम् ।।56।।

sarva-karmāṇy api sadā kurvāṇo mad-vyapāśhrayaḥ
mat-prasādād avāpnoti śhāśhvataṁ padam avyayam

sarva—all; *karmāṇi*—actions; *api*—though; *sadā*—always; *kurvāṇaḥ*—performing; *mat-vyapāśhrayaḥ*—take full refuge in me; *mat-prasādāt*—by my grace; *avāpnoti*—attain; *śhāśhvatam*—the eternal; *padam*—abode; *avyayam*—imperishable.

My devotees, though performing all kinds of actions, take full refuge in Me. By My grace, they attain the eternal and imperishable abode.

In the previous verse, Shree Krishna explained that through bhakti, the devotees enter into full awareness of Him. Equipped with it, they see everything in its connection with God. They see their body, mind, and intellect as the energies of God; they see their material possessions as the property of God; they see all living beings as parts and parcels of God; and they see themselves as His tiny servants. In that divine consciousness, they do not give up work, rather, they renounce the pride of being the doers and enjoyers of work. They see all work as devotional service to the Supreme, and they depend upon Him for its performance.

Then, upon leaving their body, they go to the divine abode of God. Just as the material realm is made from material energy, the divine realm is made from spiritual energy. Hence, it is free from the defects of material nature and is perfect in every way. It is *sat-chit-anand* i.e., full of eternality, knowledge, and bliss. Regarding His divine realm, Shree Krishna had said in verse 15.6: 'Neither the sun nor the moon, nor fire can illumine that supreme abode of Mine. Having gone There, one does not return to this material world again.'

The various forms of God have Their own personal abodes in the spiritual realm where They engage in eternal loving pastimes with Their devotees. Those who perfect their selfless loving service towards Him go to the abode of their worshipped form of God. Thus, the devotees of Lord Krishna go to *Golok*; those of Lord Vishnu go to *Vaikunth*; the devotees of Lord Ram go to *Saket Lok*; the worshippers of Lord Shiv go to *Shiv Lok*; those of Mother Durga go to *Devi Lok*, and so on. The devotees who reach these divine abodes, having attained Him, participate in His divine pastimes that are imbued with the perfection of the spiritual energy.

चेतसा सर्वकर्माणि मयि सन्न्यस्य मत्परः ।
बुद्धियोगमुपाश्रित्य मच्चित्तः सततं भव ।।57।।

chetasā sarva-karmāṇi mayi sannyasya mat-paraḥ
buddhi-yogam upāśhritya mach-chittaḥ satataṁ bhava

chetasā—by consciousness; *sarva-karmāṇi*—every activity; *mayi*—to me; *sannyasya*—dedicating; *mat-paraḥ*—having me as the supreme goal; *buddhi-yogam*—having the intellect united with God; *upāśhritya*—taking shelter of; *mat-chittaḥ*—consciousness absorbed in me; *satatam*—always; *bhava*—be.

Dedicate your every activity to Me, making Me your supreme goal. Taking shelter of the Yog of the intellect, keep your consciousness absorbed in Me always.

Yog means 'union', and *buddhi yog* means 'having the intellect united with God'. This union of the intellect occurs when it is firmly convinced that everything in existence has emanated from God, is connected to Him, and is meant for His satisfaction. Let us understand the position of the intellect in our internal system.

Within our body is the subtle *antaḥ karaṇ*, which we also refer to colloquially as the heart or the etheric heart. It has four aspects to it. When it creates thoughts, we call it *mana* or mind. When it analyses and decides, we call it *buddhi* or intellect. When it gets attached to an object or person, we call it *chitta* or the subconscious mind. When it identifies with the attributes of the body and becomes proud, we call it *ahankār* or ego.

In this internal machinery, the position of the intellect is dominant. It makes decisions, while the mind desires in accordance with those decisions, and the *chitta* gets attached to the objects of affection. For example, if the intellect decides that security is the most important thing in the world, then the mind always yearns for security in life. If the decision of the intellect is that prestige is the source of happiness in life, then the mind keeps yearning, 'prestige...prestige...prestige.'

Throughout the day, we humans control our mind with the intellect. That is why anger flows downward. The CEO shouts at the director. The director does not shout back because the intellect realises that it will cost him the job; instead, he vents his anger at the manager. The manager controls himself, despite feeling vexed with the director; but finds release by shouting at the foreman. The foreman takes it out at the worker. The worker purges his frustration on the wife. The wife shouts at the children. In each case, the intellect decides where it is dangerous to get angry and where it does not have repercussions. The example illustrates that as human beings, our intellect possesses the ability to control the mind.

Thus, we must cultivate the intellect with proper knowledge and use it to guide the mind in the proper direction. This is what Shree Krishna means by *buddhi yog*—developing a firm conviction of the intellect that all work and all things are meant for the pleasure of God. For such a person of steadfast intellect, the *chitta* easily gets attached to God.

मच्चित्तः सर्वदुर्गाणि मत्प्रसादात्तरिष्यसि ।
अथ चेत्त्वमहङ्कारान्न श्रोष्यसि विनङ्क्ष्यसि ।।58।।

mach-chittaḥ sarva-durgāṇi mat-prasādāt tariṣhyasi
atha chet tvam ahankārān na śhroṣhyasi vinaṅkṣhyasi

mat-chittaḥ—by always remembering me; *sarva*—all; *durgāṇi*—obstacles; *mat-prasādāt*—by my grace; *tariṣhyasi*—you shall overcome; *atha*—but; *chet*—if; *tvam*—you; *ahankārāt*—due to pride; *na śhroṣhyasi*—do not listen; *vinaṅkṣhyasi*—you will perish.

If you always remember Me, by My grace you shall overcome all obstacles and difficulties. But if, due to pride, you do not listen to My advice, you will perish.

Having advised Arjun what to do in the previous verse, Shree Krishna now declares the benefits of following His advice and the repercussions of not following it. The soul should not think that it is independent of God in any way. If we take full shelter of the Lord, with the mind fixed only on Him, then by His grace, all obstacles and difficulties will be resolved. But if, out of vanity, we disregard the instructions, thinking we know better than the eternal wisdom of God and the scriptures, we will fail to attain the goal of human life, for there is no one superior to God, nor is there any advice better than His.

यदहङ्कारमाश्रित्य न योत्स्य इति मन्यसे ।
मिथ्यैष व्यवसायस्ते प्रकृतिस्त्वां नियोक्ष्यति ।।59।।

yad ahankāram āśhritya na yotsya iti manyase
mithyaiṣha vyavasāyas te prakṛitis tvāṁ niyokṣhyati

yat—if; *ahankāram*—motivated by pride; *āśhritya*—taking shelter; *na yotsye*—I shall not fight; *iti*—thus; *manyase*—you think; *mithyā eṣhaḥ*—this is all false; *vyavasāyaḥ*—determination; *te*—your; *prakṛitiḥ*—nature; *tvām*—you; *niyokṣhyati*—will engage.

If, motivated by pride, you think, 'I shall not fight,' your decision will be in vain. Your own nature will compel you to fight.

Speaking in a chastising tone, Shree Krishna now delivers a word of caution. We should not think we have complete liberty to do what we wish. The soul does not lead an independent existence; it is dependent upon God's creation in many ways. In the materially bound state, it is under the influence of the three gunas. The combination of gunas creates our nature, and we are compelled to act according to its dictates. Hence, we do not have absolute freedom to say, 'I will do what I like.'

We have to choose between the good advice of God and the scriptures or the compulsions of our nature.

There is an anecdote regarding one's nature:

A soldier retired after thirty years of service and returned to his hometown. One day, he was standing in the coffee shop drinking a cup of tea, when a friend thought of a practical joke. He screamed from behind, 'Attention!' Responding to that command had become a part of the soldier's nature. Involuntarily, he dropped the cup from his hand and put his hands by his side.

Shree Krishna warns Arjun that by nature he is a warrior, and if, out of pride, he decides not to listen to good advice, his Kshatriya nature will still compel him to fight.

स्वभावजेन कौन्तेय निबद्धः स्वेन कर्मणा ।
कर्तुं नेच्छसि यन्मोहात्करिष्यस्यवशोऽपि तत् ।।60।।

swbhāva-jena kaunteya nibaddhaḥ svena karmaṇā
kartuṁ nechchhasi yan mohāt kariṣhyasy avaśho 'pi tat

swabhāva-jena—born of one's own material nature; *kaunteya*—Arjun, son of Kunti; *nibaddhaḥ*—bound; *svena*—by your own; *karmaṇā*—actions; *kartum*—to do; *na*—not; *ichchhasi*—you wish; *yat*—which; *mohāt*—out of delusion; *kariṣhyasi*—you will do; *avaśhaḥ*—helplessly; *api*—even though; *tat*—that.

O Arjun, that action which out of delusion you do not wish to do, you will be driven to do it by your own inclination, born of your own material nature.

Continuing His words of warning, Shree Krishna further elaborates on the previous theme. He says, 'Due to your *sanskārs* of past lives, you have a Kshatriya nature. Your inborn qualities of heroism, chivalry, and patriotism will compel you to fight. You have been trained in past lifetimes and in this one, to honour your duty as a warrior. Is it possible for you to be inactive when you see injustice being meted out to others in front of your eyes? Your nature and inclinations are such that you vehemently oppose evil wherever you see it. Therefore, it is beneficial for you to fight in accordance with My instructions, rather than be compelled by your nature to do the same.'

ईश्वरः सर्वभूतानां हृद्देशेऽर्जुन तिष्ठति ।
भ्रामयन्सर्वभूतानि यन्त्रारूढानि मायया ।।61।।

īśhvaraḥ sarva-bhūtānāṁ hṛid-deśhe 'rjuna tiṣhṭhati
bhrāmayan sarva-bhūtāni yantrārūḍhāni māyayā

īśhvaraḥ—the Supreme Lord; *sarva-bhūtānām*—in all living beings; *hṛit-deśhe*—in the hearts; *arjuna*—Arjun; *tiṣhṭhati*—dwells; *bhrāmayan*—causing to wander; *sarva-bhūtāni*—all living beings; *yantra ārūḍhani*—seated on a machine; *māyayā*—made of material energy.

The Supreme Lord dwells in the hearts of all living beings, O Arjun. According to their karmas, He directs the wanderings of the souls who are seated on a machine made of material energy.

Emphasising the dependence of the soul upon God, Shree Krishna says, 'Arjun, whether you choose to obey Me or not, your position will always remain under My dominion. The body in which you reside is a machine made from My material energy. Based upon your past karmas, I have given you the kind of body you deserved. I too am seated in it, and am noting all your thoughts, words, and deeds. So, I will also judge whatever you do in the present, to decide your future. Do not think you are independent of Me in any condition. Hence Arjun, it is in your self-interest to surrender to Me.'

तमेव शरणं गच्छ सर्वभावेन भारत ।
तत्प्रसादात्परां शान्तिं स्थानं प्राप्स्यसि शाश्वतम् ।।62।।

tam eva śharaṇaṁ gachchha sarva-bhāvena bhārata
tat-prasādāt parāṁ śhāntiṁ sthānaṁ prāpsyasi śhāśhvatam

tam—unto him; *eva*—only; *śharaṇam gachchha*—surrender;

sarva-bhāvena—whole-heartedly; *bhārata*—Arjun, son of Bharat; *tat-prasādāt*—by his grace; *parām*—supreme; *śhāntim*—peace; *sthānam*—the abode; *prāpsyasi*—you will attain; *śhāśhvatam*—eternal.

Surrender exclusively unto Him with your whole being, O Bharat. By His grace, you will attain perfect peace and the eternal abode.

Being dependent upon God, the soul must also depend upon His grace to get out of its present predicament and attain the ultimate goal. Self-effort will never suffice for this. But if God bestows His grace, He grants His divine knowledge and divine bliss upon the soul and releases it from the bondage of material energy. Shree Krishna emphasises that by His grace, one will attain eternal beatitude and the imperishable abode. However, to receive that grace, the soul must qualify itself by surrendering to God. Even a worldly father will not hand over all his precious possessions to his child until the child becomes responsible enough to utilise them properly. Similarly, the grace of God is not a whimsical act; He has perfectly rational rules on the basis of which He bestows it.

If God does not follow rules while bestowing grace, people's faith in Him will break. Let us say, for example, that there is a father who has two sons. He instructs both of them to work hard in the paddy field as it is the cultivation season. One son toils and sweats it out in the blazing sun all day long. In the night when he returns, the father says, 'Well done, my son. You are obedient, hard-working, and loyal. Here is your reward. Take Rs 1,000 and do what you like with it.' The second son does nothing—he lies in bed all day long, sleeping, drinking, smoking, and abusing his father. At night, suppose the father says, 'Never mind, after all, you are also my son. Here is Rs 1,000; go and enjoy yourself with it.' The result of this will be that the first son's motivation to work hard will be smothered. He will say, 'If this is my father's reward system, then why should I work? I will also do nothing, for I will receive the Rs 1,000 in any case.' Likewise, if God grants His grace without our qualifying for it, all those who became saints in the past will complain, 'What is this? We strived for many lifetimes to purify ourselves and then we became recipients of God's grace, but this person received it without making himself eligible. Then our effort for self-improvement was meaningless.' God says, 'I do not behave in this irrational manner. I have an eternal condition on the basis of which I bestow My grace. And I have declared this in all the scriptures.' The *Śhwetāśhvatar Upanishad* states:

yo brahmāṇaṁ vidadhāti pūrvaṁ
yo vai vedānśh cha prahiṇoti tasmai
taṁ ha devaṁ ātma-buddhi-prakāśhaṁ
mumukṣhur vai śharaṇam ahaṁ prapadye (6.18)

'We take shelter of that Supreme Being who created Brahma and others. It is by His grace that the soul and intellect get illumined.' The Shreemad Bhagavatam states:

mām ekam eva śharaṇam ātmānaṁ sarva-dehinām
yāhi sarvātma-bhāvena mayā syā hy akuto-bhayaḥ (11.12.15)

'O Uddhav! Giving up all forms of mundane social and religious conventions, simply surrender unto Me, the Supreme Soul of all souls. Only then can you cross over this material ocean and become fearless.'

Shree Krishna also stated in verse 7.14 of the Bhagavad Gita: 'My divine energy, maya, consisting of the three modes of nature, is very difficult to overcome. But those who surrender unto Me cross over it easily.'

The Ramayan also says:

sanamukha hoi jīva mohi jabahīṅ,
janma koṭi agha nāsahiṅ tabahīṅ

'The moment the soul surrenders to God, its account of sinful deeds in endless past lifetimes is destroyed by His grace.'

In the above verse of the Bhagavad Gita, Shree Krishna has reiterated the principle of the necessity for surrendering to God to receive His grace. The details of what it means to surrender are explained in the *Hari Bhakti Vilas*, *Bhakti Rasamrita Sindhu*, the *Vayu Puran*, and the *Ahirbudhni Samhita* in the following manner:

ānukūlyasya saṅkalpaḥ pratikūlyasya varjanam
rakṣhiṣhyatīti viśhvāso goptṛitve varaṇaṁ tathā
ātmanikṣhepa kārpaṇye ṣhaḍvidhā śharaṇāgatiḥ

(*Hari Bhakti Vilās* 11.676)

The above verse explains the six aspects of surrender to God:

1. To desire only in accordance with the desire of God: By nature, we are His servants, and the duty of a servant is to fulfil the desire of the master. So as surrendered devotees of God, we must make our will conform to the divine will of God. A dry leaf is surrendered to the wind. It does not complain whether the wind lifts it up, takes it forward or backward, or drops it to the ground. Similarly, we too must learn to be happy in the happiness of God.

2. Not to desire against the desire of God: Whatever we get in life is a result of our past and present karmas. However, the fruits of the karmas do not come by themselves. God notes them and gives the results at the appropriate time. Since God Himself dispenses the results, we must learn to serenely accept them. Usually, when people get wealth, fame, pleasure, and luxuries in the world, they forget to thank God. However, if they get suffering, they blame God for it, complaining, 'Why did God do this to me?' The second aspect of surrender means to not complain about whatever God gives us.

3. To have firm faith that God is protecting us: God is the eternal Father. He takes care of all living beings in creation. There are trillions of ants on planet earth, and all of them need to eat regularly. Do you ever find that a few thousand ants in your garden have died of starvation? God ensures that they are all provided for. On the other hand, elephants eat mounds of food every day. God provides for them too. Even a worldly father cares and provides for his children. Why then should we doubt whether our eternal Father, God, will take care of us or not? To have firm faith in His protection is the third aspect of surrender.

4. To maintain an attitude of gratitude towards God: We have received so many priceless gifts from the Lord. The earth that we walk upon, the sunlight with which we see, the air that we breathe, and the water that we drink, are all given to us by God. In fact, it is because of Him that we exist; He has brought us to life and imparted consciousness in our soul. We are not paying Him any tax in return, but we must at least feel deeply indebted for all that He has given to us. This is the sentiment of gratitude.

The reverse of this is the sentiment of ungratefulness. For example, a father does so much for his child. The child is told to be grateful to his father for this. But the child responds, 'Why should I be grateful? His father took care of him, and he is taking care of me.' This is ingratitude towards the worldly father. To be grateful towards God, our eternal Father, for all that He has given to us, is the fourth aspect of surrender.

5. To see everything we possess as belonging to God: God created this entire world; it existed even before we were born and will continue to exist even after we die. Hence, the true owner of everything is God alone. When we think something belongs to us, we forget the proprietorship of God.

For example, let us say that someone comes into your house when you are not at home. He wears your clothes, eats food out of your refrigerator, and sleeps on your bed. On returning, you ask indignantly, 'What have you been doing in my house?'

He says, 'I have not damaged anything. I have merely used everything properly. Why are you getting annoyed?'

You will reply, 'You may not have destroyed anything, but it all belongs to me. If you use it without my permission, you are a thief.'

Similarly, this world and everything in it belongs to God. To remember this and give up our sense of proprietorship is the fifth aspect of surrender.

6. To give up the pride of having surrendered: If we become proud of the good deeds that we have done, the pride soils our heart and undoes the good we have done. That is why it is important to keep an attitude of humbleness: 'If I was able to do something good, it was only because God inspired my intellect in the right direction. Left to myself, I would never have been able to do it.' To keep such an attitude of humility is the sixth aspect of surrender.

If we can perfect these six points of surrender, we will fulfil God's condition, and He will bestow His grace upon us.

इति ते ज्ञानमाख्यातं गुह्याद्गुह्यतरं मया ।
विमृश्यैतदशेषेण यथेच्छसि तथा कुरु ।।63।।

iti te jñānam ākhyātaṁ guhyād guhyataraṁ mayā
vimṛiśhyaitad aśheṣheṇa yathechchhasi tathā kuru

iti—thus; *te*—to you; *jñānam*—knowledge; *ākhyātam*—explained; *guhyāt*—that secret knowledge; *guhya-taram*—still more secret knowledge; *mayā*—by me; *vimṛiśhya*—pondering; *etat*—on this; *aśheṣheṇa*—completely; *yathā*—as; *ichchhasi*—you wish; *tathā*—so; *kuru*—do.

Thus, I have explained to you this knowledge that is more secret than all secrets. Ponder over it deeply, and then do as you wish.

A secret is that information which is not accessible to a majority of the people. Most of the laws of physics were a secret until a few centuries ago, and many still continue to remain so. Spiritual knowledge is profound and not realisable through direct perception. It needs to be learnt through the guru and the scriptures. Hence, it is described as secret. In the second chapter, Shree Krishna had revealed knowledge of the soul, which is *guhya* or secret knowledge. In the seventh and eighth chapters, He explained knowledge of His powers, which is *guhyatar* or more secret. In the ninth and subsequent chapters, He revealed knowledge of His bhakti, which is *guhyatamam* or most secret. In the present chapter, verse 55, He revealed that He can be known in His personal form only by bhakti. Shree Krishna is now concluding the Bhagavad Gita. Having spoken most of the verses in the eighteen chapters, including imparting the most secret knowledge to Arjun, He now leaves the choice in Arjun's hands. He says, 'I have revealed to you profound and confidential knowledge. Now the choice is in your hands.'

Lord Ram made a similar statement to the residents of Ayodhya. He invited them all for His discourse. In it, He explained to them the purpose of human life and the way to accomplish it. In the end, He concluded:

nahiṅ anīti nahiṅ kachhu prabhutāī,
sunahu karahu jo tumhahi sohāī (Ramayan)

'The advice I have given to you is neither incorrect nor coercive. Listen to it carefully, contemplate over it, and then do what you wish.'

This free will to choose between available alternatives has been given to the soul by God. The freedom of choice is not infinite. One cannot decide, 'I choose to be the most intelligent person in the world.' Our choices are limited by our past and present karmas. However, we do possess a certain amount of free will; we are not machines in the hands of God. Sometimes people question that if God had not given us free will, then we would not have done any evil. But then we would not have done anything good either. The opportunity to do good always comes with the danger of doing evil. More importantly, God wants us to love Him, and love is only possible when there is a choice. A machine cannot love because it does not have any freedom of choice. God created us with free will and provided us with choices so that we may choose Him and thereby exercise our love for Him. Even the all-powerful God cannot force the soul to love and surrender to Him; this decision must be made by the soul itself. Here, Shree Krishna is calling Arjun's attention to his free will and asking him to choose.

सर्वगुह्यतमं भूयः शृणु मे परमं वचः ।
इष्टोऽसि मे दृढमिति ततो वक्ष्यामि ते हितम् ।।64।।

sarva-guhyatamaṁ bhūyaḥ śhṛiṇu me paramaṁ vachaḥ
iṣhṭo 'si me dṛiḍham iti tato vakṣhyāmi te hitam

sarva-guhya-tamam—the most confidential of all; *bhūyaḥ*—again; *śhṛiṇu*—hear; *me*—by me; *paramam*—supreme; *vachaḥ*—instruction; *iṣhṭaḥ asi*—you are dear; *me*—to me; *dṛiḍham*—very;

iti—thus; *tataḥ*—because; *vakṣhyāmi*—I am speaking; *te*—for your; *hitam*—benefit.

Hear again My supreme instruction, the most confidential of all knowledge. I am revealing this for your benefit because you are very dear to Me.

A teacher may know the deepest secret, but he does not necessarily reveal it to the student. Before sharing it, he considers many things, such as the preparedness of the student to receive it, comprehend it, and benefit from it. In the beginning of the Bhagavad Gita, Arjun was bewildered by the problems facing him and asked for guidance from Shree Krishna. The Lord enlightened him with great care and consideration, uplifting his understanding, little by little, through the eighteen chapters. Having seen Arjun receive the message so well, Shree Krishna now feels confident that he will be able to grasp the final and most profound knowledge as well. Further, He says *iṣhṭo 'si me dṛiḍhamiti*, meaning, 'I am speaking this to you because you are My very dear friend. So, I care for you deeply and sincerely desire your best interest.'

मन्मना भव मद्भक्तो मद्याजी मां नमस्कुरु ।
मामेवैष्यसि सत्यं ते प्रतिजाने प्रियोऽसि मे ।।65।।

man-manā bhava mad-bhakto mad-yājī māṁ namaskuru
mām evaiṣhyasi satyaṁ te pratijāne priyo 'si me

mat-manāḥ—thinking of me; *bhava*—be; *mat-bhaktaḥ*—my devotee; *mat-yājī*—worship me; *mām*—to me; *namaskuru*—offer obeisance; *mām*—to me; *eva*—certainly; *eṣhyasi*—you will come; *satyam*—truly; *te*—to you; *pratijāne*—I promise; *priyaḥ*—dear; *asi*—you are; *me*—to me.

Always think of Me, be devoted to Me, worship Me, and offer obeisance to Me. Doing so, you will certainly come to Me. This is My pledge to you, for you are very dear to Me.

In chapter 9, Shree Krishna had promised Arjun that He would reveal to him the most secret knowledge, and then had gone on to describe the glories of bhakti. Here, He repeats the first line of verse 9.34, asking him to engage in His devotion. By developing deep love for Shree Krishna and having his mind always absorbed in exclusive devotion to Him, Arjun will be assured of attaining the supreme destination.

A perfect example of someone completely absorbed in devotion was King Ambarish. The Shreemad Bhagavatam describes:

sa vai manaḥ kṛiṣhṇa-padāravindayor
vachāṁsi vaikuṇṭha-guṇānuvarṇane
karau harer mandira-mārjanādiṣhu
śhrutiṁ chakārāchyuta-sat-kathodaye

mukunda-liṅgālaya-darśhane dṛiśhau
tad-bhṛitya-gātra-sparśhe 'ṅga-saṅgamam
ghrāṇaṁ cha tat-pāda-saroja-saurabhe
śhrīmat-tulasyā rasanāṁ tad-arpite

pādau hareḥ kṣhetra-padānusarpaṇe
śhiro hṛiṣhīkeśha-padābhivandane
kāmaṁ cha dāsye na tu kāma-kāmyayā
yathottamaśhloka-janāśhrayā ratiḥ (9.4.18–20)

'Ambarish absorbed his mind on the lotus feet of Shree Krishna; he used his speech in glorifying the qualities of God, his hands in cleaning the temple, and his ears in hearing the divine pastimes of the Lord. He engaged his eyes in seeing the deities; he used his limbs in serving those who were engaged in devotion, his nose in smelling the fragrance of the Tulsi (holy basil) leaves offered at the feet of the Lord, and his tongue in tasting prasad (food sanctified by offering to God). He utilised his feet for walking to the holy abodes, and his head in offering obeisance to the lotus feet of God. He offered all paraphernalia, such as garlands and sandalwood, in the service of God. He did all this, not with some selfish motive, but only to attain the selfless service of Lord Krishna, through purification.'

The instruction to wholeheartedly engage in devotion is the essence of all the scriptures and the summum bonum of all knowledge. However, this is not the most confidential knowledge that Shree Krishna referred to, for He has already mentioned this earlier. *He now reveals this supreme secret in this next verse.*

सर्वधर्मान्परित्यज्य मामेकं शरणं व्रज ।
अहं त्वां सर्वपापेभ्यो मोक्षयिष्यामि मा शुचः ।।66।।

sarva-dharmān parityajya mām ekaṁ śharaṇaṁ vraja
ahaṁ tvāṁ sarva-pāpebhyo mokṣhayiṣhyāmi mā śhuchaḥ

sarva-dharmān—all varieties of dharmas; *parityajya*—abandoning; *mām*—unto me; *ekam*—only; *śharaṇam*—take refuge; *vraja*—take; *aham*—I; *tvām*—you; *sarva*—all; *pāpebhyaḥ*—from sinful reactions; *mokṣhayiṣhyāmi*—shall liberate; *mā*—do not; *śhuchaḥ*—fear.

Abandon all varieties of dharmas and simply surrender unto Me alone. I shall liberate you from all sinful reactions; do not fear.

All along, Shree Krishna had been asking Arjun to do two things simultaneously—engage his mind in devotion and engage his body in fulfilling his material duty as a warrior. He thus urged Arjun not to give up his Kshatriya dharma, but to do devotion alongside with it. This is the principle of karm yog. Now, Shree Krishna reverses this teaching by saying that there is no need to fulfil even material dharma. Arjun can renounce all material duties and simply surrender to God. This is the principle of karm sanyas. Here, one may question that if we give up all our material dharmas, will we not incur sin? Shree Krishna tells Arjun not to fear; He will absolve him from all sins and liberate him from material existence.

To comprehend this instruction of Shree Krishna, we need to understand the term dharma. It comes from the root word *dhṛi*, which means *dhāraṇ karane yogya* or 'responsibilities, duties, thoughts, and actions that are appropriate for us'. There are actually two kinds of dharmas—material dharma and spiritual dharma. These two kinds of dharmas are based on two different understandings of the 'self'. When we identify ourselves as the body, then our dharma is determined in accordance with our material designations, obligations, duties, and norms. Hence, serving our physical parents, fulfilling responsibilities to society, and nation—are all part of material dharma. This is also called *apara dharma* or material dharma. This includes the dharma as a Brahmin, Kshatriya, etc. However, when we identify ourselves as the soul, we have no material designations of varna (social class) and ashram (status in life). The soul's Father, Mother, Friend, Beloved, and resting place are all God. Hence, our one and only dharma becomes loving devotional service to God. This is also called *para dharma* or spiritual dharma.

If one leaves the material dharma, it is considered a sin due to dereliction of duty. But if one leaves material dharma and takes shelter of spiritual dharma, it is not a sin. The Shreemad Bhagavatam states:

devarṣhi-bhūtāpta-nṛiṇāṁ pitṝīṇāṁ
na kiṅkaro nāyam ṛiṇī cha rājan
sarvātmanā yaḥ śharaṇaṁ śharaṇyaṁ
gato mukundaṁ parihṛitya kartam (11.5.41)

This verse explains that there are five debts for those who do not surrender to God: to celestial gods, to sages, to ancestors, to other humans, and to other living beings. The varnashram system includes various procedures for releasing ourselves from these five kinds of debts. However, when we surrender to God, we are automatically released from all these debts, just as by watering the roots of a tree, all its branches, twigs, leaves, flowers, and fruit automatically get watered. Similarly, by fulfilling our duty to God, we automatically fulfil our duty to everyone. Hence, there is no sin in renouncing material dharma if we are properly situated in spiritual dharma. In fact, the ultimate goal is to engage completely and wholeheartedly in spiritual dharma. The Shreemad Bhagavatam states:

ājñāyaivaṁ guṇān doṣhān mayādiṣhṭān api svakān
dharmān santyajya yaḥ sarvān māṁ bhajeta sa sattamaḥ
(11.11.32)

'I have given innumerable instructions regarding the performance of bodily dharma in the Vedas. But those who realise the shortcomings in these, and renounce all prescribed duties, to simply engage in My devotional service, I consider them to be the best *sādhaks*.' In the Ramayan, we read how Lakshman renounced all material duties to accompany Lord Ram in the forest. He said:

guru pitu mātu na jānahu kāhū, kahahu subhāū nātha patiyāū
more sabahiñ eka tuma swāmī, dinabhandhu ura antarayamī

'O Lord, please believe me, I do not know any teacher, father, mother, or any other relative. As far as I am concerned, You, the Saviour of the fallen and the Knower of the heart, are my Master and my Everything.' Similarly, Prahalad said:

mātā nāsti pitā na 'sti na 'sti me swajano janaḥ

'I do not know any mother, father, or relative (God is everything to me).'

In the Bhagavad Gita, Shree Krishna gives Arjun sequentially higher instructions. Initially, He instructed Arjun to do karm i.e., his material dharma as a warrior (verse 2.31). But material dharma does not result in God-realisation; it leads to the celestial abodes, and once the pious merits are depleted, one has to come back. Hence, Shree Krishna next instructed Arjun to do karm yog i.e., his material dharma with the body and spiritual dharma with the mind. He asked Arjun to fight the war with the body and remember God with the mind (verse 8.7). This instruction of karm yog forms the major portion of the Bhagavad Gita. Now at the very end, Shree Krishna instructs Arjun to practise karm sanyas i.e., renounce all material dharma and simply adopt spiritual dharma which is love for God. He should thus fight, not because it is his duty as a warrior, but because God wants him to do so.

But why did Shree Krishna not give this instruction to Arjun earlier? Why did He seem to extol just the reverse in verse 5.2 when He stated karm yog superior to karm sanyas? Lord Krishna clearly explains this in the next verse.

इदं ते नातपस्काय नाभक्ताय कदाचन ।
न चाशुश्रूषवे वाच्यं न च मां योऽभ्यसूयति ।।67।।

idaṁ te nātapaskyāya nābhaktāya kadāchana
na chāśhuśhruṣhave vāchyaṁ na cha māṁ yo 'bhyasūtayi

idam—this; *te*—by you; *na*—never; *atapaskāya*—to those who are not austere; *na*—never; *abhaktāya*—to those who are not devoted; *kadāchana*—at any time; *na*—never; *cha*—also; *aśhuśhrūṣhave*—to those who are averse to listening (to spiritual topics); *vāchyam*—to be spoken; *na*—never; *cha*—also; *mām*—towards me; *yaḥ*—who; *abhyasūyati*—those who are envious.

This instruction should never be explained to those who are not austere or to those who are not devoted. It should also not be spoken to those who are averse to listening (to spiritual topics), and especially not to those who are envious of Me.

It was explained in the previous verse that if one is situated in loving devotion to God, there is no sin in giving up material duties. However, there is one problem with this instruction. If we have not yet become established in love for God, and we prematurely give up material duties, we will be neither here nor there. Thus, karm sanyas is only for those who are qualified for it. And what we are qualified for is determined by our guru who knows our capabilities and the stringency of the paths. If a student wishes to become a graduate, it will not do to directly go and attend the graduation ceremony. We will have to begin studying sequentially from grade one. Similarly, a vast majority of people are eligible for karm yog, and it would be a great folly for them to prematurely take karm sanyas. It is better to instruct them to fulfil their material dharma and practise devotion alongside. That is why, in this verse, Shree Krishna says that this confidential teaching given by Him is not for everyone. Before sharing it with others, we should check their eligibility for this teaching.

This word of caution applies specifically for the confidential teachings of the previous verse, and in general, for the entire message of the Bhagavad Gita. If it is explained to someone who is envious of

Shree Krishna, that person may respond, 'Shree Krishna was very conceited. He kept asking Arjun to glorify Him.' By misunderstanding the teachings, the faithless listener will be harmed by the divine message. The *Padma Puran* also states:

aśhraddadhāne vimukhe 'py aśhṛiṇvati
yaśh chopadeśhaḥ śhiva-nāmāparādhaḥ

'By giving transcendental instructions to those who are faithless and averse to God, we cause them to become offenders.' Hence, Shree Krishna describes the disqualifications for listeners in this verse.

य इदं परमं गुह्यं मद्भक्तेष्वभिधास्यति ।
भक्तिं मयि परां कृत्वा मामेवैष्यत्यसंशयः ।।68।।

ya idaṁ paramaṁ guhyaṁ mad-bhakteṣhv abhidhāsyati
bhaktiṁ mayi parāṁ kṛitvā mām evaiṣhyaty asanśhayaḥ

yaḥ—who; *idam*—this; *paramam*—most; *guhyam*—confidential knowledge; *mat-bhakteṣhu*—amongst my devotees; *abhidhāsyati*—teaches; *bhaktim*—greatest act of love; *mayi*—to me; *parām*—transcendental; *kṛitvā*—doing; *mām*—to me; *eva*—certainly; *eṣhyati*—comes; *asanśhayaḥ*—without doubt.

Amongst My devotees, those who teach this most confidential knowledge perform the greatest act of love. They will come to Me, without doubt.

Shree Krishna now declares the consequence of properly preaching the message of the Bhagavad Gita. He says such preachers first attain His *parā bhakti* and then attain Him.

The opportunity to engage in devotion is a special blessing of God, but the opportunity to help others engage in devotion is an even bigger blessing which attracts the special grace of God. Whenever we share something good with others, we benefit from it too. When we share whatever knowledge we have with others, by grace, our own knowledge increases as well. By often giving food to others, we never go hungry ourselves. Saint Kabir said:

dāna diye dhana nā ghaṭe, nadī ghate na nīra
apane hātha dekha lo, yoṅ kyā kahe kabīra

'Wealth does not decrease by giving in charity; a river does not become narrow, though people take water from it. I am not saying this without basis; see it for yourself in the world.' Thus, those who share the spiritual knowledge of the Bhagavad Gita with others receive the highest blessing themselves.

न च तस्मान्मनुष्येषु कश्चिन्मे प्रियकृत्तमः ।
भविता न च मे तस्मादन्यः प्रियतरो भुवि ।।69।।

na cha tasmān manuṣhyeṣhu kaśhchin me priya-kṛittamaḥ
bhavitā na cha me tasmād anyaḥ priyataro bhuvi

na—no; *cha*—and; *tasmāt*—than them; *manuṣhyeṣhu*—amongst human beings; *kaśhchit*—anyone; *me*—to me; *priya-kṛit-tamaḥ*—more dear; *bhavitā*—will be; *na*—never; *cha*—and; *me*—to me; *tasmāt*—than them; *anyaḥ*—another; *priya-taraḥ*—dearer; *bhuvi*—on this earth.

No human being does more loving service to Me than they; nor shall there ever be anyone on this earth more dear to Me.

Of all the gifts we can give to others, the gift of spiritual knowledge is one of the highest because it has the capacity to transform the recipient eternally. King Janak had asked his guru, 'The transcendental knowledge you have bestowed upon me is so precious that I feel deeply indebted to you. What can I give you in return?' Guru Ashtavakra replied, 'There is nothing you can give that will relinquish you from your debt. The knowledge I gave was divine, and all that you possess is material. Worldly objects can never be a price for divine knowledge. But you can do one thing. If ever you find someone who is thirsty for this knowledge, share it with him.'

Shree Krishna states here that He considers the sharing of the knowledge of the Bhagavad Gita as the highest loving service one can render to God. However, those who lecture on the Bhagavad

Gita should not feel they are doing something very great. The proper attitude of the teacher is to see oneself as an instrument in the hands of God and to accord all credit to the grace of the Lord.

अध्येष्यते च य इमं धर्म्यं संवादमावयोः ।
ज्ञानयज्ञेन तेनाहमिष्टः स्यामिति मे मतिः ।।70।।

adhyeṣhyate cha ya imaṁ dharmyaṁ saṁvādam āvayoḥ
jñāna-yajñena tenāham iṣhṭaḥ syām iti me matiḥ

adhyeṣhyate—study; *cha*—and; *yaḥ*—who; *imam*—this; *dharmyam*—sacred; *saṁvādam*—dialogue; *āvayoḥ*—of ours; *jñāna*—of knowledge; *yajñena-tena*—through the sacrifice of knowledge; *aham*—I; *iṣhṭaḥ*—worshipped; *syām*—shall be; *iti*—such; *me*—my; *matiḥ*—opinion.

And I proclaim that those who study this sacred dialogue of ours will worship Me (with their intellect) through the sacrifice of knowledge; such is My view.

Shree Krishna had repeatedly told Arjun to surrender his intellect to Him (verses 8.7, 12.8). This does not imply that we stop using the intellect; rather, it means we utilise our intellect to the best of our ability in fulfilling His will for us. From the message of the Bhagavad Gita, we understand what His will is. Hence, those who study this sacred dialogue worship God with their intellect.

श्रद्धावाननसूयश्च शृणुयादपि यो नरः ।
सोऽपि मुक्तः शुभाँल्लोकान्प्राप्नुयात्पुण्यकर्मणाम् ।।71।।

śhraddhāvān anasūyaśh cha śhṛiṇuyād api yo naraḥ
so 'pi muktaḥ śhubhāñl lokān prāpnuyāt puṇya-karmaṇām

śhraddhā-vān—faithful; *anasūyaḥ*—without envy; *cha*—and; *śhṛiṇuyāt*—listen; *api*—certainly; *yaḥ*—who; *naraḥ*—a person; *saḥ*—that person; *api*—also; *muktaḥ*—liberated; *śhubhān*—the auspicious; *lokān*—abodes; *prāpnuyāt*—attain; *puṇya-karmaṇām*—of the pious.

Even those who only listen to this knowledge with faith and without envy will be liberated from sins and attain the auspicious abodes where the pious dwell.

Not everyone has the intellect to comprehend the deep imports of the dialogue between Shree Krishna and Arjun. Here, Shree Krishna reassures that if such people merely hear with faith, they will also benefit. God is seated within them; He will note their sincere endeavour and reward them for it.

A story about a disciple of Jagadguru Shankaracharya, called Sananda, illustrates this point:

Sananda was illiterate and could not comprehend his guru's teaching as the other disciples could. But when Shankaracharya delivered the discourse, he would listen with rapt attention and great faith. One day, he was washing his guru's clothes on the other side of the river. It was time for the class, and the other disciples requested, 'Guruji, please begin the class.'

Shankaracharya replied, 'Let us wait; Sananda is not here.'

'But Guruji, he cannot understand anything,' the disciples urged.

'That is true; still, he listens with great faith and so I do not wish to disappoint him,' said Shankaracharya.

Then, to show the power of faith, Shankaracharya called out, 'Sananda! Please come here.'

On hearing his guru's words, Sananda did not hesitate. He ran on water. The story goes that wherever he placed his feet, lotus flowers sprang up to support him. He crossed over to the other bank and offered obeisance to his guru. At that time, a *stuti* (verses in praise) of the guru emanated from his mouth in sophisticated Sanskrit. The other disciples were amazed to hear this. Since, lotus flowers had bloomed under his feet, his name became 'Padmapada,' meaning, 'the one with lotus flowers under the feet.' He became one of the four main disciples of Shankaracharya, along with Sureshwaracharya, Hastamalak, and Trotakacharya.

In this verse, Shree Krishna assures Arjun that even those who merely hear the sacred dialogue with great faith will gradually become purified.

कच्चिदेतच्छ्रुतं पार्थ त्वयैकाग्रेण चेतसा ।
कच्चिदज्ञानसम्मोहः प्रनष्टस्ते धनञ्जय ।।72।।

kachchid etach chhrutaṁ pārtha tvayaikāgreṇa chetasā
kachchid ajñāna-sammohaḥ pranaṣhṭas te dhanañjaya

kachchit—whether; *etat*—this; *śhrutam*—heard; *pārtha*—Arjun, son of Pritha; *tvayā*—by you; *eka-agreṇa chetasā*—with a concentrated mind; *kachchit*—whether; *ajñāna*—ignorance; *sammohaḥ*—delusion; *pranaṣhṭaḥ*—destroyed; *te*—your; *dhanañjaya*—Arjun, conqueror of wealth.

O Arjun, have you heard Me with a concentrated mind? Have your ignorance and delusion been destroyed?

Shree Krishna has taken the position of being Arjun's teacher. It is natural for the teacher to enquire whether the student has grasped the subject or not. Shree Krishna's intention of asking the question is that if Arjun has not understood, He is ready to re-explain or go into further details.

अर्जुन उवाच ।
नष्टो मोहः स्मृतिर्लब्धा त्वत्प्रसादान्मयाच्युत ।
स्थितोऽस्मि गतसन्देहः करिष्ये वचनं तव ।।73।।

arjuna uvācha
naṣhṭo mohaḥ smṛitir labdhā tvat-prasādān mayāchyuta
sthito 'smi gata-sandehaḥ kariṣhye vachanaṁ tava

arjunaḥ uvācha—Arjun said; *naṣhṭaḥ*—dispelled; *mohaḥ*—illusion; *smṛitiḥ*—memory; *labdhā*—regained; *tvat-prasādāt*—by your grace; *mayā*—by me; *achyuta*—Shree Krishna, the infallible one; *sthitaḥ*—situated; *asmi*—I am; *gata-sandehaḥ*—free from doubts; *kariṣhye*—I shall act; *vachanam*—instructions; *tava*—your.

Arjun said: O Infallible One, by Your grace my illusion has been dispelled, and I am situated in knowledge. I am now free from doubts, and I shall act according to Your instructions.

At the outset, Arjun was faced with a bewildering situation and confused about his duty in the situation. Overwhelmed with sorrow, he had sat down on his chariot, given up his weapons. He had confessed that he could find no remedy to the grief that attacked his body and senses. But he now finds himself completely transformed and announces that he is situated in knowledge and no longer perplexed. He has given himself to the will of God and will do exactly as Shree Krishna has instructed. This was the impact of the message of the Bhagavad Gita upon him. However, he adds *tvat prasādān mayāchyuta*, meaning, 'O Shree Krishna, it was not just Your lecture, but Your grace that dispelled my ignorance.'

Material knowledge does not require grace. We can pay the educational institute or teacher and receive knowledge in exchange, but spiritual knowledge can neither be purchased nor sold. It is bestowed through grace and received through faith and humility. Thus, if we approach the Bhagavad Gita with an attitude of pride, 'I am so intelligent. I will evaluate what the net worth of this message is,' we will never be able to comprehend it. Our intellect will find some apparent defect in the scripture to dwell upon, and on that pretext, we will reject the entire scripture as incorrect. There have been so many commentaries on the Bhagavad Gita and innumerable readers of the divine message in the last five thousand years, but how many people have become enlightened like Arjun? If we wish to truly receive this knowledge, we must not merely read it, but also attract Shree Krishna's grace with an attitude of faith and loving surrender. Then, by His grace, the true purport of the Bhagavad Gita will be revealed to us.

सञ्जय उवाच ।
इत्यहं वासुदेवस्य पार्थस्य च महात्मनः ।
संवादमिममश्रौषमद्भुतं रोमहर्षणम् ।।74।।

sañjaya uvācha
ity ahaṁ vāsudevasya pārthasya cha mahātmanaḥ
saṁvādam imam aśhrauṣham adbhutaṁ roma-harṣhaṇam

sañjayaḥ uvācha—Sanjay said; *iti*—thus; *aham*—I; *vāsudevasya*—of Shree Krishna; *pārthasya*—Arjun; *cha*—and; *mahā-ātmanaḥ*—the noble-hearted soul; *saṁvādam*—conversation; *imam*—this; *aśhrauṣham*—have heard; *adbhutam*—wonderful; *roma-harṣhaṇam*—which causes the hair to stand on end.

Sanjay said: Thus, have I heard this wonderful conversation between Shree Krishna, the Son of Vasudev, and Arjun, the noble-hearted son of Pritha. So thrilling is the message that my hair is standing on end.

In this way, Sanjay comes to the end of his narration of the divine discourse of the Bhagavad Gita. He refers to Arjun as mahatma (great soul), as he has heeded the advice and instructions of Shree Krishna, and hence has become eminently wise. Sanjay now remarks how amazed and astounded he is on hearing their divine dialogue. The hair standing on end is one of the signs of deep devotional fervour. The *Bhakti Rasamrita Sindhu* states:

stambha sveda 'tha romāñchaḥ svara bhedo 'tha vepathuḥ
vaivarṇyamaśhru pralaya ityaṣhṭau sāttvikāḥ smṛitāḥ

'The eight signs of devotional ecstasy are: becoming stupefied and motionless, sweating, hair standing on end, choking of the voice, trembling, colour of the face becoming ashen, shedding tears, and fainting.' Sanjay is experiencing such intense devotional sentiments that his hair is bristling with divine joy.

One may ask how was it possible for Sanjay to hear this dialogue that took place on a far-off battlefield. He reveals this in the next verse.

व्यासप्रसादाच्छ्रुतवानेतद्गुह्यमहं परम् ।
योगं योगेश्वरात्कृष्णात्साक्षात्कथयतः स्वयम् ।।75।।

vyāsa-prasādāch chhrutavān etad guhyam ahaṁ param
yogaṁ yogeśhvarāt kṛiṣhṇāt sākṣhāt kathayataḥ svayam

vyāsa-prasādāt—by the grace of Ved Vyas; *śhrutavān*—have heard; *etat*—this; *guhyam*—secret; *aham*—I; *param*—supreme; *yogam*—Yog; *yoga-īśhvarāt*—from the Lord of Yog; *kṛiṣhṇāt*—from Shree Krishna; *sākṣhāt*—directly; *kathayataḥ*—speaking; *svayam*—himself.

By the grace of Veda Vyas, I have heard this supreme and most secret Yog from the Lord of Yog, Shree Krishna Himself.

Shree Krishna Dwaipayan Vyasadev, also known as Sage Ved Vyas, was the spiritual master of Sanjay. By the grace of his guru, Sanjay had been blessed with the power of clairvoyance, i.e., to know all that transpired on the battleground of Kurukshetra while he sat in the royal palace of Hastinapur. Here, Sanjay acknowledges it was by his guru's mercy that he got the opportunity to hear the supreme science of Yog from the Lord of Yog Himself, Shree Krishna.

Ved Vyas, the author of the *Brahma Sutras*, the eighteen Puranas, the Mahabharat, and other scriptures was a descension of God and possessed all the clairvoyant powers himself. Thus, he not only heard the conversation between Shree Krishna and Arjun, but also the one between Sanjay and Dhritarashtra. As a result, he included both conversations while compiling the Bhagavad Gita.

राजन्संस्मृत्य संस्मृत्य संवादमिममद्भुतम् ।
केशवार्जुनयोः पुण्यं हृष्यामि च मुहुर्मुहुः ।।76।।

rājan sansmṛitya sansmṛitya saṁvādam imam adbhutam
keśhavārjunayoḥ puṇyaṁ hṛiṣhyāmi cha muhur muhuḥ

rājan—King; *sansmṛitya saṁsmṛitya*—repeatedly recalling; *saṁvādam*—dialogue; *imam*—this; *adbhutam*—astonishing; *keśhava-arjunayoḥ*—between Lord Shree Krishna and Arjun; *puṇyam*—pious; *hṛiṣhyāmi*—I rejoice; *cha*—and; *muhuḥ muhuḥ*—repeatedly.

As I repeatedly recall this astonishing and wonderful dialogue between the Supreme Lord Shree Krishna and Arjun, O King, I rejoice again and again.

A spiritual experience gives a happiness that is far more thrilling and satisfying than all the material joys put together. Sanjay is rejoicing in such happiness and sharing his experience with the blind Dhritarashtra. Reflecting and remembering the wonderful dialogue, he is feeling divine bliss. This indicates the sublimity of the knowledge contained in this scripture and the divinity of the leela (pastimes) that Sanjay was able to witness.

तच्च संस्मृत्य संस्मृत्य रूपमत्यद्भुतं हरेः ।
विस्मयो मे महान्राजन्हृष्यामि च पुनः पुनः ।।77।।

tach-cha sansmṛitya sansmṛitya rūpam aty-adbhutaṁ hareḥ
vismayo ye mahān rājan hṛiṣhyāmi cha punaḥ punaḥ

tat—that; *cha*—and; *sansmṛitya sansmṛitya*—remembering repeatedly; *rūpam*—cosmic form; *ati*—most; *adbhutam*—wonderful; *hareḥ*—of Lord Krishna; *vismayaḥ*—astonishment; *me*—my; *mahān*—great; *rājan*—king; *hṛiṣhyāmi*—I am thrilled with joy; *cha*—and; *punaḥ punaḥ*—over and over again.

And remembering that most astonishing and wonderful cosmic form of Lord Krishna, great is my astonishment, and I am thrilled with joy over and over again.

Arjun was blessed with the vision of the cosmic form of the Lord which is rarely seen even by the greatest yogis. Shree Krishna told him that He was showing him the universal form because Arjun was His devotee and friend, and thus very dear to Him. Sanjay also came to see that cosmic form because he was fortunate to be a part of the divine pastimes as the narrator. There are times when an unexpected grace comes our way. If we utilise it properly, we can progress rapidly in our sadhana. Sanjay is repeatedly contemplating upon what he saw and flowing in the current of devotion.

यत्र योगेश्वरः कृष्णो यत्र पार्थो धनुर्धरः ।
तत्र श्रीर्विजयो भूतिर्ध्रुवा नीतिर्मतिर्मम ।।78।।

yatra yogeśhvaraḥ kṛiṣhṇo yatra pārtho dhanur-dharaḥ
tatra śhrīr vijayo bhūtir dhruvā nītir matir mama

yatra—wherever; *yoga-īśhvaraḥ*—Shree Krishna, Lord of Yog; *kṛiṣhṇaḥ*—Shree Krishna; *yatra*—wherever; *pārthaḥ*—Arjun, son of Pritha; *dhanuḥ-dharaḥ*—the supreme archer; *tatra*—there; *śhrīḥ*—opulence; *vijayaḥ*—victory; *bhūtiḥ*—prosperity; *dhruvā*—unending; *nītiḥ*—righteousness; *matiḥ mama*—my opinion.

Wherever there is Shree Krishna, the Lord of all Yog, and wherever there is Arjun, the supreme archer, there will also certainly be unending opulence, victory, prosperity, and righteousness. Of this, I am certain.

The Bhagavad Gita concludes with this verse delivering a deep pronouncement. Dhritarashtra was apprehensive of the outcome of the war. Sanjay informs him that material calculations of the relative strengths and numbers of the two armies are irrelevant. There can be only one verdict in this war—victory will always be on the side of God and His pure devotee, and so will goodness, supremacy, and abundance.

God is the Independent, Self-sustaining Sovereign of the world, and the worthiest object of adoration and worship. *na tatsamaśhchābhyadhikaśhcha dṛiśhyate* (*Śhwetāśhvatar Upanishad* 6.8) 'There is no one equal to Him; there is no one greater than Him.' He merely needs a proper medium to manifest His incomparable glory. The soul who surrenders to Him provides such a vehicle for the glory of God to shine forth. Thus, wherever the Supreme Lord and His pure devotee are present, the light of the Absolute Truth will always vanquish the darkness of falsehood. There can be no other outcome.

Guide to Hindi Pronunciation

Vowels

अ	*a*	as *u* in 'but'
आ	*ā*	as *a* in 'far'
इ	*i*	as *i* in 'pin'
ई	*ī*	as *i* in 'machine'
उ	*u*	as *u* in 'push'
ऊ	*ū*	as *o* in 'move'
ए	*e*	as *a* in 'evade'
ऐ	*ai*	as *a* in 'mat'; sometimes as *ai* in 'aisle' with the only difference that a should be pronounced as *u* in 'but', not as *a* in 'far'
ओ	*o*	as *o* in 'go'
औ	*au*	as *o* in 'pot' or as *aw* in 'saw'
ऋ	*ṛi*	as *ri* in 'Krishna'[1]
ॠ	*ṛī*	as *ree* in 'spree'

Consonants

Gutturals: Pronounced from the throat

क	*ka*	as *k* in 'kite'
ख	*kha*	as *kh* in 'Eckhart'
ग	*ga*	as *g* in 'goat'
घ	*gha*	as *gh* in 'dighard'
ङ	*ṅa*	as *n* in 'finger'

1 Across the many states of India, *ṛi* is pronounced as '*ru*' as *u* in p*u*sh. In most parts of North India, *ṛi* is pronounced as *ri* in K*ri*shna. We have used the North Indian style here.

Palatals: Pronounced with the middle of the tongue against the palate

च	*cha*	as *ch* in 'chanel'
छ	*chha*	as *chh* in 'staunchheart'
ज	*ja*	as *j* in 'jar'
झ	*jha*	as *dgeh* in 'hedgehog'
ञ	*ña*	as *n* in 'lunch'

Cerebrals: Pronounced with the tip of the tongue against the palate

ट	*ta*	as *t* in 'tub'
ठ	*ṭha*	as *th* in 'hothead'
ड	*ḍa*	as *d* in 'divine'
ढ	*ḍha*	as *dh* in 'redhead'
ण	*ṇa*	as *n* in 'burnt'

Dentals: Pronounced like the cerebrals but with the tongue against the teeth

त	*ta*	as *t* in French word 'matron'
थ	*tha*	as *th* in 'ether'
द	*da*	as *th* in 'either'
ध	*dha*	as *dh* in 'Buddha'
न	*na*	as *n* in 'no'

Labials: Pronounced with the lips

प	*pa*	as *p* in 'pink'
फ	*pha*	as *ph* in 'uphill'
ब	*ba*	as *b* in 'boy'
भ	*bha*	as *bh* in 'abhor'
म	*ma*	as *m* in 'man'

Semi-vowels

य	*ya*	as *y* in 'yes'
र	*ra*	as *r* in 'remember'
ल	*la*	as *l* in 'light'

व	*va*	as *v* in 'vine', as *w* in 'swan'

Sibilants

श	*śha*	as *sh* in 'shape'
ष	*ṣha*	as *sh* in 'show'
स	*sa*	as *s* in 'sin'

Aspirate

ह	*ha*	as *h* in hut'

Visarga

:	*ḥ*	it is a strong aspirate; also lengthens the preceding vowel and occurs only at the end of a word. It is pronounced as a final *h* sound

Anusvara Nasalized

ं	*ṁ/ṅ*	nasalizes and lengthens the preceding vowel and is pronounced as *n* in the words 'and' or 'anthem'[2]
ँ	~	as *n* in 'gung-ho'

Avagraha

ऽ	'	This is a silent character indicating अ. It is written but not pronounced; used in specific combination (sandhi) rules

Others

क्ष	*kṣha*	as *ksh* in 'freakshow'
ज्ञ	*jña*	as *gy* in 'bigyoung'
ड़	*ṛa*	There is no sign in English to represent the sound ड़. It has been written as *ṛa* but the tip of the tongue quickly flaps down
ढ़	*ṛha*	There is no sign in English to represent the sound ढ़. It has been written as *ṛha* but the tip of the tongue quickly flaps down

2 Sometimes nasalized and sometimes not. In many words such as *Aṁsh*, *Saṁskar*, etc. are pronounced with a nasal sound as *Aṅsh*, *Saṅskar*, etc. OR Since it is nasalized, we are using *ṅ*.

Glossary

Abhiniveśh	The instinctive urge to desire life.
Abhyās	Practice, or a concerted and persistent effort to change an old habit or develop a new one.
*Adharm*a	Irreligion.
Adhyātma	1) The individual soul, 2) Science of spirituality.
Ādiātmik	Miseries arising from one's own body and mind.
Ādibhautik	Miseries caused by other living entities.
Ādidaivik	Miseries caused by environmental conditions, such as earthquakes, floods etc.
Agnihotra yajna	A ritualistic fire sacrifice described in the Vedas.
Agni Devatā	The celestial god of fire.
Aham	Sense of the self.
Aham chetanā	Pride arising out of the sense of self.
Ahankār	1) Ego, 2) The entity created by the evolution of *mahān*.
Aiśhwarya bhakti	A type of devotion wherein the devotee is motivated to engage in devotion by contemplating upon the almighty aspect of God. The dominant sentiment in *aiśhwarya bhakti* is of awe and reverence. In such devotion, the feeling of remoteness from God and the need for maintaining propriety of conduct is always perceived.
Akarm	Inaction.
Akṣhar	Imperishable.
Anāhat nād	Sound that pervades creation and can be heard by yogis who tune in to it.
Anandmaya kośh	One of the five sheaths that covers the materially bound soul, consisting of the ego that makes one identify with the tiny bliss of the body-mind-intellect mechanism.

Anant	Without an end, unlimited.
Anant Shesh	The divine ten thousand-headed serpent on whom Lord Vishnu resides.
Ananya bhakti	Exclusive devotion.
Annamaya kośh	One of the five sheaths that covers the materially bound soul; it consists of the five gross elements (earth, water, fire, air, and space).
Antaḥ karaṇ	Colloquially referred to as the heart; it consists of the mind, intellect, subconscious mind, and the ego.
Antar kumbhak	Holding the breath in the lungs after inhalation. The outgoing breath gets suspended in the incoming breath during the period of suspension.
Aṇu	Tiny.
Apara dharma	The social aspect of religion, including duties towards parents, friends and relatives, society, etc.
Apauruṣheya	Not created by any person.
Apān	A type of pran, it is responsible for controlling the function of elimination of urine and faeces.
Arpaṇam	Dedicating and mentally delivering works to God.
Aryan	A person established in goodness, a perfect gentleman.
Asat	Temporary.
Aṣhṭa sattvic bhav	Physical symptoms of devotional absorption such as becoming stupefied, sweating, horripilation, choking of the voice, trembling, complexion becoming ashen, shedding tears, and fainting that sometimes manifest.
Ashtang yog	The eight-fold process of Yog propagated by Sage Patanjali.
Asmitā	Pride.

Ashram	1) One of the four phases of life, 2) Place similar to a monastery where dedicated spiritual practitioners reside.
Āstik Darshans	Schools of thought that accept the authority of the Vedas.
Asura	A demon.
Atma	The real self or 'soul' that is spiritual in nature and which imparts consciousness to the body.
Atmāhuti	*See Atma samarpaṇ.*
Atma jnana	Knowledge limited to that of the self.
Ātma-krīḍa	One who performs pastimes with his or her own self.
Ātmārām	One who rejoices in the self and has no need of anything external.
Ātma-ratī	One who is attracted to his or her own self.
Atma samarpaṇ	Offering one's soul to God.
Avatar	Descension of God or His special powers on earth.
Avatārī	The source of all the Avatars, Shree Krishna.
Āveśhāvatār	A person in whom God's special powers descend and act through.
Avidyā	Ignorance within.
Avidyā shakti	The aspect of the material energy that puts the soul into illusion.
Bāhya kumbhak	Keeping the lungs empty after exhalation; the incoming breath gets suspended in the outgoing breath during the period of suspension.
Bhagavan	The Supreme Lord, who is the possessor of infinite opulences.
Bhakta vatsaltā	God's love for his devotees.
Bhakti	Devotion to God.
Bhakti yog	The science of uniting with God through Divine Love.
Bhakti yogi	One who practises bhakti yog.
Bhāṣhya	Commentary.

Bhav	Sentiment.
Bhog	Material enjoyment.
Bīja	1) Impurities of the heart, 2) Seed.
Bīja mantra	The seed mantra.
Brahmacharya	The practice of celibacy.
Brahmacharya ashram	The first stage of life, in the varnashram system, from birth till the age of twenty-five.
Brahma-jnana	Knowledge of the Supreme.
Brahma Lok	The abode of Brahma, the highest abode in the material universe.
Brahman	The formless aspect of God, which is without Names, Virtues, and Activities.
Brahma Vidyā	The science of God-realisation.
Brahmin	Person who has a preponderance of the mode of goodness. They are predisposed towards teaching and worship.
Buddhi	Intellect.
Buddhi yog	The science of controlling the mind by the intellect.
Chatur-bhuj roop	Four-armed form of God.
Chatuḥśhlokī Bhāgavat	The original form of the Shreemad Bhagavatam that God whispered into Brahma's ears prior to creation.
Chitta	The subconscious mind.
Daityas	Demons.
Dānavas	Demons.
Darshan	1) Philosophic text written by a sage, 2) Divine vision.
Dās	Servant.
Dāsoham	Sentiment of servitude, 'I am the servant of God.'
Dāsya bhav	The sentiment of servitude towards God as one's Master.
Devatā	Celestial god.
Devi Lok	The divine abode of Mother Durga, located in the *Paravyom*.

Dhām	Abode.
Dharma	Responsibilities, duties, thoughts, and actions that are appropriate for a person.
Dhārmic	Of or related to Dharma.
Durga	The feminine form of God, who oversees material creation and is worshipped as the divine Mother of the universe.
Dwāpar yug	Era that precedes Kali yug, consisting of 864,000 years.
Dveṣh	Hatred.
Dwitīya Purush	*See* Garbhodakshayi Vishnu.
Gandharvas	Celestial beings who sing beautifully.
Gāṇḍīv	Arjun's bow.
Garbhodakshayi Vishnu	An expansion of Maha Vishnu who resides at the bottom of each material universe.
Golok	The divine abode of Shree Krishna, which exists in the spiritual realm, beyond this material world.
Gopis	The village maidens who resided in Braj when Shree Krishna displayed His leelas there five thousand years ago.
Govardhan Leela	Shree Krishna's famous pastime upon earth, in which He lifted the Govardhan Hill on the little finger of His left hand, to protect the residents of Braj from the rain caused by Indra.
Gṛihastha	Household.
Gṛihastha ashram	The second stage of life in the varnashram system, which is regular married life, from the age of twenty-five to fifty.
Gunas	Modes of nature.
Guru	A God-realised teacher of spirituality.
Hansa	1) The swans, 2) A category of spiritual practitioner, who can perceive God within everything and hence does not get attached.
Hanuman	An ardent devotee of Lord Ram who possesses the form of a divine monkey in his pastimes. He is an expansion of Lord Shiv.

Hatha Yog	A system of sadhana based on physical practice and the force of willpower for preparing the body and mind for meditation.
Hiraṇyagarbh	Primordial from of material energy.
Hlādinī Shakti	The bliss-giving power of God.
Indra Devatā	The king of heaven, who is the celestial god of rain.
Itihās	The two historical texts of Indian civilisation, Ramayan, and Mahabharat.
Jagat	World.
Jagadguru	Spiritual Master of the world; similar to the Pope in Christianity.
Japa	Chanting of mantra or name of God on rosary beads.
Jīva	Living being.
Jīvan mukt	One who is liberated even while residing in the body.
Jīva shakti	Soul energy of God.
Jivatma	Individual soul.
Jnani	1) Person of knowledge, 2) One following the path of jnana yog.
Jnana	Knowledge.
Jnana-kāṇḍ	The section of the Vedas containing philosophic knowledge.
Jnana tripuṭī	Triad of knowledge which includes the knower, the object of knowledge, and knowledge.
Jnana yog	The system of Yog in which the emphasis is on knowing the self, which is considered as non-different from God.
Kaamdev	Cupid.
Kāla	Time.
Kali yug	The present era on the earth planet. This was preceded by *Dwāpar yug*, *Tretā yug*, and Satya yug.
Kām	1) Desire, 2) Lust.
Kalp	One day of Brahma comprising of thousand cycles of four yugas.

Karanodakshayi Vishnu	The form of Lord Vishnu, commonly called Maha Vishnu, who resides in the causal ocean and from whom all the infinite universes come forth.
Karm	Work in accordance with the prescribed rules of the Vedas.
Kāraṇ śharīr	The causal body, consisting of the account of karmas from endless past lives, including the *sanskārs* (tendencies) from previous lives.
Karm Dharma	One's ritualistic and bodily duties according to the Vedas.
Karmi	One who performs karm.
Karm-kāṇḍ	1) Ritualistic ceremony, 2) Section of the Vedas dealing with ritualistic ceremonies and duties.
Karm sanyasi	One who renounces worldly duties and engages only in spiritual practice.
Karm tripuṭī	Triad of action which includes the doer, the instrument of action, and the act itself.
Karm yog	The practice of uniting the mind with God even while doing one's obligatory duties in the world.
Karm yogi	One who practices karm yog.
Kartritwābhimān	The ego of being the doer.
Kashi Vidvat Parishat	The supreme body of Vedic scholars in the city of Kashi (highest seat of Vedic learning).
Kauravas	Descendants of Kuru; the term primarily refers to the hundred sons of Dhritarashtra.
Kirtan	The singing of names, virtues, and pastimes of God, usually done in a group.
Kshatriya	Person with a preponderance of the mode of passion mixed with a smaller amount of the mode of goodness and inclined towards administration and management.
Kṣhetra	The field of activities of the embodied soul, i.e., the body.
Kṣhetrajña	The knower of the *Kṣhetra*, the soul.

Kshirodakshayi Vishnu	The expansion of Lord Maha Vishnu, who resides at the top of every universe.
Kṣhīr Sāgar	Abode of Kshirodakshayi Vishnu, located at the top of every universe.
Kuber	The treasurer of the celestial gods.
Kumbh Mela	A mass Hindu pilgrimage of faith in which devotees gather at a sacred river for a bath in the river. It is held every third year at one of the four places by rotation, viz. Haridwar, Allahabad, Nasik, and Ujjain.
Kundalini	A power that resides at the base of the spine, like a coiled serpent. When it begins rising up the spinal column, it bestows various material mystic abilities.
Kusaṅg	Association that makes one's mind worldly.
Leela	A divine pastime enacted by God in His personal form.
Lok	Abode or planet.
Lord Kapil	A descension of God; he revealed the *Sānkhya* system of philosophy and also taught the glories of bhakti yog.
Mādhurya bhav	The sentiment of worshipping God as one's Soul-beloved.
Mahajan	A great knower of religious principles. The Bhagavatam mentions twelve such great personalities, viz. Brahma, Sage Narad, Lord Shiv, the four Kumars, Bhagavan Kapil (son of Devahuti), Svayambhuva Manu, Prahalad Maharaj, Janak Maharaj, Grandfather Bheeshma, Bali Maharaj, Shukadev Muni, and Ved Vyas.
Maha pralaya	The great cosmic dissolution at the end of Brahma's life, wherein the entire creation merges back into Maha Vishnu's body.
Mahān	The entity created by evolution of prakriti.
Maha Vishnu	*See* Karanodakshayi Vishnu.

Maha yug	A cycle of four yugas, consisting of Satya yug, *Tretā yug*, *Dwāpar yug*, and Kali yug.
Mānasī sevā	Serving God in the mind.
Mānav	Human being.
Manomaya Kośh	It is the mental sheath, one of the five sheaths that cover the soul in the materially bound state.
Manu	The progenitor of humankind. We are presently in the era of the seventh Manu, who is called Vaivasvat Manu.
Maya	The material energy from which this world is created. It also puts souls, who are forgetful of God, into illusion, and makes them transmigrate in the cycle of life and death.
Maya shakti	*See* Maya.
Māyā-viśhiṣhṭ brahma	An atheistic opinion about Shree Krishna, considering him as a lower grade of the Supreme Divinity, due to contact with the material energy.
Meru	A mountain in the celestial abodes famed for its rich natural resources. It is believed to be the axis around which many heavenly bodies rotate.
Mimansa	One of the six philosophical treaties. It was written by Sage Jaimini and describes ritualistic duties and ceremonies.
Mithyā	Non-existent.
Moksha	Liberation from material bondage.
Naimittik Pralaya	This is the dissolution of all the abodes up to *Mahar Lok* at the end of Brahma's day.
Naiṣhkarmya-siddhi	The state of actionlessness.
Narad	A celestial sage, who roams the three worlds and was the guru of many great personalities.
Narak	Hellish abode.
Narayan	The form of Vishnu that resides eternally in the divine realm called the *Vaikunth*.

Nar-Narayan	The twin descensions, where Nar was a perfected soul and Narayan was the Supreme Lord.
Nididhyāsan	Internalising a concept with firm faith.
Nirākār	Not possessing material form.
Nirguna	Not possessing material qualities.
Nirvana	*See* moksha.
Nirviśheṣh	Not possessing material attributes.
Niṣhedh	Directives not to perform certain actions.
Nitya baddha	Souls bound under the spell of maya since eternity.
Nitya karm	Routine activities for bodily maintenance like eating, bathing, etc. plus daily Vedic rituals such as *Sandhyā Vandan.*
Nitya pralaya	Daily dissolution of our consciousness that takes place when we fall into deep sleep.
Nitya siddha	The eternally liberated soul who has never been under the spell of maya and has, therefore, resided in the divine realm of God since eternity, participating in God's divine pastimes.
Nrisingh	The half man-half lion descension of Lord Vishnu.
Om	The sound that pervades the material universe and can be heard by yogis who tune into it. It is added in the beginning of many Vedic mantras as the seed mantra. It is also a name for the formless aspect of God.
Pandavas	The sons of Pandu, viz., Yudhishthir, Bheem, Arjun, Nakul, and Sahadev.
Pañcha jnanendriya	The five knowledge acquiring senses—eyes, ears, nose, tongue, and skin.
Pañcha karmendriya	The five working senses—hands, legs, voice, genitals, and anus.
Pañcha kleśhas	The five defects of the material intellect—*avidyā, asmitā, rāga, dweṣha,* and *abhiniveṣha.*

Pañcha kośhas	The five sheaths that cover the materially bound soul—annamaya kosh, pranamaya kosh, manomaya kosh, vijnanamaya kosh, anandmaya kosh.
Pañcha mahābhūta	The five gross elements in creation—earth, water, fire, air, and space.
Pañcha tanmātrā	The five subtle elements of creation—taste, touch, smell, sound, and sight.
Pāp	Sin.
Parā bhakti	Divine Love.
Para dharma	The spiritual duty of a person, which is devotion to God.
Paramatma	The Supreme Soul aspect of the Lord who resides in all living beings.
Paramhansa	An elevated soul who effortlessly sees only God everywhere.
Paramparā	1) Social or family custom or tradition, 2) Disciplic succession.
Param Purush	The Supreme Lord.
Paravyom	The divine sky of the spiritual realm, containing the eternal abodes of the different forms of God, such as *Golok, Saket Lok, Vaikunth Lok, Shiv Lok, Devi Lok*, etc.
Pariṇām vāda	A school of thought believing that God has transformed into the world.
Peepal tree	Sacred fig.
Phalgu vairāgya	Renunciation motived by the desire to run away from difficulties.
Prakriti	The primordial form of material energy.
Pralaya	Dissolution.
Pran	A subtle life force energy that pervades the breath and varieties of animate and inanimate objects.
Pranamaya kośh	The life airs sheath, consisting of the five life airs.
Praṇav	*See* Om.

Pranayam	Breathing exercise for controlling the breath and assimilating pranic energy.
Prārabdh karma	The destiny one is allotted at the time of birth, based on past karmas.
Prasad	Grace of God. Specifically, food offered to God, which is then accepted by devotees as His grace.
Prasthān Trayī	Three points of commencement for understanding Vedic thought. These are the Upanishads, the Brahma Sutras, and the Bhagavad Gita.
Pratham Purush	*See* Maha Vishnu.
Pratyāhār	Control of the mind and senses from chasing the objects of the senses.
Preya	Happiness that initially appears to be sweet but becomes bitter in the end.
Puja	Worship.
Pūrak	A part of the pranayam exercises, in which the lungs are filled by drawing the breath into them.
Purushārth	Actions performed by exercising one's freedom of choice.
Radha Rani	God takes on two forms in His divine pastimes—Krishna (the Energetic) and Radha Rani (His divine energy). Radha is also called the Divine Mother of the Universe, to whom all the other energies of God are subservient.
Rāga	Attachment.
Rajas	The mode of passion.
Rajo guna	The mode of passion.
Rakshasa	Powerful being who is inclined towards sensual enjoyment, revenge, and wrath.
Rasik	Devotee who is inclined to relishing the sweetness of God.
Rechak	A part of the pranayam exercises, in which the lungs are emptied of breath.

Rishi	Sage.
Rog	Disease.
Roop dhyan	Meditation upon the form of God.
Sadashiv	The original form of Lord Shiv, from whom all his other forms (eleven *rudras*) have emanated.
Sādhak	Spiritual practitioner.
Sadhana	Spiritual practice.
Sādhan siddha	These are the souls who were previously in the material realm, but they practised sadhana and attained the Supreme Lord. Now they reside in the divine realm for the rest of eternity and participate in God's pastimes.
Saket Lok	The abode of Shree Ram situated in the *Paravyom.*
Sakhā	Friend.
Sakhya bhav	The sentiment of devotion to God as one's Friend.
Sākṣhī bhav	The attitude of being the detached observer of the happenings in one's body and mind.
Samadhi	Meditative trance.
Samān	A type of *pran,* responsible for the bodily function of digestion.
Samarpaṇ	Dedication of oneself or one's works to God.
Sama Veda	One of the four Vedas. It describes God's glories as they manifest in the celestial gods, who are in charge of administering the universe. The *Sama Veda* is also the most musical and is sung in praise of the Lord.
Sampradāya	A group of practice, views, and attitudes, which are transmitted by each successive generation of followers.
Sāmpradāyic	Of or belonging to a *sampradāya.*
Samsara	The cycle of life and death.
Sanātan Dharma	The Eternal Religion.
Sañchit karmas	A person's accumulated karmas of endless past lifetimes.

Sandhyā Vandan	Set of rituals performed thrice daily (at dawn, noon, and dusk) by those who have received the sacred thread.
Saṅkalp	Resolve made by the utilisation of one's free will.
Sānkhya	Complete analytical knowledge of something.
Sānkhya Darshan	One of the six philosophical treatises in Indian philosophy, written by Sage Kapil. It makes an analytical enumeration of the entities in the cosmos.
Sānkhya Yog	System of Yog based on analytic knowledge regarding the nature of the soul and creation.
Sanskārs	Tendencies from previous lives.
Sanyas	The renounced order of life.
Sanyas ashram	The fourth stage of life, which is from the age of seventy-five onwards, where one gives up all household duties and resides in a holy place, absorbing the mind in God.
Sanyasi	One who practises sanyas.
Sarvajña	Omniscient.
Sarva-śhaktimān	Omnipotent.
Sat	1) Eternal existence, 2) Perpetual goodness and virtue, 3) Established in the performance of sacrifice, austerity, and charity.
Sat-chit-anand	Eternality, sentience, and bliss.
Satsang	Association that purifies the mind.
Sattva	The mode of goodness.
Sattva guna	The mode of goodness.
Satya yug	First of the cycle of four yugas lasting for 1.728 million years.
Śhāligrām	A special kind of fossil stone worshipped as a representation of Lord Vishnu.
Śhānt bhav	The sentiment of adoring God as our King.
Śhārīrik dharma	One's bodily duties as described in the Vedic scriptures.

Shastra	Scripture.
Shiv Lok	The abode of Sadashiv, situated in the *Paravyom.*
Śhraddhā	Faith.
Śhreya	Happiness that is unpleasant in the beginning but becomes sweet in the end.
Shree Krishna	God takes on two forms in His divine pastimes—Krishna (the Energetic) and Radha Rani (His divine energy).
Śhruti	Knowledge received through the oral tradition. It is used as another name for the Vedas.
Śhuddha bhakti	Pure bhakti, devoid of selfish desires.
Śhuddha sattva	Divine mode of goodness, distinct from the material sattva guna.
Shudras	Persons predominated by the mode of ignorance.
Siddhānt	Principle.
Siddhas	Perfected beings.
Siddhi	1) Perfection in something, 2) Mystic power accrued by yogic practice.
Smritis	Scriptures written by sages.
Soma juice	Ambrosia drunk by the celestial gods.
Sṛiṣhṭi	1) The process of unfoldment of Creation, 2) The act of releasing.
Sthiti	Maintenance of Creation.
Sthūl śharīr	Gross body.
Stuti	Eulogising prayer to God.
Sutra	Aphorism.
Sūkṣhma śharīr	Subtle body.
Suṣhumṇā	The main pranic channel situated inside the spinal column.
Swa-dharma	One's duty as an individual, based upon one's nature, profession, and stage in life.
Swānśh	Expansions of Shree Krishna, who are non-different from Him.

Swarg	The celestial abodes within the material world, which have far greater facility for enjoyment than the earth planet but are not beyond the cycle of life and death.
Tamas	The mode of ignorance.
Tamo guna	The mode of ignorance.
Tānpurā	A stringed Indian musical instrument, resembling a guitar.
Tapasvī	Ascetic.
Tat	Brahman.
Tattva jnana	Knowledge of scriptural concepts and principles.
Tilak	A religious (or decorative) mark on the forehead made by a certain thin paste or colour in a particular style according to one's religious tradition.
Tretā yug	Second of the cycle of four yugas, consisting of 1.296 million years.
Tri-gunas	Three modes of material nature, viz., sattva, rajas, and tamas.
Triguṇātīt	Transcendental to the three modes of material nature.
Trikāl-darśhī	One who has knowledge of the past, present, and future.
Tṛitīya Purush	*See* Kshirodakshayi Vishnu.
Tulsi	Holy basil.
Tyāg	Renunciation of fruits of action.
Upanishads	Philosophical texts that constitute a section of the Vedas.
Upāsanā-kāṇḍ	Section of the Vedas dealing with different kinds of worship.
Vaikunth Lok	The divine abode of Lord Vishnu in the spiritual realm, beyond the material world.
Vānaprastha ashram	The third stage of life, which is from the age of fifty to seventy-five, in which one practises detachment while living in the household.

Varna	The four social classifications according to occupations in Vedic society.
Varnashram dharma	The system of prescribed duties in accordance with one's profession and status in life.
Varun Devatā	The celestial god of the ocean.
Vayu Devatā	The celestial god of the wind.
Vedant	One of the six philosophical treatises in Indian philosophy, written by Ved Vyas.
Vedas	The eternal knowledge of God that He manifested at the beginning of creation, and which was passed down from master to disciple through hearing, and finally divided and written in four books—*Rig Veda*, *Yajur Veda*, *Sama Veda*, and *Atharva Veda*.
Ved Vyas	Descension of God who revealed, compiled, and wrote many scriptures.
Vibhinnānśh	The differentiated parts of God. These are the souls, who are the part of His *jīva shakti*.
Vibhūti	Opulence.
Vidhi	The directives to perform certain activities or follow certain rules.
Vijnanamaya kośh	It is the intellectual sheath, one of the five sheaths that cover the soul in the materially bound state.
Vipassana	A Buddhist technique for developing detachment. Rigorous training is undertaken to reach this state of clarity and precision, ultimately leading to equanimity and destruction of self-will.
Viparyaya	Reversals of knowledge under material illusion.
Virāṭ Purush	The personality of God encompassing the entire material creation.
Vishwakarma	The celestial architect.
Viśhwaroop	The universal form of God.

Vrindavan	The land in Mathura district, India, where Lord Shree Krishna displayed His divine pastimes during His descension upon earth five thousand years ago.
Yajna	Sacrifice.
Yakṣha	Semi celestial beings who exude power and wealth.
Yamdoot	Servants of the god of death.
Yamraj	The celestial god of death.
Yog	1) Union with God, 2) System that unites the soul with God.
Yogmaya	Divine power of God.
Yukt vairāgya	Renunciation through seeing the whole world as the energy of God. Such practitioners do not see what they possess as belonging to them and do not wish to enjoy it for themselves. Instead, they are motivated by the desire to serve God with whatever He has given to them.

Appellations in the Bhagavad Gita

For Shree Krishna

Achyut	—	the infallible one
Arisudan	—	the destroyer of the enemies
Bhagavan	—	the Supreme Divine Personality
Govind	—	He who gives pleasure to the senses, He who is fond of cows
Hrishikesh	—	the Lord of the senses
Jagannivas	—	He in whom the entire universe resides
Janardan	—	He who looks after the public
Keshav	—	the killer of the demon named Keshi
Keshinisudan	—	the killer of the demon named Keshi
Madhav	—	the husband of *Yogmaya*
Madhusudan	—	the killer of the demon named Madhu
Purshottam	—	the Supreme Divine Personality
Varshneya	—	He who belongs to the Vrishni clan
Vasudev	—	the son of Vasudev
Vishnu	—	the Supreme Lord Vishnu
Yadav	—	He who was born in the Yadu clan
Yogeshwar	—	the Lord of Yog

For Arjun

Anagha	—	the sinless one
Bharatarshabha	—	the best of the Bharatas
Bharata Sattama	—	the best of the Bharatas
Bharata Shreshth	—	the best of the Bharatas
Dhananjay	—	the conqueror of wealth
Gudakesh	—	the conqueror of sleep
Kapidhwaj	—	he whose flag is adorned with the insignia of Hanuman
Kaunteya	—	the son of Kunti
Kiriti	—	he who wears a diadem
Kuru Nandan	—	the joy of the Kurus
Kuru Shreshth	—	the best of the Kurus

Mahabaho	— the mighty-armed
Pandava	— the son of Pandu
Parth	— the son of Pritha, Kunti
Parantapa	— the scorcher of foes
Purushavyaghra	— the tiger amongst men
Savyasachin	— the one who can shoot arrows with both hands

Subject Index

Abode of God, 8.20, 10.42, 15.6, 18.56
Absolute Truth, 16.8, 17.27
Action
  superior to inaction, 3.33
  compared to inaction, 4.17–18
  do not bind if dedicated to God, 4.41
  purify even the wise, 18.5
  its five factors, 18.13–14
  of three kinds, 18.23–25
Advaya jnana tattva, 18.20
Ambarish, 18.65
Anger, 2.62, 4.10, 16.1–4
  its consequences, 2.63, 16.21
Arjun, 1.20, 1.38–39, 1.47, 2.4–5, 2.35
  questions by him, 2.54
Aryan, 2.2
Asceticism, 5.28–29, 6.17
Ashtang yog, 8.9–10
Ashwatthama, 1.38–39
Aśhvatth tree *see* Nature of the world
Atma jnana, 7.29
Attachment, 13.8–12
  can be good or bad, 1.28
  its cause, 2.62
  to God is liberating, 2.64
Austerity, 16.1-3, 17.5–6,
  of body, speech, and mind, 17.14–16
  according to the gunas, 17.17–19
Avatar, 4.7–9, 9.11
Bhagavan, 10.14, 12.2, 15.18–19
Bhakti (Devotion)
  enslaves God, 1.21–22
  five sentiments (*bhāvas*) of devotion, 4.3, 11.45
  bhakti yog is the highest yog, 6.47
  ananya (exclusive devotion), 9.22, 11.55
  only means to know God, 8.22, 11.52–54, 18.55
  with any item or action, 9.26–27
  reforms even sinners, 9.30
  devotional ecstasy, 11.14
  aiśhwarya and *mādhurya*, 11.45
  leads to Bhagavan realisation, 12.2
  higher than jnana, 18.54
  by absorbing all the senses in God, 18.65
Bheeshma, 1.10, 2.4, 2.6, 11.26–27
Bliss *see* Happiness
Body
  made from mud, 2.18
  compared to city of nine gates, 5.13
  requires maintenance, 6.16
Brahma, 10.6, 11.43
Brahmacharya see Celibacy
Brahma jnana, 7.29
Brahman, 7.24, 8.3, 12.1–5, 13.13, 15.19, 18.51–53
  personal form is the basis, 14.27
Brahmin, 18.41
Buddhi yog, 2.39, 2.41, 3.1–3, 18.57
Causal body, 2.28
Celestial abodes, 2.42–43, 9.21
Celestial gods, 3.11, 4.12, 7.20–23, 9.23-24
Celibacy, 6.14, 8.11
Chanting *see* Kirtan
Chariot model, 3.43
Charity, 16.1–3, 17.20–22
Cleanliness, 16.1–3
Compassion, 16.1–3
Conscience, 3.36
Contentment, 12.13–14
Creation, 7.4, 8.18, 9.7-9
  abodes in material realm, 8.16
  prakriti is the womb, 14.3–4
Cosmic form, 11.3–5
Death, 10.34
  remembering God, 8.5–6
Deity worship, 4.9
Demoniac nature, 16.4–5
Desire, 2.55, 2.62, 2.64, 13.7

cannot be quenched, 2.58
sublimating it, 2.59
its cause, 2.62, 3.37
of the five senses, 2.67
shrouds the intellect, 3.38
slaying it brings peace, 3.41
Determination, 6.24–25, 12.13–14, 16.1–3
according to the gunas, 18.33–35
Devatās see Celestial gods
Descension *see* Avatar
Devotees
of four kinds, 7.16
qualities of, 12.13–19
Dharma *see also* Duty
para and *apara*, 2.31, 18.66
should do one's natural duties, 3.35, 18.47
Dissolution, 7.6, 8.19, 9.7–8
Divine Love, 7.18, 18.54
Divine vision, 11.48
Dronacharya, 1.2–11, 2.4, 11.26–27
Duty, 2.31, 3.19–21
should not be renounced, 18.7–8
fulfilling it leads to perfection, 18.45
Vyadha Gita, 18.46
Ego (*see also* Pride), 2.71
Equanimity, 2.10, 2.48, 5.19–20, 13.8–12, 14.22–25
example of Prahalad, 12.18–19
Equality of vision, 5.18, 6.8–9, 6.29, 6.32, 13.29
Exclusive devotion *see also* Bhakti—*ananya*
Faith, 3.31–32
in guru, 4.39, 18.71
grows with knowledge, 7.19
created by God, 7.21
first step in spiritual path, 9.3
science also requires it, 17.2
based on nature of the mind, 17.3
Fear, 12.15, 16.1–3
Food *see also* Vegetarianism, 17.7–10
Forgiveness, 12.13–14, 13.8–12, 16.1–3
Free will, 5.15, 18.63
Gayatri mantra, 10.35
God (*see also* Shree Krishna)
both personal and formless, 4.6, 12.1
not tainted by activities, 4.14
seeing Him everywhere, 4.24
ocean of bliss, 6.21
Supreme Energetic, 7.5
beyond sense perception, 7.25
His qualities, 8.9–10
all-pervading, 9.4, 13.14
possesses personal form, 9.11
beyond the intellect, 10.10
opulences of God, 10.18, 15.12
possesses contradictory attributes, 11.47, 13.13-15
Golok see Abode of God
Grace, 7.29, 10.10, 11.48, 11.52–53, 18.58
is based upon rules, 18.62
Greed, 2.62, 2.71, 16.1-3, 16.21
Gross body, 2.28
Gunas, 14.5, 17.1–22, 18.37–40
transcendental to them, 14.19–25
devotion takes us beyond, 14.26
Guru, 13.8–12
necessity, 2.7
how to approach, 4.34
faith in him, 18.71
Hanuman, 1.20
Happiness
God is an ocean of it, 6.21
nature of God's happiness, 2.15
its four kinds, 6.28
of the soul is in God, 15.9
according to the gunas, 18.36–39
Human form, 2.40, 5.23
Humbleness *see* Pride
Inaction (*Akarm*), 3.5, 4.17, 18.49
in action, 4.18
cannot give up all activities, 18.11
Intellect, 2.41, 12.8
characteristics of a surrendered intellect, 18.66
according to the gunas, 18.29–32

Jagadguru, 4.2
Janak, 2.6, 3.20–21, 4.2, 18.54, 18.69
Jesus, 2.13, 12.15, 13.19, 16.14–15
Jīvan Mukt, 2.72
Jīva Shakti, 4.24, 7.5, 13.20
Jnana yog, 9.15, 12.2, 12.5
  qualification to enter it, 9.32
Karn, 11.26–27, 11.34
Karm Sanyas
  compared to karm yog, 5.2, 5.26
  non different from Yog, 6.2
  compared to *tyāg*, 18.1–2
  qualifications, 6.3, 18.67
Karm yog, 2.47, 3.4, 5.2, 6.3, 8.7
  does not impede performance, 2.50
  definition, 3.7
  sets a good example for society, 3.20–21
  compared to Karm sanyas, 5.2
  examples of great karm yogis, 5.4
  dedicating works to God, 5.8-12
Karma, 11.20
  destroyed by the fire of knowledge, 4.37
  God is like the umpire, 5.15
Kirtan, 9.14, 10.9
Knowledge, 5.15-16
  ascending and descending processes, 4.1
  leads to devotion, 4.33, 7.19, 10.7
  two kinds of knowledge, 4.38
  according to the gunas, 18.19–22
  comes by grace, 4.39, 18.73
Kośhas see Sheaths
Kripaluji Maharaj, 4.2
Krishna *see* Shree Krishna
Kshatriya, 18.41, 18.43
Kṣhetra, 13.1–2, 13.6
Lamentation, 2.11, 2.27, 6.30, 12.17
Law of Karma, 3.27, 4.11, 7.26, 9.28-29, 16.16
Liberated souls
  Vedas do not apply to them, 3.17
Liberation, 2.72
Lust, 3.37, 3.40
  gateway to hell, 16.21
Maha Vishnu *see* Vishnu
Maya, 7.4, 7.13–14
  is beginningless, 13.20
Meditation, 6.12–15, 6.24–26
  roop dhyan, 6.15
  importance of practice, 6.26
  process, 6.26
Mimansa, 13.5, 18.3
Mind, 6.5–6, 12.13–14, 16.1-3
  diseases of, 2.62
  how to cleanse it, 4.10, 9.30–31
  cause of bondage and liberation, 5.5, 12.8
  can be enemy or friend, 6.6
  difficult to control, 6.34–35
  its four aspects, 6.5
Misery, 6.23
  also has a purpose, 8.15
Mithyā, 2.16
Modes of material nature *see* Gunas
Nature of the world, 2.16
  like a mirage, 2.55
  no happiness in it, 5.22
  compared to *aśhvatth* tree, 15.1–4
Nitya karm, 3.8
Non-violence (Ahimsa), 1.36–37, 2.19, 13.8–12, 16.1–3
Om, 8.13, 17.23
Parā Bhakti see Divine Love
Paramatma, 12.2, 13.23, 13.28–29, 15.17, 15.19
Param Purush, 10.12–13, 13.20, 18.19
Prakriti *see* Maya
Pralaya *see* Dissolution
Pranayam, 4.29–30
Prasad, 3.13, 4.31
Preaching, 18.68–69
Preya, 16.22, 18.37
Pride, 13.8–12, 16.1–4, 16.13–15
  of being the doer, 5.8–9, 18.15–16, 18.62
Puranas, 13.5
Purush (*see also* Soul), 13.22, 18.19
Radha (Radha Rani), 7.25, 9.13, 11.50
Rebirth *see* Transmigration

Relationship with God, 9.18, 15.7
Renunciation (*Vairāgya*) (*see also* Karm sanyas), 16.1–3, 18.5–12
  false renunciants, 3.6
  of two kinds: *phalgu* and *yukt*, 5.4, 6.2
  through work in devotion, 5.6
  according to the gunas, 18.7–9
Reincarnation *see* Transmigration
Resentment, 16.16
Rituals, 2.53, 9.20
Roop Dhyan, 6.15
Rudra *see* Shiv
Sacrifice *see* Yajna
Sādhaks
  of three kinds, 4.40
  fate if unsuccessful, 6.37-45
  follow variety of paths, 13.25–26
Sadhana, 6.10–13
  requires repeated practice, 6.35, 12.9
  of various kinds, 13.25–26
Saint
  God is their Doer, 7.10
  beyond the three gunas, 14.21–26
Saintly nature, 16.1–3, 16.5
Samadhi, 2.53, 6.21-22
Sānkhya, 2.39, 3.3–4, 18.3, 18.19
Sanyas *see* Karm sanyas *and also* Renunciation
Saubhari, 2.60
Self, 2.12–13, 2.25–26, 15.10–11
  perceived through purified mind, 6.20
Selfless devotion *see* Divine love
Service
  intrinsic nature of the soul, 15.5
Sexual activity, 7.11
Shiv, 1.35, 10.23, 10.42
Sheaths, 13.6
Śhraddhā see Faith
Shree Krishna (*see also* God)
  divine pastimes, 3.23
  divine birth, 4.5
  Cause of all causes, 7.7, 10.8, 11.38
  basis of formless Brahman, 7.24, 14.27
  Source of all Avatars, 10.8
  Shree Krishna, a sweet form of God, 11.24
Śhreya, 16.22, 18.37
Shudra, 18.41, 18.44
Siddhi, 7.3
Sin
  why do we commit it?, 3.36
Spiritual Master *see* Guru
Soul, 2.12
  where does it reside, 2.17
  is eternal, 2.20
  is immutable, 2.24
  inconceivable to our intellect, 2.25
  is the non-doer of actions, 3.27
  energy of God, 7.5
  oneness and difference with God, 7.5
  kṣhetrajña, 13.2
  exists in plants as well, 13.27
  savors the world through the body, 15.9
  cannot be perceived by scientists, 15.10, 15.11
Sthita Prajña, 2.54, 2.57, 18.54
Subtle body, 2.28
Supreme Soul *see* Paramatma
Supreme Divine Personality, 10.15
Surrender, 4.11, 7.14, 18.62
Thoughts, 17.16
Time, 8.17, 9.7–8
Transmigration, 2.13, 2.22, 15.8
  how it is decided, 8.5–6
Truthfulness, 16.1–3
Universal form *see* Cosmic form
Vaishya, 18.41, 18.44
Varnashram System, 4.13, 18.41–44
Vedant, 13.5
Vedas, 10.22, 11.18, 13.5, 15.15
  divided in three sections, 2.42–43
  their goal, 2.46
  breath of God, 3.15
Vedic rituals *see* Rituals
Ved Vyas, 7.2, 10.37, 11.48, 13.5, 18.75

Vegetarianism, 3.13, 17.8
Vipassana, 2.14
Vishnu (*see also* God), 8.18, 10.8, 11.37–38
Western philosophers, 18.23
Women respected in Vedic tradition, 1.41
Work (*see also* Duty)
  without attachment to results, 2.38, 2.47, 2.50–51
Yajna, 16.1–3
  liberates from maya, 3.9
  as duty toward God, 3.10
  pleases celestial gods, 3.11
  kinds of sacrifice, 4.25–30
  according to the three gunas, 17.11–13
Yog (Yoga), 6.1
  its practice, 6.10
  various kinds, 9.15
  Bhakti essential in all paths, 13.19
Yogi *see Sādhaks*
Yogkṣhem, 9.22
Yogmaya, 7.25, 9.5, 9.13
Yudhishthir, 1.16, 2.27, 18.46

Index of Verses Quoted in the Commentary

Vedas

deśhe kāle upāyena dravyaṁ, 9.32
ekasmin vijñāte sarvamidaṁ, 7.29
mā hinsyāt sarvā bhūtāni, 1.36–37, 2.19, 18.3
sūryastapati tejasendraḥ, 13.18
yajño vai viṣhṇuḥ, 3.15
ya ātmani tiṣhṭhati, 10.20

Yajur Veda

tasya no rāsva tasya no dhehi, 10.10, 11.48
kurukṣhetraṁ deva yajanam, 1.1

Taittīrīya Āraṇyak

ūrdhvamūlaṁ arvākśhākhaṁ vṛikṣhaṁ, 15.1

Rig Veda

apaśhyaṁ gopāṁ anipadyamānamā, 9.11
atapta tanurnatadā mośhnute, 17.14
bhūrbhuvaḥ swaḥ tatsaviturvareṇyaṁ, 10.35
ko addhā veda ka iha prāvochat, 10.2
pādo 'sya viśhwā, 10.42, 15.5
puruṣha evedaṁ sarvaṁ, 6.9, 9.4
tadviṣhṇoḥ paramaṁ padaṁ, 2.72, 4.35
yaṁ kāmaye taṁ taṁ ugraṁ, 10.8

Māṭhar Śhruti

puṇyena puṇya lokaṁ nayati, 2.38
bhaktirevainaṁ nayati, 11.54, 13.19

Subāl Śhruti

divyo deva eko nārāyaṇo, 9.18

Upanishads

Bṛihad Āraṇyak Upanishad

ahaṁ brahmāsmi, 4.27
asya mahato bhūtasya, 3.15
ayam agnir vaiśhvānaro, 15.14
dwe vāva brahmaṇo rūpe, 4.6
etasya vā akṣharasya, 8.11
niḥśhvasitamasya vedā, 13.5
sa eṣha neti netyātmā, 10.10
sa vā eṣha mahān aja, 2.20

Chhāndogya Upanishad

āchāryavān puruṣho vedaḥ, 4.34
āhāra śhuddhau sattva śhuddhiḥ, 17.7
sarvaṁ khalvidaṁ brahma, 7.5, 13.14
sa vā eṣha ātmā hṛidi, 2.17
tattvamasi, 4.27

Gopāl Tāpani Upanishad

dwibhūjaṁ mauna mudrāḍhyaṁ, 9.11
kṛiṣhṇa eva paro devas, 15.18
yo 'sau paraṁ brahma gopālaḥ, 15.18

Īśhopanishad

andhaṁ tamaḥ praviśhanti, 6.16
īśhāvāsyam idam sarvaṁ, 6.9, 7.5, 9.4
nainaddevā āpnuvan pūrvamarṣhat, 10.2
tad ejati tan naijati taddūre, 13.16

Kaṭhopanishad

anyachchhreyo 'nyadutaiva preyaste, 18.37
ātmānagvaṁ rathinaṁ viddhi, 3.43
bhayādasyāgnistapati bhayāt, 11.23
chetanaśhchetanānām, 10.22
iha chedaśhakad boddhuṁ, 2.40
indriyāṇi hayānāhurviṣhayānsteṣhu, 3.43
indriyebhyaḥ parā hyarthā, 2.25

na jāyate mriyate vā vipaśhchin, 2.20
naiṣhā tarkeṇa matirāpaneyā, 7.26
nāyamātmā pravachanena labhyo, 7.29
parāñchi khāni vyatṛiṇatsvayambhūḥ, 2.67, 15.7
sarve vedā yat padamāmananti, 11.18, 15.15
śhravaṇāyāpi bahubhiryo na, 2.29
śhreyaśhcha preyaśhcha, 18.37
tameva bhāntamanubhāti sarvaṁ, 13.18
ūrdhvamūlo 'vākśhākha eṣho, 15.1
vijñānasārthiryastu manaḥ, 4.36
yadā sarve pramuchyante kāmā, 2.55

Kenopanishad

iha chedavedīdatha satyamasti, 2.40
yachchakṣhuṣhā na paśhyati, 18.15–16
yachchhrotreṇa na śhṛiṇoti, 18.15–16
yadvāchānabhyuditaṁ yena, 18.15–16
yanmanasā na manute, 18.15–16
yasyā mataṁ tasya mataṁ, 10.10
yat prāṇena na prāṇiti, 18.15–16

Muṇḍakopanishad

avidyāyāmantare vartamānāḥ, 2.42–43
dvā suparṇā sayujā sakhāyā, 13.23
eṣho 'ṇurātmā, 13.34
nāyamātmā pravachanena labhyo, 11.52–53
parīkṣhya lokānkarmachitānbrāhmaṇo, 2.52
samāne vṛikṣhe puruṣho nimagno, 13.23
tadvijñānārthaṁ sagurumevābhigachchhet, 2.7
upāsate puruṣhaṁ ye, 13.19
yaḥ sarvajñaḥ sarvavidyasya, 7.26

Praśhnopanishad

eṣha hi draṣhṭā spraṣhṭā, 18.14
hṛidi hyeṣha ātmā, 2.17

Śhaṇḍilya Upanishad

śhauchaṁ nāma dwividhaṁ, 13.8–12

Śhwetāśhvatar Upanishad

ajāmekāṁ lohita-śhukla-kṛiṣhṇāṁ, 18.40
anantaśhchātmā viśhwarūpo hyakartā, 10.19
apāṇipādo javano grahītā, 13.15
bālāgraśhatabhāgasya śhatadhā, 13.34
bhoktā bhogyaṁ preritāraṁ cha, 2.16
eko devaḥ sarvabhūteṣhu, 9.4, 12.2, 13.28
jñājñau dwāvajā vīśhanīśhāvajā, 2.12
kṣharaṁ pradhānamamṛitākṣharaṁ, 2.16, 7.5
māyāṁ tu prakṛitiṁ, 7.14
navadwāre pure dehī, 5.13
na tatsamaśhchābhyadhikaśhcha, 7.7, 11.43, 18.78
puruṣha evedaṁ sarvaṁ, 7.5
sahasraśhīrṣhā puruṣhaḥ, 11.23
sanyuktametat kṣharam, 2.16, 13.24
tamīśhwarāṇāṁ paramaṁ, 10.3
yasmāt paraṁ nāparamasti, 10.15
yasya deve parā bhaktiryathā, 4.39, 13.19
yo brahmāṇaṁ vidadhāti, 18.62

Taittirīya Upanishad

ānando brahmeti vyajānāt, 5.21
raso vai saḥ, 2.59, 6.21
so 'kāmayata bahu, 2.16
tasmadvā etasmādātmana ākāśhaḥ, 7.4
yato vācho nivartante, 7.26
yato vā imāni bhūtāni, 10.20

Puranas

Ādi Puran

gītvā cha mama nāmāni, 7.18

Bhaviṣhya Puran

dānamekaṁ kalau yuge, 17.20

Brahma Vaivarta Puran

yathā tvaṁ rādhikā devī, 9.13
viruddha dharmo rūposā, 13.15

Devi Bhagavat Puran

aiśhwaryasya samagrasya dharmasya, 10.14

Garuḍ Puran

chakradharo 'pi suratvaṁ, 2.55
ūrdhvaṁ gachchhanti sattvasthā, 16.16

Nārad Puran

durlabhaṁ mānuṣhaṁ janma, 9.21
na devaḥ keśhavāt paraḥ, 11.41–42

Padma Puran

ānanda mātra kara pāda, 5.21
aśhraddadhāne vimukhe 'py, 18.67
brahmavidyāhamatulā yogiṁ, 18.55
dāsa bhūtamidaṁ tasya, 2.47, 15.5
na deśha niyamastasmin, 9.32
sarve pūrṇāḥ śhāśhvatāśhcha, 4.7
yannakhenduruchirbrahma dheyaṁ, 7.24, 14.27
yastu nirguṇa ityuktaḥ, 4.6, 14.26

Shreemad Bhagavatam Puran

ahaṁ bhakta-parādhīno, 1.21–22, 6.47
aham evāsam evāgre, 11.41–42
ahamevāsamevāgre nānyadyatsadasat, 9.19
aho imaṁ paśhyata, 2.60
ājñāyaivaṁ guṇān doṣhān, 2.46, 18.66
anādyavidyā yuktasya puruṣhasyātma, 4.34
anityānātma duḥkheṣhu viparyaya, 12.8
asyāpi deva vapuṣho, 9.11
ātmārāmāśh cha munayo, 18.54
āvirāsīd yathā prāchyāṁ, 4.9
barhāpīḍaṁ naṭa-vara-vapuḥ, 18.54
bhakti-yogena manasi, 7.2
bhaktyāhamekayā grāhyaḥ, 8.22, 11.54
bhavān hi sarva-bhūtānām, 13.28
brahman parodbhave kṛiṣhṇe, 10.20
chetaḥ khalvasya bandhāya, 12.8
daivāt kṣhubhita-dharmiṇyāṁ, 14.3–4
devarṣhi-bhūtāpta-nṛiṇāṁ, 18.66
dharmaṁ tu sākṣhād, 4.16
dravyaṁ karma cha, 13.17
ete chāṁśha kalāḥ puṁsaḥ, 10.8
gṛiheṣhv āviśhatāṁ chāpi, 3.9
gṛihītvāpīndriyair arthān yo, 5.4
gūḍhaṁ paraṁ brahma, 9.11, 11.51
harirhi sākṣhādbhagavān, 10.20
janma-karmābhidhānāni santi, 4.7
kṛite yad dhyāyato, 9.14
kāmaṁ bhavaḥ sva, 18.54
kāyena vāchā manasendriyair, 9.27
kevalānubhavānanda svarūpaḥ, 5.21
kṛipaṇo yo 'jitendriyaḥ, 2.49
kṛiṣhṇamenamavehi tvam, 10.20, 12.2
mām ekam eva śharaṇam, 8.14, 18.62
muktānām api siddhānāṁ, 6.47
mukunda-liṅgālaya-darśhane, 2.61, 18.65
na veda kṛipaṇaḥ śhreya, 2.49
na jātu kāmaḥ kāmānām, 2.58
naiṣhāṁ matis tāvad, 4.34
na sādhayati māṁ, 11.54, 13.19
nāyaṁ deho deha-bhājāṁ, 5.23
na hi kaśhchit kṣhaṇam, 3.5
niśhamya bhīma-gaditaṁ, 11.46
nirviṇṇānāṁ jñānayogaḥ, 4.27
pādau hareḥ kṣhetra, 2.61, 18.65
patraṁ puṣhpaṁ phalaṁ, 9.26
sapadi sakhi-vacho, 11.26–27
sarva-bhūteṣhu yaḥ, 4.24
sattve pralīnāḥ svar, 14.18
satya jñānānantānanda mātraika, 6.21
satya-vrataṁ satya-paraṁ, 17.26–27
sa vai manaḥ kṛiṣhṇa, 18.65
sāttvikaḥ kārako 'saṅgī, 18.28
sāttvikaṁ sukhamātmotthaṁ, 6.28
sā vidyā tanmatiryayā, 4.28, 10.32, 11.38, 13.25
śhṛiṇvatāṁ sva-kathāṁ, 13.26

śhuchau deśhe pratiṣhṭhāpya, 9.32
swayambhūr nāradaḥ śhambhuḥ, 2.6
sukhāya karmāṇi karoti, 2.51
tam adbhutaṁ bālakam, 4.9
tasmād guruṁ prapadyeta, 2.7
tāvat karmāṇi kurvīta, 3.25, 18.47
tāvat pramodate swarge, 9.21
tene brahma hṛidāya, 4.2, 11.43
tvatto jñānaṁ hi, 15.15
tvayopabhukta-srag-gandha, 4.31
vadanti tat tattva, 12.2, 15.19, 18.20
vayaṁ tu na vitṛipyāma, 10.18
vāsudeva-paraṁ jñānaṁ, 2.46
vāsudeva-parā vedā, 2.46, 11.18
vilajjamānayā yasya, 9.5
yajño 'haṁ bhagavattamaḥ, 3.15
yaṁ pravrajantam anupetam, 6.31
yan manyase dhruvaṁ, 2.28
yasya chchhando mayaṁ, 2.7
yasyāsti bhaktir bhagavatyakiñchanā, 12.15
yatrāvatīrṇo bhagavān paramātmā, 9.11
yat-pāda-paṅkaja, 4.14
yat pṛithivyāṁ vrīhi-yavaṁ, 2.62
yathā taror mūla, 9.23
yāvad bhriyeta jaṭharaṁ, 16.12
yo vā anantasya guṇānanantān, 10.19
yudhi turaga-rajo-vidhūmra, 2.6

Skand Puran

archite deva deveśhe, 3.11
nyāyopārjita vittasya daśhamānśhena, 17.20

Vishnu Puran

aṅgāni vedāśhchatvāro, 10.32
āyurvedo dhanurvedo, 10.32
eka-deśha-sthitasyāgnir, 7.5
viṣhṇuśhaktiḥ parā proktā, 7.25

Itihās

Ramayan

ānanda sindhu madhya tava vāsā, 6.21
baṛeñ bhāga mānuṣha tanu pāvā, 9.21
brahma rām teṅ nāmu baḍa, 6.15
chidānandamaya deha tumhārī, 7.25
eka bāra raghunātha bolāe, 18.63
eka bharoso eka bala, 8.14
ehi bidhi jaga hari āśhrita rahaī, 13.21
guru binu bhava nidhi tarai na koī, 2.7
guru pitu mātu na jānahu kāhū, 18.66
hari ananta hari kathā anantā, 10.19
inhani bilokata ati anurāgā, 18.54
jauṅ sapaneṅ sira kāṭai koī, 2.19, 13.21
jākī sahaja svāsa śhruti chārī, 9.16–17
jāneṅ binu na hoi paratītī, 7.19
jāsu satyatā teṅ jaḍa māyā, 9.9
jimi pratilābha lobha adhikāī, 2.62
jo ānand sindhu sukharāsī, 5.21
kalijuga kevala hari guna gāhā, 9.14
kalijuga kevala nāma ādhārā, 10.25
karama pradhāna bisva kari rākhā, 11.20, 16.16
kāmihi nāri piāri jimi, 15.9
mānas roga kachhuka maiṅ gāe, 2.62
milahiṅ na raghupati binu anurāgā, 8.22, 11.54
more sabai eka tumha swāmī, 5.2, 9.18
nahiṅ anīti nahiṅ kachhu prabhutāī, 18.63
nema dharma āchāra, 8.28
para upakāra bachana mana kāyā, 5.25
prema bhagati jala binu raghurāī, 4.10
pragaṭa chāri pada dharma ke, 17.20
rāmahi kevala premu piārā, 13.19
rākāpati ṣhoṛasa uahiñ tārāgana samudāi, 5.16, 10.21
rām atarkya buddhi mana bānī, 7.26, 10.10
rām brahma chinamaya abināsī, 13.28
rām eka tāpasa tiya tārī, 4.8

saba kai mamatā tāga baṭorī, 9.18
samaratha kahuñ nahiṁ doṣhu gosāīṁ, 4.14
sanamukha hoi jīva mohi jabahīṁ, 18.62
sevahiṁ lakhanu sīya raghubīrahi, 5.19
sīyā rāmamaya saba jaga jānī, 4.35, 6.9
so dāsī raghubīra ki, 7.14
swargahu swalpa anta dukhadāī, 9.21
tanu binu bhajana veda nahiṁ varanā, 6.16
ulaṭā nāmu japata jagu jānā, 9.30

Adhyātma Ramayan

avikārī vā vikārī, 9.14

Vālmīki Ramayan

ekaikasyopakārasya prāṇān dāsyāmi, 4.11
piśhāchān dānavān yakṣhān, 5.11
tvamomkāraḥ parātparaḥ, 11.41–42

Mahabharat

ahanyahani bhūtāni gachchhantīha, 2.27
ātmanaḥ pratikūlāni pareśhāṁ, 18.23
gūhitasya bhaved vṛiddhiḥ, 16.17
yo na kāmayate kiñchit, 5.19

Darshan Shastras

Nyaya Darshan

jātasya harṣhabhayaśhoka sampratipatteḥ, 2.22
stanyābhilāṣhāt, 2.22

Patanjali Yog Darshan

abhyāsa vairāgyābhyāṁ tannirodhaḥ, 6.35
brahmacharya pratiṣhṭhāyāṁ, 6.14
ṛitambharā tatra prajñā, 5.24
samādhisiddhirīśhvara praṇidhānāt, 4.28, 6.21
śhrutānumāna-prajñābhyām, 4.38
sthira sukhamāsanam, 6.12–13

Brahma Sutra/Vedant Darshan

achalatvaṁ chāpekṣhya, 6.12–13
avirodhaśhchandanavat, 2.17
ānandamayo 'bhyāsāt, 6.21
āsīnaḥ sambhavāt, 6.12–13
dhyānāchcha, 6.12–13
guṇādvā lokavat, 13.34
jño 'ta eva, 18.14
kartā śhāstrārthavattvāt, 18.14
viśheṣhānugrahaśh cha, 10.11
vyaktireko gandhavat, 2.17

Smritis

Manu Smriti

bhūtaṁ bhavyaṁ bhaviṣhyaṁ, 13.5, 16.24
māṁ sa bhakṣhayitā 'mutra yasya, 17.10
satyaṁ brūyāt priyaṁ brūyān, 17.15
ṛitvikpurohitāchāryair mātulātithisaṁśhritaiḥ, 1.38–39
vidyāt taṁ puruṣhaṁ param, 11.41–42
yatra nāryas tu pūjyante, 1.41

Parāṣhar Smriti

kṣhatriyoḥ hi prajā, 2.33

Saints, Devotees, and Philosophers

Jagadguru Shree Kriapaluji Maharaj

Bhakti Śhatak

bandhan aur mokṣha kā, 4.33, 5.5
brahma lok paryanta sukh, 7.18
'jīvu' 'māyā', dui śhakti haiñ, 7.5
jo hari sevā hetu ho, soī karma bakhān, 11.38, 13.19
karm yog aru jñāna sab, 8.22

mana hari meṅ tana jagat meṅ, 3.7
māyādhīn malīn mana, 13.8–12
sabai sarasa rasa dwārikā, 11.45
sarvaśhakti prākaṭya ho, 15.19
sarvaśhakti sampanna ho, 15.19
sarvaśhakti sanyukta ho, 15.19
śhaktimān kī śhaktiyāñ, 7.25
satya ahinsā ādi mana, 9.31
sau bātana kī bāta ika, 15.5
tīna rūpa śhrī kṛiṣhṇa ko, 15.19

Prem Ras Madirā

dekho dekho rī, gwāla bālana yārī, 11.24
nakha dhāryo goverdhan, 11.24

Radha Govind Geet

hari kā viyogī jīva, 5.29
jaga meñ raho aise govind radhe, 12.18–19
sarva śhāstra sāra yaha govind rādhe, 15.15

Sadhana Bhakti Tattva

mana ko māno śhatru, 6.6
sochu mana yaha karm, 5.2

Sadhana Karu Pyāre

jagata te mana ko haṭā kara, 12.9

Chanakya

ātmavat sarva bhūteṣhu, 6.9

Neeti Sutra

nirutvāhād daivaṁ patita, 18.14
utsāhavatāṁ śhatravopi vaśhībhavanti, 18.14

Jeev Goswami

Parmātma Sandarbh

śhaktitvenaivāṁśhatvaṁ vyañjayanti, 13.20

Kalidas

Raghuvanśh

sa viśhwajitam ājahre, 3.9

Kabir

dāna diye dhana nā ghaṭe, 18.68
jaba maiṅ thā taba hari nathīṅ, 13.8–12
jahañ jahañ chalūñ karūñ parikramā, 9.27, 11.55
jo karai so hari karai, hota kabīr kabīr, 3.28
mana na raṅgāye ho, 3.6
mālā pherata yuga phirā, 4.33
mālik itanā dījiye, 12.18–19
nindak niyare rākhiye, 5.11
sumiran kī sudhi yoṅ karo, 8.7
tīra talavāra se jo laṛai, 18.4
ūñche pānī na ṭike, 16.13–15

Narad, Devarshi

Nārad Bhakti Darshan

anyāśhrayāṇāṁ tyāgo, 8.14
loka hānau chintā na kāryā, 6.30
nāradastu tadarpitā khilāchāratā, 9.27
tat prāpya tad evāvalokayati, 6.27
tat sukha sukhitvam, 7.18
yatprāpya na kiñchidvāñchhati, 12.17

Nārad Pañcharātra

eka deśhasthitasyāgnirjyotsnā vistāriṇī, 6.29
vāsudevaḥ praḥ prabhuḥ, 11.41–42

Madhvendra Puri

sandhyā vandana bhadramastu, 2.53

Rahim

denahāra koī aur hai, 18.17

Roop Goswami

Bhakti Rasāmṛit Sindhu

ādau śhraddhā tataḥ, 9.3
kleśhas tu pāpaṁ tadbījam, 9.2
nāma-līlā-guṇadīnām, 9.14
śhāstre yuktau cha nipuṇaḥ, 4.40

stambha sweda 'tha romāñchaḥ, 11.14, 18.74
yaḥ śhāstrādiṣhvanipuṇaḥ, 4.40
yo bhavet komala śhraddhaḥ, 4.40

Sanatan Goswami

Hari Bhakti Vilās

ānukūlyasya saṅkalpaḥ, 18.62
tulasī-dala-mātreṇa, 9.26

Shankaracharya

Prabodh Sudhākar

kāmyopāsanayārthayantyanudinaṁ... 18.54
śhuddhayati hi nāntarātmā, 4.10

Śhārīraka Bhāṣhya

guru vedānta vākyeṣhu dṛiḍho, 3.32, 4.39
mūrtaṁ chaivāmūrtaṁ dwe, 12.1
vivekino viraktasya śhamādiguṇa, 9.32
yā vāsudeve anīśhvarāsarvajñāśhaṅkā, 4.5
yāvat gururna kartavyo, 4.34

Śhāṇḍilya

Śhāṇḍilya Bhakti Darshan

gavāṁ sarpiḥ śharīrasthaṁ, 8.22

Tulsidas

āju jo harihiṅ na śhastra gahāūñ, 2.6
brahma jñāna jānyo nahīṅ, 3.20–21
jiba jiba te hari te bilagāno, 3.17
na maiṅ kiyā na kari sakauṅ, 7.10
To Rahim: aisī denī dena jyuñ, 18.17

Yamunacharya

Śhrī Stotra Ratna

mama nātha yad asti, 5.11
yadāvadhi mama chetaḥ, 5.24

Vidyaranya

Pañchadaśhī

mana eva manuṣhyāṇāṁ, 5.5, 12.8
tatpādāmburu hadvandva sevā, 4.34

Other Scriptures

Brahma Samhitā

aṅgāni yasya sakalendriya, 18.20
ānanda-chinmaya-rasa, 15.6
goloka-nāmni nija-dhāmni, 15.6
īśhwaraḥ paramaḥ kṛiṣhṇaḥ, 7.7, 9.11, 11.38
yasyaikaniśhvasita kālamathāvalambya, 10.8

Charak Samhitā

śharīra mādhyaṁ khalu, 6.16

Chaitanya Charitāmṛit

ataeva kāma-preme bahuta antara, 7.18
bhakti mukha nirīkṣhaka, 8.22
jīva-tattva śhakti, kṛiṣhṇa-tattva śhaktimān, 4.24, 7.5
jīvera svarūpa haya, 4.23
kabhu swarge uṭhāya, 15.3–4
kāmera tātparya nija-sambhoga kevala, 7.18
kṛiṣhṇa bhuli 'sei jīva, 15.3–4
kṛiṣhṇa sūrya-sama, māyā haya andhakāra, 6.23
śhraddhā śhabde viśhwāsa, 3.32
swayaṁ bhagavānera karma, 10.8
tāñhāra aṅgera śhuddha kiraṇa-maṇḍala, 14.27

Tantra Bhagavat

ahankārāt tu samsāro, 13.30

Tantra Sār

yajño yajña pumāṁśh chaiva, 3.15

Vaiśhampāyan Samhitā

sarva dharma bahirbhūtaḥ, 9.14

Yog Vāsiṣhṭh

kartā bahirakartāntarloke vihara, 5.8–9, 13.30

Guru Granth Sahib

hari sama jaga mahañ vastu nahiṅ, 13.19

The Bible

Be sure your sin...(*Numbers 32:23*), 16.16
Blessed are the pure...(*Matthew 5:8*), 4.10
Do to others...(*Luke 6:31*), 18.23
Do unto others … (*Matthew 7:12*), 13.8–12
Father, forgive them...(*Luke 23:34*), 12.15
For dust thou are...(*Genesis 3:19*), 2.18
For where your treasure...(*Matthew 6:21*), 10.9
In the beginning...(*John 1:1*), 8.13
Malachi 4:5, 2.13
Mark 12:30, 13.19
Matthew 11:13-14, 2.13
Matthew 17:10-13, 2.13
We walk by faith...(*2 Corinthians 5:7*), 9.3
To be born in sound body...*Wisdom of Solomon(8:19-20)*, 2.13
When you are invited...(*Luke 14:10-11)*, 16.13–15
You shall love the Lord... (*Deuteronomy 6:5*), 13.19

Dhammapada

na kahāpaṇa vassena, 3.39

Tao Te Ching

Instead of trying to be the mountain, 16.13–15

Sukti Sudhakar and Other Sayings

āmle kā khāyā aur baḍoṅ kā kahā, 18.37
ek peḍa do pakṣhī baiṭhe, 6.5
eke satpuruṣhāḥ parārthaghaṭakāḥ, 16.13–15
kuraṅga mātaṅga pataṅga, 2.67
mārane vāle ke do hāth, 15.17
vindhya na īndhana pāiye, 11.34
rātrirgamiṣhyati bhaviṣhyati, 2.66
yā chintā bhuvi putra, 16.11

Other Books by the Author

7 Divine Laws to Awaken Your Best Self

7 Mindsets for Success, Happiness and Fulfilment

Science of Healthy Diet

Spiritual Dialectics

The Science of Mind Management

Yoga for the Body, Mind, and Soul

Books for Children

My Wisdom Book

Essence of Hinduism

Festivals of India

Healthy Body Healthy Mind: Yoga for Children

Inspiring Stories for Children (set of 4 books)

Mahabharat

My Best Friend Krishna

Ramayan

Saints of India

Let's Connect

If you enjoyed reading this book and would like to connect with Swami Mukundananda, you can reach him through any of the following channels:

Websites: *www.jkyog.org*, *www.jkyog.in*, *www.swamimukundananda.org*

Swami Mukundananda Exclusive community (SMEx): *www.smexclusive.org*

YouTube channels: 'Swami Mukundananda' and 'Swami Mukundananda Hindi'

Facebook: 'Swami Mukundananda' and 'Swami Mukundananda Hindi', 'The Bhagavad Gita'

Instagram: 'Swami Mukundananda' and 'Swami Mukundananda Hindi'

Pinterest: Swami Mukundanada - JKYog

Telegram: Swami Mukundananda

Twitter: Swami Mukundananda (@Sw_Mukundananda)

LinkedIn: Swami Mukundananda

Podcasts: Apple, Google, SoundCloud, Spotify, Stitcher

JKYog Radio: TuneIn app for iOS and Android

JKYog App: Available for iOS and Android

WhatsApp Daily Inspirations: We have two broadcast lists. You are welcome to join either or both.

USA: +1 346-239-9675
India: +91 84489 41008

To subscribe for Bhagavad Gita verse of the Day:

WhatsApp: www.holy-bhagavad-gita.org
Telegram: Gita Daily Verse
Email: www.holy-bhagavad-gita.org

Online Classes:

JKYog India: www.jkyog.in/online-sessions
JKYog USA: www.jkyog.org/online-classes

Email: deskofswamiji@swamimukundananda.org

To bring the message of *The Holy Bhagavad Gita* or Swami Mukundananda to your organisation—as Google, Intel, Oracle, Verizon, United Nations, Stanford University, Yale University, IITs and IIMs have done—please write to deskofswamiji@swamimukundananda.org